Madness Unchained

Madness Unchained

A Reading of Virgil's Aeneid

Lee Fratantuono

LEXINGTON BOOKS

A division of
ROWMAN & LITTLEFIELD PUBLISHERS, INC.
Lanham • Boulder • New York • Toronto • Plymouth, UK

LEXINGTON BOOKS

A division of Rowman & Littlefield Publishers, Inc.
A wholly owned subsidiary of The Rowman & Littlefield Publishing Group, Inc.
4501 Forbes Boulevard, Suite 200
Lanham, MD 20706

Estover Road
Plymouth PL6 7PY
United Kingdom

Copyright © 2007 by Lexington Books

All rights reserved. No part of this publication may be reproduced, stored in a retrieval system, or transmitted in any form or by any means, electronic, mechanical, photocopying, recording, or otherwise, without the prior permission of the publisher.

British Library Cataloguing in Publication Information Available

Library of Congress Cataloging-in-Publication Data

Fratantuono, Lee, 1973–
  Madness unchained : a reading of Virgil's Aeneid / Lee Fratantuono.
    p. cm.
  Includes bibliographical references and index.
  ISBN-13: 978-0-7391-1237-3 (cloth : alk. paper)
  ISBN-10: 0-7391-1237-6 (cloth : alk. paper)
  ISBN-13: 978-0-7391-2242-6 (pbk. : alk. paper)
  ISBN-10: 0-7391-2242-8 (pbk. : alk. paper)
  1. Virgil. Aeneis. I. Title.
  PA6825.F774 2007
  873'.01—dc22   2007009279

Printed in the United States of America

⊖™ The paper used in this publication meets the minimum requirements of American National Standard for Information Sciences—Permanence of Paper for Printed Library Materials, ANSI/NISO Z39.48–1992.

DIS MANIBUS

Seth Benardete
New York University
14 November, 2001

Gerard Lavery
The College of the Holy Cross
21 January, 2005

Robert Carrubba
Fordham University
12 December, 2005

sunt lacrimae rerum, et mentem mortalia tangunt.

- Virgil, *Aeneid* 1.462

Contents

Acknowledgments	ix
Ad Lectorem	xi
Introduction	xiii
I: *Arms and the Man*	1
II: *All Fell Silent*	37
III: *After It Seemed Best*	75
IV: *But the Queen*	99
V: *Meanwhile Sure Aeneas*	131
VI: *So He Spoke, Weeping*	163
VII: *You Also, Dying*	205
VIII: *As Turnus Raised*	233
IX: *And While These Things*	263
X: *The House of Olympus*	291
XI: *Dawn Left the Ocean*	321
XII: *As Turnus Sees*	367
Select Bibliography	405
Index	419
About the Author	427

ACKNOWLEDGMENTS

This book owes much to ideas that arose during work on my Fordham dissertation commentary on Book 11 of the *Aeneid* in 2001-2002. The late Professor Robert Carrubba directed that thesis with wisdom and erudition. Professors Harry Evans and George Shea offered valuable criticism and advice as first and second readers. But my coming to terms with the *Aeneid* came only after a close study of its rightful sequel, Lucan's *Bellum Civile*, in a Monday evening graduate course with Professor Seth Benardete at New York University in the spring of 1998. That seminar studied a book of Lucan's baroque horror show week after week (ignoring the hour, too, until the entire book was completed); Benardete was as much at home in Latin imperial epic as in Greek poetry or philosophy, and he taught his students much about Lucan, Ovid, and Virgil through those insightful readings each week. More than anything, he taught us to read complete works at a reasonably rapid pace, so as to appreciate better the whole effect of the poet's workmanship and artistic craft. Benardete provided much assistance to my work between 1998 and 2001. His death in November of 2001, as I was finishing my Virgil commentary, came as a blow to all of us who had the pleasure of studying the classics under him.

This book was written shortly after the untimely deaths in 2005 of two other formative influences on my studies: Professors Robert Carrubba and Gerard Lavery, the latter a fellow Fordham classicist and undergraduate professor of mine at Holy Cross. Professor Lavery taught me the fundamentals of Roman Republican and Imperial history, Lucretius, and Tacitus during his final years on Mount Saint James before his 1995 retirement.

This book is dedicated to the memory of all three men. *Requiescant in pace.*

I owe a special debt of gratitude to a number of colleagues at various institutions who have helped me and my work over the last few years in diverse ways: at Ohio Wesleyan, Donald Lateiner, my senior in classics, who has provided a most congenial place both to study and teach the classics; at Holy Cross, my *alma mater*, Blaise Nagy, Ann Batchelder (*optima magistra*), Thomas Martin, Kenneth Happe, John D.B. Hamilton and William Ziobro; at Boston College, Father David Gill, S.J., Dia Philippides, and Jack Shea; at Fordham, Robert Penella; at New York University, David Sider; at the City University of New York, Jennifer Roberts, Jacob Stern and Joel Lidov; at the University of Dallas, Stephen Maddux, David Sweet, and Robert Dupree; at Hamilton College, Mary McHugh, and at the College of New Jersey, Holly Haynes. At Ohio Wesleyan, I am grateful to faculty colleagues in other departments who have made the process of finishing this book easier by their friendship: Danny Vogt, Margaret Fete, Sean Kay, David Caplan, Bob Olmstead, Katie Hervert, and Bob Flanagan.

At Ohio Wesleyan, I am also indebted to several of my Latin and mythology students and classics majors, who were helpful in so many ways as this book was completed: Michael McOsker (now of the University of Michigan), Samantha Nevins, Aycan Garip, Jennifer Alta Dansie, Sarah Brown Ferguson, Marie

Jaquish, and Louisa Hoffmann. I am also grateful to Tyler Travillian of Boston University, and Rebecca Longtin, for their usual incisive criticism.

Special thanks are also due to the patient and helpful editors at Lexington Books, especially Patrick Dillon, Sarah Fell, Julia Loy, and Serena Krombach.

But, most personally, this book would not have been finished on time without the great assistance of Andrea, impish Muse.

Lee Fratantuono
William Francis Whitlock Professor of Latin
Ohio Wesleyan University
Delaware, Ohio
29 September, 2006
Michaelmas

AD LECTOREM

The Latin text of Virgil that has been printed in this book is the Oxford Classical Text of Hirtzel, *P. Vergili Maronis Opera*, Oxford, 1900. Hirtzel's OCT was "replaced" by R.A.B. Mynors' 1969 (corrected, 1972) edition. As might be expected with an author whose text is as reasonably secure as Virgil's, the differences between Hirtzel and Mynors are exceedingly few, especially if one does not consider editorial decisions on punctuation, or whether *Manes* (*et sim.*) should be capitalized. Hirtzel's text is out of copyright; Oxford University Press considered it appropriate to charge several hundred pounds Sterling for the right to print the Mynors text for the several hundred lines quoted in this volume, which has induced me to cite Hirtzel without apology. Below I have noted the (few) significant divergences of Hirtzel's text from Mynors' that are not discussed separately in my chapters.

1.2

Mynors *Laviniaque* for *Lavinaque*: Virgil wants to highlight from the beginning Aeneas' conquest of *Lavinia*, the erotic object of struggle for both him and Turnus. *Pace* Mynors and Goold's new Loeb text, *Laviniaque* should stand for the evocation *ab initio* of Aeneas and Turnus' future would-be prize. The "Lavinian shores" Aeneas will obtain points forward in the poem to his winning of Lavinia from Turnus.

2.433

Mynors *vitavisse vices Danaum* for *vitavisse vices, Danaum*: Hirtzel takes *Danaum* with *manu*, Mynors with *vices* (probably better), though it is attractive to take the genitive with *manu* rather than interpret it as Aeneas' own hand.

8.533 *ego poscor Olympo* for *ego poscor. Olympo*

Mynors is probably right to take Olympus with what precedes rather than what follows, though it is tempting to leave *ego poscor* as a simple declarative statement with emphatic pronoun subject and no agent; this passage is a rare instance of Aeneas asserting his own first person rights (cf. his blaming Pallas for the killing of Turnus at the end of the poem); immediately after underscoring his own identity with *ego*, Aeneas supplies evidence for his assertion by citing his divine mother, sent down from Olympus.

INTRODUCTION

The Roman epigrammatist Martial advised against reading Virgil's *Aeneid* after gambling during the Saturnalia.[1] Martial felt that the winter holiday festivities called for something more lighthearted than Virgil's poem of war. I disregarded his advice during the Christmas season of 1995-1996, and read one book of the poem a day as a sort of Virgilian twelve days of Christmas, and I have repeated that nativity tradition yearly ever since.[2]

Indulging in a slow haste though the entire poem has a pleasure all its own. The reader is able to sense more keenly Virgil's elucidation of his grand themes. A swift march from Book 1 to Book 12 (and Virgil advances inexorably to his end, with eyes always fixed on how the poem will conclude) reveals the structure of the *whole* more clearly. Connections between books, episodes, even individual lines become part of an elaborate web made stronger and simpler in its elegance with every reading. Virgil's most important interlocking rings in the *Aeneid* are his wordplay with the Latin verb *condere* (1.5 *conderet* and 12.950 *condit*) and his descriptions of the poem's two main characters, Aeneas and Turnus (1.92 and 12.951 *solvuntur frigore membra*): these two rings frame the entire poem. *Condere* means both "to found" and "to bury." In Book 1, the imperfect subjunctive *conderet* describes the anticipated action of Aeneas in founding Rome. In Book 12, the present indicative *condit* describes the burial of his sword in Turnus' chest.[3] The poem begins with Juno furious with the Trojans and determined to stop their founding of Rome; it ends with the "founding," as Aeneas inherits Juno's fury and kills his rival. In Book 1, *solvuntur frigore membra* describes Aeneas' limbs, chilled with the fear of doom during the great storm that overwhelms his ships. In Book 12, the same phrase describes the dying Turnus. Numerous smaller rings of composition work together to help anchor the structure of a massive, complex work of poetic genius. Further, the second half of the poem both expands upon and forces a reappraisal of the poem's first six books.

Unfortunately, due in part to the exigencies of time, most Latin classes on the *Aeneid* (both the traditional secondary school senior year Advanced Placement Virgil curriculum and college advanced Latin courses) do not aspire to read the entire poem. Indeed, the principal prejudice in classroom study of the *Aeneid* has been to pretend that the second half of the epic does not exist; this lamentably misguided pedagogical approach to Virgil has only relatively recently been remedied to some extent by alterations to standard syllabuses and the publication of several commentaries on Books 7-12.[4] One can find a vast number of "schoolboy" editions of *Aeneid* 1-6 from the late nineteenth and early twentieth centuries, while comparatively few editions of the poem's second half were prepared. At the time of the writing of this chapter, astonishingly, no full English scholarly commentary yet exists on the crucial last and longest book of the *Aeneid*, and Book 11, the penultimate in the tragedy of Virgil's war in Italy, remains entirely ignored by the Latin Advanced Placement curriculum.[5] (Virgil himself started something of this trend, however unwillingly; Augustus is said to have been so eager to hear the poem that he demanded readings of selected books while Virgil was still in the long process of composition and refinement).[6] More than one medieval commentary on the poem ignores or virtually ignores the entire second half; even Henry's enormous *Aeneidea* begins to show fatigue with the poem's second half, certainly by Book 9.[7] Besides the odd phenomenon of not finishing the poems one starts, this neglect of the second half of the *Aeneid* is at direct variance, as we shall explore later, with Virgil's own declaration that the second half of his *magnum opus* is the greater of its two parts.[8] Virgil would perhaps feel that his deathbed wish for the whole thing to be burned is validated every time even advanced students of the original Latin ignore what he considered the more important part of the whole. Taking something of the opposite approach, some have felt that the poem certainly should not end where it does in Book 12; Mapheius Vegius thoughtfully supplied a thirteenth book.[9] Refusal to read the entire second half of the poem, or even supplementation of the second half with an extra book, stems ultimately, I would contend, from a dislike of the contents of Books 7-12.

The title of this book is *Madness Unchained: A Reading of Virgil's Aeneid*; it offers one man's interpretation of the epic after a decade of more or less continuous study.[10] It takes for granted the idea that the *Aeneid* of Virgil was intended to offer reflection on the momentous changes that took place in Roman government and life in the last years of the tumultuous first century B.C., as Octavian assumed complete control of the Roman state and initiated his *Pax Augusta*.[11] The *Aeneid*—written in the context of the birth of the Augustan principate and the end of the Roman civil wars after Octavian's defeat of Antony and Cleopatra—is a literary response to the tumultuous political changes Virgil and his contemporaries lived through. Virgil's moment in history was fraught with numerous complications that weighed heavily on thoughtful, literary men; his *Aeneid*—in its totality, with due privilege given to the very half of the poem that he labeled the greater work—is his testimony to how he viewed the Rome of his age.

Virgil's times were tinged with an odd combination of tremendous relief, hope for the future, and a gnawing sense of anxiety and worry. The Roman Republic had suffered from civil wars almost constantly for a century. Octavian's victory and governmental reorganization marked the end of internecine strife for Rome. But no one could be certain that the cycle of civil war was truly over, and, even if Octavian—soon to be "Augustus"—could truly inaugurate a new age of tranquility for the empire, Rome had no guarantee that he could establish a lasting, permanent peace. Any joy at the dawn of the Augustan principate was tinged with fear and dread for what might come to pass for Rome.

Years of peace allow for the calm expression of the poetic mind and the nurturing of the artist's voice. Horace (65 B.C.-8 B.C.), Virgil's close personal friend, probably published his collection of three books of *carmina* (the "Odes") in 23 B.C., at the age of forty-two. Horace's *carmina* are deeply imbued with a spirit of reflection on the nature of the Augustan principate. The collection prominently highlights Octavian's defeat of Cleopatra at Actium in 31 B.C. (*carmen* 1.37 *Nunc est bibendum*). Octavian was consul every year from Actium to the publication of the three books of Horace's *carmina*. After Actium and the mopping up operations that followed it, Octavian returned to Rome in 29 B.C. and closed the doors of the temple of Janus: the civil wars were over at long last. In 27 B.C. he restored much of the old Republican apparatus, and in return received the honorific title *Augustus*. Due to his careful management of what was in effect a monarchy, it is difficult if not impossible to decide when the Republic dies and the Empire begins for Rome: Augustus may have ended the civil wars and brought peace and prosperity to Rome, but somewhere along the way through the slaughter and turmoil of Marius and Sulla, Caesar and Pompey, and finally Octavian and Antony, the Roman Republic had died.

Virgil had introduced Horace to the literary circle of Augustus' friend Maecenas.[12] Together the two men produced the greatest poetic achievements of the Augustan Age. Virgil's *Georgics* were likely finished in 29 B.C., the year Octavian returned to Rome after the Antony and Cleopatra debacle. The close of the *Georgics* celebrates the peace and quiet Octavian's foreign campaigns allowed on the home front for a writer whose deeds of daring would be not martial but literary:

> fulminat Euphraten bello victorque volentis
> per populos dat iura viamque adfectat Olympo.
> illo Vergilium me tempore dulcis alebat
> Parthenope studiis florentem ignobilis oti,
> carmina qui lusi pastorum audaxque iuventa,
> Tityre, te patulae cecini sub tegmine fagi. (4.561-566)

> *The victor thunders over the Euphrates in war and gives*
> *laws to willing people and fashions a path to Olympus.*
> *Sweet Parthenope was nurturing me, Virgil, in that time,*
> *as I was flourishing in the pursuits of an ignoble leisure,*
> *I who first, daring, played the songs of shepherds in my youth,*
> *O Tityrus, as I sang of you under the cover of a spreading beech tree.*

The end of the *Georgics* ties together the poet's most recent accomplishment with his first published work, the *Eclogues*, which open with an address to the shepherd Tityrus. But in the context of Virgil's triple poetic achievement, the *Aeneid* offers the most sustained treatment of the problems raised by the Augustan principate. It has only one rival for extended poetic commentary on Octavian's reign: Ovid's *Metamorphoses*, a work that is not a sequel to the *Aeneid*, but rather stands out proudly as an anti-*Aeneid*, a rival to Virgil's vision of Augustan Rome.[13]

It is highly probable that Horace alludes to the creation of the *Aeneid* in his celebrated *propemptikon* ode to Virgil (*carmen* 1.3), where he describes his friend setting off on a sea journey, a perilous undertaking that proves how foolhardy we mortals are; we continue to try to climb the heights of heaven (like the giants of mythology), and thereby do not allow Jupiter to put down his thunderbolts.[14] Horace, it seems, knew better than to try to explain the Augustan principate through epic verse. His *carmen* 1.3 is probably one of the earliest surviving pieces of literary reflection on the *Aeneid*. Horace's description of an imagined sea journey is not only an image of Virgil's setting out to compose the *Aeneid*, but also a response to Virgil's own storm at sea that will fatefully set Aeneas on his course to Carthage and Dido at the beginning of Book 1. Most probably about three years before Horace's ode, in 26 B.C., Propertius hauntingly asserted that something greater than the *Iliad* was being born (*carmen* 2.34.91-92).[15]

After finishing the bulk of the work of composition, Virgil departed for Greece and Asia Minor, intending to spend three years in revision of his masterpiece. Augustus met Virgil in Athens, and the two men returned together to Italy (an appropriate final sea journey for the author of the *Aeneid*); Virgil died at Brundisium, apparently of fever, on 20 September, 19 B.C., and the work fell into the hands of his literary executors and the rich afterlife or *Nachleben* it has enjoyed (and sometimes suffered) that stretches to our own day and the present pages.

Those who read the *Aeneid* are being disobedient to Virgil's will. As we have already noted, Virgil wanted the *Aeneid* burned.[16] He was a perfectionist, we can be sure, and his premature death in 19 B.C. came before he could apply the *ultima manus* to his masterpiece. As we shall see, besides concerns about the imperfect state of the poem, Virgil may well have been concerned that much of his point in writing the *Aeneid* might well be lost on its audiences. Like all great poems, the *Aeneid* is open to many and sometimes conflicting interpretations. All who truly love the poem will arrive at heartfelt conclusions about the ambiguities, vagaries, perplexities, and outright paradoxes the poem offers its readers (and listeners!).

Once we have decided to disobey Virgil and set out to read his epic, then, we must carry out our intention completely and read the entire poem. The chapters of this book aim at presenting an analysis of the *Aeneid* that moves episode to episode through the epic, letting the text speak for itself. So while someone might consult these chapters for commentary on Dido, or Palinurus, or Amata, or Mezentius, I would urge the reader to move continuously through them from beginning to end.[17] I presume the corresponding book of Virgil's poem has been read, either in Latin or in English translation, before my chapter is studied. In accord with Virgil's own announcement that the second half of the poem is the *maius opus*, I have given fuller and more detailed attention to Books 7-12.

In Book 1 of the *Aeneid* we are shown a glimpse of divine life: Jupiter offers solace to his daughter Venus by means of a prediction of Rome's future greatness and a peaceful empire: empire without end and the imprisonment of Madness. In Book 12, the poem's hero Aeneas will surrender to Madness in the epic's final lines; Fury is the poem's single most dominant image. The madness Aeneas exhibits in the very last lines of the poem is parallel to the wrath of Juno at the poem's outset. By the end of the poem, the audience knows that Juno's wrath has accomplished much. Because Aeneas' wrath comes in the poem's final lines, we are unable to see its consequences. We are left with the frozen image of Aeneas' killing of Turnus. The Trojan prophet Helenus had told Aeneas to make sure he always venerated Juno most especially (so as to assuage her rage); Aeneas takes the admonition quite seriously: he worships Juno by taking on the weight of her furious madness. The anticipatory subjunctive *conderet* of the poem's proem will come to terrible fruition in the indicative *condit*, the "founding" act of murder that concludes the epic. In the middle of the poem, during Aeneas' education in the underworld, we shall learn that the Augustus of Rome's future will not be the reincarnation of *Aeneas* (or, for that matter, his father Anchises or son Ascanius). In *Augustus*, then, we may envision the end of history: the establishment of perpetual peace and the suppression of Madness. Such a vision would most assuredly not come to fruition for Rome (though Virgil himself, of course, could not predict the future with certainty). The poet chose to end his work not with a triumphal scene in heaven (Venus is conspicuously absent from the end of the *Aeneid*), but with his mad hero's sword buried in his enemy's chest. The *Aeneid* proudly announces history's dream; Virgil leaves us at the end of Book 12 with a sudden jolt that wakes us from the dream. We move from the prediction of Augustus' empire of peace in Book 1 to the horror of the *Aeneid*'s ending in Book 12. Augustus had certainly restored peace to Rome, though fears for the future (both Augustus' and beyond) were understandable; the end of the *Aeneid* does nothing to calm them. Once the poem is over, the weary reader can try to seek renewed rest and quiet slumber (with due gratitude to Augustus for providing the peace that allows for such leisure as writing poetry or enjoying it). The present moment was one of tranquility for Virgil and his contemporaries; just how long the calm would last was unknown. After a sufficient passage of time (and how short it would prove to be), the Roman principates of Tiberius, Caligula, Claudius and Nero would allow the true inheritor of Virgil's poetic mantle, Lucan (A.D. 39-65), to set the stage for his own verse exposition of Rome's nightmare.[18]

Notes

1. *Epigrammata* 14.185 *Accipe facundi Culicem, studiose, Maronis, / ne nucibus positis "arma virumque" legas.*

2. I would also recommend that all students and lovers of Virgil read the *Aeneid* through at least once at a reasonably rapid pace, perhaps even in a day or weekend. The poem must be viewed as a whole; its complex problems of interpretation require the forest to be viewed, even if later individual trees beckon for closer examination. Such is the method of reading Seth Benardete used in Florence, Italy with the *Iliad* while mulling over his Chicago dissertation. Students at Ohio Wesleyan heard the *Aeneid* recited overnight and into the early morning by a series of speakers in a Virgil Vigil in March of 2006.

3. On this crucial verb, see JAMES, "Establishing Rome with the Sword: *Condere* in the *Aeneid*," *The American Journal of Philology* 116 (1995), pp. 623-637.

4. Cf., for example, Vincent Cleary's comment on a reprint of Fordyce's Oxford commentary on Books 7-8: "most secondary teachers will not teach these books in Latin" (in "*Aeneidea*: Important Work on the *Aeneid*, 1984-1987, for Secondary School Teachers," *Vergilius* 33, 1987, p. 104). Happily, the long pattern of neglect of the poem's greater half has been reversed.

5. We eagerly await Richard Tarrant's Cambridge commentary on Book 12.

6. Books 1, 4, and 6 (according to Donatus' *Vita*). The citation names three of the most popular books and omits Book 2, powerful and popular but clearly lacking Virgil's *ultima manus*.

7. HENRY, *Aeneidea: Critical, Exegetical, and Aesthetical Remarks on the Aeneis, with a personal collation of all the first class Mss., upwards of one hundred second class Mss., and all the principal editions* (4 vols.), London-Dublin, 1873-1892.

8. 7.45 *maius opus moveo.*

9. PUTNAM, ed., *Maffeo Vegio: Short Epics*, Cambridge, Massachusetts, 2004; BRINTON, *Maphaeus Vegius and His Thirteenth Book of the Aeneid*, London, 2002 (reprint of the 1930 Stanford University Press original). Many early editions of the *Aeneid* printed Vegio's thirteenth book as if it were Virgilian—a tribute less to Vegio's talent than to the audacity of Virgil's editors.

10. Besides similarity of title, this work shares some basic intentions with DI CESARE, *The Altar and the City: A Reading of Virgil's Aeneid*, New York, 1974, though it reaches several different conclusions and has attempted to be rather more comprehensive in its analyses. This sort of systematic study of the *Aeneid* owes much to the work of QUINN, *Virgil's Aeneid: A Critical Description*, London, 1968; CAMPS, *An Introduction to Virgil's Aeneid*, Oxford, 1969; ANDERSON, *The Art of the Aeneid*, Englewood Cliffs, 1969. Curiously, all three men are strangely unwilling to draw many cohesive conclusions about the poem as a whole. In the same vein, though less useful, is GRANSDEN, *Virgil's Aeneid*, Cambridge, 1990 (and note the much improved second edition "by" S.J. Harrison (2004). On Books 2, 5, 8, and 12, PUTNAM, *The Poetry of the Aeneid: Four Studies in Imaginative Unity and Design*, Cambridge, Massachusetts, 1965, is essential reading for any student of Virgil.

11. I have deliberately refrained from aiming this book at any particular audience. My hope is that anyone seriously interested in Virgil—whether Advanced Placement student or senior Latinist—will find something of profit here, either in studying new issues or revisiting old and favorite problems.

12. See Horace *Sermones* 1.6.55, with Palmer's notes.

13. For Virgil's life in general, see JACKSON-KNIGHT, *Roman Vergil*, London, 1944, pp. 52-98, and LEVI, *Virgil: His Life and Times*, London, 1998. "There is a pressing need to restore Virgil's poetry to the true, unglamorized history of his own times." If the message of the *Aeneid* is that Madness has been unchained, then the message of the *Metamorphoses* is that Madness has been transformed. Lucan, following the lead of Virgil in sequel, will present in the *Pharsalia* Madness Triumphant. Interestingly, both Ovid and Lucan will focus on the figure of Julius Caesar as the summit of their reflections, and not Augustus.

14. Horace's ode also contains one of Latin literature's greatest literary tributes to a friend: he calls Virgil *animae dimidium meae*, "one half of my soul." See further CLARK, "Horace on Vergil's Sea-Crossing in *Ode* 1.3," *Vergilius* 50 (2004), pp. 4-31.

15. On the immediate reception of Virgil's epic see BOYLE, "The Canonic Text: Virgil's *Aeneid*," in his *Roman Epic*, London-New York, 1993, pp. 79-107.

16. *Egerat cum Vario, priusquam Italia decederet, ut siquid sibi accidisset, "Aeneida" combureret; at is facturum se pernegarat; igitur in extrema valetudine assidue scrinia desideravit, crematurus ipse.* The standard text of the Virgilian lives is HARDIE, *Vitae Vergilianae Antiquae*, Oxford, 1966; the most recent text (with translation) is in the revised Loeb Classical Library edition of ROLFE, *Suetonius: Volume II*, Cambridge, Massachusetts, 1997. Hardie's Oxford Classical Text of the ancient lives was originally published together with the *Appendix Vergiliana* in a combined OCT (1957), then separated once the Appendix was revised (1966, reprinted 1967), and finally allowed to go out of print, so that the Loeb edition is now the most convenient Latin text.

17. The same advice is given by Robert Cruttwell in the preface to his 1946 Oxford volume *Virgil's Mind at Work: An Analysis of the Symbolism of the Aeneid*, one of the more perceptive and intriguing studies of the poem from the mid-twentieth century, a book that deserves more attention from Virgilians, despite its occasionally bizarre associations; note Arthur Stanley Pease's quite negative review in *The Classical Journal* 44.3 (1948), pp. 225-226.

18. The translations provided are my own; they do not aspire to any literary quality whatsoever, but are meant to serve the reader without Latin. The quality of the translation, in fact, will hopefully spur the reader to learn Latin. Virgil, in my view, is well nigh untranslatable, which is why I have refrained in the bibliography from suggesting any particular English version, since recommending translations can often be an exercise in deciding between more or less offensive or even odious betrayals of the original Latin. Since the majority of users of the book will have some (if not extensive) Latin, I have refrained from translating every last Latin reference in the text and notes. In the notes, I have also cited some standard commentaries by the author's last name only. I have not hesitated to cite important Virgilian scholarship in languages other than English.

Chapter I

Arms and the Man

The first three words of the *Aeneid* make a bold declaration, one of the most awe-inspiring in world literature. Each of Virgil's first three words is laden with literary implications of great significance:

Arma virumque cano[1]

Arms and the man I sing

The man, of course, will be Aeneas; of this there can be no doubt. The "arms" are a bit less specific, a bit ambiguous. An attractive idea is to relate the poem's opening two words (which set the theme for the entire epic) to the opening two words of Homer's *Iliad* and *Odyssey*. The *Odyssey* opens with clear reference to the resourceful Greek hero who reached his home in Ithaca after an absence of twenty difficult years:

Ἄνδρα μοι ἔννεπε, Μοῦσα, πολύτροπον

Sing to me of the man of many ways, O Muse

The *Iliad* is Homer's epic of the wrath of Achilles, greatest of Greek warriors at Troy, and its terrible consequences:

Μῆνιν ἄειδε, θεά, Πηληϊάδεω Ἀχιλῆος

Goddess, sing of the wrath of Achilles, the son of Peleus

Virgil is audaciously challenging Homer. Virgil's *one* poem will accomplish, and surpass, what Homer achieved in *two* epics. Indeed, the first half of the *Aeneid* will be Virgil's *Odyssey*, and the second half his *Iliad*. Virgil has reversed the order of the Homeric epics.

There is no surprise when we hear Virgil announce that he will be singing of a man, Aeneas, who is meant to evoke memories of Odysseus. To be sure, the one is Trojan and the other Greek, but as we read the first half of the *Aeneid*, the parallels will be easy enough to recognize; the first half of the *Aeneid*, though vastly different from the *Odyssey*, has many of the same colorful and magical episodes that so enchant the readers of Homer's poem. Part of the splendid adventure of a long sea journey over mysterious waters will be the tragic romantic interlude in North Africa, where Aeneas will live for a year of amorous pleasure with Dido, an episode with precedent in the *Odyssey* that Virgil will rework in a very different style for his own purposes.

But what, then, are we to make of the first word of the poem, *arma*? If the first half of the poem is Virgil's *Odyssey*, then the second half is his *Iliad*, and Virgil himself will announce in Book 7 that the second half is greater than the first. If the first half of the poem is about the man Aeneas, who like the man Odysseus will embark on a long sea journey across perilous waters as he travels homeward, so the second half of the poem, we may expect, will be concerned with the wrath of another Greek hero from Troy, Achilles. The understudied Books 7-12 will retell the *Iliad*'s account of the devastating anger of the greatest of the Greek heroes. The word *arma*, "arms" or "weapons," refers to the war Aeneas will fight when he finally arrives at his fated destination in Italy. The message of the second half of the *Aeneid*, we shall see, will be greater than the message of the first half. It will be nothing less than the most profound reflection we have on the nature of the Augustan regime in Rome, written by a man who saw all too clearly what the coming of Augustus' peace meant both for Rome and Italy.

The first verbs of the *Iliad* and the *Odyssey* are imperatives. The poet calls on the Muse to sing the epic subject of his poem. The first verb of the *Aeneid* is an assertive first person singular, present indicative active.[2] The Muse will not be invoked until line 8 of the justly famous proem to our epic:

Arma virumque cano, Troiae qui primus ab oris
Italiam fato profugus Laviniaque venit
litora—multum ille et terris iactatus et alto
vi superum, saevae memorem Iunonis ob iram,
multa quoque et bello passus, dum conderet urbem
inferretque deos Latio—genus unde Latinum
Albanique patres atque altae moenia Romae.
Musa, mihi causas memora, quo numine laeso
quidve dolens regina deum tot volvere casus
insignem pietate virum, tot adire labores
impulerit. tantaene animis caelestibus irae? (1.1-11)

Arms and the man I sing, who came first from the shores of Troy
to Italy by fate as an exile, and the Lavinian shores—
that man was much buffeted on both land and the deep
by the power of the ones above, on account of the mindful wrath of savage Juno,
and he suffered many things also in war, until he could found a city
and bring his gods to Latium—whence the Latin race
and the Alban Fathers and the walls of lofty Rome.
Muse, recall to me the reasons, with what divine power having been offended,
or sorrowing over what, did the queen of the gods compel the
man who was outstanding in virtue to undergo so many misfortunes,
to draw near to so many labors. Can heavenly minds have such great anger?

Aeneas came from Troy to Italy and the Lavinian shores after he had endured numerous trials both on sea and on land. He was an exile from Troy; he came to Italy by fate (1.2 *fato* with *Italiam*). The cause of Aeneas' troubles was Juno's anger. Jupiter's sister and wife is the first goddess our poem mentions.[3] The opening of the *Iliad* blames Apollo (a sun god) for the anger that erupts between Achilles and Agamemnon. The opening of the *Odyssey*, somewhat in parallel, mentions the sun god Helios; Odysseus made it home to Greece, but he did not save his companions, since they ate Helios' cattle (later, we learn that Poseidon is Odysseus' implacable foe).

Juno, then, is a crucial deity in the *Aeneid*; she appears at the poem's beginning and near its ending, framing the poem with the image of her wrath and its quelling. The poem opens with her anger seething and ready to erupt in dreadful violence.[4] Juno has several reasons for her anger, as we soon learn; during the judgment of Paris that opened the entire epic history of the Trojan War, Juno had been slighted in the contest for the apple of beauty that Discord had cast forth at the wedding of Peleus and Thetis, Achilles' parents. Juno's husband Jupiter had abducted another Trojan prince, Ganymede, for a homosexual affair. But beyond these intensely personal slights, Juno is aware that the city Aeneas will found in Latium is destined one day to destroy her favorite city in the world: Carthage. Desperate to try to save her beloved land, Juno is determined to prevent the Trojans (whom she hates already for the aforementioned reasons) from settling Rome and setting in motion the historical timeline that will end in Carthage's eventual sacking. In one sense, Virgil's epic is the story of the metamorphosis of Juno's wrath from these opening scenes of Book 1 through well into the twelfth and last book. The *arma*, in one sense, refers to the wrath of Juno, which will prove so central to the causation of the war that dominates the second half of the poem.

The *Aeneid* opens with the cry of a man who does not understand fully the ways of the immortals. Can any heavenly one be so angry, he asks, that they would so violently oppress a man who is outstanding for his faithfulness and loyalty to family and the gods? The question that ends the proem of the *Aeneid* is one of the many eternal reflections in the epic that have served to make the poem a timeless classic. For the first of many times in the poem, a question is asked that has what we may unashamedly identify as universal resonance. Virgil's question is also connected to his predecessor in the Latin literary tradition, Lucretius. For the Epicurean author of the *De Rerum Natura*, the immortals are utterly detached from human concerns. No Lucretian goddess could ever be as irritated over the fate of mortal cities as Virgil's Juno.[5]

We are left, then, with a clear enough contrast between the pious Aeneas and the wrathful Juno. A Roman audience of Virgil's day would have no sympathy whatsoever for Carthage, Juno's favored city. All the sympathy of the listener to this proem rests with Aeneas. But, on the other hand, we are left with the troublingly ambiguous first word of the poem, *arma*.

As we have noted, *arma* does not neatly accord with the "wrath of Achilles" from Homer's *Iliad*. In fact, the *Aeneid* opens with two mentions of the wrath of

Juno; Juno's *ira* certainly recalls Achilles' wrath more than the vague *arma*; perhaps the slights Juno has suffered can even be compared to Achilles' feelings at the beginning of the *Iliad*. As he will so often, Virgil has created an ambiguous, mysterious scenario; no poet, I would argue, does this as often or as well. Just what will be our subject in this poem? Will Juno alone be the wrathful one whose rage we sing? Answers will be forthcoming, but for the present, as is his wont, Virgil is satisfied with introducing the puzzle.[6] By the second half of the poem, we shall see the question of "whose wrath?" shifting back and forth, now Turnus', now Aeneas'. Likewise, Aeneas will suffer the delusions of madness in the first half of the poem. Juno will remain prone to anger throughout the epic, until near the end of the last book, when her rage will be handed over to the man who here is so sympathetically introduced at the poem's outset.

Because of Juno's wrath and its consequences, the founding of Rome was no easy accomplishment:

tantae molis erat Romanam condere gentem. (1.33)

So great a task it was to found the Roman race.

The Trojan ancestors of Rome are happy when we first meet them, because they have embarked on what they thought would be the last leg of their journey, the voyage from Sicily to Italy. Juno is enraged at the progress they are making; at once she visits Aeolus, lord of the winds—the Trojans are at sea, sailing toward their Roman future; they must be harassed.

The sea played a great role in the life of another figure whose image will lurk throughout the *Aeneid*, Augustus. The naval victory at Actium signaled the end of the last civil war: Antony and Cleopatra's defeat there and final loss at Alexandria soon after began the period of the Augustan Peace. Until his death in A.D. 14, Rome would remain largely at peace, certainly free of the cycle of bloody civil war the preceding century had seen. For Virgil and the Romans of his day, there was, of course, no certainty that Augustus' reign would prove to be so calm and serene. History seemed to be on the side of those who feared continued bloodshed. The *Aeneid* (unlike the Homeric epics), was a commissioned poem. At the very outset of his reign, Augustus wanted a literary epic to enshrine not so much the founding of Rome as the *restoration* of Rome as a city secure in peace and the rule of law. But the reality of Roman history compelled Virgil and his fellow literary Romans (Horace, Propertius) to wonder: what exactly had happened with the accession of Augustus? First, would his plans work? Would civil war really end for good and all, and would the horror of Marius vs. Sulla, Caesar vs. Pompey, Octavian vs. Antony, really be put to rest? But second—and more darkly—if the Augustan Peace did last, and Rome really did see a renaissance—what would happen after Augustus' death? After all, in everything but appearance the reign of Augustus marked the end of the Roman Republic and the beginning of the Roman Empire (i.e., the return of the Roman Monarchy). No monarch, however benign, can guarantee his own succession.

This second problem—admittedly less immediate than the first—will seriously haunt the pages of the *Aeneid*. Virgil's *Aeneid*, then, cannot be fully understood or appreciated outside of its historical context. It must be interpreted in the light of the reality of the early, formative years of Augustan Rome.

If Virgil meant to challenge Homer, he succeeds in his first "Homeric" episode. Aeolus is borrowed from Book 10 of the *Odyssey*, where Odysseus, fresh from his adventures with the Cyclops, has arrived at the home of the wind god and is sent on his way with favorable winds. After his companions foolishly unleash the full fury of the winds while Odysseus slumbers, they are driven back to Aeolus' floating island. The wind god dismisses Odysseus and his men, convinced that they must be cursed, and after a week they arrive at the home of the Laestrygonians, violent cannibal giants who attack them.

The brief Homeric episode of the winds becomes the first episode in the *Aeneid* and the proximate cause of Aeneas' detour to Carthage. Juno visits Aeolus and makes her appeal; the Trojans have been defeated and are trying to carry their conquered city away to Italy:

gens inimica mihi Tyrrhenum navigat aequor
Ilium in Italiam portans victosque penatis. (1.67-68)

*A race hateful to me is sailing the Tyrrhenian Sea
carrying Troy and the conquered Penates into Italy.*

The Penates (the word is connected to *penitus*, "deeply," and *penus*, "larder") were the spirits of the household, concerned with the innermost, most sacred part of the Roman home. How Roman religion adopted them is uncertain; Virgil's explanation has become the traditional one. The theme of the conquered Penates of Troy will recur throughout the early sections of the *Aeneid*. The Penates are also the first of many anachronistic religious details in the poem; both the Trojans and the native Italians they will find at the end of their long sea journey are already imbued with many of the traditions of Roman religion.

Juno is a marriage goddess, and she promises Aeolus the beautiful nymph Deiopea as his reward for inciting the winds against the Trojans (in Homer he is married already, with children). Aeolus complies, of course; we could not have expected such a minor god to challenge his better. The scene is memorable (more so than its Homeric model); we learn much about Juno's character in this scene, and are left with a clear picture of even the very minor character Aeolus (who will not reappear in the poem). Juno's actions here are the first in a long series of attacks she will launch on the Trojans; those actions will reach their climax in Book 7, the book that opens the terrible war in Italy. The storm here ends the happy day of travel the Trojans had been enjoying; we meet Aeneas for the first time in the epic, the captain of this now imperiled band. Virgil's introduction of Aeneas is striking; the Trojan leader is terrified by the storm:

extemplo Aeneae solvuntur frigore membra. (1.92)

At once the limbs of Aeneas were loosened with a chill.

The "man" has been introduced at last, his limbs trembling with the chill of dread. He addresses heaven, lamenting that the fortunate were those who died at Troy, those who had been saved from this tempest. As the first mention of the poem's putative hero, the line is important and must be remembered; Virgil will test our memory at the very end of the epic.

The north wind strikes Aeneas' flagship as he cries out. The south wind hits three other ships from the Trojan fleet and flings them against the *Arae*, the "Altars," bits of rock in the sea somewhere near Sicily that cannot be precisely identified.[7] Some have argued that the significance of the geographical detail is the sacrifice imagery "altars" evokes; according to this interpretation, Aeneas and his men are like sacrificial victims on the altar of Juno's wrath, as it were; this certainly fits with Juno's concerns that men might not worship her if she were seen as powerless (1.48-49). The east wind drives three other ships into shoals and sandbars. One ship, conveying Orontes and his Lycians (Trojan allies), is overwhelmed by a wave, the loss of its helmsman, and a whirlpool: a powerful sort of ascending tricolon of nautical terror. The moment is one of Trojan disaster; Virgil's comment is not without black humor:

apparent rari nantes in gurgite vasto,
arma virum tabulaeque et Troia gaza per undas. (1.118-119)

Men appear swimming here and there on the vast sea,
the arms of men, and ship planks, and Trojan wealth are scattered on the waves.

Trojan arms and men are scattered alike on the vast sea. Virgil names some other Trojan sailors: Ilioneus, Achates, Abas and Aletes (the first two significant, the others not) all suffer the loss of their ships. We have met Aeneas; now we begin to meet his companions. Most of them will remain a somewhat shadowy, not to say mysterious bunch throughout the poem (not entirely unlike their leader). Virgil sometimes draws his minor characters crisply and clearly (Aeolus); other times he leaves us with a dim view.

Neptune, appropriately enough, is aware of the storm in his realm; he also, somehow, knows the cause:

nec latuere doli fratrem Iunonis et irae. (1.130)[8]

Nor did the tricks and wrath of Juno escape the notice of her brother.

Neptune realizes the ultimate cause of the ferocious storm, but his angry address to the winds does not mention Juno, only Aeolus:

. . . illa se iactet in aula
Aeolus et clauso ventorum carcere regnet. (1.140-141)

> ... let Aeolus boast in his courtyard
> and rule over the winds in their enclosed prison.[9]

Diplomatically, Neptune focuses his blame on the lesser god; throughout the *Aeneid*, Neptune takes the side of Aeneas and the Trojans, though always with a certain circumspect detachment. Here the sea god quells the storm, and in a beautiful description of how lesser marine gods remove the beached ships from their rock prisons, Virgil introduces the first simile of the poem:

> ac veluti magno in populo cum saepe coorta est
> seditio saevitque animis ignobile vulgus;
> iamque faces et saxa volant, furor arma ministrant;
> tum, pietate gravem ac meritis si forte virum quem
> conspexere, silent arrectisque auribus adstant. (1.148-152)

> *And just as when often among a great people*
> *sedition arises, and the ignoble crowd rages in its heart;*
> *and now torches and rocks fly (Madness hands out the weapons);*
> *then, if by chance they have seen some solemn and meritorious man,*
> *they are silent, and stand with ears pricked up.*

This first simile uses concepts the poet has already made central to his epic: *arma* and *pietas*. Neptune is the faithful, trustworthy and respected man, while torches and rocks serve as ready weapons in a crowd once sedition arises and violence breaks out. This is the first appearance in the *Aeneid* of *furor*, "madness;" it will not be the last.[10] What sedition has broken out here? Virgil has already mentioned how Neptune understood his *sister*'s wrath and tricks; Jupiter, we shall soon enough learn, is also supportive of the fated arrival of the Trojans in Italy. The sedition would seem to be among the family of the gods; Neptune will appear later in the poem to perform a similar favor for the sea-bound Trojans, though at a blood price. Moreover, for the Romans of Virgil's day *seditio* would raise the specter of the century of civil war they had just experienced. In Neptune's quelling of the sea storm there is a faint glimpse of Augustus Caesar at Actium.[11] Neptune is the first appearance in the poem of the power of rational order over madness. The fight between Juno and Venus over the fate of Aeneas, even Juno and Jupiter, is a divine image of Rome's own seemingly eternal problem with civil war.

Aeneas reaches the shore in North Africa with seven ships. Achates is with him; Antheus, Capys, and Caicus (new names) are all missing (Caicus will be the first Trojan to respond to Turnus' opening military maneuvers during the Italian war at 9.35). Aeneas strikes down seven stags to feed his weary men.[12] He has recovered from his storm-induced emotions, and addresses his men with memorable, powerfully calming words:

> "O socii (neque enim ignari sumus ante malorum),
> o passi graviora, dabit deus his quoque finem.

vos et Scyllaeam rabiem penitusque sonantis
accestis scopulos, vos et Cyclopia saxa
experti: revocate animos maestumque timorem
mittite; forsan et haec olim meminisse iuvabit.
per varios casus, per tot discrimina rerum
tendimus in Latium, sedes ubi fata quietas
ostendunt; illic fas regna resurgere Troiae.
durate, et vosmet rebus servate secundis." (1.198-207)

"O comrades (nor, truly, are we ignorant of evils),
O you who have suffered worse things, the god will also grant an end to these.
You have approached the froth of Scylla and the
loudly sounding crags, you have experienced the Cyclopean rocks;
recover your courage and send away sad fears:
perhaps, one day, it will be pleasing to remember even these things.
Through various fortunes, through so many crucibles
we are heading for Latium, where the Fates offer a quiet home;
there it is right for Troy to rise again.
Be strong, and preserve yourselves for favorable things."

Aeneas recalls their Odyssean trials with the monstrous Cyclopes and Scylla. Aeneas knows they are headed to Latium in central Italy, where he expects a "quiet seat" and the resurgence of the kingdom of Troy. His words are effective, but their prediction of the Trojan rebirth will not exactly come to pass, as we shall see much later in the poem. Discreetly and sensitively, Aeneas does not mention the wars he already knows will have to be fought in Italy, instead preferring to speak of the "quiet home" that the peninsula offers.

Aeneas has been faking his calm, assured stance:

Talia voce refert curisque ingentibus aeger
spem vultu simulat, premit altum corde dolorem. (1.208-209)

Such things did he say with his voice and, sick with great anxiety,
he faked hope with his face and suppressed his profound sorrow in his heart.

His men dine on the feast he has procured for them, and after the venison and the wine they had managed to salvage from what they had obtained in Sicily and carried on ship, they begin to discuss their numerous missing companions. Orontes (whose disaster has already been related) is missing, as are Amycus, Lycus, Gyas and Cloanthus (more new names). *Pius* Aeneas laments for his men (Virgil takes care to show a leader's concern for his lost men). This juncture is a peaceful interlude in a largely tense and violent poem; it is not happy, since the fate of the missing Trojans hangs heavily over the supper, but it is calm.

The next episode in Book 1 is one of the key moments in the entire poem: the colloquy between Venus and her father Jupiter. Together with Jupiter's conversation with his wife Juno in Book 12, it serves to bookend the *Aeneid*. We know that Juno is angry because of the report that the Trojan castaways are to found the anti-Carthaginian Rome; now we shall learn the details behind this report from the Father of gods and men himself.

Jupiter gazes down at Libya and is troubled.[13] He is a latecomer to the games his wife has been playing; he knows the storm and the African landing are mere digressions from the forward thrust of the Trojans' fate. Venus, Aeneas' mother, is even more upset.[14] Her beautiful eyes are full of tears as she speaks to her father. Apparently Jupiter had already promised that the Trojans, the descendants of Teucer, would be parents to the Romans, the very same Romans who would one day rule the world. Troy has been ruined, and Venus has pinned her hopes on Aeneas' line; she mentions the fate of Antenor, another Trojan who had journeyed to Italy, where he founded Padua and lived in quiet retirement, content to be alive and safe.[15]

Venus' speech is framed by two complaints: she and her Trojan children are being punished on account of two things, Italy and anger:

cunctus ob Italiam terrarum clauditur orbis? (1.233)

Is the whole world to be closed off on account of Italy?

navibus (infandum!) amissis unius ob iram
prodimur . . . (1.251-252)

*On account of the wrath of one, with our ships lost (unspeakable!)
we are betrayed . . .*

Presumably the Trojans are denied a home anywhere because Juno keeps delaying them from arriving at their fated home in Italy. Since Juno cannot defeat their ultimate fate, only delay it, "on account of Italy" the whole world is closed off to them. The expression is strange. Towards the end of Venus' speech there is a parallel expression: "we are betrayed," she laments, "because of anger" (the recurring theme of *ira* we have seen). *Italy* is Juno's anger, and Juno's anger is Italy; Italy means the furthering of the day when Troy will be reborn and Carthage soon after destroyed. Like her uncle Neptune, Venus does not explicitly name her enemy Juno, only obliquely.

The speech ends with a rhetorical question. "Is this the honor due to faithfulness?" Aeneas' quality of *pietas* is offered as an indignant end to a mother's plea; a recurring theme of the early part of Book 1 has been that Aeneas and his Trojans do not seem to deserve their troubled fate. While this may be true, it is also a theme of the opening scenes of the *Aeneid* that one can take just pride in having achieved victory after suffering numerous trials. This was the point behind Aeneas' comment to his exhausted men that "one day, perhaps it will be pleasing to remember even these things."

Venus, goddess of love and sensuality, has made an appeal to her father; Jupiter responds with a smile and a kiss, before beginning a much lengthier speech designed to alleviate her cares. His first promise (in accordance with preordained fate) is that Venus will see the city and walls of Lavinium and will bring Aeneas up to heaven as a god:

> ... cernes urbem et promissa Lavini
> moenia, sublimemque feres ad sidera caeli
> magnanimum Aenean (1.258-260)

> ... *you will see a city, and the promised walls of*
> *Lavinium, and you will bear high to the stars of heaven*
> *great-hearted Aeneas*

This basic promise is not new, but a reaffirmation at a time of apparent defeat for Venus' progeny. Ironically, we shall learn later that Aeneas' future deification will deprive him of a place in the dramatic solemnity of the procession of souls of future Roman worthies in the underworld.

The second revelation Jupiter makes is that Aeneas will wage a great war in Italy, smash fierce peoples, and give institutions as well as walls to his people:

> bellum ingens geret Italia populosque ferocis
> contundet moresque viris et moenia ponet. (1.263-264)

> *He will wage a great war in Italy and will*
> *smite ferocious peoples; he will give customs and walls to men.*

Jupiter next blithely passes over the fact that Aeneas will (probably) die only three years after his victory at the end of the *Aeneid*, an important feature of the tradition that is, perhaps, often forgotten by readers of the epic.[16] Ascanius,[17] his son by the Trojan Creusa, will rule for roughly thirty years and move his kingdom from Lavinium to Alba Longa.[18] There his successors will reign for three hundred years, until the time comes for Ilia (whose name simply means "the Trojan girl") to be impregnated by Mars and give birth to Romulus and Remus, who will be suckled by a she-wolf.[19] Romulus will found "the walls of Mars" and name the *Romans* after his own name. In turn, the Romans will be given *imperium sine fine*: "empire without end" (1.279). Jupiter's vast sweep of more than three centuries offers a quick version of the foundation legend of Rome. In the prefatory four lines sometimes affixed to the *Aeneid*, Virgil's abrupt *arma* is expanded by *horrentia Martis*. Virgil will sing of the "bristling arms of Mars." Rome will be founded by twin sons of Mars; small wonder that Rome's history has been one of warfare. Besides the war god, Rome's ancestors include his sometime lover, Aeneas' mother Venus, the goddess of love; between love and war, Rome's violent history is easily understood. No wonder that Lucretius would include an urgent prayer for Venus to ask her lover Mars to bring peace to the Roman Republic near the beginning of his Epicurean gospel, the *De Rerum Natura*; whether he believed his "prayer" could be efficacious (however heartfelt and sincere) is another issue altogether. Jupiter predicts that Romulus and Remus will be in heaven together, where they will administer laws: this prophecy might well be a prediction that even Aeneas and Turnus will one day be united in heaven, having been reconciled in the afterlife—though this dream (wishful thinking) is certainly absent from the close of Virgil's poem.[20]

The more interesting part of Jupiter's speech, however, is its long conclusion. Venus is afraid that Juno has been hindering her beloved son and his men. Jupiter assures his daughter that Juno will come around to reconciliation with fate. This seems improbable given the events of the poem so far, but what follows is even more shocking:

> ... veniet lustris labentibus aetas
> cum domus Assaraci Phthiam clarasque Mycenas
> servitio premet ac victis dominabitur Argis. (1.283-285)

> ... *an age will come with the sacred years gliding by*
> *when the house of Assaracus will press down Phthia and famous Mycenae*
> *in slavery, and will hold dominion over conquered Argos.*

Not only will Juno be placated, but the house of Assaracus will enslave Phthia, home of Achilles, and Mycenae, home of Agamemnon, and will also rule over Argos, which Virgil had already noted (1.24) was the "dear" city Juno had fought for at Troy. The mention of both Achilles and Agamemnon early in the first book of the *Aeneid* evokes the great conflict between the two men in the first book of Homer's *Iliad*: the Romans will conquer both great Greek homelands in the course of history. And, next, there comes a passage that has been vexed by another magnificent Virgilian enigma:

> nascetur pulchra Troianus origine Caesar,
> imperium Oceano, famam qui terminet astris,
> Iulius, a magno demissum nomen Iulo.
> hunc tu olim caelo spoliis Orientis onustum
> accipies secura; vocabitur hic quoque votis.
> aspera tum positis mitescent saecula bellis;
> cana Fides et Vesta, Remo cum fratre Quirinus
> iura dabunt; dirae ferro et compagibus artis
> claudentur Belli portae; Furor impius intus
> saeva sedens super arma et centum vinctus aënis
> post tergum nodis fremet horridus ore cruento. (1.286-296)

> *A Trojan Caesar will be born from a beautiful origin,*
> *who will fix the Ocean as his empire's border, and the stars as his fame's,*
> *a Julius, his name descended from great Iulus.*
> *Without anxiety, you will receive this man at some point in heaven*
> *laden down with the spoils of the East.*
> *Then the harsh centuries will become gentle once wars have been put aside;*
> *hoary Faith and Vesta, and Quirinus with his brother Remus*
> *will give laws; the grim Gates of War will be closed with*
> *tight iron bars; wicked Madness will be inside,*

*sitting on top of savage arms, its hands bound behind its back
with a hundred brazen knots, and it will seethe, horrible with its bloody mouth.*

The passage is of supreme importance for understanding much of what will unfold as the central problem of the *Aeneid*, namely the problem of the Augustan succession.[21] The prediction is for a Caesar to be born, one who will spread his empire to the River Ocean (the ends of the earth), who will win Eastern spoils and one day be received by Venus, like his ancestor Aeneas, as a god in heaven, one who will be called upon by his Romans with votive offerings. He will be born from a "beautiful" origin because Venus is his distant ancestor. Wars will cease and impious Madness (the very opposite of Aeneas, we may think) will be chained up, sitting on top of its savage arms and seething with bloody mouth. The main import of the passage, even with the problems we shall dispense with in a moment, is clear: civil wars will cease. This was the main announcement of glad tidings for the advent of Augustus' regime. This is the second time Virgil has mentioned *furor*, "Madness," and here it should indeed be capitalized, Madness is personified as some wraithlike demon. In this Caesar we are reminded of the simile of the man who quelled the *furor* of the mad crowd; the Jovian prediction extends far past the mythological "present" of the poem to Virgil's own day and the poem's own reception in the nascent Augustan Rome.

The madness / anger / arms theme has frequently recurred since the putative first word of the poem. We still do not know precisely what that *arma* meant. The vexed tradition of the poem's actual opening reflects uncertainty about how so major a poem should open, even on the part of its author, let alone his literary executors. We are still bothered by the ambiguities that first word raised, but we have learned much already, especially through this prophecy. Virgil announced that his song would be of "arms" and the "man," and the learned audience immediately thought of Achilles' wrath and Odysseus' return (itself wrathful, insofar as the suitors were concerned). But at once Virgil moved on to the wrath of Juno. Here Jupiter announces that Juno will be reconciled and Madness will be chained up after the peaceful establishment of the Augustan program. The first half of the *Aeneid* may indeed be Virgil's *Odyssey*, but the preeminent, *greater* work, the song of madness, casts its poetic spell everywhere, even from the beginning. We may now begin to see why Virgil has reversed the order of the Homeric epics. The greater work must be treated last, lest the second half of the epic whole be less significant than the first (as far too many schools and commentators have treated it), but so great is its theme that it permeates even the first half of the poem, even more so than the spirit of the *Iliad* hangs over the *Odyssey*.

The great ambiguity of Jupiter's prophecy is the identity of the *Iulius* of line 288. The entire announcement of future Roman greatness and peace can be ascribed to Augustus Caesar, but many scholars (following Servius) find here a clear reference to Julius Caesar. Augustus was a member of the *gens Iulia* by adoption, but it is persuasive to argue that mention of "Julius" (especially the repeated *Iulius . . . Iulo* framing the line, which emphasizes the name of the clan) would immediately recall the man who fell on the Ides of March in 44 B.C., not Augustus. Virgil must have been aware that the ghost of Julius Caesar haunted these lines, even if the Eastern triumphs Jupiter mentions most dramatically refer to the reclaiming in 20 B.C. by Augustus of the standards Crassus had lost to the Parthians at Carrhae, and even if the main thrust of the passage is on the coming of peace (i.e., the *Pax Augusta*). The man of the poem's first simile, the bringer of peace and tranquility after years of uncertainty and bloodshed, is embodied in Augustus (not Julius, whose death was violent and immediately set off another round of civil strife).

Both Julius and Augustus were would-be autocrats, but where Julius had failed miserably and was assassinated in the Senate, as it met. Augustus triumphed and reigned supreme until A.D. 14, when he died of natural causes at seventy-six. The *Aeneid* was written at a time when the memory of civil war was alive and well; the verb *mitescent* in line 291, centrally placed, is poignant: it is an inchoative verb, denoting the beginning of a state of being; the ages will then begin to soften, Virgil says, once wars have been placed aside. Both Julius and Augustus fought wars, but only with the coming of Augustus will they finally be put aside. Or so at least went the hope.

So we have a major Virgilian ambiguity. Augustus had been adopted by Julius Caesar, his great-uncle, on 13 September, 45 B.C., in Caesar's will, and his adoption casts a pall over this passage.[22] Virgil does not let us reflect on the greatness of Augustus without allowing a shadow of Julius to fall over the passage. The question of which Caesar line 288 refers to cannot be answered definitively, just as Virgil wished it; what is important is that the Julian ghost haunts the Augustan home. Nor is Virgil done with this important topic; he will revisit it later, as is also his wont, at another key moment in the poem.[23]

Virgil's contemporary Livy (59 B.C.-A.D. 17) probably finished the first pentad of his monumental Roman history *Ab Urbe Condita* around the same time Virgil was deeply engaged in work on the *Aeneid* (c. 27-25 B.C.).[24] His first book opens with Aeneas and Antenor. Aeneas is a *profugus*, an "exile", at the start of both works; in Livy Aeneas will move directly from Troy to Macedonia to Sicily to Italy, without any Carthaginian complications.

We move instantly, without pause, to Jupiter's sending of his son Mercury to Carthage.[25] Venus, we must assume, is content with her father's news. We learn that Jupiter's sending of Mercury is meant to prevent Dido, the Carthaginian queen, from keeping Aeneas and his Teucrians from her borders:

. . . ne fati nescia Dido
finibus arceret. (1.299-300)

. . . lest Dido, ignorant of destiny,
should keep them away from her borders.

The Carthaginians "put aside their ferocious hearts," because the god wills it. The queen, in particular, is pacified by Mercury's spell. These brief details are redolent with the spirit of Roman attitudes toward the Carthaginians; they are a violent people, prone to savagery. The queen in particular is calmed; this could be taken to mean that Dido, leader of this Phoenician (Punic) band, is the most savage of them all. There has been no Venusian magic yet, no falling in love; the passage is devoted to Punic violence and Jupiter's attempt to quell it. The Trojans are in no state to leave and sail to Italy on their own. They need time to repair their ships and provision themselves. As we shall soon learn, the hitherto calm shore of North Africa holds danger for the shipwrecked.[26]

Aeneas, ever *pius*, spends the night bereft of sleep and eager for first light. At dawn he goes out with Achates to seek information about the country and, perhaps, their lost friends. He hides the fleet (a wise precaution) before setting out armed with his faithful friend. His mother, fresh from her visit to Jupiter and apparently buoyed by the word she has received, intercepts him. She has found time to change her clothes:

> cui mater media sese tulit obvia silva
> virginis os habitumque gerens et virginis arma
> Spartanae, vel qualis equos Threissa fatigat
> Harpalyce volucremque fuga praevertitur Hebrum.
> namque umeris de more habilem suspenderat arcum
> venatrix dederatque comam diffundere ventis,
> nuda genu nodoque sinus collecta fluentis. (1.314-320)

> *His mother came right up to him in his path*
> *having the face and bearing of a virgin and the arms of a*
> *Spartan virgin, or just as Thracian Harpalyce tires out*
> *her horses or outruns the swift Hebrus in flight.*
> *For on her shoulders according to custom she had slung her handy bow*
> *as a huntress, and given the wind her hair to blow around,*
> *naked up to her knee, and having collected the flowing folds of her*
>   *garment with a knot.*

Venus is disguised as Diana, or at least some nymph-like follower of Diana.[27] Diana is usually attended by a coterie of young women, fellow huntresses; Venus asks her son if he has seen any of her sisters, her fellow denizens of the world of the hunt. Aeneas has no answer for his lying mother, and he wonders if the beautiful girl in front of him is either Diana or some nymph of the local area. He promises sacrificial offerings in thanksgiving if she can identify the land and peoples where the Trojan exiles have landed.

No two goddesses are as opposite as Venus and Diana. The sylvan setting, of course, is the sort of place where one might expect to find the patron virgin of hunting. Virgil compares the huntress Venus to a Spartan maiden (that is, a warlike girl) or to "Thracian Harpalyce" (also warlike, from the savage wilds of northern Greece). No text prior to the *Aeneid* survives to tell us more about who this Harpalyce might be.[28] Servius *auctus* tells the story that she was the daughter of a Thracian monarch who apparently annoyed his people enough for them to kill him; his daughter was raised alone in the woods and was killed after raiding livestock for food. Her death led to violence; there was a fight over who owned the last animal she had stolen, and the skirmish led to several deaths. In consequence, her grave became a site for mock battles; apparently her death caused the curse of violence that led to the first fight, and the mock battles were meant to be expiatory rites at her grave, intended, it would seem, to appease her violent nature. Much about the significance of the Harpalyce narrative here will come to light only late in the poem, in Book 11, where Virgil finishes what he starts here with the great tragic drama of his heroine Camilla.[29] Like Camilla, Harpalyce was noted for her swiftness (Servius notes that she could evade cavalry, another linkage to the equestrian Camilla).

"Harpalyce" is Greek for "snatcher she-wolf." Venus had just heard about Romulus and Remus, "happy in the tawny pelt of the wolf," suckled as would-be lupine offspring after they had been exposed to death in the elements. The Harpalyce detail Virgil introduces here is not mere Hellenistic or Alexandrian poetic embellishment, but links this story allusively to the speech Venus has just heard. This is not mere ornamental detail by a learned poet; rather, the carefree, flighty Venus has been inspired by her father. He had mentioned the she-wolf of Romulus and Remus at a moment of great solemnity in his speech to her, and she at once remembered Harpalyce, an infant girl who had been reared (perhaps) by a she-wolf. Playfully, she has disguised herself as if Harpalyce, a violent girl (as befits the violent Carthaginian coast of North Africa), and a huntress, similar to Diana. Diana was not necessarily connected to the story of Harpalyce, but she is the patroness of huntresses, and when Virgil returns in Book 11 with Camilla to complete the ring he starts here with Harpalyce, Diana will move to center stage. In the *Aeneid*'s divine scheme, Diana is presented as firmly on the Italian side (for reasons we shall consider later).[30] Venus' playful mockery of her opposite here is symbolic of that conflict on the immortal plane. Similarly, Dido (who will soon be introduced with heavy ironies of Diana and Diana-like women) will contrast with Camilla later in the poem. Virgil may have borrowed the story of Harpalyce from Callimachus (there is no substantial evidence for her outside the *Aeneid* and Servius' commentary). Less likely is that Servius invented the details of the story merely in reminiscence of Virgil's Camilla; the notes about the theft of livestock and the expiatory mock battles at her grave are likely the preservation of an otherwise lost story. The Harpalyce lore may represent a belief in lycanthropy (as her name reveals); in Book 11, as we shall see, Virgil will model his Volscian heroine Camilla on both the Amazon Penthesilea and the lycanthrope Harpalyce.

Venus lies and denies her divinity; she identifies herself as a Tyrian girl before launching into an explanation of the land and its new inhabitants. Dido had been married in Phoenicia to the wealthy Sychaeus.[31] Her brother Pygmalion was the Tyrian ruler and a vicious criminal; *furor* (1.348) came between him and Sychaeus. Impious (like the Madness we have been assured will be chained with the coming of the Augustan Peace), Pygmalion killed Sychaeus at an altar. He lied to his sister, assuring her that her husband was alive and well; in a dream,

Sychaeus visited his grief-stricken bride and revealed his murder and how he had been left unburied (an especially terrible fate in antiquity). Sychaeus urged his widow to flee Phoenicia, revealing the secret location of some of his wealth; together with a large number of Tyrians who either hated or feared Pygmalion, Dido outfitted ships and escaped by sea. They bought land in North Africa from the Libyan natives and established their city. Venus ends her address by asking Aeneas to identify himself; the mother intends to continue to delude the son (though for the sake of the narrative the trick allows Virgil to introduce his hero's background story briefly and powerfully).

Aeneas describes the storm that has led to his Carthaginian detour and succinctly identifies himself to his already knowing mother:

sum pius Aeneas, raptos qui ex hoste penatis
classe veho mecum, fama super aethera notus.
Italiam quaero patriam et genus ab Iove summo. (1.378-380)

I am faithful Aeneas, and I carry with me the Penates
that were snatched from my enemy; my fame is known above the ether.
I seek Italy as a native land and my race descended from highest Jove.

These are the Penates, the household gods, that Juno had indignantly told Aeolus were being led from the defeated Troy into Italy; Aeneas casts them in as positive a light as he can, almost as if they were spoils of victory: Penates "snatched" from the enemy. The three lines are a marvelous declaration of who Aeneas is and how he identifies himself, with an eye both to the past and the future. We further learn that Aeneas had twenty ships before the recent sea disaster. Venus at last interrupts her son (she knows everything already, after all).[32] She announces the safety of twelve ships (one has been lost, as we could surmise from the description of Orontes' fate during the storm); she further reveals an omen of twelve swans flying safely after "the bird of Jove" (an eagle) had disturbed them.[33] Aeneas had said he was seeking the race that was descended from highest Jove (a reference to his ancestor Dardanus' descendants who are already in Italy). Now Venus mentions Jupiter (albeit in the odd context of the vicious bird that has upset the lovely swans). By these subtle touches Virgil emphasizes the shadow that Jupiter's consolatory speech has cast over this scene. When Aeneas says he is seeking a race from highest Jove, he means not only his ancestor's descendants in Italy, but also the future Romans whose father he will be.

And, for those who note such things, Aeneas' declaration of his *pietas* and deliverance of the Trojan Penates comes at exactly the midpoint of Book 1 (378x2, or the 756 lines in the book).[34]

Venus tells her son to go to the very threshold of the queen, Dido. Her departure from Aeneas is swift, but as she departs her ambrosia-scented hair gives forth the full perfume of its odor, her hiked-up skirt flows down fully, and (mysteriously) her divinity is revealed. Aeneas advances to the Tyrian city, but not before reproaching his mother; apparently this is not the first time she has teased her son. The normally playful goddess had been disturbed by the troubles her son was facing on account of the storm; once comforted by Jupiter, her playful nature returned. Her son is not so much comforted by his mother's brief revelations as annoyed by her mendacious visit. Only in Book 12 shall we learn that Venus' lighthearted demeanor and easygoing calm might be premature.

Before leaving him to his journey, Venus takes care to envelop her son and Achates in a mist, lest anyone be able to touch them, delay them, or ask why they are coming. Herein there is a strange paradox. We know already that the Carthaginians are potentially violent; soon we shall have confirmation of the fear that drove Jupiter to send Mercury down to soften their Punic hearts. Venus has told her son to go to Dido; she does not seem terribly concerned about Tyrian hospitality, but she does wrap the two men in the mist of invisibility. Most probably she merely wishes to get them to Dido's court as quickly as possible, without the interception one might expect of someone trying to enter the royal presence. In any case, once Aeneas arrives in their city, he sees a nascent Carthage with laws, magistrates and a senate (1.426)—not to mention theater arts (1.427-429). Aeneas had said that the blessed and lucky were those who had died at Troy; now he proclaims fortunate those who see their walls rising for them. Like bees, the Carthaginians busy themselves with their building projects.[35] What a contrast with the violent race that had inspired Jupiter to send his son Mercury on precautionary measures, and perhaps moved Venus to wrap her son in mist! As we shall see, the Carthaginians' main problem is with foreigners, not themselves.

Aeneas and Achates can freely travel through the city, and they arrive at its very center, the "old" neighborhood where the Tyrians had first landed. Here the Carthaginians had excavated on the site of the sign Juno had given them: the head of a fierce horse, a portent of their equine and martial prowess. Dido built a temple to the goddess on this spot, splendid in bronze. At this very place, heavy with the irony of Juno's presence, Aeneas has a strange reaction as he enters the goddess' temple:

hoc primum in luco nova res oblata timorem
leniit, hic primum Aeneas sperare salutem
ausus et adflictis melius confidere rebus. (1.450-452)

In this grove, for the first time, the new circumstance
softened his fear, here first Aeneas dared to hope
for salvation and to have greater confidence in a time of affliction.

As we shall be able to confirm later in the poem, Aeneas should not be taking solace or comfort in entering a temple of Juno. Perhaps the fact that his mother had advised him to seek out Dido has convinced him that all is suddenly well among the immortals, that all are now united behind his successful settlement in Italy; he has also been advised, we shall learn later (3.435-440), to reverence Juno carefully to ensure a safe arrival at Italy (but, we should note, his Carthaginian detour was never foretold to him). What he next sees on the walls of the temple should chill him. Appropriately enough, Juno's temple is decorated with scenes from the Trojan War that are, overall, less than celebratory of Aeneas' people. First come the sons of Atreus, Agamemnon and Menelaus, then Priam, Troy's ill-fated last monarch, and, to complete another ascending tricolon, Achilles, savage to them both. Aeneas stops and cries out to Achates:

> constitit et lacrimans, "quis iam locus," inquit, "Achate,
> quae regio in terris nostri non plena laboris?
> en Priamus. sunt hic etiam sua praemia laudi,
> sunt lacrimae rerum et mentem mortalia tangunt.
> solve metus; feret haec aliquam tibi fama salutem." (1.459-463)

> *He halted, and, crying, said, "Achates, what place is there,*
> *what region on earth, which is not full of our labor?*
> *Behold, Priam! Here also praise has its own rewards,*
> *there are tears for deeds, and mortal things touch the mind.*
> *Let go your fear: this fame will bring you salvation of some sort."*

Before we analyze this passage and what follows closely, it should be admitted that line 462, in any context, is the most beautiful line in Virgil.[36]

At the moment Aeneas utters these words his mind is overcome by the idea that even here in North Africa the news has already arrived of the epic battle at Troy (how many years have passed?).[37] Especially since the designers of this temple were from Phoenicia, closer to the Troad than Libya, this should not be so surprising; later we also learn that Dido knows much of the story from the visit of Teucer, Ajax's half-brother by Hesione and Telamon, to the court of her father Belus in Phoenicia (1.619-626). Aeneas takes solace from the fact that here, in this strange new land, there are tears; mortal affairs touch the mind. Aeneas ends his brief address with the assurance to Achates that this reputation of theirs, this news of Troy, will bring salvation (in other words, here there are people who understand human tragedy).

But the reality is now exposed more clearly, after the emotional outburst:

> . . . animum pictura pascit inani. (1.464)

> . . . *he nourishes his mind on the empty picture.*

The painting is not only empty because it lacks life, but because its images do not accord with Aeneas' optimistic interpretation. The first episode is solace enough for a Trojan: their young army presses hard, and the Greeks flee (1.467). But then the Trojans fall back as Achilles advances (1.468). Next, Diomedes, son of Tydeus, is awash in the blood of Rhesus, Thracian ally of Troy (1.469-473). Then Troilus, son of Priam (no match for Achilles) is dragged off to his doom by his own horses (1.474-478). The Trojan women supplicate Pallas Athena, but she turns her gaze away from them in rejection (1.479-482).[38] The climax, brief but effective, comes as Achilles drags the greatest Trojan warrior, Hector, around the walls of the city three times before *selling* (a non-Homeric detail that increases the pathos of the scene) his dead body to Priam for gold (1.483-484). Aeneas groans loudly, overcome by grief; he sees himself, the Eastern host of Memnon from Ethiopia, and, in an elegant coda very much in Virgil's style, Penthesilea, the Amazon queen, who came so late in vain to help the beleaguered city (1.488-493).[39] The mention of Penthesilea is a distant foreshadowing of Camilla in Book 11, who will fulfill the Penthesilea-role of coming late to a lost cause; Camilla will have affinities with both Harpalyce and Penthesilea.

The pictures follow the story of the fall of Troy to the very point where Aeneas' story in Book 2 will begin; Aeneas himself will paint the rest of these pictures, as it were, when he tells the story of what happened after the Ethiopian and Amazonian allies came in vain to Priam's aid. Aeneas knows that the pictures of Memnon and Penthesilea presage the final chain of events leading to the sacking of the city; the sum total of the pictures, especially in the situational context of Juno's temple, should not be consolatory to a Trojan. These are images set up not as memorials of human compassion, but as triumphant records of the victories of Juno's beloved Greeks over the enemy she so hates. In the first excitement of seeing the early scenes from the war that so changed his life, the images of Agamemnon, Menelaus, Priam, and Achilles, it is as if Aeneas momentarily forgot the dreadful context of this artwork. It is significant that Virgil's extended description of the pictures in Dido's temple comes *after* Aeneas' beautiful and powerful, though ultimately quite misguided reaction to them. The scene is one of increasing horror as Aeneas surveys the paintings in their terrible order, before he finally cries out after seeing the desecration of his friend Hector's body:

tum vero ingentem gemitum dat pectore ab imo. (1.485)

Then indeed he gave a mighty groan from deep in his breast.

The pictures might have been fitting to help rouse Carthaginian morale during the Punic Wars; they celebrate the worst degradation of the Trojans. Aeneas stares fixed and agape at these images as Dido finally enters the temple and interrupts his tour of her art gallery.[40]

Dido's entrance into the temple is the occasion for another great simile. Dido, as we already know, is a widowed queen. Strange, then, it might seem, for Virgil to compare her to Diana, the virgin huntress:

regina ad templum, forma pulcherrima Dido,
incessit magna iuvenum stipante caterva.
qualis in Eurotae ripis aut per iuga Cynthi
exercet Diana choros, quam mille secutae
hinc atque hinc glomerantur Oreades; illa pharetram

fert umero gradiensque deas supereminet omnis
(Latonae tacitum pertemptant gaudia pectus):
talis erat Dido, talem se laeta ferebat
per medios instans operi regnisque futuris. (1.496-504)[41]

The queen, most beautiful Dido, proceeded into the
temple, accompanied by a great crowd of youths,
just as on the banks of Eurotas and through the heights of Cynthus
Diana exercises her choirs, she whom a thousand
Oreads crowd round from this side and that, having followed her; and advancing
that goddess carries a quiver on her shoulder and towers over all the rest;
and joys touch the silent heart of her mother Latona:
such was Dido, in such a manner did she carry herself
through their midst, attentive to the work and the future kingdom.

As often, the ancient commentators miss the point. The grammarian Probus felt that no image had been lifted more inopportunely from Homer; Virgil's Diana simile comes from Homer's description of Nausicaa, the Phaeaecian princess, playing with her girlfriends (*Odyssey* 6.102-109).[42] Nausicaa and her maiden companions are like Artemis and her coterie of young virgins. The point, of course, is what we have just read about Venus' disguise. Venus disguised herself as a Diana-like woman to see her son, and here Dido enters the temple and is described with an inappropriate simile. Dido may be a widow, but she is no virgin; Diana is not a builder of cities, but a denizen of the forest glades and remote haunts of wild animals. Dido is no true Diana, despite her current appearance. After the simile, Virgil describes Dido's apportioning of tasks for the construction projects in her young capital; Dido is the Carthaginian lawgiver, not the virgin huntress. As with his depiction of Venus, Virgil has given us a beautiful fraud; on the surface we see one picture, aesthetically pleasing, while the reality is far different.[43] Linking the two mendacious images are the pictures on the walls of the temple, which also, initially, seem to please Aeneas and give him cause for renewed hope, when in reality they celebrate the worst moments in Trojan history, and serve to glorify the goddess who so hates his people. Likewise, though we have been warned by the precautionary actions of Jupiter (and even of Venus) that the Carthaginians are potentially violent and dangerous to strangers, we have so far seen only the peaceful, even *Roman* (1.426 *sanctumque senatum*!) life of a new settlement. We now see something very different, something that accords with the darker side of Carthage. Dido, like Venus, is not what she seems; Diana has nothing to do with either of them. Camilla and the real Diana will balance this fakery in Book 11.[44] In Virgil's ethnography, then, Carthage is the land of deceit and perfidy; Italy is the homeland of truth and honor.

Suddenly, Aeneas and Achates, still cloaked in mist, see Antheus, Sergestus, Cloanthus, and the other Trojans they had feared lost in the storm. Their companions enter amid a great throng of Carthaginians, begging pardon; they are supplicants before the judgment seat of Dido. Ilioneus speaks for them. Apparently, they have beached their broken ships somewhere apart from Aeneas' seven, and in a less fortuitous place; the Carthaginians have fired their vessels. Ilioneus assures Dido that they have not come as invaders, but as a conquered people seeking a mysterious new home in the west, in Italy. Ilioneus explains how the sudden storm drove them to the African coast, and then asks what race could be so barbarous as to attack shipwrecked travelers and forbid their safe landing. Ilioneus does not know if his king Aeneas is still alive, but he promises that there is also the Trojan Acestes, a lord in Sicily, who would repay kind treatment of this exile band. Ilioneus closes his speech with an appeal that they be allowed to repair their fleet and set sail either for Italy or, if Aeneas and his son are truly dead, at least for Sicily and Acestes' lands.

Dido's reply, to be sure, is worthy of a noble queen. She argues that the fiery attack on the ships was necessitated by the circumstances of her young kingdom, which presumably needs to be on guard against possible invasion at a vulnerable moment in its development (though, arguably, a shipwrecked band of Trojans would be no obvious threat). Dido agrees to help them sail off either for Italy or Sicily, or, in a lavish promise, to let them settle in Carthage:

Tros Tyriusque mihi nullo discrimine agetur. (1.574)

Trojan and Tyrian will be managed by me with no distinction.

It is a sad line (in light of later Roman history), however oddly at variance with the demonstrated violent tendencies of her people; would a contemporary Roman, though, think of Cleopatra, eager to control (*agetur*) Romans? Dido wishes to see Aeneas, and promises to send scouts, at which point Achates eagerly remarks to Aeneas that everything is safe, just as Venus had foretold. The mist suddenly vanishes, and Aeneas is revealed in a state of divine beauty: his mother has enhanced his appearance.[45] The goddess of love and beauty cannot resist using her standard repertoire of tricks; already her natural inclinations are at play, and she is eager to make her son as physically appealing as possible, especially in the presence of the beautiful young widow. Aeneas' introductory words to Dido are no less ebullient than the queen's:

semper honos nomenque tuum laudesque manebunt,
quae me cumque vocant terrae. (1.609-610)

*Always your honor, and name, and praises will remain,
whatsoever the lands that call me.*

The promise will not be fulfilled.

Presents are sent to the shore, and preparations are made for a banquet.[46] Aeneas is thinking paternally (1.643-644 *patrius consistere mentem passus amor*), and he sends Achates out to bring Ascanius to the temple, now that he knows all is safe. Consistently thus far in the poem, Aeneas has been depicted as the man of fatherly *pietas*. His cognomen *pius*, as we shall see in his own recollection of the night Troy fell, was largely rooted in the great (and very Roman) image of his rescue of his father and son from the doomed city of Troy.[47] In this powerful triad we see the first notes of Virgil's overarching concern in the *Aeneid*: the problem of the Augustan succession. At the time the *Aeneid* was being written, Augustus had ended a century of civil war, and Rome could breathe more easily for the first time in many years. While maintaining a veneer of continuing Republican government, Augustus was firmly in charge of what was now a *de facto* monarchy. But in one crucial area he was to find failure: ensuring his succession. According to one tradition Aeneas, as we already know, will live only three years after where the end of Virgil's poem leaves off. But at least he would have Ascanius (who would rule another thirty years after his father's death). Augustus, in the end (after Virgil's own death) would live much longer than Aeneas. But he would have no Ascanius, as we shall see. For now, the succession theme is quietly introduced, in Virgil's customary subtle and painstaking manner:

omnis in Ascanio cari stat cura parentis. (1.646)[48]

Every concern of the dear parent was focused on Ascanius.

Connected to this theme of the succession is the theme of Madness, which we have been assured (by no less than Jupiter himself) will be chained up at some future point (i.e., the Augustan Peace). Indeed, in Virgil's own day there *was* peace—assuming Augustus himself remained benevolent (and this was by no means assured). But there was legitimate fear for the succession, the intense and profound fear that Madness would return. By the time Lucan would write what is, thematically, the sequel to the *Aeneid* (his *Bellum Civile*) the madness would have returned in the form of Nero. After Augustus' death, in fact, Rome would only have to wait twenty-three years to see a Caligula. Is Jupiter wrong, then? No, insofar as Jupiter is equal to Fate, and Fate can never be wrong. But "yes," if Lucretius, Virgil's poetic predecessor, was right and there are no gods, no Fate, no predestined future for people or nations, or at least no gods who care for our fate.[49]

Aeneas asks Achates to bring specific gifts back to Dido's court, in exchange for her generosity. One of the gifts is the covering Helen of Sparta wore when she sailed off to become Helen of Troy (1.649-652). Virgil lingers over its description lest we pass over it; Dido's gifts were the stock offerings of epic poetry, but Aeneas' have significance. We are reminded of the cause of the war at Troy; Aeneas may not appreciate the irony of its grim evocation of Helen.[50]

We have seen a strange dichotomy in Dido's new city, an unsettling mix of warm, indeed overly familiar, welcome juxtaposed with violent repulsion of the Trojan ships, unsatisfactorily explained as the tactic the Carthaginians are forced to employ against all newcomers, even the obviously weak and shipwrecked. Jupiter had softened their hearts (which would explain the reception we have just seen). Venus cannot help herself where sexual attraction is concerned, and she enhanced the beauty of her son before he met Dido. Venus had been calmed by her father's assurances, but her calm is short-lived. She now fears the perfidious Punic race:

> quippe domum timet ambiguam Tyriosque bilinguis,
> urit atrox Iuno et sub noctem cura recursat. (1.661-662)

> *Indeed, she fears the duplicitous house and the double-speaking Tyrians, terrible Juno burns her, and her anxiety recurs at nighttime.*

Part of the goddess' concern is the fact that Carthaginians cannot be trusted (Virgil's audience would appreciate this, of course), and Juno has been quiet for too long.[51] But there is also Venus' own nature. A creature of emotional intensity and sexual drive, she cannot remain calm and sedate for too long. Her concern is justified, as her father's actions have shown; Venus may be inclined to irrational fears, but Jupiter never is. Venus works with the tools of her trade. At this point in the narrative she decides that it would be better if Dido fell in love with Aeneas; her beautification of her son has already foreshadowed this next, fateful step. A rational thinker might point out any number of reasons why this decision of Venus is fraught with danger; then again, we are left with the impression that Dido might well not need Venus' help to fall madly in love and lust with her new visitor. At the very least, Venus' actions do not help the situation. In a strategic blunder that would make Juno proud, Book 1 closes as it began, with a goddess delaying Aeneas from his settlement in Italy. Juno comes out the wiser of the two divine women in this book; she wants Aeneas to get to Italy as slowly and torturously as possible, while Venus wants to see the happy settlement of her son. Venus' actions now do not serve that ultimate goal.

Venus summons her son Cupid, Aeneas' half-brother.[52] She cites Juno's hostile actions up to this point, and makes an interesting observation:

> nunc Phoenissa tenet Dido blandisque moratur
> vocibus, et vereor quo se Iunonia vertant
> hospitia; haud tanto cessabit cardine rerum. (1.670-672)

> *Now Phoenician Dido holds and delays him with enchanting words, and I am afraid to imagine where Juno's hospitality is leading; scarcely will she cease at so critical a moment.*

It is almost as if Venus credits Juno with Aeneas' warm reception in North Africa. Her words put Juno at the heart of Dido's actions, and her use of the adjective *blandis* is hardly complementary to Dido; neither is the verb *tenet*. Would a Roman audience have already begun to think of Mark Antony in the grip of Cleopatra's Egypt? Here, in Venus' misguided and unnecessary amatory attack on Dido, the reader is allowed to begin to form a personal response to Virgil's

Dido. Her life has been one of unquestioned difficulty thus far. She lost her husband violently and was forced to flee to a hostile land. She has successfully established a new city under the patronage of Juno. If she fell in love with Aeneas on her own, few today would condemn her, even if, as we shall learn later, she had pledged herself to the memory of a dead husband. Indeed, Virgil has drawn a sympathetic portrait thus far, one that has attracted many to the beautiful and vulnerable character he has crafted so carefully and with such heartfelt attention.

But what would a Roman audience of Virgil's own day think? She is Carthaginian. She is Cleopatra. If Virgil sought to present her positively, he set up a difficult task for himself. The ostensible cause for Roman-Carthaginian enmity will be the curse she invokes later in the poem, when Aeneas leaves her. But already the poet has defined the Carthaginians as violent; her gracious welcoming of the Trojans can be ascribed to *Jupiter*'s intervention (one of so many divine interventions at important junctures in the *Aeneid*). Venus shares her father's view of Carthaginians, and, as we have noted already, uses her specialty to overcome Carthaginian violence: Dido must *love* Aeneas, and quickly. Perhaps (probably?) it would have happened naturally, on its own. But Venus, impetuous, is impatient as well as worried:

> ... capere ante dolis
> ... ne quo se numine mutet. (1.673-674)

> *... to seize her first with trickery*
> *... lest she change herself through some divine agency.*

If Jupiter could change Punic hearts, so can Juno. So Venus *must* strike first. Her reasoning is logical, even if shortsighted. The prevention of one potential problem will cause numerous others.

Cupid is to impersonate Ascanius. Venus will secret her grandson away to Cythera, or perhaps Idalium. Virgil is careful even with seemingly unimportant details; Venus is not the sort of goddess who worries about the specifics of plans, anymore than she thinks through their likely consequences. Cupid does not speak, but silently obeys his mother's orders. Venus finally chooses Idalium for Ascanius' divinely inspired lengthy slumber.[53] Throughout this passage, Virgil makes sinister use of Latin's vocabulary of happiness. Dido is most happy (1.685 *laetissima*), Cupid steps lightly in his glad rejoicing (1.690 *gaudens*), the disguised Cupid is happy as he walks with Achates to Dido's temple (1.696 *laetus*). Indeed, *laetus* will recur as an important keyword in association with Dido much later in the poem.[54] Everyone is happy right now, but Venus should be fearful for the outcome of this scheme. Indeed, once the banquet begins and the god Cupid arrives, all is lost for Dido; she is now described quite differently, with no joyful associations:

> praecipue infelix, pesti devota futurae,
> expleri mentem nequit ardescit tuendo
> Phoenissa, et pariter puero donis movetur. (1.712-714)

> *And, in particular, the unlucky woman, now doomed to her future destruction, is not able to satisfy her mind, and the Phoenician woman burns just by looking at him, and she is moved both by the boy and the presents.*

Dido is moved both by Cupid and the gifts Aeneas had ordered brought to her court (which include the fateful veil Helen wore when she went to Troy with Paris). There is a touch of Virgil's authorial criticism of the female here; women are moved by presents, especially fine ones like Helen's *velamen*. This theme will recur in his study of a very different woman much later in the poem. It is another quiet, important detail; the gifts, in fact, move Dido just as much as the god Cupid; Venus cannot be blamed for everything.[55]

Dido calls for a heavy cup, inlaid with jewels and gilt, a cup that her father Belus and his ancestors before him had used. She invokes Jupiter, asking him to make this day happy (he already has, by his intervention); she calls on Bacchus and Juno, the first because she is taking a draught of wine, the latter because Juno is the special patroness of Carthage (there is also, perhaps, a faint foreshadowing of Juno as marriage patroness: the love between Aeneas and Dido is advancing). The queen offers a libation and takes her drink. She offers it to Bitias (otherwise unknown) and challenges him to drain it.[56]

Iopas, taught by Atlas himself, now sings an astronomical song.[57] Arcturus, that is, Boötes, the starry keeper of the Bear (*Ursa maior*), is the first subject of Iopas' song, and the implications are ominous; Arcturus' rising and setting were associated with storms. The book opened with one tempest, and at its end another is brewing. Iopas was taught by Atlas, and not surprisingly his next song is of the Hyades, the Rainy Ones, sisters of the Pleiades and daughters of Atlas; the song continues its stormy imagery. The Triones are next, that is, *Ursa maior* and *Ursa minor*. In myth they had their origin in the complex story of Callisto. We can be sure that Virgil had access to far more Callisto-lore than we possess; the most famous surviving version of her story is Ovid's, where Callisto was a companion of Diana (indeed, her favorite) who was raped by Jupiter; Diana had no tolerance for Callisto's involuntary loss of her virginity and subsequent pregnancy and banished her from her presence. She was changed by Juno's wrath into a bear; her own son, Arcas, would have killed her had Jupiter not intervened. The two celestial bears were compared to oxen yoked to a wagon, and so were called *triones*, which in Latin properly meant oxen plowing the land; there was some confusion, apparently, over whether Arcas was the Bear-watcher or the Lesser Bear.[58] Iopas was trained by Atlas; when Jupiter sends Mercury later in the poem to warn Aeneas that he must leave Dido's Carthage (4.238-251), Mercury will catch sight of Atlas as he wings his way down to North Africa: the ring started here will be complete.

Iopas' song is not simply a learned, indeed Hellenistic or Alexandrian adornment to Dido's banquet. Nor is Iopas merely present to satisfy the Homeric precedent of having a singer at a banquet (e.g., Demodocus in Book 8 of the *Odyssey* with his celebrated account of Ares and Aphrodite). On the simplest level, Iopas' song portends the storm that will soon engulf Dido and Aeneas. Further, the song's scientific concerns (why are the winter days short and summer days long?) are reminiscent of Lucretius, Virgil's Roman poetic master.[59] But on another level, Virgil has ringed his description of Dido with two allusions to Diana. The first, as we observed above, was striking and unmistakable; it was also inappropriate for a description of Dido. The second, Iopas' allusion to the myth of Callisto, is more subtle, like all of the dark undertones to this ostensibly happy banquet. Callisto was driven from Diana's presence through no fault of her own; Dido too will give up any Diana-like lifestyle she may be living. In one sense, the reason for this loss of the Diana-like mode of living is the trickery of Venus. But, in another sense, Dido was never Diana-like; the *sine qua non* for Diana's patronage is virginity. Diana is a patroness of young girls; a married woman, even made a widow, cannot be a suitable devotee of the virgin goddess of the hunt. These themes will recur in the poem, most dramatically in Virgil's introduction of the Diana and Camilla story in Book 11. For the present, at the very least the Diana-frame to the Dido story in Book 1 gives the narrative of Aeneas' reception in North Africa a disquieting tone. All is not as it seems (and we know this because we can assume that Dido's pleasant welcome to Aeneas is the result of Jupiter's softening of the Carthaginians' hearts). Punic emotions, Cupid-as-Ascanius, and Dido's Diana-like description all help to build up an atmosphere of sinister foreboding and nervous tension.

Dido asks Aeneas about the war at Troy. She asks about Priam, Hector, Memnon, Diomedes, and Achilles; significantly, all of this is lore she already knows, as her paintings in the temple prove.[60] She is already madly in love with Aeneas:

infelix Dido longumque bibebat amorem. (1.749)

Unlucky Dido was drinking deep of love.

She does not know of his adventures on Troy's last night, and certainly does not know of the adventures he and his men experienced after their flight from the city; in this regard he will complete her temple's artwork. Her only reliable source of information had been Teucer, the half-Greek, half-Trojan son of Ajax's father Telamon and the war bride Hesione, daughter of Priam. Now she will hear from a great Trojan hero about what happened on that fateful night. She knows that it has been seven years since the city fell (1.755-756). Her comment about the year has bothered critics; in Book 5 (626) Iris, in the disguise of a Trojan woman at the behest of Juno, will mention (inconsistently) that it is now the seventh year after the destruction of Troy. After all, the *Aeneid* was left unrevised.[61]

So ends the first book of Virgil's epic. We are left knowing that Aeneas will now tell the background story that we crave along with Dido; Homer had left the story of Troy's fall to other poets, and now Virgil will complete the tale. Book 1 has accomplished its main goal of introducing the major themes of the entire epic; for the next two books the action of the present will be suspended as we hear of the near-legendary past. As the first book ends, the reader is left with no reasonable doubt that the situation between Dido and Aeneas will end badly. Virgil introduced Aeneas to us on the deck of his flagship, his limbs shaken by fear on account of Juno's storm; as the first book ends, Aeneas is in the position of war-weary veteran, urged by his dinner companions to recount his martial adventures. The first third of the poem is dominated by Aeneas' relationship with Dido; even the lengthy digression of the second and third books is situated within the overshadowing context of Dido's banquet. We shall learn much about Aeneas and his character in the next two books, but only at table with Dido and her court. Augustus had easily ignored the allure of Cleopatra; Aeneas at Carthage reminds us of Antony at Alexandria, far more than he evokes any image of Octavian in the crucible of Cleopatra's seductive charms during his campaigns in the East.

Virgil did not have to put such emphasis on the role of Dido in the foundation legends of Rome. Gnaeus Naevius, the Campanian poet of the third century B.C., wrote a poem in the Saturnian meter on the First Punic War (264-241 B.C.).[62] It was circulating in Virgil's day; the date and reason for its eventual loss is unknown, and it survives only in the slenderest fragments. Macrobius (fifth century A.D.) claims in his *Saturnalia* (6.2.31) that entire passages from the *Aeneid* were lifted from Naevius. Whether Aeneas even landed in Carthage, let alone had a love affair with Dido (or her sister, Anna), is unclear from what little survives of Naevius. But neither Livy, as we have observed, nor Dionysius of Halicarnassus, working at almost the same time as Virgil, give Aeneas a Carthaginian sojourn. Indeed, Macrobius also notes that the story of Dido and Aeneas is a lie that the *Aeneid* managed to foist successfully on the world (5.17.5)—a wonderful expansion, if true, of the mendacious atmosphere that surrounds Carthage in Book 1. Odysseus had been delayed by the immortal Calypso, but the tragedy of Dido and Aeneas trumps Homer's ultimately insignificant (in the sense that it has no lasting consequences) and episodic delay in his hero's homecoming. We are left to wonder why Virgil felt the need to let the Dido and Aeneas love story occupy so much of his poem, and at its very beginning, so that we get to know his hero almost as if at Dido's side; we learn of him together with her, and form long-lasting images of his character from his experiences with her, especially in Book 4. And, further, the Roman audience of Virgil's day would have the fresh memory of Antony and Cleopatra and the tragic results their love affair had brought to Rome.

So if Aeneas were supposed to evoke Augustus (which would be neat and understandable), Virgil has taken a circuitous and strange route to his goal. Those who would wish to link Aeneas with Augustus at this point in the poem have a difficult task; the ambiguity of Jupiter's prophecy earlier in this book (who is the Julius?) has now been embodied by Aeneas: he reminds us of Mark Antony or Julius Caesar at Cleopatra's court far more than he evokes Augustus. For the moment, deep in the heart of Dido's Carthage, we are quite far from

Italy and Rome. Juno is no doubt happy, just as she will be at the end of Book 12, though for very different reasons.

Notes

1. We know that the opening *Arma Virumque Cano* (v = u) is an acrostic for *Ab Urbe Condita* and even Augustus (c and g are equivalent letters), thanks to the brilliant observation of FROESCH, "*Arma virumque cano.* Beobachtungen zu Eingangsworten der *Aeneis,*" *Anregung* 31 (1991), pp.309-312.

2. It is true that there was epic precedent for Virgil to use a first person singular (cf. the opening of the *Ilias Parva*), but the *Aeneid*'s clear binary structure most directly responds to Homer's *Iliad* and *Odyssey*, which open with imperatives addressed to the Muse, not first person declarations by the poet. The "Little Iliad" included some of the material Virgil covers in his Fall of Troy narrative in Book 2. See further M.L. WEST, *Greek Epic Fragments*, Cambridge, Massachusetts, 2003, and DAVIES, *The Epic Cycle*, London, 1989. It is possible that the first three words of the *Aeneid* challenge the entire tradition of epic poetry surrounding the Trojan War. But even in Virgil's own day, no one fancied Arctinus a Homer.

3. On Juno in the *Aeneid* see further BAILEY, *Religion in Vergil*, Oxford, 1935, pp. 129-132. On the gods in general in the *Aeneid* FEENEY, *The Gods in Epic: Poets and Critics of the Classical Tradition*, Oxford, 1991, is essential reading; note also COLEMAN, "The Gods in the *Aeneid,*" *Greece and Rome* 29 (1982), pp. 143-168, and WILLIAMS, *Technique and Ideas in the Aeneid*, New Haven, 1983, pp. 17-39. One of the most important debates on Virgil's immortals are whether or not they are mere literary tropes—in other words, did a god really toss Palinurus off Aeneas' flagship, or did he merely fall asleep? Feeney neatly demolishes the whole idea of allegorical tropes.

4. Virgil no doubt would have wanted his completed, published epic to be read in linear fashion, but we also know that he probably did not write the poem in such a straightforward way. Instead, he worked on separate sections as he wished, not composing everything in order, and sometimes soliciting advice from small audiences of invited guests at difficult or vexing points. Related to these general remarks on Virgil's method of composition is the report (Donatus, Servius) that "our" Book 1 was not actually the *original* Book 1. The poem opens, after all, in what has been called *in medias res,* "in the middle of the action," with the announcement of Juno's wrath and its devastating consequences for the sea-bound Trojans. The testimony of Aelius Donatus (the fourth century A.D. grammarian and teacher of Saint Jerome) in "his" ancient life (almost certainly Suetonian) is that our Book 1 was originally the third book, giving an order of Book 2, Book 3, Book 1, and Book 4. We have no way of knowing if the story is true, though there is no good reason for it to have been invented after Virgil's death; in any case, we can be certain that Virgil eventually decided that the books should stand in their present order. The framing of the story of Troy's fall and the subsequent wanderings in the Mediterranean with the tragedy of Dido creates a beautiful unity for Books 1-4, the poem's first third. We have noted that the second half of the poem has often been neglected, and that Virgil himself recognizes a twofold division for his poem. But there are other patterns. Books 1-4, 5-8, and 9-12 will also form neat units, as we shall see. Less neatly, but still perceptibly, there are affinities between the odd and even numbered books, and even between the "penultimate" books, 5 and 11, and the ultimate books, 6 and 12. Contiguous books of the *Aeneid* tend to be closely linked as well. The effect of these affinities is to provide a remarkable coherence and tightly constructed unity to the poem. Virgil is a master of using even the most seemingly minor episodes to provide dramatic foreshadowing of major events; the minor episode casts its spell over the major and the reader's interpretation is thereby seemingly effortlessly manipulated by the poet

magician. See further DUCKWORTH, "The *Aeneid* as a Trilogy," *Transactions of the American Philological Association* 88 (1957), pp. 17-30, and especially HARRISON, "The Structure of the *Aeneid*: Observations on the Links between the Books," *Aufstieg und Niedergang der Römischen Welt* II.31.1 (1980), pp. 359-393. Note also KEHOE, "Was Book 5 once in a Different Place in the *Aeneid*?," *The American Journal of Philology* 110 (1989), pp. 246-263.

5. For Lucretius' theology, see further BAILEY, *Lucretius De Rerum Natura* (3 vols.), Oxford, 1947, pp. 66-72.

6. Interestingly, there is an ancient controversy over the opening of the *Aeneid*. Both "Donatus'" life and Servius' commentary tell us that Virgil's literary executors removed the original opening of the poem:

ille ego, qui quondam gracili modulatus avena
carmen, et egressus silvis vicina coegi
ut quamvis avido parerent arva colono,
gratum opus agricolis, at nunc horrentia Martis
arma virumque cano

I am that one, who once turned my song on the graceful
reed, and, having left the woods, next I compelled the
neighboring fields to obey their tiller, though he be greedy,
a work pleasing to farmers, but now of Mars' bristling
arms and the man I sing

The lines, whatever their provenance, give a literary biography for Virgil, author of the *Eclogues* and the *Georgics*. Hirtzel was willing to print them in his 1900 Oxford Classical Text; by 1969 Mynors was unwilling even to mention them in his apparatus, and indeed no modern editor prints them. At least in comparison to the *Iliad* and the *Odyssey*, Virgil's epic opens with an intensely personal *cano*, which these lines amplify; they also offer some explanation for the ambiguous *arma* with which the poem opens; the Iliadic wrath of Achilles is here replaced explicitly by the war in Italy between Aeneas and Turnus. As Servius observed, many contemporary students of the *Aeneid* wondered why the poem begins with *arma*, for the reasons we have already noted; James Henry was bothered enough by the abrupt beginning of the poem to write many pages defending these four introductory, explanatory lines. The question of their authenticity cannot be definitely solved; for the main arguments see further AUSTIN, *P. Vergili Maronis Aeneidos Liber Primus*, Oxford, 1971, pp. 25-27; note also KENNEY, "That Incomparable Poem the *Ille Ego*?," *The Classical Review* N.S. 20.3 (1970), p. 290. As with the infamous Helen passage in Book 2, these lines ultimately occasion the question of who wrote them, if not Virgil? Once Virgil's authorship is acknowledged, their existence becomes a moot point in light of what we know to be the unrevised nature of the poem. Among the many reasons Austin and others offer against them, I would add that *arma* works better if left less precisely defined. See also THEODOROKOPOULOS, "Closure: The Book of Virgil," in MARTINDALE, ed., *The Cambridge Companion to Virgil*, Cambridge, 1997, pp. 160-162.

7. Virgil's geography seems vague, as we end up moving from Sicily to North Africa rather abruptly; see further BLEISCH, "Altars Altered: The Alexandrian Tradition of Etymological Wordplay in *Aeneid* 1.108-112," *The American Journal of Philology* 119 (1998), pp. 599-606, and O'HARA, "Callimachean Influence on Vergilian Etymological Wordplay," *The Classical Journal* 96.4 (2001), pp. 370-372.

8. On Neptune in the *Aeneid* see further Bailey, *Religion in Virgil*, Oxford, 1935, pp. 118-121.

9. The winds, of course, are literally enclosed: *clauso ventorum carcere*: syntactic enactment.

10. 1.150, 1.294, 1.348, 2.244, 2.316, 2.355, 4.91, 4.101, 4.333, 4.501, 4.697, 5.659, 5.670, 5.801, 6.102, 7.386, 7.406, 9.760, 10.63, 10.905, 12.601, 12.680 and 12.832: most frequently in Book 4, not surprisingly, and not at all in the quietly reflective Books 3 and 8.

11. On the poem's first simile see further HORNSBY, *Patterns of Action in the Aeneid: An Interpretation of Vergil's Epic Similes*, Iowa, 1970, pp. 20-21, and, on Virgilian similes in general, ROSS, "The Similes of Virgil's *Aeneid*," *Classicum* 33 (1997), pp. 22-29.

12. See further STALEY, "Aeneas' First Act," *Classical World* 84.1 (1990), pp. 25-38. Staley sees much symbolism in Aeneas' stag hunt; just as the death of Sylvia's stag will bring chaos to Latium, so the killing of the stags here is a precursor of the violence between Rome and Carthage: overly subtle, but perhaps right.

13. On Jupiter in the *Aeneid* see further HEINZE, *Virgil's Epic Technique* (trans. Harvey and Robertson), Berkeley-Los Angeles, 1993, pp. 236 ff., POSCHL, *The Art of Vergil: Image and Symbol in the Aeneid* (trans. Seligson), Ann Arbor, 1962, pp. 16-17, and Bailey, *op. cit.*, pp. 132-143.

14. On Venus in the *Aeneid* see further Heinze, *op. cit.*, pp. 27 ff. and 378 ff., Bailey, *op. cit.*, pp. 126-129, and Wlosok, *Die Göttin Venus in Vergilis Aeneis*, Heidelberg, 1967.

15. Antenor is largely irrelevant to the *Aeneid*; he plays no role in its action in Italy. Aeneas was not, strictly speaking, the *first* to arrive in Italy from Troy; Virgil's *primus* at the opening of the poem must refer to the ultimately unimportant settlement of Antenor; Aeneas was the first Trojan whose coming to Italy meant anything. But the character is problematic. There was a tradition that Antenor survived the fall of Troy because he helped betray it to the Greeks (Aeneas himself would not be spared this accusation).

16. On the tradition of Aeneas' death and the Augustan poets' response to it, see KEPPLE, "Arruns and the Death of Aeneas," *The American Journal of Philology* 97 (1976), pp. 344-360, especially pp. 358 ff., and NADEAU, "The Death of Aeneas: Vergil's Version (and Ovid's): An Insight into the Politics of Vergil's Poetry," *Latomus* 59 (2000), pp. 289-316. In Dionysius of Halicarnassus (1.64), after three years in power Aeneas' body vanishes during a resurgence of conflict with the Rutulians; some, Dionysius reports, assumed the gods had taken him up to heaven, while others felt the body had been lost in the River Numicius. In Livy (*Ab Urbe Condita* 1.2) his end is even more mysterious (there is no real explanation of his death). But Livy also connects the location of his death/burial with the Numicius. Virgil does not clearly define Aeneas' future; 6.764 *tibi longaevo*, of Aeneas' age when Lavinia bears him Silvius, seems to imply a long life beyond the narrative of the *Aeneid*.

17. Virgil says that Ascanius, "to whom know the cognomen Iulus has been given," will rule at Alba Longa for thirty years; he was called "Ilus" ("the Trojan") while Troy still stood. It is entirely unclear where and when Aeneas' son acquired multiple names, but the mention of Iulus and *cognomen* emphasizes the origin of the Julian *gens*. See further Austin on 2.563. Virgil is not forthcoming with allusions to the tradition that Aeneas died in battle at the Numicius, a stream near the Tiber (see, e.g., Livy *Ab Urbe Condita* 1.2.6).

18. The poem's proem had showcased the "Alban Fathers" (1.7). Ascanius was the traditional founder of Alba Longa, which was apparently located near the current papal summer residence at Castel Gandolfo. The line of Alban kings was marred, not

surprisingly, by civil strife between Numitor and his brother Amulius. Numitor's daughter was Rhea Silvia, who was forced into Vestal virginity by Amulius to prevent avenging offspring. The twins Romulus and Remus were sired by Mars, and eventually restored Numitor to his rightful throne. Rome was then founded as a separate city with a settlement on the Palatine Hill.

19. On Mars in the *Aeneid* see further Bailey, *op. cit.*, pp. 109-117.

20. See further HERSHKOWITZ, *The Madness of Epic*, Oxford, 1998, p. 122, and INDELLI, "The Vocabulary of Anger," in ARMSTRONG et al., *Vergil, Philodemus, and the Augustans*, Austin, 2004, pp. 103-110. Indelli is right that *violentia* is applied only to Turnus in the *Aeneid* (10.151-152), not Aeneas. But the reader is left at the end of Book 12 with the vision of the mad Aeneas taking his vengeance on Pallas' killer—not on one word two books before.

21. *Inter alios*, see GRIEBE, "Augustus' Divine Authority and Vergil's *Aeneid*," *Vergilius* 50 (2004), pp. 35-62, especially pp. 47-49.

22. See further Suetonius *Divus Iulius* 83 (with Butler and Cary's note), and, on Octavian's probable appointment as *magister equitum*, Dio 43.51.7. Caesar's son by Cleopatra, Caesarion, did not appear in the will; see also CROOK, LINTOTT, and RAWSON, eds., *The Cambridge Ancient History IX: The Last Age of the Roman Republic: 146-43 B.C.*, Cambridge, 1994, p. 466.

23. For enthusiastic argument that Virgil is referencing Julius, not Augustus, see DOBBIN, "Julius Caesar in Jupiter's Prophecy, *Aeneid* 1," *Classical Antiquity* 14 (1995), pp. 5-41. For the opposite view, see KRAGGERUD, "Which Julius Caesar? On *Aen.* 1.286-296," *Symbolae Osloenses* 67 (1992), pp. 103-112. But Virgil's ambiguity must stand.

24. See further LUCE, "The Dating of Livy's First Decade," *Transactions of the American Philological Association* 96 (1965), pp. 209-240.

25. On Mercury in the *Aeneid* see further Bailey, *op. cit.*, pp. 117-118.

26. On the introduction of Dido here see FARRON, *Vergil's Æneid: A Poem of Grief and Love*, Leiden-New York-Cologne, 1993, p. 132.

27. On Diana in the *Aeneid* see further Bailey, *op. cit.*, pp. 157-162, and FRATANTUONO, "Diana in the *Aeneid*," *The New England Classical Journal* (2005), pp. 101-115; see also WILHELM, M.P., "Venus, Diana, Dido and Camilla in the *Aeneid*," *Vergilius* 33 (1987), pp. 43-38, and DE GRUMMOND, "The Diana Experience: A Study of the Victims of Diana in Virgil's *Aeneid*," *Collection Latomus: Studies in Latin Literature and History* VIII (1997), pp. 158-194. Virgil starts his examination of these opposite female types (both immortal and mortal) very early in the poem. His sympathies, one grows to suspect, are with Diana and Camilla (at least in light of Rome's Italian future), despite a very sympathetic treatment of Dido. For the work of Julia Dyson on Diana *Nemorensis*, her cult at Aricia, and the implications of her rites for the poem's climax, see my note below on Turnus' death scene. Better is GREEN, "The Slayer and the King: *Rex Nemorensis* and the Sanctuary of Diana," *Arion* Ser. 3.7 (2000), pp. 24-63; note also PASCAL, "*Rex Nemorensis*," *Numen* 23.1 (1976), pp. 23-39.

28. Foundational is ARRIGONI, *Camilla: Amazzone e Sacerdotessa di Diana*, Milan, 1982, pp. 16-19; note also ANDERSON, "Venus and Aeneas: The Difficulties of Filial Pietas," *The Classical Journal* 50.5 (1955), pp. 233-238. Just as there appear to have been two Atalantas, so there seem to have been two (if not more!) Harpalyces; what these stories all have in common is not so much confusion over different female characters as the portrayal of conflicted adolescent females—what may have been genuine mythological confusion serves the author's purpose in presenting his characters. On Parthenius of Nicaea's account of the "other" (non-Virgilian) Harpalyce, a victim of

incest and bird-metamorphosis, see LIGHTFOOT, *Parthenius of Nicaea*, Oxford, 1999, pp. 446-451. Besides Virgil, we are reliant on the mythographer Hyginus *Fabulae* 193 for any further mention of the *huntress* Harpalyce; Hyginus adds the detail that Neoptolemus, the son of Achilles, attacked Harpalycus and was driven off by the young Harpalyce (perhaps inspired by the tradition of how Penthesilea had fought Achilles and been killed—the son had less luck against the Amazonian). Virgil uses these different traditions to great effect in his depiction of Camilla, who operates simultaneously in different worlds. It seems highly unlikely that Virgil invented either the huntress Harpalyce or Camilla; he has rather melded diverse material to create a complex composite. On the possible lycanthropy of Harpalyce and Camilla the commentators seem to have been asleep. Is there a hint of incest in the stories of all of these troubled girls? Where did Hyginus get the detail about Neoptolemus' encounter with Harpalyce? Was he really just imitating the Achilles-Penthesilea story?

29. The introduction of Harpalyce here as precursor of Camilla is an outstanding example of Virgil's love of anticipatory craftsmanship and his expectation that his readers have good memories; see further Williams, *op. cit.*, pp. 67-75.

30. Virgil's Diana is not Homer's Artemis with respect to her loyalties; cf. *Iliad* 5.447-448, where Artemis helps heal Aeneas after his encounter with Diomedes, and especially 21.470 ff., the comic scene of Hera boxing Artemis' ears. In Virgil, Diana's main concern will be Camilla (to whom she has a loyalty that transcends any concerns about Trojans or Italians).

31. There was a tradition that he was Dido's uncle (Justin "Trogus" 18.4.5); Virgil is silent on the "repugnant detail" (AUSTIN, *P. Vergili Maronis Aeneidos Liber Primus*, Oxford, 1971, p. xvii).

32. Less likely is that Venus cannot stand seeing her son aggrieved (so Austin ad loc.); her mood in this passage is one of lighthearted whimsy, not maternal sympathy.

33. See further HARDIE, "Aeneas and the Omen of the Swans," *Classical Philology* 83 (1988), pp. 195-205.

34. On Aeneas' *pietas* see JOHNSTON, "Piety in Vergil and Philodemus," in Armstrong et al., *op. cit*, Austin, 2004, pp. 163-165, and, more generally, BOYANCE, *La Religion de Virgile*, Paris, 1963, pp. 58-82, and GALINSKY, *Aeneas, Sicily, and Rome*, Princeton, 1969, pp. 3-62, with reference both to literature and art. Boyancé remains the finest single treatment of religion in Virgil.

35. The simile (1.430-436) is practically lifted from *Georgics* 4.162-169; see further Hornsby, *op. cit.*, pp. 48-49.

36. See further BRIGAZZI, "Verg., *Aen.* 1.462 *sunt lacrimae rerum*," *Prometheus* 12 (1986), pp. 57-71; he thinks the tears are in the painting.

37. Three? *Seven*? See further below on the *septima aestas*.

38. On Pallas Athena/Minerva in the *Aeneid*, see further Bailey, *op. cit.*, pp. 152-157, and WILHELM, M.P., "Minerva in the *Aeneid*," in WILHELM, R.M., and JONES, *The Two Worlds of the Poet: New Perspectives on Vergil*, Detroit, 1992, pp. 74-81.

39. Virgil is reticent about Aeneas' depiction in the picture; was it the scene from *Iliad* 5 of Diomedes nearly killing him, and Apollo shielding him from harm? In any case, Virgil will evoke the bad luck of Achilles vs. Diomedes later in the poem.

40. On the pictures in Dido's temple, see further WILLIAMS, "The Pictures on Dido's Temple," *The Classical Quarterly* NS 10 (1960), pp. 145-151, reprinted in HARRISON, *Oxford Readings in Vergil's Aeneid*, Oxford, 1990, pp. 37-45, CLAY, "The Archaeology of the Temple to Juno in Carthage," *Classical Philology* 83 (1988), pp. 195-205, LOWENSTAM, "The Pictures on Juno's Temple in the *Aeneid*," *Classical World* 87.2 (1993), pp. 37-49, and BOYD, "*Non Enarrabile Textum*: Ecphrastic Trespass and

Narrative Ambiguity in the *Aeneid*," *Vergilius* 41 (1995), pp. 71-92, especially pp. 76-79. Lowenstam and others argue that Virgil is not explicit about whether these are paintings or sculptures, but Virgil's *pictura* leans heavily toward painting. For sympathetic commentary on Aeneas' Book 1 adventures in Carthage, see CONSTANS, *L'Enéide de Virgile*, Paris, 1938, pp. 54-70.

41. On this simile see further Hornsby, *op. cit.*, pp. 8 and 89, PIGON, "Dido, Diana, and Penthesilea: Observations on the Queen's First Appearance in the *Aeneid*," *Eos* 79 (1991), pp. 45-53, and POLK, "Vergil's Penelope: The Diana Simile in *Aeneid* 1.498-502," *Vergilius* 42 (1996), pp. 38-49.

42. On the Homeric simile see GARVIE, *Homer: Odyssey VI-VIII*, Cambridge, 1994, p. 107.

43. Williams ad loc. argues that Virgil is depicting Dido "most sympathetically" here with his comparison to Diana. But, as so often in Virgil, the beauty of the verse and the perfection of the images the lines fashion must not blind us to their contextual realities. The great poet does not carelessly insert similes. This use of exquisite poetic art to express disquieting realities is a technique Virgil borrowed from his beloved Lucretius, who used beautiful poetry to teach the difficult, often grim truths of Epicureanism.

44. Both Dido and Camilla were a major inspiration for imitators of Virgil; for Dido's *Nachleben* see especially DESMOND, *Reading Dido: Gender, Textuality, and the Medieval Aeneid*, Minneapolis-New York, 1994.

45. On the similes describing Aeneas' beautification see Hornsby, *op.cit.*, pp. 93 and 103.

46. Line 636, *munera laetitiam dii*, is the first half-line in the poem, on all of which see further SPARROW, *Half-Lines and Repetitions in Virgil*, Oxford, 1931, and WALTER, *Die Entstehung der Halbverse in der Aeneis*, Giessen, 1933; for a more modern appraisal, see BALDWIN, "Half-Lines in Virgil: Old and New Ideas," *Symbolae Osloenses* 68 (1993), pp. 144-151. Most probably this line is an imperfectly finished stopgap; *dei* (for Bacchus) perhaps gives the best sense, but we cannot be sure, and the ancient critics may be right to take *dii* as genitive of *dies*, with the whole line standing in apposition to the preceding description of bulls, lambs, and ewes.

47. On Virgilian *pietas* see HANDS, *Charities and Social Aid in Greece and Rome*, Ithaca, 1968, pp. 87 and 112.

48. Venus echoes the same sentiment herself when she sends Cupid to impersonate Ascanius, whom she calls *mea maxima cura* (1.678).

49. See also Hershkowitz, *op. cit.*, pp. 68-124. Hershkowitz argues that Juno turns the *Aeneid* from a Jovian poem of *fata* to a Junonian poem of *furor*. But Virgil's point is that Rome's *fatum* is *furor*. Her conclusion that Aeneas and Turnus present a sane/mad dichotomy is also not without difficulties. For a comprehensive and superlative study of the issues of family and inheritance under Augustus, see SEVERY, *Augustus and the Family at the Birth of the Roman Empire*, New York-London, 2003.

50. So Austin notes, who correctly observes that the garment has "an ominous association." Presumably Aeneas does not reveal the veil's provenance.

51. On the perfidy of the Carthaginians, and Dido herself, see STARKS, "*Fides Aeneia*: The Transference of Punic Stereotypes in the *Aeneid*," *The Classical Journal* 94.3 (1999), pp. 255-281.

52. The best commentary on Venus' manipulations of Dido in *Aeneid* 1 is KHAN, "The Boy at the Banquet: Dido and Amor in Vergil, *Aen.* 1," *Athenaeum* 90 (2002), pp. 187-205.

53. Venus does not want Ascanius to show up suddenly and spoil the deceit (1.682 *mediusve occurrere possit*), but she also does not want him to know about her trick

(1.682 *ne qua scire dolos*). Partly this is simply so he does not ruin the trick, but perhaps there is also a shade of the idea that the ultimate hope of the race should not be sullied with knowledge of his grandmother's duplicitous nature. Aeneas knows it; we have already heard from his own words that his mother likes to trick him with disguises; Ascanius is to be spared the experience of his grandmother's mendacious games. The theme is folkloric; so Solomon will build the temple, because David has too much blood on his hands, and Joshua will lead the Israelites into the land of promise, because Moses was disobedient but once; cf. 2.717-720.

54. Cf. also 1.732 *laetum* and 1.734 *laetitiae dator*.

55. Austin ad loc. argues incorrectly that the boy is named first because "he is more important than any of the gifts." The crucial word is *pariter*.

56. Servius identifies Bitias as a Carthaginian naval commander, and Iopas, her bard (1.740-741), as an African king and suitor of Dido (but he may actually be talking about Iarbas, whom we shall meet in Book 4). For the amusing nature of this scene, see LLOYD, "Humor in the *Aeneid*," *The Classical Journal* 72.3 (1977), pp. 250-257, especially pp. 253-254. Not all of Lloyd's scenes are as amusing, however, as his article argues.

57. See further BROWN, "The Structural Function of the Song of Iopas," *Harvard Studies in Classical Philology* 93 (1990), pp. 315-334, LITTLE, "The Song of Iopas: Aeneid 1.740-746," *Prudentia* 24 (1992), pp. 16-36, and BROWN, "The Homeric Background to a Vergilian Repetition," *The American Journal of Philology* 111 (1990), pp. 182-186. *Contra* Brown see HANNAH, "The Stars of Iopas and Palinurus," *The American Journal of Philology* 114 (1993), pp. 123-125. Was Iopas from Joppa?

58. Virgil also alludes to the story in the *Georgics* (1.138 *Pleiades, Hyadas, claramque Lycaonis Arcton*); Arcturus is the brightest star in Boötes. Ovid has two accounts of the myth (*Metamorphoses* 2.405 ff. and *Fasti* 2.155 ff.). In the *Metamorphoses*, Callisto is tricked by Jupiter, who disguises himself as Diana. The son, Arcas, is snatched up with his mother to heaven, where they begin their lives as constellations, the *Triones* who are not allowed to dip below the horizon into the ocean at the command of Juno. In the *Fasti*, for 11 February Ovid points out the constellations *Ursa Maior* and *Arctophylax*, "the Guardian of the Bear," also known as Boötes, and tells the same story; Arcas was changed into the constellation at the moment he would have slain his mother. Ovid, therefore, reflects the astronomical confusion over just who Arcas was; in the *Metamorphoses* he and his mother are the plough-oxen, while in the *Fasti* he is the Bear-watcher. In Book 3 of the *Aeneid* (516-517), Aeneas' helmsman Palinurus sees the Triones and Orion; Virgil seems to have thought that the Triones were Callisto and her son, while Boötes was Orion. On Callisto/*Ursa maior* as star guide, cf. Propertius *carmen* 2.28a 23-24 *Callisto Arcadios erraverat ursa per agros: / haec nocturna suo sidere vela regit*, with Enk's notes.

59. The passage directly echoes *Georgics* 2.475-482 and 490:

> me vero primum dulces ante omnia Musae,
> quarum sacra fero ingenti percussus amore,
> accipiant caelique vias et sidera monstrent,
> defectus solis varios lunaeque labores;
> unde tremor terris, qua via maria alta tumescent
> obicibus ruptis rursuque in se ipsa resident,
> quid tantum Oceano properent se tinguere soles
> hiberni, vel quae tardis mora noctibus obstet.

But first may the Muses, who are sweet before all else,

whose sacred things I bear (struck as I am with great love for them),
accept me, and show me the ways of heaven and the stars,
the different eclipses of the sun and labors of the moon,
whence there are tremors on land and in what way the deep seas swell
with their barriers broken and again sink back on themselves,
why winter suns hurry so fast to dip themselves in the Ocean,
or what delay obstructs the slow nights.

felix qui potuit rerum cognoscere causas.

Happy is he who was able to understand the nature of things.

Virgil has ended Book 1 of his epic with a direct allusion to his tribute to Lucretius in the *Georgics*. On the one hand, this is an act of homage to the Latin poet for whom he felt the greatest affinity; on the other hand, it expresses the attitude of Virgil the scientist, who explores in the verses of the *Aeneid* the nature of the Augustan principate. Virgil will return to Lucretius, at the crucial midpoint of his epic, where the themes of the Augustan succession and the Lucretian view of the universe will return.

60. Servius ponders what Virgil meant by the *Diomedis equi* here. On the one hand, as the murals in the temple depicted, Diomedes took the horses of Rhesus before they could eat of Trojan grass. On the other hand, Diomedes took horses from Aeneas himself (*Iliad* 5.251-351) after seriously, indeed almost fatally, wounding him; Aphrodite had to come and help her son. After she was wounded by Diomedes and dropped Aeneas, Apollo saved him. The passage illustrates how difficult it is to make Trojan War allusions without recalling less than glorious moments for the Trojan Aeneas; surely the very painting of Diomedes reminded Aeneas of his nearly fatal encounter with the Greek warrior. Small wonder the Latins will try to secure an alliance with Diomedes in Book 11.

61. For thoughts on the "seventh summer" inconsistency, see DYSON, "Septima Aestas: The Puzzle of *Aen*. 1.755-6 and 5.626," *The Classical World* 90.1 (1996), pp. 41-43.

62. KENNEY and CLAUSEN, eds., *The Cambridge History of Classical Literature, Volume II Part I: The Early Republic*, Cambridge, 1982, pp. 59-60.

CHAPTER II

ALL FELL SILENT

Books 2 and 3 form a cohesive whole; the opening line of Book 2, *conticuere omnes*, forms a ring with the closing line of Book 3, *conticuit tandem*; we move from the silence of the Trojan-Carthaginian audience as Aeneas begins his lengthy account of his adventures to the silence of Aeneas once he finishes his reminiscences of the last several years. Book 2 is full of incident and action; indeed, the even-numbered books of the *Aeneid* have a well-deserved reputation for their emotional intensity. All moderns are indebted to Virgil for what has become the definitive account of the fall of Troy. The same ground would be covered in even more detail by the imperial Greek poet Quintus of Smyrna in his (*circa* third century A.D.) *Posthomerica*, itself most probably heavily indebted to *Aeneid* 2, but it is Virgil whose poetic vision has remained the memorable norm for the story of Troy's *Götterdämmerung*. As we have noted, in a very real sense Aeneas here finishes the rest of the portraits for Dido's temple to Juno. Book 2 was not one of the books Virgil himself is said to have read for Augustus (it shows telltale signs of rough and unfinished composition); in any case, the book has had a long history down to the modern age as one of the most popular in the epic. In some ways, it has been *too* successful in its power and vivid descriptive force; many a class of young Latinists has labored over the vocabulary and syntax of Virgil's splendid description of the death of Laocoon and his sons, perhaps at the expense of appreciating the overall context of the book's powerful imagery. All are indeed silent, and will remain silent for two books; it is important to remember that it is Aeneas alone who tells the story of these events.[1]

The Oxford commentary of R.G. Austin (1964) is perhaps the most exemplary of his four editions; Nicholas Horsfall now promises (2006) a Brill volume.

Dido has asked Aeneas to relive his worst horror (2.3 *infandum . . . renovare dolorem*). He begins his dramatic story at once with the mention of the horse; significantly, a horse's head had been Juno's sign for where her temple should be built in the center of Carthage (1.441-445).[2] Minerva assists in the construction of the horse (she too had been slighted by Paris' judgment); the Greeks feign a votive offering for their safe return to their homelands. The horse is a symbol of prowess in war; just as the image of a horse's head had signaled the extreme prowess in battle of the Carthaginians, so will this horse signal the Greek conquest of Troy.[3] The Greeks hide on the island of Tenedos and leave behind the wooden horse with its deadly contents. Thymoetes wants it brought inside for unknown reasons (innocent or traitorous); Capys (perhaps the Capys of 1.183) wants it either burned or drowned in the sea, or at least examined more closely. Virgil now introduces one of his most memorable characters, the ill-fated Laocoon, who makes one of the most famous and memorable comments in the poem:

> quidquid id est, timeo Danaos et dona ferentis. (2.49)
>
> *Whatever it is, I fear the Danaans, even when they bring gifts.*

Laocoon is right, of course, in suspecting that the horse bodes ill for Troy. He hurls a spear at its flank, which causes it to resound in an echo, thereby revealing its hollow interior. Troy is fated to fall, however, and Aeneas blames Troy's fate on divine intentions:

> et, si fata deum, si mens non laeva fuisset,
> impulerat ferro Argolicas foedare latebras,
> Troiaque nunc staret, Priamique arx alta maneres. (2.54-56)
>
> *And, if the fates of the gods, if their intention had not been hostile,*
> *truly he would have impelled us to befoul the Argive hiding places,*
> *and now Troy would be standing, and you, lofty citadel of Priam, would still remain.*

Indeed, what are we to make of the "fates"? The Latin word *fatum* is etymologically from *fari*, meaning, "to speak." An oracle might speak forth the "fate" of a man or a nation, but the ultimate "fate" of anyone is death. So *fatum* in Latin often simply means the end of life. Thus far in the epic, Juno has represented the fight against fate. Ultimately, she is fighting the *fatum* of Carthage, which is its doom at the hands of the Romans of Aeneas' future and Virgil's past. The way to save Carthage is to ensure that Rome will never be built; so Juno fights against Rome's *fatum*, which most proximately is its initial foundation, and, more distantly, the *imperium sine fine* that Jupiter has promised his daughter (1.279). That "empire without end" had not yet been achieved in Virgil's own day, though the recovery of the standards from the Parthians, especially if amplified by Augustan propaganda, must surely have helped point to some future Roman hegemony over the entire known world; the *Aeneid* does not envisage any end for Rome.[4] We already know some things about Aeneas' fate, also thanks to Jupiter's magisterial address to Venus; once he settles in Italy, he will perhaps be dead within three years (1.265-266). Dido's fate can already be guessed; twice Virgil has called her ill-starred (1.712, 1.749). At some level Juno must know that she cannot prevent the fate of the Trojans to found their new city in Italy. Jupiter has told Venus that even Juno will be reconciled to the founding of Rome (1.279-282); the reasons for her sudden change of heart, as we have noted, will not be revealed until near the very end of the poem.

Jupiter himself is virtually akin to fate (cf. Helenus' words at 3.375-376). He not only knows the future thrust of world history (as do all the other immortals), but he has no apparent problem with it, and he never struggles against it in some frustrated act of resistance to the inevitable course of history. In this detachment he comes across as rational and sober; the emotionalism of his wife and daughter contrast greatly with his calm assurances in Book 1. It is important to note and remember that Virgil does not neatly explain the exact relationship between *Fatum* (capitalized or not, singular or plural) and Jupiter, anymore than he explains clearly how free will coexists with fated destiny. All we can say with certainty is that Virgil's Jupiter never tries to resist the decrees of fate, and that there is indeed room for a person's personal choices, even in the context of an oppressively predetermined fate.[5]

One of the agents of Troy's fate is now introduced: the lying Sinon. Willingly, Sinon has allowed himself to be captured by Trojan shepherds, uncertain about whether he will face instant death or be spared long enough to weave his deceitful web. Aeneas holds the Greeks in contempt as treacherous liars:

accipe nunc Danaum insidias et crimine ab uno
disce omnis. (2.65-66)

Hear now of the treachery of the Danaans, and from the crime of one learn of them all.

By learning of Sinon, Aeneas assures the Carthaginians, you will know what all Greeks are like. Such racial reflections must be examined through the lens of Virgil's own day, especially as his hero speaks to a Carthaginian audience. Would a contemporary Roman think Carthaginians were more notoriously deceitful than the Greeks of yesteryear? Virgil's half-line here, intentional or not, is very effective; Book 2 has the most unfinished lines of any book in the poem, which points to the especially imperfect completion of this section of the poem.

Sinon introduces himself as a man without a country; neither the Greeks nor the Trojans will welcome him, he laments.[6] The Greek most known for trickery and deceitful wiles was Odysseus, and Sinon brilliantly (and ironically) identifies himself as a victim of Odyssean inveiglement. The Greeks had executed Palamedes ("the clever one", reinforcing the idea Aeneas has introduced of expert Greek machinations). Palamedes had been an enemy of Odysseus ever since he forced him to leave Ithaca and join the expedition to Troy; according to one tradition he had exposed Odysseus' feigned madness by placing the infant Telemachus in the path of his father's plough.[7] Later, to exact his revenge, Odysseus forged a letter from Priam to Palamedes that implicated Palamedes as a traitor to the Greeks. Palamedes was stoned to death in consequence. This unjust death was the reason his father Nauplius put up false beacons to wreck the Greek fleet; Virgil identifies Belus as Palamedes' father for reasons that are unknown (he must not be confused with Dido's father Belus).[8] Sinon's whole story is a lie, and contains lies within lies; he blames Palamedes' attempt to end the war for his own unjust condemnation and death (2.84). The Trojans, after all, would not necessarily be privy to events in the Greek camp.

The story continues. Sinon had been a relative of Palamedes, sent at a young age by his father to train under him. Sinon claims that he threatened to take his vengeance on Odysseus for his master's unjust death. At this moment in his deceitful yarn, Sinon leaves off from his tale just as he mentions that Odysseus finally joined in nefarious league with Calchas, the Greek seer. The Trojans, of course, press him to continue his mesmerizing mendacity.

In a touch of flattering credit to Trojan resistance, Sinon reveals that the Greeks often wanted to flee the site of their ten year stalemate of a war; they fashioned the horse, apparently, as an offering to the gods to hasten their departure with favorable winds. Storms continued to buffet them, and finally they sent Eurypylus to seek an oracle. The response came that they needed a sacrifice to balance the killing of Iphigenia at the outset of the expedition. Odysseus summoned Calchas, who for ten days remained silent and refused to identify who should die. Finally, with Odysseus shouting demands for a name, Calchas doomed Sinon. The preparations were set in motion for a blood sacrifice; somehow Sinon managed to escape his bonds and flee towards Troy as a helpless supplicant.

Events are moving swiftly for Troy; Sinon's ultimate goal is to persuade the Trojans to receive the wooden horse within their walls. Interestingly, we are given no real sense by Aeneas of where he was during all of these crucial deliberations. The Trojans had been divided on what to do with the horse, the Trojans had taunted Sinon when he was first captured, and the Trojans eventually pity him and agree to spare his life after they hear his tale of woe. The first person verbs remind us throughout the narrative that Aeneas is a part of the action, but he remains an anonymous face in the crowd. As we have noted, the entire drama of this last night of the war unfolds at the setting of Dido's banquet. By this artifice, Virgil ensures that the events of this book are not mere detachable episodes, however technically magnificent and poetically brilliant. No, they are integral to his story; at some point in the conception of the structure of the *Aeneid* he decided that Aeneas must visit North Africa and, once there, recall the great events of Troy's demise, but only within the context of Dido's banquet.

The Trojans have granted Sinon his life; now they wish to know more about the horse. Sinon has already briefly alluded to it (even incorrectly identifying it as of maple wood, not pine, which Austin correctly surmises is a deliberate error by Sinon to make his story appear the naïve story of a not altogether learned or knowledgeable young man).[9] And so Sinon begins the final, climactic part of his grand lie. Odysseus and Diomedes had stolen the Palladium, a sacred image of Pallas Athena that apparently guaranteed Troy's safety. The image of the goddess was set up in the Greek camp, and at once Athena withdrew her favor from the Greeks. Flames shot forth from the statue's eyes (2.172-173). Salty sweat ran down its limbs. Three times the statue appeared to come to life as the goddess herself appeared in it (2.174-175). Calchas orders that the Greeks flee at once and seek omens at Argos, before bringing the Palladium back to Troy. The Greeks have fled homeward, and will be back soon enough, back again for the fight once Athena has been appeased. The horse, meanwhile, has been left as an expiatory offering to atone for the offense to the goddess. This is a bit of suspenseful climax on Virgil's part:

hanc pro Palladio moniti, pro numine laeso
effigiem statuere, nefas quae triste piaret. (2.183-184)

*Having been warned, they set up this effigy in place of the Palladium,
in place of the offended deity, which could expiate the unspeakable baleful thing.*

Sinon had already mentioned the horse:

... saepe illos aspera ponti
interclusit hiems et terruit Auster euntis.
praecipue cum iam hic trabibus contextus acernis
staret equus toto sonuerunt aethere nimbi. (2.110-113)

*... often a harsh storm at sea hemmed them in, and the southwest wind
terrified them as they tried to depart;
especially when now the horse woven with maple beams was
standing here, the clouds thundered throughout the whole upper air.*

What exactly was the horse doing then? Was it an offering to end the storms, which failed? The two versions of horse explanation do not accord (and it seems highly improbable that Sinon is being deliberately inconsistent, unless he has become so arrogant in his successful lies that he has decided to prove just how credulous these Trojans can be). The horse is so huge, Sinon explains, because the Greeks wanted to be sure it could not be drawn easily into Troy's walls; if it should enter the city, it would not only safeguard the city (like the Palladium it is replacing), but (appropriately enough for a horse) be a symbol of the successful attack the Trojans could launch on Greece itself. But if the Trojans destroy the horse, their act will spell doom for their city.

Sinon achieves his goal; the Trojans swallow the whole dose of deceit. The immortals are now ready to give evidence to support further Sinon's deception. Laocoon, now revealed to be a priest of Neptune, is sacrificing a bull at an altar. Presumably he is seeking the god's help in uncovering the Greek tricks he suspects. Two serpents appear, from Tenedos, where the Greek fleet is hiding. The terrible sea monsters swim straight for the shore and do not stop when they reach land. First they attack and begin to feed upon Laocoon's two young sons in grisly feast. Laocoon tries to help his sons, but the serpents turn their massive coils against him; he is horribly crushed to death, and his cries reveal that he has *become* the bull he was in the process of slaughtering:

clamores simul horrendos ad sidera tollit:
qualis mugitus, fugit cum saucius aram
taurus et incertam excussit cervice securim. (2.222-224)

*At the same time he raised shouts to the stars that made us shudder,
like the bellowings a wounded bull raises when it
flees the altar and shakes the uncertain axe from its neck.*

Laocoon had not finished sacrificing his bull when the serpents struck (the imperfect *mactabat* at 202 is inchoative); now the gods will take their sacrifice from him and his sons. The serpents, their bloody meal over, seek rest under an image of Minerva herself in the citadel of Troy. Sinon must have been right; the goddess has punished the man who dared to raise a weapon against the horse that has been identified as her propitiatory offering. The simile's description is grisly; the axe hangs from the neck of the sacrificial animal, strong enough to have pierced the flesh and be embedded, but not strong enough to remain fixed: it wobbles in gruesome "uncertainty" (224 *incertam*).

Virgil did not invent Laocoon. He appears in the epic cycle and a lost tragedy of Sophocles. Later writers did not necessarily agree with Virgil's details of what must have been a web of conflicting stories even by the Augustan Age. Even the most unenthusiastic students of classical art history are familiar with the Hellenistic group depicting the slaughter of Laocoon and his sons; the scene was a highly popular theme for the visual arts in antiquity, and Virgil's description is more than probably inspired by something he saw; we may again consider the continuation Aeneas is offering to the scenes he saw painted on the temple walls; Laocoon's death would be a most fitting continuation of the queue of Trojan ignominies.[10]

The crucial fact in this scene is the beginning of the divine assault on Troy, which will explode in a full frenzy of immortal violence later (2.604-620). So doomed is Troy that even Neptune's priest is savagely assaulted at his seaside altar. Laocoon's exact divine job is not altogether clear in the tradition. In Virgil he is plainly identified as a priest of Neptune; this is fitting for Virgil's scene painting, which demands an altar on the beach for the serpents to attack suddenly and readily in a shocking burst of hideous violence. Laocoon's end, and that of his sons, comes fast and furiously. Others (Servius for one) say that Laocoon was actually a priest of Apollo. Perhaps this would not do for Virgil's purpose, since Apollo was so important a god for the Augustan regime. The shocking murder of an Apollonian priest at prayer would not work, at least not so early in the poem (there will be other times for devotees of Apollo to die in this epic), and certainly not so public, dramatic, and atrocious a murder (during a sacrifice); the death of Panthus (2.429-430) will be far more honorable (and, in any case, Panthus' death is not as stunningly horrible as Laocoon's). Servius is, as usual, eager to explain apparent inconsistencies and errors in Virgil; he proposes that Laocoon was indeed a priest of Apollo, and was chosen by lot to conduct sacrifices to Neptune after the previous occupant of the job had been killed for not successfully keeping the Greek invasion fleet from the Trojan beaches. Another suggestion he offers is that Neptune did not object to the killing of his priest, since he never forgave the Trojans for their perfidy when Laomedon refused to pay him for his work in building their walls. This scene, nonetheless, is one of divine conflict; one goddess is indeed sending her familiars against another divinity's priest. The penultimate book of the poem will have a similar scene to ring this one, with another devotee of Apollo dying ignominiously; here Minerva is indirectly attacking Neptune, while there Diana will, in effect, attack

Apollo.

The horse enters the city. Some divine power still feels sympathy for Troy; the horse becomes stuck four times while moving over the very threshold of the city, and each time it will not budge, the sound of the armed men hidden inside echoes:

> instamus tamen immemores caecique furore
> et monstrum infelix sacrata sistimus arce. (2.244-245)
>
> *Nevertheless we continue, heedless and blind with madness,*
> *and we place the unlucky portent in the hallowed citadel.*

The Trojans are "blind with madness," and the victim of their rage is themselves. Cassandra, Priam's daughter, finally appears. Virgil momentarily misleads us:

> tunc etiam fatis aperit Cassandra futuris
> ora dei iussu non unquam credita Teucris. (2.246-247)
>
> *Then too Cassandra opened her mouth with future fates,*
> *she who by order of the god was not ever believed by the Teucrians.*

Until the negative, we might for a moment forget that Cassandra had been cursed; she can never be believed. The Trojans veil the temples of the gods with festal fronds; they are celebrating their own requiem.

Night falls: the last for Troy. The Greeks advance against the city in naval array while Sinon unloosens the pine bars of the horse to let out his fellow Greeks; he had artfully pretended to forget that the horse was made of pine, not maple; Virgil's detail about the *pinea claustra* (2.258-259) reminds us of the cunning lie. Aeneas proclaims that Sinon is under the protection of divinities hostile to Troy:

> ... fatisque deum defensus iniquis
> inclusos utero Danaos et pinea furtim
> laxat claustra Sinon. (2.257-259)
>
> *... and, defended by the hostile fates of the gods,*
> *Sinon secretly loosens the Danaans enclosed in the belly*
> *and the pine bolts.*

Artfully, Virgil keeps the identity of this defended man ambiguous until the last word of the sentence; the import of his sentiment is that the lying Sinon does not deserve any immortal protection. The Greeks exit the horse; Odysseus is there, and the son of Achilles, and Menelaus; they slaughter the guards on night watch and open the gates of Troy to let in their comrades who have arrived by sea from Tenedos, just as Minerva's serpents had arrived earlier thence to slay Laocoon before he could spoil Sinon's treacherous game. Minerva had helped craft the horse; she has sent both snakes and horse to destroy Troy and achieve her vengeance for the slight she had suffered at the judgment of Paris. Small wonder that Juno had invoked her example in her early rhetorical complaint that she alone was not permitted to avenge slights (1.39-45); she complained that Pallas Athena could slay Ajax, son of Oileus, in retribution for how he had dragged Cassandra out of her temple in Troy. Now Minerva plays a major divine role in the destruction of Troy.

Aeneas has been absent from the narrative thus far; like most of the other Trojans, he is in peaceful slumber, his last in his own home. The ghost of Hector appears to him, the first in a series of visions that explain his destiny as would-be savior of Troy's destiny (2.270-297).[11] Hector is the first denizen of the underworld Virgil will present to us; he will not reappear in Aeneas' descent to Avernus, but he is the first casualty of the Trojan War we meet *post mortem*.[12] The apparition of Hector is appropriately grisly; he appears as he did when he was dragged by Achilles' chariot around the walls of Troy. Hector's appearance befits his urgent message to Aeneas; Virgil has decided to indulge in appropriate poetic license (after all, Hector's body was purified before his funeral rites, after Priam had successfully ransomed it, even if we allow for no posthumous glorification of the appearance of those who are in the Elysian Fields, where perhaps we are safe in assuming that Hector has found a home).

Hector's message is succinct; the city has been infiltrated fatally, and there is no one who can save it. Had Troy been able to be preserved, Hector himself would have done it. There have been allied attempts to defend Troy since Hector's death (Memnon and his Ethiopians, Penthesilea and her Amazons), but they have been mere delaying tactics, it seems; the end came, strategically, when Hector died. Homer, at any rate, seems to have felt this way, though his *Iliad* is not principally concerned with the fate of a city or a people. The *Iliad*, as we have noted, is concerned with the wrath of Achilles. The ultimate victim of Achilles' wrath in Homer's epic is Hector, whose burial ends the poem.

Indeed, Hector's dream arrival is *Homer*'s arrival, in a sense. Virgil's announcement of the apparition echoes Ennius' description of Homer's nocturnal visit to him:

... maestissimus Hector
visus adesse mihi (2.270-271)

... there seemed to be present to me
Hector the sad

visus Homerus adesse poeta (*Annales* fr. 1.3 Skutsch)

The poet Homer seemed to be present

Virgil's depiction of the mutilated Hector is a direct evocation of the horrors described in Homer (*Iliad* 22.395 ff.).[13]

The *Iliad* is a reflection on learning how to die when you would rather live. Achilles goes into battle and slays Hector, though he knows that his own death will not come long after. His wrath abates at the end of the epic; if it is good and salubrious for a man to learn how to curb his wrath, then Achilles learns his lesson by the end of the *Iliad*; there is sufficient time before his own inevitable death for him to show mercy to Priam and hand over the broken body of his son Hector. The point the *Iliad* wishes to make at its close is how much the violent Achilles can accomplish in the brief span of time between Hector's savage death and his own fate.[14]

The *Odyssey*, in contrast, shows how a man must live on when sometimes the travails and turmoil of life might cause him to yearn for death. This has been the Homeric model Aeneas has followed from the moment we met him on the deck of his ship, lamenting the blessed fate of the dead at Troy who had not lived to see the horror of the storm. The same emotions will soon return full force in the heat of battle. The Greeks of Homer's day had no sense of national unity and pride to compare even with the stasis-prone Romans of Virgil's day; Odysseus must go through a gauntlet of trials to reach his wife and son, while Aeneas will leave his wife behind to contract a dynastic marriage and found a new city; his son is important mainly for the succession (albeit, a reason that we have already noted was quite paramount in Augustus' mind). The *Odyssey* also shows an alternative path to glory in contrast to the vision of Achilles' noble sacrifice of his own life at a young age. Odysseus' long journey home offers a reward of its own: in Virgil's vision of "homecoming," Aeneas experiences a reversal of Odysseus' model. The Greek had left the site of a foreign war and traveled home to his wife and child; Aeneas leaves his home (and his wife) and travels to a foreign land to seek a new foundation.

The implications of these Homeric associations, especially the theme of madness that will dominate the second half of the poem, will not become fully clear for some time. For now, as we continue to learn more about Virgil's *vir*, we may make some brief observations as we pause to ponder Hector's ghostly appearance.

We have observed that it is difficult to link Aeneas with Augustus at this early point in the poem. But what of Aeneas and Odysseus, his Homeric model for the first six books? Homer's Calypso cannot compare with Dido. When first we meet Odysseus in Calypso's control, he is crying because he cannot proceed on his way home to Ithaca (*Odyssey* 5.149-158). Indeed, he spends his days groaning over his entrapment, a far cry from Aeneas' attitude in Carthage, as we shall see. When Calypso finally dismisses Odysseus, he makes her pledge an oath by the Styx that she will not sabotage his seaborne departure; what a contrast to the curse Dido will place on Aeneas and his descendants. The image of Odysseus, alone and depressed on Calypso's shore, has not yet appeared in Roman dress.

Hector's visit in a dream is the beginning of Aeneas' fated future. Aeneas' greeting of his dead friend will be echoed later in the poem:

... quibus Hector ab oris
exspectate venis? (2.282-283)

... *from what shores do you come,
O Hector, you who have been awaited?*

venisti tandem, tuaque exspectata parenti
vicit iter durum pietas? (6.687-688)

*Have you indeed come at last, and has your piety,
Awaited by your parent, conquered the difficult road?*

The second context is Aeneas' father Anchises' reception of his son in the underworld. There it will be Aeneas who makes a dreamlike voyage across the river of death to visit a figure from his past. There, as we shall see, Aeneas will receive further instructions about his destiny. For now, just as the Greeks stole the Palladium, so Aeneas will make his departure with the "fillets of Vesta" and the sacred fire (2.296-297), handed over to him, as it were, by Troy's final great defender. It is a dream, to be sure; no image of Vesta will be subsequently mentioned. The actions of a dream cannot be pressed too far; Hector is entrusting the Trojan protector deities to Aeneas, and that is what matters.

The action of the actual city invasion has a roughly tripartite division: 1) the events before the arrival at Priam's palace, 2) the slaughter in the royal enclosure, 3) the events surrounding Aeneas' rescue of his own family. Thus Virgil directs the action on increasingly smaller units: city, royal family, and finally Aeneas' own family.

Aeneas wakes up; we learn that his father Anchises has a house in the outer suburbs, as it were, of the city.[15] He hears the destruction from his roof; it is as when fire or water destroys fields and flocks, and the unknowing shepherd listens to the ominous noise from a high rock.[16] Aeneas is now shepherd of his people, just as Hector had been; the shepherd is also *inscius*, "unknowing," just as Dido was at the end of the first book (1.718). There the word had its true force, since Dido was unaware of Cupid's great assault on her heart. Here it is less clearly applicable to Aeneas, who unlike the shepherd of the simile surely realizes what the sound of arms implies; Hector, after all, has revealed the news of the invasion. The adjective's force must be that Aeneas, now shepherd of his people after Hector's passing over the mantle of Trojan protector, is unaware and uncertain of how exactly he is to defend his family and exile band (let alone where he is to lead them). Any momentary confusion, however, is soon dispelled by how fast the Greek advance approaches:

tum vero manifesta fides, Danaumque patescunt
insidiae. (2.309-311)

*Then truly the truth was clear, and the treachery of the
Danaans began to become apparent.*

First Deiphobus' house is mentioned; he had been Helen's husband after the death of Paris. Aeneas will meet him not on this night, but in the underworld of Book 6, where he will be as mutilated as Hector just was in the dream. Besides Helen's new husband's house, Virgil mentions Ucalegon's (311-312).[17] Aeneas' reaction to the fiery devastation of his city is instinctive:

> arma amens capio; nec sat rationis in armis,
> sed glomerare manum bello et concurrere in arcem
> cum sociis ardent animi; furor iraque mentem
> praecipitat, pulchrumque mori succurrit in armis. (2.314-317)

> *Mindless I take up arms; nor is there sufficient reason in arms,*
> *but my courage burns me to gather a force for battle and to*
> *rush to the citadel with my companions; madness and anger*
> *drive my mind headlong, and the thought enters my mind that it is*
>   *beautiful to die in arms.*

These famous lines mark the beginning of a long digression during which Aeneas will engage in some small scale fighting during the invasion, and will learn (for our sakes, and Dido's, as much as his) the fate of the Trojan royal family (at least Priam's tragic end). Madness has provoked Aeneas to fight, and even be ready to die, with his Trojan brothers; Hector's words are forgotten for the time being. There is no mention as yet of Aeneas' thoughts for his wife, son, and father. No Homeric hero would condemn Aeneas for his behavior here; his words are redolent with sentiments they all would understand and approve.

Laocoon had been killed while praying on Troy's beach; now Aeneas will meet the priest Panthus, sacred to Apollo. Panthus is carrying sacred and precious things:

> sacra manu victosque deos parvumque nepotem
> ipse trahit cursuque amens ad limina tendit. (2.320-321)

> *He was dragging the sacred things in his hand, and the conquered gods,*
> *and his little grandson, and, mindless, was hastening in his course to the threshold.*

Like Aeneas, Panthus is "mindless" in the frenzy of this sudden and unforeseen nocturnal invasion. The commentators here have noted some confusion. Panthus arrives at Aeneas' door; Aeneas is able to secure a summary of what Hector had already told him. Virgil does not describe Panthus' handing over of the *sacra* he is holding, and indeed the "small grandson" Panthus is safeguarding is never heard from again. Aeneas' reaction to Panthus is to rush off to battle. Roland Austin takes pains in his commentary to explain how here Panthus gives to Aeneas the Penates, the sacred household gods of Troy, the holy treasures that will, indeed, have arrived at Aeneas' house by the end of this book (2.717) when Aeneas finally leaves with his father and son. Austin is following a weighty tradition in his conclusion: Servius, Augustine, the medieval *Excidium Troiae*, and

Heinze: all agree that Panthus, the priest of Apollo, is now delivering the Penates. As for the boy, Austin sentimentally concludes, as have others, that he is a "pathetic prolepsis" for Aeneas' own son.

But Virgil's point is that even after this encounter with Panthus, Aeneas rushes off into battle, ready to die; his words to the comrades in arms he finds outside his house express the same sentiment he felt before he met Panthus:

> ... moriamur et in media arma ruamus. (2.353-355)
>
> *... let us die, and let us rush into the midst of arms.*

Perhaps the household gods were magically transferred to his father's house; perhaps Panthus is the one who hands them over here. But Aeneas has not changed even after two encounters, one waking and one sleeping, with messengers of Troy's ruin. Even the presence of the unnamed boy with Panthus does not stir Aeneas to think of Ascanius, who is asleep inside the house his father now leaves. There is no shame at all in Aeneas' flight from Troy, but he does have certain obligations now both to city and family.

Panthus declares that Troy is finished and that Jupiter has transferred everything to Argos. Sinon is mentioned one last time (2.329); he is now spreading not lies but fire. Aeneas' explanation of his own actions now is interesting:

> talibus Othryadae dictis et numine divum
> in flammas et in arma feror, quo tristis Erinys
> quo fremitus vocat et sublatus ad aethera clamor. (2.336-338)
>
> *By such words from the son of Othrys and by the power of the gods*
> *I am carried off into flames and arms, where the grim Fury*
> *and the roar of battle calls me, and the shout raised to the upper air.*

"Mysterious," as Austin rightly notes. What does Aeneas mean by the *numen divum*?[18] The words of Panthus move him into the flames and arms; this much at least makes obvious sense. Some have argued that the meaning must be that the divine power of the gods has willed the destruction of Troy (true enough), and that Panthus has just mentioned Jupiter's decision to end the war with Greek victory (also true). But Aeneas says that he was borne off into flames and arms by the words of Panthus *and* the divine power of the gods, almost as if it were their will that he rush into battle. Peerlkamp was so bothered by the phrase that he simply deleted it, but of course the words must stand, and we must ferret out their possible meanings.

Numine divum is *Aeneas*' explanation of his actions. What would Dido imagine, reclining and listening to this account? Would she wonder why Aeneas had not fled at once with his son, whom she has been cradling in her arms (as she at least thinks)? Is Aeneas offering an explanation for his actions, which Servius rightly calls *mala desideria*?

Aeneas is joined by fellow Trojans, including one Coroebus. The tradition behind this young lover of Cassandra is vexed. According to Homer (*Iliad* 13.363-401), Othryoneus of Cabesus had come to Troy with a promise for Priam: he would see to the expulsion of the Greeks, if only he might marry Cassandra.[19] Idomeneus of Crete killed him, insulting him with the taunt that he could have the most beautiful daughter of the son of Atreus, if he would now make common cause with the Greeks. It is unclear how much of this story lies behind the lore about Coroebus; Quintus of Smyrna conflates the two men in his version. Aeneas tells the young assembly (the first men he will lead into battle in this poem) that the gods have abandoned the burning city:

> una salus victis nullam sperare salutem. (2.354)
>
> *There is one hope for the conquered: to hope for no salvation.*

The sentiment drives the youths even madder with frenzy to fight and die:

> sic animis iuvenum furor additus. (2.355)
>
> *So was madness added to the courage of the youths.*

A lupine simile (the first of four in the poem) describes the young Trojan warriors:

> ... inde, lupi ceu
> raptores atra in nebula, quos improba ventris
> exegit caecos rabies catulique relicti
> faucibus exspectant siccis, per tela, per hostis
> vadimus haud dubiam in mortem mediaeque tenemus
> urbis iter. (2.355-360)[20]
>
> > *... then, like wolves*
> > *or raptors in the dark fog, whom the terrible frenzy of*
> > *the stomach has driven on, and the pups left behind await them*
> > *with dry throats, through weapons, through the enemy we*
> > *go into scarcely doubtful death and we hold a path*
> > *through the middle of the city.*

The wolves are hungry, and so are their young, but for what? Perhaps for some final acts of vengeful slaughter against the Greeks who have destroyed their future? This might explain the wolves, but what of the cubs who have been left behind? Surely Ascanius is prominent among them? What does he hunger for on this night? Book 11 will have another wolf simile to balance this one, as we shall later see; there Arruns will be compared to a wolf that has just killed a shepherd or a bullock. He has slain Camilla, and in awareness of his dangerous, audacious deed, he slinks off like a wolf with tail between its legs, seeking shelter and safety. That simile comes at the end of the action, while this one comes at the beginning. There the wolf (Arruns) will be killed; here Aeneas only, it seems, will survive. These wolves act in the night; Arruns' wolf will strike in broad daylight. The simile here is Virgil's, but he has *Aeneas* deliver it in the context of his speech to Dido's court; does Aeneas think his son hungers most for the food of revenge his father can now prepare for him?

Urbs antiqua ruit (2.363), Aeneas declares; his words are reminiscent of the first description of Carthage, *urbs antiqua fuit* (1.12). By Virgil's own time, both cities had been destroyed. Trojans fall dead everywhere, even some Greeks do not survive their night of success; the dead even fall at the thresholds of the gods (2.364-366). Small wonder that even Panthus, Apollo's priest, will soon die; the gods have indeed fled, and will soon be revealed as participating in the destruction that was but presaged in Minerva's sending of the serpents to kill Neptune's priest. Edgar Allen Poe would have been pleased by Aeneas' summary of the night of blood and fear:

... crudelis ubique
luctus, ubique pavor et plurima mortis imago. (2.368-369)

... *everywhere there is cruel grief,*
everywhere fear and a great image of death.

If the Trojans had any sort of reputation for trickery and deceit, Odysseus and the stratagem of the horse have matched them. The Trojans with Aeneas have no chance of victory, and at this juncture they follow Coroebus' advice and decide to make use of the unfortunate arrival of Androgeos and some Greek companions.[21] They will end up slaying the outnumbered Greeks and stealing their arms; so disguised, they will deal death to numerous Greeks before their element of surprise is lost. After the tale of Sinon and the horse, Aeneas need feel no shame in recounting this episode to Dido. Androgeos is *inscius* (2.372), just as Aeneas was earlier. He quickly realizes that he and his men have fallen in with Trojan warriors. He is compared to a man who has stepped on a snake, another of Virgil's typical expansions of a Homeric simile (*Iliad* 3.33-37). In Homer, Paris retreated from the sight of Menelaus; Hector immediately upbraids him for his cowardice.[22] In Homer's simile, the man merely *sees* the snake (just as Paris had merely seen Menelaus); in Virgil, the man *presses* on the snake. This is not precisely what Androgeos did; Virgil has increased the power and force of the simile, once again making the Homeric original more deadly serious. Both Paris and Menelaus would leave their single combat alive; Androgeos and his men are finished in barely four lines (2.382-385). Fortune has indeed smiled on Aeneas' first labor.

Coroebus at once suggests that they follow the path the "first fortune" has shown them: the time has come for the changing of their arms. For Coroebus, the fortune or luck of the Trojans has been to obtain a selection of Greek weapons and armor. Androgeos was the only Greek named in the brief encounter; Coroebus puts on his helmet and takes his sword. He is the leader now, not Aeneas; like the original owner of the arms, he will soon die. The young men are happy (2.395 *laeta*) as they don the arms; once again, the adjective is used in an ominous context.

The action continues:

vadimus immixti Danais haud numine nostro. (2.396)

We proceed, mixed in with the Danaans, scarcely under our own divine power.

The *numina* of Troy have departed, and the Trojans are now wearing arms that are under the protection of Greek *numina*. The phrase links back to the *numine divum* that explained Aeneas' battle frenzy above (2.336). Neither *numen* has been authentic. Like the wolves to which they have already been compared, the Trojans slaughter many in the blind night.

Virgil is obviously concerned with the issue Coroebus raises when he suggests the wearing of Greek arms: *dolus an virtus*, trickery or virtue? Coroebus would not have raised the issue (even to dismiss it at once) if it were not on his mind, and probably the minds of Aeneas and the other Trojans. Trickery and deceit have been a part of war, one might assert, from the beginning; who can claim that their side has always abstained from trickery? Certainly neither Greeks nor Trojans in Virgil's vision; there is no moral high ground for anyone to claim in the terror of this night. Admirers of Aeneas and the Trojans should enjoy the ambiguities of the present; they will come into sharper relief once we finally arrive in Italy.

Juno had lamented, as we have noted, that Pallas Athena was able to take her vengeance on Ajax, the son of Oileus, who had snatched Cassandra from her temple in Troy and raped her. The pathetic scene of Cassandra at the image of the goddess, about to be dragged off by Ajax the Locrian, was a favorite in art; the whole story was known to cyclic epic.[23] Juno had mentioned Ajax' mad frenzy (1.41 *furias*); now Coroebus is described by Aeneas as maddened at the sight of his beloved's imminent rape (2.407 *furiata mente*). Coroebus rushes in to try to help Cassandra; Aeneas and the other Trojans assist him, heedless of the risk. For the first time they are assaulted by Trojans who do not recognize them due to their Greek arms.

The next sequence is the most desperate fighting Aeneas will endure on this night. Coroebus and the Trojans actually manage to rescue Cassandra, only to find that much of the Greek army seems to be concentrated on them: Agamemnon and Menelaus, Ajax son of Oileus, the Dolopians as a whole. They are like winds clashing over sea and land; the storm strikes land and sea just as the disguised Trojans are being struck by their own men as well as by the Greeks.[24] Coroebus dies first, as befits the brave but foolhardy leader of this hopeless fight; his death at an altar further confirms the abandonment of the city by the gods, a theme that has been constant since the death of Laocoon at his beachfront altar. Ripheus had been a mere name in life (2.339, 2.394), but in death he receives a typical Virgilian epitaph; no Trojan had been more just, though the gods did not spare him. Panthus now dies:

> ... non te tua plurima, Panthu,
> labentem pietas nec Apollinis infula texit. (2.429-430)

> *... your frequent piety did not shield you, Panthus,*
> *and the fillet of Apollo did not cover you.*

Lucretius would have been proud of these lines. Indeed, all the religious trappings of the fall of Troy would have been have appreciated by Virgil's poetic mentor.

Aeneas is not the only survivor of the catastrophe; along with Iphitus and Pelias he escapes to Priam's palace. He swears to the dead Troy that he did not act out of cowardice in this departure; indeed, he is right, and any tradition that he was less than heroic in his exit from the city is thoroughly put to rest by Virgil. On the contrary, he should be making his departure from the ruins, and if he is to be criticized, it will be for his apparent forgetfulness of Hector's words. Indeed, his oath recalls Hector's:

> testor, in occasu vestro nec tela nec ullas
> vitavisse vices Danaum et, si fata fuissent
> ut caderem, meruisse manu. (Aeneas at 2.432-434)

> *I call you to witness in your destruction that I did not avoid*
> *the weapons or any blows of the Danaans, and, if the fates had allowed it,*
> *I would have merited to fall by the deeds of my own hand.*

> sat patriae Priamoque datum: si Pergama dextra
> defendi possent, etiam hac defensa fuissent. (Hector at 2.291-292)

> *Enough has been given to our country and to Priam; if Pergamum*
> *had been able to be defended, it would have been defended by this hand.*

Right after he makes his prayer, Aeneas proceeds to Priam's home, despite Hector's admonition that enough has been done for Priam (who is doomed). Aeneas' deeds, the dead Hector realizes, are purely the work of madness; if Troy had been able to be saved, he would have done it with his own hand. Aeneas declares that if it had been so fated, he would have died in the debacle over Cassandra and Coroebus, so fiercely did he fight. Careful, too, is Aeneas' choice of verb to describe his exit: the passive voice 2.434 *divellimur*, "we are torn away" (from the scene of fighting) preserves his full dignity.

Despite this strong assertion, when he arrives at Priam's enclosure, Aeneas declares that the fighting there was so horrific that it was as if there were no fighting, no deaths, anywhere else in the city. His hyperbole comes off as a bit much after the dramatic oath he has just sworn, but his oath had to come immediately after the most fighting he will do on this night. He will be a mere spectator of the drama in Priam's palace, not a participant.

The palace is under siege, with a hopeless defense that only delays the inevitable breakthrough. Aeneas knows of a rear entrance; Virgil allows us to picture the whole scene in our mind, even if we would be at a loss to draw precisely what we see; the entire narrative of Books 2 and 3 is an oral response to what Dido has had painted on the walls of Juno's temple, and much of what Virgil writes in these books, as we have noted, is a response to some of the most popular images of the visual arts, both sculpture and painting. Significantly, the so-called postern gate Aeneas uses is the entrance Andromache used to use to bring the boy Astyanax to see his grandparents. Yet again we are reminded of a helpless youth (and one doomed to die), and yet again we are reminded of Hector's ghost; it should be Hector rushing through the secret gate to mount the battlements and lead the defense, but instead Aeneas continues his tour of the devastation. His disobedience to Hector's orders allows him to give firsthand accounts of the episodes Dido knows only by hearsay, and so in this it serves the narrative purpose, besides continuing to emphasize his surrender to madness: he is entering a burning house now, as it were, with no mortal hope of escape.

Another unfinished line (468) ushers in the transition between the action on the roof and the sudden appearance of Achilles' son Pyrrhus, who will orchestrate the next, and most terrible, section of the drama in the palace.[25] Pyrrhus is another name for Neoptolemus (unknown to Homer); he had been one of the Greeks named in the horse (2.263; cf. *Odyssey* 11.505-537). He was the son of Achilles and Deidamia, and may have been the killer of Astyanax (so the *Ilias Parva*), and possibly Polyxena.[26] Some have noted that the abrupt transitions from section to section reflect the unfinished state of the poem. But the effect of the less than smooth movements between sections well suits the confused nature of the night, and further reinforces the painting-like nature of Aeneas' recitation; we are deep into one of the most episodic sections of the whole poem, as befits Virgil's response to Homer's *Odyssey*.

Pyrrhus, "red as fire," enters with gleaming bronze, as befits his fiery appearance; he is the living embodiment of the conflagration that has overtaken Troy:

qualis ubi in lucem coluber mala gramina pastus,
frigida sub terra tumidum quem bruma tegebat,
nunc, positis novus exuviis nitidusque iuventa,
lubrica convolvit sublato pectore terga
arduus ad solem, et linguis micat ore trisulcis. (2.471-475).[27]

Just as when a snake comes into the light, having fed on bad herbs,
a snake that the chill winter was holding swollen under the earth,
and now it is new, with its skin sloughed off and shining in its youth
as it rolls over on its slippery back, with its chest upraised,
reaching high for the sun, and its mouth flickers with a triple-forked tongue.

It is one of the best and most appropriate similes in Virgil. Its origin lies in

Homer's description of Hector before his fateful encounter with Achilles (*Iliad* 22.93-96), where the Trojan hero is compared to a snake.[28] Several of Virgil's lines are borrowed and adapted from his description of the hazards of a lurking water snake in the *Georgics* (3.425-439).[29] Pyrrhus has arrived suddenly on the scene. He is not only the living embodiment of fire, but also the mortal incarnation of the sea serpents that had traveled from Tenedos at Minerva's behest to slay Laocoon. The simile's emphasis is on the coming into battle of Achilles' son. He can be nothing but a monster in Aeneas' retelling of the murder of Priam; he is an incomplete version of his father, lacking the understanding of the ways of mercy that Achilles seems to gain by the end of the *Iliad*. His entourage of men, appropriately enough, comes to hurl fire; this night has been illuminated by the dominant image of the Greeks burning the city. Virgil takes care to name Pyrrhus' Achillean entourage of Periphas and Automedon (his father's charioteer); the son may have the trappings of his father, but he lacks much his sire had learned.

Virgil now paints the death *tableau* after Pyrrhus breaks through the barred door with powerful anaphora and alliteration:

apparet domus intus et atria longa patescunt;
apparent Priami et veterum penetralia regum,
armatosque vident stantis in limine primo. (2.483-485)

The interior of the house appeared and the long courtyards were opened;
the inner chambers of Priam and the old kings appeared
and they see armed men standing on the first threshold.

The last line must mean (as most critics take it) that Pyrrhus' party sees armed guards on the inside; Virgil changes the scene immediately with 2.486 *At domus interior*, where he describes the panic in the palace. The three lines of description are the poetry of suspended action; time is frozen as the palace is finally exposed to the serpent enemy. Pyrrhus the snake had sloughed off his old skin; now he has torn the covering off the royal residence. The "first threshold" (485) evokes the image of the infancy of life (cf. 6.426-429).

There were bars, and there were the final bodyguards of the royal family, but the work is now that of a butcher. Pyrrhus has his father's force (2.491 *vi patria*); Priam's son Paris had succeeded in killing Achilles, but now the son will finish the slaughter his father began when he killed Hector. The whole scene slowly and carefully describes what happened so rapidly; the battering ram takes down the door and the guards are killed. Now that no barriers exist between killers and royal victims, Aeneas describes the flood of Greeks as being more powerful than a swollen river that has burst its floodgates; the river takes away livestock along with their stables. Aeneas had set out with his fellow Trojans like wolves hunting stealthily in the night; Pyrrhus and his Greeks are a force of nature that sweeps away animals as well as their homes. Our eyewitness Aeneas can report that he himself saw Neoptolemus, and Hecuba, and Priam; one hundred daughters and daughters-in-law are also there (reminding us of the absent men who are either dead or dying throughout the falling city). We know the names of the most important of Priam's fifty sons from our extant epics; the mythographers were not satisfied until they could list all of them. Priam is befouling the fires he had kindled on the altars; the ever-present theme of religious profanation returns; he has apparently been wounded in the initial onslaught.

Like Aeneas, Priam is ready to die (2.511 *moriturus*).[30] Virgil paints one image of the final end of Troy's monarch; there were many traditions. Cyclic epic had defined the altar of Zeus as Priam's place of death; others preferred to imagine Priam executed on the grave of Achilles, his head mounted on a pike that Neoptolemus carried about (a grisly possibility Virgil's account does not exclude).[31] The city will fall for good and all with its head. Resistance to Aeneas in Latium will end, we know, with the death of Turnus in the last lines of Book 12; the only enmity that does not die with its originator in all of Virgil is Carthage's hatred for Rome, which will be born soon enough through Dido's curse. (Indeed, even in the underworld the dead Dido will show the eternal nature of that hatred by her silence in Aeneas' presence). Virgil's description of Priam's end is horrific, but more restrained than some depictions; more than one vase painting shows Neoptolemus smiting Priam with the dead body of Hector's son Astyanax.

The altar that will mark Priam's death is unidentified by Virgil, but elsewhere named (Servius, et al.) as a dedication to Jupiter Herceus, Jupiter of the Courtyard. A laurel tree is near it, shading the altar and the Penates that are on it. The poet has made this a very Roman altar; we might pause to ask just what households gods Aeneas is supposed to carry out from Troy, just as we did when Panthus appeared at Aeneas' home carrying Penates earlier. Has Priam's altar already been stripped of its Penates in face of invasion (highly unlikely, given the present text)? Which Penates did Panthus have with him when he arrived at Aeneas' house (his own?) Does Aeneas end up taking the Penates of his own house alone (I suspect so)? Poetry does not usually solve such pedantic speculations; for now, the scene is the most sacred spot in Troy, soon to be the scene of horrific violence. Hecuba and her daughters are now like doves caught in a storm, and they cling to the images of the gods around the altar. We have not met Aeneas' wife yet; Priam's queen Hecuba sees her husband's brave but foolish attempt to fight as he dons his armor. Hecuba's remark that this is not the time for the aid of weapons, not even if Hector himself were present, hearkens back to Hector's ghost and its assurance to Aeneas that if he could not save Troy, no one could; Hecuba takes her son's analysis a step further: not *even* Hector could now save Troy.

Pyrrhus enters, chasing Polites, another prince of Troy. The prince is felled by a spear in the sight of his parents. The son's gore stains the father's face (2.539 *foedasti . . . vultus*); the line recalls Aeneas' words to Hector's ghost:

... quae causa indigna serenos
foedavit vultus? (2.285-286)

... what unworthy cause has befouled
your serene visage?

In the half-wakeful state of a dream, Aeneas had not at first realized why Hector looked so bloody; what had been seen of the son in a vision is now seen in the living reality of the father. Achilles had restored one son to him for an honorable burial; Neoptolemus has slaughtered another and stained the father with filial blood. Priam's words to Pyrrhus are sharp, but the son of Achilles has the most memorable verses of the sequence:

cui Pyrrhus: "referes ergo haec et nuntius ibis
Pelidae genitori. illi mea tristia facta
degeneremque Neoptolemum narrare memento.
nunc morere." (2.547-550)

*To whom Pyrrhus replied: "You will bring these things and go as a messenger
to my father, the son of Peleus; remember to tell him of my baleful deeds and
how degenerate Neoptolemus has become;
Now die."*

He drags Priam to the altar (2.551 *traxit*), just as Panthus dragged his unnamed grandson to the house of Aeneas (2.321 *trahit*), and just as Andromache used to bring Astyanax to see his grandfather and her father-in-law (457 *trahebat*). The verb has shifted from present to imperfect to false perfect (aorist); Priam is as good as dead, we know Astyanax will soon die, and we can assume Panthus' grandson will die. Priam's face had been splattered with blood; now he slips in the gory pool before the altar. Pyrrhus had entered the enclosure "gleaming" (2.470 *coruscus*); now he will draw his gleaming sword to dispatch Priam (2.552 *coruscum*). Virgil has been shifting the lens on his study of Troy's fall, more a painter of scenes than a chronicler; he makes his final, dramatic shift now:

... iacet ingens litore truncus,
avulsumque umeris caput et sine nomine corpus. (2.557-558)

*... The huge trunk lies on the shore,
and the head torn from the shoulders, and the body without the name.*

Suddenly we are on the Trojan beach, and we might picture the Greeks sailing away. Servius was the first to record that this image was borrowed from the death of Pompey, beheaded at the behest of the eunuch Pothinus and the court of Ptolemy after he had fled to Egypt after the disaster at Pharsalia.[32] The image of a Roman hero lying dead on the shores of Egypt, the victim of Eastern treachery and degeneracy, must have occurred to Virgil's listeners as they heard of Priam's fate. One Roman worthy had fallen to the brother; another, Mark Antony, would fall to the sister, Cleopatra. We cannot be sure what reasons Virgil had for such echoes and images, anymore than we can know why a fleeting geographical detail might recall a line of Callimachus, or a moment of high emotional tension might suddenly evoke a lighthearted moment in Catullus. In some cases, we may be stretching too far to find explanations. But, like Pompey, though Priam was the "enemy," he did not deserve his fate. If we are to find Pompey in these lines, all the pathos that Priam's death has occasioned must now, at the end, be felt for Pompey. Virgil has ended his masterful mythological death *tableau* with a recent memory of pain and sorrow for Rome. Lucan, unlike Virgil, would have the advantage (or disadvantage) of seeing the principate unfold; he would choose for *his* reflection on Rome's relationship with *Furor* the civil war between Caesar and Pompey, which for him marked the ascendancy of Caesar and the decline of the Republic. His account of Pompey's death was perhaps inspired by this scene (*Bellum Civile* 8.667 ff.). It does not matter that the master poet compels the pedant to wonder how Aeneas knows about the headless corpse on the beach and to wonder when and if he saw it.

Finally, Aeneas is inspired by this slaughter to remember his father, wife, and son:

> ... subiit cari genitoris imago,
> ut regem aequaevum crudeli vulnere vidi
> vitam exhalantem; subiit deserta Creusa
> et direpta domus et parvi casus Iuli. (2.560-563)
>
> ... *the image of my dear father entered my mind,*
> *as I saw the king, a man of my father's age, giving up*
> *his life with a cruel wound; deserted Creusa entered my mind,*
> *and the ransacked house, and the fate of small Iulus.*

We have waited long for this passage, and it has come at last after the climax of Trojan horror. Aeneas freely says he deserted his wife; the adjective he uses to describe his son increases our awareness of his family's helplessness. Aeneas, too, has been deserted. His companions have either jumped to the ground or to the fire; their king's death has driven them to suicide when they see they have no chance.

Now comes one of the most vexing problems in all Virgilian scholarship.[33] The fifth century Medicean manuscript, containing the entire *Aeneid*, and the fourth or fifth century Palatine, which has most of the poem, both omit lines 2.566-588, and they are the best manuscripts we possess. Servius and Tiberius Claudius Donatus, our oldest surviving commentaries, both ignore these lines. Servius Danielis preserves them, along with the information that Virgil's literary executors Varius and Tucca removed them, principally because they depict Aeneas prepared to kill a defenseless woman, Helen, and secondarily because in Book 6 Deiphobus, Helen's last husband, will more or less report that Helen was at home when he suffered his brutal end (6.511-527). Besides a remark in Servius' preface that this passage, like the so-called opening lines of the poem (*Ille ego*), are examples of how Varius and Tucca emended the *Aeneid* at the order of Augustus, who ordered the removal of "superfluous" things, we have *no* further evidence of the authenticity or lack thereof of these lines. They were included in the (Roman) first printed edition of the *Aeneid* (1473), and no modern editor has been brave enough to excise them; Mynors brackets them, with neutral commentary, in his Oxford Text.

We must believe Servius Danielis, who had no reason to lie. They are Virgil's own words, and his executors removed them from the poem in an early act of literary criticism. We have more reason to trust their inclusion than we do the *Ille ego* lines "1-4" of Book 1, where Donatus reports that the grammarian Nisus (first century A.D.) had merely heard that they had been cut by Varius; further, it is one thing to eliminate four introductory lines that may have been meant as a frontispiece or prefatory remark, and quite another to remove an entire passages from Aeneas' recounting of Troy's last night. No, the main reason they must have so offended Virgil's first readers is their depiction of Aeneas, ready to kill a woman. Deiphobus, by tradition Helen's last husband after the death of Paris, will reveal more about this last night to Aeneas in the underworld (6.494-547).

Aeneas would not have seen Helen, were not the raging fires of Troy's destruction bringing everything to light. The fires have increased in intensity; earlier the disguised Trojans were in part successful because of the night's relative darkness (2.397 *caecam . . . noctem*). The fires Helen enkindled now reveal her. She has taken refuge at an altar as a supplicant; of all the characters so far in the book, she alone will be successful in her prayers, and with good reason; Venus favors her. The goddess' interruption of Aeneas' frenzied urge to take vengeance on Helen shows concern for both of them; Venus does not wish to see Helen killed, and she is eager to see Aeneas get her former lover Anchises and her grandson Ascanius out of the ruined city. It is true that Virgil's geography is vague at the beginning of this scene. Aeneas was on the roof, gazing down at the violence below. He catches sight of Helen, who is hiding at the *limina Vestae*, "the threshold of Vesta," crouching at the altar (2.574 *aris . . . sedebat*). Later (2.632 *descendo*) we learn that he has finally left the roof. As we have noted already, the transitions between these episodes are not necessarily finely polished to satisfy a nitpicker who is looking for inconsistency. Once again, the narrative is somewhat suspended, to allow for the expansion of thoughts that might take mere seconds in reality. Aeneas' friends have been so terrorized by the slaughter of the royals that some have committed suicide (2.566); Aeneas had no mad urge to join them, because for him the deaths of Priam and Polites finally triggered memory of his own vulnerable family. He looks for a way to descend safely:

erranti passimque oculos per cuncta ferenti. (2.570)

to the one wandering and bearing his eyes through all things everywhere.

A beautifully balanced line: Aeneas roams the rooftop, moving back and forth; we must imagine that Pyrrhus' troops are ransacking the area around the altar of Jupiter where Priam died, and that Aeneas has moved to another sector of the palace enclosure. He sees Helen, who, understandably, fears both Trojans and Greeks now, and especially her deserted husband Menelaus (2.572 *deserti coniugis iras*). Troy is in flames, and now fire begins to burn in Aeneas' heart:

> exarsere ignes animo ... (2.575)
>
> *fires blazed up in my heart ...*

The sight of Priam moved him to remember his own family; the sight of Helen drives him back once more into madness. Is Helen to survive and return home with Trojan escort, while Priam dies in misery? Aeneas intends to take righteous vengeance on the cause of the war:

> ... sceleratas sumere poenas. (2.576)
>
> *... to exact criminal penalties.*

Helen is the criminal, and Aeneas will take "criminal penalties" from her: a transferred epithet, and an extraordinary use thereof. These are Aeneas' own words; in a fit of what we can call madness he has decided that it is right and proper to kill Helen. This crucial scene (which some would have us pretend is the mysterious work of some anonymous hack) will be echoed at the climactic moment of the entire epic:

> ... Pallas te hoc vulnere, Pallas
> immolat et poenam scelerato ex sanguine sumit. (12.948-949)
>
> *... Pallas sacrifices you with this wound, Pallas*
> *exacts the punishment from criminal blood.*

Aeneas is again speaking: this time it is Turnus who is in his grasp, and no Venus will intervene to keep Aeneas from surrendering to his frenzy and rage. Turnus had asked to be spared, and had invoked the plight of his own aged father, Daunus; surely such an appeal to filial *pietas* would move Aeneas. When Aeneas sees the armor of his dead young friend Pallas, the friend Turnus had slain, he is driven to take vengeance; at some level, no doubt, he knows that his action is questionable, and he deflects some of the onus of guilt by the effective anaphora *Pallas ... Pallas*: it is Pallas who is sacrificing Turnus on the altar, as it were (*immolat*), not Aeneas. Aeneas has rejected Turnus' plea, but he casts himself in the role of agent of Pallas' posthumous revenge. Here, with Helen, he also realizes that his vengeful act would be questionably appropriate:

> ... namque etsi nullum memorabile nomen
> in feminea poena est nec habet victoria laudem (2.583-584)[34]
>
> *... indeed, even if there is no memorable name*

for killing a woman and this victory does not bring praise.

This scene will also be echoed, though more faintly, in Arruns' attack on Camilla. He is also willing to receive no glory for his deed, so long as the woman dies:

> ... haec dira meo dum vulnere pestis
> pulsa cadat, patrias remeabo inglorius urbes. (11.792-793)

> *... provided that this dire pest fall by*
> *my wound, I shall return to my father's cities without glory.*

Arruns will kill Camilla; his return home will be denied. Aeneas will not kill Helen, and he will find a new home in Italy. Books 2 and 11 provide a closed ring that centers on the death of young women. Helen and Camilla are vastly different, but both their actions lead to the deaths of many Trojans; Venus successfully protects Helen, while Diana will not prevent Camilla's death, but will ensure her honorable burial and the death of her killer, Arruns.

Aeneas describes his mind's turmoil; he has reservations about the killing of a woman, but he is sure he will be praised for having killed the one woman who now is hateful to both sides. The Latin here is quite difficult:

> exstinxisse nefas tamen et sumpsisse merentis
> laudabor poenas, animumque explesse iuvabit
> ultricis fama, et cineres satiasse meorum. (2.585-587 Mynors)

> *Nevertheless I shall be praised for having destroyed the unspeakable*
>   *woman and for*
> *having exacted the punishment she deserved, and it will be pleasing to*
> *have filled my mind with the reputation of an avenger, and to have*
>   *satisfied the ashes of my own.*

The problems of line 587, most likely, will never be solved definitively. The general sense is clear: it will please Aeneas to fill his heart with vengeance and to satisfy the ashes of his ancestors (again, the emphasis of this night is on the fire that is consuming Troy). The madness that has led to the flames of Troy has spread to Aeneas (2.575 *exarsere ignes animo*); now he seeks a way to provide solace to his dead fellows. *Meorum* is a crucial word; this delay to deal with Helen has, once again, distracted Aeneas from his own family, who are not yet ash.

The principal problem in line 587 with the Latin is that the Servian manuscripts all read some form of *fama* (either genitive/dative or accusative; Mynors prints *famam*). The simplest solution is to interpret the line as meaning that Aeneas will be pleased to have filled his spirit with the reputation of an avenger, and (thereby) to have satisfied the ashes of his ancestors (changing forms of *fama* to forms of *flamma* only makes a hellish line even worse; Hirtzel prints *flammae*). Helen is clinging to the altars of Vesta, the hearth goddess; Hector had specifically shown an image of Vesta to Aeneas in his dream visit (2.296). This passage, then, links to the one before and forms a ring that is centered on the household goddess *par excellence*; again, the theme is Aeneas' abandonment of his own home. Rather than taking vengeance on the cause of the war at the goddess' shrine, he should be saving his family.

Venus appears for the second time in the poem to her son.[35] She has no time now for tricks and subterfuge; she manifests herself in a pure light, in contrast to the horrible light of the Greek fires (2.590 *pura per noctem in luce*); finally the light of the gods will, in some small way, illumine Troy's final evening. The so-called Helen episode from Servius is now over, but the appearance of Venus here, in a passage whose authenticity no one questions, creates problems of continuity for those who would insist on excising lines 567-588.

"nate, quis indomitas tantus dolor excitat iras?
quid furis?" (2.594-595)

*"Son, what great sorrow rouses your unconquered anger?
Why do you rage so?"*

These lines lose much of their force if they are deprived of their proper context. It has been argued that this small passage was inserted by Virgil to give even more justification for Aeneas' flight. But the problem has not been Aeneas' eagerness to leave Troy: quite the opposite. Venus asks the questions we might wish Aeneas had considered far earlier than he did: are Creusa and Ascanius alive? Venus reminds Aeneas that the Greek battle lines are prowling about everywhere (2.599 *errant*), just as he has been looking around on the roof for a safe descent (2.570 *erranti*). Indeed, Venus reveals that only her protection has saved Aeneas' family thus far. Venus assures Aeneas that it is not her beloved Paris or Helen who are to blame for this night, but the gods; she now unveils reality, the celebrated image of the immortals destroying Troy. Their divine destruction is compared to the action of farmers who work together to cut down an aged ash tree high on the mountains; these celestial woodsmen are planting the seeds of Rome by cutting down the ancient tree.[36] The simile is left technically incomplete, another possible sign of the imperfect nature of the poem and, perhaps, this book in particular; but the hasty style and rapidly shifting images accord well with the events of the night and Aeneas' dramatic recitation of them at table. Aeneas, understandably, has had no thought during his adventures on this final night that he could actually help to save Troy; his fighting earlier in the evening was the mad frenzy of a man ready to die in the flames of his homeland, and during the entire episode in the royal palace he had no sudden urge to throw himself down and die for Priam; indeed he had the curious stance of a somewhat detached observer: he had followed Coroebus during the rescue of Cassandra, but during Pyrrhus' onslaught he was nearly immobile.

Aeneas' own escape from Priam's palace is magical; Venus protects him as both weapons and flames give way before him (2.632 *ducente deo*, instead of *dea*, has caused needless concern).[37] His first thought upon his arrival home is the safety of his father Anchises, whose entrance into the poem's action is not unlike his son's in Book 1; there Aeneas had praised as blessed the dead at Troy, and now Anchises reflects that flight and exile are for the young and strong, not the old and feeble. His aged and tired demeanor contrast sharply with the eternal loveliness of the goddess who has just send Aeneas homeward; Dido had asked if Aeneas were indeed that one who had been born of Venus and Anchises (1.617-618). Anchises has seen Troy sacked before (Heracles had destroyed it when Laomedon refused to pay him for his construction work). Anchises' reluctance to leave is understandable (he has, as yet, no divine knowledge about his son and grandson and their special destiny); the son, though, has inherited some of the father's willingness to surrender to apparent disaster. Like Aeneas' companions who had flung themselves into the flames to die with their king, Anchises threatens to kill himself:

ipse manu mortem inveniam; miserebitur hostis
exuviasque petet. facilis iactura sepulchri. (2.645-646)

*I myself shall find death with my own hand: the enemy will show mercy
and seek spoils. Easy is the tossing aside of burial.*

The first phrase could mean suicide in his very home; the immediate mention of the Greek enemy has been taken to mean that Anchises (like Priam) intends to rush out and die in battle. This seems unlikely; Anchises is in no mood for fighting now, hopeless cause or not. He means that the Greeks will find him and "pity" him (sarcasm): they will seek spoils from his corpse. He then makes an even more wry comment about burial. His words will be echoed later in the poem:

Tros Anchisiade, facilis descensus Averno. (6.126)

Trojan son of Anchises, easy is the descent to Avernus.

The Sibyl is assuring the Trojan son of Anchises that the descent to the underworld (where he will meet his father in the Elysian Fields) is easy; the return is the labor. Anchises' words here are also paralleled by the haunting words of the dead man at the end of Horace' enigmatic Archytas Ode (*carmen* 1.28):

quamquam festinas, non est mora longa; licebit
    iniecto ter pulvere curras. (1.28.35-36)

*Although you hasten away, the delay is not long; it will be permitted
    for you to run off, after having thrown dust on me three times.*

In Horace's ode, the full horror of what the loss of burial meant to the ancients (so well known from Sophocles' *Ajax* and *Antigone*) is central to his poem's emotional resonance. Aeneas had already shown his ability to imagine the unburied body of Priam on the coast of Troy; now we see more clearly and fully why Hector had appeared to Aeneas in the bloody, gory visage of the unburied hero, tied to Achilles' chariot: Anchises does not care about his own burial, but Aeneas will not allow his father to experience what he just described of his king. Anchises is hateful to the gods; he had boasted of his love affair with Venus, in consequence of which Jupiter had almost destroyed him on the spot with a thunderbolt.[38] Anchises does not know what Aeneas has already seen (though he could, no doubt, imagine it); soon enough (2.662 ff.) Aeneas will relate what he has witnessed.

Aeneas, Creusa, and their servants urge Anchises not to destroy everything with himself (for they will not be willing to abandon him), not to surrender to the death that is pressing on him (both from the encircling Greeks and his own resolution to commit suicide). His refusal to reconsider is the next event that drives Aeneas to madness; he rushes for arms and desires to die like his father:

rursus in arma feror mortemque miserrimus opto. (2.655)

Again I am borne off into arms and, most wretched, wish to die.

Salvation in extreme circumstances lies with the sword (as Dido herself will illustrate); death is the answer Anchises' frustrating obstinacy provokes in his son. The emotions are understandable, but the question Aeneas immediately asks has an answer:

nam quod consilium aut quae iam fortuna dabatur? (2.656)

For what plan or what fortune now was at hand?

Delay follows delay in the execution of Hector's order to get out of the city. Aeneas, in despair, asks his mother if she saved him thus far only so that he might see Pyrrhus burst in and slaughter *his* own family. Aeneas calls for arms so that he might rush out into battle again and die with at least some vengeance for the loss of his family; he hopes to kill as many Greeks as possible before he is at last cut down. The individual reader will decide what to make of Aeneas in these scenes. A Roman would fully appreciate his unwillingness to defy the will of his father and forcibly rescue him. A Roman would understand Anchises' wish to face death: both Stoic and Epicurean, in fact, would smile at his words (indeed, Servius notes that Anchises' blithe dismissal of the need for burial was an Epicurean sentiment). Divine intervention is necessary at this juncture, even if the multiplication of divine interventions might begin to weaken faith in a mortal hero.

Creusa stops Aeneas in the doorway. She is ready to die along with her husband, and asks him to take them with him if he is rushing off to instant death.

But, she asks, if he has any hope of finding some salvation with his sword, will he not remain and guard his own house? Creusa had been absent from Aeneas' first hasty departure from home. Now she appears with all the emotional intensity of a wife holding a child at the doorway of a beleaguered dwelling. The gods do not demand that Aeneas decide what to do: they send a portent of immense significance, one which once again focuses the poem's emphasis on the crucial matter of the succession (the Augustan succession):

> cum subitum dictuque oritur mirabile monstrum
> namque manus inter maestorumque ora parentum
> ecce levis summo de vertice visus Iuli
> fundere lumen apex, tactuque innoxia mollis
> lambere flamma comas et circum tempora pasci. (2.680-684)

> *When suddenly a portent arises, wonderful to relate;*
> *for behold, between the hands and sad faces of his parents*
> *a light wisp of flame was seen to pour forth light from*
> *the topmost head of Iulus, and the flame, harmless in its touch,*
> *licked his soft locks and grazed around his temples.*

Iulus' head bursts into flame. Apparently *apex* here means a tip of flame; later it will be used to describe Aeneas' helmet and crests, which send off flames like comets in the night (10.270-271) as he advances against his enemies under the protection of the gods (the very same helmet and crests will be struck down by Messapus at 12.492). Elsewhere *apex* is used by Virgil to describe the immense Atlas (4.246), the famous portent of the bees in ancient Latium (7.66), and the olive headpieces with woolen tufts worn by the ancient Salii (8.664). The fire that shoots up from Ascanius' head here will be echoed by the flames from Aeneas' helmet/head in battle, and indeed by the flames from Augustus' on the shield Vulcan will forge for Aeneas (8.680-681). Lavinia's head, too, will burst into flame (7.71-80), a portent of war, to be sure, but also of her role as the wife of Aeneas in Latium.

The fire portent, then, is not uncommon in the *Aeneid*, but among mortals it is limited to the soon-to-be "royal family" in central Italy of Aeneas, Ascanius, and Lavinia, as well as their descendant Augustus. But its first appearance in the poem, and at a crucial moment for Aeneas, is evocative of the succession worry. For once, a character is happy with good reason; Anchises alone recognizes the portent and gives thanks to Jupiter. This is the first divine sign that Anchises has received concerning the positive destiny of his young family beyond the devastation being wrought in Troy. Aeneas has had two superhuman announcements of his mission, Hector's and Venus'. Anchises, significantly, changes his mood completely (and without lapse) after the one portent (older and wiser?). True, he asks Jupiter to confirm the sign: as the commentators have noted, the reason for this is not to assuage any remaining hesitations, but to follow the prescriptions of augury; the first omen had not been granted in response to any human prayer. The second will come as a result of Anchises' imprecation. Virgil is not concerned to prove yet again that Aeneas had full justification to leave Troy; he shows here an important contrast between the father and the son. After Aeneas saw Hector in a dream, it took him an uncomfortable amount of time to think of his father, wife, and child; Anchises' change of mood is appropriately rapid.

Jupiter answers Anchises' ritually prudent prayer and thunders on the left. The omen is Roman; the Greeks, and indeed the "barbarians," considered the right side to be the lucky one. Jupiter sends a shooting star. This star is echoed by the simile of the comet (not strictly the same astronomical phenomenon, but close enough for poetry's purposes) that describes the flames shooting from Aeneas' helmet and crests in Book 10; an identical, mysterious portent of a shooting star phenomenon will occur in Book 5 (522-528) during the funeral games for Anchises: the Sicilian king Acestes will shoot his arrow into the air during the archery contest, seemingly without purpose, and it will erupt in a flame that streaks the sky. That portent is one of the most mysterious in the *Aeneid*; what could such an apparently important sign foretell? Perhaps there is some real link between its occurrence at Anchises' funeral games and the sign given on Troy's last night that Ascanius will succeed Aeneas. Some have seen a connection to the comet that heralded Julius Caesar's apotheosis, while others, less fanciful and more historically grounded, have considered the tremendous role Sicily, especially Acestes' own city of Segesta, would play in the struggle against Carthage: this may well be right. But the matter must remain a Virgilian puzzle.

hic vero victus genitor se tollit ad auras
adfaturque deos et sanctum sidus adorat. (2.699-700)

*Here, conquered at last, my father raised himself to the breezes
and addressed the gods, and adored the holy star.*

Anchises is "truly conquered." The theme of the conquered Penates and conquered city of Troy is at last turned into a positive development: every step now brings Rome closer. Anchises' first prayer now is that the gods of his homeland will preserve his house and his grandson (again, the succession theme). He now asserts that Troy is under the *numen* of the gods; their divine power will make a future for his household.

Aeneas' action now was an immensely popular subject in ancient art (even parody). Aeneas could not forcibly take his father and carry him off, but now he will lift up the weight of his ancestral Troy on his shoulders.[39] Indeed, Anchises is his first concern:

quo res cumque cadent, unum et commune periclum,
una salus ambobus erit. (2.709-710)

*Wheresoever events may lead, joined and common will be the danger,
and there will be one salvation for both.*

The next lines have rightly occasioned question and commentary, not always fruitfully:

> . . . mihi parvus Iulus
> sit comes, et longe servet vestigia coniunx. (2.710-711)
>
> . . . let small Iulus
> be my companion, and let my wife observe my tracks from afar.

The passage has rightly occasioned question (not to say surprise and even outrage). As usual, some who have been justly troubled by Aeneas' seemingly strange instruction for his wife have tried to emend the text because they did not like what it says. Servius' explanation is that a large group would be an obvious target for the Greek occupiers. Austin thinks that the instruction for Creusa is "sensible in itself," but his judgment does not altogether calm the curious reader. Williams is right: this plan will indeed lead to disaster for Creusa; some will mechanically argue that Aeneas must marry Lavinia in Italy, and so Creusa must be removed from the scene: now will do just as well as later. We shall try to explicate what Virgil's intentions in this passage might be by examining closely what takes place next.

Aeneas addresses his household servants; he identifies a familiar location outside the city:

> est urbe egressis tumulus templumque vetustum
> desertae Cereris, iuxtaque antiqua cupressus
> religione patrum multos servata per annos;
> hanc ex diverso sedem veniemus in unam. (2.713-716)
>
> For those who depart from the city there is a mound and an old
> temple of the deserted Ceres, and next to it an ancient cypress
> preserved for many years by the religion of our fathers;
> from different places we shall come to this one spot.

The implications of Aeneas' choice of location are ominous. There is a cypress, which was associated with death; the temple is of the "deserted Ceres," a reference to the abduction of Ceres' daughter Proserpina by the god of the underworld.[40] It is probable that the reason for the meeting place is its remote, hidden location; temples of Ceres were apparently supposed to be constructed in remote and isolated places.[41] "Deserted" certainly evokes the long decade of the war, but the reference to Ceres' daughter's disappearance is unmistakable. Indeed, Creusa will be the lone casualty this sad cypress will mourn. The adjective "deserted" echoes Aeneas' first thought of his wife (2.562 *desertae Creusae*), and serves as an ill-omen.

Aeneas tells his father to pick up the Penates (2.717); the sacred objects that had been entrusted to Aeneas earlier on this night are finally ready to be evacuated. Aeneas claims that he cannot touch them until he has washed in a running river; this is the folkloric theme of the hero who cannot do something because of ritual impurity. Is it overly subtle to imagine that Aeneas is giving a justification for why he has not yet seen to the safe departure of his family and the household gods, the departure Hector had enjoined on him over four hundred lines before? After all, practically speaking, Aeneas cannot carry his father, lead his son, and be expected to carry the Penates; he needs no religious explanation for what human anatomy compels him to do.

The departure begins according to Aeneas' instructions; Creusa follows behind, as she had been instructed:

pone subit coniunx. (2.725)

His wife followed behind.

The adverb *pone* is rare in Latin; it means Creusa was behind Aeneas, but it does not indicate how close or how far (did Creusa interpret *longe* as loosely as possible?) Aeneas has been afraid of nothing thus far, because he has been alone or, at least, never with a family member; now he is afraid for his father and son (though not his wife, apparently):

... pariter comitique onerique timentem. (2.729)

... equally fearful for his companion and his burden.

The father is on his back and the son is following at the best pace a small boy can be expected to muster; Aeneas is defenseless and unable to protect against any assault. The specific mention of his father and son, without notice of his wife, reinforces the theme Virgil has already started; we wondered for much of this book why Aeneas was not heeding Hector's instructions; now, at a moment of great suspense in the narrative, we feel even more intensely a sense of disquiet at Aeneas' *modus operandi*.

We now enter a dream world again:

iamque propinquabam portis omnemque videbar
evasisse viam, subito cum creber ad auris
visus adesse pedum sonitus (2.730-732)

*"And now I was drawing near to the gates, and I seemed
to have finished the course, when suddenly there came to
my ears a frequent sound of advancing feet."*

Aeneas hears something: the sound of pursuers. Anchises can visually confirm Aeneas' aural evidence; he can see the bronze shields of the enemy (the bronze gives them away, while the Greeks cannot see the relatively small party as it tries to flee). The language Aeneas uses to describe the sound he hears (2.732

visus adesse) is the same language he used to describe Hector's ghost's apparition earlier on this long night; the narrative has come full circle. Aeneas must now describe the mysterious loss of his wife:

> hic mihi nescio quod trepido male numen amicum
> confusam eripuit mentem. (2.735-736)
>
> *Here some unfriendly divine power I know not what*
> *snatched my mind away from me and confused it.*

Aeneas' words recall Anchises' hopeful, happy prayer before they had set out:

> ... sequor et qua ducitis adsum,
> di patrii; servate domum, servate nepotem.
> vestrum hoc augurium, vestroque in numine Troia est. (2.701-703)
>
> *... I follow and am present wherever you lead,*
> *gods of my native land; preserve my home, preserve my grandson.*
> *This is your augury, and Troy is in your power.*

Anchises asked the gods of his fathers to protect his home, and, in particular, his grandson; he credits them with the omen of the shooting star, and announces that Troy is in their protection. They will indeed grant his prayer (and Jupiter's speech to Venus in Book 1 confirmed that for us long ago), and certainly the comet-like omen was sent from above as a sign of this favored destiny. But, as we shall only learn much later, Troy is truly finished on this night; the new city in Italy will not be Trojan, but Italian.

Aeneas has begun the account of his wife's disappearance by assigning blame to some "badly friendly" (that is, "unfriendly") divine power; the periphrasis shows that the divine power is indeed friendly, since it has preserved Aeneas, his father, and his son, but "badly" friendly, because he blames it for his confusion before the loss of his wife (the words *male and amicum* are deliberately separated; cf. 4.8 *male sana*, of Dido). There is a tone of reproach of the gods. The divine power snatched away his mind and confused it (*confusam* is probably proleptic). Similarly, he had blamed divine power (2.336 *numine divum*) when he initially disregarded Hector's admonition. He explains that he was off the well-traveled roads; he and the others had begun to hurry on in the night as they heard the Greeks coming (they are no phantoms), and were now outside, on their way to the distant temple. Aeneas does not realize Creusa is missing until he arrives at the temple; she is, in fact, the only one absent from their party. Aeneas begins to upbraid both gods and men (surely someone from the household was with her, or saw her); he declares to Dido's court that he saw nothing crueler in all the events of the night than his wife's loss (crueler, in part, because it is the principal reported event of this night of which he is not an eyewitness).[42] He hides his father, son, and companions, and then goes back into the city, armed, in the hope of finding Creusa.

Aeneas is recounting a moment of intense emotional loss and pain. He asks if it were fate that took Creusa away, or was it that she wandered from the path, or perhaps became tired (2.738-739). He blames some deity for confusing him (otherwise he would have detected her departure); at the moment he detected her absence, he was not sure whether her disappearance had been fated (that is, by divine will), or was an accident of nature (not that the difference, in the end, matters much). The point is that he blames heaven for her loss as much as himself; not surprising, since he knows he is open to potential criticism.

Divine power must surely be guarding Aeneas; he revisits, amazingly, his own home (which is in flames), Priam's palace (which is under guard with its booty), and sees the captive youths and their mothers. He cries out for Creusa again and yet again (we are still in the midst of scenes that cannot be pushed too far for their realism). And, now, Creusa's ghost appears to balance Hector's from before:

infelix simulacrum atque ipsius umbra Creusae
visa mihi ante oculos et nota maior imago. (2.772-773)

The unhappy image and shadow of Creusa herself
was seen before my eyes, and an image greater than was known before.

This is a waking image, and so more dramatic and frightening than Hector's nocturnal apparition; Aeneas' hair stands on end and his voice catches in his throat (2.774), just as it will when he encounters the dead Polydorus in Thrace (3.48).[43] Creusa addresses her husband and asks why he is indulging in so much grief; she confirms that it was the will of heaven (2.777 *numine divum*) that she not accompany her husband out of Troy. She specifically names Jupiter; he has not sanctioned her safe egress (2.779 *fas* shows that it is practically a religious imperative). Hector had predicted a long sea journey; Creusa now adds the detail that the goal is Hesperia, where the gentle Lydian Tiber flows amidst fertile soil. Generalizing prophecy has given way to particularizing; the Tiber is Lydian because the Etruscans allegedly had a Lydian origin. Aeneas most probably has never heard of the Tiber. Creusa predicts flourishing success (2.783 *res laetae*; "happy days" is not quite right), a kingdom, and a princess. Creusa urges Aeneas to forget her; at least she will not be a war prize for the Greeks. Before urging Aeneas to guard the son who is hers as well as his, she makes a mysterious remark:

sed me magna deum genetrix his detinet oris. (2.788)

But the great mother of the gods holds me on these shores.

The Great Mother Goddess is Cybele, a deity of Asia Minor whose principal cult sites were in Troy's environs in Phrygia.[44] In Greece she was quickly associated with Demeter. She had to make an appearance in Rome, given the legendary

Trojan origins of the city; her cult was admitted in 204 B.C. during the time of the city's worst fears about Hannibal's encroachment. But her cult was always somewhat suspect in Rome; her associations with castrated eunuch priests and orgiastic rites are exactly the sorts of things Jupiter will assure Juno are not to follow the Trojans into Italy; Roman citizens were not practitioners of Cybele's frenzied liturgies.

Aeneas now knew for certain that it had been the will of heaven (what he called "fate") that he was to lose Creusa. But the *numen* (2.777) of the gods responsible for Creusa's departure is not to be identified too closely with the *numen* Aeneas blamed for his confusion before her disappearance (2.735). Two separate events have run together; on the one hand there was the incontrovertible will of the gods that Creusa vanish, and, on the other, Aeneas' wrongheaded instruction that she walk far off behind him. Aeneas does not recognize (or wish to acknowledge) that the original error on his part was his wrongheaded, strange command to his wife. But surely that command was no more inexplicable than the inordinately long amount of time, with repeated fits of madness, which it took him to see to the safety of his entire family. A god may have snatched Creusa, and a god may have confused Aeneas, but if a god also told him to instruct his wife to follow "at a distance," he does not seem to recognize or acknowledge it. Virgil need not have had Aeneas tell his wife to follow at a distance, but he did, and Aeneas does not come off the better for it. Like his mother, Aeneas sometimes behaves inexplicably.

Creusa, then, has been sacrificed; room had to be made for Lavinia in Italy (and Dido in Carthage), and she is the first of several blood offerings (usually near the ends of books) to further Rome's destiny. If we can link Cybele and Ceres, then Creusa is an offering to the "deserted" goddess; Cybele/Ceres now holds her in her native land. Three times Aeneas tries in vain to grasp the ghost, just as he will try to embrace his father's much later in the underworld (in imitation of Odysseus's attempt to embrace the ghost of his mother in the underworld; cf. *Odyssey* 11.204-214). There is more at work here than mere consideration of plot convenience and the necessary disappearance of Creusa. Aeneas' wife, originally, had been named Eurydice; Virgil could not resist the appeal of an Orpheus and Eurydice-like story to close his Troy-tale.[45] Virgil had already told the myth of the famous lost wife in the *Georgics* (4.453-529). Ceres' daughter Proserpina, queen of the underworld, had ordered Eurydice to follow Orpheus to the underworld by walking behind him (4.487 *pone sequens*); Virgil has repeated the same image in his Creusa's disappearance. Madness overcame Orpheus (4.495 *furor*), his Eurydice lamented; he looked back at her before they had safely escaped. Aeneas does the opposite, and Creusa is lost. Orpheus disregarded a condition that seemed either purposeless or full of possible treachery (why have his wife walk behind him, unless this is some trick of Prosperina's?) Creusa obeyed an inexplicable instruction of her husband, and is also lost. In some versions Eurydice escaped with Aeneas; that would not do for Virgil, who intended to invest so much energy in his hero's Carthaginian love affair. Aeneas must have a wife in Troy, and, for Virgil's purposes, that wife must die; the image of Orpheus and Eurydice must have been irresistible. But once that connection is made, the blame of Orpheus can be transferred to Aeneas, no matter how sad and poignant the story, or how beautifully it is told.[46] Creusa's stay with Cybele distantly foreshadows the coming suppression of Troy in favor of Italy. Aeneas' seemingly inexplicable act has furthered Rome's destiny in more ways than one.

The night is far spent; the day draws near, in a sense the first one for Rome. Just as at the end of Book 6, when, after trying to grasp his father, Aeneas will instead see the line of future heroes of Rome, so now after trying to grasp his lost wife, he returns to the shore and finds that the number of Trojan refugees has increased during his absence. He is now responsible not only for his own household, but also for the vast bulk of Troy's exiles. Through the loss of his wife, he has been transformed from guardian of a small family to father of a nation.

cessi et sublato montis genitore petivi. (2.804)

I departed, and having lifted up my father I sought the mountains.

The family picture had been complete when Aeneas made his exit from Troy, but Creusa had followed. Now the picture is painted again, with the inconvenient Trojan wife gone from the scene. Lucifer, the Morning Star, rises over Mount Ida, the sacred mountain of Cybele; the Morning Star is the planet Venus.[47] As we shall see, Virgil will echo this passage much later in his epic (8.585-591), when he describes the departure of the young Pallas (Aeneas' *surrogate* son) with Aeneas and Achates as they march off to the war in Italy (and Pallas' doom). There Virgil will compare the departure of Pallas to the shining of the Morning Star (Pallas is the bright hope of the Trojans at war). Pallas will die in battle; the hopeful passage with which Virgil ends his catalogue of Trojan horrors here in Book 2 will be echoed later, only to presage the untimely, premature death of the youthful Pallas (again, the Augustan succession motif is central). Ascanius is part of the departure now, with Aeneas and Anchises, but he is protected and safe; Pallas will depart with Aeneas and Achates in Book 8, but with fatal consequences.

Slightly more than half of Aeneas' total story is over; the essential elements of the Roman succession are now in place. We are very far from the world of the *Odyssey*, though that will at once change; we have seen repeatedly and with crystal clarity that Aeneas is given to fits of madness, and that the immortals (excluding Juno, at least) are thus far unfailingly supportive of the thrust of fate that will lead to the walls of lofty Rome (though sometimes, as with Venus, their good intentions lead to more problems than they envisaged). Virgil will allow us to rest for a while after the relentless horrors of this book. But the sleep will be brief, and the waking hell.

Notes

1. On Book 2 as a whole, see especially PUTNAM, *The Poetry of the Aeneid*, Cambridge, Massachusetts, 1965, and also KNIGHT, *Vergil's Troy: Essays on the Second Book of the Aeneid*, Oxford, 1932.
2. On Virgil's story of Troy's fall as tragic theater, see J.A. EVANS, "*Aeneid* 2 and the Art of Theater," *The Classical Journal* 58.6 (1963), pp. 255-258.
3. For a convenient summary of the main points on the Wooden Horse, see AUSTIN, *P. Vergili Maronis Aeneidos Liber Secundus*, Oxford, 1964, pp. 34-36.
4. Mark Antony lost tremendous resources in Parthia; living hostages from his campaigns joined Crassus' standards as symbols of Roman humiliation. For Octavian's (sensible) diplomacy with Parthia in the period after Actium, see Dio 51.18.2-3; for the much-publicized return of the standards see *Res Gestae Divi Augusti* 29.2, Dio 54.8.1-2, and Suetonius *Divus Augustus* 21.3. Rome was essentially given a free hand in Armenia and Parthia an understanding that the Euphrates would serve as the *de facto* border between the respective spheres of influence.
5. See further Bailey, *op. cit.*, pp. 204 and 228-232.
6. On the deceptive story that now begins, see LYNCH, "Laocoon and Sinon: Virgil, *Aeneid* 2.40-198," *Greece and Rome* 27 (1980), pp. 173-177, and MOLYNEUX, "Sinon's Narrative in *Aeneid* II," *Latomus* 45 (1986), pp. 873-877.
7. Hyginus *Fabulae* 95.2; see also Apollodorus *Library* 3.7.
8. The hanging of the false beacons was the subject of Sophocles' fragmentary *Nauplius Pyrkaeus*; see also Euripides *Helen* 766-767 and 1126-1131 (with Dale's notes) and Apollodorus *Library* 2.1.5.
9. On the horse's wood see LOSADA, "Maple, Fir, and Pine: Vergil's Wooden Horse," *Transactions of the American Philological Association* 113 (1983), pp. 301-310.
10. Austin's commentary on this book gives a full survey and bibliography of Laocoon lore (pp. 94-99).
11. On dreams in the *Aeneid*, see especially STEINER, *Der Traum in der Aeneis*, Bern, 1952.
12. Aeneas' visit to Hades will be strangely devoid of any contact with famous heroes of the Trojan War from either side. Virgil thereby shows the finality of the break with Homeric epic his *Aeneid* seeks to effect.
13. See CLARK, "The Reality of Hector's Ghost in Aeneas' Dream," *Latomus* (57), 1998, pp. 832-841, and, on the entire passage, KRAGELUND, *Dream and Prediction in the Aeneid: A Semiotic Interpretation of the Dreams of Aeneas and Turnus*, Copenhagen, 1976. Kragelund offers subtle and careful analysis of Aeneas' dream encounter with Hector.
14. Ingmar Bergman's 1957 film *The Seventh Seal* touches on something of the same theme, albeit in a medieval, Scandinavian, Christian setting; his knight Antonius Block uses his brief respite to prove to himself that while God either does not exist or does not care for mortals, man is capable of finding meaning in heroic acts. Like Homer's Achilles (or, for that matter, Virgil's Turnus), Block is doomed to die. When he realizes his one chance at survival—victory in the most famous chess match in cinema—is lost, he uses his little remaining time to save a young family by distracting Death. The context is quite different from that of the classical epics; the timeless theme is the same.
15. 2.300 *Anchisae* is the poem's second mention of Aeneas' father (cf. 1.617 *Anchisae*, where Dido asks if the man before her is indeed the son Venus bore for Dardanian Anchises). Virgil's first mention of both father and son is oblique.

16. On the shepherd simile see further Hornsby, *op. cit.*, pp. 13, 15, 22, 24, 31, 36, 64, 91, and 101; Virgil has adapted it from *Iliad* 4.452-456 of a shepherd hearing the crash of winter torrents in a valley; Virgil has added the fire, and made the anonymous shepherd of Homer the main character in his drama. Cf. 4.69-73.

17. For perceptive analysis of a seemingly insignificant detail (are there any in Virgil?), see BLISS, "Ucalegon and the Scaean Gate," *Vergilius* 42 (1996), pp. 50-54.

18. See further Fowler on Lucretius *De Rerum Natura* 2.168 *deum sine numine*.

19. Janko comments on the Homeric passage: "...Othruoneus' terms for Kassandre's hand forfeit our sympathy: it is greedy to offer no gifts, but only a promise to repel the Greeks. Her other suitor, Koroibos, was no less stupid."

20. See further Hornsby, *op. cit.*, pp. 9, 63, and 92.

21. On Androgeos see RAUK, "Androgeos in Book Two of the *Aeneid*," *Transactions of the American Philological Association* 121 (1991), pp. 287-295. Rauk makes too much of the eventual Trojan decision to make no distinction between *dolus* and *virtus*; after the Wooden Horse, all bets are off, as it were.

22. Kirk ad loc. speculates that the anonymous man in Homer's simile may be a shepherd.

23. Cf. *Odyssey* 4.502, where the Lesser Ajax is already "hated by Athena." According to Proclus' summary of the *Iliupersis*, Ajax was almost stoned to death by the Greeks for his disgraceful treatment of Cassandra, but he saved himself by taking refuge at Athena's altar; the goddess dealt with him later at sea.

24. On the brief simile see further Hornsby, *op. cit.*, pp. 22 and 38.

25. For a persuasive argument that Aeneas is to be identified with Neoptolemus (cf. 2.479 ff. and 12.577), see MOSKALEW, *Formular Design and Poetic Language in the Aeneid* (*Mnesmosyne* Supplement 73), Leiden, 1982, pp. 152-155.

26. Pausanias 10.25.5-27.2 describes murals at Delphi, one of which shows Andromache with Astyanax; Neoptolemus, Pausanias notes, personally wanted to kill the son of Hector. See further M. L. WEST, *Greek Epic Fragments*, Cambridge, Massachusetts, 2003, pp. 134-139.

27. On this simile see further KNOX, "The Serpent and the Flame: The Imagery of the Second Book of the *Aeneid*," *The American Journal of Philology* 71.4 (1950), pp. 379-400 (reprinted in COMMAGER, *Virgil: A Collection of Critical Essays*, Englewood Cliffs, 1966, pp. 124-142), and Hornsby, *op. cit.*, p. 61.

28. Snakes in Virgil, as in Homer, are "vicious and courageous," though not necessarily at the same time (see Richardson on *Iliad* 22.93-97).

29. See further BRIGGS, "Lines Repeated from the *Georgics* in the *Aeneid*," *The Classical Journal* 77.2 (1982), pp. 130-147, and, more generally, his *Narrative and Simile from the Georgics in the Aeneid*, Leiden, 1980.

30. On the death of Priam see further WILLIAMS, "Vergil's Tragic Vision: The Death of Priam," *The Classical Journal* 72.3 (1978), pp. 159-166, BOWIE, "The Death of Priam: Allegory and History in the *Aeneid*," *The Classical Quarterly* N.S. 40 (1990), pp. 470-481, and SKLENAR, "The Death of Priam: *Aeneid* 2, 506-558," *Hermes* 118 (1990), pp. 67-75.

31. Pausanias knows another variant where Priam was pulled from the altar and killed in the doorway. Priam's death scene was a popular subject for art (like most of the episodes from Troy's fall); see further Austin on 2.506 ff.

32. See further NARDUCCI, "Il tronco di Pompeo," *Maia* 25 (1979), pp. 317-325, and ROSSI, "The *Aeneid* Revisited: The Journey of Pompey in Lucan's *Pharsalia*," *The American Journal of Philology* 121 (2000), pp. 571-591.

33. For the best example of arguments against Virgilian authorship of the Helen episode, see GOOLD, "Servius and the Helen Episode," *Harvard Studies in Classical Philology* 74 (1970), pp. 101-168, reprinted in Harrison, *op. cit.*, pp. 60-126; see also MURGIA, "The Date of the Helen Episode," *Harvard Studies in Classical Philology* 101 (2003), pp. 148-170. The naysayers on the authenticity question should be further silenced by FISH, "Anger, Philodemus' Good King, and the Helen Episode of *Aeneid* 2.567-589: A New Proof of Authenticity from Herculaneum," in Armstrong et al., *op. cit.*, pp. 111-138.

34. Mynors prints *haec habet* for *nec habet*; here the latter reading is better, as *tamen* proves.

35. The late (fifth century?) Greek poet Tryphiodorus (*Iliupersis* 651-655) notes that Aphrodite took care to save Aeneas and Anchises from the city, and to deposit them safely in Ausonia, so that from them might come a powerful people. Understandably, Tryphiodorus calls Aphrodite "dear to Ares"—another detail emphasizing Rome's (fitting, given her history) birth from war.

36. On this simile see further Hornsby, *op. cit.*, pp. 25-26 and 79.

37. The textual problem is old and vexed the earliest commentators, and has been used as further evidence for the later (and imperfect) insertion of the Helen and Venus episodes. Williams here correctly observes that there is no problem in using the masculine for the concept of divinity, even when contextually the referent is female.

38. For the tradition of Anchises' death or near-death see Austin ad 2.649.

39. Antoine Coypel (1661-1722) completed a series of seven paintings (royally commissioned), including Aeneas carrying his father, Aeneas and Dido, Dido's suicide, Aeneas entering the underworld, Evander lamenting the dead Pallas, and the death of Turnus.

40. On Virgil's several cypresses see further CONNORS, "Seeing Cypresses in Virgil," *The Classical Journal* 88 (1992-1993), pp. 1-17.

41. See further Henry on 2.702-714 and Vitruvius *De Architectura* 1.7.2.

42. A theme of Book 2 is the Lucretian sentiment that it is pleasurable to observe the troubles of others while you yourself are safe; Dido's court can vicariously thrill to the scenes Aeneas has created. He has no ability to draw Creusa's picture, however; he saw others die, but not his own wife: perhaps a natural result of the lengthy time he spent ignoring her and his family.

43. See further KHAN, "Exile and the Kingdom: Creusa's Revelations and Aeneas' Departure from Troy," *Latomus* 60 (2001), pp. 906-915.

44. On Cybele in the *Aeneid* see further Bailey, *op. cit.*, pp. 174-177, and cf. his note on Lucretius *De Rerum Natura* 2.610 ff., Fordyce on Catullus c. 63, as well as WILHELM, M.P., "Cybele, the Great Mother of Augustan Order," *Vergilius* 34 (1988), pp. 77-101.

45. Pausanias 19, citing the cyclic epic *Cypria*.

46. See further JENKYNS, "Virgil's Women," *Omnibus* 25 (1993), pp. 1-4.

47. On the close of this book, and others, see NAGLE, "Open-Ended Closure in *Aeneid* 2," *The Classical World* 76.5 (1983), pp. 257-263.

Chapter III

After It Seemed Best

Book 3 has never enjoyed the popularity of the dramas that surround it.[1] It is as episodic as its predecessor, if not more so, and some of the adventures on the way from Troy through Greece and on to Sicily have a certain amount of action, emotion, and tension. But for the most part, Book 3 is quiet and reflective, a companion in every way to Book 5. Along with the underworld of Book 6, it is here that we feel most lost in the world of the *Odyssey*. This is the final book that is set in the past; just as Creusa died at the end of the first half of Aeneas' story, so Anchises will die at the end of the second half. By the close of Book 3, only Aeneas and Ascanius will be left alive of the original family unit that fled Troy. Book 2 covered the events of only one night; Book 3 has to survey seven years of travel (and it is a shorter book). In consequence, episodes are often time-syncopated. In fact, it takes torturous, labored effort to make the episodes of Book 3 equal seven years.[2]

Book 3 (and its companion Book 5) was supplied with Oxford commentaries by R.D. Williams (Book 3, 1962; Book 5, 1960) as part of the Oxford Virgil series. Nicholas Horsfall published a lengthy edition of Book 3 for Brill in 2006 (the third of his *Aeneid* commentaries).

For now, Anchises is the elder statesman of the exile band; he gives the order to depart Troy; it is early summer (3.8 *prima . . . aestas*). Book 3 begins and ends with Aeneas' father. Virgil does not bother with logistical details to describe the Trojan flight. Ships are ready because Virgil needs them. The first leg of the journey to "Hesperia" brings Aeneas to the coast of Thrace. The landing is swift and the first settlement established; he calls the inhabitants the "sons of Aeneas" (3.18 *Aeneadas*), a name Virgil frequently uses for the Trojans, which recalls the great opening of Lucretius' *De Rerum Natura* with its invocation to Venus, "mother of the sons of Aeneas," *Aeneadum genetrix*. On first landing in North Africa, Venus had met his mother, who was compared to *Thracian* Harpalyce. Now Aeneas takes his first step away from Troy and toward Rome here in Thrace, a warlike place where the doom of one of Priam's unfortunate sons will be recalled.

The earliest references we possess to accounts of Aeneas' sea voyage survive in Dionysius of Halicarnassus' monumental *Roman Antiquities*.[3] He was a Greek who came to Rome and began his antiquarian research under Augustus; he tells us (1.7) that he arrived at Rome when Augustus had put an end to civil war in the middle of the 187th Olympiad (c. 30 B.C.); Dionysius casts himself in the role of the intellectual who can indulge in scholarly research thanks to Augustus' restoration of peace. His complete history was in twenty books, of which we possess Books 1-11. Dionysius (1.61-62) recounts how Dardanus, the son of Zeus and Electra (daughter of Atlas) was king in Arcadia, and eventually migrated after a flood to the Troad; the story had confused and conflicting details, but in Virgil (3.167-168) we shall learn that Dardanus came not from Arcadia, but from Hesperia. Virgil wanted to have Aeneas' landing be a homecoming; Dionysius, a Greek, was interested in making Aeneas turn out to have been a Greek all along.[4]

Aeneas spent much of Book 2 in apparent disregard of Hector's dream visit; at the beginning of Book 3 he seems strangely unaware of Creusa's prophecy (3.7 *incerti, quo fata ferant, ubi sistere detur*). Such an "inconsistency" can perhaps be excused by the unrevised status of the poem, though it does trouble us; perhaps "Hesperia" was too vague an indication—most probably the Tiber, as we have noted, is unknown to Aeneas. More troubling, though, is the first episode of this book: the dead Polydorus. He was the youngest son of Priam; in the *Iliad* (407-412) he is credited with fleetness of foot, though Achilles is able to spear him in the back as he runs past. Aeneas is sacrificing a bull (which was bad luck for Laocoon) to his mother. He tries to pull some greens from a nearby mound to decorate his makeshift altar. Even after the first drips blood, he tries to pull another, and still another. The passage will be oddly echoed in Book 6 (210-211) by the celebrated capture of the Golden Bough before the descent to Avernus.

Polydorus had been sent for safe-keeping to the Thracian king, along with payment for his care; Polydorus' name is his undoing ("much gifted"), and he is robbed and killed by the king when it is clear that Troy is finished (and that nobody is left alive in Troy who would pay the ransom for Polydorus' life). Aeneas sets up requiem altars and celebrates funeral rites; the black cypress adorns the spot (3.64 *atra cypresso*), one of two links between this story and the loss of Creusa (cf. 3.48 and 2.774, repeated lines that describe Aeneas' reaction to both ghosts). The cypress that opens this book will recur at the end, as a harbinger of the death of Anchises (3.680). So Books 2 and 3 with their one story are linked by the deaths of Creusa and Polydorus. We must not be surprised that this book opens so darkly; Aeneas' destination is Hesperia and the Tiber (as Creusa told him so recently). Aeneas travels to Thrace in part because it was traditionally allied with Troy (3.15 *hospitium antiquum Troiae sociique Penates*). It is logical enough that such a long journey would have frequent stops, and that some people will be left behind at various points (cf. 3.190). But it cannot be denied that the Trojans seem strangely unaware of where they are going.

Aeneas next visits the once floating island of Delos (sometimes called Ortygia), where we can expect a prophecy from Apollo's haunt.[5] (At the end of the book, Aeneas will sight Ortygia, the island off Syracuse, which shared its name with Delos—an artful ring). Strictly speaking, Aeneas should not need an oracle or prophecy. But there was a tradition that the Trojans visited Delos, and King Anius recognizes Anchises as an old friend. The prophecy is like the creation myth of Deucalion and Pyrrha, where the survivors of the flood were told to seek the bones of their mother; a new world is to be born through these castaways, and they must seek their ancient mother:

"Dardanidae duri, quae vos a stirpe parentum
prima tulit tellus, eadem vos ubere laeto
accipiet reduces. antiquam exquirite matrem.
hic domus Aeneae cunctis dominabitur oris
et nati natorum et qui nascentur ab illis." (3.94-98)

*"Hardy sons of Dardanus, the earth that first bore you from the
stock of your parents, this same land will accept you back with its
fertile field. Seek your ancient mother.
Here the house of Aeneas will be powerful on all shores
and the sons of sons, and those who are born from them."*

Anchises, the senior authority for the Trojans, interprets this riddle as referring to Crete; Creusa's words eliminate the need for the whole episode, of course; Servius notes that the Trojans should also realize that *Dardaniae* refers to Dardanus' homeland (Italy), not Teucer's (Crete). Bulls are sacrificed to Neptune (to guard the three day trip to Crete) and Apollo (to thank him for the words they have just misinterpreted); once again, bull sacrifices will have bad results. Anchises notes that the worship of Cybele came to Troy from Crete; he thinks the *antiquam matrem* must be Cybele.[6] Just as later Romans would have their reservations about the cult of the *Magna Mater*, so here the mention of the great Mother Goddess is irrelevant and ultimately unhelpful to the Trojans; Crete is a backward step for them, not a step forward to Rome.[7] Cybele holds Creusa back on the shores of Phrygia; in a sense both Cybele and Creusa stand for the Trojan past, not the Italian, Roman future. Delos allegedly (so says Callimachus) received its name (Greek for "clear, apparent") because once it was fixed and stopped floating, it could actually be found; its prophecies, of course, did not always match the name of the island. Aeneas' fleet sails through the Cyclades and arrives at Crete, where the Trojan exiles found Pergamum. Idomeneus should be here, but Aeneas receives the report that he has left his homeland; we learn more about his fate later in this book (3.401). Almost as soon as they have landed, a plague strikes and begins striking down both man and crops.

Somewhat surprisingly, Anchises suggests they go back to Delos and learn more about what they are to do next (another reminder that they are far from the track Creusa had outlined to Aeneas, which he inexplicably keeps secret from his father and men). The time element is again compressed; on the one hand, the plague strikes fast, on the other, Aeneas had already started assigning laws and homes (3.137), while the young were planning marriages (3.136). At night, Aeneas had yet another vision; this time the Penates he has brought out of Troy appear to him and correct Anchises' misinterpretation of the Delian oracle:

mutandae sedes. non haec tibi litora suasit
Delius aut Cretae iussit considere Apollo.
est locus, Hesperiam Grai cognomine dicunt,
terra antiqua, potens armis atque ubere glaebae;
Oenotri coluere viri; nunc fama minores
Italiam duxisse ducis de nomine gentem:

hae nobis propriae sedes, hinc Dardanus ortus
Iasiusque pater, genus a quo principe nostrum. (3.161-168)

*Your dwelling must be changed. The Delian one did not persuade you
to settle these shores, and Apollo did not order you to settle in Crete.
There is a place, the Greeks call it Hesperia by name,
an ancient land, powerful in arms and in the richness of sod—
Oenotrian men cultivate it; now the report says that their
descendants have led forth an Italian race from the name of their leader:
this is the proper home for you, from here Dardanus and
Iasius your father arose, from which is the beginning of our race.*

"Hesperia" is old information; the "Oenotrian" colonists (were they winedressers?) and the name "Italy" (from the eponymous king Italus) are new pieces of the puzzle. We can assume Aeneas and the Trojans knew that Dardanus and his brother Iasius came from Italy (though we are less than certain, given the aforementioned vexed tradition). The Penates name "Corythus" and the "Ausonian" lands (3.170-171)—further geographic aid for the Trojans. Corythus was the husband of Electra and mortal father of Iasius, while Dardanus, the more important brother, was Zeus' son; "Ausonian" refers to the Aurunci, who may be the Oscans (so Servius). "Auson" was the child of Odysseus and Calypso.

Anchises reveals to Aeneas that the reason he did not think of Hesperia and Dardanus' origins there was because Cassandra had often told him that the Trojans were destined to settle in Italy, and of course no one would ever believe Cassandra's prophecies. Virgil has given Anchises the perfect explanation for his decision to go to Crete; the blame for the error rests on Aeneas, who already could have guessed that Crete was the wrong place, if he had remembered his wife's words.[8] It will be profitable throughout the poem to consider which visions Aeneas reports, and which he keeps silent; apparently the vision of his wife has not been revealed (nor the vision of Hector), while here he immediately leaps from his bed to give his father the Penates' message.

The departure from Crete is followed by a terrible three-day storm, longer than the one that drove the Trojans to Carthage, but less devastating in its consequences. Book 3 could easily have turned into a travel catalogue of all the places linked in any way to the legend of Aeneas' flight. So Virgil has decided to introduce elements of fantasy, both to color the story with mythological magic and to evoke the amazing adventures of Homer's *Odyssey*. Aeneas' next stop is south of the Greek island of Zacynthus, the "Strophades," named after the Greek verb meaning "to turn." The story went that the sons of Boreas, the North Wind, were not allowed to pursue the Harpies past this spot (so Apollonius of Rhodes); the learned audience would know that we are about to meet the infamous bird-women, as indeed Virgil at once announces (3.210-211).[9] Aeneas was at fault for the diversions so far; this interlude is the accident of an apparently natural storm.

The storm in nature is now replaced by a figurative storm; "Harpies" in Greek means "snatchers." They personify storms in both Hesiod and Homer, but their snatching extends to the Thracian king Phineus' food in Apollonius' *Argonautica*, a story that can also be traced back as far as Hesiod.[10] Virgil's "Celaeno" ("Dark One") may be his invention. Besides adding the color of folklore to Aeneas' tour of the eastern Mediterranean, the Harpies offer a page from the *Odyssey* (the encounter with the Sirens, with which they have some affinities), recast in Hellenistic style: the Harpies from Apollonius, whose Jason and Medea love affair will soon be repeated with Aeneas and Dido.[11]

Aeneas and his men land and begin to feast on the cattle and goats they find unguarded; a foolish thing, we the audience know, after the experience of Odysseus and his men with the cattle of the sun god. At once the Harpies come and ruin the Trojan meal with their droppings and terrible screeching. After moving to a more sheltered place, the Trojans suffer yet another avian attack; Aeneas now orders that they prepare to fight in the next encounter. When the Harpies come a third time, the Trojan Misenus sounds the alarm from his vantage point. (3.239)

Misenus is the second Trojan specifically named during this episode; the first was Palinurus, introduced as Aeneas' helmsman (3.202) during the storm that drove them to the Strophades. Both Misenus and Palinurus will be dead before the first half of the poem is over, and both men's deaths will be intertwined, as we shall see, with the great events that bring Aeneas to the underworld in Book 6. Their presence here quietly foreshadows their later deaths. Palinurus complained to Aeneas that he could not find his way during the storm; in Book 5, after he has been thrown overboard by the god Sleep, Aeneas' rudderless ship will make its way past the Sirens' rock (the Sirens there connect to the Harpies here). Palinurus was curiously absent from the major storm in Book 1.

The Harpies befouled the Trojans' meal (227 *foedant*; cf. 216 *foedissima*); now the Trojans try to befoul their bodies with the sword (241 *foedare*). The Harpies are immune to the iron, though the attack does drive them off in flight; they leave befouled tracks (244 *foeda*). *Foedus*, "disgusting" is the signal word for this passage. One of the Harpies, Celaeno, now addresses the Trojans.[12] She calls them the "sons of Laomedon," an insulting reference to the perjurer who caused a previous destruction of Troy. She tells them that Jupiter made a prophecy to Apollo, and Apollo relayed the news to her, the "greatest of the Furies" (252 *Furiarum . . . maxima*). Twice Celaeno names Italy as the destination of the Trojans. Then she makes a new prophecy: the Trojans will eat their own tables before they build their city:

sed non ante datam cingetis moenibus urbem
quam vos dira fames nostraeque iniuria caedis
ambesas subigat malis absumere mensas. (3.255-257)

But you will not gird the city that has been granted to you with walls
before terrible famine and the offense of our slaughter
has compelled you to consume half-eaten tables with your jaws.

Virgil did not invent the prophecy.[13] It will be fulfilled rather harmlessly in

Book 7 (107-134), when the Trojans eat some thin bread on which they have heaped their meager meal. Aeneas' son Iulus will be the one who exclaims, "We have eaten our tables!" At the time of the Harpy's prophecy Iulus would be too young to appreciate what is being said. But Aeneas announces in Book 7 that *Anchises* was the one who told him about the eating of the tables; there is no mention of the Harpies. The commentators have duly noted the alleged inconsistency. It is possible that Anchises did repeat the Harpy's prophecy to Aeneas during the long journey ahead, perhaps even in the underworld right before the prophecy was fulfilled. Soon enough, at Buthrotum, Aeneas will learn from the seer Helenus (3.394-395) that the eating of the tables is nothing to fear. Aeneas mentions the Harpy's prophecy to Helenus, but he does not specify the detail about the tables; Helenus knows the detail from other sources (Apollo?). Just as Virgil did not invent the legend of the tables, so it is not the exclusive property of the Harpy. It should also be noted that *Anchises* is the one who makes the immediate petition to the gods that they avert the Harpy's threats:

"di, prohibete minas; di, talem avertite casum
et placidi servate pios." (3.265-266)

"O gods, forbid these threats, o gods, avert such a catastrophe
and, at peace, preserve your pious ones!"

Aeneas also reveals in Book 7 that his father's mention of the tables came with an instruction to take hope and commence the first buildings in Italy; Anchises' version of the prophecy is a positive announcement of progress and advancement towards the ultimate goal of city-building, while Celaeno makes ineffectual threats:

tum sperare domos defessus, ibique memento
prima locare manu molirique aggere tecta. (7.126-127)

Then, though tired, hope for a new home, and there remember
to place your first dwellings with your hand and build them with a rampart.

After the omen is fulfilled, Aeneas pours libations to Jupiter *and* Anchises. In any case, it does not seem necessary to imagine that the Harpies were inserted late and imperfectly into the poem.

Anchises orders an immediate departure from the Strophades after the brief and unpleasant episode; there is a final, oblique reference to Palinurus (3.269 *gubernatorque*) as they leave, which rings the whole passage with mention of Aeneas' faithful and ill-starred sailor.

The next episode is of minor importance in the context of the Odyssean westward voyage of Aeneas, but held supreme significance for the Augustan regime.[14] The Trojans land at Leucas (modern Lefkada, the name of both the island and its capital city). Virgil mentions the cliffs of Leucate, on the southern tip of the island (Cape Lefkatas), where according to legend Sappho had leapt to her death for love of Phaon (it is sometimes called the "Cape of the Lady"); the cliffs are about thirty meters in height. Their white color gave the island its Greek name. The whole area looks over to the mainland and Odysseus' homeland of Ithaca (though some have argued that Odysseus' Ithaca was actually one of the islands in the vicinity). Actium is the promontory of the mainland in the extreme northwest of Acarnania. Apollo cults were located both at Leucas and Actium long before Augustus' famous battle on 2 September 31 B.C.; the promontory of Leucate was the site of a famous temple to Apollo. According to Dionysius (1.50) the Trojans visited both Leucas and Actium; Virgil conflates the two visits into one. The distances involved are not insignificant (some forty miles), but for poetry's sake Leucas and Actium can be the same place. According to Dionysius the Trojans also stopped at Zacynthus; there they held games. The games here, however, are the ones Augustus would institute in 28 B.C. to commemorate his victory over Antony and Cleopatra, the final step in achieving his Roman peace. Augustus greatly embellished the existing town of Actium into Actium Nicopolis, Actium the "City of Victory" (modern Preveza); Nicopolis had been the site of his battle camp at Actium. Virgil gives us a rare indication of the time of year; it is winter, and we can perhaps assume it is some six months after the start of the voyage, though this cannot be pressed too far:

interea magnum sol circumvolvitur annum
et glacialis hiems Aquilonibus asperat undas. (3.284-285)

Meanwhile the sun is turned around the circuit of the great year
and the icy winter blows over the waters with blasts of the north wind.

Aeneas dedicates a shield here, meant, of course, to evoke Augustus' Actian victory. Virgil will reserve his more expansive exploration of the Actium theme for Book 8, where the shield of Aeneas offers a convenient device to allow for anachronistic embellishment. The Trojans travel to the northwest, hugging the coast, until they arrive at Buthrotum (the modern uninhabited Butrinti), where Augustus intended to make a veterans' colony after Actium, in modern Albania, near the Greek island of Corcyra (modern Corfu). Augustus had borrowed the idea from Caesar, who had the same idea for his veterans after the war with Pompey. These historical associations may help underscore why Virgil considered Buthrotum an appropriate place to dwell on the theme of those who no longer need to worry about laboring on the journey: Helenus and Andromache. For these Trojans, the war and their slavery are over, but they have no future, only the past. Virgil does not characterize his central hero Aeneas as preferring this quiet, trouble-free existence, though when Aeneas leaves them, he will reflect on the positive aspects of their settled life. One theme of the book's opening had been that Troy fell in part because it was (justly) proud and even haughty: the gods take note of such things (3.2 *superbum*). Troy did not deserve its fate, in Aeneas' view (3.1-2 *gentem / immeritam*): the gods target the excessively wealthy or powerful. For this reason, Helenus' pitiful settlement will at least never have to fear invasion (3.499).[15] Helenus will instruct Aeneas on the dangers of Scylla and Charybdis, just as Circe did for Odysseus: there are few parallels to note between the two stopovers, except the very real attraction of each place (for quite different reasons) for the tired, weary wayfarer.[16]

The traditions about Helenus all agreed that he was a seer; in the *Ilias Parva* he predicted that if Philoctetes and his bow were brought to Troy, the city would fall.[17] After the war he had an unusual relationship with Pyrrhus/Neoptolemus: he was aware that Greeks were dying on their cursed return voyages, and he urged Pyrrhus to travel by land. In consequence, he was rewarded after Pyrrhus' death with Andromache for a wife (again, the chronology cannot be pressed too far). In Dionysius (1.51) the Trojans separate here; Anchises visits Buthrotum, but Aeneas makes a trip to the oldest of Greek oracles, Zeus' shrine at Dodona, which was also sacred to Dione (Aphrodite's sometime mother). Herodotus describes its origins (2.54-57), which in legend were connected with Phoenician abductions of Theban priestesses, who ended up in Dodona and Libya. According to Dionysius, it was at Dodona that Aeneas received the oracle about eating his tables.[18]

Andromache is making offerings at the cenotaph that marks where Hector's empty grave is located on the outskirts of this fake Troy.[19] The sight of Aeneas and the Trojan warriors immediately recalls to her all the horror of that last night:

ut me conspexit venientem et Troia circum
arma amens vidit, magnis exterrita monstris
deriguit visu in medio, calor ossa reliquit,
labitur et longo vix tandem tempore fatur. (3.306-309)

As she caught sight of me coming, and, mindless,
saw the Trojan arms all around, she was terrified by the great portents
and froze in the midst of her gaze, the heat left her bones,
she swooned and, after a long time, at last scarcely spoke.

The repetition of *arma amens* (2.314) recalls Aeneas' frenzy; Andromache's is of a very different sort, though no less intense. She is in such a state of confusion that she wonders for a moment if Aeneas is dead, like her husband. *Magnis monstris* nicely contrasts the portentous arrival of Trojans thought dead or far off in slavery or exile with the tiny Troy in Buthrotum. Andromache is like Aeneas in the moments of despair we have observed: she proclaims that Polyxena was blessed, since she was sacrificed on Achilles' grave rather than handed over by lot to serve a Greek master.

In the tradition, after the war Neoptolemus married Hermione, the daughter of Helen and Menelaus. Orestes killed Neoptolemus when he went to Delphi to learn why Hermione was barren. The story (like almost all Greek myth) is confused and varied (if only we had Stesichorus' *Oresteia*!), but everyone agrees that Hermione ended up married to Orestes. Neoptolemus' death closes the ring his evil slaughter of Priam started:

excipit incautum patriasque obtruncat ad aras. (3.332)

He caught him unawares and slaughtered him at his father's altar.

Servius says that Pyrrhus had built an altar to his father at Delphi (thus explaining the difficult *patrias*); Pyrrhus has suffered Priam's death, before his father's eyes. Andromache, in any case, has questions for Aeneas: what has prompted his visit? She asks specifically about Ascanius:

quid puer Ascanius? superatne et vescitur aura?
quem tibi iam Troia—
ecqua tamen puero est amissae cura parentis? (3.339-341)

*What of the boy Ascanius? Does he survive and feed on the air,
whom Troy now to you—
and does the boy have some concern for his lost parent?*

This is the only half-line in Virgil that makes no complete sense as it stands. Virgil is perhaps expressing Andromache's sudden emotion as her question about Ascanius reminds her of the horrible fate of Astyanax. More mysterious is how Andromache knows that Creusa is dead—being a seer's wife has its advantages. Helenus interrupts the conversation with his entrance and immediate invitation for the Trojans to enter his pathetic replica of Troy. Virgil has masterfully mixed the reality of all Helenus and Andromache lost with the palpable emotions as these separated countrymen are all reunited. There is a banquet, and a vague amount of time is spent in reminiscence and rest before Aeneas makes his departure, which will be preceded by a farewell prophecy.

Aeneas asks Helenus about what he faces on the journey to Italy. He credits Helenus with knowledge of the "tongues of birds," an appropriate appellation for someone who is being asked in particular about how bad the bird-woman Celaeno's threat was. He tells Helenus that he has heard how his journey is predicted to be "prosperous" (3.362 *prospera*); he credits *religio* with the auspicious news (Lucretius may have appreciated this sentiment, considering how much trouble lies ahead on Aeneas' journey, and how the Carthaginian aspects of the voyage will lead to immense trouble for Rome's history).[20] *Religio* persuaded men to do things like slit Iphigenia's throat so ships could sail; *religio* has conveniently omitted any warnings about Carthage—in fact, Venus herself has helped Juno in orchestrating the many troubles in Carthage.[21]

Helenus cannot reveal everything: he says that he can make the journey safer (3.377 *tutior*), but that the Parcae do not allow him to know everything, and, besides, Saturnian Juno does not allow him to speak. This is the first ominous mention of Juno in quite some time; perhaps there are things Helenus knows, which Juno forces him to keep secret: the important detail is that Juno wishes to make this as hard as possible, and the Fates are willing to oblige her; it is highly significant, though, that while the storm that brought Aeneas to Carthage was Juno's doing, the storm of passion in Dido's heart was Venus'. And, in the end,

Juno will score a great victory in the ultimate resolution of the epic. For the present, Helenus' prophecy is detailed (the longest so far), and quite in the mortal realm: no ghost of Hector or Creusa, no Penates in a dream speak now.

Principio Italiam (3.381): of course the prophecy begins with Italy, and Italy will be sighted before this book closes. The opening word, *principio*, will be echoed in Book 6 (724 *Principio*) when Anchises begins his great revelation of the purgatorial process of reincarnation that so mystifies Virgil's underworld vision. Helenus' speech is a practical one; Anchises will offer philosophy and theology. The first piece of (rather mundane) information now is Italy's great distance, and the second is the rough outline of what must be traversed first: Sicilian waters, Ausonian waters (i.e., the Tyrrhenian Sea), the "infernal lakes" (i.e., the Lucrine and the Avernian, with their links to one of the traditional entrances to the underworld), and Circe's Aeaean island, whose location was the subject of quite varied speculation in antiquity. After a geography guide, Helenus announces a major portent: the white sow with her thirty white offspring, located near a river and oak trees (Aeneas might now remember the Tiber, which Helenus does not name; the river god Tiberinus will complete this prophecy, as it were, much later, once Aeneas arrives in Latium). Significantly, Helenus names Apollo (3.395) as the god who will be present for the Trojans in their difficulties; this is the Apollo we have just met obliquely in Aeneas' landing at Leucas and Actium, the Apollo of the Augustan regime whose protection of Octavian granted the naval victory over Antony and Cleopatra, a symbol of the triumph of Roman rationality over Eastern madness. Apollo makes few direct appearances in the *Aeneid*; his is a mysterious divine presence, mentioned here and there, and never at great length. In Book 6, his prophetess, the Sibyl, will conduct Aeneas safely to his father Anchises for the grand vision of Rome's future worthies. In Book 11, he will play a similarly mysterious yet important role in helping to vanquish one of the Trojans' deadliest foes. He is the god of prophecy (cf. 3.434), a natural patron for Helenus.

The geography lesson now expands, as Helenus explains why the Trojans must take the long route around Italy, rather than the short and expeditious trip to the eastern coast of the peninsula. First he mentions the landing of the "Narycian Locrians" (the modern Lokrida), Greeks from the eastern part of Locris on the mainland, opposite Euboea (famous for Thermopylae). Narycium was the traditional birthplace of Ajax, son of Oileus; his destruction at sea by Minerva has been mentioned, as well as the reason (1.41, 2.414), and here Virgil gives a sequel to his brief allusions to the lore. Aeneas knew already that Idomeneus had left Crete upon his return; now Helenus reveales that he is in Calabria, besieging the Sallentini.[22] Philoctetes rounds out the tricolon of Greeks who are in southern Italy's *Magna Graecia*: Virgil is alluding to the tradition of how had Helenus announced to the Greeks the prophecy about Philoctetes and his bow at Troy.[23]

Helenus now establishes the traditions of Roman religion. Aeneas is to make sure to pray with a veiled head, to prevent any "hostile face" (407 *hostilis facies*) from upsetting the rites. The awesome significance of Actium was passed over briefly, and so too is this quick statement about Roman religion, which is almost awkward in its placement here, though perhaps it reflects the typically mysterious style of prophecies and oracular pronouncements; it does form a ring with the solemn injunction below (3.435-439) to reverence Juno always. Helenus shifts back to geography (3.410 *ast*) and urges Aeneas not to brave Pelorus, the northeastern tip of Sicily, the site of the modern Straits of Messina: Aeneas is to sail around the entire island instead. Once, Helenus says, Sicily and the mainland were joined (and, at the dawn of the twenty-first century, proposed plans to rejoin Messina with its opposing city, Reggio Calabria, have attracted both positive and negative attention). The detour will allow Aeneas to avoid what Odysseus faced: a choice between Scylla on the right and Charybdis on the left.

In Homer (*Odyssey* 12.85-100), Scylla has six heads, each one with three rows of teeth. Virgil's Scylla has a woman's beautiful body and a mortal face, but with the dolphin tails that befit a sea monster, as well as a lupine midsection. Odysseus survived an encounter with both Scylla (who took six of his men) and Charybdis; the encounters are separated in Homer by the fateful eating of Helios' cattle and the subsequent loss of Odysseus' remaining companions. Aeneas will avoid both terrors. Having cheated death, he will make his way to the Italian coast (3.440 *finis Italos*) and proceed to Cumae, the "divine lakes," and the "sounding woods of Avernus" (3.441-442), where he will meet the Cumaean Sibyl, a priestess of Apollo. Cumae (the modern Cuma) is about sixteen kilometers northwest of Naples, and was the oldest Greek colony on the Italian mainland. The Cumaean Sibyl was one of ten sibyls officially "recognized" by the Roman polymath Varro (who died in 27 B.C., sometime during the composition of the *Aeneid*). In some sources the Sibyl was able to speak without Apollonian inspiration; this would not do for Virgil's Augustan epic: it was Augustus who transferred the famous collection of Sibylline books to Apollo's temple on the Palatine. Aeneas is given precise instructions by Helenus on how to consult the Sibyl: he must command her to speak on her own, and not merely have her write the oracles in order on leaves that will be blown around by the slightest breeze. It is the Sibyl who will announce what Aeneas will face in Italy: both the peoples (3.458 *Italiae populos*) and the wars.

Once the prophecy is finished, Helenus presents Aeneas and his men with gifts, which include cauldrons from Dodona, a nod to the tradition that Aeneas had consulted the famous oracle there while Anchises went to Buthrotum alone, and the arms of Neoptolemus: Aeneas had been helpless to stop Pyrrhus' slaughter from Priam's rooftop, but now he wins something of a personal victory over Achilles' son, however hollow—like the entire existence of Helenus' replica of Troy. Virgil rarely, if ever, allows "traditional" lists of gifts to become mere collections of ornamental epithets and irrelevantly allusive virtuosity.

Anchises gives the order to sail. Curiously, at this last moment, Helenus makes an address to Anchises. He announces the land of Ausonia (3.477 *ecce tibi Ausoniae tellus*), which is far off, indeed, as he had already warned Aeneas in his prophecy:

longa procul longis via dividit invia terris. (3.383)

A long pathless way divides you with long tracts of land.

Did Helenus know that Anchises would not live to see the promised landing at Cumae?

Poignantly, Andromache's farewell gifts for Aeneas include a Phrygian cloak for Ascanius, who reminds her so strongly of her dead son, partly because (we learn here) they were the same age. Aeneas' valediction to Andromache and Helenus has the faintest hint of weariness; the promised Ausonia is always receding back, always just over the next horizon, as it were (3.496-497).[24] Aeneas promises that if he ever reaches the Tiber (the river his wife had mentioned to him), he will link Hesperia and Epirus linked together as kindred lands: he will make one Troy (3.504-505 *unam / Troiam*) from the two. Such promises must be read closely; Augustus founded Nicopolis (which is not exactly in the vicinity of Buthrotum), to be sure, and Servius thinks Aeneas' injunction to his grandsons to take care to fulfill his wish is a reference to Augustus, but what Aeneas promises here will not be fulfilled, strictly speaking, since, as we learn so much later, Troy is truly finished, and Rome will be Italian.

Indeed, one of the problems faced by Virgil in composing his *Aeneid* was the fact that Augustan Rome was not Trojan. The explanation Virgil offers is that Jupiter promises Juno almost at the end of the poem that the new city to be born, that city she knows will one day destroy her beloved Carthage, will not be Trojan (12.836 *subsident Teucri*). This explains the disappearance of Trojan customs, dress, and language (of course in epic, everyone always speaks the same language). The Trojans will intermarry and be mixed with the Ausonians only in blood (12.835 *commixti corpore tantum*). Trojan custom and sacred paternal rites will be added (12.836-837 *morem ritusque sacrorum / adiciam*) to the Latin ways: this explains the existence at Rome of customs associated with Troy (including, for example, the cult of the *Magna Mater* from Phrygia). Juno leaves Jupiter's presence happy and content; the poem began with a speech from Jupiter to his daughter and ends with a speech from Jupiter to his wife, where the *entire* truth is revealed. Venus is nowhere at the end of the *Aeneid*; one wonders what her reaction to Jupiter's final speech and promise to his wife would be.

So this tension between the Trojan and the Roman (i.e., the native Italian, the Latin, the Ausonian) runs like an undercurrent throughout the poem. It only becomes a dramatic, climactic revelation in Book 12, when the poem has but a hundred and twenty some lines left. Below it manifests itself subtly and quietly, with the omen of the four white horses, which both is and is not meant for the Trojans.

According to some traditions (as Dionysius records), Anchises died at Onchesmus, on the coast parallel to the northern tip of the island of Corcyra. Here was the traditional point of departure for the Trojans from the Greek mainland. In Virgil, the story changes: the Trojans sail north, hugging the coast, until they reach the point that offers the shortest trip to Italy. Helenus had forbidden the Trojans from trying to settle on Italy's eastern shores, where the Greeks returning from Troy have already established nascent colonies. They stop at Acroceraunia (apparently a Virgilian invention in the tradition), a mountainous region of modern Albania ("Thunder Mountains"), just as the sun is setting. They rest, and sleep overtakes them; only Palinurus, the helmsman, is awake just before midnight, as he takes note of the constellations and the winds. When he sees that all is calm, he gives the order that the Trojans should break their brief camp and make a night voyage.

Virgil has invented the landing at Acroceraunia for his own mysterious purposes. Once again, Palinurus appears, and once more, the narrative is full of details that will only become important later. In Book 5, after so much has happened both in Carthage and Sicily, Palinurus will again be awake on deck just before midnight, when everyone else is asleep (5.835-837). The stars he sees here in Book 3 are exactly the ones Iopas sang about after Dido's banquet, before Aeneas began his long story (cf. 3.515-517 and 1.744-746).[25] Palinurus will die just before the Trojans land on the west coast of Italy near Cumae; here he is mentioned in an identical context just before they catch sight of the eastern coast. Indeed, Acroceraunia is a brief interlude for Virgil to give a brief solo stage to Palinurus. The reader cannot suspect anything ominous or foreboding; indeed, our memory will be tested when we return to the Palinurus story at the end of Book 5, after so much emotion has been spent in Carthage. But even without foreknowledge, we would rightly wonder why the Trojans have stopped here. There is possible significance for Virgil's story in the name "Thunder Mountains," which is difficult to explicate (see below). Why, too, has Virgil delayed the death of Anchises? A clue is how Anchises at once makes a prayer when Italy is sighted (3.528-529). In the tradition, Anchises did not live to see the Italian coast. Virgil has granted him that wish, just as Helenus had intimated (*Ecce tibi Ausoniae tellus*). Virgil also wishes to save Anchises' death for the end of the book, another death to dominate our thoughts as a book ends. At crucial moments in the narrative, mortals die as sacrifices for the advance of fate. So Orontes died on the "Altars" (1.109 *Aras*) during Juno's storm, so Creusa has died before Troy could be abandoned, so Astyanax has died instead of Ascanius, so Anchises will die near Drepanum (Greek for "sickle"), cut down, as another victim, and both Palinurus and Misenus will die so close to the (Italian) goal. All of these Trojan deaths in the first half of the *Aeneid* are sanctioned by divine will, as apparent blood offerings demanded for reasons mortals cannot fathom; the deaths in Italy will be of a different sort.

Three times Achates shouts out the cry of "Italy" (3.523 *Italiam. Italiam*; 3.524 *Italiam*). Three times Anchises will announce "war" (3.539 *bellum*; 3.540 *bello . . . bellum*) when the Trojans see not a white sow, but four white horses, an omen, Anchises declares, of the war Helenus has predicted: Italy will mean savage war for the Trojans, before there can be any hope of a peaceful and lasting settlement. The horse has appeared in two ominous contexts so far; on the Trojan coast it represented Greek invasion and victory, and in North Africa it was an indicator of the future military dangers of Carthage (i.e., to Rome). Here the meaning is changed somewhat. Wars still lie ahead, to be sure, but Anchises notes that horses can be yoked, and so he gives a positive reading to the first portent on Italian soil. The Trojans land here, at the modern Castro, the ancient site of the *Castrum Minervae*, a famous temple to Athena in Calabria said to have been founded by Idomeneus. Strictly speaking, the Trojans have violated Helenus' prescription to flee the eastern shores of Italy. The commentators excuse the landing here by noting the religious nature of the layover: the Trojans burn sacrifices both to Minerva and Juno, first veiling themselves according to Helenus' injunction. But they do not see the omen of the white sow that will appear near the Tiber in its appointed place; instead they see the unpredicted omen of the white horses, which they should not have seen, had they followed Helenus' instructions.

The Trojans land here out of excitement and impatience. Minerva has spelled doom for the Trojans thus far in the poem, and the unauthorized stop at her temple does allow for appeasement of both her and Juno. The Trojans know they cannot stay long on these shores, these new homes for the Greeks (3.550 *Graiugenumque domos suspectaque linquimus arva*). The portent of the white horses has been connected to Roman triumphal processions, where four white steeds would draw the general's chariot, and indeed Anchises' interpretation of the omen may point to this:

sed tamen idem olim curru succedere sueti
quadrupedes et frena iugo concordia ferre:
spes et pacis. (3.541-543)

But, nevertheless, the same horses are accustomed to come at some time
beneath the car and to bear the reins in harmony under the yoke:
there is also hope of peace.

We should not push the implications of this vision too far; it has mixed connotations, but we ought not to forget that the Trojans have not adhered to the strict letter of Helenus' advice, though quite understandably, given the well-deserved excitement of the first glimpse of Italy. Anchises interprets the omen correctly, but the evocation of the Roman triumphal procession belongs to Italy, not Phrygia.

In Dionysius the Trojans landed at Lacinium and dedicated a bowl that could still be seen in Augustus' day (Virgil alludes briefly to this tradition when he mentions the "Lacinian promontory" the Trojans see as they sail away). This entire scene balances Anchises' mistaken reading of the Delian oracle; here he reads the signs correctly, and with appropriate haste the Trojans leave the Greek lands of Italy. All of these events, including the attempted supplication of Juno, occur before the storm with its far reaching consequences; the propitiatory rites to Lacinian Juno will be ineffective.

We arrive at Sicily and the horror of Charybdis with surprising speed; the geography cannot be examined too closely, and Virgil is still rapidly painting scenes as he has Aeneas unfold his long story to Dido's court. Mount Etna is spotted, on the Sicilian shore. Here, at the fiery volcano, Virgil turns to another classic episode from the *Odyssey*: the one-eyed giant Cyclopes.[26] This sequence is overshadowed by a palpable sense of Aeneas and Odysseus almost just missing each other in their westward Mediterranean travels. The chronology, as so often in this book, cannot be pressed too far (it has only been about three months since Odysseus was here, we learn later). Aeneas will meet a member of Odysseus' crew and just catch a glimpse of the monsters Odysseus fought so memorably (*Odyssey* 9.105-566). Immediately after his adventure with the Cyclopes, Odysseus comes to the wind god Aeolus; the narrative in Virgil also links round, since reasonably soon after his Cyclops adventure comes the storm that will bring Aeneas to Dido and the "present" of the end of Book 1 and the beginning of Book 4. Aeneas is chasing Odysseus, in a sense; the first part of the poem is devoted to Aeneas' journey and the education it brings him; Virgil has conflated the Odysseus and Telemachus strands of the *Odyssey* into one story, where Aeneas can aspire to be both father and son. Everything in the first half of the epic is aimed at the landing in Italy and the great war that will erupt there, a war in which Aeneas will (perhaps) have his chance to move into another heroic role, that of Achilles.

Just as the Trojans had spent part of a night on Acroceraunia, the "Thunder Mountains," so now they will spend a night in the shadow of Etna. All was quiet and calm on the first excursion; on this trip, the night is spent in wonder at the terrible noise from the volcano. We are in a place of primeval terror; the giant Enceladus, the story goes, was thrust under Etna during the Gigantomachy. In his brief description of Etna's eruptions (3.570-582)—some have unjustly condemned it for excess—Virgil gives another nod to Lucretius, who also described Etna (*De Rerum Natura* 6.639-702), and at much greater length. A didactic poem survives (the *Aetna*), which was traditionally included among the alleged Virgilian juvenilia; its actual date of composition and author are unknown.[27] As at Acroceraunia, there is no real reason for the Trojans to have stopped in the shadow of Etna (indeed, arguably it is a strange place for a night's rest).

Here Aeneas' band of travelers takes on a castaway, the Greek Achaemenides.[28] The passage has sometimes been criticized; in many ways it reads like a doublet of the Sinon story, though with a very different import (Achaemenides is no liar). There is no prior evidence for the story; it is likely a Virgilian invention. Odysseus brought none of his men home with him to Ithaca; all died somewhere or other on the journey. Virgil gives Aeneas a chance to save one. This passage, in fact, marks the end of all Trojan hostility toward the Greeks; in the underworld, some Greek ghosts will run in fear at the sight of the armed (and living) Aeneas, but in effect the Trojan War is over once Aeneas leaves Buthrotum (indeed, in Book 11, Diomedes will refuse to come and help the Latins). We might surmise that Odysseus, certainly recklessly, would not flee from the possible adventure of the Cyclopes; for Aeneas this is a relatively minor episode on the journey, a leftover, as it were, from Homer's table. The episode also continues the undercurrent in this book of Greek disasters after Troy (a theme of the *Odyssey*); Aeneas and his men can take some consolation in the change of fortune their invaders have suffered.

The Homeric story is retold. Achaemenides saw two men smashed and eaten; Homer says six men died, but Achaemenides is emphasizing what he himself saw (3.622 *vidi egomet*). The Cyclops Polyphemus is the living version of Etna (3.632 *eructans*, 3.576 *eructans*). The Trojans had not been able to see during the night where all the loud noise was coming from (3.584): Etna and the Cyclopes (Achaemenides says there are a hundred of them, though he is perhaps embellishing out of terror) have blended into one. Virgil had noted how Enceladus the giant was the mythological explanation for the stories about Etna's eruptions; the Cyclopes had already been localized around Etna by Virgil's time (Euripides), and the association allowed Virgil to make an appropriate juxtaposition between the world of natural science and the world of mythological fancy.[29] Indeed, Etna itself bellows when Polyphemus raises his cry once the Trojans try to escape with Achaemenides (3.674 *curvisque immugiit Aetna cavernis*). The other Cyclopes rush out to see what the commotion is when they hear Polyphemus, and Virgil describes their appearance on the shore with the only simile of this book:

... quales cum vertice celso
aëriae quercus aut coniferae cyparissi
constiterunt, silva alta Iovis lucusve Dianae. (3.679-681)[30]

... *just as when on a lofty height
airy oak trees or cone-bearing cypresses
stand, in the deep forest of Jove or the grove of Diana.*

This simile has not received much attention—odd, considering how particularly Virgil has showcased it at the end of this one book of the poem in which he has consciously eschewed them.[31] The oak is sacred to Jove; the oracle at Dodona has been mentioned briefly already as a traditional stop for the exile Trojans. Diana's cypress recalls the cypress at the altar of the deserted Ceres at the end of Book 2.

The mention here of the "grove of Diana" evokes her temple in the wooded grove at Aricia (modern Ariccia). Aricia, some twenty-five kilometers southeast of Rome, was the birthplace of Augustus' mother. The priest of the cult of Diana there was a runaway slave who achieved his office by murdering his predecessor (the so-called *Rex Nemorensis*); the story formed the starting point for Frazer's celebrated *Golden Bough*. Diana (the "bright one") eventually received a cult at Rome, on the Aventine, traditionally under Servius Tullius. Hecate, a complex goddess unknown to Homer, was associated with both Persephone and Artemis; in the myths of Persephone's abduction she is sometimes a helper in the search and sometimes another daughter of Demeter who assists in retrieving Persephone from the underworld.[32] Hecate was a goddess of the crossroads (because tombs were often by the roadside, and she guarded the entrance to Hades?), and the Latin epithet *Trivia*, "the three ways," came to be applied to Diana in her triple incarnation: on earth as the huntress, in the sky as the moon, and in the underworld as Hecate. In the *Iliad* Artemis was sympathetic to the Trojans; in the *Aeneid* she is largely disinterested: when her favorite Camilla is going to die, Diana enjoins her nymph Opis to kill whoever it is who slays Camilla, Trojan or Italian. Still, her rare appearances in the *Aeneid* incline more to the Latin / Italian side than the Trojan; she is already in her role as a major goddess of the ancient Latin League, and she will never do anything to hurt the Latin cause—on the contrary, she is the patroness of one of the protomartyrs of Italy, Camilla. Given that her brother Apollo was such an important god for the Augustan regime, it is perhaps odd that the brother and sister have such muted roles in the *Aeneid* (compare their far more frequent pro-Trojan appearances in the *Iliad*);[33] Virgil is once again firmly devoted to his celebration of Italy and quiet dismissal of Troy.[34]

So Virgil has ended both Books 2 and 3 (the two halves of Aeneas' story) with ominous references to the cypress, and its associations with both Demeter / Persephone and Trivia / Diana / Hecate, and both omens will foretell major deaths, Creusa's and Anchises'. Venus mocked Diana in Book 1, and Virgil used the Diana image to underscore the confused and complex life Dido is living in Carthage. In Book 11, Diana will finally make her own appearance, and play a major role in one of the last phases of the war in Italy.

The flight from the Cyclopes is understandably rapid, and Aeneas and his crew run the risk of facing Scylla and Charybdis if they are not careful (lines 684-686 are, as Williams notes, not able to be construed without serious grammatical gymnastics that are unworthy of Virgil; the meaning is tolerable even if the lines clearly would have been revised—they perhaps show an original draft of the poem, not quite adjusted for whatever late alterations Virgil might have conjured).[35] The North Wind saves them from an Odyssean horror, and they sail past Sicilian sites Achaemenides had seen in the opposite direction when he had approached Sicily from the south. We hear no more of Odysseus' former companion after this quiet close to the Cyclopean adventure; he has served his purpose.

Virgil describes the bay of Syracuse at some length. The Sicilian emphasis of the end of Book 3 links it to the events of Book 5, which focus almost entirely on Italy's island neighbor. It is possible that we are supposed to see here, too, the origins of Sicily's enormous significance in Roman history, especially during the struggle against Carthage. Books 3 and 5 will also be linked by the figure of Anchises; Book 5 will be dominated by the games in his memory.

While circumnavigating Sicily, we are still not finished with Diana. Virgil names the island of Ortygia, the original site of Corinthian settlement in the Syracuse area. "Ortygia" was most famously a name for Delos (its association with "Quails"—Quail Island—seems to relate to the metamorphosis of some nymph, or possibly even Diana's mother Latona, into a quail). Ortygia, famous for its spring, was the reported location of Arethusa's fountain. The nymph Arethusa had been pursued by the river-god Alpheus from Elis in southern Greece, and was changed into a fountain. Alpheus pursued her relentlessly, under the sea, and eventually mingled his waters with hers on Ortygia. The fountain was famous (it even gave its name to a classics journal). Here, "as ordered," Aeneas venerates the "great divine powers" of the place, Diana certainly. The Trojans then pass the very rich soil of Helorus (Greek for "marsh," as Virgil tells us at 3.698 *stagnantis*, a typical Virgilian play on words with Greek, and useful for the non-Hellenists in both his ancient and modern audiences). They then pass Pachynus (Sicily's southeastern tip) and Camerina, "never to be moved" (a marsh that provided both disease and protection against external invasion), and the Geloan fields that announce the River Gela, areas of Sicily made famous in modern history by Patton's famous amphibious landings in 1943. Acragas is next, home of the Greek philosopher Empedocles; the Romans knew it as Agrigentum (the modern Agrigento). Aeneas apostrophizes "palmy Selinus," a reference not so much to balmy trees, but rather to the plants used in crowns for Greek athletic contests, and then passes Lilybaeum, on the western edge of southern Sicily.

Drepanum, on the western coast of Sicily, was so-called (Greek for "sickle") because it had a sickle-shaped coast. But in Virgil it becomes the place where Anchises dies, like a crop cut down at harvest—Virgil has apparently invented this place for Anchises' death, though he had varied traditions from which to select a place for Aeneas' father's demise. In some versions Anchises reached Italy; the fact that we cannot conceive of Aeneas' forthcoming love affair with Dido in Carthage with Anchises still alive says much about both father and son. If Aeneas is to visit Carthage and have a lengthy sojourn with Dido, Anchises must die; appropriately, his end comes at the very end of Book 3, before the tragedy of the fourth *Aeneid* can commence.

> ... hic me, pater optime, fessum
> deseris, heu, tantis nequiquam erepte periclis!
> nec vates Helenus, cum multa horrenda moneret,
> hos mihi praedixit luctus, non dira Celaeno. (3.710-713)

> ... *here, best father, you left me behind tired, alas!*
> *from what great perils you were snatched in vain!*
> *Nor did the bard Helenus predict this pain to me when*
> *he was warning me about many horrible things ... nor did grim Celaeno.*

Helenus, as we have noted, may well have known about this impending loss; Celaeno certainly did not. Aeneas mentions them both because he considers Helenus' prophecy one of general optimism and Celaeno's a harbinger of evil. Did Juno forbid Helenus to reveal this forthcoming tragedy to Aeneas?

Books 2-6 will all end with some sort of death or loss. Creusa and Anchises die suddenly and somewhat mysteriously. In Book 4, Dido will commit suicide. Palinurus will be lost at the end of Book 5 (we learn his complete fate in Book 6, in the underworld), and, at the close of the catalogue of future Roman historical personages, Virgil will highlight the death of Marcellus, possible heir to Augustus, in a stunning crescendo to the theme of the imperial succession. The first two deaths, Creusa and Anchises, eliminate all but the essential (so far as

Rome's future is concerned) members of the small family that fled Troy. Dido's death remains unknown to Aeneas until the underworld. The loss of Palinurus is the final sacrifice before Aeneas can land in Sicily (and, likewise, we do not learn the complete story until the underworld). Aeneas has no idea who Marcellus is (but Virgil's audience was well aware). This trend of deaths will break after Book 6, in a sense; Book 7 will end with the mention of Camilla (who is doomed to die in Book 11). No characters die at the ends of Books 8 and 9; Mezentius, Camilla, and Turnus die at or at least reasonably near (Camilla) the ends of Books 10-12, as Virgil finishes off the major Italian heroes. The schema works out more or less neatly: Books 2, 3, and 4 definitely end with the deaths of characters in the poem; 5 (Palinurus does not actually die right away), 6 (Marcellus is not a "character" in the poem *per se*), 7, 8 and 9 arguably no, and 10, 11, and 12 definitely yes; Book 1 is introductory. The "death" of Marcellus comes at the climactic midpoint of the entire poem, and is most important; Virgil showcases it. After him, the next significant losses come in Book 10 with Pallas, Lausus, and Mezentius; Pallas and Lausus continue the "Marcellus" image of the death of young worthies (a theme which will also lie behind the deaths of Camilla and Turnus).[36] The deaths in Books 2-4 are outside Italy; the deaths in 10-12 are inside. Palinurus at the end of Book 5 represents the Troy that will be lost, Camilla at the end of Book 7 (not dead, but tragically foreshadowed) represents the Italy that will be gained, but at a price; Marcellus at the end of Book 6 balances them both: the fragile future Rome.

The pattern Virgil has now set in motion with Anchises' death raises our expectations of doom as books end. Throughout Book 4 we can guess that any fatal horrors will come from Dido. Palinurus' death comes as a complete surprise (to us as well as to Aeneas). Marcellus' ends the catalogue of Rome's future in an eminently logical fashion: it must end in Virgil's own time, and his thematic obsession with the succession motif compelled him to end not with the glories of Augustus (and how easily he could have!), but with the prematurely dead heir apparent.

> Sic pater Aeneas intentis omnibus unus
> fata renarrabat divum cursusque docebat.
> conticuit tandem factoque hic fine quievit. (3.716-718)
>
> *So father Aeneas alone was relating all the fates of the gods while*
> *all were intent, and he was teaching them about his journeys.*
> *He was silent at last and here, once he reached the end, was quiet.*

Aeneas is *pater* now that Anchises is dead; the quiet close of the book (*quievit*) is tinged with a reminder of the last sorrow.[37] He has lost wife, father, and homeland; Dido has lost husband and homeland, and has no child to comfort her. When Book 4 opens, there will be no narrative close to the banquet, no dismissal of the Trojans and Carthaginians as the night draws to a close; instead the poem will at once thrust us into the tragedy of the queen. Virgil is now ready to begin the final chapter of the first act of the *Aeneid*. It will be his shortest book, though one of his most powerful; we read it not to learn the end of the love story of Aeneas and Dido (we can already guess), but to understand something of the ways of fragile, tortured mortals.

Notes

1. On this book in general, see LLOYD, "*Aeneid* III, A New Approach," and "*Aeneid* III and the Aeneas Legend," *The American Journal of Philology* 78 (1957), pp. 133-141 and 382-400, HERSHKOWITZ, "The *Aeneid* in *Aeneid* 3," *Vergilius* 37 (1991), pp. 69-76, and especially PUTNAM, "The Third Book of the *Aeneid*: From Homer to Rome," *Ramus* 9 (1980), pp. 1-21 (a useful accompaniment to his *Poetry of the Aeneid*). This article, and several others of Putnam, is most conveniently found in his *Virgil's Aeneid: Interpretation and Influence*, Chapel Hill, 1995. On Aeneas' journey to Italy in general note HORSFALL, "Aeneas the Colonist," *Vergilius* 35 (1990), pp. 8-26.

2. On the chronology of the *Aeneid* see MANDRA, *The Time Element in the Aeneid of Vergil: An Investigation*, Williamsport, 1934. Mandra's book (a Columbia dissertation) is a well-intentioned and extremely useful detailed chronology of the events of the poem; it is not without some overly subtle (not to say perverse) speculations about the passage of days. Virgil was not writing a diary.

3. On the mythohistory of the Trojan foundation of Rome, see PERRET, *Les Origines de la légende troyenne de Rome*, Paris, 1942, a still useful and beautifully written summary of the problems and evidence.

4. See further GRUEN, *Culture and National Identity in Republican Rome*, Ithaca, 1992, pp. 6-51.

5. On Delos as an oracular site, see DEN ADEL, "Apollo's Prophecies at Delos," *Classical World* 76.5 (1983), pp. 288-290.

6. See further HARDY, "*Antiqua Mater*: Misreading Gender in *Aeneid* 3.84-191," *The Classical Journal* 92.1 (1996), pp. 1-8.

7. For an intriguing argument on the symbolism of Crete in the *Aeneid*, which raises the idea that Crete's new Pergamum represents the threat of a city of free will in opposition to a city of fate, see ARMSTRONG, "Crete in the *Aeneid*: Recurring Trauma and Alternative Fate," *The Classical Quarterly* N.S. 52 (2002), pp. 321-341. More important for Virgil, though, is probably the point that Crete represents the fallen Minoan empire; like Troy, Minos' Crete is not destined for rebirth, since it is an image of past, not future victories.

8. See further QUINT, "Painful Memories: *Aeneid* 3 and the Problem of the Past," *The Classical Journal* 78.1 (1982), pp. 30-38. Quint ignores Cassandra's role in Anchises' misreading of the oracle.

9. On the Harpies see RABEL, "The Harpies in the *Aeneid*," *The Classical Journal* 804. (1985), pp. 317-325, KHAN, "The Harpies Episode in *Aeneid* 3," *Prometheus* 22 (1996), pp. 131-144, and STUBBS, "Vergil's Harpies: A Study in *Aeneid* III," *Vergilius* 44 (1998), pp. 3-12. *Pace* Rabel, it is difficult to characterize the Harpies as "innocent settlers" whose way of life has been disrupted by Trojan pirates.

10. For the Hesiodic Harpies see M.L. West on *Theogony* 266-267.

11. Virgil will save mention of the Sirens themselves for 5.864, during the eerie and enigmatic Palinurus episode, where their presence is very effective and appropriate.

12. Celaeno's name (the "Dark One," appropriate both for a Harpy as the personification of a storm cloud and the messenger of a baleful prophecy) has not received much comment (see Horsfall ad 211 for a convenient summary). Is there any connection between Celaeno and Poseidon, the parents of Lycus ("Wolf"), and the Harpies, Harpalyce (the snatcher she-wolf), and Camilla? See further p. 373 n. 49 below, and Apollodorus *Library* 3.10.1 and Hyginus *De Astronomia* 2.21 (*ex Celaeno Lycum . . . natum*).

13. See Williams and Horsfall for complete references.

14. On the Actium visit in the context of Aeneas' "mythological" journey westward, see especially STAHL, "Political Stopovers on a Mythological Travel Route: From Battling Harpies to the Battle of Actium," in STAHL, ed., *Vergil's Aeneid: Augustan Epic and Political Context*, London, 1998, pp. 37-84.

15. Dante catches the mood of Buthrotum perfectly: "The people for whom the sea opened were dead before Jordan saw its heirs; and those who did not endure toil to the end with Anchises' son gave themselves to a life without glory." (Singleton's translation of *Purgatorio* 18.133-138). See further SAYLOR, "Toy Troy: The New Perspective of the Backward Glance," *Vergilius* 16 (1970), pp. 26-28.

16. On Virgil's sad look at the past and comparison with the glories of Rome's future, see BETTINI, "Ghosts of Exile: Doubles and Nostalgia in Virgil's *parva Troia* (*Aeneid* 3.294ff)," *Classical Antiquity* 16.1 (1997), pp. 8-33.

17. Apparently he appeared at the very beginning of the Troy cycle as well; in the *Cypria* he predicted what would happen if Paris gave in to Aphrodite and accepted Helen as his "wife."

18. On the traditions surrounding Dodona and ancient epic, see GWATKIN, "Dodona, Odysseus, and Aeneas," *The Classical Journal* 57.3 (1961), pp. 97-102. Virgil no doubt thought that a harpy was the most appropriate source of a baleful oracle about hunger.

19. See further GRIMM, "Aeneas and Andromache in *Aeneid* III," *The American Journal of Philology* 88 (1967), pp. 151-162.

20. For the opposite view (Virgil as anti-Lucretian), see especially WARDEN, "*Patria praecepta*: Lucretius and Vergil in the Underworld," *Vergilius* 46 (2000), pp. 83-92. Essentially, Warden's view is a recast optimistic reading of the *Aeneid*: there really is an underworld in Virgil, "Acherusian temples" are not a figment of the imagination, and Aeneas has a glorious future. The end of Book 6 quietly rebels against such fantasies. Fundamental to the topic of Lucretius' formative influence on the "young" Virgil is GIESECKE, *Atoms, Ataraxy, and Allusion: Crossgeneric Imitation of the De Rerum Natura in Early Augustan Poetry*, Spudasmata 76, Hildesheim-Zürich-New York, 2000, which should be studied closely in conjunction with GALE, *Virgil on the Nature of Things: The Georgics, Lucretius and the Didactic Tradition*, Cambridge, 2000.

21. Lucretius *De Rerum Natura* 1.81-101.

22. Idomeneus had promised Poseidon that he would sacrifice the first thing he saw if he returned home from Troy safely; he saw his son and refused to sacrifice him, upon which the gods sent a plague on Crete. Virgil's reminiscence of this myth is the plague the Trojans suffered when they landed abortively on Crete.

23. According to the *Ilias Parva*, Philoctetes came to Troy with his bow and killed Paris (Alexander).

24. On the parallels between this farewell to the fake Troy and the funeral of Pallas in Book 11, see OTIS, *Virgil: A Study in Civilized Poetry*, Oxford, 1964, p. 365.

25. See further HANNAH, "The Stars of Iopas and Palinurus," *The American Journal of Philology* 114 (1993), pp. 123-125.

26. Useful on the subject of Etna, volcanoes, and related topics is JOHNSTON, "Under the Volcano: Volcanic Myth and Metaphor in Vergil's *Aeneid*," *Vergilius* 42 (1996), pp. 55-65.

27. The standard edition is GOODYEAR, *Incerti Auctoris Aetna*, Cambridge, 1965. Most scholars agree that the poem must predate Vesuvius' eruption in A.D. 79 (which it does not mention).

28. Note here RAMMINGER, "Imitation and Allusion in the Achaemenides Scene (Vergil, *Aeneid* 3.588-691)," *The American Journal of Philology* 112 (1991), pp. 53-71.

29. On the Cyclopes, see the important article of MONDI, "The Homeric Cyclopes: Folktale, Tradition, and Theme," *Transactions of the American Philological Association* 113 (1983), pp. 17-38.

30. On this simile see further Hornsby, *op. cit.*, pp. 26 and 80. Horsfall here misses the forest for the sake of the trees.

31. Horsfall ad loc. oddly comments: "R. D. Williams' enthusiasm for these vv. is not easily shared." *Pace* Horsfall, the comparison of the Cyclops' eye (637) to an Argive shield or Phoebus' eye (i.e., the sun) is hardly to be considered a rival for this simile's lone status in Book 3.

32. See further Hesiod *Theogony* 404-452, with M. L. West's notes.

33. Though, significantly, it will be Apollo who intervenes in Book 9 to keep Ascanius, Rome's future, out of the war.

34. Downplaying the role of both deities in the *Aeneid* allows Virgil to let them remain divine patrons of the future *Italian* Rome without making either one an overt helper or foe of Aeneas: by downplaying their presence, they are not forced to "switch sides," as it were: that dramatic reversal will be reserved for Juno, whose "reconciliation" will not be to the Trojan/Roman future but to Italian Rome.

35. The best study of this vexed section is TRAILL, "Between Scylla and Charybdis at Aeneid 3.684-686," *The American Journal of Philology* 114 (1993), pp. 407-411.

36. See further GENOVESE, "Deaths in the *Aeneid*," *Pacific Coast Philology* 10 (1975), pp. 22-28.

37. Note GEYMONAT, "Callimachus at the End of Aeneas' Narration," *Harvard Studies in Classical Philology* 95 (1993), pp. 323-331.

Chapter IV

But the Queen

Book 4 is the close of the first third of the *Aeneid*; it is divided into three sections that together form a three-act tragedy. Dido the queen is the central character of each act of the drama (4.1 *At regina*, 296 *At regina*, 504 *At regina*). This is Virgil's commentary on the origins of the conflict between Rome and Carthage. It is a commentary rooted in the realities of the civil war Virgil had just seen concluded between Octavian and Antony, with its central character Cleopatra. *Aeneid* 4 brings with it Dido's curse on Aeneas and his descendants (4.622-629), which presages the Punic Wars that were ancient history in Virgil's own day; the Augustan audience might well have noted that Aeneas left Dido in contrast to their beloved Antony's relationship with Cleopatra: Aeneas' flight meant a curse on Rome, while Antony's fidelity to Egypt's queen brought death to them both but new life for Rome.

Carthage and Cleopatra spelled some difficulty for Virgil in any wish he may have had to fashion an appealing, attractive Dido. The overwhelming majority of scholarly commentators and readers, both casual and serious, have found in their hearts tremendous sympathy for Dido and her suicidal love for Aeneas—their feelings are easily understood, given remoteness from the time and place of ancient Rome. Most would agree that Virgil's portrait of Dido allows such a sympathetic, even positive reception, and, in the end, every reader of the *Aeneid* will decide for himself how he will respond to Virgil's Dido. But some considerations might well guide our deliberation.

Virgil did not have to include this episode in the *Aeneid*. It borrows something from Homer's depiction of Odysseus with both Calypso and Circe, though few would push this too far; neither Homeric escapade has anything approaching the impact of Dido. In the underworld, Dido will ignore Aeneas in stony silence, just as Ajax did Odysseus in consequence of the judgment for the arms of Achilles, an encounter we shall study closely. But while Dido is a figure from Carthage's legendary history, there is no certain evidence that Aeneas was ever recorded as having paid a visit to Dido in North Africa; chronologies, for one thing, however loose in the *Aeneid*, must become exceedingly vague in this case: Carthage was supposedly founded centuries after Troy fell. Dido appeared in Naevius' Punic epic, but there is no proof that Aeneas visited her in Naevius' poem.

A shadowy mythology (at least from our vantage point) existed for Dido, though. She will contrast later in the poem with Camilla (for whom a similar sort of scanty evidence does *not* survive). There, too, Virgil could have avoided the character altogether. Camilla is modeled after the Penthesilea of the epic cycle (the Amazon who came in vain to save Troy in its final days), and Dido, to some extent, is also modeled after Medea in Apollonius of Rhodes' Hellenistic *Argonautica*. So besides Carthage and Cleopatra, we can add Medea to the Dido *prolegomena*: and indeed, at the end of the book, we fear for Ascanius, the future of Rome. Like her scorned Colchian model, Dido seems capable of anything, including the murder of a child. And, like Medea, she will indulge in sorcery and magic. Virgil moves from comparing her to Diana (inappropriate), then to a wounded deer (appropriate, and the opposite of the first comparison—the huntress becomes the hunted), and then to a raving Bacchant (also appropriate, and perhaps the best indication of her true nature). After all, one of the underlying themes in the *Aeneid* is not only how the gods are able to influence mortals (as Venus and Cupid do Dido), but also how they seem most likely to amplify and underscore traits and feelings already present.

Camilla will dominate one book of the *Aeneid*, and in an interesting and important battle context. Dido dominates this first third of the poem: impressive accomplishments for two characters that were not, strictly speaking, necessary to the plot. Once Virgil decided to challenge both of Homer's epics (a natural enough goal for someone writing the definitive epic poem for his time and place), at some point in the composition he decided to collapse Homer's two temptresses, Calypso and Circe, into one Carthaginian woman, Dido, who would fit well with his desire to depict Juno's implacable wrath as a divine symbol of the madness that never dies: after all, in Book 12, Juno's madness will end, while Aeneas' will just be getting started: the *arma* that started the poem will become Aeneas' arms, slaying Turnus. How these ideas germinated and crystallized, we cannot know. Virgil wanted a divinity that could embody *Furor*, and Juno, with her love for Carthage, was an irresistible choice. Book 2 showed Aeneas overcome with frequent bouts of madness as he was witness to the final night for Troy; in Book 4 Dido's frenzy duplicates the horror of the *excidium Troiae*. In Book 4, Juno will accomplish much through Dido's rage and Aeneas' Jovian summons to duty.

Aeneas winters with Dido. His delay in Carthage does not in any way reflect Octavian's behavior with Cleopatra, unless we are to imagine that Aeneas' flight from Carthage really represents Octavian's successful resistance of Cleopatra's wiles, which I cannot accept, and the important detail, as we shall see, is that Aeneas only chooses to leave Dido after Jupiter sends Mercury to order him to leave: all the prophecies, from Hector to Creusa to the Penates to Helenus, will be forgotten in short order, as Aeneas stays on in North Africa. Lurking in the background, occasionally flashing forth, there is also the role of divine intervention in the actions of Juno and Venus. Book 4 shows the two goddesses at their closest and most cooperative with each other; the full danger of the two angry, scheming women will pour forth on both Dido and all Rome in the person of Hannibal, the fulfillment of her curse of future enmity between Carthage and Italy.

When this book ends, with a third of the poem over, Rome will be no more advanced than it was at the end of Book 3, and the unborn city will have a major curse on its future, while the poem's hero will have need of divine injunction to send him on his way from Dido's arms to central Italy and Rome's conception. We have reason to be troubled, which is exactly what Virgil wants; indeed, the sympathy we feel for Dido comes in part from the role the manipulations of Venus and Juno play in her emotional state—we expect more from Aeneas. The theme of madness is clear in Dido's transformation from kind and benevolent host to savage wraith; in the case of Aeneas, it is subtler. In fact, throughout his book Virgil emphasizes Dido's madness by having Aeneas act far more quietly and calmly than he did seven years earlier when Troy fell.

And, in the final analysis, there is a similarity between Dido's appeal and that of the fake Troy at Buthrotum: the lure of the accomplished over the unaccomplished. So says Ovid's Dido to Aeneas:

facta fugis, facienda petis; quaerenda per orbem
altera, quaesita est altera terra tibi. (*Heroides* 7.13-14)

You flee the things that are done, you seek things that still must be done;
one land must be sought through the world, while another land has
  already been sought by you.

The two standard English commentaries on Book 4 are very different; Arthur Stanley Pease's monumental Harvard edition (1935) is a valuable collection of (*inter alia*) parallel passages. Austin's 1955 Oxford edition (the result of lectures he gave at Cardiff) was the first of his four commentaries on various books, and is redolent with the author's deeply felt emotion for Virgil's character study of a young (how old is she?) woman hopelessly lost in love.

Book 4 opens with Dido reeling from Cupid's effect and Aeneas' long story.[1] She has not been able to sleep, and at first light she speaks with her sister Anna, her closest confidante. After understandable words of exuberant praise for Aeneas' physical features, virtuous and brave behavior, and divine ancestry, Dido announces that she is wavering (4.22 *labantem*) in her pledge of loyalty to the memory of Sychaeus (a pledge a Roman audience would appreciate, with all the esteem Romans placed on the concept of a woman being faithful *uni viro*, "to one man").[2] Dido recognizes that breaking her oath to Sychaeus would be a "fault" (19 *culpae*), and, despite her tears, she solemnly pledges to *pudor* ("a sense of shame") that she will keep her oath—though her tears (4.30) reveal how unsteady her emotional state is. Virgil's Dido, despite Cupid's actions, is no Ovidian Apollo smitten with Daphne. She is resilient in a way a Roman could admire; she is resisting the divine interference in her life, even after the lengthy story Aeneas told gave Cupid's poison time to accomplish its mission.[3]

Anna's reply is partly the timeless analysis a sister or friend might give their loved one in this situation—how could one be expected to live as a young widow—and partly eminently practical advice: Dido is surrounded by North African enemies, not to mention the dangers her brother Pygmalion still represents. Anna's words, ironically, are framed by mention of the two goddesses who will take center stage on the divine plane in this book: Venus (4.33 *Veneris*) and Juno (4.45 *Iunone*). Will Dido know nothing of Venus? And, surely, Aeneas has arrived in Carthage under Juno's favor—true, though not in the way Anna thinks. Dido's sister is brilliantly characterized; a medieval reader of Virgil's might have recognized a Christian conception of a demon, sent with beautiful lies, mixed with truth, to tempt and confuse the paragon of virtue (the young widow who keeps faith with her dead husband). Anna is, in the final analysis, loyally and patriotically concerned with Punic glory:

> ... Teucrum comitantibus armis
> Punica se quantis attollet gloria rebus! (4.48-49)

> ... *with the arms of the Teucrians accompanying us,*
> *by what lofty deeds will Punic glory raise itself!*

Book 4 has opened similarly to Book 2, its emotionally intense partner: Anna is Sinon. Her effect is to loosen Dido's sense of shame (4.55 *solvitque pudorem*); her intentions are what moderns might call "good," though their effect is to destroy an important (Roman) concept. Pudicitia had a cult in Rome, exclusive to women who had been married but once. Anna may mean well for her sister, but her advice is fraught with offense to Roman standards of morality and noble behavior. The book will open and close with Dido and Anna; here they whisper in secret about Dido's deepest desires; at the end they will be joined together as Dido breathes her last (and Anna tells the handmaidens she will breathe in her sister's final gasp).

Dido immediately turns to religious rites and offers due sacrifices to Ceres, Apollo, Bacchus, and Juno above all (a marriage goddess, besides being Carthage's patroness). Her prayer is unstated but obvious; she wishes to marry Aeneas. Her actions are pious and dutiful. She consults the entrails of sacrificed beasts:

> heu, vatum ignarae mentes! quid vota furentem,
> quid delubra iuvant? (4.65-66)

> *Alas, ignorant minds of prophets! Do temples*
> *or vows avail a woman who is mad?*

The sentiments, once again, would please Lucretius. In this case, Dido cannot expect any help from sacrifices or the reading of omens, because she is already under Cupid's spell, and the effects are becoming more pronounced as time passes. These sacrifices are harmless and trivial in comparison with the elaborate rites she will prepare to conceal her suicide, rites that she claims are meant to end her obsessive love for Aeneas (and, indeed, by means of her suicide that is exactly what she will do). Now Virgil describes her with the first simile of the book:

uritur infelix Dido totaque vagatur
urbe furens, qualis coniecta cerva sagitta,
quam procul incautam nemora inter Cresia fixit
pastor agens telis liquitque volatile ferrum
nescius: illa fuga silvas saltusque peragrat
Dictaeos; haeret lateri letalis harundo. (4.68-73)[4]

*Unlucky Dido is burning, and she wanders through
the whole city raving, like a deer that has been shot through with an arrow,
a deer that a shepherd pierced among the Cretan groves while it was
incautious, driving it on with weapons, and he left behind the flying iron
unknowing; that deer ranges over the forests and the Dictaean
groves; the lethal shaft clings to its side.*

Cupid struck Dido, but the simile unfolds the powerful image of the *pastor . . . nescius*, who is Aeneas. The simile is parallel to the one in Book 2 (304-308) describing Aeneas' first reaction to the Greek invasion of Troy: another connection between the two books. In both instances, Aeneas is strangely unaware of his surroundings (a recurring motif). This first description of the mad (*furens*) Dido is the opposite of the simile that described her entrance in Book 1. There she was inappropriately compared to Diana; here, as we have noted, we see a more accurate image, that of the wounded deer. The huntress is now hunted. The deer was incautious, unwary, unsuspecting (*incautam*): Dido had expected to remain celibate in widowhood, and had already rejected numerous suitors, and, too, who expects a shepherd to be hunting? Further, she was not expecting Venus and Cupid to assault her. The placement of *nescius* is significant. The shepherd was apparently actively hunting (*agens telis*), and yet he did not know where he had left behind the flying iron. Virgil has muddied the waters. What exactly did the shepherd *not know*? Was he shooting arrows recklessly? Was he deliberately hunting the deer (as *agens* hints at)? Did he fire and then think he missed? Indeed, until we get to the keyword *nescius* in the last line of the simile, we have no idea the archery is not deliberate. The geographic setting of the simile (*Cresia, Dictaeos*) is a reference to the exceptional archery skills of Cretans.

The wounded deer runs off to the forests and groves; Dido wanders the city. After the simile we learn that she gives Aeneas a guided tour of the city and in the evening hosts an additional banquet and wants to hear the story of Books 2-3 again. In any case, Aeneas is apparently unaware of the extreme emotions she has for him; how can this be? Could the shepherd really have been driving on the carefree deer with weapons and then manage to strike it and not know what he had done, that he had not killed it, but only wounded it? The carefully wrought image Virgil creates shows a man who, at the very least, *should* know what effect he is having on Dido. The shepherd, however unknowing, *was* hunting; Aeneas, hunting for Ausonia, has found Dido, however unwittingly.

Dido's passion for Aeneas is *infandum* (4.85 *infandum . . . amorem*), the same word used by Aeneas to describe the sorrow of Troy's fall (2.3 *infandum . . .*

dolorem), another of Virgil's connections between the events of Books 2 and 3. At the end of this book, the flames of Dido's pyre will be a parallel for the flames that consumed Troy. She is childless (though this is not made explicit in the *Aeneid*, and Virgil gives no information about it), and Aeneas' son plays a part in her love:

> ... illum absens absentem auditque videtque,
> aut gremio Ascanium genitoris imagine capta
> detinet, infandum si fallere possit amorem. (4.83-85)

> ... *absent she hears him and sees him, though he is absent,*
> *or she holds Ascanius in her lap, captured by the image of the father,*
> *if she should be able to deceive her unspeakable love.*

These are important lines in Dido's psychology. She imagines hearing and seeing Aeneas (this is clear enough), and she holds Ascanius in her lap, seeing in him the image of his father. This is a reference to Cupid's impersonation of Ascanius (the god is gone now, his work done); Dido is either imagining that first night at the banquet, where she held Aeneas' son, or she really is holding the boy (and Rome's future) in her arms. The latter must be the case, since she does this to "deceive" (*fallere*) the unspeakable truth of her love for the father. And, of course, while all of this attention is paid to her love, the work of building Carthage (not to mention Aeneas' future city) is halted. Dido was the competent shepherd of her people; apparently without her orders and direction, the city's development is arrested—such is their dependence on the queen. When Mercury visits Aeneas later in the book (4.259-261), he will find him engaged with building projects in Carthage (i.e., Aeneas is building the wrong city). Dido, it seems, is too overcome by Cupid's curse to continue the work she was so ably directing in Book 1.

Juno revisits the scene now with all her crafty intelligence. Except for the very last scene of the book, where she frees Dido's soul from her body, this is the only appearance Juno makes in Book 4—but it is enough. Her capable skill and deeply felt emotion frames this briefest of the *Aeneid*'s books. Her goal is simple: delay in any way possible the mission of Aeneas. Venus had been afraid of the Carthaginians (reasonably so), and felt using her usual amatory tricks with Dido would protect her son and be the safest course of action. Juno has apparently been watching everything quite closely and now sees a perfect opportunity to further her own agenda: she approaches Venus with the idea that the Dido-Aeneas love story be solemnly ratified with a marriage (4.99 *pacem aeternam . . . pactosque hymenaeos*).

Venus is not so easily fooled. She has spoken to Jupiter already, and invokes his name in response to Juno's plan. She is not certain the father of gods and men will approve of the formation of one city shared by Trojans and Carthaginians. Juno does not bother to respond to Venus' objection. She dismisses the Jovian problem with the assertion that she will handle him. In the meantime, she announces the incarnation of the wounded deer simile:

> venatum Aeneas unaque miserrima Dido
> in nemus ire parant, ubi primos crastinus ortus
> extulerit Titan radiisque retexerit orbem. (4.117-119)

> *Aeneas and, together with him, most wretched Dido*
> *are preparing to go into the grove to hunt, when Titan raises*
> *tomorrow's first light and covers the world with his rays.*

The hunt planned for tomorrow is a chance for Dido to act out the imagery that has framed her story so far, ever since Venus told Aeneas about her while disguised as Diana. All the imagery that has hitherto been used to describe Dido will now come to life. Juno had used a storm to get Aeneas off his track; she will use another to disrupt the hunt and accompany their ill-omened first union. They will end up seeking shelter in the same cave where, if Juno is certain of Venus' good will, she will join them in a Roman marriage (a parallel of sorts to the marriage she promised Aeolus if he would carry out her storm orders in Book 1). Juno, in other words, has proposed that Venus agree to a nuptial union: the Jovian issue of the joined cities is something momentarily put off the agenda. Venus is not at her most intelligent:

> . . . atque dolis risit Cytherea repertis. (4.128)[5]

> . . . *and, what is more, Cytherea laughed once the trick had been discovered.*

Perhaps the goddess of love cannot resist the romantic union of Aeneas and Dido. Perhaps in *dolis repertis* there is the faintest echo of Venus' memory of how she mockingly played the Diana role in Book 1; Juno's plan will turn the chaste huntress' leisure activity into the pleasures of Venus. Venus thinks she has uncovered Juno's games, and yet she is oblivious to the reality that her assent to this scheme will do her no good. Venus' laughter, so emblematic of her nature, is misplaced.

The dawn rises on the morning of the hunt (cf. 4.129 and 11.1, "a Homeric picture," as Austin notes—in Book 11 it will begin the book that describes the deeds of Diana's true devotee, Camilla).[6] An elaborate dawn formula will also open the last day of Dido's life, making an effective link with this hunt scene (4.584-585). Dido is delaying (4.132 *cunctantem*) in her chamber; Virgil significantly calls it the *thalamus*, a word that evokes the marriage chamber.[7] Dido's horse is caparisoned in purple and gold, the same royal colors that Camilla herself will be wearing later (7.814-816). Purple and gold are colors suitable for a queen, though not for a huntress; Camilla will wear them as a Volscian war leader, having abandoned her childhood and adolescent hunting lifestyle in the forest. Camilla is a true huntress, who will conflate the worlds of hunting and warfare (to her doom); Dido here is like Venus, playing Diana.

Aeneas arrives and is compared at once to Diana's brother Apollo in a famous simile that forms a companion to the one that introduced Dido (1.498-504):

qualis ubi hibernam Lyciam Xanthique fluenta
deserit ac Delum maternam invisit Apollo
instauratque choros, mixtique altaria circum
Cretesque Dryopesque fremunt pictique Agathyrsi:
ipse iugis Cynthi graditur mollique fluentem
fronde premit crinem fingens atque implicat auro,
tela sonant umeris: haud illo segnior ibat
Aeneas, tantum egregio decus enitet ore. (4.143-150)[8]

*As when Apollo leaves behind his winter home at Lycia and the streams
of Xanthus and visits his maternal Delos and
starts up the dances, and, mixed together, the Cretans and
the Dryopes and the painted Agathyrsi crowd around the altars:
he himself over the ridges of Cynthus advances and presses his
flowing locks with leafage, shaping and binding them with gold,
and the weapons sound on his shoulders: not in any way more slowly
did Aeneas advance, and such great glory shone on his noble face.*

Once again, Virgil has crafted a beautiful poetic image that can be admired on a simple level as a piece of exquisite allusive and learned verse; Apollonius of Rhodes compared Jason to Apollo (*Argonautica* 1.307 ff.), so there was epic precedent for his Apollonian description of Aeneas (who will soon play Jason opposite Medea). In mythology Diana and Apollo were brother and sister, rarely if ever in disagreement with each other, opposites in some ways (sun/moon, day/night), similar in others (hunting). Both were responsible for the sudden deaths of the young. Just as Apollo/Arruns will have a role in the death of Camilla, so Apollo / Aeneas will even supply the weapon for Dido's suicide. In Apollo's weapons sounding on his shoulders, there is the faintest echo (cf. *Iliad* 1.46) of the Homeric god's sending of the plague on the Greeks. In the light of Roman history, what begins on this hunt will end in the greatest threats to Rome's existence, namely Hannibal and the Punic Wars, a theme that cannot be exaggerated in studying the *Aeneid*: we need look no further than Silius Italicus' Silver Age decision to compose a *Punica* that is steeped in Virgiliana; Silius was profoundly reverential to Virgil's memory—he considered it his greatest honor that he was caretaker of Virgil's tomb, and his epic unfolds the aftermath of Dido's curse.

The appropriateness of the comparison between Aeneas and Apollo only highlights the inappropriateness of Dido's to Diana. And, besides, there is the useful prominence of Apollo in a poem ostensibly devoted to the celebration of the Augustan regime.

Deer run amok (4.154-156) in a reminiscence of Dido's deer-like, maddened flight through the city. Ascanius (whose chronology and age, as we have noted, are left confused and vague throughout the poem) takes a prominent part in the hunt (4.156-159)—for the first time, Aeneas' son takes a young adult role in the poem. The storm arrives, as Juno promised, and Dido and Aeneas are driven to a cave, alone together. The nymphs howl (4.168 *ululdrunt*) at this wedding and Virgil leaves no room for doubt: this day was the first of death and the cause of evils (4.169-170). Dido had been admirably restrained in her secret love for Aeneas until this point; indeed, we may ponder what might have happened had Juno not sent her second storm on Aeneas. After the cave there is no turning back for Dido, she now calls her fault a "marriage." It does no good to debate whether what happened in the cave was a legitimate marriage or not; the witnesses were the immortals and the elemental forces of nature—it was not a *Roman* marriage, to be sure, and Virgil perhaps implies that even in her far gone state Dido retains some awareness that this is all wrong (he certainly considers it a fault):

> coniugium vocat, hoc praetexit nomine culpam. (4.172)
>
> *She calls it a marriage, with this name she conceals her fault.*

Virgil is willing to call the "marriage" Dido's *culpa*; I would emphasize the efforts Dido has made until this second divine intervention (first Venus, then Juno) to resist Aeneas. Aeneas himself is a different story. When Virgil described Cupid's imitation of Ascanius, his language was careful:

> ille ubi complexu Aeneae colloque pependit
> et magnum falsi implevit genitoris amorem,
> reginam petit. (1.715-717)
>
> *That one, after he was hanging from Aeneas' neck in an embrace,*
> *and had filled him with the love of a false parent,*
> *sought the queen.*

Cupid goes on to work his magic at erasing the memory of Sychaeus from Dido's heart (1.720); with Aeneas Virgil says only that he "satisfied the love of his false father"—Aeneas is fixated on Ascanius. There is no explicit indication that Cupid caused Aeneas to fall in love with Dido. What happened in the cave was mysterious and private; though orchestrated by the immortals, the encounter in the cave was a personal moment between Aeneas and Dido, in stark contrast to the public relationship between Turnus and Camilla later in the epic: Aeneas and Dido will now commence an intense, passionate, *private* relationship, romantic and sexual, which will alienate them from their respective peoples and delay the advance of Rome.

Odysseus' dalliances with Calypso and Circe (especially the former) remained almost entirely in the private domain. His return home to Penelope was, after all, a largely private mission; his duties and obligations to his household are not really parallel to Aeneas' obligations to the future Roman Empire.

Dido's union with Aeneas has repercussions both for Roman and Carthaginian destinies (Mercury will find Aeneas building the *wrong* city, and Dido has apparently given up on urban planning), and attracts the attention of her rejected suitors in Libya once word reaches them of her romantic guest. Virgil's depiction of the goddess Fama, "Rumor," recalls the monsters of Etna (4.179 *Encelado*, and cf. 4.181 with 3.658, of Polyphemus). Rumor is a primeval force, a sister to the giants of old and just as impossible to stop, absent divine intervention. She frequents the towered cities of the great (visiting the poor and weak less often, perhaps), and she speaks the truth, even as she clings to the false and wicked (4.188)—an important fact. She tells both lies and the truth, though the specific details we are told of her rumors here are all true enough: Aeneas came, born from Trojan blood, Dido has deigned to join herself to him in wedlock, and they are spending a winter together and forgetting the respective works of their kingdoms. Rumor is a disgusting goddess (4.195 *foeda*), reminiscent of the Harpies, and yet her revolting appearance does not change the truth of her statements, any more than the Harpy told a lie in her omen of the eating of the tables. Part of why Rumor is so hideous in appearance is because she reflects the emotions felt when uncomfortable truths are brought into the light, truths usually better left unspoken.

As might be expected, the rumors about Dido and Aeneas quickly reach Iarbas, the son of Jupiter Ammon and an unnamed Garamantian nymph. "Ammon" was the chief Egyptian god. Iarbas' plea to Jupiter is the first instance in the poem of a theme that will become more developed in the second half of the epic: stereotyped insults against Trojans:

> et nunc ille Paris cum semiviro comitatu,
> Maeonia mentum mitra crinemque madentem
> subnixus, rapto potitur. (4.215-217)[9]
>
> *And now that Paris with his half-male retinue,*
> *propping up his chin and dripping locks with a Maeonian band,*
> *takes by plunder.*

Turnus' brother-in-law Numanus Remulus will utter similar ethnic slurs during the war in Italy (9.598-620). It is profitable for moderns to consider what picture of Aeneas and his Trojans they have in their minds (Virgil is notoriously vague about actual physical appearances, despite his wealth of details). The insults against Trojan manhood stem from their worship of Cybele and her cult of eunuch priests. Iarbas is being unfair in accusing Aeneas of Paris-like actions here; the Paris image will certainly be present in the triangle of Aeneas-Lavinia-Turnus later. Jupiter hears Iarbas' prayer (though he has no interest in Dido's love life, except insofar as it impedes Rome's founding). Virgil says that Jupiter now turned his attention to the "lovers who were forgetful of a better reputation"—a direct reference to the *fama* that provoked Iarbas' petition. The "better reputation" implies that Aeneas and Dido are not behaving admirably (Dido should be preserving her faith with the dead Sychaeus, and Aeneas should be off to Italy). Just as Jupiter sent Mercury to calm the Carthaginians and soften their hearts, so now he will send Mercury as a ring to the whole Carthage episode.[10] The storm is long over, and Aeneas has had more than enough time to recover. Jupiter's words to his messenger son deserve attention:

> non illum nobis genetrix pulcherrima talem
> promisit Graiumque ideo bis vindicat armis;
> sed fore qui gravidam imperiis belloque frementem
> Italiam regeret, genus alto a sanguine Teucri
> proderet, ac totum sub leges mitteret orbem. (4.227-231)

> *Not such as this did his most beautiful mother promise*
> *him to us and twice save him from the weapons of the Greeks;*
> *but as one who would rule Italy, pregnant with empire and seething with*
> *war, and as one who would bring forth a race from the lofty blood*
> *of Teucer, and, what is more, who would send the whole word under his laws.*

The word order is important. Jupiter's point is that Aeneas was not preserved twice from Greek arms at Troy so that he could stay with Dido in luxury and love, but so that he could found the future ruling city of the world. But the opening has a far more general resonance: "it was not a man such as this that his most beautiful mother promised to us." Jupiter is more than disappointed in his favored hero. He is willing to consider the possibility that Aeneas does not care for fame and glory outside of Carthage; he therefore mentions Ascanius, who deserves the chance to fulfill his destiny. Why, Jupiter asks, does Aeneas delay among a personally hostile people (4.235 *inimica in gente*): not just *hostis*, a public enemy, but *inimicus*, a personal enemy: Jupiter, with the eye of eternity, is already looking ahead to the Punic Wars and Roman-Carthaginian enmity.

The poetic description of Mercury's descent to earth is lengthy, but not merely ornamental mythology.[11] Mercury grabs his wand, the staff by which he conducts souls to the underworld in his role as psychopomp. This is a foreshadowing of Dido's death, which will come as the not unexpected result of Jupiter's edict; Mercury sometimes summons souls, but sometimes he sends them down to baleful Tartarus (4.243 *Tartara tristia*); this will be Dido's home in the underworld. At the end of the book, Juno will pity her Carthaginian Dido and grant her soul release (and not by means of Jupiter's messenger Mercury, but by her own messenger, Iris). This present passage details Mercury's associations with Death and his brother, Sleep: Mercury was the god who put Argus, Juno's watchman, to sleep so that Io could be freed. The extended description Virgil provides of Atlas is here because of geographic location (the Atlas Mountains, broadly conceived) and because of Mercury's mother Maia, who was the daughter of Atlas. Further, the Trojan ancestor Dardanus was the son of Zeus and Electra, the daughter of Atlas: Jupiter has sent Mercury to give the soundest advice to Aeneas as Trojan leader. The extended description of the mountain-god foreshadows the important connection Atlas represents between the Trojans and the Greek allies they will find in Italy, Evander's Arcadians (8.134-142).

When Mercury finds Aeneas, he is at work on the building projects of Carthage. The detail is interesting. We had been told (4.86-89) that Dido had stopped attending to supervision of her city's construction projects. Rumor (4.194) had said that both Aeneas and Dido were being forgetful of their kingdoms. It seems Rumor was right, in the strict sense; Dido has become so lovesick for Aeneas that she cannot concentrate on her work, while Aeneas is busy working for the wrong kingdom: a Roman would rightly be filled with some trepidation at the thought of one of their great ancestors assisting with the building and strengthening of Carthage. Just as in Book 2, we are left to wonder why Aeneas has seemingly forgotten the prophecies that had sent him forth to Italy. Aeneas is wearing a Tyrian cloak Dido made for him: he has assumed Carthaginian dress (Virgil will return to the theme of ethnic customs at the end of Book 12, with the announcement of the suppression of Trojan *mores*). Mercury wastes no time with pleasantries or conversation; he attacks Aeneas (4.265 *invadit*) and conveys the substance of his father Jupiter's commands.

Aeneas' reaction to Mercury's words is fittingly irrational: he is mindless (4.279 *amens*), in the same emotional state he was when he first glimpsed the fiery destruction of Troy (2.314 *amens*). One disaster will now give way to another. To his credit, on the one hand, he is ready to leave immediately; he now *burns* with the desire to flee (4.281 *ardet*); this apparent sudden change of heart is exactly what some readers and commentators have found so objectionable. But thus far Aeneas has been largely passive; we have received little if any sense of his emotional state while wintering with Dido; we feel as if we know so very much about the Carthaginian, and so little about the Trojan. His concern over how to approach Dido is understandable, no matter what the motivation. He decides to prepare for his departure in secret (again, the path of least resistance, however wise and prudent); he also tells his men to prepare arms.[12] Aeneas has matured from the man of Troy; unlike his reactions to the crises in Book 2, here, after some initial self-deliberation, he gives crisp and sound instructions to his men. His conflict is restricted to his mind; he does not rush out headlong into danger now. Significantly, Aeneas' men are "happy," indeed "joyful" (4.295 *laeti*) as they carry out his orders. Subtly, Virgil has conveyed the state of mind of the Trojan guests (we may compare Odysseus' men at Circe's house). This sojourn has been a private one for Aeneas. They are ready, indeed eager, to make their way to their promised homes. So ends the first act of the tragedy.[13]

Dido had held Ascanius in her arms, trying thereby to satisfy her desire to hold Aeneas (4.85 *infandum si fallere possit amorem*); her efforts failed, in large part thanks to Venus and Juno, and now she cannot be deceived by Aeneas' secrecy (4.296 *fallere quis possit amantem?*). Rumor, *impia* (like Madness), visits Dido now and informs her of the preparations: again, the goddess may be foul and loathsome, but the report is true. Dido had offered libations to Bacchus (4.58 *Lyaeo*, the "loosener" after the effects of wine); now she is compared to a raging Bacchant, she rushes on in violent frenzy (4.302 *Thyias*, a "violent rusher") and we are thrust into the terrifying world of Euripides' *Bacchae*, with all the violently gory associations of the climax of that tragedy:

> saevit inops animi totamque incensa per urbem
> bacchatur, qualis commotis excita sacris
> Thyias, ubi audito stimulant trieterica Baccho
> orgia nocturnusque vocat clamore Cithaeron. (4.300-303)[14]

> *Helpless in mind she rages and cries like a Bacchant through*
> *the whole city, as if set on fire, like some Thyiad when,*
> *once the Bacchic cry has been heard, the biennial orgies rouse her up*
> *and Cithaeron calls her with a shout.*

We are far from Diana and her sylvan haunts. After a recovery of her senses, Dido is ready to make her first speech to Aeneas.

Dido wins a victory over Aeneas in the ensuing games of rhetoric. Aeneas cannot have much to say; he is obedient to the will of the gods and his Roman destiny, though unwillingly (see below on 4.361). Here Dido's opening sentiments express the ultimate outcome; she is already expecting death (4.308 *moritura*). Interestingly, Dido blames Aeneas for the fact that her Tyrians now hate her (4.321 *infensi Tyrii*); Mercury found Aeneas working on building projects in Carthage, but we must imagine that Dido's attention has hardly been fixed on her people and their burgeoning city. Aeneas has ruined Dido's relationship with her neighbors, her own people, and he has stolen away the sense of shame and modesty (4.322 *pudor*) that she previously boasted was her greatest virtue. Dido wishes that she had at least had a son with Aeneas, a child who could remind her of her great love; this wistful longing reflects the earlier episode where she had held Ascanius in her arms and pretended she was holding Aeneas.[15] His response is marked by brevity (4.333 *pauca*, 4.337 *pauca*). Before giving voice to Aeneas' response, Virgil makes clear that it was because of Jupiter (4.331 *Iovis monitis*) that Aeneas was holding his eyes unmoved (where was his gaze fixed?) and kept suppressing (4.332 *premebat*, a frequentative imperfect) his concern for her in his heart, with great effort (4.332 *obnixus*). Aeneas' speech—his only one—has received severe criticism from some (Page) and excuse and pity from others (Austin). The basic argument he makes is that he never married her:

> ... neque ego hanc abscondere furto
> speravi (ne finge) fugam, nec coniugis umquam
> praetendi taedas aut haec in foedera veni. (4.337-339)

> *... nor did I ever hope to conceal this flight*
> *in stealth (do not imagine it), nor ever did I*
> *extend the torches of a spouse to you or come into this agreement with you.*

He introduces his denial of marriage by a denial of subterfuge; he never intended to cover his flight by deceit. This is technically true; he ordered his friends to prepare their flight secretly, while he waited for the best time to approach Dido; thanks to omnipresent Rumor she anticipated his news (cf. 4.296-297 *At regina dolos . . . praesentit*). It is not, however, the most forthcoming and admirable way to begin his argument. The denial of the marriage is also true: Juno and Venus had agreed it would be a marriage, Dido thought it would be a marriage, but Aeneas technically never pledged his troth. Some might argue that Aeneas makes a weak argument into a despicable one by next arguing that if he had his own way (and we expect him to say he would stay with Dido), he would first look after Troy and the relics of his dead countrymen, Troy would still be standing, and he would be setting up a Pergamum for the defeated (4.342-344): a somewhat disjointed statement (evidence of his emotional state); he seems to conflate the cultivation of the dead Troy we associate with Helenus and Andromache with the preservation of the original Troy of Priam before the fall. Aeneas follows up his Trojan wishes with mention of Apollo's oracle that he settle in Italy (a reference to the Delian oracle from Book 3)—how can Dido begrudge the Trojans the right to pursue the same new, foreign homelands that her people have pursued? Lastly, Aeneas reveals that *Anchises* has often visited him in dreams and admonished him, besides the recent visit of Mercury that the audience has already witnessed. Somewhat ambiguous is why Aeneas mentions "Grynean Apollo" (4.345, after Gryneum in Lydia) and the "Lycian oracles." Servius says that Apollo gave his oracles at Lycia in winter, when the action of Book 4 is occurring, and at Delos in the summer. We have heard of nothing of these oracles (only Delos earlier, in Book 3), but they do serve to underscore the reality of how many clear indications of his destiny Aeneas has received. Still, it seems unsatisfactory that we have not heard of these oracles; their presence only serves to emphasize just how lost in Dido Aeneas has become.

As mentioned, it is profitable to take note of the visions and apparitions Aeneas receives and reports to others. This is the first manifestation we learn of only through Aeneas' own admission. We have no reason to doubt its veracity (and Anchises will confirm it later, in the underworld). Anchises could not have been alive for the Dido episode, and now his ghost appears to have cast its pall over the events of the first part of this three act tragedy. *Aeneas has effectively ignored Anchises*, though, until Mercury jarred him back to his obligations. But this revelation is trivial compared to the stunning conclusion of Aeneas' speech to Dido:

Italiam non sponte sequor. (4.361)

I am not pursuing Italy of my own will.

It is perhaps the most powerful "unfinished" line in all of the *Aeneid*. Irvine was right: no one would ever wish to see this line finished, and Virgil certainly wanted it noticed, and it is probably one of the "deliberate" hemistichs in the poem.[16] It summarizes the passivity of Aeneas with a devastating brutality: he was not really married to Dido, he has argued, but on the other hand he does not go to Italy of his own will; he would rather be in Troy, in any case. It does Virgil no justice for commentators to seesaw back and forth between excuse for Aeneas and excuse for Dido. Aeneas has declared his (current) state of mind, and he has made a hard stand on the past by introducing *Troy* into the equation, in addition to Dido's Carthage and Ascanius' Italy. Aeneas' concluding remark here is strange considering he had called Italy his love and his native land (4.347); apparently there he was referring to the will of divine decree, not his own. Virgil has powerfully manipulated a complex array of audience emotions, and under the whole scene lurks the recent Roman history of Antony's stay with Cleopatra (for Antony had no wish to betray or deny Rome, and would surely have called Rome his love and his country). Williams rightly notes that despite modern sentiments, Aeneas should *not* say that he will never feel shame at the remembrance of Dido (4.335)—on the contrary, he should regret the memory of his abandonment of duty. In Book 2, Aeneas' momentary lapses into madness were brief and ultimately without serious effect; they represented relatively minor delays in the furthering of his Roman destiny. His lapse in Book 4 is more disturbing because 1) it has serious consequences for Rome and Carthage, and 2) as Dido becomes the more visibly "mad" character, Aeneas' quiet calm and composed demeanor adds a new element to the equation: we can readily forgive a maddened Aeneas when he (temporarily) seems to forget a prophecy, but now we must accept an Aeneas who pursues his mission only because Jupiter says so. We are far indeed from Odysseus crying on Calypso's beach.

Dido's reply is worthy of her predecessor Medea:[17]

"nec tibi diva parens generis nec Dardanus auctor,
perfide, sed duris genuit te cautibus horrens
Caucasus Hyrcanaeque admorunt ubera tigres." (4.365-367)

*"You had no divine parent nor was Dardanus the author of your race,
treacherous one, but the horrible Caucasus bore you on
its hard crags, and Hyrcanian tigers gave you their teats."*

Some of Dido's speech is the stock rhetoric of insult and invective; some of it is a true rendition of recent events.[18] Dido mentions how she saved Aeneas' shipwrecked companions from death (4.375 *socios a morte reduxi*), which recalls how Dido saved some of the Trojans from the firing of their ships by unfriendly Carthaginians. Dido has a sense of sarcasm for the gods that an Epicurean would appreciate: evidently, she says, concerns over things like Italy stir up the gods who should be living in quiet calm, detached from mortal affairs. Evidently, she says, the gods labor to further human endeavors. Dido's first curse, so to speak, will be for Aeneas alone (as her rage builds, so will the scope of her imprecations). Like some wraith from the underworld, Dido promises that she will pursue Aeneas and be present at the moment of his death (in other words, she will be the last image in his mind before he breathes his last, and the image will not be a loving one). She threatens to pursue Aeneas with "black fires" (4.384 *atris ignibus*); this is perhaps guilt over her impending suicide and burning on her pyre (Aeneas will see the smoke from the pyre at the beginning of Book 5, and receive confirmation of her suicide when he sees her shade in the underworld, though presumably he never learns the details of her end). Aeneas, then, is to follow Italy (4.381 *I, sequere Italiam!*), while Dido will pursue Aeneas (4.384 *sequar*) even beyond the grave in a perverse and horrible mutation of her love for him. She will abandon this rage, and, what is more, find Sychaeus again for all time in the underworld—but the curse she will utter against Rome will remain.

Dido flees at the end of her attack on Aeneas, eventually collapsing, and her attendants take her back to her chamber to rest (now her chamber is called a *marble* bridal chamber, since what she thought was a nuptial union is instead now a union with death); she leaves Aeneas behind in a curious state:

linquens multa metu cunctantem et multa volentem
dicere. (4.390-391)

leaving behind the one who was hesitating very much because of fear,
though he was also wishing to say many things.

Just as Dido had delayed in her chamber before the fateful hunt (4.133 *cunctantem*), so now Aeneas is delaying. The second half of the sentence is easy to construe; Aeneas wished to say many more things to her. The first half is more difficult. Apparently he is hesitating to say or do anything more out of fear of her highly emotional state. But Virgil delays the crucial verb *dicere*; the line highlights Aeneas' trepidation and delay, two qualities that have been demonstrated consistently thus far in the poem. Austin suggests that Aeneas is afraid of giving in to his desire to stay with Dido. The Oxford text (Hirtzel or Mynors) here prints *parantem* for *volentem* (Aeneas was "preparing" to say many things). *Volentem* is the reading of one of the capital manuscripts (*M*); Austin prefers to read *parantem* ("more graphic"). I rather think *volentem* works better with *cunctantem*. But the meaning is not very different.

After Dido's departure, Virgil describes Aeneas as *pius* (4.393): he both wants to assuage Dido's feelings and avert her curses. The adjective is deliberately chosen.[19] He has a very real sense of loyalty to her, and so he wishes to comfort her; he also quite rightly wants to deflect her curse from his and his descendants. Beyond all this, he has decided to leave her, despite his mixed feelings. He has not been entirely clear and forthcoming with her (or us); he has defined his heartfelt wish to be a return to Troy and a restoration of life as it was before the Greek invasion. Where Dido fits into the equation after that is less certain, though his actions (staying with her until Jupiter's order to go) and his stated lack of personal volition in going to Italy muddy the waters. If he could not have his wish to return to a reconstituted Troy, thus far he has been content to remain with Dido, despite his mention of his people's divine right to seek a foreign home in the same way Dido and her Phoenicians had (4.346-350). Aeneas may have been externally calm in this entire exchange with Dido, but the logic of some of his conflicting remarks is ample evidence of his interior struggle, which Jupiter solves for him, against his will. He may be weakened by his great love, as Virgil says, but he will follow the decrees of the gods.

Ships were supposed to be repaired and built during the sojourn in Carthage, but the ships Aeneas' men now set out on the water still have leaves on their oars on account of the hasty flight (the half-line 400 *infabricata fugae studio* may be a deliberate trick to illustrate textually the rapid, unfinished task). Aeneas' men are compared to ants that store up food for winter.[20] The fact that the ants are described as preparing for winter, while Aeneas' men are making their hurried exit from Carthage during winter, well illustrates the lateness of the Trojan departure. The fact that they are like ants also points to their vulnerability, especially in this makeshift flight. Dido sees everything from her lofty citadel, and resolves to try again at persuading Aeneas to stay. Virgil's apostrophe reminds us of the source of Dido's *culpa*:

improbe Amor, quid non mortalia pectora cogis! (4.412)

Relentless Love, what do you not compel mortal hearts to do!

So Dido had also labeled Aeneas, Amor's half-brother (4.386 *improbe*). Carthaginian hearts had been calmed by Jupiter when he first sent Mercury to North Africa to prevent violence against the beleaguered Trojans. Dido was next assaulted by Venus and her son, when the goddess was concerned that Phoenicians could not be trusted to keep their word and remain peaceful and hospitable. Venus' assault reached a third stage when Juno proposed the "marriage" rites between Aeneas and Dido, and Venus was, amazingly, willing to consent (she was probably thinking ahead to any future enmity between Rome and Carthage; ironically, her machinations have helped to guarantee them). Besides all of this divine manipulation, Dido, like Cleopatra and Medea, cannot be expected to behave rationally.

Dido approaches Anna for help, in a ring with their conversation from the book's opening. There was a tradition (Servius preserves it from Varro) that Anna and Aeneas had been the romantic couple; this no doubt accounts for Dido's revelation now that Anna has always been the one who could approach Aeneas and know his hidden feelings. Her words carry a tone of jealous reproach, as we might expect from a scorned lover. Dido asks Anna to go as a supplicant to the "proud enemy" (4.424 *hostem . . . superbum*) Aeneas; the origins of the Punic Wars are already quite apparent: Aeneas is a *hostis*, a state enemy. Dido notes that she was not among the Greeks responsible for destroying Aeneas' city and that she was not responsible for desecrating Anchises' grave (4.426-427), an obscure legend that needed explanation even in Servius' day, the origin of which is impossible to determine. Dido has changed her request in a way that is immediately understandable to anyone ever rejected by a former lover: she is only asking for some "empty time" (4.433 *tempus inane*), a respite to learn to adjust to her new state of life. Her final words to Anna are mysterious:

> extremam hanc oro veniam (miserere sororis),
> quam mihi cum dederit cumulatam morte remittam. (4.435-436)

> *I beg you for this last favor (have pity on your sister);*
> *which, when he will have given it to me I shall pay back with interest at my death.*

When Dido dies, she will return Aeneas' favor with interest.[21] Aeneas' favor, though, would be *inane*, empty and in vain, and so will her payment at her death. Dido has probably already resolved to die if she is refused (and surely she knows Aeneas will reject this last appeal). She had previously promised a curse on Aeneas after her death. Her payment to Aeneas will be empty, because the last request he might have granted would have been an empty gesture. Aeneas had "feasted his eyes on the empty picture" (1.464) in Dido's temple, where he took comfort in images that should have offered not comfort but dread; now Dido, so close to suicide, wavering between life and death, has asked for what she knows would be an empty solace. Twice nothing is nothing, and that is what Dido is promising at her death: an improvement, at least, over her promise of *post mortem* terror and vengeance. She is fighting an epic, ultimately hopeless struggle against Cupid and his mother Venus—Rome's future parent and protector.

Anna might well have succeeded, had not "the god" (4.440 *deus*) stopped up Aeneas' "placid ears" that were open to temptation and submission even now. Because of this divine action, Aeneas is compared to a mighty oak tree (Jupiter was no doubt the "god," as the oak is his symbol), which resists the immense buffets of the Alpine winds in winter (again, a reminder of the season, especially since Dido asked for a respite during the stormy weather) and loses only a few leaves, but does not collapse:

> mens immota manet, lacrimae volvuntur inanes. (4.449)

> *His mind remained unmoved, and empty tears rolled down the face.*

The *mens* (i.e., Aeneas' mind, his intention) remains unmoved, like his eyes during his conversation with Dido earlier, and the tears fall empty, as empty as the solace of a short respite would have been to Dido in the end. Whose tears are these? Virgil would not wish an exclusive answer (*pace* his commentators, from Augustine onwards), and neither should we. In any case, they are without substance.[22] It would be perverse and very un-Virgilian, to imagine that Aeneas is faking tears here to impress upon Dido how deeply this is bothering him.

Dido wants to die (she has been called *moritura* twice already by Virgil, but now her intention is made explicit)—she prays for death. She is thoroughly terrified by the fates (4.450 *exterrita fatis*): deeply wounded by Cupid's curse, she feels she cannot live without Aeneas (and, indeed, only when dead, in the underworld, will she find peace from her agony). She begins sacred rites: the water and wine she pours out on the altar in libation change to gore, an omen of her own impending death, and another sacrifice before the coming of Rome. Why is she burning incense and conducting religious ritual? Possibly even now she is trying to sway Aeneas back to her, or perhaps she is seeking to make peace with heaven before she ends her life. Whatever the motivation, the rites do not console:

quo magis inceptum peragat lucemque relinquat,
vidit (4.452-453)

by which the more she may carry out what she has started and leave the light,
she saw (terrible omens)

"By which the more she may follow through on what has been started, and leave the light," she now sees terrible omens. The line is mysterious; the omens clearly portend her death, but were they sent so as to hasten her suicide? Do the gods want her dead quickly, perhaps before she can wreak some final havoc on the Trojan fleet as it makes it quick exit? At the end of the book, Virgil tells us that Juno took pity on Dido's soul because her death had not been deserved and was not fated; instead, it was wretched and premature. If Aeneas had never arrived in Carthage, surely Dido's future would have been different; what if he had arrived, but the gods had never intervened (and it was Jupiter who originally stepped into human affairs to send Mercury to soothe the Carthaginians' fierce hearts). Why does Dido not reveal these omens (just as Aeneas often keeps his supernatural experiences private)? Would Anna realize they portended Dido's likely suicide? The longer Dido remains alive, the more work the gods must do to keep Aeneas resolute. The gods do not *force* Dido to commit suicide (her death was not "fated," strictly speaking); she would have lived longer had she not killed herself—an obvious and yet somehow terrible logic.

Virgil also mentions Dido's memorial temple to Sychaeus, which she *used* to cultivate (4.458 *colebat*); she thinks she hears her husband's voice calling to her. She is also terrified by many sayings she remembers from Carthaginian prophets (were they predicting the future disasters with Rome?) Aeneas, too, drives her on (4.465 *agit*), just as the hunter did who wounded the deer. He pursues her, and yet she is left alone on the road, like the deer that was wounded, not killed, and then abandoned. The shepherd/hunter of the simile was unknowing, but now Aeneas is called fierce (*ferus*), because he is fully aware now of everything.[23]

Dido had earlier been compared to a raving Bacchant, one of those who killed King Pentheus and ripped him apart; now she sees herself in her dreams running in terror and flight from Aeneas, and Virgil says it is just as if *she* were Pentheus. The change is significant, and part of a profound reflection on the nature of her suicide. Dido can only escape her divinely inspired feelings for Aeneas by killing herself; before she resolved to die, she was a mad, raging, emotionally overwrought and ultimately dangerous woman, like a Bacchant. Now, as she wavers between life and death, she sees herself in the opposite role; she has run the full gamut of emotional frenzy. *She* is now pursued, by the mysterious forces, internal and quite possibly external, that seem to her to demand her death. This wavering also explains how she is further compared to Orestes, running on the tragic stage from the ghost of his murdered mother Clytemnestra with her threats of the Furies; like Orestes', Dido's actions can be understood even by those who would not be willing to call them justified, and Virgil explicitly compares her to Orestes "on stage" (4.471 *scaenis*), so as to highlight how we are in the midst of a Greek tragedy.

Dido concealed the omens from Anna, but now, having resolved to die, apparently once and for all (cf. 4.529 ff.), she outlines her plan. If Dido merely wishes to commit suicide, why does she orchestrate the baroque death *tableau* we now see unfold, replete with the spells of magic and the horror of necromancy? A small part of the reason is the comparison with the sorceress Medea, and, by extension, to highlight Dido's Eastern irrationality and make a Roman reader justly fear her. But principally there is the sacrifice ritual Dido will now undertake, with herself as the sacrificial victim. By this religious rite she will end her obsessive love (i.e., Cupid's curse), expiate her guilt for violated *pudor*, and propitiate Sychaeus' ghost. Lofty goals demand elaborate liturgy. She reveals that a Massylian priestess has been "shown to her" (4.483 *monstrata*), probably in the ominous visions she has received from the gods (if she is not lying to beguile Anna into helping her); she will seek out a priestess (4.509) who will be present at her magic ceremonies. Dido claims that this priestess (who used to guard the temple of the Hesperides at the western edge of the earth, where the golden apples were kept that were the gift of the earth to Juno when she married Jupiter) has the power to "loosen minds" and to "send cares" as she will: in the context of Dido's speech to Anna, she means the priestess can remove the curse of love from Dido's heart, but by *solvere mentes* (4.487; cf. 479 *solvat*) Dido really portends her suicide.

Much of this is inspired by Medea, then, and her part in the quest for the Golden Fleece. Dido says that she is undertaking these magical rites unwillingly:

... magicas invitam accingier artis. (4.493)

... *against my will am I girded for the magic arts.*

The archaic present infinitive passive *accingier* adds solemnity to Dido's declaration; Aeneas was not seeking Italy of his own free will, and neither is Dido resorting to magic of her own volition: the gods have portended the way; they have demanded her death, and with the full apparatus of a sacrifice: a fine way to present to an Augustan audience the elaborate death *tableau* of Cleopatra, whose suicide cheated Octavian out of a triumph. Even a Roman audience could admire what Heinze called a truly Roman heroism (*echt römischer Heroismus*); cf. Horace *carmen* 1.37:

> ausa et iacentem visere regiam
> vulto sereno, fortis et asperas
> tractare serpentes, ut atrum
> corpore combiberet venenum,

deliberata morte ferocior (*carmen* 1.37.25-29)

She dared also to gaze on her kingdom with
serene countenance, though it was in ruin, and was brave enough
to handle fierce serpents, so that she might quaff down the
black poison in her body,

more ferocious because her death was premeditated.

There is a certain shiver of fear at such bold resolution; Dido, like Cleopatra, becomes more ferocious because of how she has orchestrated her own exit. Dido was not willing to throw herself at the Trojans and follow their utmost orders in some servile lifestyle; this is parallel to Cleopatra not being willing to indulge any of Octavian's wishes for a triumph.[24] Of course, the lurid and magical details of either death only underscore the traditional Roman view about the extreme dangers of such foreign, Eastern women.

It will be pleasing for Dido to burn all her mementos of Aeneas on a huge pyre; she, of course, is a living remembrance of Aeneas. She will ignore him in the underworld because the flames of this pyre will extinguish the memory of Aeneas from her mind and body and leave him to remember her for as long as he lives, in a sort of fulfillment of her original curse on him. And so the stage is set for the third and final act of the tragedy.

The death of Dido is partly all too terribly real and partly tinged with the magic of Medean mythology. Dido had strangely said that a priestess had been "shown" to her; this priestess had once been far off at the end of the world, guarding the dragon of the Hesperides and keeping it sedate with honey and poppy (4.486 *mella soporiferumque papaver*, the opium poppy, associated with sleep, death, and the underworld because of its narcotic, soporific effects).[25] Now this mythological priestess is present at the rites, because Virgil needs one; the world of fantastic magic has entered the conventional narrative of Dido's end. The Diana motif that has marked Dido so powerfully will now come full circle; the priestess will invoke Diana in her manifestation as the death goddess:

tergeminamque Hecaten, tria virginis ora Dianae. (4.511)

and Hecate of triple form, the three faces of the virgin Diana.

The poppy, too, that the priestess offers the Hesperides dragon to keep it sluggish may connect Dido's death scene with the motif of Demeter and her abducted daughter Persephone, though this need not be pushed too far. There may be some connection between Demeter / Ceres and the controversial, mysterious "Poppy Goddess" who appears on a thirteenth century B.C. terra cotta statuette found west of Knossos on Crete and now in the Herakleion Museum. The main image Virgil presents is the ring between Dido's first entrance and her exit, and it is Diana who provides the bond, Diana who now appears in her infernal form. Yet again we are told that Dido is "about to die" (4.519 *moritura*; cf. 308, 415, and 604). Night comes, and Dido remains alive; it is unclear why there is delay now, though the delay allows Virgil to reinforce the theme of the queen's relentless love (it can only end with her death), the tragic result of Cupid's curse. On this last night of her life, the love rages yet again (4.531-532 *rursusque resurgens / saevit amor*). The feelings of love come back in another strong wave, and Dido once more wonders what to do (her resolution to die weakened by the sudden jolt from Cupid's curse).

Dido's emotions are being torn in different directions under the power of conflicting calls, now to die, now to throw herself at the Trojans, perhaps, and simply follow them and execute their every command (4.537-538 *ultima / iussa*). At the end of her soliloquy, Dido laments that it was not permitted for her to live a life without sin, in the manner of a wild beast, a strange line that has occasioned much critical comment:

> non licuit thalami expertem sine crimine vitam
> degere more ferae, talis nec tangere curas. (4.550-551)
>
> *It was not permitted for me to live an innocent life apart from the*
> *marriage chamber, in the manner of a wild beast, and to abstain from such concerns.*

The woman who will live this sort of life is Camilla, who never violated her virginity. Dido had not been a virgin, but had decided to consecrate her widowhood and live a celibate life; she was not a huntress, though, but a leader of her people and a city-builder. When we meet Camilla, she will be leading her force into battle, but her essential connection to Diana (virginity) will remain intact. Dido has not infrequent moments of lucidity in her final hours; the line even stretches back to her marriage to Sychaeus and how her love for him, in a sense, led to the conflict with her brother Pygmalion: the murder of Sychaeus was the proximate cause for her flight from Tyre. It was not in Dido's nature to be able to live alone and without marriage; in contrast, Camilla will remain a virgin throughout her life, even when she abandons the world of the hunt. Very different too is the cause for the *infant* Camilla's flight from her homeland. Throughout this book *cura* is a word Virgil uses to describe Dido's love; because she cannot truly have Aeneas, her love is a constant source of anxiety.

Aeneas, meanwhile, who is aboard his flagship, is "fixed on going" (4.554 *certus eundi*), though he has not yet made his departure. He is asleep when Mercury appears to him a dream and asks how he could be asleep at such a moment of crisis (4.560 *hoc sub casu*). We might wonder why Aeneas has so listlessly decided to delay his departure (earlier the image was one of rapid preparation); of course, we might also ask why Dido has delayed her suicide, given her earlier, apparently resolute state (the two lovers have their shared traits). Mercury tells Aeneas that Dido is resolved to die (4.564 *certa mori*, parallel to Aeneas' *certus eundi*), and warns him that if he lingers until dawn, he will see his ships burned:

> illa dolos dirumque nefas in pectore versat,
> certa mori
> iam mare turbari trabibus saevasque videbis
> conlucere faces, iam fervere litora flammis,
> si te attigerit terris Aurora morantem. (4.563-564; 566-568)
>
> *She turns over in her heart the trick and the unspeakably dire plan,*
> *set on dying*
> *and soon you will see the sea disturbed by broken timbers, and*
> *savage torches blazing, and the shores hot with flames,*
> *if Aurora should touch you as you delay on land.*

The next dawn, in other words, will contrast with the dawn that saw their fateful union in the cave (4.129; cf. 585—Virgil underscores the theme). The problem here is that Dido had not made any threats at all against the Trojans in her insomniac speech. When dawn finally comes, Dido will see the fleeing Trojans and make the threats Mercury has mentioned; she will also utter her curse that binds Rome and Carthage in eternal enmity. Mercury had said, after all, "woman is always a variable and changing thing" (4.569-570 *varium et mutabile semper / femina*). Dido is planning no trick, no treachery; part of the tone of Mercury's speech is the prejudice of Romans against perfidious Phoenicians, and part is a simple description of the vicissitudes of a woman: today's lover is tomorrow's vengeful fury.

There is a contrast for both Dido and Aeneas between what they are *resolved* to do (die and go) and what they are actually doing (insomnia and sleep). Both their allegedly resolved actions and their actual activities are diametrically opposed. Yet again, Dido's action can be somewhat excused by divine power (Cupid)—Aeneas' is somewhat less easy to understand (Mercury certainly is frustrated with him). Virgil depicts the god Mercury in curious language:

> huic se forma dei vultu redeuntis eodem
> obtulit in somnis rursusque ita visa monere est,
> omnia Mercurio similis (4.556-558)
>
> *To him a form of the god returning appeared in sleep with the same*
> *face, and again seemed to warn him,*
> *similar to Mercury in all things*

Aeneas is asleep for the vision, and after he wakes up and stirs his companions to make their sudden departure, he addresses the god:

> quisquis es, imperioque iterum paremus ovantes.
> adsis o placidusque iuves et sidera caelo
> dextra feras. (4.577-579)

> *Whoever you are, again, hailing you, we obey your command.*
> *Be present, be peaceful to us and help our cause, and*
> *bring favorable stars with your right hand.*

Who exactly was the god? The phrase *quisquis es* need not imply a serious question about the god's identity (cf. 9.22, where Turnus knows it is Iris who is summoning him to battle, and the rhetorical *quisquis* there may point to Juno as Iris' instigator, as here it probably refers to Jupiter as the ultimate origin of the message). We can excuse Aeneas' wording of his prayer, then, though it remains interesting that Dido did not give voice to the vain threats she soon utters. When she sees the fleet sailing off, in her frenzy she calls on men who are not present to hear her to take fire and prepare a navy to pursue them (shades of Actium and Cleopatra?) No one seems to be around to hear Dido; she is already alone, as she was in her dream. We can well appreciate that this reaction of Dido's would have happened whenever the Trojan fleet finally made its departure; Mercury's prophecy was a wise enough warning, especially given the crucial detail in this scenario: Aeneas has still not left Carthage.

Did Juno send Mercury, seeking to aggravate the situation and to thereby provoke the curse of Carthage on Rome? The possibility seems doubtful, though it is strange that after the vision, Virgil says that Aeneas woke up thoroughly terrified by "sudden shades":

> ... subitis exterritus umbris. (4.571)

> ... *terrified by the sudden shades.*

The phrase, as the commentators have noted without real solution, seems odd to use for Mercury's visitation. In any case, the irrevocable step had to come, and the gods have somehow precipitated it. From a human point of view, the emotional behavior of both Dido and Aeneas is understandable; from the Roman point of view, the delays and mood changes of mortals are becoming tedious and wearisome. Dido's reaction now is thoroughly in line with her emotional state, and the consequences for Rome's future are enormous. Dido sees the Trojan fleet departing at dawn, and the same extended formula used to describe Aurora's rising will be used later in the poem, no doubt deliberately, to describe the arrival of the news of the deaths of Nisus and Euryalus, the Trojan youths who conduct a fateful night raid (cf. 4.584-585 and 9.459-460).

Dido had invoked a number of gods and divine powers when she was preparing her ritual pyre earlier. Now she invokes them again: Hecate, Juno, the Sun, the Furies—and her first curse is personal, as it was before. She prays that Aeneas may die prematurely and remain unburied (we remember Priam's headless body on the beach of Troy). As offerings at her own grave, she then calls on the Tyrians to pursue the Trojans with eternal hatred. She uses the future imperative of solemn, legal and religious authority:

> ... nullus amor populis nec foedera sunto. (4.624)

> ... *let there be no love between our peoples, no alliances.*

Finally, she summons an avenger (4.625 *ultor*) from her bones (a reference to Hannibal) that will pursue the Trojans in war. Dido herself may not pursue Aeneas, but her avenger will bring terror to Aeneas' descendants. Hannibal will indeed be at the door of Rome: all the horror the invasion of Spain, of elephant armies marching over the Alps and descending into Italy, of Cannae— everything is evoked by Dido's call for vengeance. The Trojans had been compared to ants in the simile describing their dutiful flight. According to Servius, Virgil's description of the ants (4.404 *it nigrum campis agmen*) had been used by Ennius to describe elephants (he provides no context). Thus we see an evocation of Hannibal, who will descend into Italy the way Aeneas' men now flee.

Now Dido can carry out her death scene, which has all the trappings of a sacrifice ritual. Dido sends Sychaeus' aged nurse Barce to arrange the remaining preparations. Anna must lustrate herself in river water and bring the expiatory offerings (4.636 *piacula*). Dido plans to kill herself with Aeneas' sword on what she considered their marriage bed; she makes a final address to the symbols of Aeneas and their former love, which include his effigy (4.508). These constant interruptions of her determination (4.649 *mente morata* describes her wavering state perfectly) reflect the power of Cupid's spell; twice Dido says this suicide will free her from her anxiety (4.639 *curis*, 652 *curis*). Powerfully, after a recapitulation of her life and its virtues until Aeneas came, Dido evokes the same utterance Aeneas had made in a moment of tremendous madness on the night Troy fell:

> ... moriemur inultae,
> sed moriamur. (4.659-660; cf. 2.353 and 670)

> ... *let us die unavenged,*
> *but let us die.*

Dido has conflated two moments in Aeneas' first person narrative of Troy's death agonies (an allusion ignored by both Austin and Williams). As she stabs herself, she prays that Aeneas will see the smoke from the pyre as he sails away, and be filled with the omen of her suicide: her wish will be granted. Aeneas had been willing to die in a frenzy of madness, while Fate and the gods had other plans; Dido is also willing to die in a frenzy of madness, which was in accord with Fate and the will of the gods—and in these final moments she finds rationality at last in her self-release from Cupid's spell. The power of having Dido unknowingly quote Aeneas with her dying words reflects the obsession the spell has wrought in her; despite her curse of vengeance, she will die unavenged, since she will not live to see Aeneas and his Trojans punished by Hannibal.

Fittingly, once Dido dies Rumor will make its last appearance, as it runs like a Bacchant (4.666) through the city, announcing the news of Dido's suicide—and once again, the Rumor is true. Rumor is a Bacchant because the people who spread the word of the death of their queen are not quietly whispering (as no doubt they were when the gossip was of Dido's love affair), but instead they are in the madness of grief; their behavior is like that of the inhabitants of an invaded city (4.669-671). Virgil has once again linked the horrors of Books 2 and 4. Without their leader, the Carthaginians are now at the mercy of Iarbas, who in some versions of the legend apparently invaded Carthage after Dido's death. Anna's rushing to her dying sister's side will be echoed in Book 11 by the appearance of *Acca*, Camilla's closest friend, though in a quite different context. Camilla will die in full view of both her army and those who watch the combat from the walls of Latium's capital city; Dido dies in relative privacy, and it is Rumor who makes her death public.[26]

Book 4 reaches its emotional climax with the death of Dido, a scene of contrasting horrors: the madness in the city, where Dido has abandoned her people by her death, and the more personal madness at the suicide couch, where Dido has abandoned her sister.[27] Aeneas has safely sailed away from the North African coast, but his Trojans carry with them the promise that an avenger will arise from the ashes of Dido's pyre and wreak vengeance on Rome. Juno, as Book 4 closes, is all-powerful; she has accomplished much in the shortest book of the epic. The closing of *Aeneid* 4 is one the most moving in all Latin poetry. It should be read and read again by all who think that Virgil is but a poor imitator of Homer:

> Tum Iuno omnipotens, longum miserata dolorem
> difficilisque obitus Irim demisit Olympo
> quae luctantem animam nexosque resolveret artus.
> nam quia nec fato merita nec morte peribat,
> sed misera ante diem subitoque accensa furore,
> nondum illi flavum Prosperina vertice crinem
> abstulerat Stygioque caput damnaverat Orco.
> ergo Iris croceis per caelum roscida pennis
> mille trahens varios adverso sole colores,
> devolat et supra caput adstitit. "hunc ego Diti
> sacrum iussa fero teque isto corpore solvo":
> sic ait et dextra crinem secat: omnis et una
> dilapsus calor atque in ventos vita recessit. (4.693-705)

> *Then all-powerful Juno, having taken pity on the long sorrow*

BUT THE QUEEN 125

and the difficult death, sent Iris down from Olympus
so she could free the struggling soul and the tightly-bound limbs,
since Dido was not perishing by the decree of fate, and not by a deserved death,
but miserable, before her time, and aflame with sudden madness,
and Proserpina had not yet snatched a blond lock of hair from her head
and condemned her head to Stygian Orcus.
Therefore Iris flew down through the sky, dewy with her saffron wings,
dragging a thousand different colors as she faced the sun,
and she stood over Dido's head. "Having received my orders, I snatch
this lock as sacred to Dis, and release you from your body:"
so she spoke, and she cut the lock with her right hand: at once all the
warmth left her body, and her life departed into the winds.

Juno is all-powerful, and she has satisfied herself in the present with delaying Aeneas and in the future with the promise of hell on earth for the Romans during Hannibal's invasion of Italy. Dido's death was the result of intense divine intervention (Venus and Juno, female divinities); in Book 11, Camilla's death will similarly result from divine action (Apollo and Jupiter, male divinities). In neither case is the victim entirely sympathetic and without flaw—quite the contrary. Juno's actions here reflect her deep love for Carthage and its founder, despite her willingness, in fits of madness, to sacrifice Dido in the midst of her raging campaign against Aeneas and the Trojans. Now that she has satiated her fury (for a moment at least), she can indulge in a scene of pity and mercy that comes in complete contrast to the image of the goddess we have seen thus far. Books 2-4 have all closed with deaths that in more or less significant ways have mentioned Diana/Prosperina: the temple of the deserted Ceres with its cypress that presaged Creusa's death, the lone simile of Book 3 with its cypresses in Diana's grove that presaged Anchises', and now the funeral ritual of Prosperina's cutting the lock of Dido's hair (the most dramatic of all the death scenes). The heat (4.705 *calor*) of Dido's passion is finally over; in suicide, Dido has finally found an escape from the passion she could not quell. Iris is the rainbow that has come after the storm of Dido's love has finally ended.[28]

Aeneas had escaped Troy with minimal impact on his future destiny; the same is not true for his flight from Carthage: the departure from Troy brought him closer to the dawn of Rome, while the departure from Carthage introduces the horror of the Punic Wars into his future.[29] He has replicated his previous experience, especially in his loss of another woman, his second "wife," in a real (if not literal) sense. During the exodus from Troy he had the support of his father (whom he carried on his shoulders as a parent and guide to be treasured and safeguarded); the loss of Anchises has been keenly felt in Carthage. The first third of the *Aeneid* is now over, and we have seen ample evidence of the difficult labor of founding Rome that had been predicted at the start of the poem (1.33). The next third of the epic is the intense phase of Aeneas' education as Roman progenitor. During the course of Books 5-8, Aeneas will learn dramatic and comprehensive details about the future destiny of his Trojans. The first third of the epic has set up the problem: madness must be subdued and chained for all time, the madness that has manifested itself so often in Books 2 and 4. The second third of the poem will now show the way to that Augustan Peace that promises the hope of salvation from fury, of redemption from madness. The last third will reveal the results of that education, and offer Virgil's final words on the future of the Augustan principate and the Roman Empire.

Notes

1. On Dido's transformation from leader of her people to lovesick, mad woman, see KEITH, "*Tandem Venit Amor*," in HALLETT and SKINNER, eds., *Roman Sexualities*, Princeton, 1997, pp. 297-299.

2. For Dido's praise of Aeneas' various qualities and the criteria for choosing a spouse, see TREGGIARI, *Roman Marriage*, Oxford, 1991, p. 87.

3. On Dido's erotic wound, see MOORTON, "Love as Death: The Pivoting Metaphor in Vergil's Story of Dido," *Classical World* 83.3 (1990), pp. 153-166.

4. On this simile see further Hornsby, *op. cit.*, pp. 6, 60, 91, and 134-135, O'HARA, "Medicine for the Madness of Dido and Gallus," *Vergilius* 39 (1993), pp. 12-24, especially pp. 13-20, MORGAN, "Dido the Wounded Deer," *Vergilius* 40 (1994), pp. 67-68, THORNTON, "Vergil's Injured Deer Motif in the *Aeneid*," *Latomus* 55 (1996), pp. 389-393, CHEW, "*Inscius Pastor*: Ignorance and Aeneas' Identity in the *Aeneid*," *Latomus* 61 (2002), pp. 616-627, and cf. 4.465-466, where he simile is fulfilled in Dido's dream world. Both Books 2 and 4 have similes that depict Aeneas as a shepherd at a moment of great emotional turmoil.

5. On Venus' smile see KONSTAN, "Venus' Enigmatic Smile," *Vergilius* 32 (2000), pp. 18-25.

6. The entire opening of Book 11 will be clouded by remembrances of Book 4, especially during the funeral rites for Pallas. Just as Book 11 opens with a dawn formula, so one will occur at the end (11.913).

7. On Dido's delay see SEGAL, "Dido's Hesitation in *Aeneid* 4," *The Classical World* 84.1 (1990), pp. 1-12. Dido's hesitation is probably comparable to the Golden Bough's (4.133 *cunctantem*, 6.211 *cunctantem*). As we shall see later, the Bough hesitates because Aeneas did not follow the Sibyl's instructions; Dido hesitates *in the bridal chamber* (*thalamo cunctantem*) to highlight the fatal significance of this marriage. Dido's marriage to Aeneas may also carry shades of the folklore motif of the woman who is doomed if she marries (Atalanta). In any case, Dido is strong-willed (like Camilla); Cupid's action does not seem to have been sufficient to destroy her, as the scene between Juno and Venus shows.

8. On this simile see further Hornsby, *op. cit.*, pp. 93-94.

9. *Subnixus* is better than *subnexus* (*pace* Hirtzel, Mynors, Henry, and others); Iarbas imagines Aeneas' effeminate and elaborate headdress as propping up his weak head.

10. On the two visits of Mercury to Carthage, see "Leaving Dido: The Appearance(s) of Mercury and the Motivations of Aeneas," in BURDEN, ed., *A Woman Scorn'd: Responses to the Dido Myth*, London, 1998, pp. 105-127.

11. Essential reading on this passage is JONES, "*Aeneid* 4.238-278 and the Persistence of an Allegorical Interpretation," *Vergilius* 33 (1987), pp. 29-38. Jones argues against any attempt to view the gods of Book 4 as mere allegories for the characters' states of mind. "[Aeneas] does not what he would, but what he must. When he says to Dido, "*Italiam non sponte sequor*," we should believe him even though the queen cannot." Jones does not, however, explore the ramifications of Aeneas' actions for the father of Rome.

12. 4.290 *arma parent*, which some have strangely taken to mean "tackle" *vel sim*. But Williams ad 4.11 is right; ambiguous words should be taken with their usual meaning, unless the context forbids it (strangely, in this passage Williams prefers to imagine the *arma* are not weapons). Aeneas is very well aware of what Dido and her people are capable. Still, Virgil so delights in such vague expressions, where it suits him; 4.299 *armari classem*, Rumor's report to Dido, may imply harmless outfitting of ships. Cf. 5.15

arma, where the word clearly refers to the tackling, and there see Williams (Oxford edition), who suggests that Virgil may have been the first to use *arma* of a ship's rigging.

13. For a good analysis of the important scene of Aeneas' reaction to Mercury's orders, see STARR, "Aeneas the Rhetorician," *Latomus* 62 (2003), pp. 36-46.

14. On this simile see further Hornsby, *op. cit.*, p. 94.

15. For the possibility that Dido's childlessness is a retort to those who accused Caesar (rightly) of having fathered a child with Cleopatra (Caesarion, "Little Caesar"), see BARRETT, "Dido's Child: A Note on *Aeneid* 4.327-330," *Maia* 25 (1973), pp. 51-53, and GRIFFIN, *Latin Poets and Roman Life*, London, 1985, p. 184. But did anyone seriously doubt Caesar's peccadilloes in Alexandria? If there is allegory here (doubtful), DREW, *The Allegory of the Aeneid*, Oxford, 1927, p. 83 is likelier to be right: "Sidonian" Dido stands for "Scribonia," whom Octavian divorced on the day their daughter Julia was born.

16. IRVINE, *The Loves of Dido and Aeneas*, Oxford, 1924, is an edition of Sir Richard Fanshawe's (seventeenth century) translation of Book 4 with brief notes and a useful appendix on that idiosyncratic obsessive of Virgilian lore, James Henry. It was part of the same postwar Oxford (Basil Blackwell) Virgil series in green boards that produced the Fowler editions of passages from Books 7, 8, and 12, the Butler Book 6, and a few monographs.

17. "The most eloquent character in the *Aeneid* is Dido." (HIGHET, *The Speeches in Vergil's Aeneid*, Princeton, 1972).

18. And, of course, one of Virgil's poetic inspirations here is Ariadne's rebuke of the (absent) Theseus in Catullus (c. 64.154 *quaenam te genuit sola sub rupe leaena*).

19. For a compelling study of this passage, see FARRON, "*Pius Aeneas* in *Aeneid* 4, 393-6," *Collection Latomus: Studies in Latin Literature and History* VI (1992), pp. 260-276.

20. On this simile see further Hornsby, *op. cit.*, p. 50. The main point of the simile is the fortune of the Trojans, who have stayed too long in Carthage; ants in nature know better than to wait this long for winter provisioning. Hornsby sees the ants as destructive influences on Carthage, but this seems unlikely from a Roman perspective. Virgil is concerned about the seasons, not Carthaginian booty (4.404 *praedam*).

21. On these notoriously difficult lines, see MURGIA, "Dido's Puns," *Classical Philology* 82 (1987), pp. 50-59, and CASALI, "Staring at the Pun: *Aeneid* 4.435-436 Reconsidered," *The Classical Journal* 95.2 (1999-2000), pp. 103-118.

22. For the simile of the oak tree, see further Hornsby, *op. cit.*, pp. 26, 80-81, and 84. The image must be understood in its context, which is immediately after the gods strengthen Aeneas' placid will.

23. Note KREVANS, "Ilia's Dream: Ennius, Virgil, and the Mythology of Seduction," *Harvard Studies in Classical Philology* 95 (1993), pp. 257-271.

24. On Cleopatra's suicide, with survey of the ancient evidence, see BOWMAN, CHAMPLIN, and LINTOTT, eds., *The Cambridge Ancient History X: The Augustan Age*, Cambridge, 1996, pp. 63-65. While I agree that Cleopatra was intended for Octavian's triumph and outwitted him with her suicide, I suspect that Octavian made use of her "victory" for his own propaganda: she looked all the fiercer because even in defeat she was able to assert some sort of triumph of her own (cf. Horace's *deliberata morte ferocior*).

25. Henry's typically discursive note on his own enjoyment of honey and poppy treats in Austria is not to be missed; it should be read with his note on the Sibyl's tasty treat for Cerberus (6.419-423).

26. Silius appropriately has Hamilcar dictate to his young son Hannibal a solemn oath against Rome in the very spot where Dido is said to have committed suicide (*Punica* 1.81-119).

27. Virgil's depiction of Dido and Anna owes much to Sophocles' portrayal of Antigone and her sister Ismene.

28. Henry's notes on the close of Book 4 are not to be missed (conveniently quoted in part by Austin on 705).

29. On Aeneas and Dido as symbols of Carthage and Rome, see FARRON, "The Aeneas-Dido Episode as an Attack on Aeneas' Mission and Rome," *Greece and Rome* 27.1 (1980), pp. 34-47, especially p. 39.

Austin ends his commentary on Book 4 with a beautiful note, very much in his sensitive and sympathetic style of Virgilian reflection: "Dido's bright day is done, and all the heat and fury of her tragedy is fallen to nothing, ending quietly at the last. It is the end of the 'first act' of the *Aeneid*. Henry's epilogue here should be read by all who (in his words) dare to feel that the exercise of their intellectual faculties in the ennobling, exalting, purifying contemplation of the grand, the beautiful, and the pathetic, whether in the poetical, philosophical, or manuplastic creations of the master spirits of mankind, is not, cannot be, of the nature of sin." Guillemin remarks well: "Le rôle de Didon comporte aussi un point délicat. Comme Médée qui fuit la maison paternelle et égorge vaisseau de Thésée, comme la Tarpéia de Properce, qui livre la citadelle dont son père pas oublié; la conscience de la belle Carthaginoise la torture et le remords la ronge." (GUILLEMIN, *Virgile: Poète, Artiste, et Penseur*, Paris, 1951, p. 261). In allowing his readers to shed any tears over Dido at the close of Book 4 and the first third of his epic, Virgil shows his calm and masterly control of his poetic landscape. There will be time enough later for him to introduce a similar and yet quite different woman, who will contrast dramatically with the Carthaginian lover of Aeneas. In several aspects of her character, Virgil's Camilla will remind us of his Dido. Both women will die violently; Camilla, in contrast to Dido, will become Italy's heroine.

Chapter V

Meanwhile Sure Aeneas

Book 5 is a companion to Book 3.[1] After the introductory material of the first book, Books 3 and 5 alternate with 2 and 4 in their relative visceral intensity. Like Book 3, the fifth book of the *Aeneid* has been underappreciated by some readers and critics. Despite the book's rather discursive and quiet atmosphere, it does have moments of dramatic intensity and great power. The same could be said of Book 3 (especially the encounter with Andromache and the report of Anchises' death). But when we compare Book 5 to its companion, we feel a great sense of narrative urgency; the poem is ever hastening to its close, even if the journey sometimes seems slow and winding. Book 5 is the first book of the second third of the poem, and introduces themes and ideas that will find their culmination and climax in the revelations of Books 6 and especially 8; Books 6 and 8 will be quiet and reflective interludes between the fires that threaten Aeneas' ships toward the end of Book 5 and the war in Italy that begins to rage in Book 7. At the same time, in the twofold division of the poem between *Odyssey* and *Iliad*, Book 5 is a "penultimate book" that immediately precedes the power and vigor of the events of the "final" books, 6 and 12.[2] In this regard it has affinities with Book 11. Like the preceding Books 2-4, it will end with a death, that of the helmsman Palinurus. Book 5 complements Book 3 in its emphasis on Anchises, whose funeral games are the dominant theme for more than half its verses. In this Book 5 represents a departure from the Odyssean model we have observed; the funeral games for Anchises are modeled after Homer's description of the games for Patroclus in *Iliad* 23. In some ways, Book 5 is the most moving and powerful of all; it casts a peculiar spell over the audience, especially during the narrative of Anchises' memorial rites and Palinurus' loss, and it rewards careful re-readings.

Virgil could easily have designed games for the funeral of Pallas in Book 11, since Pallas fulfills the Patroclus role in his *Iliad*. But as yet another of the many linkages between Books 5 and 11 that we shall observe, he decided instead to insert an anniversary game narrative in Book 5 (Anchises has been dead for a year), rather than have any memorial athletic events in Book 11 for the young Pallas. In this Virgil has departed from his Homeric model in a significant way. In his conception of the progress of the *Aeneid*, he decided against having any possible lightening of the emotional mood in what could be called his saddest book, Book 11, and instead transferred the game scenes to his happiest book, Book 5. For it is in this book that Aeneas is perhaps at his happiest and most relaxed in the entire poem. That mood will be interrupted by Juno's orchestration of the burning of the ships and the subsequent death of Palinurus, though neither event will have significant or lasting consequences for the Trojans. Games would have been thoroughly out of place in the epic structure of Virgil's

Iliad; for him, the Achilles-Hector combat will come in the final scenes of the poem, another departure from Homeric precedent that allows him to underscore the absence of any scene corresponding to the granting of Hector's body to Priam after his death and his corpse's desecration. It is true that even in Book 5, there are some ominous foreshadowing of future disaster (Palinurus' drowning, even Nisus and Euryalus' night raid in Book 9). But for the most part, all is happiness. Unlike the happier moments in Book 3, the narrative of Book 5 is never rushed, despite the narrative urgency. We are able to savor the relaxed atmosphere and even comic humor at some points in the athletic competitions. We never feel pressed to board ship for the next destination. We learn much about Aeneas in this book, much about his son Ascanius, and much about the nature of the immortals. For once in this poem, there is time to let the story unfold at a peaceful, discursive pace; especially after the demands Book 4 makes on its readers' emotions, the quiet rest is welcome, though the calm has a deceptive nature too: in some odd and peculiar way tears come most naturally for the audience in Book 5. We understand why it is "wrong" to stay with the walking dead in Buthrotum in Book 3, and the sexually tempting Dido in Book 4. We wish we could stay in Sicily, in the moment of happiness the games offer.

Virgil quite possibly invented the story of a love affair between Aeneas and Dido, or at least amplified the existing tradition in ways previously unexplored. Similarly, there is no extant record of a tradition of a *second* Trojan visit to Sicily. Not everyone agreed that Anchises had died anywhere near Sicily, in fact, and no one whose work survives has a record of the Sicilian revisit depicted in Virgil's Book 5. Ring composition was dear to Virgil's heart, and the rings often overlap (Books 1-6 vs. 7-12, 1-4 vs. 5-8 and 9-12, 5 and 11, 6 and 12, 2 and 4, etc.). But besides the parallels between Books 3 and 5, Virgil has found in Sicily the only place where the action of the poem can quietly subside without sacrificing realism and verisimilitude. The calm and relaxed atmosphere of this book could never have occurred in Greece, North Africa, or Italy upon landing. Sicily had previously been a place of danger and disaster (the Cyclopes, Anchises' death); here it serves the cause of peaceful interlude. Ascanius, too, will have a chance to be developed as a character; his equestrian show in Book 5 will be his first role of leadership in the poem, and provides a happy contrast to his previous presence at the hunt in Carthage, where first he showed any maturation from being an infant or a toddler. Venus will reappear and once again be nervous for her beloved Trojans; the appeal she makes to her uncle Neptune for calm seas and an uninterrupted voyage from Sicily to Italy will introduce the book's closing episode of Palinurus and his seemingly purposeless death. And, as we might well predict, even in the repose of Book 5, the fury of Juno will manifest itself, however ultimately ineffectively. The beauty of Book 5 is best appreciated, as we have noted, after frequent *rereading*; it has a subtle power that is absorbed slowly and over time.

It is winter, and the north wind is raging; Dido had suggested deferring departure until the spring. The stormy north wind provides a dark and ominous mood, which is only enhanced by the fiery glow from Dido's fire that the Trojans see in their hasty flight. They are aware of what a raving woman might do (just as Mercury had warned Aeneas in a dream that women can change their moods so quickly), and they fear the worst. Virgil notes that the love between Dido and Aeneas had been *pollutus* (5.5-6 *amore polluto*), a word that is difficult to translate precisely, and whose import is mysterious and delightfully ambiguous. How exactly was their love "polluted"? The Trojans are surely aware that Dido felt betrayed and abandoned, that her love affair with Aeneas had been desecrated by his departure. But there is also a sense, however faint, of the inappropriateness of their love, which Dido herself knew so well, the betrayal of Sychaeus' memory; a love affair that should never have started has had the consequences we should have expected. It does not matter if Aeneas was right in saying that they were never married; it suffices that Dido thought they were. Aeneas himself is "sure" (5.2 *certus*) as he sails ahead to his destiny; the real power of Dido's temptation came from proximity, and except for the scene in the underworld when he meets her, Aeneas will never mention her again (though Virgil will). It is true that he has responded to the will of the gods and answered their call; he has agreed to fulfill the dictates of fate and destiny (though unwillingly).

Another storm strikes the Trojan fleet; not every tempest can be blamed on Juno. Dido was right that this was not the season to attempt flight by sea; the storm will send Aeneas on a detour to Sicily. The language is almost exactly the same as the description of the storm after the departure from Crete (another place the Trojans should not have visited); that storm had driven them to the Strophades and the adventure with the Harpies, while this one will have less sinister consequences (3.192-200). Palinurus had been unable to control his rudder in that storm; the same will be true now (5.8-12). Book 5 will open, then, with the helmsman whose death will be the subject of the book's closing. He calls on Neptune, asking what the god is preparing; the answer, we shall learn much later, is Palinurus' own death, which Neptune will announce near the end of the book to Venus. Palinurus' trust in following Fortune wherever she leads (5.22-23) will be echoed later by the first change of fortune in the book, when Juno provokes the burning of the Trojan fleet (5.604 *Hic primum Fortuna fidem mutata novavit*). The previous Trojan visit to Sicily had been full of danger and sadness (Polyphemus and the death of Anchises); this landing will be an opposite experience. This is the only storm in the *Aeneid* that does not have ominous consequences; Palinurus knows that Aeneas' half brother Eryx once settled in Sicily, and Aeneas here mentions Acestes, the son of a Sicilian river god and the nymph Segesta; Acestes had been exiled from Troy by the lying Laomedon. Acestes had been credited early in the poem (1.195) with the wine that provided some comfort to the Trojans after they had been beached on the Carthaginian coast; this earlier visit with him was not mentioned in Book 3 (another possible mark of the unrevised state of the poem).[3] The first and second occurrences of Book 5's key word *laetus* ("happy") describe the arrival of the tired Trojans at Sicily and Acestes' reception of them (5.34, 40). Acestes is dressed in a Libyan bear skin (the commentators since antiquity have had great fun arguing about the existence of bears in Africa in antiquity), the deeper significance of which, if any, is hard to determine.[4] He has weapons, but the bear pelt and arms immediately identify him as a hunter; these Sicilians do not live with the same fear of their neighbors Dido did. The Trojans seem to go to sleep at once (an indication of the status of Acestes' kingdom as a place of rest and security).

At dawn we learn why Aeneas had been called *pius* (5.26) as this scene began: he announces the year anniversary of Anchises' death and burial. Anchises had been mentioned in Book 4 when Aeneas revealed to Dido that his father had visited him in dreams and urged his flight from Carthage; Dido was responding to the revelation of this dream visitation when she used the appeal that she had never disturbed Anchises' ashes in desecration of his grave. Anchises' absence was keenly felt throughout the book; now he returns to center stage, as the backdrop for the whole story about to unfold. Aeneas sees divine purpose in the storm that has brought them to Sicily; it has allowed them to pay the honors due to the dead in the actual place of death and burial (5.55 *ad cineres ipsius et ossa parentis*). The Trojan honors to the dead Anchises commemorate a baneful event, but the honor is "happy" (5.58 *laetum* yet again): happy because they allow the Trojans to show their piety to the dead, happy because the anniversary finds the survivors together on friendly land, close to the dead. Aeneas here announces the foundation of a key feature of future Roman religion: the rites paid to dead ancestors at the *Parentalia*, which was celebrated on 13 to 21 February. The feast closed with the *Feralia*, when families would bring offerings to the graves of their dead. Ovid describes the solemnities and credits their origin with Aeneas' offerings for his father's ghost (*Fasti* 2.533 ff., where see Bömer's commentary). These ceremonies find their Christian parallel in the traditional rites for the octave of All Souls' Day in November, when cemeteries are traditionally lustrated and special indulgences granted for prayer on behalf of the dead during an octave of eight days. Aeneas calls for a similar octave observance here, after which, on the ninth day, athletic contests will be held: a ship race, a foot race, an archery contest, and a boxing match. The origins of this are Homeric: Hector's funeral preparations take up nine days (*Iliad* 24.784). Aeneas' plans for Anchises' memorial of "nine days" is Virgil's etiology for the *novendiales*, an ancient novena of prayer (which has modern parallel in the solemn obsequies for a dead pope, which are still called the *Novendiales* and are marked by nine days of Requiem Masses after his death). The dead were cremated on the eighth day and buried on the ninth.

In the immediate aftermath of Aeneas' announcement of anniversary rites for Anchises, Virgil gives the first indication of Ascanius as a leader:

hoc puer Ascanius, sequitur quos cetera pubes. (5.74)

So did the boy Ascanius, whose example the rest of the youth followed.

Especially at the grave of Anchises, we are reminded that now Aeneas is the father and Ascanius the son; the succession motif has advanced another step. There is a procession to the gravesite, where libations of wine, milk, and blood are poured. Purple flowers (violets perhaps) are thrown over the mound (5.79); this act will be remembered in the underworld, when Anchises announces that he wishes to throw purple flowers over the grave of the young, dead Marcellus (6.883-884), a scene which offers a powerful contrast to Aeneas' memorial act here: Anchises may have died before the landing in Italy, but he has at least died in the natural order of aging, unlike the prematurely dead Marcellus, whose death carries such resonance in the theme of the imperial succession. The tradition held that Ascanius would be king in Alba Longa for thirty years; the fears in Virgil's time were not over the long dead past, but the living present of Augustus and the question of his replacement. All the solemnity of the Roman rites for the dead are prefigured here, and Aeneas receives his due reward for his piety: the appearance of the serpent on the burial mound (5.84-93). Aeneas is not sure whether this serpent represents the *genius* of the place or the spirit of his father. The *genius* was a divine being, a procreative spirit, the double, as it were, of a man. Divinities and localities also had geniuses. The *genius* was particularly associated with the head of a family, the Roman *paterfamilias*, a word so deeply rooted in Roman religion that the archaic genitive form *familias* was never abandoned. Worshipping the genius of the ultimate Roman *paterfamilias*, the emperor, would become an obvious extension of this cult.

Manes (5.99) is a mysterious and difficult word. In poetry it can often simply mean "the realm of the dead." The *Manes* are Roman ghosts, who sometimes wander the world seeking their due rites (so Ovid in his description of what happened once upon a time when the *Parentalia* rites were neglected).[5] Aeneas sacrifices animals over the mound and calls on the ghost of Anchises. He is unsure whether the snake represented the *genius* of the place or the ghost of his father, but the omen is obviously a propitious one; the Trojans are happy (5.100 *laeti*) as they offer food to the gods before feasting at the grave. Book 11 will also open with rites for the dead, for both Trojan and Italian casualties, among them most especially Pallas' requiem: the mood there is completely different from the present scene. Indeed, how differently we respond to the "delays" of Book 5: we feel that Rome's future is quietly and softly being advanced, not as dramatically as in moments like the granting of Aeneas' shield or the great procession of future Romans in the underworld, but advanced nonetheless. This tone of quiet urgency contrasts strongly with the delays of Book 4.

The horses of Phaëthon, the "Bright One," usher in the ninth dawn: an appropriate image for a day of games, even if there will be no chariot race *per se*.[6] Happy (5.107 *laeto*) crowds gather for the announced competition. The prizes are set up in the middle of the assembly, and a trumpet announces the beginning of the games; similarly Achilles set out the prizes before Patroclus' funeral games to commence the competition (*Iliad* 23.258-261). The first contest will be a ship race, a change from Homer's chariot race that is eminently fitting for the

"Odyssean" half of the *Aeneid*.⁷ For once Aeneas' fleet is not in danger from storms or Carthaginian fire; the mood is relaxed and the excitement palpable as the naval race begins. Rome's advance continues even in the details of the crews; Mnestheus the Trojan will be the forebear of Memmius the Italian (5.117), a nod to Lucretius again, whose patron was Memmius; less likely is a nod to Catullus' pro-praetor Memmius in Bithynia. Sergestus is most famous as the traditional forebear of Catiline; Cluentius is best known to students of Cicero's speech. He captains the *Scylla*, a reminder of the monster they avoided in Book 3. This is the first extended scene in the poem that shows the Trojans at rest, with no ominous background (as at the banquet in Dido's Carthage); it is a natural place to begin to unfold the lineages of Rome's great patrician families. Except for the first, the Memmii, whose presence is an obvious homage to Lucretius, the others are mysterious; it is tempting to see in Sergius a nod of honor to Catiline (especially if Drances in Book 11 was meant to be an evocation of Cicero—though at 8.666-669, on Aeneas' shield, Virgil will depict Catiline suffering in Tartarus).⁸ In any case, the Roman families that mattered in Virgil's day may not be the same for us.

Aeneas fixes a young oak tree on a small jutting sea rock to mark the turning point in the race; the oak is a nod to Homer (*Iliad* 23.328). Like royalty, the contestants are outfitted in gold and purple, the colors Dido wore to her hunt with Aeneas; again, how different is this day. In case we did not know our Homer, Virgil describes the beginning of the boat race with a chariot simile. "Not so headlong did chariots snatch the plain . . . " (5.144-145), says Virgil: he proudly surpasses Homer. The mood is all excitement and rejoicing; in Homer, the chariot race began with a dark reference to Aeneas: Diomedes was riding with the horses he had stolen from Aeneas, who nearly died in battle with the son of Tydeus (*Iliad* 5.290-346). In Homer, Apollo had saved Aeneas from Diomedes after the wounded Aphrodite had dropped her son; in the chariot race, Apollo cheats by disturbing Diomedes' lash (lest he win with Aeneas' Trojan horses). Athena intervenes, however, to help her favorite; Diomedes wins.

Gyas' Chimaera takes the early lead, followed closely by Cloanthus' Scylla, which is hindered (appropriately enough) by its size.⁹ The Pristis (an obscure type of sea monster) and the Centaur struggle together, trading third place back and forth. Gyas is nervous because of Cloanthus' hot pursuit; he urges his helmsman Menoetes to hug the turning point more closely to ensure victory. Menoetes is more cautious and disregards his captain's dangerous advice; Cloanthus takes the tight opening on the left and passes Gyas. In rage, Gyas flings Menoetes overboard. Here Virgil foreshadows how Sleep will cast Palinurus overboard at the end of the book; all is comedy here, while all will be deadly serious there. We know Menoetes is fine enough at once; Virgil has the Trojans laugh with good humor as he tries to sit on the rock, only to slip off into the water again. The trouble on deck slows Gyas' ship; Sergestus and Mnestheus have a chance now to contest the second place. Virgil describes Mnethesus' strategy. He offers a prayer to Neptune: let the victor be the one the god favors. He states obliquely the real intention of his prayer: it would be a shameful thing to come to the finish line last. The god gives no answer, but mere chance (5.201 *casus*) does: as Sergestus approaches the rock, he beaches his ship. Mnestheus, happy in any event (5.210 *laetus*), sails ahead and beats not only Sergestus' wrecked ship but also Gyas' huge Chimaera, now harder to navigate without Menoetes. The flight of Mnestheus' ship past the other two is described as the easy glide of a dove in the open air, after it had been frightened out of its home.[10] The dove here presages the target-dove of the archery contest below; the dove's smooth flight in the air is appropriate to Mnestheus' ship. Less fitting, it would seem, is the description of the dove's terror (5.215 *exterrita*) after its sudden disturbance from its home. The simile here is not really comparable to the brief dove simile in Book 2 that described Hecuba and her daughters huddled in fright (2.515-517). The simile here must be a foreshadowing of the archery contest, where Mnestheus will hit the rope and free the terrified dove (5.507-512); the simile of the dove will become incarnate, and the dove there will also be terrified when Hippocoon strikes the mast where it is tied as the target (505 *timuitque exterrita*, echoing this passage).

Mnestheus had been talking only of not coming in last; now the excitement of his success makes him think even of victory. The crowds watching the contest stir him on in his efforts (5.227-228). His earlier prayer had been flawed; he wanted victory, but did not ask for it directly; he made no promise of a gift in return (*do ut des*). Cloanthus knows religious ritual better; he promises a sacrifice to the gods of the sea if he wins: a bull to be killed on the beach, its entrails scattered on the water. The image of the bull sacrifice on the beach recalls Laocoon's disastrous seaside experience; that ominous image has been replaced by the happy (2.236 *laetus*) Cloanthus. Is it fanciful to connect the flawed prayer of Mnestheus (sire of the Memmii), and the advantage he gained by mere chance, with Lucretius? In any case, the whole apparatus of marine divinities comes forth to help Cloanthus win: the Nereids, and Phorcys ("the old man of the sea"), and especially Portunus, a god of harbors.

There are prizes for everyone, as it turns out; the chief prize is a cloak (5.250 *chlamydem*) that is decorated with the scene of Ganymede's abduction by the eagle of Jupiter. The scene is depicted in some detail.[11] We see Ganymede hunting deer on leafy Mount Ida. Virgil says that this is the Ganymede who was snatched by Jove's armor-bearer, the thunderbolt-carrying eagle; apparently the cloak also shows the boy's aged watchers raising their palms to the sky in vain, and the hunting dogs barking at the air. What is the significance of this scene? The rape of Ganymede was one of the main reasons Juno had been incensed at the Trojans (1.28). Its mention here is understandable enough as a significant scene from Trojan history. Still, its overtones in the context of the *Aeneid* are somewhat ominous; in Book 9, we shall learn that Nisus, the ill-fated homosexual lover of Euryalus, came from Mount Ida (9.176-178). Note that in contrast to the sinister undertones of the end of Book 1, the implications of trouble in Book 5's narrative of the games only make sense after we read the Nisus and Euryalus episode in Book 9. We can predict trouble in the confused web of Venus, Juno, Aeneas, and Dido; we can see nothing truly ominous here without the benefit of hindsight.

Sergestus has somehow managed to save what is left of his beached ship and sail it in the relatively short distance to shore. Aeneas is happy (5.283 *laetus* again) that Sergestus and his ship have safely arrived in the harbor, and he grants him a prize as well: a woman skilled in the arts of Minerva, Cretan Pholoe and her twin sons at the breast—another nod to Homer's chariot race (the *first* prize there was a woman and a tripod). Sergestus' broken Centaur is described as a snake that has been wounded by a bronze wheel (another reference to a chariot, probably) or a traveler on foot (a reference to the forthcoming foot race).[12] The "snake" may be seriously wounded, but it wins what had been the first prize in Homer—after all, in some ways he manages to accomplish the most difficult task of all the contestants in getting the ship back. Still, the simile seems somewhat strange after the prominent and positive depiction of the serpent that appeared on Anchises' burial mound. The snake can perhaps be expected to die (5.275 *seminecem*); but more probably the simile is trying hard to emphasize the tremendous skill it took (5.270 *multa . . . arte*) to bring the ship home, against all hope and odds. The art is all the more impressive if the job was next to impossible to complete. Just as Mnestheus' dove simile points forward to the archery contest with its climactic and mysterious omen, so Sergestus' snake looks back to the portent at the grave. From the old man who would not leave the burning city of Troy, Anchises has become a powerful symbol of Roman respect for their ancestors, the genesis of the rites of the *Parentalia*, the future announcer of Rome's glory in the underworld. The wounded snake is compared specifically to the broken oars of Sergestus' boat (5.280); a passerby has left it on a rock, just as the ship had been smashed against the goal post. The snake is burning with rage (5.277 *ferox ardensque*); Virgil had not explicitly described Sergestus' reaction to his shipwreck, though we can guess. When the ship crashes on the rock, the sailors immediately begin the work of freeing it (5.207-209); their actions reflect their desire to get the ship underway as quickly as possible:

consurgunt nautae et magno clamore morantur (5.207)

The sailors rise up, and they are delayed with a great shout

The sailors then take up tools to try to dislodge the ship from its rock prison. The exact meaning of *magno clamore morantur* has been disputed; it most naturally would seem to mean that they are delayed, shouting loudly (both complaints and commands). Williams thinks *morari navem* was a technical term that described stopping a ship and holding her steady by reversing the oar movement so she stops moving in any one direction; but the context (not to mention lack of parallels for such a use of *moror*) seems to argue against this interpretation; the point, as the simile makes clear, is that the sailors are upset (like the snake), and they at once try to dislodge themselves from the rock, like the snake on the road. The ship is dashed, after all, against the goal post; the sailors rise up to grab the poles they will need to free their craft.

The foot race is described next, and, in accord with the overall balance of the games, the description is briefer than the boat race, just as the boxing match will be elaborated in contrast to the archery contest. None of the contestants in the boat race have any significant role in the *Aeneid*, but the foot race introduces Nisus and Euryalus, who participate in the doomed night raid that is explored at great length in Book 9 (176-502). Their deaths come with an added layer of shock when we remember the amusing misadventures of this contest. Virgil has taken great pains to make sure we know his young war dead before they meet their end. Unlike the first contest, blatant cheating (by Nisus on behalf of his friend) will mark the foot race; this unfair act foreshadows Nisus' heroic unwillingness to abandon Euryalus in Book 9 when he might have saved his own life. The contrast between the two scenes could not be greater, and helps to underscore further the horror of their deaths. Still, as we shall see in the later scene, their characters are not without flaws: the first of these is revealed here in Nisus' willingness to cheat, even if on behalf of his friend. Palinurus had been introduced in Book 3, and he will die at the end of this book; Virgil prepares to finish one ring even as he introduces another to replace it, which enriches his epic with a wonderfully interlocking structure.

Nisus is the older of the two young men, and he is said to have a "faithful love" (5.296) for the boy Euryalus; this first and defining fact of his life comes immediately after Virgil's detail that Euryalus was notably handsome and in the first bloom of youth. In the *Iliad*, there is no definitive indication either way that Achilles and Patroclus had what we might call a homosexual relationship; from classical antiquity onwards, though, some have assumed this to be true.[13] For Aeneas and Pallas, too, there is no clear indication in Virgil of such a relationship. "Homosexual relationship," in any case, is a potentially problematic label: it certainly meant different things to different people at different times in the histories of Greece, Rome, and our own day; we are on safe ground, though, if we define it as sexual relations between partners of the same gender. Rome did not wholly approve of sexual relationships between males.[14] All we can safely say is that Nisus and Euryalus certainly evoke classic Greek homosexuality, that is, the pursuit of attractive young boys on the cusp of manhood for sexual relationships. Most interesting is Virgil's use of the adjective *pius* to describe Nisus' love. It emphasizes the great devotion of the one for the other; it never has negative connotations in Virgil. There is no question that Virgil has tremendous sympathy for these two young Trojans, as we shall see in the narrative of their final hours. Indeed, his memorial apostrophe to them (9.446-449) is among the most explicit authorial declarations of praise for any characters in the poem. Roman invective against "homosexuality" is focused on males who allow themselves to be penetrated, males who play the woman's role, as it were, in sexual encounters. So no Roman adult male could pursue a freeborn Roman boy with impunity (what he did with his slaves was another matter altogether).[15] Roman invective against the effeminate male finds its home in the *Aeneid* in the taunts of both Iarbas in Africa and Numanus Remulus in Italy (the latter comes soon after the Nisus-Euryalus episode in Book 9). Nisus and Euryalus are not Romans; they were not bound by any Roman social conventions (and their deaths do remove them from the future foundations in Italy).[16] Like Camilla, a woman who fights (and evokes Amazons), Nisus and Euryalus, in all likelihood lovers (who evoke Greek homosexuality), must die to the past before the coming of Rome.

But all the horror of their inevitable end is far off as Aeneas presides at the start of the foot race. Besides Diores, a surviving son of Priam, Salius and Patron are also contestants; the former is from Acarnania (the region around Buthrotum), the latter from Tegea in Arcadia, also the home of the fleet-footed Atalanta in Ovid's Calydonian boar hunt (*Metamorphoses* 8.317-323, where see Hollis' notes). Balancing the two Greeks are two Sicilians, Helymus and Panopes, friends of Acestes who were accustomed to forest life (so also Camilla will be noteworthy in particular for her swift running). There are other participants, who remain unnamed. The Homeric foot race was much smaller (*Iliad* 23.740-797, with the Lesser Ajax, Odysseus, and Antilochus). Aeneas invites the assembly to turn the attention of their "happy minds" (5.304 *laetas . . . mentes*) to the new contest. The prizes are announced (quite different from Homer's), both for all the runners and for the first three to cross the finish line. The winner will receive a horse and the second place an Amazon's quiver with Thracian arrows (the Amazons were vaguely located to the northwest of Greece, in the traditionally warlike and rough region of Thrace). Together with the parallel of swift running, these first two prizes foreshadow the cavalry battle in Book 11, which will be dominated by the figure of Camilla. The Trojans have an Amazon quiver in part because Penthesilea had come in the last days of the war to help Priam; in Virgil the "Amazon" will be fighting on the other side (and both Camilla and Atalanta have Amazonian associations). This sort of foreshadowing, as we have seen, is very much in Virgil's style, and reflects a highly polished degree of completion for an unrevised poem, and is indeed a mark of his legendary perfectionism.

Nisus is the early favorite, just as Ajax, son of Oileus, was in Homer.[17] Nisus' speed surpasses the winds or a thunderbolt; Virgil has nodded to the tradition that Ajax (Nisus' Homeric counterpart) was killed by a blast of lightning from Minerva (1.39-45), an image he highlighted prominently at the very beginning of the poem. Salius and Euryalus follow him in order; surely Virgil's three half-lines about Euryalus (5.294 and 322, and 9.467) were meant to highlight the ill-fated young man; certainly in Book 9, Virgil wants us to remember this race. Helymus and Diores come next; the latter is almost ready to overtake the former. Nisus slips in the blood of some sacrificial animals. In Homer, Ajax similarly slips (and Homer cannot resist the detail that his face fell into the gore; cf.

9.332-333)—but only after Odysseus had uttered a prayer to Athena for help in winning. Nisus reasons that he can at least help his young lover; he starts to rise up and blocks Salius, knocking the runner over and thereby giving the prize of victory to Euryalus; Helymus and Diores come in second and third. Salius is rightly incensed at the cheating (5.342). Virgil has transferred to his foot race the arguments between Menelaus and Antilochus in Homer's chariot race (*Iliad* 23.540-611, itself a profound study of Greek character, replete with moving considerations of respect and honor). Aeneas does not agree to change the order of the prizes—instead he grants the pelt of a huge lion to Salius as a consolation prize. Nisus sees a chance here to share in Aeneas' generosity; Euryalus had cried when he thought he might lose his first prize (5.343), while Nisus shows the filth that has stained his face and limbs from where he slipped. Aeneas laughs and gives him a shield that was torn down from the sacred doorpost of a temple of Neptune, apparently by the Greeks (5.360 *Danais* is somewhat ambiguous; it is probably a dative of agent, meaning the Greeks tore it down). But where was the shield, and how did Aeneas get it? Some commentators think it was torn down and brought to Troy by a Greek as a sort of good luck charm; others think it was torn down from a Trojan temple and mysteriously made its way back into Trojan hands (this seems unlikely). Whatever the original provenance, the gift has ominous undertones; a shield torn down from a temple is not an auspicious present.

The boxing match that comes next has its origin in Homer's brief description of a similar contest (*Iliad* 23.653-699). On the one hand, Virgil's pugilistic bout balances the ship race in length; on the other hand, Virgil decided to let the boxing contest be his comment on a theme Homer developed in the first book of the *Iliad*: the outstanding prowess of men who have lived long and seen many generations of warriors (1.247-272). The aged Nestor of Pylos responds to the quarrel between Achilles and Agamemnon by reminding them that in his youth he knew men who could destroy any of the great heroes among the Greeks of the present day. Dares is a fierce opponent and dangerous foe, but old Entellus had been taught by Eryx, Aeneas' brother on his mother Venus' side. Eryx had died in mortal boxing combat with Hercules on these very shores in Sicily, when Hercules had been returning from one of his labors. Entellus has Eryx' boxing gloves—they are stained with blood and gore. Even the gloves and former pupil of the loser from an ancient contest will be enough to win in this lesser day. In the midst of the athletic competitions in memorial of a fallen hero from yesteryear, Virgil has injected the Homeric, indeed Hesiodic theme of the decline of the ages. The theme is appropriate as a response to Dares' boasting as he comes forward in boastful arrogance. Dares had boxed at the funeral games for Hector, where he vanquished one Butes, a descendant of Amycus of Bebrycia, a character from the opening of Book 2 of Apollonius' *Argonautica*.[18] Amycus had been a son of Poseidon and a nymph; he compelled all travelers through his realm to box with him (they usually died). Polydeuces accepted his challenge on behalf of the Argonauts and permanently ended his inhospitality. Dares also fought regularly as Paris' sparring partner. Dares, then, is a "second generation" fighter; he can boast a proud lineage and frighten others of his own generation—Entellus, though, has seen better.

Virgil's boxing competition is the least lighthearted of the four events of these games. The match is liminal; it juxtaposes representatives of the old and the new. This theme lies behind much of the action of the *Aeneid*: even among the generation that fought at Troy, many of the greatest warriors (Achilles, Ajax, and Hector, most prominently) are dead. Others who survived (Diomedes) will refuse to participate in further warfare, content with genteel retirement. And, long before those dead and retired heroes, there was a generation that is still a living memory for old men like Entellus, as it was for the recently dead Anchises. It is easy, and reasonable, to transfer this theme to Roman mythology and history. Certainly for the imperial succession theme, such thoughts are fitting. Boxing is a fitting metaphor for the decline of men; it was a deadly serious sport in Roman times, a contest of almost unbelievable brutality.[19] It would have been next to impossible for Virgil to have depicted it with the same humor and lighthearted revelry that characterized the boat and foot races.

Acestes, too, represents the older generation with its long memory. He cannot brook the arrogance of Dares, and it is he who goads Entellus to fight. Entellus has to be encouraged; part of the myth of the declining ages is that the older does pass away before the younger. He does not rise up on his own. Virgil has already called Acestes a "hero" (1.196); now Acestes reminds Entellus that he had once been the strongest of heroes (5.389 *heroum . . . fortissime*). Eryx may have died at Hercules' hand, but Acestes can still call him a "god" (5.391 *deus*). Dares wants his prize at once; Entellus has prizes, we learn, stored up in his home—prizes from a greater age. And, we learn, Entellus has not lost his love of praise and his desire for glory. He is, quite simply, older and weaker. For that reason alone he has abstained from accepting Dares' challenge. His victory, then, will come as a surprise to himself most of all. Entellus also declares that he is not interested in prizes (as he will prove at the end of the contest, when he sacrifices the steer). Dares' interest in taking his reward at once is another sign of the younger generation's degeneracy. For glory alone will Entellus fight, and as a late reminder to the young of what they are not. Almost as if by magic, Entellus is able to throw forth his boxing gloves into the middle of the assembly. Dramatic necessity compels the gloves to be ready at hand for this moment. Pathetically, Dares at once retreats from his previous arrogance. The mere sight of the gloves is enough to frighten him off. Even Aeneas, significantly identified as "the son of Anchises" (5.407 *Anchisiades*, and cf. 5.424 *satus Anchisa*) can but touch and examine them; he too is of the younger generation that cannot fight as of old. The gloves themselves, of course, are nothing compared to the arms of the victor, Hercules, which Entellus saw when he watched the previous boxing match on this exact spot. Eryx had been no match for Hercules; his student Entellus had marked one decline, and now Dares signals an even greater one. Dares does not even respond to Entellus' offer to fight without Eryx's gloves; Aeneas brings out regular gauntlets for the two of them, and it as if Dares is now caught in something beyond his control; at this point he has no choice but to fight. The beginning of the fight, in fact, seems to lend some restored courage to Dares' spirit; as the two men assume their fighting stances, each one is unafraid (5.427 *interritus*). Men were bigger once upon a time; the ensuing fight contrasts the artful, nimble skill of the younger, more vigorous man with the massive bulk of the older, slower man (5.430 and 442); we are filled with wonder at the thought of what such a huge man could have done in his healthy youth. As in Homer, so in Virgil one contestant will fall; Entellus lands a heavy blow in the air after the faster Dares anticipates it, and his collapse is compared to a tree on Ida in the Troad or in Erymanthian Arcadia (a reference to Hercules, one of whose canonical labors was to kill the Erymanthian Boar). Frequent connections are made between Entellus and Acestes (who helps him to his feet): both men are labeled *gravis* on account of their size, presumably (5.387 of Acestes, 437 and 447 of Entellus), and Acestes is Entellus' equal in age (452 *aequaevum*). Like Acestes in Book 1, Entellus is identified explicitly as a "hero" (453 and 459 *heros*). Indeed, he is most signally identified in this passage as the *gravis heros*, here proving that while the old generation is feeble and a pale imitation of its former self, it is not wholly dead yet, and can still win a victory and the glory of praise. So great, in fact, has been the decline in heroic ability that even an aged, weakened member of the past generation can defeat this braggart younger warrior.

Entellus has to be stopped; he could easily kill Dares as he rains down blows on him like hail on a rooftop (5.458-459). He is described with words that evoke bitter rage (462 *saevire . . . acerbis*). When Dares had boasted of his prowess, Entellus had not been provoked to fight (Acestes had to rouse him to defend the honor of their generation). Now, as he has seen how even in his weakened state, he can batter this fast young (braggart) warrior, he is filled with contempt. Aeneas interrupts the fight and advises Dares of what he no doubt has already determined—the gods are at work here:

non viris alias conversaque numina sentis?
cede deo. (5.466-467)

Do you not feel another sort of strength, and a changed divine power?
Yield to the god.

Has some god inspired Entellus' strength? Is Entellus' strength godlike in comparison to Dares'? In the end it matters little; the point is that Dares cannot compete—and neither can anyone else present, by extension. As representatives of this younger, inferior generation, now Dares' age mates come and carry him off (5.468 *aequales*).[20] Entellus' knees had been slow as the fight opened (431-432 *tarda genua*); now Dares' are "sick" (468 *genua aegra*). The difference between "slow" and "sick" marks the distinction between the two men at the beginning and now the end of the contest. Dares is in no condition to receive his second place prizes, which his friends take for him: the sword and helmet that a warrior might wear—an ironic prize for this defeated boxer. Entellus takes just pride in the revelation of his strength: he reminds the Trojans of what strength he had when he was *younger*. He then smashes his right fist into the head of the steer; Eryx's gloves had been covered with brains and blood, and now these lesser gloves will be stained with the blood of the bull. Entellus offers the bull as a sacrifice to Eryx: a better life (5.483 *meliorem animam*) in place of the death of Dares. This is Entellus' final insult over the defeated younger man: the bull would have been a greater foe. *Pace* Servius and others, Entellus is not concerned with the kindness of offering a dead bull instead of Dares ("better" in the sense of preserving human life). Entellus would have killed him, had Aeneas not intervened.

The mood of the book remains bright enough (though notably Virgil does not use the adjective *laetus* throughout the boxing episode). But the younger generation of Trojans, future progenitors of Rome, have learned a valuable lesson, important enough for Homer to introduce it in the first book of the *Iliad*, when the fateful quarrel between Achilles and Agamemnon first erupted. Once again, Virgil has adapted an episode borrowed from Homer in exceptionally skillful and profound ways.

The final contest of the games is the archery competition, another imitation of Homer (*Iliad* 23.850-883), a briefly described event in both poets, but in Virgil the context for a major event: the portent of Acestes' arrow shot. The goal, as in Homer, is a dove tied to the mast of a ship. In Homer there are but two contestants; in Virgil several. Hippocoon wins the first lot for the shooting order; he is probably the brother of Nisus, who is identified in Book 9 as the son of Hyrtacus (cf. 5.492 *Hyrtacidae* and 9.406 *pater Hyrtacus*). Mnestheus makes his second appearance at the games (and so Virgil links the beginning and end of the contests, as also by having the dove tied to a *ship*'s mast). Virgil strangely describes Mnestheus as a victor who had received an olive wreath (not mentioned earlier as a prize for second place)—the point may be to emphasize Mnestheus' prominence as a repeat contestant in another event. Pandarus' far less famous brother Eurytion (known only from this passage) is also present; his brother had been ordered by Athena to break the truce by shooting Menelaus (*Iliad* 4.86-140)—presumably skill in archery was a family trait. Acestes draws the final lot. Here Virgil has linked together the boxing match and the archery contest. Both will be won by older men of a preceding generation. Both men will perform more gloriously than their younger competitors. The contest follows a logical progression: Hippocoon strikes the ship's mast, Mnestheus breaks the cord and frees the bird, and Eurytion kills it as it flies off, "happy" (5.515 *laetam*) in its flight—an ironic use of the book's favorite word. Acestes would seem to have no function left in the competition. What happens next is exceedingly mysterious:

> hic oculis subitum obicitur magnoque futurum
> augurio monstrum; docuit post exitus ingens
> seraque terrifici cecinerunt omina vates.

namque volans liquidis in nubibus arsit harundo
signavitque viam flammis tenuisque recessit
consumpta in ventos: caelo ceu saepe refixa
transcurrunt crinemque volantia sidera ducunt. (5.522-528)

Here a sudden portent is cast before them, destined to be a
great augury; the mighty outcome taught this,
and terrifying prophets sang late omens.
For as the shaft was flying among the liquid clouds it was burned up
and marked its path with flames and, once consumed,
vanished into the thin winds: as when the flying stars, unloosened
from the sky, often run across it and drag their locks.

Some preliminary considerations need to be offered here. Acestes' arrow bursts into flame and is consumed in the air. In the immediate context of Book 5, this fire omen comes soon before the burning of the ships, a disaster that is relatively quickly averted by a rainstorm sent from heaven that puts out the flames. Most of the criticism on this passage has focused on the meaning of the shooting star to which the burning arrow is compared; some have seen an allusion to the famous comet of 44 B.C. that was considered a sign of the apotheosis of Julius Caesar, while others have insisted that the omen here must have something to do with Acestes—perhaps a reference to the future glory of his home, Segesta, which would aid the Romans so much during the First Punic War.[21] It can sometimes be unwise to assume that Virgil shared our modern views on the relative importance of various characters in his poem; readers today might well consider Acestes too insignificant in the general scheme of the *Aeneid* for such an elaborate portent.[22]

Aeneas certainly considers the portent a happy one that somehow points out Acestes in particular (5.531 *laetum . . . Acesten*). In this archery contest, Virgil's key word *laetus* describes both the dove before its death and Acestes, who now receives the prizes of first place, with no objection from Eurytion, the technical winner. We are told that seers sang the "late omens" after some "great outcome": the seers are labeled *terrifici*, "terrifying," a term that elsewhere is used in Jovian weather contexts (4.210 *terrificant*, the related verb, where Iarbas asks Jupiter if thunder and lightning terrify us in vain, and 8.431 *terrificos*, also of Jupiter's terrifying lightning bolts, which the Cyclopes are busy forging when Venus visits them to seek arms for Aeneas). The only other use of the word is a description of the terrifying noise of a bull (12.104 *terrificos*), which describes the ferocity of Turnus as he is stirred by Amata to battle. It is at least possible, given both the proximity of this omen to the firing of the ships, and the use of similar vocabulary in contexts connected to Jupiter in his storm god capacity, that we are to connect Acestes' omen with the imminent disaster for the Trojans of the firing of their ships.

A shooting star image also marked the portent of Iulus' future glory in Book 2 (692-698; cf. 2.697 *signantem* and 5.526 *signavit*).[23] Here we have the best evidence to connect the portent of the Sicilian games with Julius Caesar's comet (comets and shooting stars are not the same thing, but in ancient epic poetry, they just might qualify as equivalent phenomena). The comet appeared at a time of incredible tension between Antony and Octavian, just after Caesar's assassination, when it was very unclear whether or not civil war would erupt at once between the two rivals. Caesar had established games in honor of his divine progenitor Venus, and they were eventually moved to July, his own birth month, probably by Octavian in 44 B.C., the first summer after Caesar's death. There was certainly a comet in 44 B.C. (Chinese sources buttress the Roman evidence!)—and it seems likely that the comet seen in Rome in July of 44 B.C. was one of the luckiest events in the life of the young Octavian, at one of the most perilous times in his life.[24] It is very attractive to connect the portent here with the comet of Caesar and its enormous impact on Octavian's life, though difficulties remain (most especially the fact that the role of Acestes in the omen would then be nearly irrelevant, unlike the centrality of Iulus to both the portent and its future fulfillment in Book 2—Aeneas' son is the living symbol of the imperial succession). This omen is immediately followed by the very Roman solemnity of the *lusus Troiae*, the equestrian exhibition presided over by Ascanius himself. Both Julius and Augustus Caesar revivified this ancient ceremony, whose origins are misty; it may have had an Etruscan source. The shooting star omen in Book 2 confirmed the portent of Ascanius' burning hair. As we shall see below, once Aeneas' fleet is fired by the Trojan women at the instigation of Juno, it will be *Ascanius first* (5.667 *primus et Ascanius*) who rides off to see what has happened: have the Trojans been attacked by some new enemy? This book is Ascanius' real debut as the heir apparent (cf. 5.74 above). He moves from the dutiful world of leading the youths at the memorial rites for Anchises, to his role as captain of the host for the *lusus Troiae* (a proud display of the future strength of the race), and finally to the honor of being the first to charge off and investigate the burning ships.

For Acestes' role in the omen, there may be significance in the fact that the prize he is given by Aeneas is a decorated bowl that was once a gift for Anchises. The Segestan king is a living memorial of Anchises' generation. Neither he nor his friend Entellus could have been expected to triumph in their respective contests. The honor shown to Acestes by the omen (followed by the equestrian pageantry of the following scene with the Trojan youth) links the generations in an eminently Roman style. Anchises' bowl has now been brought to the land that holds his bones and has passed into the hands of one of his age mates, a man beloved by the Trojans as a longtime ally and trusted friend.

Romulus was said to have disappeared mysteriously in a storm (cf. Livy *Ab Urbe Condita* 1.16); does the shooting star portent presage Romulus' apotheosis? We should also note the portent of thunder in a clear sky and a strange "lightning cloud" upon arrival at the Tiber in Book 7 (141-143), which is heralded by the Trojans as a sign of the appointed time and place to found their walls.

Aeneas sends the "son of Epytus" (probably the same Epytus who was one of his comrades in arms on the night Troy fell; cf. 2.340) to bring forth Ascanius, who has been preparing for the *lusus Troiae*, the "game of Troy." The elaborate horsemanship the young people will here display will find its terrible parallel in the cavalry battle before the walls of the Latin capital in Book 11, one of the many correspondences between the two books. Here the Trojan youths perform a show of martial splendor and ancient virtue; there the Trojans will attempt a cavalry assault as a feint to cover Aeneas' planned infantry march over difficult terrain. Neither Aeneas nor Ascanius will participate in the deadly serious equestrian exercises of Book 11; it will be the Volscian heroine Camilla who will dominate the field. There, as here, Jupiter will intervene to save the Trojans: here by sending rain to rescue the Trojan fleet from Juno's fire, there to save the Trojans from Camilla's *aristeia*. There are also parallels between the audience that marvels at seeing the *lusus Troiae* and the crowds that will marvel to see Camilla both on her entrance into Laurentum and at her death. The solemnity of the mock skirmish in Book 5 will be overwhelmed by the real battle of Book 11. Ascanius and his young charges enter: each one is wearing some sort of garland (the exact force of 5.556 *tonsa coma pressa corona* cannot be determined; it must mean they are wearing some sort of trimmed leaf crown on their heads) and they have both spears and a decorative necklace of gold; some have quivers. Thirty-six boys participate, divided into three groups of twelve each.

At the outset of the ship race, Virgil introduced the future patrician families of Rome by marking their descent from the captains of the four ships. Here, too, the leaders of the three equestrian contingents are connected to future noble families of Rome. The first group is led by "a little Priam" (5.563-564 *parvus . . . Priamus*), apparently the son of Polites, who had been so horribly murdered before his father's eyes on Troy's last night. Another ring then is closed, and most joyfully, as the first contingent advances. Atys is next, the founder of the *gens Atia*, the family of Augustus' mother Atia: Virgil has linked the first family of Troy with the new first family of Rome. Atys, too, is noted as a particularly close friend of Iulus': Virgil thereby connects the *gens Iulia* with Augustus. Apparently there are three trainers (*magistri*) for each group, as well as the three leaders (*ductores*), though some commentators have taken them to be one and the same.

The last contingent is led by Iulus himself. Here Virgil dramatically changes the mood of proud joy and Trojan rejoicing, as he prepares for the narrative of the firing of the Trojan fleet. He notes that Iulus is riding on a horse that had been given by Dido as a pledge of her love and a memorial. Virgil used almost the same words (5.572 *esse sui dederat monumentum et pignus amoris*) to describe the bowl that Thracian Cisseus had given to Anchises (5.538 *ferre sui dederat monumentum et pignus amoris*). Cisseus (in Virgil at least, though not in Homer) was Hecuba's father. A gift from Hecuba's father to Anchises is harmless; a gift from Dido carries tremendously ominous significance (cf. 9.266, of the gifts offered by Ascanius to Nisus and Euryalus). Its appearance here shocks us out of the relaxed mood of the parade. The Sicilian youths of Acestes ride on last, after the three main Trojan bodies.

Elsewhere, too, Virgil is interested in Dido's gifts. In Book 11, when Pallas is buried, Aeneas will use one of two cloaks that Dido had woven for him (72-77); at a moment of intense pain for Aeneas, Virgil recalls Dido. The two cloaks were no doubt meant for Aeneas and *Ascanius*; Aeneas' decision to bury Pallas in one of them will be a sign of his feelings for the young, dead warrior, and marks a tragic moment for the imperial succession. In Book 9, Iulus will promise Nisus a bowl that Dido had given to the Trojans (266), another disturbing omen.

The son of Epytus gives the signal with a shout to begin the exercises; those who think (with difficulty) the trainers and the leaders are different must imagine Epytides standing somewhere off to the side and directing the exercises. The actual mock battle is easy enough to visualize from Virgil's Latin; the boys split into two groups and then turn round to charge each other; the only mystery is where the leaders go (presumably they stay in the center, hopefully out of the path of the charging cavalry). Two similes describe the ensuing complex and vaguely described maneuvers of circular motion and artfully simulated cavalry war: the Cretan Labyrinth and the swimming of dolphins.[25] The labyrinth image presages the artwork we shall soon see on the doors of Apollo's temple at Cumae (6.9-33). The significance of that scene will be discussed in its place, but for now the labyrinth image recalls the sacrifice of the young Athenian tribute youths to the Cretan Minotaur, and the search for their savior and liberator Theseus, who represents the imperial successor who can save the youth of Rome from further civil bloodshed. The dolphins presage the magical deliverance of the Trojan fleet in Book 9 (114-122). There, Turnus will have threatened to fire the ships when Ascanius and the others (in Aeneas' absence and at his order) refuse to go out on the plains and meet Turnus in battle. Cybele protested that the ships had been hewn from pine on her sacred Mount Ida; Jupiter agreed that they could therefore be saved. After Turnus' attempted firing of them, they were changed into mermaids, whose swimming is compared to that of dolphins.[26]

Dolphins at sea offer a strange comparison for young warriors on horseback; Virgil wants to connect the dots between the different fates of the Trojan ships. Their plight during the storm in Book 1 was the first crisis in the poem and the first time we met Aeneas and his men; later in this book, Jupiter will send rain to save them, and in Book 9, they will experience their last salvation, a magical transformation also sanctioned by Jupiter. Dolphins also appear on Aeneas' shield (8.673-674), where they anticipate the fleet that will soon be saved. So while the dolphins anticipate the firing of the ships that is about to spoil the mood of the book (though only temporarily), ultimately they signify the frequent intervention of the gods on behalf of their beloved Trojans. The legendary friendliness of the dolphin to man makes their appearance a calming and comforting presence amid trials.

This equestrian display, Virgil declares, was instituted at Alba Longa by Ascanius, where it was celebrated by the "old Latins," the *Prisci Latini* (5.596-603), and passed on to the Romans. All the grandeur and venerable spectacle of Roman glory are summed up in these concluding lines that connect the Trojan past to the Augustan present. But Virgil will allow little time for us to indulge in the comfort and pride of the moment.

Juno has been silent since she took pity on Dido and released her soul from its body. She had succeeded in doing much to further her anti-Trojan cause in Book 4; now, after a brief respite, she returns, again sending Iris, just as she had done at the end of Book 4. The compassionate Juno of that scene has completely reverted to a more recognizable goddess. Virgil says that "Fortune" changed its course here (5.604), but he quickly enough identifies the cause. Iris immediately travels down to the coast, where she sees the Trojan women, who have been segregated from the men during the athletic competition. They are mourning both for the dead Anchises and for the long and tiring sea journey that has taken them so far from a sure home. Once again, the goddess will not have to do very much to work her will; the Trojan women have been excluded from the celebratory rituals that have memorialized Anchises. They have been left alone for a lengthy period of time on the shore of the sea, which they view as a tangible sign of their seemingly endless travels. Iris throws herself into their midst, just as soon she will throw the first firebrand with her right hand (5.619 *conicit*, 643 *iacit*, and cf. 662 *coniciunt*). She disguises herself as one Beroe (unknown outside Virgil), the wife of one Doryclus (another shadowy figure). Iris' argument evokes the same image as Helenus and Andromache in their fake Troy; why should the Trojans continue sailing on and on without respite, when they have a perfectly acceptable home in Sicily? (Her declaration that it is the "seventh summer" since the fall of Troy does not accord with 1.755—a mistake that no doubt would have been corrected in a more thorough revision of the poem). Just as there was an imitation Simois and Xanthus at Buthrotum, so Iris/Beroe asks if she will ever see those Trojan rivers, immediately before she urges the burning of the ships—they can find substitute rivers, in other words, in Sicily. Why Iris lies about a vision of Cassandra is unclear; the Trojan seeress had been cursed and was never believed until it was too late. Virgil provides a nice touch in the suggestion that the fire to burn the ships should come from Neptune's altar; the lord of the sea had quelled Juno's storm in Book 1.

Beroe is an old woman: she is the female equivalent of the older generation that had seen the past and retained a living memory of it. But there is a still older woman, Pyrgo (5.644 *maxima natu*), who had nursed many of Priam's children. She reveals the ruse: she can recognize even the disguised signs of the goddess (helped along, of course, by the fact that she had just been with the sick Beroe). The Trojan mothers are doubtful; they are not sure whether they are more in love with the idea of staying in Sicily and ending their travels or moving ahead to the promised home in Italy. These Trojan women will find their parallel in Book 11, when the women of the Latin capital will watch the cavalry battle unfold beneath them from the safety of the towers and battlements; like these women, they will not have participated in the main event of the day. When they see Camilla's example of heroism, they are spurred on to defend their city and begin to hurl weapons down from the heights. Iris / Beroe does not bother to defend the indefensible; she instead uses divine action: she leaves their sight in a reverse epiphany, and it is clear that the portent of her divine departure stirs the women to choose the fiery option: they are driven on by the divinely inspired madness that is Juno's hallmark:

tum vero attonitae monstris actaeque furore
conclamant (5.659-660)

Then indeed the women began to shout, having been troubled by the portents and driven on by madness

Somehow the Trojan Eumelus (not mentioned again) discovers the fire and brings news to the crowd at Anchises' grave and the *lusus Troiae* assembly. Just as they had seen the portent of the flaming arrow of Acestes, so now they see the black ash floating in a cloud of smoke. Ascanius had been "happy" (5.667 *laetus*) in leading the Trojan young men; the contrast is profound as he charges forth and shows that the virtue he had prefigured in the equestrian display can be put to swift practical use. Ascanius is still in a transitional stage between youth and adulthood; the trainers try to restrain him, but he forces his way on and speaks his first words in the poem, the same words Lucan would use at the beginning of his *Bellum Civile*: "what madness?" (cf. 6.670 *quis furor* and *Bellum Civile* 1.8). Just as Lucan asks why Romans are killing Romans, so Ascanius asks the women (and how quickly he gets to them) why they are burning their own ships (as opposed to Argive camps). "Behold, I am your Ascanius!" he shouts out to them (6.672-673 *en ego vester / Ascanius!*). This is Ascanius' first action in defense of his future; he will be shielded and protected very closely later (so great is the risk to the succession). But here he proves his mettle, and moves without pause from the pageantry of a sham battle to the terrible reality of the fiery sabotage of the precious ships that will convey him to his new home and destiny. Ascanius' presence shatters the madness that had seized the Trojan women; his presence is like a divine epiphany in its own right. He throws forth his helmet, just as Iris had thrown the first firebrand. His brief words and action are sufficient to end their frenzy. Of course, the bulk of Juno's work is already finished; the madness of the women may subside, but the destructive fire is still eating (5.683 *est*) the ships.

It will be Aeneas who takes the next step. He tears his garments and speedily raises his palms to heaven and invokes the gods (the historical infinitives express well his haste). He prays to Jupiter, who is all-powerful because he can presumably thwart Juno's malignant actions easily (besides being a rain god). Aeneas makes a bold prayer. He wants Jupiter either to save the fleet from fire or to kill him with a thunderbolt. After the happiness of the vast majority of this book, Aeneas has no tolerance for a new disaster; it seems not to have occurred to him that building new ships in Sicily could remedy this Junonian setback. The prayer has barely been uttered (5.693 *vix haec ediderat*), when Jupiter the storm god answers it with a sudden thunderstorm and heavy downpour. Four ships are destroyed, because there had been four altars to Neptune that had provided most of the firebrands (5.639-640). Each altar has taken one ship as a sacrifice; the women have thus completed their own (warped) sacrifice rituals in memory of Anchises. The sacrifice of the ships to the fire of Neptune's altars links this scene with the forthcoming sacrifice of Palinurus at the insistence of the sea god.

Presumably mortals do not always notice dramatic portents and manifestations of divine power. Despite the rescue of the ships, Aeneas is torn between staying in Sicily and moving ahead to his destiny in Italy. This renewed sense of listlessness is not terribly surprising, given that so recently Aeneas had told Dido he was going to Italy against his own will. Still, we can feel uncomfortable hearing yet again about his consideration of abandoning the mission. How different was the reaction of Ascanius to the news of the fire! The younger generation, it would seem, can sometimes outdo their parents; in Book 5 Virgil juxtaposes the decline of the heroic generations with the bright promise of Rome's future as embodied in Ascanius—only to dash those hopes with the death of Marcellus at the end of Book 6.

A representative of the older generation, the age of Anchises, appears now at this critical juncture. Athena herself had taught Nautes, the "Sailor." Nautes' plan (revealed by the goddess) is that Aeneas should give the aged (5.715 *longaevosque senes*) a home here with Acestes, a new settlement in Sicily. This plan marks another step in the transition of generations that has been a major theme of this book. The future belongs to the young; just as Ascanius had been bold and daring in racing to the fired ships, so the old, having had their last triumphs in the victories of Entellus and Acestes, will now have a lasting home. Their Sicilian home does not carry the same sense of purposelessness that we saw in Buthrotum, where Hector's empty grave and the conscious effort to mimic the destroyed home city conveyed a sense of perverse nostalgia and pitiful clinging to the past.

Aeneas now receives a third confirmation of what he should be doing. Despite the divine rainstorm, and the inspired words of Nautes, he is still troubled (5.720). He receives a dream visit from his father Anchises. Appropriately, towards the end of this book that has been dominated by the image of the dead father, Anchises gives his son yet more assurances about the future. Jupiter has sent him (5.726); Anchises can confirm that the rain had been sent by Jovian command. Fate has worked out a plan through the frailty of Aeneas' fears and even the madness of Juno: the old will stay behind in Sicily. The honor shown to the dead Anchises has also been a tribute to the old and infirm, the feeble and weak who had once been the great glory of Troy. For the first time, we learn that Aeneas is to fulfill another Odyssean model: he will visit the underworld, for the express purpose of communicating with his father in person. We learn what we might have guessed: Anchises is in Elysium, among the blessed, not with the grim mass of souls. Anchises mentions the Sibyl; Helenus had already predicted that Aeneas would consult the Sibyl in Cumae and learn about the coming war in Italy (3.441-460). It is midnight when the dream vision vanishes, like smoke, Virgil says, that flees into thin air (5.740 *tenuis auras*)—the same image as the flame from the arrow in Acestes' portent, which receded into the thin winds (526-527 *tenuis ventos*).

When Aeneas rises from sleep, awakened by the ghost of his father, he laments that he cannot embrace the man whose absence he so keenly feels. He next offers incense and "holy meal" (5.745 *farre pio*) to Vesta and the Lar of Pergamum. Here perhaps we see the belief that the *Lar* was a ghost. Clearly in Virgil the hearth is an acceptable dwelling place and cult site for the Lar, in this case the Trojan Lar who represents all the dead spirits from the doomed city. Here the vision of the ghost of Anchises leads seamlessly to the mention of ancestral spirits. Whatever his emotional state, Aeneas is always fastidious in the proper execution of liturgical rites; this is the *pietas* he owes to the gods.

Aeneas informs Acestes and the others of the decision he has made in concert with the gods; the souls of those who do not need great praise (5.751 *animos nil magnae laudis egentis*) will be left behind in Sicily. Entellus had fought in the boxing match for praise alone; he sacrificed his prize bull. The older generation has proven its worth and, in fact, the superiority it has over the younger; it has no further need to display its prowess. Nor must we imagine that families have been divided by gender lines here; the Sicilian foundation will not include only Trojan women (any more than we should be amazed, as some commentators have been, when we encounter Trojan matrons later in the poem). The number of people who stay in Sicily is great; they have survived difficult phases of the journey, but they will be spared the supreme challenge of the war in Italy. Acestes has no Buthrotum here, but a miniature Rome: he has a senate and a forum (5.758), the first mentions of these classically Roman features in the context of *Aeneas*' future settlement (as opposed to Dido's Carthage), and another example of Virgil's subtle introduction of strands of Roman glory in his epic. A temple is erected for Venus on Mount Eryx; besides the famous temple on Eryx itself, there were two ancient temples to *Venus Erycina* in Rome, one outside the Colline Gate and the other on the Capitoline. L. Porcius Licinus, consul in 184 B.C., had vowed the former during war with the Ligurians; Q. Fabius Maximus Dictator vowed the latter in 217 B.C. after the Roman disaster at Lake Trasimene.[27] Mount Eryx itself, some seven hundred and fifty meters high, was a traditional landmark for sailors (perhaps there is some echo of this in the aged "Nautes" who first urges a settlement in Sicily). The modern Erice, some sixty-five kilometers from Palermo (ancient Panormus), has a view that can stretch even as far as the Tunisian coast of North Africa. The great mountain overlooks the harbor at Cape Drepanum, and thus overshadows the place of Anchises' death. A priest is also assigned to the burial mound of Anchises; the portent of the snake at the book's opening thus now receives its closing ring with the provision for the perpetuation of a hero cult for Aeneas' father. Virgil is not interested in defining this deification of Anchises, but the implications are clear.

The nine days devoted to the rites in memory of Anchises are now duplicated with nine days of rejoicing and feasting that mark the establishment of the new settlement and the imminent departure of the Trojan young for their new home. The weather, with its placid winds and gentle south breeze, announces the time for sailing to the mainland. The sadness of the separation is understandable and great; the women who had once burned ships in madness are now momentarily fortified with the courage to boast of their willingness to go to Italy—but Aeneas and Acestes know better. More sacrifices are conducted, this time to Eryx and the Tempests—the religious ceremonial of the closing scenes of Book 5 is intense and detailed; the Trojans have had more than enough experience of storms and delays, and there is a palpable sense that finally the long journey is approaching its last leg. The sacrificial entrails and libations of wine are poured into the water to propitiate the marine gods as Aeneas sails off. The ship race at the book's opening is here subtly evoked; the Trojans compete with each other (5.778 *certatim*) as they leave harbor. Certainly the wealth of pious and dutiful religious rites should provide sufficient protection for the Trojans. But as the final sailing to Italy commences, more sorrow remains in sight for Aeneas.

Venus has not appeared in the poem since her encounter with Juno in Book 4, where the fate of Dido was effectively sealed (4.90-128). Laughter-loving Venus had last been seen smiling at the discovery of some or another trick. True to her nature, she is frivolous and capricious; she appears as she wishes, and her relationship with her son is frustrated by her frequent choice not to communicate openly and directly. The visit she makes to Neptune as Book 5 ends is fitting; she has had ample experience of Juno's rage. Like the fire that had eaten away at the Trojan vessels (5.683 *est*), Juno has eaten away the Phrygian capital, and thoroughly (5.785 *exedisse*); Venus complains, with some embellishment, that Juno has even been pursuing the ashes and bones of Troy's dead. Virgil had asked at the outset of his epic if the gods could possibly have such intense anger that they would force a man such as Aeneas to undergo so much pain (1.10-11). Venus expresses a similar sentiment:

... causas tanti sciat illa furoris. (5.788)

... *let her know her own reasons for such great madness.*

Venus, of course, is not being as theologically profound as Virgil had been; she is interested in persuading Neptune that Juno has no good reason to be pursuing the Trojans in fury and rage. Venus summarizes neatly Juno's activities in Books 1 and 5 (she omits, of course, all mention of the troubles Aeneas suffered in Carthage because of her own amorous schemes): she notes the storm that drove Aeneas to North Africa and the recent burning of the ships, that is, destruction with both water and fire. Her complaint that the Trojans have now been forced to leave people behind because of the four lost ships is a nice touch, very much in keeping with her cajoling manner with her uncle Neptune, though another exaggeration. She knows, too, that Aeneas' divinely approved fate is to reach the Tiber and Laurentum; her speech ends with a fittingly coy remark:

> si concessa peto, si dant ea moenia Parcae. (5.798)
>
> *If I seek things that have been granted, if the Fates grant these walls.*

Neptune, we may imagine, is not immune to his niece's charms; he notes his affinity with her as a sea deity (a reference to her birth in Hesiod out of the sea foam following the castration of Sky). We know already of the help Neptune has given the Trojans; his first appearance in the poem (1.124-147) was to calm Juno's storm. He alludes to the incident late in the *Iliad* (20.158 ff.) where he saved Aeneas from Achilles. Interestingly, Neptune notes that Aeneas was no match for Achilles in strength (5.809 *nec viribus aequis*); early in Book 6, Aeneas will learn from the Cumaean Sibyl that he must face another Achilles in Italy, a clear reference to Turnus (89-90). Neptune is no mere tool for Venus' manipulation, either; he notes (5.810-811) that he saved Aeneas despite his desire to destroy the city because of Laomedon's perjury. Neptune readily agrees that the port of Avernus (the lake of the dead) will be open safely to Aeneas. "One only" does he demand as a price:

> unus erit tantum amissum quem gurgite quaeres;
> unum pro multis dabitur caput. (5.814-815)
>
> *Only one will be lost, whom you will seek in the water;*
> *one head will be given for the many.*

The half-line is almost certainly deliberate.[28] The anaphora (*unus, unum*) and strong, ninefold alliteration of *u* give the line power and a chilling creepiness. The first clue to the eerie close of the book comes with 5.813 *Averni*; Aeneas has been granted safe passage to the underworld, in other words: a fine lead-in to the narrative of Book 6, but an omen, also, of Palinurus' imminent death.

For reasons we can scarcely fathom, Venus is happy (5.816 *laeta ... pectora*) as Neptune closes his speech and prepares for a suitably dramatic exit, befitting the marine master and echoing his calm gliding over the waters after he calmed the storm in Book 1. Venus does not bother to ask who the one sacrifice must be; true, from Jupiter's prophecy she already knows Aeneas and Ascanius will survive to arrive safely in Italy, but her lack of reaction to Neptune's condition is noteworthy. Neptune's retinue of sea deities is largely ornamental, though it also provides a suitable contrast between the world of mortals and that of the gods, besides increasing suspense: who will die? One clue is given as to the manner of the sacrificial offering: Palaemon (5.823 *Inousque Palaemon*) was the son of Ino; both mother and son threw themselves into the sea to avoid the mad husband and father Athamas (perhaps *Pala*emon presages *Pali*nurus).

Aeneas is also somewhat happy (5.828 *gaudia pertemptant mentem*), though his mind is anxious (827 *suspensam*), in the sense of poised between joy and sorrow, and joy is (perhaps) winning out. It is a subtle description of a man who has known intense pain, often from sudden and unexpected events. *Princeps ante omnis* (5.833) ("first before all") is Palinurus, who leads the fleet out from Sicily. Soon it is midnight, and all are asleep, except the one who will soon die.

Palinurus had been introduced in Book 3 (202), where we noted the foreshadowing of his end. His death had been a part of the traditional Trojan lore; Dionysius of Halicarnassus tells the basic story (1.53.2).[29] Servius says that there was a pestilence in Sicily, and that an oracle revealed that it would not end until the ghost of Palinurus had been placated, on which account a grove and cenotaph were erected. The Palinurus story will be concluded, appropriately enough, in Virgil's underworld (where we shall examine the alleged inconsistencies in Virgil's narrative). This final scene of Book 5 is the most memorable and lasting of all the extant traces of Palinurus lore. Book 5 is the longest book of the poem thus far; despite the genuinely peaceful moments that extended over more than half the book and in which we have lingered so calmly (not to mention the drama of the firing of the ships), it is Palinurus we remember best from this section of the poem. He has his parallel, too, in Book 11, though in a very different setting (as so much of that book perverts and subverts what happens here). There it will be Arruns who dies mysteriously, and after the direct intervention of a god. Palinurus is a logical choice for Neptune's sacrifice; with the god as navigator, there is no need for a mortal helmsman, however dutiful (Virgil is also evoking Circe's notice to Odysseus that he will need no pilot to guide his ship to the underworld; cf. *Odyssey* 10.503-507). Palinurus' death is also modeled on Odysseus' loss of Elpenor in *Odyssey* 10-11, though the difference between the drunken somnolence of the Greek and the divinely wrought somnolence of the Trojan is enormous.

Palinurus' death scene opens in an atmosphere of eerie creepiness, then, that any horror writer would pay dearly to match:

> cum levis aetheriis delapsus Somnus ab astris
> aëra dimovit tenebrosum et dispulit umbras,
> te, Palinure, petens, tibi somnia tristia portans
> insonti (5.838-841)

> *When Sleep glided down lightly from the ethereal stars*
> *and moved the dark air and dispelled the shadows,*
> *seeking you, Palinurus, and carrying baleful sleep to you*
> *though you were innocent*

Virgil conveys all the necessary information. Palinurus is innocent; in the case of a helmsman, this is sufficient proof of his wakefulness; he may be tired, but he is not going to succumb to sleep (those who seek some naturalistic explanation for what is about to happen do violence to Virgil's straightforward vision). Palinurus' innocence contrasts with Neptune's decree and Venus' lack of concern; there is no good reason that demands Palinurus' death (again, there will be a difference when we meet Arruns). The sleep the god brings is not peaceful and restful, but baleful, for it will spell his death. Apostrophe is used just infrequently enough in Virgil for it to have power in passages such as this one; later poets would overindulge in the device and ruin its power (especially Lucan).[30]

Sleep, disguised as Phorbas (the specific person does not matter; all that is needed is for Palinurus to recognize him and suspect nothing), urges Palinurus to sleep and let him take the rudder. Palinurus scarcely lifts his eyes (5.847), an action that has been interpreted in various ways since antiquity: is he too tired, or is he resolutely intent on his steering? If he is tired, he nonetheless makes a lengthy reply: Palinurus knows that the sea is fraudulent, that calm water can become stormy in mere moments. No matter how tired he is, his devotion will not allow him to surrender the rudder to another. Those who think Palinurus is drifting off (especially of his own accord) must explain why he now holds his eyes on the stars and is fixed to the rudder, clinging to it tenaciously (5.852-853). Sleep, the brother of Death, has no time for this sort of sense of obligation and duty. He has a wand that is drenched in the dew of Lethe (another underworld body of water), not to mention soporific Stygian might (to match the Avernian harbor Neptune had mentioned). Lethe was the river of forgetfulness, and Styx the river the dead had to cross (the problem Palinurus will face in Book 6, where ironically the helmsman cannot navigate his last river). Palinurus must forget his duty and fall asleep (ultimately in death); Lethe will do the first, and Styx the second. Even after Sleep shakes the wand over his head and lets the underworld water drip down over him, Palinurus still resists (5.856 *cunctanti*). He is barely asleep when Sleep throws him overboard: the rudder (no longer needed, thanks to Neptune) is torn off—such was Palinurus' grip on it. He finally wakes up as he is thrown off the ship—and he calls out to companions who cannot hear him. Sleep disappears into thin air, his work done. The Trojan fleet sails on safely, past the rocks of the Sirens.[31] The weather is calm because of Neptune's protection; this is in part a nod to the windless calm Odysseus enjoys as he approaches the Sirens' abode. Circe is Siren-like; the mention of the Sirens recalls in part Circe's announcement to Odysseus that he would have no need of a rudder.

Palinurus' (nocturnal) encounter with the god Sleep also removes him (as does the natural experience of sleep) from the "normal" experience of life: Virgil's haunting description of the god seeking out Palinurus (8.840 *te, Palinure, petens*) was inspired by Catullus' description of Bacchus' approach to Ariadne after she had been abandoned by Theseus on Naxos:

te quaerens, Ariadna, tuoque incensus amore (*carmen* 64.253) *seeking you, Ariadne, and set on fire by love for you*

The contexts are very different, but both Palinurus and Ariadne are experiencing a divine visitation, and in both cases the recipient of the visitation is removed from the natural world (though with very different results; the water Palinurus splashes into will welcome him back all too firmly into the "real" world).

The Sirens are another nod to the *Odyssey* (12.39 ff.)—but here they have special resonance. Virgil says that once (5.865 *quondam*) they were a problem for sailors, a place of death that was white with many bones. "Then," (866 *tum*), that is, on this night, the rocks were sounding with constant surf—another reason Palinurus was not heard when he cried out, besides the fact that his friends were enjoying one of the calmest nights of sleep they had experienced in a long time. Aeneas has been "chasing" Odysseus throughout the Mediterranean; Servius, among others, records the tradition that the Sirens killed themselves after Odysseus successfully escaped them—in any case, their rocks have claimed one last victim. Aeneas had been tense before the voyage, and now, just as his flagship approaches the Sirens' rock (5.864 *adeo . . . subibat*, of the fleet), he senses that the boat lacks its navigator and is drifting. Very quickly, Aeneas gains control of the boat (only a pedant asks how, given that the rudder went overboard with Palinurus—in any case, the rudder is not the *sine qua non* for controlling a ship). Aeneas is ignorant of the real cause of Palinurus' death; his accusatory lament is deeply ironic:

"o nimium caelo et pelago confise sereno,
nudus in ignota, Palinure, iacebis harena." (5.870-871)[32]

*"O you who trusted too much in the heavens and the serene sea,
Palinurus, you will lie naked on an unknown shore."*

If this ending for Book 5 really was the result of Virgil's *post mortem* editors' transfer of the authentic last two lines to the beginning of Book 6, we owe them a debt of gratitude: it is the superior ending (they acted "prudently," as Mynors notes laconically).

In her dialogue with Neptune, Venus had alluded to Virgil's own question: why indeed are the gods so angry? Neptune's response was to demand yet another seemingly purposeless tragedy: why indeed did Palinurus have to die? The death of Palinurus balances that of Anchises at the end of Book 3; despite prophecies and revelations, Aeneas had been given no indication that he would lose either his father or his helmsman, and indeed as we move into the underworld he will complain once again that he had not been warned (cf. 3.708-714 and 6.337-346). With Palinurus' death, every book so far except the introductory first one has ended with the loss of someone close to Aeneas: wife, father, lover, and now helmsman (a deeply felt loss, too, in this Odyssean story of the sea). Sleep, we later learn, did not *directly* kill Palinurus; the helmsman does make it to the shore of Italy, where he is killed by inhospitable Italians—but the role the god played in his loss is clear and unmistakable.

It is conceivable that in his death scene for Palinurus Virgil wished to evoke the memory of Octavian's naval disaster off Cape Palinurus in 38 B.C. Horace had perhaps been there, with Maecenas:

> non me Philippis versa acies retro,
>   devota non exstinxit arbos,
>   nec Sicula Palinurus unda. (*carmen* 3.4.25-28)
>
> *The battle line turned back at Philippi did not kill me,*
>   *nor the accursed tree,*
>   *nor Palinurus in his Sicilian wave.*

Octavian had lost most of his fleet in two storms off the cape; these lines may allude to that disaster. Virgil's calm sailing past the cape contrasts greatly with the stormy reputation of this area off the Lucanian coast: in the same vicinity, a small Roman naval detachment had been wrecked during the First Punic war in 253 B.C.[33] The etiology of the modern Capo Palinuro is very much in Virgil's style (cf. the opening of Book 7 with the loss of Aeneas' nurse at Caieta; the two losses frame Virgil's underworld book).

Book 5 ends, too, with the imagined horror of a naked, unburied man lying on the shore. This evokes Virgil's description of Priam's fate (2.557-558), and has affinities with the deaths of Mezentius, who will ask Aeneas for burial and not receive an answer (10.900-906), and Turnus, whose death will end the poem (in striking contrast to the *Iliad*, which ends with the *burial* of Hector, not his death). Book 5 ends darkly, as befits the prelude to the descent into the underworld. Like Book 4, this book has represented delay, though of a very different sort; while Rome's future was in no way advanced during the stay with Dido (except for the coming horror of the Punic Wars, which marks a perverse advance in Roman destiny), we have seen much of the religious and patriotic fervor of Rome in its nascent stages here on Sicilian shores, a sort of whetting of our appetite for the founding of a permanent settlement in Italy. But any indulgence in a triumphal celebration of Rome's future was lost in the fires of Juno's rage and now the waters of Palinurus' loss. Virgil could well have accelerated his hero's arrival in Italy and the shores of Cumae. But instead he has lingered over many themes and allowed his audience more time to ponder questions he has raised in his narrative. He will provide answers to those questions now, among the dead. Virgil's classroom is hell, and his teachers are ghosts.

Notes

1. Besides Putnam's chapter in *Poetry of the Aeneid*, on Book 5 see also GALINSKY, "*Aeneid* 5 and the *Aeneid*," *The American Journal of Philology* 89 (1968), pp. 157-185, and HOLT, "*Aeneid* V: Past and Future," *The Classical Journal* 75 (1979-1980), pp. 110-121.

2. See further FRATANTUONO, "The Penultimate Books of Virgil's *Aeneid*," *Maia* (2005), pp. 33-36. The keyword of Book 5 is *laetus*, while the keyword of Book 11 is *maestus*: the happiness experienced in Book 5 will never be felt again by the Trojans during the epic. There is joy in Book 8, but all joy there is overshadowed by the pall of the war that starts in Book 7; Aeneas may receive a tour of the future site of Rome in Evander's Pallanteum, but the tour comes while he is seeking allies to further his cause against Turnus and the other Italians.

3. Cf. 1.195, 550, 558, and 570.

4. See TOYNBEE, *Animals in Roman Life and Art*, Ithaca, 1973, p. 94. Perhaps the Libyan bear skin is a subtle hint of how the danger in Carthage has been temporarily averted, though the curse from North Africa remains. Book 5 is, in part, such a happy interlude in the *Aeneid* because the shadow of Anchises hangs heavily over the book. One cannot imagine Aeneas falling in love with Dido and staying so long with her, neglectful of his *Roman* mission, with Anchises alive; so in Book 5, the memorial for Anchises, Aeneas and the Trojans are safe from the threat of Dido (and Carthage); she will return, however briefly, to haunt Aeneas in hell.

5. *Fasti* 2.547 ff.

6. A reference to the ill-fated child of the sun would be utterly inappropriate here (though note that at 6.659 Elysium is located underneath the Eridanus River, where Phaëthon's sisters were said to have wept themselves into amber); the "Bright One" is simply the sun (see further Williams ad loc.)

7. See further HARRIS, *Sport in Greece and Rome*, Ithaca, 1972, pp. 128 ff., and FELDHERR, "Ships of State: *Aeneid* 5 and Augustan Circus Spectacle," *Classical Antiquity* 14 (1995), pp. 245-265.

8. For the old idea (whose origin is unknown) of Drances as allegory for Cicero, see MCDERMOTT, "Drances/Cicero," *Vergilius* 26 (1980), pp. 34-37.

9. For connections between Gyas' Chimaera and Turnus' helmet, and the possible evocation of *Gigas* ("giant") in *Gyas* and the theme of gigantomachy, see NICOLL, "Chasing Chimaeras," *The Classical Quarterly* N.S. 35.1 (1985), pp. 134-139.

10. On this simile see further Hornsby, *op. cit.*, pp. 55-56.

11. See PUTNAM, "Ganymede and Virgilian Ekphrasis," *The American Journal of Philology* 116 (1995), pp. 419-440, and *Virgil's Epic Designs: Ekphrasis in the Aeneid*, New Haven, 1998, especially pp. 55-60 and 64-74.

12. On this simile see further ROSE, "Vergil's Ship-Snake Simile (*Aeneid* 5.270-281)," *The Classical Journal* 78.2 (1982), pp. 115-121, and Hornsby, *op. cit.*, pp. 62-63. Hornsby sees in the snake's wound the "final scotching of the snake" and the end of the horrors the snake represented earlier in the poem. But the snake is not a universally evil portent in the *Aeneid*, as the fresh memory of Anchises' snake proves.

13. Homer is not explicit about the nature of the relationship; see further DOVER, *Greek Homosexuality*, Cambridge, Massachusetts, 1978, p. 53.

14. For an introductory overview of this complex topic, see further WILLIAMS, *Roman Homosexuality: Ideologies of Masculinity in Classical Antiquity*, Oxford, 1999. Williams offers judicious and carefully considered analysis of the surviving evidence,

though not all his conclusions are to be accepted. Best on this topic is OLIENSIS, "Sons and Lovers: Sexuality and Gender in Virgil's Poetry," in Martindale, *op. cit.*, pp. 294-311 (with bibliography on the general topic): "unlike Greece, Rome never sanctioned sexual love between free men. Heterosexual unions figure alternative futures; Dido and Lavinia embody lands where Aeneas may plant the seeds of his new city. Homoeroticism is not rooted in this way in Rome's master narrative; it contours the plot but remains ultimately extraneous to it."

15. On Roman homosexuality see LILJA, *Homosexuality in Republican and Augustan Rome*, Helsinki, 1983, and MACMULLEN, "Roman Attitudes to Greek Love," *Historia* 31 (1982), pp. 484-502.

16. See further FITZGERALD, "Nisus and Euryalus: A Paradigm of Futile Behavior and the Tragedy of Youth," in MARTYN, ed., *Cicero and Virgil: Studies in Honour of Harold Hunt*, Amsterdam, 1972, pp. 114-137, PAVLOCK, "Epic and Tragedy in Vergil's Nisus and Euryalus Episode," *Transactions of the American Philological Association* 115 (1985), pp. 207-224, and MAKOWSKI, "Nisus and Euryalus: A Platonic Relationship," *The Classical Journal* 85.1 (1989), pp. 1-15.

17. Nisus' Homeric antecedent Ajax may point to his forthcoming doom; both early favorites end badly; like Ajax, who is incapable of moving from the past into a new future, so (the homosexual) Nisus will be another Trojan sacrificed to the Roman future.

18. For analysis of the episode and its Greek antecedents, see SENS, "The *Dementia* of Dares: *Aen.* 5.465," *Vergilius* 41 (1995), pp. 49-54.

19. "Boxing naturally lends itself to simple violence, and in the ancient world its object was to inflict damage as directly as possible." (PLASS, *The Game of Death in Ancient Rome: Arena Sport and Political Suicide*, Madison, 1995, p. 57; see also p. 40).

20. On Dares' near fatal wounds, see MATZ, "Expectorating Blood and Teeth: Vergil, *Aen.* 5.469-470," *The Classical World* 87 (1994), pp. 310-311.

21. See further LAWLER, "The Significance of Acestes' Flaming Arrow, *Aeneid* 5.522-528," *Vergilius* 34 (1988), pp. 102-111, which provides useful comparison of the passage to other flame and arrow episodes in the poem, but somewhat disappointingly does not offer any new appraisal of the omen's mysterious import.

22. Still, one suspects such a signal omen portends more than Segesta's future founding, *pace* BRIGGS, "The Similes of *Aeneid* 5," in Wilhelm, R.M., and Jones, *op. cit.*, pp. 157-166.

23. There may be significance in the fact that the shooting star has been "wrested" (5.527 *refixa*) from the heavens, just as the shield Nisus wins after tripping in the foot race had been "wrested" (5.360 *refixum*) from Neptune's temple. But Virgil, like all Latin poets, often repeats words in close sequence without apparent reason.

24. See further the important volume of RAMSEY and LICHT, *The Comet of 44 B.C. and Caesar's Funeral Games*, Atlanta, 1997. But Williams on 523-524 is right: the games of July, 44 B.C., were not necessarily *ludi funebres* for Caesar (as Servius asserts).

25. For the labyrinth and the dolphins see further Hornsby, *op. cit.*, pp. 52-53.

26. On dolphins see Toynbee, *op. cit.*, pp. 205-208. The Romans were particularly struck by how friendly the marine mammal was to man; cf. Pliny the Elder *Historia Naturalis* 9.26, Pliny the Younger *Epistulae* 9.33 with Sherwin-White's notes, and Chilver's note on Tacitus *Historiae* 2.86.14 (note the misprinted conflation of the citations from the two Plinys there).

27. See further PLATNER and ASHBY, *A Topographical Dictionary of Ancient Rome*, Oxford, 1929, pp. 551-552, with many ancient citations.

28. On the sacrifice of Palinurus (in place of Aeneas), see HARDIE, *The Epic Successors of Virgil: A Study in the Dynamics of a Tradition*, Cambridge, 1993, pp. 32-

33, and NICOL, "The Sacrifice of Palinurus," *The Classical Quarterly* N.S. 38 (1988), pp. 459-472.

29. Misenus, a sort of doublet of Palinurus whose death and burial will be described in Book 6, is also briefly mentioned by Dionysius (1.175), as is Aeneas' nurse Caieta, whose death will be noted at the beginning of Book 7.

30. Young poets easily succumb to such excesses in their exuberant enthusiasm for powerful devices.

31. See further GRESSETH, "The Homeric Sirens," *Transactions of the American Philological Association* 101 (1970), pp. 203-218.

32. Aeneas provides a very Hellenistic, epigrammatic epitaph for Palinurus; see further BRUSS, "Famous Last Words: *Aeneid* 5, 870-71 and the Hellenistic Cenotaphic Epigramme," *Latomus* 64 (2005), pp. 325-225. Palinurus' ultimate fate will not be revealed until Book 6; the epitaph here, however, will remain all too appropriate. See further LATTIMORE, *Themes in Greek and Latin Epitaphs*, Urbana, 1962, pp. 199-202.

33. Polybius 1.39.6, with Walbank's note. Walbank observes that only Orosius among our sources locates the disaster off Capo Palinuro. For full commentary, see further NISBET and RUDD, *A Commentary on Horace: Odes Book III*, Oxford, 2004, ad loc. Augustus established two major naval bases after Actium, one at the western end of the Bay of Naples (Cape Misenum) and the other at Ravenna; see further BOWMAN et al., eds., *The Cambridge Ancient History X: The Augustan Empire, 43 B.C. to A.D. 69*, Cambridge, 1996, pp. 383-384.

Chapter VI

So He Spoke, Weeping

Roland Austin died only a few days after he had finished his Oxford commentary on *Aeneid* 6 (which was published posthumously in 1977)—a fitting end for one of the most sensitive and intelligent of Virgil's many critics. Book 6 marks the close of the first half of the *Aeneid*. Aeneas finally arrives in Italy, and this time permanently; the action of this book and the entire second half of the poem will be concentrated in a relatively small geographical area, in contrast to the vast sweep of the eastern and central Mediterranean that has been Virgil's stage thus far. In the tripartite division of the *Aeneid*, Book 6 has affinities with Book 8: in both books, Aeneas receives the most complete information in the poem about the future of Rome. As a conclusion to his *Odyssey*, Virgil has adapted Homer's account of Odysseus' visit to Teiresias in the underworld (Books 10-11). Virgil's vision of hell is more expansive and detailed; in the larger context of the *Aeneid*, this is no mere heroic adventure to represent some sort of ultimate journey or the conquest of death. Anchises summons Aeneas to the land of the dead in a dream at the end of Book 5; in the fields of Elysium he will show Aeneas the background of the Roman destiny we have so far only glimpsed, usually through divine conversations the audience, unlike Aeneas, can observe firsthand. Book 6 has been called the climax of the poem, though in Virgil's own stated views at the beginning of Book 7, it is but the close of the lesser half of the epic. It is a book of education, not of action. Aeneas knows much at its end, and he will know even more when he receives his shield in Book 8, at the end of the second third of the poem; Virgil will highlight how the visions of the future that mean so much to us (as they did for Augustan Rome), remain so obscure and mysterious (understandably enough) to his Trojan pawn of fate. In the Middle Ages, some found in the pages of the *Aeneid* answers to all the great problems and questions of life.[1] For at least some of those questions, Book 6 will offer answers, though not always the ones we (or, for that matter, Virgil) would have liked. In Book 6, Virgil will make implicit comment on both Homer and Lucretius, the two poets who most influenced his creation of the *Aeneid*. The final scene of the book, the much-discussed episode of the Gates of Sleep, will be Virgil's quiet and devastating statement of allegiance to the poet who had taught that death was nothing to be feared, and that the fantastic stories of the underworld were unworthy of mortal belief. Book 6 will close the door, also, on Aeneas' relationship with Dido; we shall meet her again in its pages, and see how much she has changed from the raving woman who cursed the Trojans and plunged Aeneas' sword into her breast—and how little Aeneas has changed. The last night of Troy, too, will be revisited; Book 6 draws to a close everything from the poem's first half in a misty penumbra of history, mythology, and philosophy.

As we have already noted, the end of Book 5 and the beginning of Book 6 was the subject of needless question in late antiquity. The first two lines of Book 6 belong here rather than at the end of Book 5. They closely link Palinurus' death narrative and the Trojan arrival at Cumae and the underworld. The shores of Cumae are called "Euboean" (6.2) because a colony from Chalcis on Euboea had been founded there sometime in the eighth century B.C. The ominous association of the region with the realm of the dead precludes any unbridled excitement at the arrival in Italy; the Trojans are burning with desire for the Italian shore (6.5 *ardens*, the same verb Virgil used at 4.281 to describe Aeneas after Mercury's order that he flee Carthage), but the mood is solemn, and while his men seek out fire, water, and food (wild animals), Aeneas wastes no time in preparing to visit the Sibyl, who dwells near a temple of Apollo. The geography of the opening of Book 6 is vaguely defined, appropriately enough for an epic poem, and for the mysterious Sibyl. No definitive map of the landscape of Cumae can be drawn from the verses of the *Aeneid*. There are "citadels" (6.9 *arces*) over which Apollo presides, as well as a grove sacred to his sister Trivia (13 *lucos*). Apollo was a god of prophecy, and Diana in her chthonic form is an underworld goddess; in the context of the second half of the poem, their traditional presiding over the sudden deaths of the young (e.g., in war) is also evoked. Aeneas is interested in two places in particular near Cumae: those Apollonian citadels (a reference to the town's acropolis), and the huge cave (11 *antrum immane*) nearby, the modern *Antro della Sibilla*, originally dug out by the Greeks and later used as a Christian cemetery; the cave was rediscovered in May of 1932 by Amedeo Maiuri (cf. works published before Maiuri, such as Fairclough's World War I era Loeb edition, which remain vague about the cave). The nearby Lago d'Averno is a volcanic crater lake, near the appropriately named volcanic field known as the *Campi Flegrei*, the "Burning Fields." Octavian's trusted friend and admiral Agrippa (the possible historical inspiration for Aeneas' companion Achates) sought to militarize the lake in 37 B.C, and was responsible for a series of five tunnels, one of which was quite wrongly taken to be the Sibyl's cave until well into the twentieth century; certainly in the Middle Ages there was confusion: Virgil's underworld mythology was a more impressive explanation than Agrippa's naval yards for the war between Octavian and Sextus Pompey.[2] Virgil later identifies *Avernus* (6.237) as the site of the actual cave that leads into the underworld: no such cave has ever been found.[3] The Sibyl's cave at Cumae has long been confused and mistakenly conflated with the apparently invented cave at Avernus. Virgil is interested, in any case, in presenting a vision of what these well-known sites might have been like in the distant past. There are no rivers in the immediate environs of Cumae, and yet Virgil's men find them (6.8 *flumina monstrat*); whenever contemporary reality might confound the poet, he can claim he is describing the distant past.

Virgil identifies the origins of the Apollo cult at Cumae with the arrival of Daedalus after he had fled from imprisonment and forced servitude on Minos'

Crete.[4] Mythological ornamentation, once again, has serious dramatic purpose. Just as this book will end with the tragedy of the premature death of Marcellus, so here it begins with an evocation of Daedalus' loss of his son Icarus, the casualty of his winged flight from Crete to Cumae.[5] There is also a parallel between the temple to Juno in Dido's Carthage and this Apollo temple in Italy. Both are decorated with disturbing and depressing memories of the past. On Apollo's temple doors, the death of Androgeos is the first sculpture relief. Androgeos had been a son of Minos; the tradition of his death was varied (as Apollodorus records): some thought he died in Greece, fighting the bull of Marathon, while others thought he died less mythically in Athens, murdered by sore losers at the Panathenaic games. Androgeos' death was the cause of Minos' demand for living tribute from Athens to feed his Minotaur. And, indeed, the next relief shows the doomed Athenian youths, with the urn (6.22) that has chosen them by terrible lot. The Minotaur itself is next, the horrible progeny of Pasiphae's bestial love for the Cretan bull, aided by Daedalus' thoughtful wooden contraption.[6] Daedalus in a sense had created the Minotaur, and he also saved Theseus and his companions from its horror when he pitied the love Ariadne had for the Athenian hero (6.28) and showed her how to save him with the (rather obvious) trick of using a ball of thread to mark their way through the labyrinth. The last relief is missing; Icarus would have been carved last, but his father Daedalus was unable to bring himself to depict the loss of his son in art. Just as Daedalus is unable to carve his son in memorial sculpture, so Anchises, at the end of this book, will need to be prompted before describing the dead Marcellus.[7] The theme of the "unfinished picture" is also a link between this book and the beginning of Aeneas' mental revisit to Troy in Dido's temple to Juno (not to mention the end of Book 12).

The doors of Apollo's temple, with their elaborate description of the Cretan / Athenian lore about Daedalus, Theseus, Ariadne, and the Minotaur, is a literary tribute to Catullus, who had depicted the same myths on the covering of a couch at the nuptial celebration for Peleus and Thetis in his lengthiest work, the celebrated little epic ("epyllion") *Peliaco quondam* (*carmen* 64). The same poem, with its lengthy account of the abandonment of Ariadne on Naxos after Bacchus had demanded her from Theseus, was also an influence on Virgil's depiction of Dido's abandonment in Book 4. Daedalus was the ancient mortal craftsman *par excellence*; at the end of this book, Virgil will have Anchises tell his son that there will be others whose arts will be bronze and marble work (6.847-853), that is, Greeks like Daedalus; for the Romans, there will be a different *ars*, a different national vocation. The reference to Catullus here links together the very dawn of the Trojan War (the marriage of Achilles' parents and the denial of an invitation to Discord) with the Roman future, besides giving the opening of the book a troublesome color. The abandonment of Ariadne in Catullus provided poetic inspiration for Virgil's depiction of the abandonment of Dido; the horrors of both Troy and Carthage will be revisited in Virgil's underworld, as Aeneas confronts his ghosts.

Interestingly, Aeneas and his unnamed companions are not able to finish surveying the images (6.33-35); they would have thoroughly taken them all in, Virgil tells us, had Achates not arrived with the priestess of Apollo and Trivia, the Sibyl Deiphobe, the daughter of Glaucus (who, appropriately enough, was a sea god with powers of prophecy). The atmosphere is more hurried than it had been in Book 1, when Aeneas and Achates were able to feast their eyes[8] on the admittedly grim images of Troy's fall; those pictures had deep resonance for the Trojans, while the images here are, for them, mythological curiosities; they do not speak any message—a parallel to the procession of Romans at the end of the book, which says so much to Virgil's contemporary audience and to us, but so little to Aeneas, for whom it is a picture without historical context (like the Roman historical artwork we shall see on his divine shield in Book 8)—the antithesis of the pictures in Dido's temple to Juno, which drove Aeneas to tears: Virgil's hero is terribly familiar with his Trojan past, but unknowing about his Roman future. The Sibyl, indeed, rushes Aeneas; the pictures on the doors are not meant for a museum tour. She instructs the Trojans to prepare a sacrifice of seven bullocks for Apollo and seven ewes for Diana. "Seven," as Austin noted in his commentary on the close of Book 1, "was a number that seemed to come easily to Virgil's pen." The number may have had special significance to Apollo's cult, though here it seems to recall the tradition that there were seven young men and seven young women who were sacrificed to the Minotaur (Virgil mentions only the boys at 6.21-22). The deaths of the Athenian youths, so pointless and contrary to the natural order, prefigure the deaths of the Trojan and Latin youths in the forthcoming Italian war.

The Sibyl goes into an ecstasy at the very threshold of her cave (6.42 ff.) and announces that it is now the time for the Trojans to "ask for the fates" (45 *poscere fata*); the *ultimate* fates will be revealed at the end of the book, to round off this beginning of the prophetic liturgy. She summons Aeneas to vows and prayers as he begins the long process of his *katabasis* or descent. Aeneas addresses Phoebus Apollo with praises that recall his work on behalf of the Trojans: he notes how Apollo had helped direct Paris' shot that killed Achilles in his vulnerable heel (so, too, in Book 11 Apollo will direct Arruns' shot in killing Camilla, one of two places in the *Aeneid* where Camilla recalls Achilles). The first request that Aeneas makes (after the summary of past favors that form the prerequisite for a fully ritualized, liturgically correct prayer) is that the fortune of Troy not follow him any further. In one sense, this request will not come to fulfillment (and indeed, very soon Aeneas will learn that another Achilles already awaits him in Italy), while in another sense, it distantly presages the final reconciliation of Juno and Jupiter's promise to her of the decline of all things Trojan. Aeneas makes a reverential reference to the gods (and goddesses!) who have opposed Troy (Helenus had warned him to placate Juno as often as possible), and he politely asks the Sibyl to announce what he already knows (6.67 *meis fatis*) is his destined due: for the Teucrians to settle in Latium. No prayer is complete without a gift in return: Aeneas promises that he will erect a marble temple to Apollo and his sister, and set up Apollonian festival days. The references here are to the building of a temple to Apollo on the Palatine by Augustus, which was dedicated on 9 October, 28 B.C., and both to (remotely) the *ludi Apollinares* that were established in 212 B.C. and (proximately) Augustus' celebration of the *ludi saeculares*, the "Secular Games." The Palatine temple was actually a thanksgiving offering for the victory over Sextus Pompey, not the defeat of Antony and Cleopatra at Actium, which had been achieved in the shadow of Apollo's temple at Leucas (cf. 3.274-275).[9] On the occasion of the *ludi Quinquennales* in 16 B.C., Propertius composed an etiological elegy (c. 4.6) that linked the Palatine Apollo and the god who had presided over the victory at Actium—fittingly enough, even if falsely.

A *saeculum* was considered the lengthiest possible span of a mortal life, i.e., about one century. The games involved sacrifice to underworld deities at the dawn of a new generation (again, the Augustan succession motif is never absent). In 17 B.C., with his power well and firmly established, Augustus celebrated the Secular Games and commissioned a poem from Rome's poet laureate Horace to mark the occasion (the *Carmen Saeculare*). No doubt Virgil's first audiences would have connected the games Aeneas vows before the Sibyl to the games Augustus celebrated some two years after Virgil's death. A very different emperor, Domitian, would mark the (rough) century after the Augustan celebration of the games in A.D. 88. The games were dedicated to Apollo and Diana (patron deities of the young, not to mention their premature deaths).[10]

There is a place, too, Aeneas promises, for the Sibyl:

te quoque magna manent regnis penetralia nostris. (6.71)

For you also there waits a great shrine in our kingdom.

Augustus had moved the so-called Sibylline Books to his new temple on the Palatine in 12 B.C. Allegedly, the books dated back to the last days of the Roman monarchy, under Tarquin the Proud; a fire in Jupiter's temple on the Capitoline destroyed the original collection in 83 B.C. Tarquin is said to have (thoughtfully) purchased the collection of Greek hexameter oracular verses (see above on 3.440 ff.). Apparently the Sibyl of Cumae offered nine books to Tarquin, who balked at the price. She burned three and offered six at the same price, and then again three: Tarquin finally relented and paid full price for the last three. The new collection of the Augustan Age apparently lasted until the Christian general Flavius Stilicho destroyed it in the early fifth century A.D. The Sibylline Books are the origin of practice of the *Sortes Vergilianae*, a form of bibliomancy by which the future is predicted by opening pages of the *Aeneid* at random and reading the first verse one sees (Hadrian is said to have opened the *Aeneid* to discover what Trajan thought of him).[11] There were lifetime custodians of the Roman Sibylline Books (complete with expert Greek interpreters) who are also foretold here by Aeneas (6.73-74). Aeneas remembers Helenus' advice about *how* the Sibyl is to be consulted; he appeals to her to forego the usual method of writing her messages on leaves, and to speak her prophecy *viva voce* (74-76; cf. 3.443-457).

In this entire speech of Aeneas to the Sibyl, we catch one of the first images in the poem of a very different Aeneas. He is more assured, more mindful of the prophecies he has already received, more determined to pursue his Roman future. He is more self-possessed and authoritative than before; the closest he has come to this degree of calm leadership was when he first appeared out of the mist to Dido and her court. It seems as if he has been strengthened and fortified by the nearness of his future home and the solemn surroundings of this holy place.

Like Dido, the Sibyl rages as if she were a Bacchant (6.78 *bacchatur vates*); she resists the awesome power of Apollo as he fights to overcome her. Physically, she has grown in size to accommodate the god (49 *maiorque videri*, 77 *immanis in antro*). The Sibyl in the cave is a symbol of Apollo in the Sibyl. Finally Deiphobe begins her oracular responses. The first revelation is that the dangers Aeneas will face on land are more serious than everything else he has hitherto experienced. The second, related announcement is that the Trojans will have wished they had not come to Italy. The third—Aeneas already knows this, but here it is expanded at greater length—is that there will be terrible wars in Italy, a replica of the war at Troy. Helenus and Andromache have a false Troy to console them; Aeneas and his men will have to relive, as it were, the worst years of their lives. Achilles is waiting for them, too:

... alius Latio iam partus Achilles (6.89)

... *another Achilles has already been born in Latium*

Book 6 is the transition, then, from the Odyssean world to the Iliadic. Here we learn explicitly that Aeneas, who has followed the same heroic path as Odysseus in his wanderings over the Mediterranean, will *not* be Achilles in the second half of the poem. To be sure, he will sometimes evoke the great Greek hero, and an important task for those who study the second half of the *Aeneid* closely is attentive awareness of the shifting images of the two Iliadic heroes, Achilles and Hector, as they reappear in Trojan and Rutulian guise during the war in Italy. But here, on the very cusp of Virgil's *Iliad*, it is firmly Turnus who is prophesied to be the new Achilles. Juno, too, will never be absent during the war (a darker message than Helenus' pious advice to make repeated attempts to supplicate her). The Trojans will once again be in the position of Paris with Helen (though the situations are quite different); Aeneas will be the foreign husband for Lavinia, cast in the role of his countryman Paris. Turnus will not be exactly equivalent to Menelaus (he and Lavinia were never married). But the two events are similar enough to make it seem that history is repeating itself. The Sibyl ends with hopeful words, and new information:

tu ne cede malis, sed contra audentior ito

quam tua te Fortuna sinet. via prima salutis,
quod minime reris, Graia pandetur ab urbe. (6.95-97; Mynors 96 *quam* for *qua*)

*You, do not yield to adversity, but go against it more bravely
than your Fortune permits. The first path to safety,
though you would hardly believe it at all, will be opened from a Greek city.*

The first line is easy enough: Aeneas is not to yield to adversity, but to advance on more daringly . . . the future imperative *ito*, as usual, lends grave solemnity. The specific piece of new detail is that Aeneas will first find hope in Italy from a *Greek* city (a reference to the help he help he will receive in Book 8 from Evander in Pallanteum). In the second line, the relative *quam* (or *qua*) has caused difficulty. *Quam* has healthy manuscript support, Servius, and Seneca (which should settle the matter); the line would then read, "Go forward more daringly than your Fortune will allow." With *qua* (the reading of a second hand in the ninth century Bern codex, which Hirtzel prints), we must translate: "Go forward more daringly, where your Fortune will allow." The whole passage is mysterious, as we should expect from a Sibyl; she seems to be alluding in her riddling words to the whole thrust of Fortune in Aeneas' life, which has been grim and fraught with difficulties.

The Sibyl is finished; she has elaborated on the basic story Aeneas already knew. The principal new information is about the Greek city waiting to help him in Italy, and the announcement of the second Achilles: for Aeneas, this news underscores (albeit very strongly) what he already expected from the predicted war in Italy. For us, as we watch Aeneas move from *Odyssey* to *Iliad*, it complicates and confuses the heroic paradigm. The revelation is significant for the audience, but less so for Aeneas. Indeed, his first words to the Sibyl almost have the tone of a complaint; he has been cheated, in a sense, by the fortuneteller, since he already knew the outline of what she revealed. The Aeneas of earlier times, who seemingly forgot or ignored his prophecies, has changed dramatically. But now he seems unmoved by the threat of Achilles. Instead, his mind is fixated on the message he received from his father Anchises in a dream: he is to visit the Elysian Fields, and learn directly from his dead sire about his future. The Sibyl is a conduit; her information is received with barely a nod by Aeneas, who is (understandably) full of ardent longing to go to his father Anchises.

Aeneas remarks on the nearby presence of the *Palus Acherusia* (6.107 *tenebrosa palus Acheronte refuso*), the "Acherusian marsh," a lake north of Naples (the modern Fusaro), some distance south of Cumae's acropolis. Today the marsh is teeming with life (it is a center of oyster and mussel harvesting); Virgil, in his usual geographical manner, has conflated Acheron and Avernus. Aeneas uses standard mythological *exempla* to justify his desire to visit the underworld: Theseus and Hercules did it, as did Pollux and Orpheus. The first two heroes are mentioned briefly and in passing (6.122-123); Virgil has Aeneas elaborate a bit more on Pollux, who sacrificed half his life for his brother Castor, and Orpheus, who was allowed to try to rescue Eurydice. The mention of Orpheus here will be echoed when Aeneas finally reaches Elysium (6.645-648); Orpheus' failure with the dead Eurydice was in our minds when Aeneas failed to save Creusa from the burning ruins of Troy.

Facilis descensus Averno (6.126): "easy is the descent to Avernus." The Sibyl's words summarize the problem: Aeneas needs no help to go down to the underworld; after all, death comes easily enough to everyone, and the gates of Dis are open night and day to accommodate the constant flow of souls. The problem is the ascent: the Sibyl, in a sense, is speaking of returning to life after death. The ascent of souls, as we shall learn, is exactly what Anchises announces at the climax of this book. First, the Sibyl advises, there are forests everywhere around the middle of the underworld, and even if one were to get through the woods, then there is the River Cocytus, from the Greek for "lamentation," described most famously for us by Dante as the icy home of Satan, Judas, and Brutus and Cassius at the end of the *Inferno*. Still, the Sibyl knows a way.

The wonder and fantasy surrounding the Golden Bough will endure as long as anyone opens the pages of Virgil. No definitive solution for the problems it poses can ever be offered. The *Aeneid* is not a puzzle waiting to be solved by some master of riddles. This is not to say that the poem should not be closely studied and explicated: Virgil says what he says, and in the way he says it, to convey the message he wanted to offer about Rome and its future. He took his mission seriously, and we must repay the deserving poet with serious study. The Golden Bough and the Gates of Sleep frame Virgil's underworld. We are no better off today in examining the mystery of the Bough than our ancient forebears. No record of such a Bough exists in extant literature before Virgil. Servius had no certain idea what it may have meant for the poet or where Virgil may have found it, if anywhere. Modern scholars grope through their own dark wood in trying to explicate it, and labor under all the burdens imposed on them by Frazer's anthropology, Norse mythology, and Harvard school symbolism.

The Sibyl had mentioned that the underworld was ringed by trees; this detail leads to her announcement that somewhere there is a shady tree (6.136 *arbore opaca*), hidden away in a grove (139 *lucus*, and cf. 154 *lucos Stygis*), which itself is hidden in a dim valley (139 *obscuris . . . convallibus*). The tree conceals (136 *latet*) a bough, golden and with pliant stem, which is sacred to the infernal Juno, that is, to Proserpina. Many have sought to connect this grove with Diana's at Aricia (see above on 3.679-681); Virgil has already told us that there are groves dedicated to Trivia here at Cumae (6.13 *Triviae lucos*). Diana can readily be associated with Proserpina in her infernal aspect; here Virgil prefers, though, to link Prosperina with Juno, which has more relevance for Aeneas: the Bough will be another step in appeasing the angry goddess (however ineffective those attempts are). The Sibyl asserts that it is not granted (140 *datur*) to go below the earth, until the Bough has been offered to Prosperina; once the Bough is torn off, we learn that another one springs up in its place, so that it has a certain immortal quality. Here the Sibyl is close to self-contradiction; she had said that it was easy to get to the underworld, and indeed we can safely assume that Hercules, Theseus, Orpheus, Pollux (not to mention Aeneas' immediate predecessor, Odysseus) most probably never used a Golden Bough to get to Hades. She soon clarifies what she apparently meant. Once Aeneas has found the Bough, he is to "pluck" it (6.146 *carpe*). If he is called by the fates to visit the underworld, then it will yield to him (147 *si te fata vocant*). If he is not so called (*aliter*), then no strength, not even a sword's blow, will be able to pull off the Bough. Virgil's Bough, then, is not a *sine qua non* for an underworld visit; it is an offering made to the queen of hell by someone who is coming by divine destiny and personal fate. This is a visit to Anchises that is approved by the highest authorities; the Bough is the peaceable symbol of that divine approbation.[12]

There is, also, another problem. The Sibyl announces that there is an unburied member of Aeneas' fleet. We (and Aeneas) might assume immediately that this is Palinurus, though the Sibyl says that Aeneas does not, alas, know about the death she is announcing (150 *nescis*, a word Heyne and Conington missed). As Aeneas and Achates leave the presence of the Sibyl, surely the problems they discuss (160) include how Palinurus cannot be buried, and how they know of no other unaccounted for casualties. In no time they find the body of Misenus, who, together with the also ill-fated Palinurus, had been introduced to us in Book 3 (239 ff.). Misenus was part of the tradition before Virgil; like Palinurus, he gave his name to a cape (the modern Punta di Miseno), which was a major naval base for the Romans (Agrippa established one here in 27 B.C., a few years after Actium).[13] This was the scene for the famous episode during the eruption of Vesuvius where Pliny the Elder died. Palinurus had been a helmsman; Misenus summoned men to battle by clarion call. He had been one of Hector's men; Virgil notes that he was now following no less a man in Aeneas (cf. Hector's dream words to Aeneas, 2.291-292). Virgil lets us know what happened, though Aeneas and Achates will remain unaware (a parallel to the death of Palinurus). The jealous sea god Triton had drowned Misenus when he heard him play (presumably exceedingly well?) on a seashell (ironic that a marine god should kill the man who would one day give his name to a naval base). At once, the solemn funeral rites for the dead man are carried out by *pius* (6.176) Aeneas. The felling of trees for the funeral (inspired by both Homer and Ennius) will be echoed in the funerals for the Trojan and Latin dead in Book 11 (135-138).[14] Here the religious ritual is meant to pay honor to a friend and to appease his wandering soul, so that the underworld can be entered without any sort of impurity (cf. 6.150 *incestat*); in Book 11, there will be more than one corpse.

Trees and forests have been a recurring theme so far in Book 6; they provide the sort of dense, shady, ominously dark setting that Virgil wants for his underworld. Aeneas has merely to ask a question, and at once an answer is given; he wonders how he could ever find the Golden Bough in such an immense wood, and he receives a sign: two doves, birds of his mother Venus, suddenly appear to serve as his guides. The doves are leisurely and casual, like their mistress; they feed (6.199 *pascentes*) as they lead the way. The doves direct Aeneas to the "jaws of Avernus" (201 *fauces . . . Averni*); in all of these preparatory scenes for the descent, Aeneas would in actuality be traveling over difficult terrain relatively quickly: the hero can do this, especially in poetry. Sulfur exhalations (201 *grave olentis*) here were thought to be fatal to birds and to offer an etymological explanation for the Greek name of the lake, that is, "Birdless." It is here, on some tree near the lake, that the doves locate the Golden Bough for Aeneas:

> discolor unde auri per ramos aura refulsit.
> quale solet silvis brumali frigore viscum
> fronde virere nova, quod non sua seminat arbos,
> et croceo fetu teretis circumdare truncos,
> talis erat species auri frondentis opaca
> ilice, sic leni crepitabat brattea vento.
> corripit Aeneas extemplo avidusque refringit
> cunctantem, et vatis portat sub tecta Sibyllae. (6.204-211)
>
> *whence the two-colored breeze of gold shone forth through the branches.*
> *As the mistletoe, which its own tree does not sow, is accustomed to grow*
> *green with new leafage in the forest during the chill of winter,*
> *and to surround the smooth trunks with yellow fruit,*
> *so was the image of the leafy gold on the dark*
> *ilex tree, and so the foil was rustling in the gentle wind.*
> *Aeneas at once snatched it and, greedy, grabbed it*
> *as it delayed, and he carried it to the dwelling of the prophetic Sibyl.*

Few lines in Virgil have occasioned so much comment as the description of the bough and its accompanying simile.[15] We had been told the "bough" was a branch of some sort (*ramus*); now the golden breeze (the magnificent, enigmatic phrase *auri . . . aura*) shines through the "branches" (*ramos*). The doves had been said to alight on a "twin tree" (203 *gemina super arbore*); Virgil at once explains this: the Golden Bough stands out among the other boughs because it is *discolor*, that is, gold and not green. The Bough's appearance is compared to mistletoe in winter; mistletoe is a parasitic plant (hence the detail *non sua seminat arbos*). The noise that the Bough makes, a sort of "tinkling" (*crepitabat*) in the wind, comes from its gold leaf foil; Lucretius speaks of the same sort of thing (*De Rerum Natura* 4.726, one of the many nods Virgil makes in his anti-Epicurean *Nekuia* to his poetic master).[16]

Aeneas is understandably excited by the appearance of the mysterious Bough, and he eagerly (*avidus*) plucks it, as he had been told—or does he? The verb *refringere* will not permit such a translation (which has ruined this passage in many a version). Aeneas had been told to "pluck" the Bough (146 *carpe*), and now we see why: it is a mere wisp (*aura*) on the tree, incredibly fragile in appearance, delicate and precious. The Bough hesitates. Of this there can be no doubt (*pace* Austin and others); *cunctantem* is too prominent a word to ignore, or to assign a trivial meaning. The Bough hesitates because Aeneas did not follow directions, which in magical rituals are exceedingly important. Aeneas' fate is to visit his father in the underworld, and the Bough is no position to reject the child of destiny. But it can raise a protest over Aeneas' rough and forceful treatment, the implications of which Virgil deliberately leaves to the individual reader to ponder. Is there a connection between the greedy Aeneas' haste in grabbing the Bough and the change that has come over him in this book? *Re-*

fringere is not as common a verb as *carpere*; significantly, this is its only occurrence in the *Aeneid*; in Catullus (*carmen* 63.86 *refringit*) it describes the trampling of one of Cybele's lions—an appropriate image for Virgil to borrow in a description of *Trojan* Aeneas' greedy grabbing of the Bough.[17]

The discovery of the Bough comes in the midst of the obsequies for Misenus. They were the two prerequisites for a successful journey to the underworld, and Virgil rightly links them closely. The care that Virgil lavishes over the funeral is made all the more poignant by his comment at the outset that the ashes of Misenus are ungrateful (6.213 *ingrato*); the dead can offer no thanks. It is a strikingly grim remark, one that could not have been made lightly or without careful reflection (and Lucretius would approve of the sentiment). The Trojans raise the pyre; cypress is (fittingly) present yet again (216). The funeral service itself is eminently Roman, not Trojan; the abundant detail makes this a *locus classicus* for a Roman requiem. Corynaeus (otherwise unknown) performs the last duties after the cremation: he gathers the bones in a bronze urn and purifies the assembly by sprinkling them three times with an olive branch—a lustration ceremony that has survived into Christian liturgy. The richly somber details are pervaded with the sense of futility that *ingrato* casts over the entire passage.

Virgil generously lavished attention over the funeral, but an atmosphere of haste returns at once: Aeneas, he says, speedily (6.236 *propere*) attended to the orders of the Sibyl. He has been entirely fixated on visiting Anchises; everything else has been prelude to the forthcoming descent. The hero's zeal, even impatience, conflicts with the poet's deliberately discursive style: Virgil's pace here is slow, his mood pensive. The description of the cave within the crater of the volcanic lake begins. The heifers are produced for the infernal sacrifice: four, appropriately black in color, over whose foreheads the Sibyl pours a libation of wine. The Sibyl plucks the topmost hairs from between their horns and throws them on the sacrificial fires in honor of Hecate. Aeneas himself offers a black lamb to Night, the mother of the Furies, and her "great sister," identified by Servius as Tellus, the Earth. For Proserpina he offers a sterile heifer (in mythology the union of Proserpina and Pluto is usually childless). Finally, for Pluto himself, the entrails of bulls are offered on burning altars. All of this takes place at night, as we might expect; at dawn Aeneas is ready to begin the descent, now that all the ritual prescriptions are complete. Hecate makes her appearance, complete with earthquake-like phenomena and what seem to be the howls of the hounds of hell (a traditional accoutrement of the goddess, a sort of perverse version of hunting hounds for Diana). A very confident Aeneas moves after the Sibyl into the underworld with fearless step (6.263 *haud timidis . . . passibus*). She orders him to draw his sword, which is good drama for the moment, though worthless in practice (cf. 290-294 below).

Virgil now invokes both the gods of the underworld and the very shades of the dead themselves. This invocation is the second in the poem, after the proem that invoked the Muse to tell the causes of Juno's unremitting anger. It announces, if we could ever doubt it, the beginning of the most important section of the poem thus far, the climax of the first half of the epic, the slow and steady march to Anchises and the Roman future. The house of Dis is empty, as is his kingdom (6.269), a remarkable phrase, given the traditionally crowded underworld teeming with souls: Virgil highlights their emptiness and how they are devoid of life. The simile that describes the early path of the two travelers is among the most perfect in Virgil:

> quale per incertam lunam sub luce maligna
> est iter in silvis, ubi caelum condidit umbra
> Iuppiter, et rebus nox abstulit atra colorem. (6.270-272)

Just as through an uncertain moon under a malignant light
there is a path through the forest, when Jupiter hides the
sky with a shadow, and the black night stole the color from things.

The moonlight reminds us that we are in the realm of the infernal Diana; her light is "malignant," not exactly "evil" as much as unhelpful and close to useless—though it is sinister in its connotations. This simile occurs right at the very vestibule of hell. Virgil repeatedly speaks of the "jaws" of his underworld geography (cf. 6.273 *faucibus Orci* with 201 *fauces . . . Averni* and 240-241 *atris/faucibus*): Hades swallows its visitors. The guests who lodge semipermanently at the very maw of Orcus (the Roman Thanatos, a vague personification of Death; cf. our "Grim Reaper")[18] are "characters" we have met already and shall meet again in the pages of the *Aeneid*: Fear, Old Age, Hunger, and especially War, Labor, Discord and Death. There is an elm tree, in whose branches lurk False Dreams (283-284 *Somnia / vana*); they prefigure the similar *falsa insomnia* that use the Ivory Gate at the end of the book (896). Significantly, near the elm tree, at the doors of hell, we find the monsters of mythology: the Centaurs and the Scyllas (a perverse reminiscence of two of the ships in the boat race that seems so far removed now both in time and space), the giant Briareus and a monster of Lerna (perhaps a lesser relative of the fifty-headed Hydra that helps guard Tartarus later at 6.576-577), the Chimaera (another ship from Anchises' games), the Gorgons, the Harpies, and Geryon with his three bodies. The Sibyl had warned Aeneas to draw his sword as he entered the underworld; we are somewhat perplexed now when she tells him it is pointless to try to attack these "monsters," which are but phantoms. Aeneas is afraid of them at first sight (6.290 *subita trepidus . . . formidine*), not surprisingly. But why had the Sibyl wanted his sword to be drawn in the first place? The Centaurs and Scyllas are here out of homage to Lucretius, who would have approved of Virgil's locating them so near the False Dreams (cf. *De Rerum Natura* 4.732 ff.). Near these beasts of mythology is the road that leads to Acheron, Acheron that belches its sands into Cocytus (Virgil's underworld river geography cannot be pressed too far).

Just as Homer had Odysseus first meet Elpenor, who died alone and was unburied, so Aeneas' first significant encounter will be with the helmsman Palinurus. Misenus was a doublet for him; the two men had been introduced together in Book 3, and Virgil has made Misenus' solemn funeral a necessary prelude to this journey—thereby increasing the pathos of Palinurus' plight. The extended description of Charon, in Virgil a god (6.304), leads seamlessly to the pitiful souls who crowd round for a ride on his boat.

> quam multa in silvis autumni frigore primo
> lapsa cadunt folia, aut ad terram gurgite ab alto
> quam multae glomerantur aves, ubi frigidus annus
> trans pontum fugat et terris immitit apricis. (6.309-312)[19]

> *As many as the leaves that fall in the forests at the first cold of autumn,*
> *or as many as the birds that throng the land from the deep sea,*
> *when the frigid year drives them across the waters*
> *and sends them to sunny lands.*

Winter imagery surrounded the mistletoe-like Golden Bough; now winter joins late autumn (autumn in its first chill) as an evocation of death. The simile is related to *Georgics* 4.471-480, where Virgil compared the souls who were crowding round to hear Orpheus' magical song to a large number of birds hiding in the leaves after the Evening Star or some winter rain has driven them from the mountains. Birds belong in the sky; even though here the souls are compared to birds that are driven to sunny lands, the point is how the "frigid year" (winter as symbol of death) has driven them south. The image of the leaves is borrowed from the Sibyl's use of leaves to record her prophecies; the wind blows and they are gone. There are so many dead, and in the great mass of souls they seem to lose their separate identity (except, of course, when a great hero arrives and is able to pick out certain dead whom he knows). Just as the birds desire the sunny lands of the south, so the newly dead desire to cross the dark river; there is a certain perversity in this love of theirs. Unburied souls are barred from seeking passage on Charon's ship. I am not as convinced as Austin that the "sunny lands" of the birds the souls are seeking hints at Elysium; the point, more darkly, seems to be that the souls are filled with an incredible longing just to cross the river—no matter that existence waits for them on the other bank.

Aeneas asks the Sibyl to explain what he sees; she answers that he is gazing on Cocytus and the "Stygian marsh" (6.323 *Stygiamque paludem*)—more looseness with rivers. The Sibyl knows that the unburied dead must wander aimlessly for a century (the length of a new age, the extreme limit of a man's life). Aeneas does not understand the logic of this system (and neither do we); he is full of pity for the fate of the unburied dead. Finally, after more than five books, we see Orontes (and Leucaspis, "White Shield," who is otherwise unknown).[20] They are mere prelude to Palinurus.

This passage has been marred by comment on its discrepancies with the account of Palinurus from the end of Book 5. The first problem comes quickly: Palinurus is said to have been lost on the "Libyan course" (6.338 *Libyco nuper cursu*), which should naturally refer to the trip from North Africa to Sicily, not the journey from Sicily to Cumae. Either two passages composed out of order (in Virgil's usual style) were fitted together roughly and without final revision, or Virgil wants to highlight the greater importance of the departure from Carthage, not the less significant stopover in Sicily; when Anchises meets his son later in this book (6.692-694), he mentions only the dangers from the "Libyan kingdom," and makes no mention of the sojourn in Sicily. Virgil also says that Palinurus had "fallen" from the ship (6.339 *exciderat*), which is technically accurate (and matches what *Aeneas* thought, at least), though somewhat odd after the narrative of Sleep's tossing him (and the ship's rudder) overboard. Aeneas at once asks Palinurus to tell him which of the gods snatched him away from us (this is a clear allusion to the reality Aeneas still does not know); Apollo, after all, a god who had never before been found false, had apparently told Aeneas that Palinurus would safely arrive in Italy. This specific promise, as the commentators have duly noted, occurs nowhere in the *Aeneid*; Aeneas may well mean that Apollo never predicted Palinurus' death (then again, no one ever predicted the deaths of Creusa, Anchises, or Dido, either). In any case, technically Palinurus *did* reach Italy (he even says later that he reached it "safely"—6.358 *tuta*—since upon arrival he did not expect to be killed by the natives as the first casualty of the war in Italy).

Palinurus' answer, though, has occasioned the most controversy. He flatly denies that the god submerged him in the deep (6.348 *nec me deus in aequore mersit*), where the "god" must be Apollo. But Aeneas had asked "which of the gods" snatched you from us, and Palinurus does not mention Sleep; this is because he has no idea what Sleep did. Sleep appeared in the form of Phorbas; Palinurus' eyes had been fixed on the stars when the god sprinkled him with the Lethaean and Stygian waters and put him to sleep. Aeneas' helmsman is as unaware of what really happened as his master—but he *knows* Apollo was not to blame. Palinurus is aware that he took the rudder with him, both because he knows how tenaciously he was clinging to it and because he survived the fall (news now both to us and Aeneas). He survived three days of stormy nights (the helmsman became a living boat, still controlling his rudder); on the fourth day he was washed up on the coast of Italy. Some unknown race, cruel and "ignorant" (361 *ignara*), killed him with a sword and threw him back in the water; the winds have now washed his dead body up on a beach in Sicily, which make Aeneas' words at the very end of Book 5 come terribly true—though there Aeneas lamented that he did not know where the body was, and here, now, Palinurus reveals the spot. We are left with many unanswered questions, especially about the identity of Palinurus' killers (there is a faint echo of the violent reception of Aeneas' men in North Africa). But there are no serious contradictions between this passage and Virgil's account in Book 5; *Libyco cursu* comes closest to causing worry. I suspect Virgil was playing with the perspectives of the various characters, trying to highlight what they individually knew and did not know; in such a *Rashomon* game, discrepancies can seem to pile upon discrepancies. Palinurus' loss, in line with Virgil's delight in name games, presages the loss of *Pallas*, the one young son of the Arcadian Evander we are soon to meet in Book 8, when Aeneas seeks help and allies from (ironically) Greeks who live in north central Italy. The death of the helmsman was a hard blow to Aeneas, though ultimately insignificant (especially since helmsmen are not needed once sea journeys are at an end); Pallas, in contrast, is a symbol of the future hope of Rome.

Just as with Elpenor's fall from Circe's roof, so in the matter of Palinurus' untimely fate, the dead man knows his body's location. Palinurus' body is at Velia in Sicily; he begs Aeneas most powerfully (by Anchises and Iulus) that he be granted burial. This is, in a remote foreshadowing, a prefiguring of both Mezentius and Turnus and their pleas. We do not know if Aeneas buried Mezentius, and we know that he did not spare Turnus' life; here we might assume he would be more than willing to accede to Palinurus' request, but it will be forbidden. Aeneas, in fact, will not be required to make any reply; the Sibyl answers Palinurus with a strong rebuke (6.373-381) The consolation she offers is what the audience already knows, anachronistically; Palinurus *will* be buried, though not by Aeneas and his Trojans, at some unspecified future date. His name will grace the cape where his body washed up on land. This passage rounds off the beginning of Book 5; Palinurus will receive honors at his grave, just as he participated in the memorial rites for Anchises. The news makes Palinurus happy . . . *parumper* (382), only for a moment. Once again, the theme of the meaninglessness of posthumous honors for the dead has returned. Both Misenus and Palinurus now disappear from the verses of the *Aeneid*; in both instances, Virgil has noted that the honors paid to them are without substance (at least from their vantage point); the ashes of Misenus are ungrateful for the lavish funeral, and Palinurus is only soothed for a moment.[21]

Charon returns to the narrative; he has had time to pay close attention to the discussion between Aeneas, the Sibyl, and the rejected Palinurus. He gives us a mythology lesson on his bad memories of Hercules (one of whose final labors was to fetch Cerberus from the underworld) and the friends Theseus and Pirithous, who conceived the crazed notion of abducting Prosperina. Aeneas is armed (6.388 *armatus*); Charon is sure he has come to work some mischief like his heroic predecessors. The Sibyl calms Charon politely, soothing him with praise for Aeneas and assurances about the real nature of their visit: she then reveals the Bough, which silences his complaint. Virgil adds the curious detail (6.409) that Charon had not seen the Bough in a long time; this is literary Virgil at his most amusing, since he knows that there was no previous time.

The conveyance of the heavy (i.e., living) Aeneas and the Sibyl over the Styx, and their arrival at three-throated (6.417 *trifauci*) Cerberus (the "traditional" dog of the underworld, unknown to Homer, but identified by Hesiod—and with fifty heads), are both scenes of the "mythological" sort, part of a conventional enough apparatus of the underworld. Virgil's Cerberus has snakes on its neck, another apparently stock detail; the Sibyl has wisely and thoughtfully brought some drugged snack for the hungry dog (6.421 *fame rabida tria guttura pandens*—he does have three mouths, after all)—a good lesson for Pluto and Prosperina on keeping their watchdog better fed.[22]

We are now on the much-loved side of the Styx, the shore the newly dead (and the long unburied dead) want so desperately to reach. As we might have expected, the reward of their ardor is not great. We are in a sort of limbo, a place that is not Tartarus (where souls we might well call "evil" are punished), and certainly not Elysium, where we find the souls of the blessed. The first souls we meet are the infants who died on the very threshold of life (6.427 *in limine primo*); we see in this passage an influence on the patristic and medieval development of the Christian hypotheses on the fate of unbaptized infants, and even the cult of the martyred Holy Innocents, the infants of Bethlehem who were slain by Herod (and venerated yearly right after Christmas on 28 December, the English "Childermas").[23] Significantly, Virgil will use the same line both to describe the deaths of these infants and the death later of Aeneas' young friend Pallas, where the line adds tremendous sympathy for the reader who remembers his underworld scenes:

abstulit atra dies et funere mersit acerbo. (cf. 6.429 and 11.28)

The black day took them away and submerged them in a bitter death.

Next are the souls of those who were condemned to death unjustly. Minos, a judge of the underworld, presides over these cases; presumably he determines the just or unjust infliction of capital punishment, and decides who can stay here (and who goes to Tartarus?) The "innocent" (*insontes*) suicides follow (6.434-436), and conspicuously absent among them is Dido. When we finally meet the Carthaginian queen, she will be in the company of other suicides, and some of her companions could certainly be called innocent. Virgil's underworld allows for multiple categories to be appropriate for the same soul. Virgil notes that these suicides would now be more than happy to endure poverty and hard labors; Dido clearly does not share their situation. In any case, these souls cannot, it seems, go anywhere else; the Styx surrounds them with nine circles. The immortals may well be to blame for Dido's lusting after Aeneas, but her decision to commit suicide was quite her own.

Aeneas and the Sibyl now approach a related area, it would seem: the *Lugentes Campi* (6.441), the Fields of Mourning. This area is also neither Tartarean nor Elysian. As an introduction to the encounter with Dido, Virgil has Aeneas enter the (presumably eternal) home of those who died because of love. These women are based on Homer's account of Odysseus' meetings with various noteworthy women of mythology after his encounter with his mother (11.225-332). The encounter with Dido is based on Odysseus' attempted conversation with Ajax (542-564). Odysseus meets Tyro, who was deceived into a union with Poseidon (though to no apparent ill effect), Antiope, who slept with Zeus and was thereby mother of the lords of Thebes, Alcmene (Heracles' mother by Zeus), Epicaste, the mother of Oedipus, Chloris, the mother of Nestor, Leda, the mother of Castor and Pollux by Zeus, Iphimedeia, the mother by Poseidon of Otus and Ephialtes (the giants who tried to assault Olympus), Phaedra, Procris, Ariadne (killed by Artemis), Maera, Clymene, Eriphyle, and many others Odysseus has no time to name. So in Homer the "famous women" have mixed histories; only some could be called notorious.

Virgil begins from the end of Homer's list, with Phaedra, Procris, and Eriphyle. In Homer, the judge Minos appears after the appearance of the women and the great heroes (11.568-571); Virgil placed him before the women, the first of whom was Minos' own daughter, Phaedra, famous for her passion for her stepson Hippolytus. Procris was accidentally killed by her husband Cephalus (Ovid's version towards the end of *Metamorphoses* 7 is the most enduring). Eriphyle had been bribed with a necklace by Polyneices to betray her husband when he wanted to leave the expedition of the Seven against Thebes, and in consequence she was killed by her son; in Virgil she still bears her wounds (6.446). Evadne immolated herself on her husband's pyre;[24] Pasiphae has already been mentioned in the context of the doors to Apollo's temple at Cumae. Laodamia had been married, the story goes, only a day before her husband Protesilaus was called to fight at Troy; she committed suicide after the brief consolation of being granted a few extra hours on earth with her dead husband. Finally, before the appearance of Dido, there is Caeneus, once a young man, Virgil says, and now a woman again, having been changed back to "his" original form. *Caenis* (a girl) had been seduced by Poseidon; he granted her request to change her gender and grant her invulnerability. He fought against the Centaurs and ended up crushed under a huge weight of trees.[25]

Caeneus / Caenis offers one of the most sensitive treatments in ancient literature of the horror of rape. The young Caenis was so traumatized by Poseidon's violence that she sought to forsake the gender that had brought her such agony and, what is more, she requested invulnerability. The requests are designed to guarantee that no one will ever hurt Caenis, now Caeneus, again. In the tradition, the invulnerability had its limitations; Caeneus the Lapith could be killed, in a sense, after being buried under a mass of trees. He was not immortal. How could Virgil include him among those who had been "thoroughly eaten away with cruel wasting by harsh love" (6.442 *durus amor crudeli tabe peredit*)? The *durus amor*, in the case of Caeneus, must refer to Poseidon's perversion of love; *durus* and *peredit*, as well as *tabe*, refer to the lasting, permanent nature of each woman's destruction at the hands of "love." Virgil's women are very different (how could he dare to put Eriphyle and Laodamia in such close proximity?). In Virgil's vision (cf. 4.412 *improbe Amor, quid non mortalia pectora cogis?*), each of these women has been excessive and out of control in response to the sudden appearance of *Amor* in their lives. Virgil does not expect widows to fling themselves on pyres (Evadne) or prefer death to a long widowhood (Laodamia). This leads naturally to thoughts of Dido: just as few could fail to understand how she might fall in love so deeply with Aeneas, so Virgil chooses to emphasize the destructive power of *Amor* in her life. *Amor* cut short her promising young life. Caenis was destroyed by the experience of her rape (instigated by Amor's effect on Poseidon, we can assume). The horror Caenis now faces is an eternity in the shadowy female form (the souls have no bodies) that had once spelled her doom. As a Lapith fighting Centaurs (even to his death), Caeneus had sought to escape the memory of sexual violation. Now it is with him forever.

Aeneas is still in love with Dido (6.455 *dulci . . . amore*); significantly, Virgil calls him the "Trojan hero" (451 *Troius heros*): we are thrust back to the happier days in Carthage. Aeneas had left Dido unwillingly; now he meets her again, as part of his education.[26] Dido had been compared to Diana so long ago; now she is like the moon one sees, or thinks one has seen, as it rises amid clouds at the beginning of its monthly cycle (453-454): Virgil has closed the ring on her life. She was no Diana in Book 1, and she is no moon in Book 6. Aeneas at once begins to express an outpouring of emotions; was he the cause of her death? Was the news then true, that she had killed herself with a sword? (It is profitless to wonder how or when he received the definitive news of her suicide) In a restatement of his earlier, striking remark about leaving Italy against his will (4.361), Aeneas "quotes" a line from Catullus:

> invitus, regina, tuo de litore cessi. (6.460; cf. Catullus *carmen* 66.39 invita,
> o regina, tuo de vertice cessi)

> *Unwillingly, O queen, did I depart from your coast.*

In Catullus, a lock of hair laments that it has been snipped from the head of Berenice (Catullus is translating a passage of Callimachus). What does Berenice's lighthearted lock have to do with Dido and this encounter of high drama and emotion? Virgil knew what he was doing (*pace* Williams, and others); he knew his Catullus, and he wanted to recall a mock-heroic verse at this precise moment. It is a judgment on the weight of Aeneas' words. Aeneas has offered nothing new, nothing that could not be predicted; his words would be laughable, were they not so terribly detached from the reality of what has happened. He has no good answer to offer Dido for his abandonment of her, because there is no good answer to give. He did not want to leave her; that much is devastatingly true (from Rome's perspective). He left her under divine order. This is an empty consolation for Carthage's queen. He reverts here, in fact, to the Aeneas we remember so well from Book 4: the orders of the gods have compelled (6.462 *cogunt*) him to visit the underworld (almost as if it were an imposition, and certainly as if he must read his daily roster of duties before mindlessly carrying them out). His statement that he cannot believe she took his departure so badly (463-464 *nec credere quivi / hunc tantum tibi me discessu ferre dolorem*) ranks among the worst misreadings of human nature in world literature. His final appeal (she is already fleeing from him) is that *fate* (466 *fato*) has decreed this encounter to be their last chance to speak. Aeneas' choice of arguments could not have been worse; Virgil's nod to Catullus underscores the point.

Aeneas tried to soften Dido with his words, and he tried to incite tears (conative imperfects 468 *lenibat* and 469 *ciebat*). Virgil builds suspense; we might think he was actually beginning to accomplish something, until the irrefutable confirmation of her rejection of his appeal comes:

illa solo fixos oculos aversa tenebat (6.469)

That one, turned away, held her eyes fixed on the ground.

The line is modeled on the picture in Dido's temple to Juno, where the image of the goddess Pallas ignores the Trojan women and their appeal for help (1.482 *diva solo fixos oculos aversa tenebat*).[27] The picture Aeneas had so delighted in has come to terrible life. Anyone who thinks Dido still loves Aeneas has ignored 472 *inimica*: she is now his personal enemy, just as her city is now irrevocably opposed to his future settlement. Sychaeus is waiting for her: he will equal her love and will respond to her cares. He is willing to love her in a deeply emotional, even anxious way. His relationship with her had also brought sorrow (hence she had lamented that she had not been able to live like a wild animal, without the trials of human love; cf. 4.550-551). But he understands her in a way Aeneas never could. Aeneas had tried to elicit tears; now it is he who is crying and pursuing her (6.476 *prosequitur lacrimis*). He pities her as she goes away (*miseratur euntem*), while we pity him.

Virgil's circle of the dead heroes of war lacks something of Homer's nobility. There will be no Agamemnon or Achilles here (and the encounter with Ajax has been transferred to Dido). After a nod to the mythological past (some of the Seven against Thebes), Virgil names a few Trojans of minor significance—his difficulty in this scene is how to show the losing side in as solemn a fashion as Homer could show the winners. In Homer, the encounter with Achilles in particular is a chance for the poet to reflect on the choice his great Iliadic hero had made: is it worth it, in a word, to sacrifice a long and happy life for the eternal glory that follows on a young, premature death in war (cf. *Odyssey* 11.489-491)? Achilles' statement that he would rather be some hireling toiling on earth than lord of the dead is not so much a rejection of the heroic ideal as a sad commentary on the purposelessness and meaningless of the underworld realm. The Greeks, in any case, who now appear in Virgil's underworld (6.489-493), are even more shadowy and insubstantial than the roughly sketched Trojans, and they flee the sight of the corporeal Trojan hero: a small victory, one might ruefully note, of the defeated Trojan over the Greeks who once (and not so long ago) so devastated his beloved homeland.

Homer's Agamemnon could relate his shameful death at the hands of his wife and her lover; Virgil has Aeneas meet Helen's last, ill-fated husband, Priam's son Deiphobus, who was horribly mutilated on the night Troy fell.[28] As Dido's ghost drew the events of Book 4 to a close, so Deiphobus ends the narrative thread started in Book 2. We learn that Aeneas had set up a burial mound on the Trojan coast for Deiphobus (an "empty" honor—6.505 *inanem*). Deiphobus was with his wife, Helen, when the Wooden Horse entered the city; she was like a Bacchant (6.517-518) as she cheered its arrival, leading the Phrygian women in a revel. Deiphobus adds that she also held a huge flame (apparently one of the fire signals to the Greeks), and called out to the Danaans from her lofty citadel.

Some (from Servius onward) have considered Deiphobus' account here of his wife's actions to be inconsistent with the controversial "Helen-episode" in Book 2 (though one might suspect that a forger/interpolator would be familiar with the only other passage in the poem that could be compared to his invention). The account here, though, causes no serious problems with the previous material; in all the slaughter and fast-paced horror that ensued after the horse discharged its lethal cargo, Helen had become rightly concerned that she might be killed by either Greeks *or* Trojans in fury over her central role in the war. Deiphobus says that Helen betrayed him to try to curry favor with Menelaus (6.525-526); she called out to her Spartan husband and opened the doors of Deiphobus' house (after prudently removing his weapons). Did she then quickly flee the scene? Surely Deiphobus lived close to Priam, and that is where we found Helen in Book 2, crouching behind an altar.

We now learn, in an elaborate periphrasis, that it is about midday; the underworld journey has now stretched from the previous night about halfway through the next day. Aeneas is in no hurry to leave Deiphobus; the Sibyl tersely presses him to go on and, in effect, stop crying over the past (6.539 *nos flendo ducimus horas*). In Aeneas' underworld education, he has been forced to relive the worst events of the first half of the poem: Books 4 and 2, tracing his life backwards in time. Aeneas is now approaching the crossroads that lead to Tartarus and Elysium. Tartarus was lower than Hades proper (cf. 6.577-579, where Virgil quotes the tradition that it extended twice as far down as Olympus rose above the earth's surface); it was the place of punishment for the worst sorts of criminals. Virgil identifies the flaming river Phlegethon as the encircling border of the triple-walled fortress of Tartarus; its inhabitants will never escape. The Fury Tisiphone, with her bloody cloak, stands guard without sleep before it (the scrupulous note that the Furies were allegedly at the very entrance to the underworld—6.280). Aeneas is rightly terrified (6.559 *exterritus*) as he hears the groans of torture emanating from the castle. The Sibyl gives him a summary of what she learned long before from Hecate herself. Rhadamanthus is here, a sort of companion to his brother Minos' judgment over the untimely dead. The Titans are here, right where Zeus hurled them after the Titanomachy that led to his ascendance (so Hesiod and Homer agree). But with the mention of the Titans we should perhaps think not only of archaic epic but also of the mysterious literature traditionally ascribed to Orpheus.[29]

There is ample evidence in classical Greek literature that Orphic lore was both well known and voluminous. Essentially the works attributed to Orpheus fall into three categories: cosmogonic poems (i.e., theogonies), actual cult hymns (centering on Dionysus), and two miscellaneous (and very late) poems, one on the Argonauts and the other on the magic properties of stones. Of these, only the last two categories survive intact; for the first we are largely dependent on the fragments preserved by Neoplatonic philosophers of late antiquity. In the Orphic cosmogony, Zeus and Persephone had an illicit, incestuous affair: Dionysus was the offspring. Hera ordered the Titans to kill the child, who was cooked and eaten. Zeus killed the Titans with a thunderbolt; man was born from the Titanian ashes, while Zeus saved Dionysus' heart and used it to create a new Dionysus with Semele (his traditional mortal mother). Hence Dionysus can be expected to have some hearing with Persephone, his mother, on behalf of mortals. It is not certain that Virgil's mention here of the "Titans" (who were a traditional feature of any Tartarean underworld since Hesiod) would evoke thoughts of Orphism; but most probably we are now slowly entering the book's imminent, climactic revelation of the reincarnated fate of some souls.

Homer had mentioned their mother Iphimedeia; Virgil now depicts Otus and Ephialtes, giants like the Titans, who are punished forever for their rebellion against Zeus. Salmoneus is also here, like the giants, an offender against Zeus; he perhaps seems a more pathetic and sorry sight than the fearsome giants, though clearly Virgil liked the story (6.585-594), which he elaborates at unusual length (a warning to would-be Roman gods?) The giant Tityos is here stretched out over nine acres in Tartarus, with a vulture forever gnawing on his immortal liver. Homer had told the reason for the torture (*Odyssey* 11.576-581); Tityos had tried to rape Leto, the mother of Apollo and Diana. Lucretius had mentioned him, only to deny his reality (*De Rerum Natura* 3.984-994); for Lucretius, Tityos is anyone who is assailed by never-ending love. The mention of Tityos leads naturally enough to Ixion (who tried to rape Hera) and Pirithous (who tried to abduct Persephone from the underworld). These two attempted rapists have a crag forever hanging over them, and are denied the pleasure of a rich meal; traditionally these are the punishments of Tantalus (especially the latter), but in Virgil, the metaphor of the illicit love that eats away at a man and can never be fulfilled, while it never lets him rest (like the crag overhead), has proven irresistible. His underworld is no prose handbook of mythology, in any case, and it does the poet no justice to mangle his text to fit the "standard" accounts.

Next come a vast crowd of sinners whose names are mostly not recorded (adding to their misery). Some of them have the punishments traditionally ascribed to Sisyphus (rolling the rock) and Ixion (being stretched on a wheel, fiery or not); among these sinners the only named culprits are Theseus (who with Pirithous had tried to rape Persephone) and Phlegyas, the father of Coronis, who in anger at Apollo's rape of his daughter had tried to burn down the temple to the god at Delphi—the divine rape motif that started with Caenis and Poseidon continues. This is Virgil's great moral condemnation of the sins of humanity; Dante was tremendously inspired by its attempt to do the impossible (cf. 6.625-627) and enumerate all the crimes of men.

The priestess of Phoebus now tells Aeneas to hasten along his way (6.629 *carpe*); she uses the same verb of the road to Elysium as she had used of the plucking of the Golden Bough (146 *carpe manu*). Virgil wants us to remember his significant verb; here is where the Golden Bough will be quietly fixed as an offering to Proserpina. No mere ornamental detail accompanies the arrival at this gate: the Cyclopes had built the entrance to Elysium, we now learn; just as the eerie image of their silhouetted bodies against the night sky had presaged the death of Anchises (3.677-681), so here their presence marks the nearness of Aeneas' reunion with his father. This brief passage also presages the role of the

Cyclopes in their traditional place at Vulcan's forge when the divine shield will be wrought for Aeneas; that shield will have artwork that corresponds to the vision we are soon to enjoy.

Groves have so far been places of sinister and ominous underworld overtones; now all changes as Aeneas and the Sibyl pass into the groves of the fortunate (6.639 *fortunatorum nemorum*), the seats of the blessed (*sedes beatas*), the home of those we might call exceptionally good. The concept of some home for the noble dead (perhaps "retired" is a better word) is Homeric (not to say Egyptian), as we have noted (*Odyssey* 4.561 ff.). Besides Homer, there is certainly a background in Hesiod, Pindar, and Plato too, that lies behind Virgil's conception of the Isles of the Blest. Homer's afterlife is a place of finality and futility; it has no escape, and even if he did admit that the righteous might expect some pleasant, peaceful abode somewhere off in the far west at the ends of the earth, there was never a thought that those souls would ever leave that place of rest and reward. The idea that not only does some part of the human being survive (we may call it the "soul"), but that the surviving part also moves on to another life, in another body, was said to have been introduced by the shadowy sixth century B.C. philosopher Pythagoras. Where he may have borrowed the idea, if anywhere, is unknown; Herodotus thought from Egypt (*Histories* 2.123). In this last third of his death book, Virgil tries to juxtapose the Homeric and the Pythagorean; Pythagoras' theories would make no sense if suddenly thrown into the underworld of the *Odyssey*, but in Virgil they find a fitting home because of the poet's main agenda item: the revelation of the future glory of Rome, for which Pythagorean ideas about the transmigration of souls offered an irresistible conduit.

Virgil's vision of the realm of the blessed opens with a beautiful image:

largior hic campos aether et lumine vestit
purpureo, solemque suum, sua sidera norunt. (6.640-641)

*A more generous upper air clothes the fields here with
purple light, and they know their own sun and their own stars.*

There is no sun, but there is light; the glow is dazzlingly radiant, and the air of heavenly ether. How different the purple of this light will be from the sepulchral flowers of purple that will adorn Marcellus' funeral (6.884, a horrible close to the ring this purple light opens), and from the purple that robed the dead Misenus at his funeral (221). Athletic competitions, along with song and dance, mark this splendid world. Orpheus is here, too, the "Thracian priest" (6.645 *Threicius longa cum veste sacerdos*). For Virgil thus far in his career (especially in the *Georgics*), Orpheus has been the figure from mythology famous for his ill-fated love for Eurydice (an image evoked powerfully at the end of *Aeneid* 2). Because of that underworld *katabasis*, no doubt, Orpheus was considered an expert on the last things (even if he failed to save his wife). For Pythagoreans, Neoplatonists, and even Bacchic mystery cultists (because of the aforementioned lore about Dionysus and his two births), Orpheus was the philosopher-theologian *non pareil*. Orpheus is the first character in Virgil's Elysium. The Trojan progenitors are here, too—men who had been but mere names in past prophecies, Ilus, Assaracus, and Dardanus. Weapons and horses are still with their warrior owners, but the chariots are "empty" (6.651 *inanis*), a word that introduces a slight but very real note of gloom into this place of tranquil calm: they are still dead, their chariots useless. Virgil locates the Elysian Fields under the River Po (the ancient *Padus*); the Po was the generally accepted identification for the mythical *Eridanus* (659). Virgil reminds us that this is a grove, and a sweet-smelling one of laurel (Apollo's emblem) at that; the ghosts sing the *paean*, which was properly associated with Apollo.

After arriving at a section of Elysium where there are the souls of those who suffered wounds on behalf of the country, chaste priests and faithful bards, Aeneas and the Sibyl see standing out above them all a companion, as it were, for Orpheus: the mythical singer Musaeus.[30] Like Orpheus, Musaeus was connected with a body of eschatological writings; he was also linked closely to the rites of Demeter and her kidnapped daughter at Eleusis. The Sibyl asks where Anchises is; Musaeus tells her that there is no certain home here for anyone, but that if she and Aeneas really have the intention of seeing Anchises, he will escort them over a nearby ridge, where they will descend into a valley and find him. In the next lines, as Anchises is dramatically introduced (the lines enact the experience of seeing him as one crosses over a height and then descends), the entire content of the next section of the poem is neatly summarized:

At pater Anchises penitus convalle virenti
inclusas animas superumque ad lumen ituras
lustrabat studio recolens, omnemque suorum
forte recensebat numerum, carosque nepotes
fataque fortunasque virum moresque manusque. (6.679-683)

But father Anchises was gazing over the souls that were
enclosed in the green valley, souls about to go to the light above,
and he was thinking about them with zeal, and, by chance, he
was reckoning the whole number of his own descendants, and his
    dear grandchildren,
and the fates and fortunes of men, and their customs and ways.

The audience can already guess that they will soon be treated to a vision that for them is the historical past and present. Up to this point, the narrative has not differed much from an underworld Homer would have recognized; he knew about a peaceful home for the honored dead, besides the terrors of Tartarus. But now (especially the more aware the audience was of Pythagorean mysticism, as well as Orphism and Platonism) Virgil's readers have been introduced in summary to the emergence of a world Homer would not have recognized. Anchises sees his son approaching, and utters what are among the most moving lines in the poem:

"venisti tandem, tuaque exspectata parenti
vicit iter durum pietas? datur ora tueri,
nate, tua et notas audire et reddere voces?" (6.687-689)

"Have you indeed come at last, and has your piety,
awaited by your parent, conquered the difficult road?
Is it granted me to look at your face, son, and to hear and reply to a voice
   that I knowso well?"

Anchises has been expecting his son; he had been exceptionally worried during the time Aeneas was with Dido. Aeneas wants to embrace his father, just as he had wanted to embrace the ghost of his lost wife at the end of Book 2; in the same lines Virgil had used there, the son is here denied the embrace of his father, despite the lengthy conversation that will follow. Virgil has once again highlighted the more depressing aspects of continued existence after the grave. Anchises cries as he sees his son, and Aeneas is moved to tears himself.[31] Virgil has crafted one of the most moving scenes in the poem; father and son are reunited in the peaceful calm of the meadows of blessed souls; there is sorrow, to be sure, since the one man is dead and the other facing the realities of imminent war (and since the setting, however tranquil, is the underworld); Virgil is about to unfold the future of the soon to be settlement of Rome, a feat of prognostication that requires a very different underworld from Homer's.

Another grove (6.704 *seclusum nemus*) will be the stage for the explanation of what has been announced to us already in brief summary. The first detail comes in the river geography, which to this point has been characteristically vague; Lethe flows in this peaceful place (705 *Lethaeumque domos placidas qui praenatat amnem*). A simile describes the souls who crowd round here:

ac veluti in pratis ubi apes aestate serena
floribus insidunt variis et candida circum
lilia funduntur, strepit omnis murmure campus. (6.707-709)

And just as when bees in the meadows in the peaceful summer
alight on various flowers, and bright lilies are
poured round, and the whole plain murmurs with their humming.

The most immediate connection for this beautiful image is the earlier simile in the book about the leaves in late autumn (309-310); the season has now changed to the peaceful summer (*aestate serena*); it is neither too hot nor too cold, and the work of pollination heralds new life. From the bleak chill of winter, dominated by grays and whites and the lifeless visage of nature, we have moved to the sun-drenched light of new life. Aeneas does not know what to make of this scene (he had not read his *Phaedo* or *Phaedrus*, let alone Orphic fragments); Anchises casually introduces the idea of reincarnation, along with its first step: the souls must forget their past lives (something Aeneas can never do in Virgil's poem). Anchises announces explicitly that he has long wanted to reveal these souls to his son, since they are to be reborn into Roman bodies and be the future glory of Italy; Anchises wants his son to be able to rejoice (6.718 *laetere*) together with him (a scene that will never occur). Aeneas does not understand how anyone could want to return to a body after death; when this book opened, we saw a newly confident and self-assured Aeneas, who was intensely eager to visit his father. He had no expectation (no prophecy had predicted this) that he would be hearing a discourse on the transmigration of souls.[32] The student's attitude on the first day of lecture is one of astonishment; Aeneas has seen what he thinks is a perfectly fitting home and rest for souls (the meadows of Elysium). Aeneas has no desire to live a life beyond the present one, especially after all the troubles he had endured in Books 1-5. As it turns out, there will be an answer to Aeneas' confusion about the dreadful desire (6.721 *dira cupido*) these souls seem to have for new bodies—though it will not be an answer all find comforting.

Now Virgil begins the most didactic section of his heroic epic; these lines read very much as if they were written by a Lucretius—in style, if not in content. Many commentators and readers of the *Aeneid* have interpreted Anchises' explanation of the fate of the souls as a strange response to Lucretius. The language and format of Anchises' explanation of the strange phenomenon of metempsychosis, they agree, is Lucretian; the philosophy behind it, with its talk of purgatorial purification and rebirth into another body, is intensely opposed to all that Lucretius tried to accomplish in his *De Rerum Natura*. Indeed, some would assert that the revelations of *Aeneid* 6 are positively anti-Lucretian. Such views are readily understandable as Anchises begins to answer his son's question. He introduces the idea that a "breath" (6.726 *spiritus*) sustains the heavens, the earth, the sea, and the sun and moon. This *spiritus*, further, is a "mind" (727 *mens*) that pervades the entire mass of the universe and drives it on (729 *agitat*): the Latin word *mens* most basically means "intention," and the *mens* that drives the universe is purposeful. The universe is conceived of as a body, and the spirit/mind mingles itself with the body in an obviously procreative act (727 *magno se corpore miscet*): from it emerge men, animals, birds, and sea creatures. Finally, Anchises reveals that the *spiritus* or *mens* has the heavenly nature of fire (730 *igneus . . . caelestis origo*). Mortal creatures, however, have bodies, and their bodies—doomed to die—impede the eternally vigorous, celestial fire. Men have fears and longings, joys and sorrows, all on account of how their body blunts (732 *hebetant*) the *spiritus / mens*. Because of this blunting, men are effectively locked in the prison of their bodies.

Virgil has complicated what was already an uneasy syncretism of the traditional underworld (Homeric, Hesiodic) with the concept of transmigratory souls. Now he has introduced another variable: there is a fiery substance, from which all life arises, and it permeates the universe, eternal and everlasting, but it is inhibited by mortal bodies. He has taken this new variable and blended it with the complex lore about metempsychosis that was said to have been introduced to the Greeks by Pythagoras. Orphic beliefs borrowed from the Pythagorean, as did Plato's own elusive views on the nature of the human soul. This new addition to the equation, the fiery *spiritus*, is Stoic; a basic tenet of Stoicism was the idea that fire was the source of everything, and Stoic philosophy was founded on the idea that the *pneuma* (Latin *spiritus*) was the glue, as it were, that held the universe together. The *spiritus* is fiery; the Stoic philosopher Posidonius (who died in 51 B.C.), with his vision of cosmic sympathy, would have been pleased.

Having learned of the prison of the human body, we now find out what fates await some souls after death: purgatorial exercises. The general tone of the discussion of the body has been negative; the body has been called a blind prison and compared to darkness (6.734 *tenebris et carcere caeco*). Indeed, the body introduces "pests" (737 *pestes*) that do not all depart with its death, but remain almost like a cancer (738 *diu concreta . . . inolescere*). A purgatory of some sort must remove these pests over time. In this conception of necessary cleansing, by water or fire, for example, we see a *post mortem* image of the same trials human beings undergo in life, whether by storms at sea or the disaster of invaded, burning cities. Anchises sums up this purgation with a line that has meant many different things to Virgil's audiences over the centuries:

quisque suos patimur manis. (6.743)

Each one of us suffers our own family ghosts.

Austin considers this perhaps the most elusive phrase in Virgil. On the one hand, it makes reasonable enough sense; the purgatory must be individual for each soul: we each suffer our own ghosts, or, put another way, everyone is haunted by their own past. On the other hand, it is just the sort of wisp of a phrase that Virgil so cherished: it reads easily enough, until you think of all the mass of Greek philosophy, let alone daring innovations with Latin vocabulary by the poet, which lurk and yet do not lurk behind it. This phrase about suffering one's family ghosts should be read closely in light of the decision Aeneas makes to slay Turnus in the last lines of the poem (especially given the injunction Anchises is about to give his son about sparing the defeated).

At this point, the soul arrives in Elysium. Some souls—Anchises, Orpheus, and Musaeus among them—remain in Elysium for a further purification. Virgil had said that "empty" chariots (6.651) and other accoutrements of warriors were lying around on the plain; Elysium is not the ultimate, most blessed destination for the soul. In this vision of transmigratory wonder, Elysium is a resting place, albeit the best place for a wayfarer, before the soul is absorbed back into the ethereal fire whence it came. Other souls, though, must be reborn into other bodies and live another mortal life. Aeneas had asked what could possibly motivate anyone to want to live another lifespan; now he receives his answer: it is a part of a process of refinement and self-improvement. These souls spend a millennium in Elysium, after which they drink of Lethe and forget their past lives. Now without memory, they begin to desire bodies again; they want to return to the world in a new form, eager for a new chance at the game of life, hopeful for a life fraught with fewer failures than their past one(s). These are the souls who will now be on display for Anchises to point out to Aeneas. This parade of the

Roman future, together with the granting of the highly decorated shield in Book 8, marks the most complete revelation of Roman destiny that Aeneas receives in the entire poem. Virgil conceived the idea of revealing the future through a strange mixture of Homeric and ultimately Pythagorean underworld eschatology; it presents a thus far hopeful view of a future that, in defiance of the Hesiodic myth of the ages, one might even hope will represent improvement and advancement over the past. It raises a number of questions of logic and contextual coherence. Are we to imagine that the souls in Tartarus, and those who have crossed the Styx and remain forever (presumably) in Virgil's "limbo" with Dido with Deiphobus, have suffered their own *Manes* and are now forever to remain in the underworld, never to return to the ether, either after purification *in situ* or rebirth into new bodies? Indeed, does the individual purification process (*quisque suos patimur Manes*) occur at the moment of death? Reconciling the Homeric and the Pythagorean is no easy task—it is perhaps impossible. But Virgil has his own answers for us.

The glorious vision begins; it is an epiphany for Roman splendor.[33] Silvius is first; he will be born from Aeneas (in his old age) and Lavinia, his Italian wife. The forest of the dark, grim underworld has given way to the "forest" (Latin *silva*) of an early progenitor of Rome. The tradition about Silvius was vexed, and Virgil seems aware of its complications; he had not declared openly in Book 1 that Aeneas would be dead three years after winning his victory in Italy (though he had implied it; cf. 1.263-266), and here he depicts Aeneas as fathering Silvius in his old age (6.764 *longaevo*)—others disagreed about Silvius' paternity. Jupiter had said that Ascanius would rule over Alba Longa for thirty years; he is not mentioned here because neither he nor his father (not to mention Anchises) have *any place* in this procession—the significance of this will not become clear until much later. Silvius has a "pure spear" (760 *pura hasta*), which most take to mean that it has no iron tip and is a symbol of peace. Virgil derives Silvius' name from the woods in which he was born (765 *educet silvis*). Procas and Capys are shadowy names; Numitor was the grandfather of Romulus. Silvius Aeneas deserves special mention for his preservation of his ancestor's name; all of them bear the civic crown of oak leaves (772), the traditional award for someone who had saved a fellow citizen in battle. Various place names indicate where they will ring the future site of Rome with defensive citadels; the places named seem to form a sort of shield around the city.

Romulus is next, whom Jupiter had already mentioned to Venus; Rome is drawing far closer now. *Pace* some of the commentators, line 780 most naturally means that Romulus will one day be deified; the Father himself (Jupiter) is already marking him out as a supernal being (*superum . . . signat*). Rome is now imagined as founded and already extending its empire over the lands, secure on its seven hills; in an extraordinary image that we might expect from the *Trojan* Anchises as he describes her future to his Trojan son, Rome is compared to Cybele, the "Berecynthian mother" (from her sacred mountain in Phrygia). There is an undertone in Anchises' simile and the general attitude of this passage that Cybele's Rome will rectify the loss of so many sons and descendants of Priam in the fall of Troy. With triple deictic announcement, the excited Anchises now announces the man who stands truly as the centerpiece of the whole ecstatic scene: Augustus Caesar.

> ... hic Caesar et omnis Iuli
> progenies magnum caeli ventura sub axem.
> hic vir, hic est, tibi quem promitti saepius audis,
> Augustus Caesar, divi genus, aurea condet
> saecula qui rursus Latio regnata per arva
> Saturno quondam, super et Garamantos et Indos
> proferet imperium; iacet extra sidera tellus,
> extra anni solisque vias, ubi caelifer Atlas
> axem umero torquet stellis ardentibus aptum.
> huius in adventum iam nunc et Caspia regna
> responsis horrent divum et Maeotia tellus,
> et septemgemini turbant trepida ostia Nili.
> nec vero Alcides tantum telluris obivit,
> fixerit aeripedem cervam licet, aut Erymanthi
> pacarit nemora et Lernam tremefecerit arcu;
> nec qui pampineis victor iuga flectit habenis
> Liber, agens celso Nysae de vertice tigris. (6.789-805)

> ... *here is Caesar and all the offspring*
> *of Iulus that is about to come under the great vault of the heaven.*
> *Here is that man, this is he, whom often you hear promised to you,*
> *Augustus Caesar, the race of a god, who will found golden*
> *ages again through the fields in Latium once ruled by Saturn,*
> *and he will extend his empire past the Garamantians*
> *and the Indians (a land lies behind the stars,*
> *beyond the paths of the year and the sun, where sky-bearing*
> *Atlas turns the vault fixed with burning stars on his shoulder):*
> *at whose coming already now do the Caspian kingdoms*
> *shudder at the responses they receive from the gods, and the*
>   *Maeotian land,*
> *and the nervous mouths of the sevenfold Nile are in turmoil.*
> *Nor, truly, did Alcides go over so much of the earth,*
> *though he shot the brazen-footed deer and pacified the*
> *groves of Erymanthus, and made Lerna tremble with his bow;*
> *not so much land does Liber travel as a victor, when he guides his*
> *yoked team with vine-leaf reins, driving the tigers from the lofty*
>   *heights of Nysa.*

The threefold anaphora of *hic* sounds the notes of triumph for Julius Caesar's heir (and the ambiguous opening, especially since Anchises has skipped so many centuries, highlights whose heir Augustus is).[34] In the context of Rome's future and the dawn of the Augustan Age, the passage can be read as an optimistic, triumphant anthem. In the immediate context of Anchises' Neoplatonic vision, we might well note that the future Augustus will not be the reincarnation of Anchises, Aeneas, or even Ascanius. Anchises had announced that the souls destined for rebirth had to wait some thousand years (748); chronologically, at least, Virgil could have envisioned one of his triad of Roman progenitors as the future Augustus.[35] Perhaps more importantly, though, Virgil has entirely skipped the Roman Republic in his anticipation of Augustus. He will remedy that soon enough, though for now the obvious historical parallel is between Romulus and Augustus; the new ruler (not to say monarch) will give Rome a rebirth that is a hard line on the past: he will restore the Golden Age of Saturn.

The comparison made here between Augustus and Hercules will achieve greater significance in Book 8, when Aeneas hears at length the story of Hercules and the "Bad Man," Cacus (8.185-305).[36] The two specific references to Hercules here are to his canonical labors: the Cerynaean Hind, the Erymanthian Boar, and the Lernaean Hydra (what, if any, special significance there may be in the choice of these three labors is difficult to discern). The image of Dionysus, reborn, hangs over the entire announcement of soon-to-be Roman reincarnated souls. Augustus is also to be another Alexander as he extends Roman might (*imperium sine fine*). When Mercury had visited Aeneas to relay Jupiter's command for immediate flight from Carthage, Virgil had lingered over the description of Atlas at the western edge of the world (4.238-251); now mythological fancy has received historical approbation: Augustus will push forward even to a region beyond Atlas, a hitherto undiscovered land (necessitated by Jupiter's promise of empire with end: Virgil could not just list regions of the known world, however remote and exotic). No Roman of Virgil's time could have failed to recall Augustus' recovery of the standards Crassus had lost at Carrhae in 20 B.C.; allegedly the dead Crassus had been posthumously forced to participate in a grisly retelling of Euripides' *Bacchae*—now Augustus himself is Bacchus.[37] Interestingly, the direct mention of Augustus, both here in the grand vision of future worthies and later on the shield of Aeneas, helps to mitigate any negative consequences of connections between Aeneas and Augustus. If Aeneas falls somewhat short of our expectations, the restrained yet powerful mentions of Augustus here and on the shield help to remind us of the separate identities (and, by extension, qualities and potential) of either man. The one set in motion the founding of Rome by the overt help of the gods; the other restored a broken Rome by the toil and sweat of his own brow, as it were: the advantages of a skeptical age that might be less inclined to ascribe victories to the divinities.

Numa Pompilius returns us to the traditional list of early Roman kings (Augustus, significantly, interrupts the procession of future *monarchs*). Numa was said to have been taught by Pythagoras of Samos himself, which makes for a wonderfully appropriate connection between Roman history and Virgil's transmigratory philosophical speculations. Tullus (Hostilius) is here, and Ancus, and "the Tarquin kings" (6.817); the mention of the last monarchs leads into the deliciously ambiguous introduction of Brutus, the founder the Republic, and, in more recent history, the assassin of Julius Caesar:

vis et Tarquinios reges animamque superbam
ultoris Bruti, fascisque videre receptos? (6.817-818)

*Do you wish to see the Tarquin kings and the proud spirit
of Brutus the avenger, and the fasces that were recovered?*

Punctuation matters here; it is possible to take the "proud spirit" with either the Tarquin kings or the avenger Brutus, and Virgil wanted us to wonder about either implication. The establishment of the Republic in 509 B.C. is introduced quickly in these lines that announce the transfer of the power of life and death (symbolized by the *fasces*, the bundle of axes) from kings to consuls. Virgil immediately focuses on the capital authority of the consuls; he tells of how Brutus' two sons rebelled against their father and his consular authority, preferring to try to help restore the monarchy. Brutus had them killed "for the sake of beautiful freedom" (6.821 *pulchra pro libertate*), and Virgil labels him *infelix*, "unlucky" or "unfortunate" (because he was forced to order the death of his own sons). There is the usual Virgilian sympathy for tragedy here, but also a clear indication of his thoughts on the matter:

vincet amor patriae laudumque immensa cupido. (6.823)

Love of country will conquer, and immense desire for praises.

The image will be echoed in Book 11, when the women of the Latin capital see Camilla's example of death for country as she battles the Trojan cavalry:

monstrat amor verus patriae, ut videre Camillam. (11.892)

True love of country showed them the way, as they saw Camilla.

It is difficult to imagine that these are not Virgil's personal reflections on the assassination of Caesar; did Brutus save the Republic (his act did, after all, pave the way for the Augustan advent) with his dagger?

From being willing to order the death of another on behalf of liberty we move to self-sacrifice for the sake of one's country: the Decii, father and son: the father "devoted" himself (*devotio*) in 340 B.C. and the son in 295.[38] The Drusi are here as well (Augustus' wife Livia was a member of their family); the mention of Manlius Torquatus, who ordered the death of his own son for disobedience, returns us to the horrible theme of fathers killing sons. Camillus is next: he recovered the "standards" Rome had lost to the Gauls after the infamous sack of the city in 390 B.C. (another allusion to Augustus' recent negotiations with Parthia). It is possible that Virgil's Camilla is in some way meant to evoke her great namesake.

Julius Caesar could not be left out of a description of Rome's future worthies. In Book 1, Virgil had played a deliberate game of ambiguity and obscurity in Jupiter's prophecy to his daughter Venus (286-291); if you want to find Julius there, you may, though you must find Augustus, and you can certainly argue that Julius is not there at all. Here Caesar and Pompey are not even named; every member of Virgil's audience knew the story of their civil war, which would be the subject of Lucan's epic sequel to the *Aeneid* in another generation, once the imperial succession unfolded. Out of his entire life and roster of deeds, Caesar is only remembered in this passage for his war with Pompey: that civil war, between father-in-law and son-in-law, is a sort of horrible perversion of the stern devotion to duty that had led Republican fathers to kill their own sons. In the wake of the magnificent prediction of Rome's future foreign expansion under Augustus, the theme of civil war comes (as it will in Lucan) as a perpetual impediment to Rome's fated greatness: how can we advance to India and Ethiopia, when we are occupied with self-slaughter? Another suspiciously effective half-line (6.835) appeals to Caesar to throw down his sword. The whole scene is vividly active; Caesar is rushing down from the Alpine heights and the citadel of Monaco, while Pompey bears the arms of the East.[39] The evocation of the great civil war between Caesar and Pompey is troubling, but since it was all part of the forward thrust that led to Augustus Caesar, the sacrifices are more palatable; all of the grim horrors of Roman history can be accepted, one might imagine, if Augustus is to rule (the Silver Latin poet Lucan would play with this conceit in the opening of his *Pharsalia*, where all of Rome's civil strife is worth the sacrifice, if it meant that *Nero* could rule supreme in Rome).

And so the drama continues: the final defeat of "Greece" had come in 146 B.C., when Lucius Mummius sacked Corinth; in the context of a Trojan's prophecy to another Trojan, Mummius' military victory, of course, is an announcement of final revenge for the events of Book 2. Lucius Aemilius Paullus is also here; he defeated Perseus of Macedon at Pydna in 168 B.C. Dido's curse is quietly put to rest by the mention first of the Scipios, the "twin thunderbolts of war" (6.842, a borrowing from Lucretius' description of them at *De Rerum Natura* 3.1034)—Carthage would be defeated for good by the Third Punic War in 146 B.C. by Scipio Africanus Aemilianus, the "Younger" Scipio—and second by the mention of Quintus Fabius Maximus "Cunctator." Fabius the "Delayer" saved Rome early in the Second Punic War by his tactics of frustrating delay and avoidance of direct conflict with the Carthaginian military.

The Roman historians were fond of introducing "examples" (*exempla*), both good and bad, for the edification of younger generations.[40] Now Anchises offers his *Roman* son an important lesson, the most explicit set of instructions Aeneas receives in the poem:

excudent alii spirantia mollius aera
(credo equidem), vivos ducent de marmore vultus,
orabunt causas melius, caelique meatus
describent radio et surgentia sidera dicent:
tu regere imperio populos, Romane, memento
(hae tibi erunt artes) pacique imponere morem,
parcere subiectis et debellare superbos. (6.847-853)

Others will beat out breathing bronze more delicately
(I do believe it), and they will lead forth living faces from marble;

*they will plead their cases better, and trace the wanderings
of the sky with a compass and speak of the rising stars:
you, Roman, remember to rule the peoples with empire
(these will be your skills) and to impose law on peace,
to spare those who are subjected to you and to beat down the proud.*

The opening lines are easy enough to explicate: they are a powerful tribute to the Greeks, masters of bronze work, oratory and the art of rhetoric (a jibe at Cicero here?),[41] and astronomy. The Roman is to rule the world, and to establish customs (law, tradition, all the richness of *mos*) in time of peace.[42] The Roman is to spare those who are at his feet, and to beat down those who are haughty and proud. Anchises' words reverse these last two admonitions; the "sparing," of course, comes after the enemy is at one's feet. Caesar himself had cultivated a reputation for clemency toward defeated enemies; Aeneas is to learn the ways of mercy. Homer's audience would not have expected Achilles to spare Hector; Virgil has outlined the great lesson of Aeneas' schooling: he is to defeat his enemies, but spare them once they are vanquished.[43] Of course Aeneas will die without Rome having been founded; some have excused Aeneas' disregard of this injunction by arguing that it is not an address to *Aeneas* but rather to the Rome of the future. This is technically correct. But pedantry does not remove the unease of the end of the *Aeneid*.[44] And, in any case, Book 6—as a major part of Aeneas' education—is focused on the transition from *Trojan* hero (who has confronted the dark moments of his past from Books 2 and 4 in the persons of Deiphobus and Dido) to *Roman* hero: powerfully, this is the first time Aeneas is called a Roman (and by his Trojan father), and the only place in the procession where he finds a place, since, after all, metempsychosis precludes bilocation).

After such a summation, we might expect the procession to be over. There is another soul, though, for Anchises to point out, and, in fact, he is the most prominent in Anchises' description (though barely a name for most moderns): Marcellus. He towers over everyone else (6.856 *viros supereminet omnis*). The procession ends, then, with its most noteworthy figure. This is Marcus Claudius Marcellus, who had won victories over both the Gauls and the Carthaginians: he killed Virdomarus in 222 B.C., the year of the first of his five consulships, and later captured Syracuse (notwithstanding Archimedes) in 212. He was the third (859 *tertia*) and last man in Roman history to win the *spolia opima*, the "Rich Spoils," for his killing an enemy commander in battle (Romulus and Cossa had been the other two).

Although Marcellus was a great figure in Roman Republican history, we might wonder (along with Virgil's contemporary audience?) why he has been so prominently featured now, after the climax of Anchises' lesson for his son. Aeneas notices that Marcellus does not walk alone. There is a young man with him, bearing a sad face (862 *frons laeta parum*) and downcast eyes (*deiecto lumina vultu*). Anchises had not mentioned this soul. The Republican Marcellus, it turns out, has served as prolegomena for the Imperial Marcellus.

This Marcus Claudius Marcellus was the son of Octavia, Augustus' sister, and Gaius Claudius Marcellus, a former consul. Augustus had no sons of his own, and so his sister's oldest son was an obvious choice as heir and successor.[45] In 25 B.C., at the age of seventeen, Marcellus was married to Augustus' only daughter, Julia. He did not live long enough to have a child with Julia; he died of some mysterious illness at Baiae, near Naples, in 23 B.C. Augustus himself fell seriously ill and was restored to health by the ministrations of one Antonius Musa, a freedman. After Augustus was cured, Marcellus became just as sick. Musa was unable to save the younger man; Cassius Dio depicts Marcellus as a sacrifice for Augustus' renewed health (53.30).[46]

After Marcellus' death, Julia was married to Augustus' trusted admiral Agrippa. Marcellus' death was soon enough attributed by rumor and gossip to the machinations of Augustus' wife Livia (with whom he would never have a child)—certainly it is suspicious that all of Julia's children with Agrippa met untimely ends. But there can be little doubt that Marcellus had been Augustus' intended successor. Anchises lavishes attention on the ghostly boy, arguing that the gods must have decided that he would have to die young, lest Rome be too great under his direction, and that no enemy would ever have been able to withstand Marcellus, whether he advanced against them on foot or on horseback. In the misty grove where the souls exercise their desire to reenter mortal bodies (6.751 *incipiant in corpora velle reverti*), the soul of Marcellus is sad because he has some awareness of his future fate—this new life will be exceedingly brief. Anchises presages the funeral of this young worthy, Rome's best future hope:

> ... manibus date lilia plenis,
> purpureos spargam flores animamque nepotis
> his saltem accumulem donis et fungar inani
> munere. (6.883-886)

> ... *Give lilies with full hands—*
> *I shall scatter purple flowers and with these*
> *gifts, at least, heap over the shade of my descendant and fulfill an empty*
> *duty.*

Virgil here makes his final (and most powerful) allusion to the emptiness of funereal rites; *M*isenus' grim funeral was a foreshadowing of *M*arcellus' here (*M . . . s*). Misenus' death was utterly insignificant to the forward progress of the Trojans (excepting the demand that Aeneas provide the ill-fated musician with burial before his own descent into the underworld); the death of Marcellus is of supreme significance to the Augustan succession. The bright vision of Rome's future has been marred by the end of history; the benevolent monarchy of Augustus cannot guarantee its own succession, and so the vision ends with Marcellus not merely because Virgil could not prognosticate the future, but because Rome's history has ended, in effect, with Augustus and his failed efforts to guarantee a transfer of power to someone as skilled and gifted as he admittedly was; Tiberius (ironically, the first and last letters remind us of *T*urnu*s*) will not be as good a ruler as his predecessor, and we are only one *princeps* removed from Caligula.

The final section of Book 6 has earned Virgil more critical commentary than perhaps any other of his many mysteries: the Gates of Sleep.[47]

> Sunt geminae Somni portae, quarum altera fertur
> cornea, qua veris facilis datur exitus umbris,
> altera candenti perfecta nitens elephanto,
> sed falsa ad caelum mittunt insomnia manes.
> his ubi tum natum Anchises unaque Sibyllam
> prosequitur dictis portaque emittit eburna,
> ille viam secat ad navis sociosque revisit.
> tum se ad Caietae recto fert limite[48] portum.
> ancora de prora iacitur; stant litore puppes. (6.893-901)

> *There are twin gates of Sleep, one of which is said to be of*
> *horn, by which an easy exit is granted to true shades,*
> *while the other is gleaming, having been fashioned from bright ivory,*
> *but the ghosts send false dreams to the sky above.*
> *Then, when he had finished speaking, Anchises followed his son and*
>   *the Sibyl*
> *and sent them out through the Ivory Gate.*
> *Aeneas cut a path to his ships and revisited his friends;*
> *then he conducts himself to the harbor of Caieta by a straight route.*
> *The anchor is cast from the prow; the ships stand on the shore.*

Book 6 thus ends with a conclusion to the ring that had started at the close of Book 5; both books finish with Sleep—an appropriate enough theme for the dream-like nature of Book 6.

Analysis of this passage usually takes one of two directions. Either the exegete tries to find quite specific scientific, astrological, philosophical, chronological, or literary reasons why Virgil has Aeneas and the Sibyl use the Ivory Gate, or the whole matter is left as a "Virgilian enigma" (to use Austin's phrase) and left unexplained. Of these methodologies the second is wiser and superior; Virgil does not play tricks to see if his readers are adept at solving riddles. Indeed, in one sense there is no problem with Virgil's closing scene here; Aeneas and the Sibyl are not "true shades," since they are alive, and so they must use the Ivory Gate—cynical pessimists notwithstanding. The descent to Avernus, we had been told, was "easy" (6.126); the ascent back was the problem. Now we learn that for "true shades" the *exit* is easy (894 *facilis*); the book rings the descent and ascent with reflections on how relatively easy they may or may not be.

The vision that Aeneas has in the underworld cannot be called "false" either. Aeneas and the Sibyl themselves are not "true shades"—but the message Aeneas brings is true in the light of Roman history. It makes no predictions about the future, either; the vision ends chronologically with Augustus, who, as we have noted, is (significantly) placed out of proper order (in a more dramatic way than some of the other figures who are slightly shifted around for the sake of word order and meter).

No, the vision is false because in the light of *Lucretian* philosophy, the vision was and is impossible. Virgil moved from the Homeric underworld of mythological lore to the underworld of those more hopeful philosophers who envisaged some sort of fate after death besides the gloomy underworld home that Achilles lamented to Odysseus was worse than the life of some hireling on earth, no matter how lofty one's *post mortem* throne. Now, at the end, Virgil sends Aeneas and the Sibyl out through the Ivory Gate as a final nod to Lucretius in this, his most Lucretian book. Virgil, I suspect, may well have hoped that Lucretius was wrong, that death was not the end of all, that there might be some sort of continued existence beyond the grave. Aeneas is a false dream in this sense because he is a prophet of a message that cannot be true according to Lucretius' admittedly difficult truth, even if the message accords with Roman "historical" truth. We can join with Augustus and his sister Octavia in mourning Marcellus; we can rejoice in the anachronistic vision of a future we know came true. But over it all looms the message of Lucretius, which hearkens to us with its own incredibly beautiful dactylic hexameters, reminding Virgil—and his audiences for all time—that death is the end, and that any hopes raised by discourses such as Anchises' on transmigratory souls and reborn heroes are, in the end, false dreams.[49]

And, whatever the implications, it is *Anchises* (6.897) who sends his son out through the Gate of False Dreams. Did the father know how the son would, in the end, respond to his admonition to spare the defeated? Book 6 is the last time that father and son will speak in the poem; after the underworld visitation, it will be Aeneas' turn to instruct his son Ascanius in the ways of leadership, honor, and valor. In Book 12, as we shall see, Aeneas will remind his son that he should learn labor and true fortune from him, and fortune from others (12.435-440, especially 435-6 *disce, puer, virtutem ex me verumque laborem / fortunam ex aliis*). It is significant that Anchises' admonition to *his* son is a positive injunction, an imperative addressed to the *Roman* Aeneas. The imperative Aeneas will give to his son Ascanius shortly before the single combat he fights with Turnus will, in effect, be a call to remember how much Father Aeneas has suffered in the furtherance of the will of the gods. It is a rather narcissistic command that Aeneas gives his son; Aeneas is still fixed on the past, whether Troy, Carthage and Dido, or the loss of Pallas. In striking contrast, here among the ghosts of the past, his father is firmly fixed on the Roman future, just as he has been since the portent in Book 2 of the fire that enveloped *Ascanius*' head: Anchises realizes that his grandson is the true hope for the future (the succession motif). Arguable, too, one could have no better teacher of *fortuna*, the luck of the gods, as it were, than Aeneas.

So ends the first half of the *Aeneid*. Aeneas' education will be completed at the future site of Rome, and a Greek will be his teacher. Within the space of another book, the long predicted war in Italy will erupt. The close of Book 6 is quiet and calm: in the space of three lines, despite the momentous revelations of the underworld visions, Aeneas rejoins his Trojan, not Roman, companions, presumably never to tell them of what he experienced in Hades (not once will he allude to the visions he saw among the dead). He sails straight on up the coast to Caieta. As the Odyssean half of the poem ends, we have a homecoming of sorts for the Trojans: the anchors are cast and the ships stand on the beach as Aeneas arrives in port. Virgil will now give both his hero and us an education in wrath, as the *Iliad* is reborn in Italy.

Notes

1. The *Sortes Vergilianae*.
2. The temple of Apollo on the Palatine was a thanksgiving offering for the victory over Sextus Pompey, not Actium.
3. For a convenient summary of the "problem" (poets, after all, are not cartographers) see Hardie's appendix on "The Crater of Avernus" in AUSTIN, *P. Vergili Maronis Aeneidos Liber Sextus*, Oxford, 1977, pp. 279-286), MONTI, "The Identification of Vergil's Cave of the Cumaean Sibyl," *Vergilius* 40 (1994), pp. 19-34, and MONTI, "Evidence for the Sibyl's Cave at Cumae," and CLARK, "Vergil's Poetic Treatment of Cumaean Geography," *Vergilius* 37 (1991), pp. 39-68. Note also the still useful overview in RAND, *The Magical Art of Virgil*, Cambridge, Massachusetts, 1931, pp. 435 ff.
4. On Virgil's labyrinthine ecphrasis, best is PUTNAM, "Daedalus, Virgil, and the End of Art," *The American Journal of Philology* 108 (1987), pp. 173-198; see also RUTLEDGE, "Virgil's Daedalus," *The Classical Journal* 62.7 (1967), pp. 309-311, CATTO, "The Labyrinth on the Cumaean Gates and Aeneas' Escape from Troy," *Vergilius* 34 (1988), pp. 71-76. But surely there is more going on in Virgil's mind with the Daedalus/Icarus imagery than the flight from Troy. See also PASCHALIS, "The Unifying Theme of Daedalus' Sculptures on the Temple of Apollo Cumanus (*Aen.* 6.20-33), *Vergilius* 32 (1986), pp. 33-42.
5. Is there a parallel between Daedalus' fantastic decision to seek safety through airborne flight and Augustus' decision to build his principate on the hot ashes of the Republic?
6. Pasiphae will return below with Dido in the underworld; see further PIKE, "*Venus nefanda*: Dido and Pasiphae in Vergil's *Aeneid*," *Acta Classica* 36 (1993), p. 167.
7. See further CASALI, "Aeneas and the Doors of the Temple of Apollo," *The Classical Journal* 91.1 (1995), pp. 1-9.
8. 1.464 *pascit*: Aeneas and Achates "feed" on the pictures before the real banquet begins at Dido's court.
9. *Res Gestae Divi Augusti* 4.19 and Velleius Paterculus 2.81 (where see Woodman's note). The temple was begun in 36 B.C.
10. See further PUTNAM, *Horace's Carmen Saeculare: Ritual Magic and the Poet's Art*, New Haven, 2001, pp. 8-50.
11. *Vita Hadriani* 2.8. He is said to have read the passage in Book 6 about Numa Pompilius.
12. Essential reading on the Bough is SEGAL, "*Aeternum Per Saecula Nomen*: The Golden Bough and the Tragedy of History: Part I," *Arion* IV (1965), pp. 617-657 and "Part II," *Arion* V (1966), pp. 34-72.
13. Propertius *carmen* 1.11 links Misenum, the Lucrine Lake, and Charon's boat (the technical term for which was *cumba*) in creating a strangely morbid atmosphere for his attack on Cynthia's vacation trip to Baiae.
14. Virgil's felling of trees for funeral pyres here and in Book 11 is possibly inspired by Ennius *Annales* 6.175-179 (Skutsch), though it is not clear the Ennian passage describes the cutting down of trees for a requiem.
15. The classic study is BROOKS, "*Discolor Aura*: Reflections on the Golden Bough," *The American Journal of Philology* 54 (1953), pp. 260-280, reprinted in Commager, *op. cit.*, pp. 143-163. See also WEBER, "The Allegory of the Golden Bough," *Vergilius* 41 (1995), pp. 3-34.

16. *ut aranea bratteaque auri*.
17. See further D'ARMS, "Vergil's *Cunctantem (Ramum): Aeneid* 6.211," *The Classical Journal* 59.6 (1964), pp. 265-268, and AVERY, "The Reluctant Golden Bough," *The Classical Journal* 61.6 (1966), pp. 269-272.
18. Cf. 11.197 *multa boum circa mactantur corpora Morti*, where Virgil probably personifies the death god (as does Horace at c. 1.4.13 *pallida Mors*). Death in classical tradition always remained something of a figure from popular mythology, often parodied (see Dale on Euripides *Alcestis* 24-6 and cf. Petronius *Satyrica* 62.2, where Orcus is humorously described as a *miles fortis*). "Orcus" (or Orchus) appears widely in Latin literature from the earliest period. Bailey notes (*op. cit.*, p. 287): "[Death]...never in Rome attained the rank of a deity." Isidore notes: *Pluton Graece, Latine Diespiter vel Ditis pater; quem alii Orcum vocant, quasi receptorem mortium. Unde et orca nuncupatur vas quod recipit aquas. Ipse et Graece Charon (Etymologiarum Libri* 8.42). See further Campbell on Lucretius *De Rerum Natura* 5.996.
19. On this simile see further Hornsby, *op. cit.*, pp. 84-85.
20. Leucaspis' name may point to lack of experience in battle; he died, in any case, prematurely.
21. Palinurus was the one casualty Neptune demanded as the price for Aeneas' fleet's safe journey from Sicily to Italy. It is possible that in Palinurus, a sort of substitute sacrifice for Aeneas, we are meant to see a distant foreshadowing of the tradition that Aeneas drowned in the River Numicius, his body never found—a dismal end for Rome's progenitor, deified or not. For a reading of this passage, see Boyle, *op. cit.*, pp. 161-162; Boyle obliquely addresses the perennial problem of the Gates of Sleep: "The worthlessness of *fama, gloria*, and *aeternum nomen* forced upon the reader in the Misenus and Palinurus episodes functions as a precursorial criticism of the *famae venientis amore* with which Anchises inflames Aeneas before sending him through the ivory gate." But, as we shall see below, the vision of the future glory of Roman history is true, not false. Pessimistic Virgil may wonder all he wants about the Augustan regime, but he has bigger philosophical targets to address in *Aeneid* 6 than Roman imperialism.
22. The often delightful, never unimaginative Henry offers a possible recipe for Virgil's dog biscuit.
23. The poignant phrase *in limine primo* will be repeated in Book 11 (423) during Turnus' speech, where he will ask Latinus' court why they should retire from the fight "on the first threshold"—a wonderfully sardonic comment by Virgil that evokes the pathos of the prematurely dead. Cf. Prudentius' breviary hymn (*Cathemerinon* 12.125-132) *Salvete, flores martyrum, / quos lucis ipso in limine / Chrisi insecutor sustulit, / ceu turbo nascentes rosas*.
24. Cf. Propertius *carmen* 1.15.21-2 *coiniugis Evadne miseros delata per ignis / occidit, Argivae fama pudicitiae*.
25. On Caeneus/Caenis and his/her relationship to Dido, see WEST, G.S., "Caeneus and Dido," *Transactions of the American Philological Association* 110 (1980), pp. 315-325.
26. On this passage see especially SKINNER, "The Last Encounter of Dido and Aeneas: *Aen.* 6.450-476," *Vergilius* 29 (1983), pp. 12-18.
27. How did Austin miss the parallel?
28. Cf. the vestigial traces of the story in *Odyssey* 8.517 ff., and the *Ilias Parva* (his marriage to Helen) and *Iliupersis* (his death at the hand of Menelaus).
29. The standard overview of the literature is WEST, M.L., *The Orphic Poems*, Oxford, 1983; for the general background, see the still useful GUTHRIE, *Orpheus and Greek Religion*, Princeton, 1952.

30. See further WINKLER, "*Tuque optime vates*: Musaeus in Book 6 of the *Aeneid*," *The American Journal of Philology* 108 (1987), pp. 655-660.

31. 6.684-702: tear "entrainment": see Donald Lateiner's forthcoming article on ancient tears. Virgil is fond of mimetic behavior; so the youth of Troy follow Ascanius' lead in Book 5, and in Book 11, the Volscian cavalry imitate Camilla in descending from their horses.

32. For the view that Anchises is asking the question rhetorically of Jupiter, *pater omnium*, see KOHN, "*Aeneid* 6.713-723," *Vergilius* 44 (1998), pp. 28-30. The article is misguided; 6.722 *dicam . . . nate*, especially after *pater*, taken in the context of a conversation between a father and a son, does not allow us to insert a third (divine) party in the conversation. Anchises maintains his calm, recollected mood throughout the entire episode except at the beginning (when he becomes emotional after seeing Aeneas for the first time) and at the end (where he laments the death of Marcellus). There is no need for Virgil to confuse the issue by inserting a rhetorical address to Jupiter that interrupts the encounter between father and son.

33. Note especially GOOLD, "The Voice of Virgil: The Pageant of Rome in *Aeneid* 6," in WOODMAN and POWELL, eds., *Author and Audience in Latin Literature*, Cambridge, 1992, pp. 110-123.

34. Though it is not entirely certain that the *Caesar* of 789 ff. is Augustus!

35. It is true that Jupiter has predicted the deification of Aeneas, but there was no reason Virgil could not have envisioned Augustus as the reincarnation of, perhaps, Ascanius; the future apotheosis of Aeneas notwithstanding, there is still, ironically, no place in the catalogue of future Roman luminaries for the dynastic triad of A-s, A-s, and A-s: a possible rueful comment on the A-s on Virgil's own day?

36. On Hercules and Augustus see *inter alios* Camps, *op. cit.*, pp. 98-100 and 141.

37. Plutarch *Crassus* 33.

38. See Livy *Ab Urbe Condita* 8.9 and 10.28, with Oakley's notes.

39. In 1981, the *Principauté de Monaco* issued a commemorative stamp to mark the bimillennium of Virgil's death (19 B.C.-A.D. 1981); appropriately, it is inscribed with line 830 and the only mention in Virgil of the citadel of Monaco, traditionally founded by Hercules; it takes its name (Greek *Monoikos*) from the epithet sixth century B.C. Phocaean colonists gave to the nearby Ligurians, who lived on the site of the present principality: they lived apart, "as a single house."

40. On the possible reception of the *Aeneid* by the "professional pessimist" Roman historians of the late Republic, see WILLIAMS, *Tradition and Originality in Roman Poetry*, Oxford, 1968, p. 75. Virgil, however, outdid the pessimism of Sallust and Livy.

41. See further SHACKLETON-BAILEY, *Cicero*, London, 1971, pp. ix-xii. For study of the possible "appearances" of Cicero in the poem, see DYER, "Cicero at Caieta in Vergil's *Aeneid*," *Latomus* 54 (1995), pp. 290-297.

42. Virgil makes no obvious distinction in the great revelations of Book 6 between Rome/Romans and Italy/Italians (after all, in the final revelations in Book 12, Rome will be *Italian*). For the opposing view, see HABINEK, *The Politics of Latin Literature: Writing, Identity, and Empire in Ancient Rome*, Princeton, 1998, p. 75.

43. See further ZETZEL, "*Romane memento*: Justice and Judgment in *Aeneid* 6," *Transactions of the American Philological Association* 119 (1989), pp. 263-284.

44. For the opposite view, see JENKYNS, *Virgil's Experience: Nature and History; Times, Names, and Places*, Oxford, 1998, pp. 666-667.

45. Just as Ascanius is depicted in the *Aeneid* as too young to engage in extended combat (as we shall see in Book 9), so Augustus apparently had some concerns about Marcellus' fitness for immediate takeover of the principate in 23 B.C., when he faced his

serious health crisis and had to make some contingency plan for the succession. After Augustus was restored to health, according to Cassius Dio he wanted to read his will to the people to make it clear that he had named no successor; while he was sick, he is said to have handed over his ring to Agrippa, his most trusted friend; everyone was shocked, we are told, that Marcellus was not the clearly anointed successor. Virgil's depiction of Ascanius parallels Augustus' treatment of Marcellus (though Marcellus would die prematurely; this early death is reflected in the great concern for Ascanius' welfare in the *Aeneid*). According to Suetonius (*Divus Augustus* 66), Agrippa was jealous of Marcellus; Tacitus (*Annales* 1.3.1) blithely passes over the whole matter. Velleius Paterculus (2.93.1) is less enamored of Marcellus than Virgil (as we might expect, given his pro-Tiberian stance); see further Woodman's notes, and Beagon on Pliny *Historia Naturalis* 7.49. For a convenient summary of what Beagon well labels "the ambiguities of 23 B.C." see BARRETT, *Livia: First Lady of Imperial Rome*, New Haven, 2002, pp. 35-36, and SOUTHERN, *Augustus*, London-New York, 1998, pp. 119-120. Syme is wise (*The Roman Revolution*, Oxford, 1939, pp. 342-343: "Some at least of the perils which this critical year revealed might be countered if Augustus silenced rumour and baffled conspiracy by openly designating a successor. He might adopt his nephew. Such was perhaps his secret wish, perhaps the intention avowed to his counsellors. It was thwarted." On the Marcellus passage in Virgil see GLEI, "The Show Must Go On: The Death of Marcellus and the Future of the Augustan Principate," in Stahl, *op. cit.*, pp. 119-134.

46. Cf. Suetonius *Divus Augustus* 81, who notes that Augustus suffered several serious illnesses in his life, of which this was the worst. One gets the impression from Suetonius that Augustus was something of a hypochondriac; still, the death of Marcellus might well have seemed sacrificial: Augustus lived, but Marcellus died; the theme resonates through the pages of Virgil.

47. See further HIGHBARGER, *The Gates of Sleep*, Baltimore, 1940, STEINER, *op. cit.*, pp. 88-96; AMORY, "The Gates of Horn and Ivory," *Yale Classical Studies* 20 (1966), pp. 3-57; REED, "the Gates of Sleep in *Aeneid* 6," *The Classical Quarterly* N.S. 23.2 (1973), pp. 311-315; TARRANT, "Aeneas and the Gates of Sleep," *Classical Philology* 77.1 (1982), pp. 51-55, WEST, "The Bough and the Gate," Exeter, 1987 (reprinted in Harrison, *op. cit.*, pp. 224-238); COCKBURN, "Aeneas and the Gates of Sleep: An Etymological Approach," *Phoenix* 46 (1992), pp. 362-364); BRENK, "The Gate of Dreams and an Image of Life: Consolation and Allegory at the End of Vergil's *Aeneid* VI," *Collection Latomus: Studies in Latin Literature and History* VI (1992), pp. 277-294; MOLYVIATI-TOPTSI, "*Sed Falsa ad Caelum Mittunt Insomnia Manes* (*Aeneid* 6.896), *The American Journal of Philology* 116 (1995), pp. 639-652; and DOMINIK, "Reading Vergil's *Aeneid*: The Gates of Sleep (VI.893-898), *Maia* 48 (1996), 129-138. I have expressed my views on the problem in a forthcoming *Latomus* article, "A Brief Reflection on the Gates of Sleep" (2007). Virgil's Gates of Sleep are modeled on Homer's twin gates of dreams (*Odyssey* 19.562-567)—a final Odyssean nod as the first half of the epic closes. On the ludicrous notion that the text can be emended to remove the problem, see the useful retort of O'HARA, "An Unconvincing Argument About Aeneas and the Gates of Sleep," *Phoenix* 50 (1996), pp. 331-334. I am indebted to Helen Gerseny for the important reminder that it is *Anchises* who sends his son and the Sibyl out by the ivory gate.

48. For *limite* instead of *litore* (so Mynors), see Austin ad loc.

49. The classic article on the Lucretian influences on *Aeneid* 6 remains MICHELS, "Lucretius and the Sixth Book of the *Aeneid*," *The American Journal of Philology* 65

(1944), pp. 135-148; note also MELLINGHOFF and BOURGERIE, *Les Incertitudes de Virgile, Contributions Epicuriennes à la Théologie de l'Enéide*, Brussels, 1990.

CHAPTER VII

YOU ALSO, DYING

The first section of the Oxford *Aeneid* was supposed to consist of the completed editions of Roland Austin and Roger Williams.[1] With the posthumously published Austin *Aeneid* 6, the project was finished despite the editor's death—only the lack of an introduction showed the tragic circumstances of its completion. In that same autumn of 1974 when Austin died, Christian Fordyce also passed away. In 1977, his home university of Glasgow released a volume with his commentaries on Books 7 and 8. It was a time of great burgeoning interest in the second half of the poem: 1976 saw the publication of commentaries on Book 8 by Eden and Gransden, for a total of three on Book 8 in two years. Since then, most of the published commentaries on the *Aeneid* have focused on these hitherto unjustly neglected books—and now there is Horsfall on Book 7 (Brill, 2000), a very different commentary from Fordyce, and the most detailed study of the book ever published.[2]

Book 7, like 3 and 5, has been overshadowed by what surrounds it. In the tripartite division of the poem, it stands with 5 in contrast to 6 and 8; like 5 it opens quietly and peacefully if not happily, and ends darkly and ominously. Books 6 and 8 are more famous for their glorious visions of Rome's future. But Book 7 is an exciting book, a collection of varied episodes fashioned after the style of Book 1, an introductory book for Virgil's *Iliad*. It sets the stage for the second half of the poem, and very well at that. Books 6 and 7 are linked closely by the mention of Caieta (the modern Gaeta), which Virgil at once identifies now as the eternal home of Aeneas' dead nurse: another empty honor, as Virgil cannot resist noting (7.4 *si qua est ea gloria*).[3] The funeral ceremony Aeneas duly performs for his nurse brings back all the sentiments of Misenus and Palinurus, as well as Anchises' memorial games. And there is a final nod to the *Odyssey*: Aeneas and his men pass by the legendary home of the witch Circe; her presence will linger throughout the book's opening scenes. Neptune is still protecting Venus' son; he fills the Trojan sails so they do not land on the sorceress' coast: the last Odyssean danger has been evaded successfully. As Aeneas draws near to the Latin coast, he sees a grove (7.29 *lucum*); what had been associated with the underworld in Book 6 will now mark the mouth of the Tiber, the river his dead wife had so long ago presaged as his future home (2.782 *Thybris*). Aeneas, happy (7.36 *laetus*), finally arrives at the long awaited river.

Virgil now invokes the muse Erato as he announces his greater work:

Nunc age, qui reges, Erato, quae tempora, rerum
quis Latio antiquo fuerit status, advena classem
cum primum Ausoniis exercitus appulit oris,
expediam, et primae revocabo exordia pugnae.

tu vatem, tu, diva, mone. dicam horrida bella,
dicam acies actosque animis in funera reges,
Tyrrhenamque manum totamque sub arma coactam
Hesperiam. maior rerum mihi nascitur ordo,
maius opus moveo. (7.37-45)[4]

Now come, what kings, Erato, what were the times,
what was the status of affairs in Latium of old, when first
the strange army drove its fleet to Ausonian shores,
I shall unfold, and I shall call back the beginnings of the first fight.
You, goddess, you, advise your bard. I shall tell of horrible wars,
I shall tell of battle lines and kings driven by courage to the death,
and the Etruscan band, and all Hesperia driven together under arms.
A greater order of affairs is born for me,
and I set into motion a greater work.

Virgil boldly declares in the first person his intention to describe the situation in ancient Latium at the time Aeneas first arrived on their shores. He invokes Erato, the Muse of Love Poetry, in an invocation that has caused some surprise. The proem here to the second half of the poem does not mention the rivalry between Turnus and Aeneas for marriage to Lavinia. War is forecast, as so many of Aeneas' prophecies have made clear. Even if this proem had mentioned the marriage conflict, Virgil does not elaborate on any possible amatory motif in his *Iliad*; the theme would not have been appropriate, and he had already explored it in Book 4 (Apollonius of Rhodes invokes Erato at the beginning of Book 3 of his *Argonautica*, which is devoted to Jason and Medea's love). The issue of Lavinia's marriage is a major one in the first stirrings of war in this book (when Allecto visits Amata), and it will recur until the poem's last book. But Virgil does not dwell on the theme (Mapheius Vegius depicts the wedding of Aeneas and Lavinia in his "Book 13," and the anonymous author of the Old French *Roman d'Enéas* devotes far more attention to the romantic motif).[5] Part of Virgil's reticence and suppression of the theme comes from his previous depictions of Aeneas with Creusa and Dido. Lavinia is a wife of destiny and fate, of prophecy and oracle—not of love. Except for this invocation, which highlights Erato boldly and dramatically at the beginning of the self-proclaimed greater half of the poem, any Virgilian amatory concerns and reflections are analyzed subtly and quietly. After all, love and war (Venus and Mars, mythological lovers) are two sides of the same coin; any discourse on war will also be a discourse on love, lust, and the affairs of the heart. This is Virgil's justification for invoking Erato before he begins a war; in Book 1, love was everywhere, working its wiles and setting in motion a chain of events that would end with the eternal enmity between Rome and Carthage. Here, in Book 7, love will lurk behind the war that soon engulfs Troy and Italy. For Aeneas, Lavinia is the bride of destiny, not love, and so Virgil will focus instead on how Aeneas' affections for Pallas spur him on to kill Turnus, and how Turnus' affections for Camilla cause him to lose the war.[6]

The opening of Book 7, with its late invocation after the epigrammatic address to Caieta and briefly sketched Circe episode, has been taken by some to be a nod to Hellenistic Greek poetry, to Apollonius and especially his contemporary Callimachus, famous to students of literature surveys for his pursuit of brief, elegant poetic topics in a sort of rejection of lengthy epics on a single theme.[7] The second half of the *Aeneid* contains a number of almost self-contained episodes that evoke such a world and poetic aesthetic: Hercules and Cacus, Nisus and Euryalus, and Camilla. Callimachus' once voluminous output survives mostly in fragments, and it is exceptionally dangerous to develop dogmas from the relatively paltry remains of the once mammoth whole. Roman poetry was unquestionably deeply influenced by him; Catullus, Propertius, and Ovid certainly all owed him much.

The delayed invocation of Book 7 does not so much reflect any literary signatures or tricks of the poet's trade as it evokes the quiet, brief lull of the first skirting of the Italian coast and arrival at Latinus' court, before the eruption of war later in this book. As Book 6 closed, we were immersed in a trance-like state of calm as we reflected on Anchises' great revelation. As Book 7 opens, the calm continues—until the address to Erato shatters it with its reminder that the second half of the poem is not so much concerned with the just reward of labors as with the fulfillment of worse horrors: war and more war in the new homeland.

We have observed that the first half of the *Aeneid* is modeled on Homer's *Odyssey*, and the second half on his *Iliad*. This division of the poem can be defended and explained easily enough. But, as we have seen in Books 1-6, the correspondences are not exact. The same will be true for the Iliadic Books 7-12. Virgil could not have seamlessly transferred the world of the two Homeric epics to his story of the foundation of Rome out of Trojan ashes. In Books 1-6, Aeneas corresponds more or less recognizably to Odysseus, as he proceeds from the Troad to his "home" in Italy. In Book 6, as we prepared to leave the Odyssean world, we learned with Aeneas that he would be facing another Achilles in Latium. If Turnus (whom we shall soon meet) is Achilles, we might have expected Aeneas to play Hector's role. In fact, though Aeneas will sometimes evoke Hector and sometimes Achilles, the same will be true for his rival Turnus. Homeric paradigms will shift between both men—this is the main cause of the unease that develops quickly and remains dark and heavy throughout the second half of the poem.

As we begin Book 7, we naturally recall Book 1. In the opening words of that book, we observed an ambiguity: the "man" of the first line, the *virum*, clearly refers to Aeneas-Odysseus. The "arms" of the first line—the first word of the poem, *arma*—is not as easy to define. Certainly it corresponds to the *bella* (7.41-42) Virgil now names as the first element in a litany of martial tragedy: *bella, acies,* and *reges*: wars, battle lines, and kings driven to death by their courage. The wars and battle lines refer to the conflict between Aeneas and Turnus. The mention of *reges*, the kings driven to their deaths, refers principally to the great Italian leaders who will die: Turnus, who dies at the end of Book 12, is lord among them, but in time we might also think of Mezentius, who will die at the end of Book 10, and Camilla (as much a king as a queen in some ways), who will die at the end of Book 11. The *arma* of Book 1 has finally received something of an expansion and explanation. The "Etruscan band" (7.43) refers to the help the Sibyl had predicted would come, unexpectedly, from a Greek city (Evander's Pallanteum).

Juno's wrath will also return in Book 7, in imitation of Book 1; unlike her pursuit of Aeolus and his winds then, her work now with the Fury Allecto will have far more devastating consequences for Aeneas and his Trojans. *Arma*, we have noted, corresponds to the Homeric wrath of Achilles; Aeneas will indeed be like Achilles at the last crucial moment of the poem, where he decides to kill Turnus. The final "wrath" of the poem belongs to Aeneas, who inherits it, as it were, from the reconciled Juno: she passes her wrath on to him. The *Iliad* originated in Achilles' wrath over the question of war prizes and captive girls, but the heroic themes of the poem were far removed from the world of jealous romantic rivals. In the *Aeneid*, the ostensible cause of the Latin war is the question of Lavinia. She is a new Helen, but she could not be more different than her Greek model. Only in one key area is she exactly the same: a war has started over the question of who will be her husband. Aeneas, though, does not kill Turnus because of Lavinia; he kills Turnus because of the dead Pallas, just as Achilles killed Hector because of Patroclus. In this the *Iliad* can be said to have "love" as its theme, as the love of Achilles for Patroclus drives him to slaughter Hector; love's connection to madness is a question the *Iliad* and the *Aeneid* both explore. In the *Aeneid*, the rivalry between Aeneas and Turnus for the hand of Lavinia is overshadowed by the return of the Iliadic question, not to say problem, of avenging a loved one (Aeneas/Pallas).[8] Juno's wrath is not concerned with the identity of Lavinia's husband, except insofar as her marriage to Aeneas would further Rome's development, to the eventual detriment of her beloved Carthage; the *Aeneid* is an epic of the city (very unlike the *Iliad*), and Erato is in part invoked to sing of the conflict that arises over Juno's love for Carthage and resultant hatred of any foundation that will someday oppose it. Juno's rage had been effective in Book 1 insofar as it led to Aeneas' fateful delay in North Africa. In Book 7, her tactics will be far more direct and immediate in their consequences: no curses on the future, however devastating, but instead an instant war in Latium.

"Love," then, exists simultaneously on several intersecting planes throughout the second half of the *Aeneid*: there is what we shall see as the rather cold and remote feelings of Aeneas for Lavinia (not surprising, given his true affection for both his dead wife and dead lover), the more complex feelings of Turnus for Lavinia, the parallel relationships between Aeneas and Pallas and Turnus and Camilla (with their devastating consequences in Books 11 and 12), the homoerotic love of Nisus and Euryalus that will be destroyed as part of the foundation of Roman views on sexuality, the loves of Venus and Juno, so different and so opposed, the love between Mezentius and his son Lausus and Evander and Pallas, even the loves of Amata and Juturna for their beloved Turnus and the love of Camilla for her country. The second half of the *Aeneid* is concerned with *arma*. The wrath—the madness—that is represented by those "arms" is motivated by "love" in its many manifestations, just as the tale of Troy had been motivated by one type of love, and even as its individual parts, like the *Odyssey*, found their ultimate motivation in stories of love (Odysseus and Penelope). All of these diverse loves need examination; some of them are healthy and beneficial for individual and state, while others are perverse, and many more appear somewhere in between.

Virgil now begins his story of one man's descent into madness. Unlike Homer's *Iliad*, Virgil's vision of wrath will have no redemptive conclusion. At midline, almost imperceptibly, the narrative begins:

... Rex arva Latinus et urbes
iam senior longa placidas in pace regebat. (7.45-46)

... King Latinus, now an old man, was ruling
the field and peaceful cities through a long peace.

This one sentence summarizes the situation in central Italy. Latinus has been king for some time; he has been ruling (durative imperfect *regebat*) his cities in tranquility (Virgil never actually names Latinus' main, capital city; most editors call it "Laurentum").[9] Circe's presence at the beginning of the book is a nod to the (pseudo-) Hesiodic tradition (*Theogony* 1011 ff.) whereby Latinus was Odysseus' son by the witch: a deeply allusive bond between Virgil's two epics. Probably by Virgilian invention, Latinus is introduced as the son of Faunus, a vaguely defined Italian rural god, and the nymph Marica. Latinus is a descendant of Saturn, an exceptionally mysterious god who was at some very early date identified with the Greek Cronos, father of Zeus, who allegedly sojourned in Italy after his expulsion from heaven, and brought a Golden Age to Latium.[10] Latinus had no son, only a daughter, who is now ready to be married. Her principal suitor is Turnus (7.55-56), whose first identifying characteristic is his handsome appearance (*ante alios pulcherrimus omnes*)—a continuing echo of the Erato theme. We learn that Latinus' wife was strongly in favor of a marriage between her daughter and Turnus; she was trying to hasten it with a "wondrous love" (57 *miro amore*)—her fondest desire and wish is for Turnus to be her son-in-law. The Fates, however, forbid it (58 ff.).

Virgil's description of a laurel tree that had been the symbol of Latinus' first settlement (like the horse's head for Carthage) evokes Apollo at a significant moment: the original foundation of the Latins. Virgil has the king derive the name of the settlers from the tree; Latinus called them the Laurentes. A swarm of bees was seen to alight on the top of the laurel; a prophet at once took this as an omen predicting the foreign birth of Lavinia's husband: he would come from the sea, whence the bees, and arrive at the same place the bees landed, the citadel of Latinus' settlement. Soon thereafter, while performing religious rites, Lavinia's long hair burst into flames, and as she ran about in a state of terror through the palace, she scattered fire everywhere. The fiery portent was taken to presage Lavinia as the cause of war for her people. Confronted with two unmistakable and disturbing oracles, Latinus consulted his father Faunus in a shady grove (7.81-84).

The description of the mysterious oracle Latinus consults brings us back to the world of *Aeneid* 6, especially with its mention of Acheron and Avernus (7.91). We could have expected the response the king receives: he is not to marry Lavinia to a Latin husband. Foreign sons-in-law will come (a sort of poetic plural), and their grandsons will see the world under their feet. The oracle says that the sons-in-law will bring the Latin name to the stars "by blood" (98 *sanguine*), a reference to the mingling of Trojan and Latin blood, but also a definite foreshadowing of the bloody start to the union the oracle fails to mention. Interestingly, Virgil says that Latinus did not keep the oracle of his father Faunus a secret (103), but that *Fama* (Rumor once again) bore it all around that the "Laomedontian youth" (105 *Laomedontia pubes*) had arrived on the Tiber's bank. Unlike Aeneas, Latinus reveals his prophetic news; the rumor, we can be sure, quickly reaches Turnus, as well as Latinus' wife Amata (the "Loved One").

In contrast with Book 1, where by now Aeneas and his Trojans were being tossed about in a Junonian storm, Book 7 has opened calmly. The seeds of war have been planted, but Virgil takes his time with exposition, just as he did with the landing in Carthage, on which the arrival in Latium will soon enough be modeled. Aeneas had shot seven stags when he landed in Carthage, to feed and provision each of his ships; they also had wine from their first visit to Acestes. Now we have a parallel passage, where there is no hunting and no apparent store of provisions ready from Acestes' Sicily. The meal is meager and not wholly satisfying; some fruit is piled on a thin layer of wheat (no wine appears, significantly, until *after* the eating of the tables). When the Trojans consume not only the fruit but also the wheat, Iulus exclaims that they have eaten their tables—the fulfillment of the "dire" prophecy of the Harpy Celaeno in Book 3 (255-257), with its celebrated inconsistency about who exactly uttered the prophecy to the Trojans. Helenus had already assured Aeneas that the prophecy was harmless; here the Trojan leader seems to be a bit overly relieved by the state of affairs in Italy:

> haec erat illa fames, haec nos suprema manebat
> exitiis positura modum. (7.128-129)
>
> *This was that hunger, this last thing was remaining for us,*
> *which would put an end on our disasters.*

This is pure rhetorical exaggeration (especially after the prophecy's grim foreboding had been removed so long before). It is also of note that after the stunning visions at the end of Book 6, the trivial prophecy about the tables should be the one that Virgil has as the first sign at the riverbank. Aeneas is wrong, of course (as he should know from numerous earlier prophecies); the eating of the tables was far from the last (*suprema*) trial awaiting the Trojans, and, in fact, was meaningless compared to what really awaits. The parallel to this passage is the false consolation Aeneas gave his men in Book 1 (198-207), where he concealed his state of despair so well. Here his mood (and that of his men) is quite different—but the trials that await them in Italy are far greater than the dangers that lurked in North Africa.

Virgil follows the strange and unimportant portent of the eating of the tables with an altogether solemn and glorious moment: Aeneas and his men offer prayers to a variety of heavenly beings (including his father Anchises in Erebus, and—a very Roman touch—the "genius" of the place), and are rewarded with a sign of approval and favor from Jupiter: thunder and what would seem to be lightning. Jupiter, with his own hand, shakes forth a cloud that is burning with the golden rays of the sun (we must remember it is nighttime); this phenomenon is probably akin to some sort of lightning or static discharge of electricity. All is happiness and great relief, though perhaps some careful audience members with better memories will note that the feasting that follows the omen uses almost the same line as the feasting that marked Dido's banquet in Book 1 (cf. 7.147 with 1.724). And indeed, when dawn comes, the Trojans will reenact the arrival in Carthage as they begin to explore the area around the Tiber, and as Aeneas sends out a hundred (epic exaggeration) men to announce their arrival to Latinus' court.

The first settlement Aeneas makes in Italy (7.157-159) is a military camp—a quiet, precautionary beginning to the war that will soon explode. The representatives to Latinus' city see the young men outside on the plain: they are engaged in athletics and mock battles with horses, chariots, archery and boxing (a sort of miniature parallel to the Trojan contests in Sicily, but also a foreshadowing of war). Before the Trojans can arrive at the palace, a messenger has already brought the news that strangers have come: they are of course "huge" (167 *ingentis*), and they have unfamiliar dress (the first mention in Italy of the traditional Trojan costume for which Iarbas mocked Aeneas in Book 4). The scene of the Trojan reception is not a temple to Juno, but rather an old building on the city's height, the palace of Latinus' grandfather Picus, marked by a hundred columns to match the hyperbole of Aeneas' hundred messengers. Fittingly, the site is very Roman: the mention of the *fasces* (173), the *curia* for the senate (174), and the reference to the traditional meal the senators would have in the Capitoline temple after sacrifices to the triad of Jupiter, Juno, and Minerva on 13 September, the anniversary of the temple's dedication. There are cedar images of the great ancestors of Latinus, native gods of the Italian people: now we meet Italus and Sabinus, mere names, in a sense, but names invested with the future of Italians and Sabines. Janus is also here, the two-faced god, a deity who presides over the household (especially the *state* household, whose dwelling is this palace); he holds a special place in an Augustan poem, as we shall soon see, because of his presiding over the Gates of War. An extended description is given to Picus, who here has the "Quirinalian staff" and the *trabea* (7.188), a short (as opposed to a long toga) ceremonial robe; if Servius and his source (Suetonius) can be believed, there were different kinds of *trabea*, and the one for kings was purple with some white. The Quirinalian staff is a reference to a mysterious Sabine deity who was associated with Mars; when Romulus was suddenly taken up to heaven one day, he somehow became associated with Quirinus.[11] The story Virgil tells here (189-191) of Picus is that Circe struck him with her magic wand and, with a poison, turned him into a bird (the woodpecker)—the beautiful witch from Homer's *Odyssey* continues to haunt the early pages of the Virgilian *Iliad*, perhaps, if it is not too fanciful, because a major theme of the second half of the poem will be the shifting, changing Homeric roles of the main characters, Aeneas and Turnus. In any case, the frequent mention of Circe in the first scenes in Latium is made more significant by Virgil's own rejection of Latinus' Circaean parentage. Certainly the constant reminders about Circe invest the beginning scenes of Book 7 with a magical quality; the war in Italy is easy enough to predict given people like Amata and Turnus, but it will come only after the supernatural machinations of Juno and Allecto.

Latinus remembers the story of the Trojan ancestor Dardanus: at least in Virgil's version, he had been born in Italy and migrated to Phrygia. Latinus names him as a god; the early reception of the Trojans is already a true homecoming. Ilioneus, the spokesman for the Trojans from Book 1, tells Latinus that they have come to seek a paltry home (7.229 *sedem exiguam*). What is most ironic about Ilioneus' speech is the odd reference it is almost compelled to make about Dido's Carthage. Ilioneus reports that many people and nations have wanted the Trojans to join with them in an allied settlement; besides the friendly, related settlements in Buthrotum and Sicily, Ilioneus is mostly referring to North Africa (whether intentionally or not). There is a possible ambiguity, in fact, in Ilioneus' words to the court. He swears by the "fates of Aeneas" (234 *fata per Aeneae*) and his "powerful right hand" (*dextramque potentem*) that many nations have sought to accept the Trojans as allies:

> fata per Aeneae iuro dextramque potentem,
> sive fide seu quis bello est expertus et armis (7.234-235)
>
> *I swear by the fates of Aeneas and his powerful right hand,*
> *whether someone has experienced it in faith, in war, and in arms*

Armis is a brilliant allusion to a famous ambiguity in Dido's description of Aeneas to her sister Anna:

> quem sese ore ferens, quam forti pectore et armis! (4.11)
>
> *how he is carrying himself in his face, in his strong chest and arms!*

Dido could have been speaking of Aeneas' weapons, or of his physical arms; Ilioneus' words could have reference to the physical arms Dido experienced around her. Ilioneus would no doubt like very much to forget Dido; Virgil will let her recur much later, in an explicit reference at a moment of supreme emotional turmoil.

When Dido met Aeneas, if there were any sort of amatory stirring in her heart, it was imperceptible; Venus and Cupid had not yet worked their spells. Latinus, on the contrary, immediately thinks of Aeneas as the fulfillment of Faunus' oracle. Latinus sends envoys to bring Aeneas to his palace; he sends three hundred horses with them, decorated with gold and purple, the colors of royalty. For Aeneas himself, as a present, he selects a chariot and two horses that were from the breed Circe raised by mating some of her father's solar horses with a mortal mare.

Juno now appears again, for the first time since her instigation of the burning of the ships. Juno had been in Argos (one of her beloved cities, along with Carthage) and has winged her way to Sicily, where she spies on the Trojans with her farsighted vision from the promontory of Pachynus (almost as if she were hunting them). Juno's rhetorical soliloquy here is a companion to her speech in Book 1; she mentions both the Trojan War and the "fires" (7.296) the Trojans have survived; nothing has yet worked. Her speech is best summarized in its most famous line:

flectere si nequeo superos, Acheronta movebo. (7.312)

If I am not able to move the ones above, I shall rouse hell.

Juno freely admits (in contrast to her speech in Book 1) that she cannot prevent the Trojan settlement in Italy. The marriage of Aeneas and Lavinia cannot be prevented. But she can cause delay and destruction; we have thus far assumed she was working delays, but now, for the first time, she freely admits her ability and intention to wreak havoc on both Trojans and Latins (316). This father-in-law (Latinus) and son-in-law (Aeneas) evoke Caesar and Pompey; if the Trojans and Latins must be allies by fate, then Juno will make them suffer internecine strife and civil war. This, too, is the sense of Juno's terrible sort of praise of Allecto:

tu potes unanimos armare in proelia fratres
atque odiis versare domos (7.335-336)

You are able to arm brothers, though they be of one mind, for battles and to overturn houses with hatred

Juno, then, the marriage goddess, will oversee a second marriage in the poem (after the quasi-nuptials of Aeneas and Dido); she will see to it that Bellona, the war goddess, will be Lavinia's matron of honor (the marriage of Pompey to Caesar's daughter Julia failed to secure a lasting peace after Julia's untimely death). Juno's praise of Allecto for her skills in handling civil strife comes right after Anchises' appeal to Caesar and Pompey during Aeneas' Roman eschatology lesson: we know the appeal will fall on deaf ears. We had heard in Book 6 from the Sibyl that "another Achilles" was waiting for Aeneas in Latium; now we hear Juno call Aeneas "another Paris" (321)—the first foreshadowing in the poem that Aeneas will kill Turnus (just as Paris killed Achilles). Juno is, of course, no suitable source of objective information about Aeneas. But this Homeric correspondence is the first one Aeneas explicitly receives anywhere in the poem, and it comes after a similar equation has been made for Turnus at the beginning of the visions in Avernus. The notion that Venus is another Hecuba (320) who will bring forth slaughter for the Trojans might come as a shock to the laughter-loving goddess.

Juno's appeal for help to the Fury Allecto comes as a direct result of her sense of abandonment. She has no allies in heaven or on earth; therefore, odious as it may be, she will seek help from hell. In Book 1 she had the time and patience to seek help from Aeolus in a polite and mannered fashion; now in Book 7 Allecto is a living symbol of how darkened Juno's own heart has become after her overall failure (despite her major victory in helping to secure Carthage's eternal enmity for Rome). The underworld demon will be able to satisfy both of Juno's wishes, by delaying the foundation of the future city and causing the slaughter of both Trojans and Latins. And, unlike her encounter with Aeolus, Juno now sees no reason to offer presents to cajole and flatter: Allecto needs no encouragement to be set loose on the world.

As so often in the *Aeneid*, immortal beings accomplish that which is not terribly surprising to imagine (and they worsen the effects of that which they incite). Allecto's first target, understandably enough, is Amata, Latinus' wife. She has already been introduced as a partisan of Turnus, and an assault on her would wreck the royal household. Indeed, when she arrives in Amata's presence the queen is already angry and burning with rage:

femineae ardentem curaeque iraeque coquebant. (7.345)

A woman's anxieties and anger were cooking her as she burned.

Women have been angrier than men in the *Aeneid* so far (Juno, Dido, and now the introduction of Allecto and Juno's mention of Bellona);[12] Amata's cares and anger begin to burn her (*coquebant*) though she is already on fire (*ardentem*); tenses and (circumstantial) participle describe well the inceptive (and durative) nature of Allecto's assault. Just as Iris (in the disguise of Beroe) had thrown forth a firebrand to instigate the burning of the Trojan ships, so now Allecto throws a snake from her hair at Amata. Just as Juno's mood has worsened through the course of the poem, so now, at the beginning of her rage, Amata is still lucid. She tries to reason with her husband about the impending marriage; she wants no exile suitor for her daughter. She is afraid that Aeneas will repeat Paris' abduction of Helen and take Lavinia far from Italy (Juno's words are already working their way into Amata's heart via Allecto's serpent). Amata correctly points out that while the oracle of Faunus had demanded a foreign husband, so Turnus is as foreign as Aeneas; Turnus can trace his lineage back to Inachus and Acrisius, the progenitors of Argos. When we had first glimpsed Juno, she was returning from "Inachian Argos" (7.286); now the descriptive adjective acquires meaning. Juno is naturally inclined to favor Turnus because of his Argive blood, and now Turnus has another Achillean attribute: he has Greek blood.

Amata's rage reaches new heights (she is barely able to finish her words), and Virgil famously compares her to a spinning top (378-384).[13] Just as Iris had attacked the Trojan women, so Allecto's assault on Amata will impact the women of Latium. These same women will appear much later in the poem, during the cavalry battle in Book 11, where they will be inspired by the example of Camilla's death to defend their city. Amata rushes into the forest in some sort of Bacchic revelry.[14] Virgil is not precisely clear here. Amata has the "simulated divine power of Bacchus" (385 *simulato numine Bacchi*); she takes Lavinia with her and declares that her daughter is meant only for the god (like an Ariadne). Rumors circulate about the queen's action, and other women join the forest frenzy. Amata raises a burning torch of pine and sings a wedding song for Lavinia and Turnus (in her madness she shifts imperceptibly from marrying her daughter off to Bacchus to a more conventional union with Turnus). There are shades of the same fears and ghastly undertones we find in Euripides' *Bacchae*; Virgil sets the mood by saying first that Amata conceived a greater crime:

maius adorta nefas maioremque orsa furorem (7.386)

She conceived a greater, unspeakable thing and embarked on a greater madness

We are, perhaps, a bit surprised (disappointed?) when the "greater unspeakable thing" is, apparently, the taking of Lavinia into the woods and the celebration of mad, fake wedding rites now with Bacchus, now with Turnus. If we were not so convinced of Fate's immovable decrees, we should half expect Amata to slaughter Lavinia in the forest. Amata's "greater" actions echo the announcement of this book: *maius opus moveo*. Whatever troubles Aeneas faced in Books 1-6, especially 4, the second half of the poem will trump them.

Allecto's second visit is to Turnus, who is in his home city of Ardea.[15] Ardea was practically a ghost town in Virgil's day; it had once been a major port for Latium and was perhaps the base Camillus used when he set out to repel the Gallic invasion. Virgil's rare contemporary note (7.413 *sed fortuna fuit*), noting the tremendous decline of Ardea, is appropriate for a description of the capital of Aeneas' defeated foe.[16] Allecto's visit to Amata had been invisible; for Turnus she transforms herself into an aged priestess of Juno, Calybe. Her opening words are reasonable enough and calm; she makes mention of Turnus' having won Lavinia and her dowry by blood (7.423 *sanguine*), another of the several occurrences of the word in this book (13 times). The reference is obscure, and must mean some war on behalf of Latinus, though we had been told he has lived in peace for some time; it probably refers to Evander's Etruscans (7.426 *Tyrrhenas*), whom Allecto soon names as Turnus' first worthy target—Turnus will more than satisfy this first piece of hellish advice, when he kills Pallas. Allecto's order to burn the Phrygian ships is a nice touch; Juno wants those vessels destroyed.

Turnus' response to the disguised Fury shows his strength of character; he has not been affected in the least by Allecto's first approach. These are his first words in the poem, his first appearance; what a contrast from the first appearance of Aeneas in the storm of Book 1. Turnus knows the Trojans have arrived; he advises the old woman to worry about temple duties and let young men fight wars and manage peace (7.444 *bella . . . pacem*)—he is no mere warmonger. He is also somewhat prejudiced against listening to "Calybe" because she is old, feeble, and unattractive. Turnus will now see Allecto's true form. What exactly did Allecto look like before? Virgil is notoriously vague about appearances: despite often abundant and carefully chosen adjectives, it can be difficult to form a clear picture of his characters. Is it possible (or probable) that Allecto in her true appearance (despite the serpents!) is eternally young (in contrast to the old woman Turnus mocked), at least in *Virgil*'s conception of her? An (attractive) young woman with such horrific accoutrements might be far more terrifying than any withered hag. In any case, Allecto's rage (7.445 *exarsit in iras*) is linked both to Turnus' resistance of her and his mockery of her aged appearance, with which she taunts him (452-453) as she quotes his own words back at him in derision.[17]

Turnus had said he managed the affairs of both war and peace; Allecto declares that she manages war and death (7.455, another quite effective half-line). At the sight of the goddess in her true form, Turnus is frightened, indeed terrified; now he balances the terrified Aeneas on the deck of his flagship (1.92). He will wake up from this infernal dream in a cold sweat. Allecto had used a snake with Amata; now with Turnus she hurls a firebrand; the twin elements that symbolized the fall of Troy (the serpents of Laocoon and the pervasive fire that destroyed the city) have been reborn in Latium: Turnus the native Italian, with his *Greek* blood, will deal death to the Trojans as the agent of Allecto and Juno. Turnus is like Aeneas on the night Troy fell:

arma amens fremit, arma toro tectisque requirit. (7.460)

Mindless he seethes for arms, and he searches for arms on his couch
   and in his dwelling.

The madness has now settled on Turnus, and his emotional state is captured well in the first simile Virgil uses to describe him: the boiling cauldron of water. Aeneas had been first compared to Apollo in a moment of relaxed celebration (the hunt with Dido). Amata, after Allecto had goaded her, grabbed Lavinia and ran out into the woods; there a large number of Latin matrons also followed. Now

Turnus gathers the Rutulian youth around him. Allecto's presence may well have affected many in Ardea, but Virgil says the youth were moved by Turnus' handsome appearance (the second mention of this theme), his noble ancestry, and his glorious deeds (7.471-474). The Amata passage ended in madness; so does the Turnus episode, though a madness that is cloaked with martial courage (7.475 *audacibus animis*); the Rutulians are ready to dare courageous deeds of valor. The apparent contrast with Amata and her women in the woods with their simulated Bacchic rites is striking; the madness is one and of the same kind.

The madness will not come only to Italians. Allecto now moves to the Trojan side, where she will set into motion the killing of Silvia's poor stag, an episode that is almost certainly a Virgilian invention.[18]

Iulus is hunting; in Book 4, when his father had his fateful hunt with Dido, Iulus was also present (156-159). Aeneas had also been compared to an unknowing hunter/shepherd who wounded Dido, the innocent deer (68-73). Now, in parallel, the war between Trojans and Italians will start because of the shooting of another deer (this one all too real). Circumstances now are identical to Book 4. Just as two goddesses had involved themselves in Dido and Aeneas' romantic lives, so now Allecto will make sure that Iulus shoots just the right deer: Silvia's pet stag. Fordyce wonders why Virgil would give a "minor character" a name so invested in the origins of Rome (we have only recently heard of Silvius and Silvius Aeneas in the underworld vision). This is precisely the point; Silvia and her stag are symbolic of the peaceful, quiet life of the Golden Age in Italy under Saturn; the animal is wild, but he allows the rustic girl to comb his hair and wash him in a pure spring, and he returns home every night (even if sometimes a bit late—a touching detail). She adorns his head with soft garlands; he lets her pet him, and he submits to a life that straddles the wild forest and the domestic hearth. Iulus was out hunting with his dogs; it is not terribly difficult to believe that the young Trojan might shoot the deer. Allecto incites the hounds and drives them mad; we are not told that she does anything to Iulus:

> ipse etiam eximiae laudis succensus amore
> Ascanius curvo direxit spicula cornu;
> nec dextrae erranti deus afuit, actaque multo
> perque uterum sonitu perque ilia venit harundo. (7.496-499)
>
> *Ascanius also, set on fire by the love of exceeding praise,*
> *directed his shafts from his curved bow;*
> *nor was the god absent from his wandering right hand, and*
> *the point, driven with much sound, went through the womb and groin.*

Iulus' first appearance as a young man had been at Dido's hunt; later he appeared at the *lusus Troiae* in honor of his grandfather and had been the first to hasten to the shore where the Trojan women had set fire to the ships. Everything about him has been commendable, and typical of brave and daring youth. Later we shall see him eager to join in the fighting that erupts near the Trojan camp, but such a valuable living symbol of the succession cannot be risked. Here he has maddened dogs, but he too is afire with a flame of a different sort than Allecto's: he wants praise; he is in love with seeking the highest rewards for valor. Like his father with Dido, he means no harm and is unaware of the significance of what he is about to do. Some vague "god" is ready to help him; his right hand was a bit unsteady, perhaps (he is still very young)—Fordyce and others have taken *erranti* to be proleptic, in the sense of "the god was not absent so that his hand failed"—but the import of the sentence is that Iulus had help (though he was still out hunting in the first place!) The "god" is vaguely defined, probably Apollo, patron of archers (if Virgil had anyone in mind), and not Allecto. The deer is struck, mortally wounded; it makes its last homecoming to its stalls. Virgil heightens the pathos of the deer's death; it is like a supplicant (7.502) as it cries out, its groans filling the whole house. Given the succession motif, there is something deliciously satisfying and appropriate in Virgil's having *Ascanius* be responsible for the onset of war in Italy.

As with the Dido episode, the immortals have caused a disaster that is perfectly plausible; Latium suddenly has a large number of Trojans around, and they have been trampling through the forest with full hunting gear—a forest where an almost magical stag likes to rest and relax and drink from cool streams. Virgil highlights the contrast between Silvia and the farmers she cries out to for help; they are "hard" (504 *duros*) in contrast to this innocent Latin girl. Silvia cries out for help, but the rural Italians are already arriving, even without hearing her call (506 *improvisi*); Virgil says that the "savage pest" was hiding in the woods (505 *pestis enim tacitis aspera silvis*). This is Allecto, or at least her baneful influence; soon we see the Fury herself on a rooftop, where she gives the "shepherd's signal" (513 *pastorale . . . signum*) and sounds a loud note on a horn with her hellish voice. Everyone in the surrounding region hears Allecto's clarion of war: appropriately, it is heard in Diana's grove at Aricia, a reference to the conflation of Artemis (with her chthonic persona, Hecate) and the native Italian Diana (the war began in Diana's own province of forest hunting). It is heard by the Nar, a river that joins the Tiber some thirty miles north of Rome, and by the springs of Velinus (in the same vicinity). Allecto is everywhere; her influence was felt in the woods earlier when she was watching the whole drama unfold from some vaguely defined height (511 *speculis*), and then she appears on (presumably) Silvia's father's roof. Mothers hear the cry of the Fury; in the poet's context they are nervous (518 *trepidae*) because they fear for their husbands and children in a time of war. The Trojans are also summoned; they rush forth to aid Ascanius, who is the immediate target of any Latin violence (thus increasing the dramatic tenor, since he embodies the future of Rome). Aeneas is entirely absent from the war's commencement. Time is compressed (one of the Fury's main tasks is to syncopate events and bring them to their climax as quickly as possible): the rustic Italians had been grabbing whatever weapons were at hand, crude sticks and clubs; now the two sides are lined up for the first time in opposition, armed with swords and arrayed in bronze. The image Virgil uses is of a crop:

> ... atraque late
> horrescit strictis seges ensibus (7.525-526)

> ... *and broadly the*
> *black crop of drawn swords begins to shudder*

These Italians and Trojans will now interrupt the daily routine of farming and the raising of livestock to engage in warfare; the crop now is a row of swords, and the harvest will be the death that the Fury announced to Turnus was her occupation (455). In the first formal simile of the war, Virgil compares the two sides to the sea stirring under the wind; the storm of Book 1 that so devastated the Trojans and led to Carthage has now been replaced by a human storm of enormous proportions and long life, with no Neptune at the ready to quell it.

The simile of the storm at sea connects next to the first two named casualties of the war, who are named after Italian rivers: Almo (Silvia's oldest brother) and Galaesus. Almo is shot in the throat, and blood obstructs the "path of the wet voice" (7.533-534), a good example of transferred epithet and a moist extension of the water imagery that describes the war's first encounters. Galaesus is an older man who tries to reason with both sides; he evokes the anonymous man of the first simile (1.148-153) of the poem, which described Neptune's control of Juno's storm at sea: this "most just man" (7.536 *iustissimus*) will have no such success. The detail about his wealth in livestock and farmland is very much in Virgil's style, and, as usual, carries significance: these Latins and Trojans should be farming and raising animals instead of killing and dying. This same theme is revisited more explicitly after the Gates of War are thrown open: the ploughshare, sickle, and all rural labors come to a halt as Latium arms itself for martial strife.

The war's opening stages, we learn, were even for both sides (540 *aequo ... Marte*); Allecto goes to Juno and announces that the first deaths have deliberately been Latin, so that the Trojans can now have no hope for an alliance with Latinus, since they are "sprinkled with Ausonian blood" (547). Allecto is willing to go further: she wants to stir up the "neighboring cities" (549 *finitimas ... urbes*) so that they will come to join in the slaughter. For once in the poem, Juno is restrained. Her words are interesting:

> ... terrorum et fraudis abunde est:
> stant belli causae, pugnatur comminus armis,
> quae fors prima dedit sanguis novus imbuit arma. (7.552-554)

> ... *there is an abundance of terror and fraud.*
> *The causes of the war now stand, there is close fighting with arms,*
> *and new blood stains the first arms that chance gave.*

What exactly does Juno mean by "new blood has stained the arms that the first chance gave"? *Prima* could be taken either with *fors* or *arma* ("new blood has stained the first arms that chance gave" or "the first chance"); the difference is negligible, though it flows more naturally to take *prima* with *arma*. The "new blood" refers to the recent deaths that have set the war on its course. But what are we to make of the "arms" that have been given by "chance" or "fortune"? Juno's actions with Allecto have been anything but deeds of chance. No, Juno's words hearken back to Allecto's. The Fury had wanted to "scatter arms through the fields" (551 *spargam arma per agros*). Juno has forbidden any expansion of the war; the *first* arms that Fortune gave will be sufficient for Juno's purpose. Juno realizes that rage like Allecto's can quickly burn out of control; she has more limited objectives (and there is the danger that any quick and dramatic expansion of the war might arouse Jupiter's notice; this will happen much later in a different context). Indeed, Juno warns Allecto that Jupiter will not allow the Fury to roam freely in the upper air; her work for Juno has brought no reward (unlike Aeolus' work in Book 1)—one gets the impression that Allecto was almost seeking some sort of Olympian rehabilitation for helping heaven's queen. Allecto's rage, quick to spiral out of control, also serves to put Juno's quite specific rage in perspective. Juno declares that if there is any remaining "fortune of labors" (559 *fortuna laborum*), she herself will handle it; in other words, she will manage whatever ensues that can be decided by chance. Allecto departs in silence and goes to one of the jaws of Acheron, near the sulfurous lake Amsanctus (part of the Vesuvian chain)—a last nod to the underworld spirit of Book 6, in Virgil's usual style of seeking close connections between his disparate neighboring books.

Juno had told Allecto that she herself would manage whatever fortune of labors remained. We are given a glimpse of the first news of war in Latinus' palace; Turnus is present, as are men who carry in Almo and Galaesus' dead bodies. The Latins demand that Latinus declare war on the Trojans; he is as immovable as a huge rock at sea (a continuation of the ongoing water and ocean imagery that has marked the start of the war). "We are borne off by the storm" (7.594 *ferimurque procella*), Latinus finally exclaims; he will not assent to the war, but he cannot prevent it. This passage in Latinus' palace opens with Juno's hand at work:

nec minus interea extremam Saturnia bello
imponit regina manum. (7.572-573)

*Meanwhile not less did the Saturnian queen
put her final hand on the war.*

Immediately thereafter, as the Latins assemble at their king's court and demand his assent to war, nothing seems to be due to Juno's personal intervention; everything happens as we might naturally expect. After Latinus is buffeted by the cries of his people and his powerful "foreign" neighbor Turnus, we again hear more of Juno's work:

verum ubi nulla datur caecum exsuperare potestas

consilium, et saevae nutu Iunonis eunt res,
multa deos aurasque pater testatus inanis:
"frangimur heu! fatis" (7.591-594)

And in truth, when no power is given to overcome the blind
plan, and things are proceeding according to the nod of savage Juno,
the father again and again called the gods to witness and the empty breezes:
"We are broken, alas, by the fates"

Latinus, it seems, has lost his power of persuasion and reasoning; Juno is, perhaps, the proximate cause. He has no ability to persuade (or even command) the assembly; he is the opposite of Neptune with the winds in Book 1. He calls on the gods to witness that he has been broken by "fate" (*fatis*)—just as Virgil himself had first noted that the Italians in Latinus' palace were calling for a war that was "opposed to the fates of the gods" (584 *contra fata deum*). The "fate" for Lavinia is to marry Aeneas—but it is also her destiny to be the innocent cause of so many deaths before her ultimate fate can be accomplished. Juno represents both that intermediary fate and the voice of resistance to the final state of affairs. As we have observed, Juno's surrender to that final fate will not be without cost to Aeneas, his mother Venus, and his Trojans. The breezes Latinus calls on as witnesses are "empty" (593 *inanis*): they do not carry his prayers to the gods; there is a hint, too, of the recurring theme of Books 6 and 7: the gods do not answer our prayers, perhaps because they are not there, or at least they do not care about our travails—once again, a Lucretian sentiment.

Turnus will be a sacrifice, Latinus predicts—and at the end of the poem Aeneas will say that Pallas is immolating (12.949 *immolat*) the prostrate Turnus. Turnus will pay the penalty for his war and will venerate the gods with a late offering—himself. Latinus hereby foretells that the war will be long and, in the end, fatal for Turnus. Turnus had mocked Allecto when she appeared as the aged Calybe; now Latinus notes that it will be the young (typified by Turnus) who will suffer; he himself is too old to be robbed of anything but a happy death (7.598-599).

We now arrive at the most dramatic reversal of fortune between the parallel Books 1 and 7: the opening of the Gates of War, the closing of which Jupiter had predicted so long ago (1.293-296). Their opening here hearkens back to the blissful prediction of their closing in Book 1. Virgil lavishly describes the use of the *Belli portae* with anachronism: the wars that are outlined (against the Hyrcanians of the Caspian Sea, the Arabs, the Indians, and especially the Parthians) are part of the conceit of the Augustan Age. Augustus would boast in his *Res Gestae* that he had shut the gates three times (the first time after Actium). They had been open continuously from 235 B.C. and the time of the Punic Wars; a major element of Augustan propaganda was that he had fulfilled the same promise of peace Virgil has Jupiter make to his daughter Venus in Book 1 of the *Aeneid*. It is unclear whether the gates were temple doors (likelier?) or an arched gateway in the Forum; nothing remains of any possible candidate structure.

Latinus is called upon here to open the gates, and his refusal can be seen as an admirable rejection of what Virgil calls the "disgusting duties" (7.619 *foeda ministeria*) of war. Latinus has a "senate" (cf. 7.174 and 611); Virgil continues his anachronistic description of the gates of Janus by describing how the consul, ritually dressed with his toga in an old-fashioned style (612), would open the doors. Latinus' rule is monarchical, and so here he takes the role of the consul who executes senatorial decrees; his refusal to participate may be admirable, but it can also be criticized. There is an alleged inconsistency in Latinus being ordered (7.617 *iubebatur*) to open the war gates (presumably by his "senators"): he had taken no vote or sought no counsel when he announced the marriage of Lavinia to Aeneas. This "inconsistency" is precisely Virgil's point; one reason the Latins are so easily roused is that many of them agree with Turnus' argument, regardless of Allecto/Juno's influence. Juno had probably prevented Latinus from saying much in protest before; now she will brook no trouble or delay as she herself flings open the portentous gates (and surely the assembled Ausonians took strength and courage from the clearly divine opening of the doors). Juno's assumption of Latinus' duties gives the Latin war far more approbation than any consent of the king.

Five towns seem to be the center of the military preparations in central Italy: Turnus' own Ardea, as well as Atina, Tibur, Crustumerium, and Antemnae. In Dido's Carthage, the work of city life came nearly to a halt because of a love affair; the greatest danger during the sojourn with Dido was that of delay (until, of course, Aeneas finally prepared to leave her and had to face the risk of a violent attack on his fleet, which would have ironically paralleled the Carthaginian reception of his beleaguered companions). Now the cities put aside all work of the fields and begin to forge and sharpen weapons. The mention of the five towns leads to the great catalogue of Italian warriors.[19] Virgil's "Gathering of the Clans" comes as a counterpart of sorts to his procession of underworld souls at the end of Book 6, and will likewise be related to the images on Aeneas' shield at the end of Book 8. The two visions of Rome's future surround the living future of Roman Italy. Since we learn much later, in Book 12, that the "losing" side, Italy, will have the real influence over the future city (not the victorious—though dead—Troy), this procession of heroes *in part* celebrates some of Rome's ancient Italian forebears.

The catalogue of heroes comes early in Virgil's *Iliad*, in imitation of Homer's great Catalogue of Ships in the second book of his epic of war: Virgil now powerfully declares his correspondence between these Italians and the Greeks who once sailed to Troy. The "second proem" to Book 7 (641-646) invokes the Muses in almost the same language as Homer. The catalogue is artfully arranged, and much briefer than Homer's; everything comes in alphabetical order with the exception of Mezentius and his son Lausus at the beginning, Turnus and Camilla at the end, and Messapus a little before the midpoint.[20] All of these figures will play significant roles in the fighting with the exception of Messapus (who is still more important in the narrative than the other "alphabetical" heroes). The catalogue begins and ends with someone whose family was exiled.

Mezentius had been an Etruscan monarch, but, as we shall learn in Book 8, he had been driven out for his savage cruelties and had settled among Turnus' Rutulians. His son Lausus (whom Virgil describes as exceptionally handsome, second best in looks after Turnus), has a thousand men with him from Agyllina in Etruria.[21] Camilla is leading Volscians; we learn later that her father had also been exiled. Somehow, both of these young people have managed to lead significant contingents from the very lands that had expelled their fathers. Both Camilla and Lausus are linked to horses and wild animals.

Mezentius, the *contemptor divum* (7.648), appears in the tradition outside Virgil; he appeared in the (fragmentary) *Origines* of Cato the Censor (234-149 B.C.), where he is killed not by Aeneas but by Ascanius.[22] Virgil presents him wholly unsympathetically, except insofar as his son (worthy of a better father, as Virgil notes) is lovingly attached to him to the death. Mezentius is an Etruscan refugee; in Virgil's conception, the Etruscans are divided, with some supporting Aeneas (as we shall see in Book 8), and others joining Turnus. In Cato, and Dionysius of Halicarnassus, the story is different: some versions have the Etruscans coming to help the Latins after Turnus dies. The thousand Etruscan men with Lausus is not a remnant of some earlier legend, but part of the divided nature of Etruria in the *Aeneid*; Messapus' contingent below is likewise representative of the sometimes vague borders between Latin and Etruscan territory to the north of Rome. We shall learn the reasons for Mezentius' expulsion from Etruria in Book 8, when Aeneas visits Caere and the very people who drove him out (8.478-495). He is the most despicable and unlikable character in the poem, but his son Lausus' devotion to him thus serves all the more to underscore the importance of the paternal-filial relationship in the *Aeneid*.[23] Lausus has a thousand Etruscans with him; Aeneas will later assign a thousand men to accompany Pallas' dead body home to his father Evander (11.60-61): even such small and seemingly insignificant details and linkages are often a concern to Virgil.

Aventinus, the first "alphabetical" hero, is the quintessential native defender of his land, whose very name (one of Rome's hills) and parentage (his mother was the priestess Rhea, that is, Rhea Silvia, sometimes known as Ilia, the mother of Romulus and Remus) evoke the ancient Italian world. In other sources he was the grandfather of Rhea; in either case he is a blood relative of Rome's founder. His father is Hercules, fresh from Spain and the labor of capturing the cattle of Geryon; he has a shield decorated with snakes (Hercules strangled Junonian snakes in his crib) and the Hydra. The mention of Hercules here foreshadows the great Hercules and Cacus miniature epic in Book 8. The mythological spirit evoked by Hercules is continued in the mention of Coras and Catillus from Tibur (7.670-677), who come with their people as if they were cloud-born Centaurs racing down from a snowy mountain and crashing through the forests (Virgil is sensitive to the virgin, untouched quality of the land around Latium; the war eventually leads to deforestation of the worst sort, as trees are turned into funeral pyres). Aventinus had a lion-skin (like his Herculean parent); the followers of Caeculus, the founder of Praeneste (the modern Palestrina) are in wolf-skin caps. These first depictions of the native Italians emphasize the rustic, wild nature of their appearance; they are fiercely independent, self-sufficient outdoorsmen. Praeneste is about thirty-seven kilometers east of Rome, and was traditionally founded by a son of Vulcan.

Messapus is said to be Neptune's offspring (only in Virgil, but our extant sources are not exactly extensive) and to be invulnerable to fire and the sword.[24] In Virgil's catalogue he leads north Latins/south Etrurians; traditionally he was the founder of Messapia in the Italian heel. We are now some distance north of Rome, in the area of Mount Soracte (which will be important later in the war). Virgil compares his contingent of Faliscans and other Etrusco-Latins to swans singing beautifully as they return from their feeding; he also compares the armored contingent of Messapus' men to a loud flock of birds—not necessarily mutually exclusive images, but the half-line at 702 (not terribly effective) and the multiplication of bird similes probably indicates a passage Virgil had not finally revised—though it should be noted that Homer (*Iliad* 2.459 ff.) also multiplies similes (albeit not all avian) at the outset of his catalogue, and Virgil may well have been trying to evoke the same effect here. This would also explain the simile's apparent lack of particular relevance to Messapus and his men. Ennius famously claimed that he was a descendant of Messapus.[25]

Clausus leads Sabine cohorts, and his men introduce the most specific geographical designations thus far in the catalogue, as befits the ancient and close associations between Romans and the Sabine inhabitants of modern Umbria and the Abruzzi, as well as part of Lazio: *Sabina* is still the name of the region of Lazio around Rieti. Virgil beautifully evokes areas familiar to any member of his audience; the poignancy of the catalogue is that from the viewpoint of one of Virgil's contemporaries, the war in Italy is already dangerously civil, especially the more intensely one might believe in the ideal of a united Italy. Clausus is credited as the eponymous founder of the *gens Claudia*. Virgil's mention of the "ancient Quirites" (7.710 *priscique Quirites*) is based on the (false) etymology that connected the Quirites with Curenses, that is, the inhabitants of Cures, a Sabine town. One of the Sabine towns noted in this passage by Virgil is Nomentum (712); the commentators note critically that in Book 6 (773) this city's foundation was predicted in the underworld. But Virgil's catalogue is redolent with the spirit of a strangely anachronistic Italy: some of the places in it were mere names, indeed ghost towns (like Turnus' own Ardea) when the *Aeneid* was composed, but all were probably names known to Aeneas' audience and full of native Italian patriotism—not to mention the occasional bad memory of conflict and war, especially civil (some of the locations are otherwise unknown to us, and certainly reveal Virgil's antiquarian interests; probably all were at least somewhat familiar to his contemporaries). Virgil's comparison of the many Sabine warriors to the waves of the sea (7.718-719) continues the storm/water imagery of the passage (Romans were notoriously timid sailors!); the comparison to the many ears of standing corn foreshadows Camilla's hyperbolic ability to speed over crops without touching them.

Halaesus is next, an "Agamemnonian" foe for Aeneas; he and the next hero, Oebalus (now moving more quickly through the alphabet) represent the Campanian contingents; they have strange weapons (we are not entirely sure what the *aclys* and the *cateia* are—the first is apparently some kind of club, and the second possibly some sort of boomerang). Some of Oebalus' men have tree bark head coverings along with bronze weapons and shields, a mixture of almost primitive native gear with "Bronze Age" weaponry.

After Halaesus comes Ufens, leading a contingent of hunters who delight in spoils. The *Ufens* was a river in Volscian territory; the location of the river, and the details about hunting and spoils, all presage Camilla's dramatic appearance at the end of this book and at great length in Book 11. This is, as we have seen, Virgil's preferred style for introducing even seemingly secondary characters; Palinurus and Misenus were similarly foreshadowed long before they became important in the narrative. Ufens' warriors from Aequicula (7.747 *Aequicula*) were (even historically) disinclined to live in towns; Camilla has the same aversion to urban life, though she somehow still manages to have led her former countrymen successfully into war.

The strange priest Umbro now arrives; his appearance after the Camilla-like Ufens and his Aequiculi also neatly foreshadows the roles not one but two priests will play in Camilla's drama: Arruns and Chloreus are both devotees of their respective gods.[26] Ufens is a snake charmer and magician of sorts; he is also the only character in the catalogue that is explicitly marked out to die with the tricolon of pathetic fallacy Virgil uses to end his vignette so hauntingly:

te nemus Angitiae, vitrea te Fucinus unda,
te liquidi flevere lacus. (7.759-760)

The grove of Angitia has wept for you, and Fucinus with his glassy wave, and the liquid lakes.

Virbius' presence in Virgil's catalogue is exceedingly strange. The traditional story is "canonically" told in Euripides' *Hippolytus*.[27] It is most likely that Callimachus told the "sequel" to the story: Artemis actually saw to Hippolytus' resurrection (thanks to Asclepius, her brother's son); he was transported to her famous grove at Aricia and safeguarded there. The grove had a prohibition on horses; this makes perfect sense given the equine nature of Hippolytus' grisly death (mangled as he was in a smashed chariot by his own runaway horses after a sea monster sent by Poseidon had frightened them). Virgil's Virbius is (somehow) the son of the notoriously celibate Hippolytus (and, as Servius also notes, the son has the same name as the rejuvenated father). "Virbius" is, appropriately enough, the "Twice Man" (*vir bis*). If the prohibition on horses was a feature of the Diana cult at Aricia that Virgil wanted his audience to remember, then here too there is a foreshadowing of Camilla's fate: she will die during a cavalry encounter, and is closely linked to horsemanship. The cult of Diana would eventually be moved from Aricia to the Aventine in Rome (possibly the reason for

Virgil's opening the catalogue with its eponymous hero); the nymph Egeria (7.775), who is here the custodian of Hippolytus reborn, would also be venerated on the Aventine along with Diana. Virbius is like Camilla: he should perhaps have stayed in quiet anonymity in the forest; instead he is driving on his horses (prohibited in Diana's grove) to war in a subtle abandonment of a life as a favorite of Diana in her grove. In a catalogue as small as Virgil's, it is extraordinary (and not often enough appreciated) that the poet devotes such attention near the end of the catalogue to characters who presage Camilla, with whom he chose to end the procession: she will receive its most honored place, and, in a sense, represent another (this time foreshadowed) death at the end of a book, though Virgil gives no indication in Book 7 that she is doomed.

Turnus is the penultimate figure in this assembly of native Italian heroes. He stands above them all with his Chimaera-crested helmet—a terrible perversion of the harmless "Chimaera" that had sailed in the boat race in Sicily.[28] The Chimaera was a fearsome beast of mythology, but Bellerophon had vanquished it; the choice of monster points to Turnus' ultimate loss. Io and her father, the river god Inachus, adorn Turnus' shield; they are a memorial to the glories of Argos, Turnus' ancestral city and one of Juno's favorite haunts. Turnus' soldiers represent (appropriately enough for the leader of the whole Italian force) several regions in central Italy: the Argive youth are Turnus' own men from Ardea (though their title, *Argivaque pubes*, reminds us that Aeneas is once again fighting Greeks). Circe's ridge is mentioned again (7.799), a final nod to the Odyssean sorceress who has in some ways presided quietly over this book (including the transformation from peace to war). The River Ufens identifies some of Turnus' men as Volscians, which leads naturally to the beautiful heroine who leads their main contingent. There is also a connection between Io, who lost her voice and humanity when she was transformed into a heifer, and Circe, who transformed Odysseus' men into swine. The actions of Juno and Allecto have transformed all of these native Italians into raging warriors, hungry for blood (cf. 7.787-788, of Turnus' Chimaera acting all the more ferociously as the blood starts to flow on the battlefield). The Chimaera is magical (and we shall never hear of it again); it is envisioned in this brief description as practically living—and indeed it is the embodiment of Allecto's firebrand. The Chimaera is a symbol of those mythological beasts that must be destroyed as part of the arrival of a system of reason, rationality, and order; Aeneas will vanquish the ancient monster (though not without consequences for himself).

Quietly, with an affection that he makes no effort to conceal, Virgil now ends his first war book with the heroine Camilla.[29] She has aroused the fascination of many of Virgil's commentators and even imitators; the medieval French *Roman d'Enéas* expands her presence in the story lavishly, and Boccaccio thought her silence was an appropriate model for young Renaissance Italian women. Strangely, no Roman poet mentions her after Virgil (though both Ovid and Silius were inspired by her), and we have no proof of her existence before the *Aeneid*. The majority of critics thus assume she is a Virgilian invention, though the silence of surviving sources makes a weak foundation for an argument. Virgil leaves us here, at the end of Book 7, with a description that will perhaps stay in our memory: Camilla will not be mentioned again until well into Book 11. Camilla comes last here because in Book 11 her *aristeia* will mark the final major combat before Turnus must face Aeneas: the cavalry battle with Camilla's Volscian forces and Turnus' planned infantry ambush of Aeneas will mark the last best chance for the Italians to destroy the Trojans. Camilla's death will so dramatically wreck Turnus' self-control and emotional state that he will abandon his ambush and thereby lose his critical opportunity for victory. Camilla comes last here because her death (which will be marked by the same line as Turnus') will foreshadow his and point the way to his inevitable destruction. Besides these plot considerations, Virgil has a genuine affection for this alluring, enigmatic girl; he does not need to justify his privileged treatment of her:

> Hos super advenit Volsca de gente Camilla,
> agmen agens equitum et florentis aere catervas,
> bellatrix, non illa colo calathisve Minervae
> femineas adsueta manus, sed proelia virgo
> dura pati cursuque pedum praevertere ventos.
> illa vel intactae segetis per summa volaret
> gramina nec teneras cursu laesisset aristas,
> vel mare per medium fluctu suspensa tumenti
> ferret iter celeris nec tingueret aequore plantas.
> illam omnis tectis agrisque effusa iuventus
> turbaque miratur matrum et prospectat euntem,
> attonitis inhians animis ut regius ostro
> velet honos levis umeros, ut fibula crinem
> auro internectat, Lyciam ut gerat ipsa pharetram
> et pastoralem praefixa cuspide myrtum. (7.803-817)

> *Beyond these there came Camilla from the Volscian clan,*
> *leading on a line of cavalry and crowds flowering in bronze,*
> *truly a warrior. She had not accustomed her woman's hands*
> *to the distaff or the baskets of Minerva, but rather, as a virgin, she*
> *endured harsh battles and surpassed the winds in the running*
>   *of her feet.*
> *She could fly over the highest grasses of the crop and*
>   *leave it untouched,*
> *nor did she harm the tender corn stalks in her course,*
> *or she could make her way through the middle of the sea, suspended*
> *on the swelling wave, and not dip her swift feet in the water.*
> *All the youth poured forth from their dwellings and the fields,*
> *and the crowd of mothers marveled at her and gazed at her*
>   *as she passed,*
> *gasping with their spirits aroused at how a pin was binding*
> *her hair with gold, at how she was carrying a Lycian quiver*
> *and a shepherd's myrtle tipped with sharp metal.*

Fraenkel declined any extensive comment on the passage in his article on the structure of the book; instead, he quoted the lines and let Virgil speak for himself.[30] Like Penthesilea, Camilla is the last picture in the Italian catalogue (and, like Penthesilea, she will come late, and in vain, to help a beleaguered city).[31] Virgil has borrowed a story from cyclic epic (Arctinus' lost *Aethiopis*) and inserted it into his *Iliad* in a prominent place (Book 11); the catalogue offers a brief introduction to his heroine, though in the (significant) last place. Penthesilea was a Trojan ally (fighting on the "right side," then, from Aeneas' point of view); Camilla's *Italian* ethnicity highlights the civil nature of this war: she fights against Aeneas, but she is on the new "right" side. There will be some interesting differences between her introduction here and the developed story later in the epic (not to say "inconsistencies"); here Virgil's depiction is more or less clear and straightforward. Camilla is not inclined to the pursuits of Minerva (weaving and spinning), but Minerva is also known as a war goddess, and Virgil, as we shall see especially in Book 11, never denies Camilla's gender (7.806 *femineas*), even when she eschews stereotypical female pursuits (as here). Crowds of mothers and of youths come out to see her, and they are agape; she is the only figure who merits an explicit crowd reaction in Virgil's procession. In this she is reminiscent of Marcellus, the only figure in the procession of souls who elicited comment from Aeneas. The same women who see her now will see her again when she dies, and her example will spur them on to daring acts of patriotism. Quintus of Smyrna was most probably influenced by Virgil's Camilla in his depiction of Penthesilea in Book 1 of the *Posthomerica*; she too is a source of wonder as she enters Troy (Quintus greatly expands Virgil's succinct description).[32] Virgil emphasizes Camilla's tremendous speed; Ovid would borrow the same image for his Atalanta (cf. *Metamorphoses* 10.654-655), who is, in fact, modeled point by point after Virgil's Camilla. The myrtle with its metal tip might seem strange as a weapon for Camilla (the myrtle, too, is sacred to Venus), but elsewhere Virgil notes that the myrtle is suitable for spears (*Georgics* 2.447). That the myrtle is "pastoral" fits the general context of Virgil's catalogue; he has consistently emphasized the rustic, rural qualities of his Italians: they have quickly assembled for battle, leaving behind their farms (and, in this case especially) forest lives. The weapon Camilla carries is a symbol of her crossover from peace to war (though we find out later she was certainly not a shepherd in her old life). Minerva is a goddess with conflicting spheres of influence (spinning, warfare); Camilla is also in conflict, as we shall later learn (hunting, war / private, public). Virgil's first hint of Camilla's multifaceted character is his seemingly odd comparison of the young heroine to Minerva: Camilla is, and yet is not, similar to the weaving warrior goddess. Virgil says that Camilla was accustomed not to weave, but to "endure tough battles" and to surpass the winds with her speed. This is a reference not to war but to hunting, as we shall later learn more explicitly (thus there really is no inconsistency with Diana's news later that this is Camilla's first battle experience). The character is already being sketched thoroughly: Camilla will conflate hunting and warfare, with fatal consequences. There is no mention as yet of Camilla's devotion to

Diana; she appears, however, after Hippolytus' son Virbius: Diana was able and willing to save Hippolytus and give him new life, but for Camilla she will only guarantee vengeance on her killer and an honorable burial.

The name of this heroine has occasioned comment. There is a common noun, *camilla*, which occurs (very rarely) in Latin literature with the meaning of female attendant or votary of the gods (this is what Camilla will be revealed to be in Book 11). It is likely that Virgil's contemporary audience would have thought of Marcus Furius Camillus, Rome's savior from the Gauls, who had appeared in the underworld (6.825). There are also possible connections between her name, her killer's, and some contemporary Romans, which we shall examine later.[33]

Aeneas is completely absent from most of Book 7. After he sends messengers to Latinus' court (152-155), he disappears from the action (unlike his near constant presence in Book 1). Throughout the war books, Turnus will be more consistently present in battle scenes; Aeneas alone dominates Book 8, which is a quiet interlude during the violence. As with the Trojans in the *Iliad*, whenever Aeneas (Achilles) is absent the Italians are at their best; when he is present, we shall see that events take an interesting course in comparison to Virgil's Homeric precedent. Camilla and Aeneas never meet (unlike Penthesilea and Achilles in the tradition of the epic cycle).

At the close of Book 1, our emotions were suspended. We might well have anticipated that there would be disaster afoot with the machinations of Venus and Cupid, but we were left waiting and in suspense, aware that Aeneas was about to tell a long and involved story about his past experiences from Troy to Carthage that would distract our attention for some time. The horrors of Troy were yesterday's sorrows, and there is a peculiar pleasure in recalling the disasters of the past from the vantage point of a safe present (*forsan et haec olim meminisse iuvabit*). At the close of Book 7, there is no calm respite (though in Book 8 the absent Aeneas will have a restful opportunity to learn more about his future). War has now erupted in Italy, and the next book will open with Aeneas in a state of anxiety, which will lead to another dream vision and set of instructions. As in Book 4, Juno has accomplished much, though she has had plenty of suitable material to use for her own devices. We are very far from the end, and we have met new characters that—especially from a contemporary Roman perspective—are evocative of the misty mythological "history" of early Italy. Some of them are vile and reprehensible (Mezentius), while others are beautiful and alluring (Camilla). The stage has been set for what will be Virgil's masterstroke: the ultimate triumph of the Italy we have just seen on parade.

Notes

1. For the history of the "Oxford Reds," of which the Austin and Williams Virgil commentaries were a famous part, see HENDERSON, *Oxford Reds: Classic Commentaries on Latin Classics*, London, 2006.
2. On Book 7 in general, see further FRAENKEL, "Some Aspects of the Structure of *Aeneid* VII," *Journal of Roman Studies* 35 (1945), pp. 1-14 (reprinted in Harrison, *op. cit.*, pp. 253-276); PUTNAM, "*Aeneid* VII and the *Aeneid*," *The American Journal of Philology* (91) 1970, pp. 408-430 (a useful supplement to *Poetry of the Aeneid*); and FREDERICKSMEYER, "Structural Perspectives in *Aeneid* VII," *The Classical Journal* 80.3 (1985), pp. 228-237. On Books 7-12 as a whole see the seminal article of ANDERSON, "Vergil's Second *Iliad*," *Transactions of the American Philological Association* 88 (1957), pp. 17-30 (reprinted in Harrison, *op. cit.*, pp. 239-252). Note also RECKFORD, "Latent Tragedy in *Aeneid* VII, 1-285," *The American Journal of Philology* 82 (1961), pp. 252-269. On the beginning of Book 7, BOAS, *Aeneas' Arrival in Latium*, Amsterdam, 1938, remains valuable.
3. As the second half of the poem begins, Aeneas' entire family is now dead except for the all-important Ascanius (and Book 6 has just ended with the prediction of Marcellus' death, to remind us of the frailty of even young lives, especially as the poet prepares for the war in Italy). See further JENKYNS, *op. cit.*, pp. 463-467.
4. On the invocation to Erato see further TOLL, "What's Love Got to Do With It? The Invocation to Erato and Patriotism in the *Aeneid*," *Quaderni Urbinati di Cultura Classica* 62 (1989), pp. 107-118.
5. The *Roman* has been translated into English (YUNCK, *Enéas: A Twelfth Century French Romance*, New York, 1974); the most convenient Old French edition (with modern French translation) is in the *Lettres Gothiques* series.
6. Significantly, Virgil will specify that Jupiter demanded Turnus' behavior; the poem does not provide a divine excuse for Aeneas'.
7. On this vast subject, useful *inter alios* is HOLLIS, "Hellenistic Colouring in Vergil's *Aeneid*," *Harvard Studies in Classical Philology* 94 (1992), pp. 269-282, even if Hollis' target material encompasses less well known byroads of Hellenistica. Foundational now is CLAUSEN, *Virgil's Aeneid and the Tradition of Hellenistic Poetry*, Berkeley-Los Angeles, 1987.
8. Aeneas, then, will not only fail to live up to his father's injunction to spare those subjected to him, but he will also regress to the Homeric model (however Achillean) of *Iliad* 22: the death of Hector. Virgil will have no scene like that between Achilles and Priam in *Iliad* 24; he leaves us with a picture of Aeneas in rage, stabbing Turnus.
9. See especially Fordyce on 7.63.
10. See ROSIVACH, "*Latinus' Genealogy and the Palace of Picus (Aeneid* VII, 45-9; 170-191)," *The Classical Quarterly* N.S. 30 (1980), pp. 140-152, and MOORTON, "The Genealogy of Latinus in Vergil's *Aeneid*," *Transactions of the American Philological Association* 118 (1988), pp. 253-259.
11. On the extraordinarily misty and complex history of Quirinus, see DUMEZIL, *Archaic Roman Religion* (Tr. Philip Krapp), Baltimore, 1996, Volume I, pp. 246-272; as he notes, for the Augustan poets, Quirinus is Romulus deified after death, *genitor Quirinus*, and almost nothing else.
12. On Bellona in the *Aeneid* see Bailey, *op. cit.*, pp. 115-116, and cf. 8.703, where she appears during the Battle of Actium on Aeneas' shield with Mars and Discord.

13. RABEL, "Vergil, Tops, and the Stoic View of Fate," *The Classical Journal* 77.1 (1981), pp. 27-32, makes an excellent case for how Amata (and, by extension, other characters in the *Aeneid*) are not mere pawns of fate. This understanding of the actions of the immortals in the poem is important; every reflection in the *Aeneid* on free will and causation must lead in the end to the last lines of the poem and whether or not Aeneas makes a free decision to kill Turnus.

14. For a sensitive and very worthwhile discussion of this Amata passage, see CLARK, "*Regina Bacchatur*: Sexual Roles and Politics in the *Aeneid*," *The New England Classical Newsletter and Journal* 21 (1993-1994), pp. 62-67.

15. Clausen, *op. cit.*, connects the introduction of the "bold Rutulian" (7.409 *audacis Rutuli*) with the Ciceronian meaning of *audaces*: "those hostile to the *boni*, the good, respectable citizens; those who would subvert the established order by violence." Elsewhere, on the importance of noting every detail in the poem, Clausen well remarks: "Virgil's Roman reader, unlike his modern, read aloud, read slowly, and had been trained from boyhood in the discipline of rhetoric." (p. 31).

16. On Ardea see TILLY, *Vergil's Latium*, Oxford, 1947, pp. 31-53.

17. For a study of how this scene underscores Turnus' arrogance, see FOSTER, "Three Passages in Virgil," *Symbolae Osloenses* 66 (1991), pp. 109-114.

18. On Silvia's deer see further VANCE, "Wildness and Domesticity in Virgil's *Aeneid*," *Arethusa* 14 (1981), pp. 127-138; STARR, "Silvia's Deer (Vergil, *Aeneid* 7.479-502): Game Parks and Roman Law," *The American Journal of Philology* 113 (1992), pp. 435-439; Jenkyns, *op. cit.*, pp. 506 ff.; and both PUTNAM, "Silvia's Stag and Virgilian Ekphrasis," *Materiali e Discussioni* 34 (1995), pp. 107-133, and *Virgil's Epic Designs: Ekphrasis in the Aeneid*, New Haven, 1998, pp. 98-117.

19. The classic work is FOWLER, *Virgil's Gathering of the Clans*, Oxford, 1918. See also WILLIAMS, "The Structure and Function of Virgil's Catalogue in *Aeneid* 7," *The Classical Quarterly* N.S. 11.2 (1961), pp. 146-153; and SAYLOR, "The Magnificent Fifteen: Vergil's Catalogues of the Latin and Etruscan Forces," *Classical Philology* 69 (1974), pp. 249-257. Williams says little on Camilla, but he is right that her name evokes the Camilli of Roman history. Saylor focuses on Virgil's criticism of the "individualism" of Turnus (and Camilla). But the Volscian heroine will die with her mind on the victory of her side, not any personal wishes or reflections.

20. See further O'HARA, "Messapus, Cycnus, and the Alphabetical Order of Vergil's Catalogue of Italian Heroes," *Phoenix* 43 (1989), pp. 35-38.

21. Virgil's detail about Turnus' exceedingly handsome appearance evokes Homer's Paris—another of the confusions of heroic models in which Virgil delights.

22. Note Ogilvie on Livy *Ab Urbe Condita* 1.2.1 (p. 41) and p. 268.

23. The standard work is still LEE, *Fathers and Sons in Vergil's Aeneid: Tum Genitor Natum*, Albany, 1980 (though many of its conclusions are to be criticized).

24. 7.692 *quem neque fas igni cuiquam nec sternere ferro*. The detail is mysterious; Virgil does not record Messapus' fate. Figures like Messapus, who essentially cheat death, are common in world literature, often with an ironic end coming after they attempt to escape some preordained manner of dying. See further Hollis on Ovid's Meleager (*Metamorphoses* 8.445 ff.): "a magic life-token is a common element of folk-tale."

25. See Skutsch on Ennius *Annales* 524, Hardie on *Aeneid* 9.27-8, and Harrison on 10.353-354.

26. We shall address the "Arruns as priest" controversy in our analysis of Book 11. For Umbro, see PUTNAM, "Umbro, Nereus, and Love's Threnody," *Vergilius* 38 (1992), pp. 12-23.

27. For the background of the legend before Euripides, see the introduction to Barrett's Oxford edition of the play.

28. See further SMALL, "The Arms of Turnus: *Aeneid* 7.783-792," *Transactions of the American Philological Association* (90) 1959, pp. 243-252; WILLIAMS, "Turnus, the Chimaera, and Aeëtes: A Note on *Aeneid* 7.785-788," *Vergilius* 39 (1993), pp. 31-38; and GALE, "The Shield of Turnus (*Aeneid* 7.783-792)," *Greece and Rome* 44 (1997), pp. 176-196.

29. For Camilla see KOVES-ZULAUF, "Camilla," *Gymnasium* 85 (1978), pp. 182-205 and 408-436; BASSON, "Virgil's Camilla: A Paradoxical Character," *Classical Antiquity* 29 (1986), pp. 57-68; HORSFALL, "Camilla, o i limiti dell'invenzione," *Athenaeum* 66 (1988), pp. 31-51; LA PENNA, "Gli archetipi epici di Camilla," *Maia* 40 (1988), pp. 228-250; CAPDEVILLE, "La jeunesse de Camille," in MOREAU, ed., *L'initiation. Tome I: Les rites d'adolescence et les mysterès; Tome II: L'acquisition d'un savoir ou d'un pouvoir. Le lieu initiatique. Parodies et perspectives*, Montpellier, 1992; TORRAU, "Camila a virgem guerreira," *Humanitas* 45 (1993), pp. 113-136; my forthcoming *Athenaeum* article "Virgil's Camilla" (2007); BRILL, *Die Gestalt der Camilla bei Vergil*, (Dissertation) Heidelberg, 1972; and ARRIGONI, *Camilla: Amazzone e Sacerdotessa di Diana*, Milan, 1982. On Camilla's afterlife in literature and beyond, see FRATANTUONO, "*Posse Putes*: Virgil's Camilla and Ovid's Atalanta," *Collection Latomus: Studies in Latin Literature and History* XII (2005), pp. 185-193, and especially (*Idem*), "*Ut Videre Camillam*: The *Nachleben of Reckless Heroism*," *Rivista di Cultura Classica e Medioevale* 48.2 (2006). On Atalanta, whose complex mythology holds clues to Virgil's depiction of Camilla, see GANTZ, *Early Greek Myth: A Guide to Literary and Artistic Sources*, Baltimore, 1993, pp. 182, 331-332, and 335-339. Ovid plays with the idea that there may well have been two Atalantas (cf. the probable two Harpalyces), manipulating the confused traditions for his purpose, which is identical to Virgil's with Camilla: the depiction of the conflicted adolescent female. The same image can be found in the first elegy of Propertius' *Monobiblos*, where the poet addresses his lover as *Cynthia* and goes on to describe his difficult relationship with her (including allusions to Atalanta's mythology). The point for Propertius is that "Cynthia" (i.e., Diana, from her association with Mount Cynthus) is an inauspicious name for a love interest; the virgin goddess of the hunt symbolizes his unattainable, even dangerous literary *objet d'amour*. Surprisingly, the commentators have largely been asleep on this point (and its relation to the identical trick Tibullus plays with the name of his girlfriend, *Delia*, from Diana's birthplace on Delos).

30. "Rather than spoil a masterpiece in a vain attempt to paraphrase it we prefer to listen quietly to the poet's own words and, while we do so, enjoy the perfect diminuendo in which the martial rhapsody passes away and feel the intense sadness of so much grace and beauty doomed to death in battle." (Fraenkel, *op. cit.*, p. 271).

31. In imitation of Virgil's Camilla, Ovid places Atalanta last in the catalogue of hunters of the Calydonian boar (*Metamorphoses* 8.317-323). See further COURTNEY, "Vergil's Military Catalogues and Their Antecedents," *Vergilius* 34 (1988), pp. 3-8.

32. On Quintus of Smyrna and Virgil, see now GARTNER, *Quintus Smyrnaeus und der Aeneis. Zur Nachwirkung Vergils in der griechischen Literatur*, Munich, 2005.

33. For some different views on Camilla, see BOYD, "Virgil's Camilla and the Traditions of Catalogue and Ecphrasis (*Aeneid* 7.803-817)," *The American Journal of Philology* 113 (1992), pp. 213-234.

CHAPTER VIII

AS TURNUS RAISED

Book 8 of the *Aeneid* is the last in the second third of the poem, and, like Book 4, it is brief (731 lines, the second shortest in the poem). It has little in common with *il libro di Didone*, though in both books the overall thrust of the action is somewhat suspended and delayed: in Carthage it was due to Aeneas' affair with Dido, while in Latium it comes as Aeneas is told to seek the Greek allies we had first heard would assist his cause during the visit to the Sibyl at Cumae (6.96-97). During his trip to Evander's settlement, Aeneas will receive the gift of a divine shield (besides other armor and weapons), fashioned by Vulcan at the cajoling request of his wife Venus. The shield is another anachronistic device, very different from Homer's depiction of the shield of Achilles in *Iliad* 18; it allows for a reinforcement and expansion of the themes developed by Anchises in Elysium. Book 8, then, is the last stage of Aeneas' education; after this third of the poem is over, the mood of the epic will be dominated to the end by nothing but war. The shield, too, is a connection between this book and Book 7; there the Italians processed out to war, and at the end of this book the Trojan Aeneas will see his own procession, of events from Roman history. Book 6 revealed the personages of Roman glory; Book 8 will reveal the events. Book 8 also has affinities in spirit and tone with Book 5; both have extended passages of discursive calm. It has long been a favorite section of the Iliadic *Aeneid*, in part because it details Aeneas' visit to the future site of Rome, and in part because it is devoid of warfare. Book 4 was a tragedy in three acts that centered on Dido (cf. the threefold *At regina*); Book 8 shows the omnipresent, protective maternal power of Venus (8. 370 *At Venus*, 608 *At Venus*—not threefold and not marking major divisions in the book, but evoking the same spirit: Venus rules over this book, as Dido had Book 4). Like her son, Venus too has matured; her amatory games are now focused for a while on her lawful husband, and her sexuality wins Aeneas his divine arms. We are far from the manipulations of Eastern queens, and Juno is nowhere to be seen. In Books 1 and 4 she and Venus were on each other's tracks, sometimes even meeting and working together (with disastrous consequences both for Aeneas and Dido); in Books 7 and 8 they are separate. It is indeed "the most sunny and relaxed book of the *Aeneid*."[1] Book 8 was the first to receive a commentary (ed. Gransden, 1976) in the Cambridge Greek and Latin Classics series; Eden's Brill commentary and Fordyce's posthumous Oxford edition (1977) appeared with it in quick succession.[2]

The book opens with Turnus, whose image had dominated so much of Book 7. Latium is nervous (8.4-5 *trepido / tumultu*; cf. 7.638), but an oath is sworn to uphold the war on Aeneas' exile band, and the leaders of the campaign (Messapus, Ufens, and Mezentius) begin to draft soldiers from the fields (Virgil continues the image of rural depopulation and suspension of agricultural work). A message is sent to Diomedes, asking him for help (10 *petat auxilium*) and requesting analysis of what Aeneas might be expected to do; this mission will not be mentioned again until it returns (unsuccessfully) in Book 11.[3] The expedition to seek help from Diomedes is somewhat misconceived; the Latins do not offer prayers and consult oracles to learn from heaven about what they should do and what they should expect from Aeneas. Instead, they seek not only an alliance from their Greek neighbor in the far south, but also an analysis from him of what Aeneas intends by his first actions (15 *quid struat his coeptis*), and what outcome Aeneas might be eager to see (*quem . . . eventum pugnae cupiat*). These are questions better asked of a god; Diomedes can hardly supply useful information from his peaceful retirement home so far off in the south. It is known that Aeneas expects to marry Lavinia; part of the Latin mood of fear and trepidation is uncertainty over what such a union might mean: would central Italy become the home for a new Troy? When first we meet Aeneas in this book, he too is nervous and upset (like the Latins); once he falls asleep, the river god Tiber appears to him, and, after he wakes up, he performs due religious rites—the Latins are not so depicted. Of course, Aeneas—the child of destiny—need only fall asleep to receive a supernatural visitation.

Diomedes was an Argive, like Turnus; he had traditionally founded Argyripa (later Arpi) in Apulia after he had fled Greece in the mayhem after the Trojan War. Diomedes forged an alliance with King Daunus, the eponymous founder of the Daunians of northern Apulia (Turnus' father's name, we later learn, is also "Daunus").[4] Diomedes is an appropriate prospective ally for the Latins, both because of his Argive relation to Turnus and his relative proximity to the fighting. But, as we have noted already, he also nearly killed Aeneas during the Trojan War (*Iliad* 5.290-346). In the *Aeneid* he is another representative of the retired class of warriors; he has no interest in fighting Trojans, having already experienced how the gods favor Aeneas. The central god of the Augustan regime, Apollo, had saved Aeneas' life during Diomedes' *aristeia*; the Argive hero will not tempt fate again.[5]

Aeneas is in exactly the same state as when Mercury visited him with the news that he had to abandon Dido (cf. 8.20-21 and 4.285-286). The crisis of the fourth book of the *Aeneid* has been revisited; the war that had been so often predicted has come at last. As another correspondence between the past in Carthage and the present in Latium, Virgil compares Aeneas' troubled thoughts to the flickering light on a ceiling caused by the sun or moon as it strikes a bowl of water: the image is from Apollonius (*Argonautica* 3.755-759), where it describes Medea's state of nervous anticipation;[6] *Aeneid* 4 is parallel to *Argonautica* 3.[7] And, just as before with the vision of the Penates in Book 3 (147) and Dido's insomniac soliloquy sleep in Book 4 (522), so now Virgil sets a nocturnal scene: the dream visitation of Tiberinus, the Tiber river god, who comes to console Aeneas now that the war has begun. The Tiber comes as an appropriate divine visitor; Aeneas had first learned of the Latin river during his encounter with the ghost of Creusa (2.781-782), and the warlike water / storm imagery of Book 7 now gives way to the peaceful vision of the fated Tiber and the river journey Aeneas will soon take to visit Evander (a positive parallel to the negative results that will come from the Latin embassy to Diomedes). This visit to Evander has an atmosphere of suspended time; the war will wait, as it were, for Aeneas to complete his pilgrimage to the future site of Rome, and we shall enjoy the last moments of quiet calm in the poem as Aeneas tours the actual home of his long awaited destiny. Aeneas' courage and fortitude increases as older prophecies are now at last fulfilled; he still shows moments of weakness and unhappiness (cf. 8.520-523 below, where Aeneas and Achates are strangely sad). Book 8 is supposed to provide the ultimate confirmation of everything he has hitherto learned; he still must go forth and fight his war, but he has received more than sufficient divine resources, help, and information to allow him to proceed. What his mother and the other divine oracles do not prepare him for, however, is the loss of Pallas in the forthcoming slaughter.

The Tiber confirms that Aeneas has indeed found his sure and certain home (8.39 *certa domus*); he also announces that all the anger of the gods has abated (40-41, where the suspicious unfinished line *concessere deum* probably explains the river god's glaring error—this passage would no doubt have been revised). All the anger and swelling (*irae, tumor*) of the gods has most certainly *not* subsided; strangely, these sorts of inconsistencies, which must be ascribed to the unrevised status of the poem, receive less commentary than more famous but at least explainable "mistakes" like the prophecy about eating the tables. We must conclude that the Tiber is speaking *sub specie aeternitatis*; his announcement looks to the future, though the difficulties, especially for someone in Aeneas' position, remain. The Tiber announces the imminent fulfillment of the portent of the white sow with her thirty offspring; this portent had first been announced by Helenus at Buthrotum (cf. 3.390-392 and 8.43-45). The Tiber now explains the vision: it signifies the foundation of Alba (Latin for "white") Longa by Ascanius after thirty years. Besides this explanation of an old prophecy, the Tiber explains how Aeneas is supposed to seek help where he would least expect it—from a Greek settlement, Evander's Pallanteum. Prophecy continues to unfold in stages; in reality, Aeneas will find out in Pallanteum that the main body of his "native" allies will come from the Etruscan city of Caere (some four hundred Arcadians, as well as Pallas, will come from Pallanteum). The prophecy is true enough, but, as has been Aeneas' constant experience with dreams, divine visions, and oracular pronouncements, it will receive expansion once it comes to pass.

Evander (Greek for "Good Man", in contrast to the "Bad Man," Cacus, whom we shall soon hear about), is an Arcadian, from the remote and mountainous central region of the Peloponnesus in Greece, the home of Pan.[8] Arcadia was famous for the eerie rites on Mount Lycaeon, "Wolf Mountain," where human sacrifice may well have been practiced. In one version of the story, Lycaon offered Zeus human flesh to see if Zeus were really a god who could tell the difference between human and animal flesh; he was changed into a wolf in punishment (in Ovid's version at *Metamorphoses* 1.211 ff., Lycaon actually tried to kill Jupiter). Elsewhere he offers a baby as a sacrifice. Apparently those who ate the human flesh from the sacrifices on Lycaeon were changed into wolves; the Arcadians also worshipped gods in animal form (like the goat deity Pan). Apparently great fear of flesh-eating wolves and their ravaging of flocks (and threat to shepherds and farmers) became part of the source, by extension, for belief in cannibalism and lycanthropy: the cannibal human does what the wolf would naturally do. The link between Arcadia and Italy comes from the false etymological connection between the *Palatine* Hill of Rome and *Pallanteum*, a town in Arcadia named after Pallas Athena (and after whom Evander's son is named)—though note the goddess' name has a short final vowel, and the young hero's a long one (and that in some versions Pallas was Evander's grandson, or even grandfather).[9] The Arcadian lore certainly points to an ancient belief in werewolves; this lycanthropic lore is also, we shall see, at the heart of the Camilla story. The theme had already been introduced by Virgil's mention of the Thracian Harpalyce in Book 1 (316-317), the "Snatcher She-Wolf"—the theme also fits in well with some of the animal costumes of the Italian warriors we have just seen, as well as Diana's apparent sympathies for the Italian side (Virbius already, and, we learn later, Camilla herself). All of this lore fits in well with the depiction Virgil offers of the native Italians: many of them live in a world but a few steps removed from magical wonder; the metamorphoses of Circe (whose image lurked behind so much of Book 7) are part of the same sort of folkloric (in this case Arcadian) lycanthropy. Frequent mention of animal skins in this book highlights this theriomorphic lore, besides providing early Italy with the sort of primitive (that is, pure and unspoiled) atmosphere Virgil desires. The complaint that Aeneas and his Trojans have brought the conquered Penates of a now dead city to Italy will be answered by the poem's revelation that Troy will *not* be reborn in Latium—this had been a prime fear of some of the native population.

The consistent pattern in Aeneas' reception of prophecies has been their slow and steady expansion; Aeneas himself has dramatically improved in his ability to accept the news of his visions and carry out his instructions expeditiously (as opposed to his sluggish response to dreams and visions in Book 2). As soon as he wakes from the dream he at once offers due prayer to the nymphs of the river as well as Tiberinus. The "reward" for his religious piety is the vision of the sow and her young, which he sacrifices at once to Juno (he has been consistently reminded to try to placate and appease her, though so far with no luck). The journey to Evander's settlement is half a day by river, at least when the Tiber deliberately eases the passage and lessens its flood; neither the geography nor the details about the exact time of the journey can be pressed too far—the minor inconsistencies do not bother the reader, and Virgil (*pace* Mandra!) did not intend for us to arrange the events of his poem on a precise timeline. While the Latins set out on a futile expedition to a hero of yesterday's war, the divinely inspired Aeneas makes a quick visit to powerful nearby allies. This journey upriver is the final step in the *Aeneid*'s long emphasis on sea travel. The Tiber voyage is a symbol of the end of the Trojans' hitherto dangerous, even disastrous sea experiences.

At Pallanteum we are introduced to Evander's son Pallas. The name derives from his ancestral Arcadian town, though Virgil also wants to evoke the P-s correspondence between Pallas and Patroclus, Achilles' (A-s) young friend. Pallas is the foremost example in the *Aeneid* of Virgil's preoccupation with the theme of the young, untimely dead. The prime importance of the theme is the issue of the Augustan succession; every young dead hero (or heroine) is another symbol of the weakening of the possible succession to the imperial throne. Pallas will be a surrogate for Ascanius; Aeneas' blood son will be preserved from the fighting by divine ordinance, so that he is subjected to no risk. Pallas will die in his place. The death of Pallas is also the main cause for Aeneas' sacrifice of Turnus at the end of the poem, the main cause for Aeneas' lapse into madness in the final lines of the epic. As with Dido, so with Pallas the gods and oracles are silent. Much of Aeneas' path is marked out for him by "fate," but much remains for the individual to work out on his own. The immortals played an active and engaged role in the Dido episode; Aeneas will make his own choice to avenge Pallas at the poem's close.

Aeneas arrives at Evander's settlement on the day of a festival in honor of Hercules. Just as Ascanius had been the first to react boldly to the burning of the Trojan fleet, so now Pallas is the first to react to the Trojan landing on their shore. Virgil's introduction of Pallas demonstrates his courage and bravery; he may be Arcadian by blood, but he is a native Italian by birth (a fact Virgil emphasizes later when Evander notes that the Etruscans, who have been told by an oracle to seek a foreign leader, cannot accept Pallas), and he will be, in a sense, another martyr for his country's future. He has an attitude not only of daring but also of religious duty; he forbids the other Arcadians from interrupting their sacred rites to react to the Trojan arrival (8.110-111). The connection between Aeneas' Trojans and Evander's Arcadians has already been foreshadowed: they are all descended from Atlas, through his two daughters, Electra and Maia. As we have noted already, in some versions Dardanus, the Trojan progenitor, originated in Arcadia, not Hesperia; in Virgil's conception, Dardanus is a native Italian (thus fortifying Aeneas' claims to Latium), and Evander another offshoot of the Atlantids. Aeneas arrives just in time to see his own future religious and liturgical life unfold.

The mention of Hercules' rites (fortuitously being celebrated just as Aeneas arrives) has intense relevance to Rome and the Augustan program. On one level, as the Hercules-Cacus epyllion reveals, the wandering hero represents the coming of order. He is an Augustan symbol of the vanquishing of monstrosity and, indeed, evil (Cacus). Here we find the strongest link between Aeneas, the wandering hero of the *Aeneid*, and Hercules, the prototypical wandering hero of mythology. Hercules was one of the oldest foreign gods to be introduced at Rome. Apparently Cacus was originally a local, Italian god who suffered the loss of his cattle; one of Hercules' labors had been the seizing of the cattle of Geryon from Spain, and the two stories have here been conflated to suit Virgil's purpose.[10] Virgil's depiction of Cacus as a son of Vulcan neatly prepares the way for Vulcan's role in the forging of Aeneas' divine shield. Book 8 will also present the Cyclopes in a new light: they will move from being the cannibal monsters of Book 3 to being the forgers of Aeneas' arms, and likewise the terror of Vulcan's cannibal son will be replaced very soon with the god himself seduced and, however hesitant, forging Aeneas' arms. From the monstrous horror of the cannibal Cyclops and the inhospitable Cacus we shall move in the latter part of Book 8 to the divine weapons that announce Aeneas' *Roman* victory.

The contrast between Aeneas' approach to Evander and Turnus' envoys to Diomedes is striking: Aeneas emphasizes how he has come in person (8.144-145 *me, me ipse meumque / obieci caput*), as opposed to Turnus' sending of Venulus in his place. Aeneas also tells a significant lie to Evander:

gens eadem, quae te, crudeli Daunia bello
insequitur; nos si pellant, nihil afore credunt
quin omnem Hesperiam penitus sua sub iuga mittant,
et mare quod supra teneant quodque adluit infra. (8.146-149)

*The same race pursues us that pursues you, the Daunian,
cruel in war; if they drive us out, they think that nothing will prevent them
from sending all Hesperia utterly under their yoke,
and from holding the sea that flows above and the sea that flows below.*

This assertion cannot be supported by the events of Book 7. From one perspective, Ascanius had struck the first blow of the war when he shot the deer; certainly the Latins overreacted (all, of course, under the influence of Juno's Allecto). But even if the Trojans were justified in presenting themselves as the injured party, they are exiles that have only recently landed. Attacking them is not part of some Rutulian plan for Italian conquest. Aeneas' opening words to Pallas had already identified his Trojans as exiles (118 *profugos*), but as exiles from the *Latins*, who had driven them on in arrogant war (*bello . . . egere superbos*). These arguments link together; Aeneas presents himself as an exile now from the people he had just met as an exile. The lie is strange, given that Aeneas has been led to believe from past prophecies that the Arcadians will help him. It is difficult to posit a motivation or reason for Aeneas' great exaggeration here. In some sense he is now fully immersed in his fate; he has come to accept the reality of his destined mission (we are very far from the emotions of *Italian non sponte sequar*). As such, he (correctly) considers his presence in Italy to be the will of fate, and anyone who opposes him might well be accused of trying to gain control of the entire peninsula. Still, the rhetorical excess and misrepresentation of the reality is strange. Critics and commentators do not claim the same sort of unpolished, unfinished writing for Book 8 that they usually impute to Book 2, for example. Aeneas' interesting summation of events in Latium since his arrival is no doubt deliberate (as opposed to the Tiber's earlier assertion that the gods were at peace with the Trojan arrival, with its telltale half-line).

Besides the Atlantid connection between the Trojans and Arcadians, Evander remembers how he met Anchises when he was a very young man; Pallas will now have his chance to meet an older hero—with very different outcomes.[11] The sacred meal had already just been finished when Aeneas arrived, but Evander now orders the food and drink to be brought forth again; he has a lion skin for Aeneas' seat on a maple throne: like the native Italians, Evander's settlement is marked by animal skins and wood; this is no Greek or Trojan city (or, for that matter, marble Rome). Everything must point to the primitive beauty of the *future* site of marble Rome (and, of course, the glories of the Augustan building program). Rome may have moved past animal skins, but it can still venerate the memory of its primitive origins.

Evander's story of Cacus opens horribly.[12] Near the very place where he is enjoying a peaceful meal with Aeneas lie the remains of Cacus' cave dwelling. Once, men's faces were fixed to the doors as grisly monuments to his ghastly killings. The story of Cacus' theft of some of Hercules' cattle while the hero was sojourning in Latium after his return from Spain is based on the account of the newborn Hermes' trick with Apollo's cattle from the *Homeric Hymn*; Cacus knows how to conceal the telltale tracks. The defeat of Cacus by Hercules foreshadows the victory of Augustus over the Eastern powers represented by Cleopatra; the audience is not supposed to make any sort of (ludicrous) comparison between Cacus and the Egyptian queen, but the account of Hercules' defeat of a notorious pest in the mythic past is yet another foreshadowing of the Augustan Peace. Evander makes the Hercules cult an indigenous part of central Italian lore; Hercules is particularly venerated here because on this spot he defeated the man-eating, fire-breathing monster. Virgil is at great pains in Books 7 and 8 to illustrate the *native* quality of the nascent foundation of the future Rome; we are very far, mythologically and historically, from the city's actual foundation, but already the land is pregnant with the origins of Roman cult and religious practice. It should not be forgotten that the cult of the *Magna Mater*, itself an obvious mythological borrowing from Rome's Trojan parents, was viewed with suspicion.[13] Hercules' cult was Greek (though it had none of the Eastern, ecstatic elements that Rome traditionally eschewed); his ancient *Ara Maxima* in the Cattle Forum (the *Forum Boarium*) had possible connections to this story about his cattle; Evander alludes to this altar as he describes how the memorial of Hercules' killing of Cacus has been kept down through the ages. The Potitii and Pinarii were the Roman *gentes* who were originally charged with maintaining the Herculean liturgy; Virgil is so eager to bring the Roman clans into the story that he tolerates confusion between his account and the traditional version, where the cult was either initiated by Hercules himself or Evander (the two families having inherited it from either). The rites of Hercules almost parallel the *lusus Troiae* in Book 5, as Virgil anachronistically seeks to provide explanations for religious rituals current in his own day (some of which Augustus took care to revive and renew).

The story of Cacus is an epyllion, a miniature epic, of the sort Hellenistic Greek poets enjoyed and the neoteric poets of Rome cultivated (cf. Catullus *carmen* 64 on the marriage of Peleus and Thetis).[14] Cacus' story comes as the first in a series of epyllia in the second half of the *Aeneid*. The story has almost an Odyssean air to it; the first half of the poem is never far from the magic and wonder of the *Odyssey*, while in general the second half has fewer episodic details and more lengthy battle descriptions. The tale has affinities with the Homeric story of the Cyclops Polyphemus in his gore-splattered cave. Virgil never exhausts his readers with martial sequences; the epyllia in Books 8, 9, and 11 vary the mood and (especially in 9 and 11) are quite closely integrated to the plot. The story of Cacus has the vivid narrative excitement and detachable quality that mark such miniature epics; it could easily be a separate composition. The mood of the ritual that follows the story is lighthearted and happy (8.268 *laeti*, 279 *laeti*, and cf. 311 *laetus*—this is the spirit we experienced in Book 5). The celebration of Hercules includes cult hymns in his honor; the first words of the ritual song speak of how he successfully defeated the snakes his stepmother Juno had sent to kill him in his cradle (288-289), an auspicious beginning for a song in Aeneas' presence which darkly leads at once to Hercules' destruction of cities: Troy is first among them (291). The other city mentioned, Oechalia, is more allusively relevant to the immediate context. Oechalia was destroyed because its king had refused his daughter Iole to Hercules after he had promised her to anyone who could defeat him in archery; Hercules destroyed the city and took Iole in any case—she would be his last mortal wife. The destruction of Oechalia can be seen as an omen for the destruction Latinus' kingdom will suffer because Lavinia has not been handed over, as promised, to Aeneas. Indeed, much later in the war many in Italy will complain that their suffering and destruction is entirely the fault of Turnus because of the Lavinia problem. So the pair of ruined Herculean cities hearkens to the present war; Latinus' city is not going to be sacked and destroyed the way Aeneas' Troy was, however—lurking behind the "tactless" (Fordyce) mention of Troy is the final suppression of the Trojan lifestyle in Book 12. There is a brief summary of the traditional labors (at least some of them). The Hercules-Cacus epyllion has reminiscences of Virgil's underworld: when Hercules tears into Cacus' cave and exposes him for attack, Virgil compares the hero's action to an earthquake that rips open an entrance to the lower world and terrifies the ghosts with unexpected light (8.246 *trepident immisso lumine Manes*). Some of Hercules' labors evoke underworld images: Cerberus (296-297), who here is no dog to be lulled with the Sibyl's treats, but, like Cacus, sitting amid gore and dead men's bones (cf. 6.417-423), and the Hydra of Lerna, a reminder of the monsters who sit in hell's vestibule (6.282-294). All of this serves to underscore the dramatic nature of Hercules' action: his labors represent, in part, a conquering of the world of the dead, which underscores heavily his role as a symbol of the conquest of irrationality.

Pallanteum is on the site of the future Palatine in Rome, the most important of the seven hills; at its foot was the cave where the she-wolf was said to have nursed Romulus and Remus.[15] A gallery of famous Romans inhabited this hill in historical times, in the fashionable Carinian district (8.361 *Carinae*), which in Virgil's anachronistic conception is here a mere cow pasture. Evander's history lesson establishes the explanation for the rustic, even wild nature of primitive Italy: central Italy had been inhabited by men who were born from tree trunks and hard oaks (315).[16] The story goes back to Homer; in the *Odyssey* (19.163), Penelope mentions to Odysseus the stories of men being born from oak and rock;[17] the myth of Deucalion and Pyrrha and the repopulation of the earth after the flood is of the same sort. What we might call the prehistoric state of life in Italy was only civilized after Saturn came down, an exile from heaven after he had been expelled by Jupiter. Evander derives the name *Latium* from the verb *latuere*: Saturn had "hid" from Jupiter in Italy (this myth may offer further reason for Jupiter's favoritism toward the Trojans in the *Aeneid*). Evander's myth of the ages (ultimately Hesiodic) specifies the decline of the Golden Age and the coming of kings in the Silver; the kings include Thybris, a huge giant to Evander and Aeneas (people were bigger in the better past)—Thybris would be the eponymous hero of the Tiber.

Evander declares that his mother, the nymph Carmentis, and Apollo sanctioned his presence at Pallanteum. The nymph's name is derived from *carmen*, a song or spell; allegedly either she or Evander taught the native Italians the alphabet. She had an altar at the foot of the Capitoline Hill; Evander shows Aeneas the Carmental Altar (8.337-338 *aram / Carmentalem*) and Gate. Not surprisingly, Evander credits his prophetic mother with the first indication of the ultimate destiny of the Aeneadae; Fordyce wonders why Virgil did not exploit such a prophecy, but possibly Evander is exaggerating about his mother's predictions about Aeneas. The "asylum" of Romulus (342) on the Capitoline is next, followed by the Lupercal:

> ... et gelida monstrat sub rupe Lupercal,
> Parrhasio dictum Panos de more Lycaei. (8.343-344)

> ... *and under a chill crag he shows him the Lupercal,*
> *named after Lycaean Pan according to the Parrhasian custom.*

We know very little for certain about the famously obscure festival of the Lupercalia on 15 February. Evander names it after Pan Lycaeus, that is, Pan with the title of his birthplace, Mount Lycaeus; the "Parrhasian" custom is Arcadian (from a local region). Arcadian in origin or not, the Lupercalia remained alive and well for centuries of Roman history; Pope Saint Gelasius I, who is credited with a number of liturgical developments in the Roman Rite, conflated it late in the fifth century with an Eastern festival in honor of the Virgin Mary's Purification on 2 February (the Greek *Hypapante* or "Meeting" between Christ and Simeon). Other than the tradition about Romulus and the she-wolf, any other connection (if any) between wolves and the Lupercalia is unknown (the etymology from *lupus*, "wolf," is difficult to discredit); the festival probably had some connection to the protection of flocks from lupine marauders. The tradition of having the patrician *Luperci* dressed in goat skins and running around the Palatine perhaps has affinities with a number of ancient rituals that involve dressing in animal skins and thereby (possibly) imitating the animal or the god in animal form (like the goat god Pan). The striking of female bystanders in particular with goat whips has been taken to reflect some fertility ritual (especially given the late winter, February date of the feast); certainly the Romans themselves thought so. The Lupercalia will be featured on Aeneas' divine shield (8.663).

There were strange rites on Mount Soracte that had definite connection to wolf aversion (as we shall see below when Virgil introduces Arruns, Camilla's killer); it is possible that the Lupercalia partly had a similar character. So too there were also rites near Soracte in honor of Feronia, possibly a Sabine native goddess; it is quite uncertain who she was and what people did in her honor, though the Augustan Age Greek geographer Strabo notes fire-walking rites (a possible confusion with the attested fire-walking rites in honor of Apollo on Soracte). Some of her denizens are fighting with Turnus (7.800 *et viridi gaudens Feronia luco*); Evander names her later in this book as the mother of a monster he defeated in his youth (8.564).[18] Book 8 is where Virgil gives the most lavish attention to archaic Roman religion; his antiquarian interest in part reflects the attention Augustus paid to the restoration of lapsed cults and the renewed organization of Roman religion. Augustus' ability to pay close attention to matters of religion also reflects the peaceful nature of his reign (which allowed for greater literary productivity, an issue already of concern to Lucretius).[19] None of the religious atmosphere of Book 8 is overtly Trojan, of course; this reflects the reality of Roman religion in Virgil's day (and historically).

The Argiletum (8.345-346) was near the Quirinal Hill; Virgil connects it fancifully with the "death of Argus" (*Argi-letum*), a guest of Evander's who tried to kill him (the same theme as the story of Lycaon and Zeus, or, for that matter, Cacus and his inhospitable ways). The Tarpeian Rock (347) offers a classic example of anachronistic nomenclature; Tarpeia betrayed the Capitolium to the Sabines during the days of Romulus, and paid with her life for her treachery.[20] The whole area, then, is invested with a solemn religious aura; even now it bespeaks its sacred, golden (348 *aurea*) future. Just as when Evander had welcomed Aeneas to a meal outside with a lion skin and maple "throne" (175-178), so now as he welcomes him inside his small, modest dwelling he invites him to rest on a bear skin and leaves (378): everything is ready for the thrust of history to manage its development. Evander's words to Aeneas as he enters the house have occasioned much comment:

   aude, hospes, contemnere opes et te quoque dignum
   finge deo, rebusque veni non asper egenis. (8.364-365)

*Dare, o guest, to disdain riches and fashion yourself as also
worthy of the god, and do not come harshly to poor circumstances.*

Evander reminds Aeneas (and future Romans) to despise riches and be satisfied with little; the admonition to fashion himself so as to be worthy of "the god" is more problematic. The Stoic Seneca took the passage as a reference to the philosophical doctrine of submitting oneself to the divine essence that rules the world (*Epistulae* 18.12 ff. and 34.11), but coming as it does right after a remembrance of how Hercules entered the very same dwelling (8.362-363) after he had killed Cacus, it seems (especially in the context of a warning about riches) to be a polite apology for the poor setting: it was good enough for Hercules, in other words, and so also for Aeneas (as *rebusque veni non asper egenis* explains). Aeneas enters, and the narrow doorway can barely accommodate the hero's large body (366-367 *angusti . . . ingentem*).

Virgil has crafted a pattern in the *Aeneid*: the immortals appear from time to time, sometimes at obviously critical junctures, other times at apparently peaceful moments of repose. Sometimes, where we might expect a particular god's epiphany, Virgil disappoints us. Venus (as befits her frivolous, often careless personality) is the usual example. She has not entered the narrative since the end of Book 5, when she ensured the safe sailing of the Trojans (at least almost all of them) from Sicily to Cumae. She was absent from the outbreak of the war. Now she visits her husband Vulcan, thoroughly terrified (8.370 *exterrita*) by the threats of the Latins and the tumult of war, just as Thetis visited Hephaestus in the *Iliad* to beg arms for her son Achilles (18.369 ff.). Vulcan is not completely sympathetic; he hesitates (8.388 *cunctantem*) before succumbing to his unfaithful wife's sexual charms. Virgil never uses *cunctantem* without significance: at 4.390 it describes Aeneas, hesitating to say more after Dido's attack on him. At 6.211 it describes the Golden Bough, hesitating in the face of Aeneas' greedily grabbing it. At 7.449 it describes Turnus, stunned by the revelation of the Fury Allecto's true appearance. At 12.940, most importantly of all, it will describe Aeneas in the crucial moment where he hesitates to consider Turnus' plea for mercy. Here, for reasons Virgil does not explicate, Vulcan hesitates before agreeing to forge divine arms for Aeneas. Thetis, in contrast, uses no sexual wiles in the *Iliad*; nor does she have to resort to them: Hephaestus is happy to grant her request.

Venus' ability to move her husband is like a lightning bolt through a cloud (8.391-392). The image is Jovian; Jupiter's will lurks behind his daughter's appeals.[21] The simile of the lightning bolt also connects to the real lightning bolts Vulcan's Cyclopes are forging for Jupiter when he visits them at their island forge (426-432). Now Vulcan is immediately transformed by his wife. Neptune had assured Venus that he could have done much for the Trojans had she only asked (5.800-815); here we see the successful results of her entreaty of another male god. In Book 5, Neptune was in control of his own realm; he was the one who soothed the happy heart of the goddess. Now it is happy Venus who rejoices in her tricks and is aware of her beauty and its power (8.393). After assuring Venus that he will do as she wishes, the two immortals embrace and Vulcan willingly falls asleep in her arms—an evocation of the ending of Book 5, where Palinurus' unwilling slumber came after the appeal of Venus to Neptune. Palinurus' sleep killed him; Vulcan's slumber emasculates him. Virgil describes the god as he rises at midnight after a brief slumber in his wife's arms: the time has come to pay the price for his abbreviated peaceful pleasure, and the poet illustrates what has happened to him in brilliant imagery, with one of the richest similes in the poem:

Inde ubi prima quies medio iam noctis abactae
curriculo expulerat somnum, cum femina primum,
cui tolerare colo vitam tenuique Minerva
impositum, cinerem et sopitos suscitat ignis
noctem addens operi, famulasque ad lumina longo
exercet penso, castum ut servare cubile
coniugis et possit parvos educere natos:
haud secus ignipotens nec tempore segnior illo
mollibus e stratis opera ad fabrilia surgit. (8.407-415)

Then, when the first quiet had driven away sleep at the
midpoint of the night's waning course, at the hour when a woman,
on whom it has been imposed to spend her life at the distaff and
with humble Minerva, rekindles the ash and the sleeping fires,
adding night to her labor, and she works her handmaids until
dawn at the long skeins of thread, so that she might be able to preserve
her husband's bed chastely and raise her small sons:
scarcely otherwise, and not more slothful at that hour,
did the powerful fire god rise from his soft bed to his craft work.

First Virgil describes the time of night: it is midnight, the hour when a woman rises to the works of Minerva, the distaff and the wool for spinning.[22] She works at night with her servant girls, so that she might demonstrate her chastity and be able to raise her young sons—the eminently Roman concept of the woman who can be found at midnight dutiful and faithful to her family (most famous from Livy's description of Lucretia before her rape).[23] After seven lines of elaborate description (where the reader wonders if this really is just a beautiful, poetic periphrasis for "midnight"), Virgil finally reveals his purpose: Vulcan is like the woman who must rush to her loom. He has been emasculated by his wife's sexual wiles and seduction. The image of the distaff of Minerva echoes Virgil's description of Camilla, who (though a woman) was not interested in spinning and weaving (7.805-806). It is particularly biting that Virgil calls Vulcan *ignipotens*, "Powerful in Fire" (8.414, 423, 628, 710, 10.243 and 12.90—the epithet appears first in Virgil, and is Virgil's technical term for Vulcan in his role as forger of Aeneas' arms): the great god of the forge has been so easily vanquished by a short romantic interlude with his beautiful wife. The woman in the simile is a widow (as is Vulcan, in a sense, since Venus is so often absent and unfaithful): it has been imposed on her (by her husband's death) to earn her living and raise her children. The contrast between the Roman widow, *univira*, that is, devoted to one man, and the cuckold husband whose wife does as she pleases, is powerful and striking (and comes as no credit to Aeneas' mother). So Vulcan also acts under compulsion, however pleasant. From the soft bed (*mollibus e stratis*) that symbolizes Venus' own works, Vulcan must rise to his own chores (*opera ad fabrilia*) as a craftsman and worker. The young children, in this case, symbolize Aeneas; the son needs his parents' divine arms, just as the children depend on their widowed mother's work to eat. Achilles' arms in the *Iliad* had timeless reflections on human life (the city at peace and the city at war); Aeneas' will have quite specific relevance to Roman history.

In Book 3 (569 ff.), the Cyclopes were exclusively depicted as Odyssean, cannibalistic horrors. Virgil now turns to the Hesiodic model of the Cyclopes as dutiful forgers of Jupiter's thunder and lightning weaponry (*Theogony* 139-146 and 501-506). Elsewhere in the Greek tradition the Cyclopes became (naturally enough) Vulcan's helpers (Callimachus *Hymns* 3.46-79). Virgil now introduces the Cyclopes in this busy, factory-like role—no longer are they the fearsome, independent monsters of Homeric lore. The two conceptions serve Virgil well: Venus' cajoling is followed by the placating of all nature, as it were (cf. Lucretius *De Rerum Natura* 1.6-9). Even Venus' lover Mars' chariot will have to wait for Aeneas' shield (8.433-434)—a reminder that Book 8 offers a quiet moment of peace in the Italian war, a suspended narrative. The volcanic island where the Cyclopes and Vulcan work (Volcania, the modern Vulcano) was near Aeolus' traditional home (Lipare; cf. 416 and 455): the Aeolian geography recalls Juno's visit to the wind god for a favor in Book 1. What had been a region of fear and ill omen when the Trojans were first approaching Sicily has now become the source of Aeneas' shield; the Cyclopes have been transformed in Virgil's epic, as it were, from monsters silhouetted on a beach in Book 3 to obedient laborers in Book 8. This too represents the coming of order and the rule of rational thought; the untamed Sicilian beasts of Book 3 are now employed, and they work in the service of heroes who will execute the will of the gods.

Unlike the god, Evander and Aeneas get to rest until morning, when the Arcadian king rises and puts on a panther skin (460), continuing the Arcadian animal motif; twin dogs accompany Evander as he leaves his dwelling. Significantly, Aeneas is already awake and in the company of the *son* Pallas (466 *filius Pallas*); after only a brief visit, the young hero is already seen as a filial companion to the Trojan hero, who is walking also with his faithful friend Achates (Ascanius was not brought on this journey); Virgil is deliberately playing with the shifting label of Pallas as Evander's and, now, *Aeneas*' son. The description of Aeneas' morning walk with Pallas, where he meets Evander (who has come to meet him), is a subtle and powerful introduction to Virgil's theme of Aeneas' surrogate son.

Aeneas had been told to expect military aid from a Greek city. Evander laments that his own forces are weak (they are in a more or less constant war with the Rutulians); he is at pains to assure Aeneas, however, that the visit to Pallanteum was indeed the will of fate (8.477 *fatis huc te poscentibus adfers*): he can offer the help of Agylla, an Etruscan town later more famously known as Caere. Mezentius had been king there, until his savage cruelty and penchant for inventive tortures had led his people to expel him.[24] The former victims of Mezentius' terror are eager to get their hands on their escaped king (who has taken refuge with Turnus); somehow, as we have already learned, Mezentius' son Lausus has managed to lead a thousand men from Agylla to support the Latin alliance under Turnus (7.647-654). In the catalogue of Italian heroes, Mezentius and his son came first. This inconsistency (of a sort) perhaps points to a civil war in Etruria; some people have apparently decided they are willing to march against the Trojans with Mezentius. The Etruscans, it seems, have received the same sort of divine injunction Latinus heard: choose a foreign leader. They send emissaries to ask the Arcadian Evander to join them; he refuses because of age. Pallas is not eligible to be their "foreign" leader since his mother is Sabellian and thus he has native Italian blood. Evander identifies the Etruscan king as Tarchon (8.506); in Book 11 (725 ff.) Jupiter will rouse him up to repulse Camilla and end her bloody slaughter of Trojan warriors.[25]

Virgil nowhere makes explicit that there is any Etruscan civil conflict. In Book 11, it will not be entirely clear if the Etruscan Arruns who kills Camilla is fighting on her own side for Turnus, or is one of Tarchon's men. The thousand men under Lausus who march with Mezentius in Book 7 could represent poetic extravagance; but it remains possible, if not provable, that the Etruscans are divided between Mezentius and Tarchon.[26] Poetic extravagance and exaggeration does not mean we must pretend the thousand men with Lausus do not exist; as we have noted, there is a parallel to Camilla, who (as we learn later) is somehow leading some of the very same Volscians who expelled her father. Unlike her father Metabus, though, Mezentius is marching with his son and their contingent, and will play a major role in the fighting.

Aeneas is somewhat troubled by the news that he must go to Agylla. Evander offers him two hundred cavalry, and Pallas has two hundred more; it is not entirely clear why Aeneas and Achates are discomfited. The commentators rightly wonder about Aeneas' downcast (8.522 *tristi cum corde*) state; some see a foreshadowing of Pallas' death, especially since Aeneas' mood seems to sour right after Evander entrusts his son to him for military apprenticeship. A likely reason for Aeneas' grim mood is the news that he has to go on yet another mission (however brief); he had been led to believe that help would come from Evander's Pallanteum, and now he finds he must go elsewhere to augment the four hundred Arcadian cavalry. In any case the bad mood is quickly dispelled: Venus sends an auspicious sign: thunder and lightning from a clear sky, the sound of the Etruscan trumpet, and the appearance of Aeneas' finished divine arms in the sky.

Once the portent of the thunder and lightning is observed, Aeneas publicly and proudly responds (how far we have come from his earliest reactions to omens):

> obstipuere animis alii, sed Troius heros
> agnovit sonitum et divae promissa parentis.
> tum memorat: "ne vero, hospes, ne quaere profecto
> quem casum portenta ferant: ego poscor Olympo.
> hoc signum cecinit missuram diva creatrix,
> si bellum ingrueret, Volcaniaque arma per auras
> laturam auxilio.
> heu quantae miseris caedes Laurentibus instant!
> quas poenas mihi, Turne, dabis! quam multa sub undas
> scuta virum galeasque et fortia corpora volves,
> Thybri pater! poscant acies et foedera rumpant." (8.530-540 Mynors)

The others stood aghast in their thoughts, but the Trojan hero
recognized the sound and the promises of his goddess mother.
Then he called out, "Do not, do not, my friend, seek out
what outcome this portent announces: I am sought by Olympus;
my goddess mother sang forth that she was about to send this sign,
if war were close at hand, and she announced she was about
to bring Vulcan's arms to me through the air for my help.
Ah, what great slaughters are looming for the miserable Latins!
What penalties you will pay to me, Turnus! How many shields
of men, helmets, and strong bodies will you turn over under your waves,
father Tiber! Let them seek battle lines and break their agreements."

Aeneas' opening words are almost an acknowledgment of his future apotheosis; there is no prophecy in the text of the *Aeneid* where Venus promises any weapons to her son, so we must assume (as elsewhere) that there have been other divine visitations. Aeneas rightly interprets the vision of the arms in the sky as an announcement of the future destruction of his Latin opponents. These are the first words Aeneas utters against the Latins, and the first time he mentions Turnus. He uses language that evokes the threats he himself heard from Dido in Book 4 (cf. 8.538 *quas poenas mihi, Turne, dabis* and 4.386 *dabis, improbe, poenas*). His prediction that the Tiber will run with the shields, helmets, and bodies of dead men is a reminiscence of his lament during the storm in Book 1 that the lucky had died at Troy, where the River Simois swept away their corpses (cf. 8.540 and 1.101). Aeneas has taken two of the worst moments in his travels from Troy (Dido's raging speech and Juno's storm) and turned them into a forecast of death for Turnus and many of his Latins. This is the most confident and self-assured Aeneas we have seen in Virgil's epic; he had been absent from the earliest stages of the war, and is still safe in Pallanteum—but he has already declared his intention to repay Turnus for breaking the treaty. His final words, "let them demand battle-lines and break treaties," is a succinct summation of his thoughts on the war, and connects to the misrepresentation of the truth with which he introduced himself to Evander (8.146-149). Aeneas blames the war on the Italians, who have broken their word to him. He has good reason to assert this position, though (as with any tragic conflict); the situation in central Italy is hardly black and white. His cry also summons the god to witness that he has not called the Latins to war. Fittingly, he ends his acknowledgment of the omen with ritual and sacrifice.

Aeneas chooses some of his best men from his boats; the rest he sends downstream to bring news to Ascanius, whose absence is at last made explicit. Aeneas prepares to travel to Tarchon's Etruscan realm; his departure is accompanied by fearful mothers (556-557), just as the Latin mothers were so fearful when they heard Allecto sounding the clarion for war (7.518, and cf. 8.592-593). The Arcadian mothers know that Aeneas is taking several hundred of their young men off to fight Turnus' forces. Evander gives a hint of the same theme that dominated the boxing match in Book 5 with Acestes and Entellus: once upon a time he defeated a Geryon-like monster, Erulus, who was born of a goddess (Feronia) and had three bodies and three lives to be snuffed out. Erulus is mentioned nowhere else in extant literature; Evander is reminiscing about how he was once like Hercules and defeated monsters who were far more challenging and dreadful than human warriors of the present like Mezentius or, for that matter, Turnus. Evander can do nothing now because of his age and feeble body; he is also afraid for Pallas (and rightly so). He does not wish to live long enough to hear any future report that his son is dead. His wish here that he might die before he learns of Pallas' possible death will not be granted. Aeneas had predicted deaths on the Latin side (and indeed there will be many); he offers no guarantee or even consolation to Evander that he will protect or guard his son. Aeneas' bold threat to the Latins will be fulfilled—but in part at the price of Pallas' life. Aeneas and Achates lead the procession out of Pallanteum, and Pallas is in the middle; Virgil uses a beautiful simile to describe the young hero that points to Pallas' role as a possible successor to Aeneas and that highlights the futility of divine favor:

> qualis ubi Oceani perfusus Lucifer unda,
> quem Venus ante alios astrorum diligit ignis,
> extulit os sacrum caelo tenebrasque resolvit. (8.589-591)
>
> *Just as when the Morning Star, drenched in the wave of Ocean,*
> *whom Venus loves before all the other fires of the stars,*
> *has lifted up his holy head to the heaven and scattered the darkness.*

Book 8 marks an expansion in the succession theme. Pallas is the Patroclus of Virgil's *Iliad*, but he is also a symbol of worthy rulers of the future city of Rome. There is not so much a competition between the fated Ascanius (founder of Alba Longa) and Pallas, who is fated to die in battle, as there is an evocation of Marcellus. Augustus brought him along for the Cantabrian War in 26-25 B.C.

in northern Spain; the brief victory Augustus enjoyed would end in 22 B.C. (the year after Marcellus' death) with another Cantabrian rebellion. But before that, Augustus shut the gates of the Temple of Janus. Agrippa would manage the Roman response to a further Cantabrian revolt in 19 B.C. (the year of Virgil's death); finally in 13 B.C. Augustus would see the Senate consecrate the *Ara Pacis* in Rome.[27] Pallas is a type of Marcellus; the point of comparison with Ascanius is not some question over who would be the better successor or who is Aeneas' favorite, but rather the fact that Pallas will die before he can pursue any possible Roman destiny. Virgil could not kill Ascanius, but he could dispense with Pallas; in his own time, Augustus did not have the guarantee of a worthy son and heir to follow him: Pallas' death will evoke the horrible tragedy of Marcellus. So Pallas will begin his own education in war with Aeneas, who will be unable to break the epic pattern started by Achilles' loss of Patroclus. Pallas represents the bright hope of the Morning Star Lucifer; Venus favors him before all others because he symbolizes the Augustan succession. He now raises his head to the sky and removes the darkness. But his light will last only a day. The image of Lucifer had appeared at the very end of Book 2 (801-802), where the rising of the Morning Star over Mount Ida was a sign of Venus' divine favor at one of the worst moments for Aeneas and his Trojan exiles. Here it has a less auspicious symbolism; Aeneas has acquired his promised allies in Etruria, but the most important of them will soon enough be dead.

When Aeneas arrives at Caere with Pallas, Achates, and his other men, he comes upon a grove (a typical *locus amoenus*) that was consecrated to Silvanus by the Pelasgians, Greek immigrants to the region who are represented as pre-dating the Etrurians. Silvanus never received any official public cult in Rome; he was a forest deity (as his name would indicate) of a decidedly local nature, perhaps a protective spirit of woodlands. Virgil is at pains to show that Aeneas is already on the side of the native Italians (what were Pelasgians doing worshipping an Italian nature spirit?) and already growing accustomed to the new, non-Trojan religion of Italy. Even though the war has barely begun, already Italians (complete with their religious practices) are siding with Aeneas.

Soon after Aeneas and his men arrive in the Silvanian grove, the Trojan hero is alone by a cool spring. His mother Venus will visit him in the same type of secluded valley that Anchises had inhabited in Elysium to show the future heroes of Rome (cf. 8.609 *valle reducta* and 6.703). The two visions are parallel; the shield of Book 8 puts the crown on the revelations of Book 6. We are now very far from the time when Venus would playfully dress in a disguise to visit her son in the woods; the change that we have observed in Aeneas, his discernible maturity and advancement, is rewarded by the direct approach of Venus to present the shield, which she rests under an oak, Jupiter's tree (8.616 *quercu*); as we have observed, Virgil has dropped hints along the way that Jupiter approved of the granting of this divine armor and weaponry.

Aeneas' helmet is belching out flames (620 *flammamque vomentem*), just like Turnus' Chimaera. His sword is "fate-bearing" (*fatiferum*), because it will bring both death (Turnus' fate) and a partial fulfillment of Aeneas' own fate (the gods have charged him with setting Rome's foundation; his decision to kill Turnus will be his own). His breastplate is bloody because of its bright red color, but also because it portends the bloody deaths of so many. It gleams like the sun through a cloud (622-623 *qualis cum caerula nubes / solis inardescit radiis longeque refulgent*); in a sense Pallas was the Morning Star, and Aeneas is the sun. The shield's story is *enarrabile*: it cannot be told.[28] This adjective will form a ring with Aeneas' unknowing state at the end of the book (730 *ignarus*); the hero can rejoice in the magnificent artwork and careful craftsmanship, but he cannot understand or tell of what the shield shows. On one level he is unknowing of what he sees because (unlike Virgil's Augustan audience) he cannot predict or appreciate the future. On another level, the contemporary audience is unknowing of the ultimate consequence of the images on the shield that they saw (possibly even participated in) during their own recent past. They can rejoice in the glorious victories of the present that have wrought peace and new hope, but without Jovian consolation about the future.

Unlike Aeneas at the end of the book, Vulcan is not ignorant of the predictions of bards and prophets (627 *haud vatum ignarus venturique inscius aevi*). "Italian affairs and the triumphs of the Romans" (*res Italas Romanorumque triumphos*) are the subject of the shield's images, the entire race of the future offspring of Ascanius and the wars they fought in order. Troy, then, is nowhere; even Aeneas is absent. The shield's introduction emphasizes his role as a conduit—an important one, to be sure, but a conduit nonetheless. It is Ascanius whose name appears prominently as Virgil commences his description of the shield. Fittingly, given the Arcadian animal imagery that has prevailed in Pallanteum, the first thing we see on the shield is the she-wolf, who is tenderly licking Romulus and Remus, fashioning them (8.634 *fingere*) for the future, as it were—molding them as lupine offspring (who, not surprisingly, will be hungry and rapacious for territory). Immediately after the mention of the she-wolf suckling the twin founders of Rome, the shield depicts the snatching of the Sabine women during a vaguely defined celebration of games: the abducted (635 *raptas*) women are the first prey for the Roman wolves. Thus begins the first war on the shield: Romulus against Titus Tatius, the Sabine leader from Cures. Men from Sabine Cures were seen preparing to march against the Trojans (7.710); Aeneas will fight his own war against the paragons of Italian strictness and severity (8.638 *severis*). The end of the war is depicted; it shows Romulus and Tatius together, making a sacrifice; Virgil's war in Italy will not end so peacefully and amicably.

Mettus (Mettius in Livy) Fufetius is next; he was an Alban dictator (so the chronology started by mention of Alba Longa's founder Ascanius is continued). His famous mendacity (644 *viri mendacis*) to Tullus Hostilius, Rome's third king, was legendary; in Livy (1.28) he is the first and last Roman example of execution by "drawing" (torn apart by two four-horse chariots)—the historian is quick to note that in all other cases the Romans can boast of being more merciful than other nations. Mendacity like Mettus' is the worst form of civil war, which is in itself a betrayal of the united nation. Mettus cannot even remain loyal to his own side. Virgil's wish (incapable of fulfillment in *present* time) for Mettus is an apostrophe not only to the mutilated liar but, in some sense, to future Romans: "if only you were remaining true to your words." The imperfect subjunctive *maneres* (643) reflects both the vividness of the picture and its contemporary application, even if the use of the imperfect subjunctive in a "retrospective command" is attestable in Latin (though rare after Cicero).[29]

Mettus' treachery is followed by the nascent city's resistance to Etruscan attempts (under Lars Porsenna) to reinstate Tarquin the Proud. Porsenna was king of Clusium, one of the traditional twelve cities of the Etruscans. What really happened between him and Rome is contradictory and confusing. In Tacitus (*Historiae* 3.72) we learn that Rome surrendered to him. The far more famous version is Livy's (2.9), whereby Porsenna withdrew when he saw how fiercely the Romans would fight for their liberty; Virgil follows the same tradition. Soon after the attack on Rome, whatever its outcome, Porsenna sent his son Arruns to attack Aricia (the site of Diana's sacred grove)—this is almost certainly part of the historical lore that lies behind Arruns' killing of Camilla, Diana's favorite, in Book 11. In Livy's history, the fifth book (the end of the first "pentad") relates the role of Camillus in saving Rome from the Gauls; Camillus had been tried and exiled the year before (391 B.C.) the Gallic sack of Rome (Camilla's father, we learn in *Aeneid* 11, had been exiled by his Volscian subjects); Livy says (5.33) that a man from Clusium, Arruns, invited the Gauls to cross the Alps into Italy—further historical clues to the likelihood, which we shall examine later more closely, that Camilla's killer Arruns is one of the Etruscans fighting on Turnus' side, and that his shooting of Camilla and frightened, rapid flight from the battlefield is an act of treachery. The historical Marcus Furius Camillus was also involved in Roman conflicts with the Volscians (Camilla's people), who were not completely subjugated until the late fourth century B.C.; Camilla is, after all, an enemy of Rome's ultimate progenitor Aeneas—but it is likely that her name evoked the romanticized history of Furius Camillus' salvation of Rome from the Gauls more than any Volscian threats to Rome.

"Cocles," ("One-Eyed") that is, Horatius Cocles, held the Sublician Bridge against Lars Porsenna until it could be destroyed by the Romans behind him; Cloelia was a Roman girl given to Porsenna as a hostage who escaped and swam the Tiber (as did Cocles) to escape the Etruscans (cf. Livy 2.9-13). Both are obvious examples of Roman *virtus* and courage in the face of death. The Capitolium, or Tarpeian Citadel (8.652 *Tarpeiae . . . sedis*) is also on the shield, with Manlius standing guard in front of it. Marcus Manlius "Capitolinus" (so-called because of his defense of the Capitol from the Gauls) was allegedly roused from sleep by a goose (depicted here in silver on the shield), who alerted him to the Gallic attack on the Capitol (Livy 5.47). The goose was sacred to Juno—she will indeed come round to the defense of Rome before the end of the poem.

The Salii, or "leaping (*salire*) priests" of Mars, and the Luperci, have already been mentioned in this book; the Salii were participants in the Arcadians' Hercules rituals (8.285-286), and the Lupercal is mentioned on Aeneas' tour of the Palatine (343-344). In reality there were two teams of Salii, one devoted to Mars, the other to the deified Romulus (Quirinus); the first team oversaw the transition from peace to war, while the second managed the shift from war to peace.[30] The Salii have their traditional insignia: woolen headpieces and shields that had fallen from heaven; allegedly they were modeled after a shield sent down from heaven (presumably by Mars, their patron)—one had fallen from the sky and served as the model for eleven more. Their origin, apparently (at least the Martian Salii), is to be found during the traditionally peaceful reign of Numa Pompilius (cf. Livy 1.20.4), when Rome was able to devote itself to the development of religious rituals and law.

These religious rites constitute the conclusion of the shield's scenes from archaic Roman history.[31] The "history" of the shield (as befits a mysterious, ancient work of art) is spotty and idiosyncratic; there is a general progression from monarchy to republic, which is summed up well in the willingness of the children of Aeneas to rush to their deaths for freedom:

Aeneadae in ferrum pro libertate ruebant. (8.648)

The Aeneadae were rushing onto the sword for the sake of freedom.

Besides the saving of Rome from the Gauls, Aeneas' shield depicts two main episodes from the Roman Republic; Catiline and Cato represent their respective stories in obvious contrast and comparison, as good and bad *exempla* for future Romans. Lucius Sergius Catilina, made famous for his conspiracy by both Cicero and Sallust, is paying a distinctly Promethean punishment for all time, hanging on a rock in the underworld; Marcus Porcius Cato Uticensis, a Pompeian, had earned his noble reputation by committing suicide in Africa in 46 B.C. rather than accept clemency from Caesar. Virgil says that "between all these things" (8.671 *haec inter*) the swelling sea was depicted, a golden sea, but with silver dolphins playing in blue water that has white billows:

haec inter tumidi late maris ibat imago
aurea, sed fluctu spumabat caerula cano,
et circum argento clari delphines in orbem
aequora verrebant caudis aestumque secabant. (8.671-674)

Among these scenes the golden image of the swelling sea flowed broadly,
but the blue water was foaming with white waves,
and bright dolphins were sweeping the seas all around in a circle,
and they were cutting the tide with their tails.

In this sea, the Battle of Actium is depicted. The world of nature (symbolized by the sea and the dolphins) is the backdrop for the establishment of the Augustan order. The colors are vividly appropriate for the setting; the image of the water is gold because of the shield's metal; the very waves off Actium are also gold (677 *auro*). The divine shield is so magnificently and realistically wrought that you can *see* the blue and white of the billowing waves, despite the gold. Aeneas' fleet will be compared to dolphins (9.117 ff.) once they are saved from Turnus' flames and turned into mermaids; the artful swimming of dolphins also describes the complex equestrian movements of the *lusus Troiae* (5.594-595); the young participants of that display of horsemanship are the progenitors of the naval soldiers at Actium.

The scenes from Roman history are on top of the shield, and the underworld with Catiline and Cato are at the bottom; Augustus' victory at Actium is in the middle. The underworld pictures are a reminiscence of Anchises' revelation in Elysium at the end of Book 6. Like Anchises, Cato is in Elysium (presumably not to be reincarnated), and is administering laws (670)—the souls in the blessed seats of Elysium do not need a judge or ruler, but Cato is their revered lawgiver all the same. Catiline is in Tartarus, a symbol of the ultimate fate of all notoriously wicked Romans, it would seem (is he here as a ghost for Sulla?) The scenes at the top of the shield, from Rome's early centuries, are almost as interesting for what they omit as for what they depict. They have something in common, too, with the scenes from the underworld. The Carthaginians are nowhere in the scenes of warfare and strife. Except for Manlius defending the Capitol from the advancing Gauls, all the images are of conflicts between Rome and her immediate neighbors, future fellow citizens and denizens of the Italian peninsula. The underworld's two exemplary figures (one bad, one good) are also both victims (in different ways) of *civil* strife. Even Manlius, who defended the Capitol and saved it from the Gallic invasion, had a short-lived glory that ended with *civil* strife: he died in 385 B.C. or 384 B.C., probably executed for alleged revolt or tyrannical aspirations to kingship. Virgil depicts Manlius on the Tarpeian Citadel (8.562); this was the traditional place where he was flung to his death on the charges of kingly aspirations.[32] What actually happened to Manlius in the late fourth century is not definitively known; we have no certain way of knowing if Virgil followed the same traditions as Livy, given the positive nature of his brief appearance on the shield. Actium too, which we are about see unfold on the shield, was an eminently civil conflict—but the image of Cleopatra with her Egyptian gods identifies it as a decidedly foreign war on this work of art. Some have seen the shield as critical commentary on the Augustan regime; I think any such criticism is exceedingly muted, and, as elsewhere, I see Virgil accepting the undeniable benefits of the *Pax Augusta*: the (quite legitimate) fears the poet has are for the succession (i.e., the future), not Augustus (the present).

What is clear from the shield's artwork depictions is that Actium, the central image, represents the settlement of all Roman history. The images on the shield depict dark moments from Rome's past as well as bright moments of pride. The shield was announced as a canvas for Italian history (8.626 *res Italas*), and Augustus Caesar on one side drives on the Italians with the Senate, the people, and the Penates—a new Aeneas, as it were, saving Rome from the *other* side (678 *hinc*... 685 *hinc*), Mark Antony and Cleopatra. Aeneas had seen the two promontories of Leucas in his travels (3.274 ff.); Virgil conflates Leucate and Actium (both of which had temples of Apollo)—this is not merely poetically acceptable imprecision, since Leucate itself was a theater of the campaign against Antony. Actium represents the image of a Roman who has succumbed to an irrational Eastern queen in obstinate betrayal of his Senate, people, and household gods (which Augustus carries with him). Actium represents what Aeneas himself almost succumbed to—he was saved only by the intervention of Jupiter (even Venus seemed utterly unconcerned that her son was spending so much time at leisure in Carthage). Actium represents the combination of domestic and foreign strife in one package (something that the conflicts of Marius and Sulla and Caesar and Pompey essentially lacked). In the past, the East and outlying areas of the Roman world might have served as backdrops for Rome's internecine squabbles; at Actium, a Roman took up arms in league with a foreign queen against a brother Roman.[33]

Both Anchises and Aeneas had been given renewed strength to pursue their destiny when, at a moment of resignation and serious depression, the infant Ascanius' head was seen to erupt in flames (2.679-686). Augustus' head is also sending forth flames of fire from both temples; his "father's star" (8.681 *patrium sidus*) appears over his head. This is usually understood as a reference to the famous comet that was visible at Augustus' funeral games in honor of Caesar; in the context of the *Aeneid*, the omen connects with the flames on Ascanius' head that appeared so early in the labors of Rome's foundation. Agrippa, Octavian's faithful admiral, is also depicted in a prominent place.[34] Agrippa is wearing the *corona navalis*, the "naval crown," which he had won in 36 B.C. for his defeat of Sextus Pompey—he was already a fearsome naval opponent by the time he met Antony at Actium. Augustus therefore has behind him the strength of the portent of fire and the accomplished career of the Roman Agrippa; Antony has "barbarian wealth" and "various arms" (8.685 *ope barbarica... variisque Antonius armis*), a denigration of his (in reality) significant Roman force, which even included Roman senators—Augustan propaganda needs to forget that as quickly as possible. Anthony has abandoned his city, and his Roman forces are not at all mentioned on the shield; this discreet omission of historical reality in one sense serves Augustus' revisionism (the campaign was about Cleopatra, not a fellow Roman)—but it also highlights the betrayal of Rome by those Romans who would side with the East against Augustus' *Italian*-only force (again, 8.678 *Italos* is prominent). Cleopatra is viewed on the *shield* as the most threatening menace to Rome since the Gallic invasion of the fourth century; the obvious omission is Carthage—Virgil has already covered that theme thoroughly in Books 1-4, and Cleopatra is another Dido.

Antony is supported by the "peoples of the Dawn" (686 *Aurorae populis*); this is poetic historical embellishment on the one hand, but most importantly for the immediate context, it recalls the Ethiopian Memnon (the son of Aurora) and his forces. Memnon came late to try to help Troy; the image was one of the last on the walls of Dido's temple at Carthage (1.489 *Eoasque acies et nigri Memnonis arma*). Aeneas is not only Augustus in the complex allegories of the *Aeneid*, but also Antony; he spent the first third of the book walking in Antony's shoes, as it were, and at the end of the poem, despite his victory, we shall hear news of Troy's ultimate defeat by Italy—the victor at Actium. Antony carries with him Egypt and Bactra (the latter is more poetic exaggeration that serves its purpose well), and, of course, the real cause of the war:

... sequiturque (nefas) Aegyptia coniunx. (8.688)

... *and following (unspeakable) there was the Egyptian wife.*

As Fordyce observed, the Roman poets of the Augustan Age never identify Cleopatra by name.[35] In Virgil's depiction, Cleopatra is calling on her native gods with a *sistrum* (8.696), a noisy, rattling instrument; she does not yet see the two snakes that are behind her.[36] The reference is to her eventual suicide at Alexandria, traditionally by the bite of an asp. But in the context of the *Aeneid*, the reference is partly to the death of Laocoon, when two snakes from the sea writhed their way to the shore and devoured him and his sons (2.199 ff.)—another subtle reference to a reversal of roles for Aeneas and his Trojans in this depiction of Italian victory (this explains why Virgil names twin snakes, while all the extant historical sources name only one).[37] Cleopatra was not in the midst of the fighting at Actium; again, it is not simply stereotyped Augustan propaganda that compels Virgil to depict her in the heart of the fray, but the view that Cleopatra was to blame for the whole mess between the two Romans.[38] So also the Roman gods who are named first as standing beside Octavian's fleet are Neptune (in his capacity as pacifier of the sea, a role Augustus helps fulfill in this battle), Venus (ever protective of her beloved Romans), and *Minerva*, who sent the snakes to kill Laocoon, and who in Roman religion was part of the Capitoline triad with Jupiter and Juno. Mars and Bellona are there as well, of course, along with Discord (the ultimate cause of the Trojan War), and the Furies (we must not press their appearance too far and think of Allecto; they make stock appearances in scenes of violence). The Furies and Discord, indeed perhaps even Bellona (who became conflated at some point with an Eastern deity and was associated with ecstatic, self-flagellating, bloody rituals), are equal opportunity destroyers.[39]

Apollo, of course, is the final Roman protector god at Actium. He bends his bow from his vantage point at his temple on the promontory. A tricolon of foreign enemies of Rome is stricken with fear: all Egypt, every Arab, and all the Sabaeans (the Shebans of the modern Yemen in south Arabia). The appearance of Apollo frightens Cleopatra so much that she gives up the fight and sets sail for home, pale at the prospect of her future death (8.709 *pallentem morte futura*). She is contrasted with Augustus himself (714 *At Caesar*); again, Antony is carefully and deliberately omitted from the scene of defeat. Augustus did celebrate a triple triumph two years after the battle, in August of 29 B.C.; Virgil says he dedicated three hundred temples—his patron was more modest (twelve temples according to *Res Gestae* 19, with a further eighty-two restored). Just as Virgil announced the shield's *Italian* history (8.626), so it is to the Italian gods (715 *dis Italis*) that Augustus dedicates his many religious shrines. Augustus' devotion to religious duty, of course, is parallel to Aeneas' careful observation of religious prescriptions, in obedience to the advice of Helenus most particularly. The Actium ecphrasis is by far the most developed on the shield; just as the waters almost come to life, so the scene seems to move with living figures, as opposed to the static scenes of history and the underworld that surround it. The passage is somewhat equivalent to the paintings on Dido's temple walls, which depicted the Greek defeat of the Trojans; while that was a votive offering to Juno; this shield is the future of Rome and the image of Aeneas' victory.[40]

The conquered tribes who are imagined as walking in triumphal procession represent the extreme borders of a fancifully conceived Augustan Empire: the "race of the Nomads" refers to North Africa's Atlas region, while the Lelages and the Carians were in Asia Minor. The Geloni are notoriously difficult to locate precisely; they were certainly Scythians. The Morini (8.727) were a Belgian tribe west of the Rhine; they and the German Suebi (not mentioned here) were subdued in 29 B.C. The Araxes is a river in Armenia that flows into the Caspian Sea; the Dahae were to its east. They are *indomiti* (728), which is historically true; it is unclear what Virgil's intention was in using the inappropriate epithet for a "conquered" tribe. Augustus' actual foreign policy was far more sedate than the extravagances of passages such as the shield would imply; Antony himself had tried to launch an invasion of Parthia in 36 B.C. and failed—Augustus' more diplomatic approach to the Roman Far East was more successful. In the Augustan view of foreign policy, one can label "conquered" that which does not attack or threaten to attack Rome.

Aeneas picks up the shield in exact imitation of how he had picked up his father; Book 2 ended with Aeneas picking up the past, and Book 8 ends with Aeneas picking up his future. He understood fully what his burden was then; this burden is unknown to him (8.730 *ignarus*). It is very much in Virgil's style that the moments of greatest triumph and glory should be followed almost at once with a darker hint. That darker hint is usually not inexplicable; it never forces us to make any drastic conclusions about Virgil's treatment of his hero: the poet prefers to use his creative tricks subtly and quietly. So the Bough hesitates, but not because Aeneas is not fated to visit the underworld; and likewise Aeneas exits the underworld through the Ivory Gate, in part because he is, quite unavoidably, not a true shade (because he is alive). Here Aeneas is unavoidably ignorant of the anachronistic shield that means so much to Virgil's contemporaries and his future audiences. We have observed that over the course of now two-thirds of the *Aeneid* Virgil's hero has become noticeably more confident and self-possessed in his undertakings. This change started at the end of Book 5, when the ships were fired; that ring will close very shortly at the beginning of Book 9, when (in Aeneas' absence) Turnus will try to burn the Trojan fleet and Cybele will save them with Jupiter's consent. When the ships were about to be destroyed in Book 5, Aeneas in despair implored heaven for aid; Jupiter immediately sent a saving rain. Palinurus' death was a setback for Aeneas (again unknowing, at first, of what had really happened). Aeneas was still troubled in Book 6 when the Sibyl advised him that one of his men remained unburied; that potential stumbling block was also quickly removed, and throughout the book Aeneas showed signs of a resolute boldness we had not seen before. This confidence reached a climax when Aeneas first saw the weapons from heaven gleaming in the sky; he saw them as a sign that portended slaughter for the Latins and the punishment (i.e., the death) of Turnus. But confidence and boldness have nothing to do with understanding of the future, and at the ends of Books 6 and 8 Aeneas sees visions he cannot possibly be expected to comprehend (however much they may fill him with a renewed sense of purpose and invigorated strength). This ignorance of Aeneas is understandable and no discredit to the hero; what he does at the ends of Books 10 and 12 will be different: in Book 10 we shall see the worst character in the poem, Mezentius, defeated and killed. He will beg Aeneas for burial—there will be no reply. We have no idea what becomes of Mezentius' body; it is likely, as we shall see, that Aeneas' men come forward to stab it in ritual slaughter at the beginning of Book 11. What happens at the end of Book 12 is crystal clear, and in direct conflict with Anchises' command to Aeneas at the end of Book 6 to spare those who are subjected to him (perhaps significantly, the images on the shield do not show the deaths of Antony or even Cleopatra—in history Octavian was excused from having to deal with either potential prisoner by their convenient suicides).[41] Of course it is possible that Anchises was speaking beyond his son, to some future "Roman." This interpretation (conveniently) absolves Aeneas of any onus of reproach for killing Turnus at the end of the poem. But the *Aeneid* is in large part the epic of Aeneas' education and what he does with that education. Rome's mythological progenitor is first addressed *as a Roman* in Elysium.

The close of Book 8 marks the end of the second third of the poem, which we have identified as the four books of Aeneas' education. The first four books set up the problem of the entire poem and served as introductory matter; the last four will resolve the problem the first four posed and thus serve as the poem's conclusion. The first four presented Dido as a threat to Aeneas' future; the gods saved him. The last four will focus on Turnus as the threat to Aeneas' future; the gods will save Aeneas, of course, insofar as they will remove any chance of Turnus' victory (especially in Book 11)—but they will not save Aeneas from himself in the poem's final lines. Books 5-8 have revealed the future to a man who cannot understand it; in this Aeneas is poignantly and tragically like Augustus, who could achieve victory in the present and set the stage for a lasting and secure future—but who could not foresee what the future would hold. In this comparison Augustus has the more tragic lot of the two figures; Aeneas might not understand the future, but at least he was ignorant of a future the audience understands, in whose glories they could take some comfort, especially in moments of anxiety. Augustus could not foretell the future; no oracles or divine visitations could enlighten him as to the outcome of his program. If previous Roman history were a clue to the future, he might well have grave concerns. This Augustan ignorance is the (equally innocent) parallel to the ignorance of Aeneas in these closing lines of Book 8. There is rejoicing in the present, and rightly so, for both Aeneas and Augustus. What the future held for the Roman principate is known to modern audiences, who therefore bring more knowledge to their reading of the *Aeneid* than Virgil's contemporaries could, and who thereby prove the worst fears of Virgil and his fellow Augustan Romans to have been well-founded indeed.

Notes

1. Jenkyns, *op. cit.*, p. 518.

2. One of the best articles on the book is WIESEN, "The Pessimism of the Eighth *Aeneid*," *Latomus* 32 (1973), pp. 737-765.

3. On Diomedes' complicated history after the Trojan War, see Homer *Odyssey* 3.191-192 (Nestor refers to Diomedes' safe homecoming); Lycophron *Alexandra* 592-632 (Diomedes' problems with his wife Aegialeia and his settlement in southern Italy), Apollodorus *Library* 6.9 (the unfaithfulness of his wife); and also TRACY, "Vergil and the Nostoi," *Vergilius* 14 (1968), pp. 36-39.

4. Daunus is the name of one of Lycaon's Arcadian sons who ended up in Italy along with two of his brothers, of Turnus' father, and of the Apulian king who graciously welcomed Diomedes; the connection between the three obviously related men is difficult to discern.

5. See further PAPOIANNOU, "Vergilian Diomedes Revisited: The Re-Evaluation of the *Iliad*," *Mnemosyne* 53 (2000), pp. 193-217.

6. See further Hunter's notes on *Argonautica* 3.755-765.

7. Hornsby, *op. cit.*, pp. 100-102, compares this simile with the image of Turnus at 7.460-466 as a pot of boiling water. Hornsby is right that "Aeneas has passed beyond the condition Turnus is now in, for his "darkness" of wrath occurred at the fall of Troy"—but the last lines of the poem will change all that.

8. Useful (with full bibliography) is PAPAIOANNOU, "Civilizer and Leader: Vergil's Evander and his Role in the Origins of Rome," *Mnemosyne* 56 (2003), pp. 680-702.

9. On the Evander traditions see further OGILVIE, *A Commentary on Livy, Books 1-5*, Oxford, 1965, pp. 51 ff.

10. Cf. Propertius *carmen* 4.9, with Hutchinson's notes.

11. For a helpful expansion of much of the work done on Aeneas/Pallas and Nisus/Euryalus as homoerotic pairs, see LLOYD, "The Evander-Anchises Connection: Fathers, Sons, and Homoerotic Desire and Vergil's *Aeneid*," *Vergilius* 45 (1999), pp. 3-21. More generally, see PAVLOCK, "The Hero and the Erotic in *Aeneid* 7-12," *Vergilius* 33 (1992), pp. 72-87.

12. See especially GALINSKY, "The Hercules-Cacus Episode in *Aeneid* VIII," *The American Journal of Philology* (87) 1966, pp. 18-51; and, more generally, his *The Herakles Theme*, Oxford, 1972, in particular pp. 131-149 (reprinted in Harrison, *op. cit.*, pp. 277-294).

13. Though note that Augustus dedicated a temple to the *Magna Mater* on the Palatine (it was destroyed by fire in A.D. 3); see *Res Gestae Divi Augusti* 4.19. The issue of her cult is connected to the reception of the *idea* of Troy in Augustan Rome; Suetonius *Divus Julius* 79.3 records that Julius Caesar intended to move the capital of the Republic/Empire from Rome to Troy; the idea may well have been revived in the early years of Augustus in more or less drastic forms. See especially Nisbet and Rudd, *op. cit.*, pp. 35-8. It is not at all impossible (*contra* Fraenkel, and G. Williams) that the Augustan program envisaged some revival of the site of Troy, especially in conjunction with a major revival of the cult of Cybele, and that the Augustan poets (at least Virgil and Horace) warned against it. See also FRAENKEL, *Horace*, Oxford, 1957, pp. 257 ff. The whole matter is of intense concern to Virgil.

14. Though note that Augustus dedicated a temple to the *Magna Mater* on the Palatine (it was destroyed by fire in A.D. 3); see *Res Gestae Divi Augusti* 4.19. The issue of her cult is connected to the reception of the *idea* of Troy in Augustan Rome; Suetonius *Divus*

Julius 79.3 records that Julius Caesar intended to move the capital of the Republic/Empire from Rome to Troy; the idea may well have been revived in the early years of Augustus in more or less drastic forms. See especially Nisbet and Rudd, *op. cit.*, pp. 35-8. It is not at all impossible (*contra* Fraenkel, and G. Williams) that the Augustan program envisaged some revival of the site of Troy, especially in conjunction with a major revival of the cult of Cybele, and that the Augustan poets (at least Virgil and Horace) warned against it. See also FRAENKEL, *Horace*, Oxford, 1957, pp. 257 ff. The whole matter is of intense concern to Virgil.

15. The classic study on Aeneas' visit remains FOWLER, *Aeneas at the Site of Rome*, Oxford, 1918.

16. On this passage see further THOMAS, *Lands and Peoples in Roman Poetry: The Ethnographical Tradition*, Cambridge, 1982, especially pp. 98 ff.; and see H.B. Evans' review in *The Classical Journal* 80.3 (1985), pp. 265-267, for important criticism. Evans rightly points out that Thomas ignores the revelations of Jupiter to Juno in Book 12.

17. "A peculiar expression, found in a number of different contexts in Homer and Hesiod." (RUTHERFORD, *Homer, Odyssey, Books XIX and XX*, Cambridge, 1992, p. 156).

18. See further DUMEZIL, *op. cit.*, pp. 414 ff.

19. *De Rerum Natura* 1.40-43.

20. Cf. Propertius *carmen* 4.4, with Hutchinson's notes.

21. On this simile see further Hornsby, *op. cit.*, pp. 106-107; Hornsby sees an evocation of Dido and Aeneas here, but Jupiter is the main figure hiding behind the comparison.

22. Note here SMOLENAARS, "A Disturbing Scene from the Marriage of Venus and Vulcan: *Aeneid* 8.370-415," *Vergilius* 50 (2004), pp. 96-107, especially pp. 103-105.

23. *Ab Urbe Condita* 1.57-58.

24. The Etruscans were justified in their rage; for the intriguing idea that Virgil modifies the noun *furiae* when the cause of the fury is legitimate (8.494 *furiis surrexit Etruria iustis*), see THOMAS, "*Furor* and *Furiae* in Virgil," *The American Journal of Philology* 112 (1991), p. 261.

25. On Tarchon see NIELSON, "*Tarchon Etruscus: Alter Aeneas*," *Pacific Coast Philology* 19 (1984), pp. 28-34. Both Tarchon and Arruns serve as proxies for Aeneas in Book 11.

26. Fordyce notes on 8.506 that "Virgil is vague about the status of Tarchon—in 555 he is *rex Tyrrhenus*—and about the polity of Etruria in general."

27. For Augustus' wars in Spain and their aftermath, see *inter alios* Cassius Dio 44.5, and Livy *Ab Urbe Condita* 28.12.

28. For the intriguing thesis that Aeneas' shield was modeled after the shield of Athena *Parthenos*, see COHON, "Vergil and Pheidias: The Shield of Aeneas and of Athena Parthenos," *Vergilius* 37 (1991), pp. 22-30. For an analysis of the motifs of fire and metal in the *Schild-Bild*, see SCULLY, "Refining Fire in *Aeneid* 8," *Vergilius* 46 (2000), pp. 93-113.

29. See Fordyce on 8.643.

30. For a comprehensive survey of the Salii and their *ancilia* (shields), see DUMEZIL, *op. cit.*, pp. 146, 166 and 276-277.

31. For the juxtaposition of scenes of Roman religious ritual and threatening foreign invasions, see Littlewood on Ovid *Fasti* 6.186 (Oxford, 2006).

32. See Livy *Ab Urbe Condita* 6.14-20, with Oakley's notes. "Manlius' models are identified as would-be tyrants at the start. Though his motives were a declamatory topic, no other surviving narrative seems to have treated him so ambiguously: in Dio he even

occupies the Capitoline. If he is presented positively, it is exclusively in the context of the Gallic war." (KRAUS, *Livy, Ab Urbe Condita, Book 6*, Cambridge, 1994, p. 205). See also WALSH, *Livy: His Historical Aims and Methods*, Cambridge, 1961, pp. 250 ff. (on the saving of the Capitol from the Gauls).

33. Cf. Manilius *Astronomica* 1.914-918.

34. For a convenient overview of the actual battle, see CARTER, *The Battle of Actium*, London, 1970. On Virgil's Actium, see THOMAS, "Le Sens synbolique de la bataille d'Actium (*Eneide*, VIII, 671-728)," *Euphrosyne* 19 (1991), pp. 303-308.

35. On Egypt's most famous queen, see VOLKMANN, *Cleopatra: A Study in Politics and Propaganda*, London, 1968; GRANT, *Cleopatra*, New York, 1972 (still a worthwhile introductory biography, well-written and comprehensive); and WYKE, "Augustan Cleopatras: Female Power and Poetic Authority," in POWELL, ed., *Roman Poetry and Propaganda in the Age of Augustus*, London, 1992, pp. 98-140.

36. The *sistrum* was an instrument associated with Eastern cults, specifically Isis worship (Isidore thought its name derived from the goddess'); cf. Ovid *Amores* 2.13.10 (with McKeown's note), and especially Lucan's celebrated attack on Egypt (guilty of the blood of Pompey, who was savagely murdered by agents of Cleopatra's brother Ptolemy), especially *Bellum Civile* 8.832; Manilius mentions Isis' sistrum in combat with the Roman fleet at Actium.

37. For exhaustive summary of the surviving evidence, see TRONSON, "Vergil, The Augustans, and the Invention of Cleopatra's Suicide—One Asp or Two?," *Vergilius* 44 (1998), pp. 31-50.

38. George Shea has suggested to me the intriguing possibility that Dido represents Cleopatra at Alexandria, and Camilla Cleopatra at Actium. But— notwithstanding fanciful propaganda—Cleopatra's lack of martial activity at Actium argues against any correspondence between Camilla and Cleopatra.

39. On Bellona's Eastern origins and the crazed liturgies in honor of Ma-Bellona see further Murgatroyd, and Maltby, on Tibullus *carmen* 1.6.43 ff.).

40. Propertius may have been inspired by this ecphrasis in his etiological account of the origin of Augustus' temple to Apollo on the Palatine (*carmen* 4.6), which was later mistakenly thought to be a thanksgiving offering for Actium. See further GUNTHER, ed., *Brill's Companion to Propertius*, Leiden-Boston, 2006, pp. 375 ff., and Hutchinson's notes ad carm.

41. It is just possible that in Virgil's silence about what Aeneas does with the bodies of Mezentius and Turnus we are meant to see a faint echo of Octavian's fortune in not having to deal with a living Antony or Cleopatra.

Chapter IX

AND WHILE THESE THINGS

Book 9 of the *Aeneid* opens the third and final section of the poem, and has affinities with both Books 1 and 5. In all three books Aeneas' fleet is in serious jeopardy; Book 9 also returns to the Nisus and Euryalus story arc that had begun in Book 5. Book 9, like Books 1 and 5, is episodic; it moves from scene to scene with a freshness and vigor that gives it great excitement. Some have felt that Virgil did not have the stomach for war narrative and that in consequence he did everything he could to delay any accounts of bloodshed and fighting. That view is demonstrably false, as we shall see; the last third of the *Aeneid* does not refrain from presenting war's horrors in all their bloody reality. The episodic "digressions" (especially the Nisus and Euryalus epyllion in this book and Camilla's background story in Book 11) serve important narrative functions. Even the fantastic transformation of Aeneas' ships into mermaids (which has been criticized by many as inappropriate to the style and flavor of the Iliadic *Aeneid*) has an important message, which becomes increasingly clear and central to the action as the last third of the epic unfolds: Jupiter, in the name of Rome's fated destiny, will intervene dramatically to favor and ensure the victory of Aeneas (just as Juno will try her best to help Turnus and resist the decrees of fate). This book begins with Juno sending Iris to inform Turnus of Aeneas' absence from the Trojan camp and the opportunity he now has to strike hard; at the book's ending (one of the most complex and important closures in the poem) she will be unable to give Turnus strength as he single-handedly takes on the Trojans inside their own camp, because Jupiter sends Iris down to warn her that Turnus must finish the retreat he has already started (another important divine intervention).

Cambridge University Press has something of a series on the second half of the poem (Books 8, 9, 11, and a forthcoming 12); of the existing volumes, the most excellent is Philip Hardie's commentary on Book 9, which incorporates valuable comments from Fordyce's never published edition of the book.

While Aeneas rightly delights in the revelation of the shield's artwork, Juno visits Turnus via Iris. She had been completely absent from Book 8; Virgil continues his pattern of alternating the work of Venus and Juno in furthering their disparate goals. Turnus had appeared at the very beginning of Book 8; now he appears at the start of Book 9, and we learn what he has been doing during the time Aeneas was in Pallanteum (9.1 *Atque ea diversa penitus in parte diversa*). The force of *penitus* at midline is strong; Aeneas has been safely absent in a distant, secluded valley (8.609 *valle reducta*) near Caere; now we learn of Turnus' parallel actions.[1] (Aeneas will be completely absent from this book, just as Turnus was largely absent from Book 8). Turnus too is in a valley, sitting in a sacred vale in a grove of his great-great-grandfather Pilumnus. In a passage of

Varro quoted in Augustine's *De Civitate Dei* (6.9.2), Pilumnus is a protector god of marriage, in particular of newborn children; he is one of the gods invoked as a protector of new mothers. At the start of Book 9, Virgil thus portrays Turnus in the context of Roman religion. Pilumnus is his ancestor; any possible connection beyond that is difficult to discern. Perhaps there is some echo of the ostensible cause of the war, namely the prospect of marriage between Turnus and Lavinia. The contrast between Turnus' appearance at the beginnings of Books 8 and 9 is great. There he was raising the battle cry, while here he is sitting quietly in a holy grove. Despite the visit from the Fury Allecto, Turnus is capable of calm and reflective moments. In some sense, the pattern we saw with Aeneas early in the poem will now be repeated with Turnus. Juno sends Iris to announce to Turnus two things. She apprises him of the battle situation (Aeneas has abandoned his camp and ships to seek help in Pallanteum and Etruria), and, in consequence, Turnus should seize the opportunity to deal Aeneas' forces a mortal blow. Turnus has been delaying (9.14 *omnis moras*) for unknown reasons; perhaps, like Aeneas, he has been debating exactly what to do now that war has been declared. Turnus has already been visited by Allecto, but he does not know who sent Iris; the omen is a mysterious one to him, obviously divine (16 *adgnovit*, i.e., he recognizes Iris), but he does not know its provenance. His declaration is perhaps reckless:

... sequor omina tanta,
quisquis in arma vocas. (9.21-22)

... *I follow such omens,*
whoever you are who call me to arms.

If Turnus is being reckless, though, in his zealous willingness to follow an unknown omen, then we must also note that Aeneas was less than zealous (cf. 4.360 *Italiam non sponte sequor*) in his willingness to follow a destiny that had been far more explicitly defined than Turnus'. Turnus is *audax* (9.3) while he sits in his grove; so too was Pallas (8.110) when he first saw the Trojans approach Pallanteum. Fairclough's "gallant" is not a good translation, but the label is not exclusively negative either. It is a frequent epithet for Turnus (cf. 7.409, 7.475, 9.126, 10.276, also his sister Juturna at 12.786, and the Rutulians at 9.519); at 5.67 it describes (neutrally) a potential contestant in Anchises' memorial games, and at 11.812 the wolf (Arruns) that has just killed Camilla. At 7.114 it describes the jaws of the Trojans, about to devour their "tables" in fulfillment of the Harpy's prophecy. Ascanius uses it (9.625) when he asks Jupiter to smile upon his "bold undertakings" in defense of the Trojan camp (undertakings the gods will stop). So it is not exactly the case that everyone described as *audax* in the poem will die or would have died had they given in to *audacia*, but it is certainly a key adjective in describing Turnus (fittingly, since he is fighting against divinely ordered fate). And, certainly, neither Turnus nor Aeneas has a monopoly on madness in this poem. Turnus concludes his private time in the sacred grove with prayer: he offers many entreaties to the gods, and heaps up the heavenly ether (9.24 *oneravitque aethera*) with his vows. Whether his prayers will be answered is another issue altogether. Virgil's concern at the beginnings of Books 8 and 9 has been to show two very different sides of Turnus.

As we observed in Jupiter's speech to Venus in Book 1, the father of gods and men predicted a future time that would be so peaceful that Romulus and Remus would be together in heaven as lawgivers (1.292-293), a future peace that contrasts greatly with how the *Aeneid* actually ends, where we are left to hope that one day Aeneas and Turnus will be similarly reconciled "brothers" in an immortal afterlife overseeing their beloved Italy. As we move through the last third of the poem, we shall frequently encounter material for comparison between Aeneas and Turnus. Both characters are deeply flawed and commit atrocities in the Italian war. Lurking behind their conflict is the dread specter of civil war (the major theme of the Romulus and Remus story, and Rome's history for the whole century before Virgil and Augustus).

We can understand at once, from the first announcement of the military movements of the Italians, the fact that they will lose. In his simile to describe the cavalry and infantry of Messapus, the sons of Tyrrhus, and Turnus himself, Virgil compares the Italians to the Nile or the Ganges. We are at once thrust back into the world of the shield, where Augustus vanquished the Egyptian forces of Cleopatra, and we can imagine the "Nile" of Messapus and Turnus soon hoisted on some placard in Aeneas' triumphal procession. However, the Nile is also described as hiding itself:

cum refluit campis et iam se condidit alveo. (9.32)

when he flows back from the fields and buries himself in his channel.

This is exactly the opposite of what the Italians are actually doing as they advance over the open plains. Virgil has confused the situation, as is his wont; the Nile is said to flow back and hide itself in the poet's simile, but the *Teucrians* see the Latins rising over the plain (34 *insurgere campis*). They do not see what we are told. The audience is here reminded, at the outset of formal military operations, of what it already knows: Turnus' cause is doomed. Aeneas also knows that he will win (it is not entirely clear how many of his prophecies he has revealed to his men). But Virgil will play on another level: what would have happened minus divine intervention. This theme will grow in importance steadily until Book 10, when, at the outset of the book, in the poem's only divine council, Jupiter essentially forbids divine involvement and interference in the war. Jupiter will break his own edict in Book 11, during a military engagement that could have spelled doom for the Trojans. Book 12 will present further complications in the theme of divine intervention, culminating in Aeneas' personal decision to kill Turnus.

The simile is jarringly inappropriate for two other reasons. It describes the Ganges and the Nile not merely in retreat, but even *peaceful* retreat (9.30 *sedatis amnibus*, 31 *per tacitum*). It also uses the flow of water to describe what the Trojans themselves see as the black cloud of dust kicked up by many horses and warriors on the plain (33-34 *hic subitam nigro glomerari pulvere nubem / prospiciunt Teucri ac tenebras insurgere campis*). Again, Virgil emphasizes the difference between what the audience sees and what Aeneas' men (soon to be trapped in their camp) see from their position. Aeneas could not possibly understand the Battle of Actium on his shield, and here his men do not grasp the truth behind the Latin movements: they understandably think that they are about to be attacked and hemmed in without their leader, but in reality, in the long view, they have won and the Latins are as doomed as Antony and Cleopatra's vessels at Actium. The false comparison of dust kicked up over a plain to peaceful water echoes the message of the shield. The artwork is beautiful and awe-inspiring in gold, silver, and the effect of living color, but the reality of warfare is very different indeed. The mention of rivers vaguely presages the attempt to fire the Trojan fleet, which is hemmed in by mounds and river waters (70 *aggeribus saeptam circum et fluvialibus undis*)—again, with a change of sides.

Caicus at once calls out for the Trojans to mount their defensive positions on the ramparts of their camp. Aeneas' order that the Trojans should not leave camp while he is absent was certainly sound and prudent strategy; he has no idea what Turnus' plans are (any more than Turnus knew where Aeneas was until Iris visited him), and he cannot risk a rout while he is securing allies. The Trojans inadvertently started the war with the shooting of Silvia's stag. Now the other side will commence operations. The Trojans are both ashamed and angry (9.44 *pudor iraque monstrat*) at Aeneas' orders in the face of Turnus' threat. Turnus has no such orders, and he outpaces his men as he rides up to the city so quickly that his arrival is unexpected (49 *improvisus*). His horse is Thracian in part because of the traditionally fierce and wild character of some of their inhabitants (particularly the mountain dwellers), and the belief that if they actually learned how to unite, they would be invincible.[2] The darker reference of the Thracian horse is to the ill fated Rhesus and *his* famous Thracian horses at Troy. Like Laocoon before him, Turnus throws a spear at the Trojans: the prime reference in the context of the *Aeneid* is to the ill-fated Trojan priest, while historically Turnus' action is eminently Roman: fetial priests would traditionally cast the spear of war into the territory of the enemy. Virgil's emphasis is on Turnus' frustration. He wishes to fight, and it is arguable that if the Trojans were to disobey Aeneas' instructions and agree to engage in combat on the plain, they might be seriously discomfited. Thus begins a major theme of the Iliadic *Aeneid*: Turnus' frustrated wish to fight Aeneas immediately. Turnus has not been patient for very long; the action of the beginning of Book 9 occurs while Aeneas is in Pallanteum. The Latin view of the Trojans' obedience to Aeneas' orders is clear: they consider it cowardice (9.55 *inertia corda*). Turnus sets out alone on horseback to find some way into the Trojan camp. Virgil compares him to a wolf that is stalking a sheepfold:

ac veluti pleno lupus insidiatus ovili

cum fremit ad caulas ventos perpessus et imbris
nocte super media: tuti sub matribus agni
balatum exercent, ille asper at improbus ira
saevit in absentis, collecta fatigat edendi
ex longo rabies et siccae sine sanguine fauces:
haud aliter Rutulo muros et castra tuenti
ignescunt irae; duris dolor ossibus ardet. (9.59-66)[3]

*And just as when a wolf lies in wait by a full sheepfold
and seethes at the pens, enduring winds and rains
during the middle of the night, and the lambs, safe under their
mothers raise their cry; the wolf, fierce and reckless in his anger
rages against the absent lambs, and the built-up frenzy to eat
tires him out after a long time, and his throat is dry without blood:
scarcely otherwise did the fires begin to burn for the Rutulian as
he watched the walls and the camps; and the sorrow burned in his
  hard bones.*

Once again, Turnus is like the Aeneas we knew far earlier in the poem; the simile is borrowed from Book 2 (355-360), where Aeneas and the Trojans with him had decided to rush into arms and die bravely on their city's horrific last night. The image was different there; the wolves of Book 2 were hungry, and so were their pups (2.357-358 *catulique relicti / faucibus exspectant siccis*): here Turnus is all alone, with no mention of any lupine children—the only offspring in the comparison here are the lambs who are safe in their mothers' care at home. The Trojans were angry because they could not get out and fight the insulting Latins; Turnus is angry because he can find no way inside to kill the sheep. This wolf will not suffer rain; Aeneas' ships will be saved this time by a more dramatic divine intervention than before. Lupine Turnus is said to be "lying in wait" (*insidiatus*, which means to lie in ambush)—this is a foreshadowing of the decisive encounter in Book 11, where Turnus will lie in wait to intercept Aeneas' infantry once he has received word that Aeneas' plan is to move ground forces over difficult terrain under cover of a cavalry assault: the simile's specific comparison of Turnus to a wolf lying in wait will not reach total fulfillment until Book 11. The presence of a Trojan settlement (*muros et castra*) in territory Turnus considers part of his sphere of influence is also a goad to his burgeoning anger.

Turnus' anger has been stirred by the refusal of the Trojans to accept his challenge of battle. Aeneas is absent and unable to accept any potential offer of single combat, and Turnus is hardly racing off to intercept Aeneas and his new allies in Etruria. His rage will now be compounded by Jupiter's willingness to intervene a second and final time to save the Trojan ships from fire. This is the third and final crisis for Aeneas' navy. The storm in Book 1 and the fire in Book 5 cost valuable ships, which were, admittedly, able to be refashioned in Carthage and Sicily respectively. Now the ships are no longer needed; Turnus assumes that he can drive the Trojans in flight away from Italy, and his decision to burn the ships signals his attention to trap them and hunt them down like the wolf he is (and indeed, this will be his analysis of their fate after they lose their ships to divine action).[4] The decision to fire the ships is a mark of Turnus' frustration; it also introduces a recurring theme of the last books, namely the stalling of any direct engagement between Turnus and Aeneas. Aeneas was inexplicably absent from the war narrative in Book 7. In Book 8 he was away with Evander. In this book he is absent. In Book 10 he will return, but for various reasons the fateful clash between the two opponents will be delayed. In Book 11 neither Aeneas nor Turnus will be central to the action. Book 12 will be the march to single combat. So the pattern is: Book 7 Turnus, Book 8 Aeneas, Book 9 Turnus, Book 10 Turnus *and* Aeneas, Book 11 *neither* Turnus *nor* Aeneas (at least in the battle sequences), and Book 12 Turnus *and* Aeneas. This creates a balanced pair of rings: Books 7-9, which begin and end with Turnus, and Books 10 and 12, which portray both characters together in the action for most of the time, with Book 11 as a strange interlude (an interlude that, as we shall see, serves to underscore Virgil's view of divine intervention between the two opponents).

Virgil dramatically announces the saving of the ships with an address to the Muses. This is the third such address in the poem, and only the second that is made to all the Muses; it must signal a tremendously significant moment in the poet's mind.[5] Venus, Aeneas' mother, is not involved; Turnus will mention her (9.135) when he notes that the Trojans have fulfilled their fate and Venus' wishes sufficiently just by reaching Italy's shores. We now learn of action on the divine plane that had been concealed from us (and Aeneas) before. Cybele (conflated often with Rhea, Cronus' wife and Zeus' mother) had visited her son while Aeneas was still in the Troad, outfitting his ships. She had asked that the ships be spared any danger from storms (she had no reason to suspect fire, presumably, at any point during the forthcoming journey). Jupiter, we learn, had not agreed that Aeneas should have such an easy time on the journey, but he did agree that when Aeneas had no more need of the ships any surviving vessels would be saved. As is typical with prophecies, the news was not complete; Jupiter did not foretell the episode of the burning of the ships (after all, he is not omniscient about the future, and he had no idea what his wife might try to do in Sicily). Creusa's ghost had told Aeneas in Book 2 that Cybele was holding her back in her native land (788); that is the only shred of connection between Cybele's recollection here and her actions there. Cybele represents the patronage of Troy, while Venus is more particularly the patroness of Aeneas' (male) family unit of Anchises and Ascanius.

Cybele's voice is heard by both the Trojans and the Rutulians (9.112-113). When she tells them that Turnus will set the entire ocean on fire before he touches her ships, we are reminded of Juno's restraint of Allecto (7.551 ff.) before she could set the entire world on fire with her rage. The ships become marine goddesses, just as Neptune had been assisted by sea deities in Book 1 when he quelled the storm and rescued most of the fleet. Messapus is the progeny of Neptune; it is not surprising that the great terror of the son of the sea god (9.123 *conterritus*) should be pointed out first. The Tiber itself is afraid and flows backward.[6] Turnus is the only one who is not cowed by the miracle.[7] His words here will be echoed in Book 12:

> ... nil me fatalia terrent,
> si qua Phryges prae se iactant, responsa deorum (9.133-134)

> *... matters of fate do not terrify me in any way,*
> *though the Phrygians boast of oracles from the gods*

> ... non me tua fervida terrent
> dicta, ferox; di me terrent et Iuppiter hostis. (12.894-895)

> *... your hot words do not terrify me,*
> *fierce one; the gods terrify me, and Jupiter is my enemy.*

The two passages neatly encircle Turnus' fate. At the beginning of Book 9 (especially in Aeneas' absence), Turnus is afraid of nothing. He is convinced that he can win in an even fight with the Trojans (i.e., a fight without divine intervention). In his bluster he reckons that perhaps he can even go so far as to challenge the clear will of at least some of the immortals (he seems to think that Jupiter has taken away Trojan salvation by depriving them of their ships). By the end of Book 12, he will have contempt for Aeneas: he will realize that the gods have interfered again and again in the war and that he has no chance, and to the end he will declare that he does not fear Aeneas, only the gods (especially Jupiter, his enemy). Turnus seems to think that it is his fate to destroy the Trojans (9.137 *exscindere gentem*, "to cut down their race completely"); he must think this at least in part because of the visitations he has received from Allecto and Iris, though, of course, neither messenger told him that he would be guaranteed victory.[8] Turnus does not misread their words. He adds extended meanings, to his doom.[9] The metamorphosis of Turnus from Book 7 to Book 12 (which parallels Aeneas' from Book 1 to Book 6) is that of a man who slowly comes to the realization that he has no chance of winning due to the decrees of fate and the gods.[10] Aeneas' metamorphosis, on the other hand, is that of a man who (however slowly) corrects his marked tendency to ignore and forget about his revealed destiny. Turnus considers it his fate to destroy the Trojans the way the Greeks once did (this fits his role as the new Achilles the Sibyl predicted). Sarcastically, he imagines the Trojan reply:

> "sed periisse semel satis est": peccare fuisset
> ante satis, penitus modo non genus omne perosos
> femineum. (9.140-141)

> *"but to have perished once is enough." If only it had been enough*
> *to have sinned once before, and not to have hated so thoroughly the*
> *entire race of women.*

The exact meaning is difficult to construe. In response to the plaintive lament Turnus envisages for the Trojans, his response is a wish in past time incapable of fulfillment: if only it had been sufficient for the Trojans to have sinned before, and not to have hated so thoroughly and deeply (*per-*, *penitus*) the entire race of women (meaning, if only they would have learned to stop stealing other people's wives or intended wives). Aeneas reasoned that he was not married to Dido; Turnus thinks he is *de facto*, if not *de iure*, married to Lavinia.[11] Turnus sees himself as more than a second Greek conqueror of Troy. For him, there will be no need of Odyssean tricks and subterfuge. There will not even be a need for divine arms (9.148 *non armis mihi Vulcani*). This is a reference not to Aeneas' divine arms (Turnus has not been told about the gifts), but to Achilles' arms from *Iliad* 18: he will not need any such presents from a divine patron. Turnus' mention of both Neptune (145) and Vulcan (148) is ironic given the aid both gods have rendered to the Trojans.

Purple and gold had marked Dido's hunt, where a storm forced Aeneas to take shelter with Carthage's queen in a cave. Now purple and gold crests mark the seven hundred Italian soldiers who set up a siege of the Trojan camp. They have little regard for the Trojans, and so they indulge in wine and lie around on the grass at leisure and in games. Their behavior is understandable given the Trojan refusal to fight, but points to a terrible comeuppance. Mnestheus is one of the Trojans Aeneas had appointed to lead his forces in case of trouble in the camp; he had been the second place winner in the boat race in Book 5, and his introduction here leads to the long narrative of the night raid of Nisus and Euryalus, previously contestants in the foot race. Nisus and Euryalus' plan has an utterly noble genesis; Nisus knows that people in the Trojan camp have been eager to inform Aeneas of the Rutulian siege, and word must somehow be sent through the enemy lines to Pallanteum.

The Nisus and Euryalus epyllion is the first of two episodes in the *Aeneid* where Virgil draws on characters already briefly introduced and greatly expands their roles in his poem. There are several parallels between the Nisus-Euryalus and Camilla epyllia. Virgil's narrative is based on Homer's so-called Doloneia in *Iliad* 10, the night action of Odysseus and Diomedes (while Camilla is based on the Penthesilea of cyclic epic). Ultimately both stories are concerned with the untimely deaths of the young. Nisus and Euryalus are loyal to the Trojan cause, but they are most clearly defined by their strong, indeed homoerotic, love for each other. Camilla is loyal first and foremost to the Italian cause (significantly, her dying words will be instructions to Turnus on what he must do next); she has abandoned, as we shall learn, the forest life she had enjoyed in her early youth as one of Diana's favorites.[12] The death of all three will have profound impact on their respective sides. Camilla, as we shall learn, was a huntress; so was Nisus' (probable) mother Ida (appropriately named after the sacred Trojan height); Virgil's description is not altogether clear:

Nisus erat portae custos, acerrimus armis,
Hyrtacides, comitem Aeneae quem miserat Ida
venatrix (9.176-178)

*Nisus was the guardian of the gate, most keen in arms,
the son of Hyrtacus, whom the huntress Ida had sent to
Aeneas as a companion*

Virgil will use the same trick later to describe Camilla right before her death, where we learn that the warrior has not left behind her huntress lifestyle:

> hunc virgo, sive ut templis praefigeret arma
> Troia, captivo sive ut se ferret in auro
> venatrix, unum ex omni certamine pugnae
> caeca sequebatur. (11.778-781)

This one the virgin was blindly following as a
huntress, him alone out of the whole struggle of the fight,
uncertain whether she should hang the Trojan weapons in
a temple, or dress herself in captive gold.

Was "Ida" Nisus' mother? If so, what was a (presumably virgin) huntress doing with a child? Was she raped? Is Ida actually the mountain, and if so, is *venatrix* a rather striking epithet that identifies Ida as a popular haunt for hunters? Ida was the mountain where Ganymede was snatched by Jupiter (5.252). Nisus has, in a sense, snatched Euryalus as his Ganymede. Ganymede had been hunting when he was abducted. Camilla's hunt during the cavalry battle of Book 11 will be inappropriate because she is in a war, not a hunt. She is faithful to her vow of virginity (which is why Diana still favors her, notwithstanding her abandonment of the forest). Nisus and Euryalus will soon depart for what will become an inappropriate hunt of their own. After the deaths of Nisus and Euryalus, as we shall see shortly, there is ample cause for tremendous grief in the Trojan camp (their bodies will be desecrated by the Italians); immediately thereafter the Volscians—who are led by Camilla, though she is not named—lead the first charge (9.505) to assault the Trojan camp. Camilla's death also causes tremendous grief and discomfiture (and, as we shall see, deprives Turnus of his best chance to win the war). Virgil bestows one of his highest honors on Nisus and Euryalus, a powerful apostrophe that promises their undying memory (446-449), while the death of Camilla will spur the women of Latium to risk their lives for their country. Diana's hunt was the most inappropriate place possible for Aeneas and Dido to consummate their union. Nisus and Euryalus, as well as Camilla, would all have been better off remaining hunters. All of them, too, have traits that would not have been acceptable at Rome: the image of a woman in battle would have evoked Cleopatra for the Romans, and if they had been Roman citizens, Nisus would not have been able to pursue Euryalus sexually. The Trojans are not the only side in this war with homosexual lovers in their army; in Book 10, Cydon (who is paying more attention to his lover Clytius than to battle) will escape Aeneas' *aristeia* when seven of his fellow fighters defend and cover his escape from the fray (324-332).

Nisus is not sure whether the gods have inspired him with a burning desire (9.184 *ardorem*) to leave the camp and accomplish some great deed, or if *dira cupido*, some "terrible desire," is to blame. In Book 6 (373, 721), the phrase *dira cupido* described the ardent desires of the dead: Nisus (and his young friend and lover) are as good as dead before they even set out on their night raid. In Hades,

Palinurus had a terrible desire, an unspeakable wish, to cross the Styx without burial. Aeneas wonders what terrible desire could possibly motivate anyone to want to return to a mortal body and live another life. The associations, then, are ominous; we know Nisus and Euryalus are doomed. We learn that the Trojans have been offering prizes to anyone brave enough to risk the journey to Pallanteum; Nisus says that he will be satisfied with fame, if the Trojans give to Euryalus what they are promising for the hazardous mission (9.194-196). Once again, Nisus is thinking of Euryalus, whom he helped by cheating in the foot race. Seeking spoils will also be a dangerous thing in the Iliadic *Aeneid* (as Camilla will discover). Arruns will be satisfied merely with returning safely home, provided he is able to kill Camilla; he will get only part of his wish, just as Nisus will get his fame, but not the prizes he had been willing to give to his beloved.

Euryalus assertively boasts that his courage is "scornful of the light" (9.205 *est hic, est animus lucis contemptor*); during their slaughter of sleeping Latin soldiers Nisus will observe that they must stop since "light, our personal enemy" (355 *lux inimica*) is approaching, and it will be the glimmering light of the moon that betrays them (373). Once Euryalus is surrounded by the enemy, Nisus will offer a prayer to Diana that he may "disturb the mass of men around his friend" (409 *turbare globum*)—she will perhaps grant the prayer, though after the Latins decide to kill Euryalus, Nisus will break forth from his cover and die along with Euryalus' killer. Whether Diana answered the prayer and guided Nisus' shafts is for the individual reader to decide; it would not have been terribly difficult for him to shoot the Latins from his hiding place. Indeed, the glimmering light that betrayed Euryalus could well be taken as the action of the moon goddess (or, of course, as a Lucretius would argue, "just" the moon and no goddess at all). Nisus is concerned because the dawn is approaching (355), but in reality it will be a ray of moonlight that glints off the helmet Euryalus steals from a corpse (373).[13]

Nisus and Euryalus, then, have several similarities to Camilla, and several differences. They disobey Aeneas' orders by leaving camp (though the other Trojans, especially Ascanius, sanction it); Camilla not only carries out Turnus' orders, but also urges her commander to continue the plan after she has been mortally wounded. Significantly, all these doomed youths are hunters (245). We shall now examine the story of Nisus and Euryalus as it unfolds.

Nisus responds to Euryalus' eager willingness to seek glory by saying that if he were to encounter serious difficulty, he would wish for his young lover to survive, asking only that he might be buried (his body perhaps bought back from the Latins), or that he might receive funeral offerings at a cenotaph (like Hector at Buthrotum). He is especially concerned that he might be a source of pain for Euryalus' mother, should his young friend die. This concern foreshadows the appearance of Euryalus' mother at the end of the story, and it also serves as a doublet for the Aeneas-Pallas-Evander emotional triad that will open Book 11, when Aeneas must face Evander after the death of the young Arcadian hero. The plot demands that Euryalus' mother be one of the women who decided to follow

Aeneas from Sicily; 9.217 *ausa* is an exaggeration. Euryalus will hear none of this; he calls Nisus' excuses "vain" or "empty" (219 *inanis*). They go at once to seek "the king" (223 *regem*, and cf. 227 *regni*), a striking word to describe Ascanius that has not received much notice—this will be Ascanius' first opportunity to be a true leader. Book 9 is especially concerned with the role of Aeneas' young son in military affairs—especially how he has to be kept safe from harm.

Their plan is to fetch Aeneas and bring him back, and they expect that there will be great slaughter in the process (understandable, if they were actually able to break through the enemy position and reach their absent leader). In reality, the great slaughter they foretell will be the result of their own nocturnal indulgence; Aeneas will have nothing to do with what soon becomes a night raid of indiscriminate slaughter. They have seen Pallanteum, dimly, from their hunting trips; just as Camilla conflates fighting and hunting, so will these two young Trojans. In the end, this conflation will be a major cause of their deaths (in the Camilla epyllion, two gods will help take down the Volscian heroine). Ascanius promises the two young heroes a pair of silver cups, two tripods, and two talents of gold (appropriately doubled prizes for the two men). The final gift (266) will be a bowl Dido had given the Trojans; the drinking cup has ominous implications because it was a gift from the ill-fated Carthaginian queen, and the last word of the line—*Dido*—has sinister overtones. Dido's curse continues to haunt the Trojans. Besides all this, there will be Turnus' horse and arms, and Latinus' kingdom, and twelve matrons. Ascanius, in his first task as Trojan leader, has all the hyperbolic zest of an inexperienced, neophyte king. Nisus had foresworn any presents and offered them to Euryalus; now he remains silent as Ascanius promises to Euryalus in particular that he will keep him at his side in the future, both in peace and in war.

Euryalus is not interested in prizes. He cares first and foremost for his aged mother, who had been mentioned earlier by Nisus.[14] Ascanius responds to Euryalus' filial concern with a solemn oath (9.300 *per caput hoc iuro*) that he will grant the same things to Euryalus' mother and to his race that he has just promised to Nisus and Euryalus. He promises that she will be like Creusa to him, different only in name. The promise Ascanius makes is motivated by the best and most noble of intentions; the reality of keeping the promise is more complex: does Euryalus have a brother or male relative to inherit these vows? He has no son. The extravagance and illogic of the entire passage describes well the young leader as he vows rewards for the first time to men of heart and courage, one of whom is his own age—again, the succession motif keeps Ascanius from going on this mission himself, and Euryalus (like Pallas) will die in part as a proxy for Ascanius. Virgil makes clear that Ascanius is too young to handle such affairs (311 *ante annos animumque gerens curamque virilem*); he is the same age as Euryalus, though, who will now go forth to risk and lose his life. Enough tears fall during the entire section to leave the audience with no doubt as to the outcome (251, 293, and 303).

As Nisus and Euryalus leave camp, Ascanius gives them the instructions they are to bring to Aeneas.[15] The breezes scatter them, and the young pair does not hear them. They are overly zealous and overly eager for this mission; their recklessness here as they disregard Ascanius' orders will be contrasted by Camilla's death orders, where she will give clear instructions to her closest friend, Acca, about what Turnus is to do next—instructions that will be disregarded. The night mission is already a partial failure; its main purpose, the conveyance of information to Aeneas about the Rutulian siege, has been forgotten already. The two young men depart in the shadow of the night:

Egressi superant fossas noctisque per umbram
castra inimica petunt, multis tamen ante futuri
exitio. (9.314-316)

*Having departed, they cross the trenches and, through the
  shadow of the night,
seek the enemy camps, destined nevertheless first to be
  the source
of future destruction for many.*

The passage is somewhat strange. The enemy camps are viewed with deep, indeed personal (*inimica*) hostility—Virgil is again describing the emotions of the two young heroes as they set out. In part their reckless slaughter of the sleeping Rutulians will be the result of their intensely personal feelings about the enemy. There is a clear sense in the arrangement of *inimica . . . tamen* that before anyone from the camp can kill them, they will kill many from the camp. When we first read *inimica*, we think of Nisus and Euryalus' reaction to the Rutulians; when we come to *tamen*, we think of the opposing side: the Rutulians also have a very personal distaste for the Trojans.[16] The *inimica* camps will be echoed later by the *inimica* light that Nisus correctly warns against. But before their deaths, Nisus and Euryalus will indulge in copious slaughter.

Nisus' instructions to Euryalus as they see the Rutulians lying around asleep from too much wine are startlingly similar to Aeneas' instructions to Creusa as they fled the burning city of Troy. He tells Euryalus to guard him from the back, at a distance (9.322 *longe*), while he himself leads the way in a broad path of slaughter for his young friend. The first victims are Rhamnes, an augur, and Remus together with his entourage (the latter with an appropriate name for an early casualty). Rhamnes is presumably "proud" (324 *superbum*) because he was asleep in an unprotected position (but so was everyone else). The slaughtered are depicted as victims of their self-indulgence (though Virgil cannot resist the black humor of noting that had Serranus decided to play games until dawn instead of just late into the night, he would have survived). The scene changes dramatically when Virgil reverses course and introduces real pathos for the victims: Nisus is like a lion driven mad by hunger, and he is assaulting a gentle flock of sheep that has been rendered mute by terror (339-341). This is a counterpart to the description of Turnus as the wolf prowling around the sheepfold. The madness spreads; Euryalus was supposed to guard Nisus' rear, but instead he too begins an indiscriminate slaughter of his own, as he is set on fire and rages terribly (342-343 *incensus / perfurit*). One victim, Rhoetus, is actually awake; he cowers in fear behind a large drinking vessel, but as he stands up (to run away or to attack?), Euryalus stabs him in the chest. Euryalus is the more careless killer; Nisus, we are told, is "hot" for his grim task (*fervidus*), but is stealthy (*furto*). Indeed, Nisus decides the killing is excessive (*nimia*) and being carried out gratuitously, out of perverse desire (*cupidine*). He knows that the "hateful light" (*inimica lux*) is drawing near—this must be the dawn. Like the camps that Virgil had described as hateful, as personal enemies, so Nisus views the dawn that will expose them to a waking enemy army. As a foreshadowing of the cause of their ultimate fate, we first learn that the two men left behind many rich spoils. At once, however, we learn that Euryalus did take spoils from the augur Rhamnes, as well as a helmet of Messapus'—the men who have been killed were Messapus' (351), but an important detail is that Euryalus has *not* taken spoils he has truly earned: he did not kill Messapus.

The cavalry led by Volcens now appear. They are carrying a reply either to Turnus the king (*regi*) or from the king (*regis*, that is, probably Latinus). Despite the case that can be made for *regis* (Servius Danielis says all good manuscripts have it, which would seem to mean we have no good manuscripts), *regi* is better: Latinus has more or less gone silent at this point so early in the war, and it seems strange to imagine that perhaps Turnus has sent a message to him asking what they should do at dawn. More likely, the cavalry are a night patrol ensuring no sudden return of Aeneas or activity from the Trojan camp. The horsemen see Nisus and Euryalus turning to the left (371 *laevo . . . limite*): the left side was lucky for Romans—not so for these two Trojans (later, at 9.468, the Trojans have set up their rampart on the left side, *in parte sinistra*, since the Tiber covers their right). The helmet Euryalus has carelessly put on his head (an emblem of a false victory) now betrays him:

et galea Euryalum sublustri noctis in umbra
prodidit immemorem radiisque adversa refulsit. (9.373-374)

and the helmet, in the glimmering shadow of the night,
betrayed forgetful Euryalus and shone forth as it faced the moon's rays.

What light betrayed him, the coming dawn or the moon? The adjective *sublustris* ("glimmering," as of soft light) gives no definitive clue (it is extremely rare, and does not occur before the Augustan poets); the light may be the first glint of dawn. The moon is mysterious, and so is its action here.[17] The cavalry patrol knows this territory, and they know exactly how to hem Nisus and Euryalus inside the dense forest where they try to make their escape. Nisus successfully evades the patrol, but Euryalus is afraid and burdened by spoils. Hardie sees the flight to the forest as a return to the adolescent world of hunting the two young men once enjoyed, but if so, Euryalus is not at ease in the woods (admittedly understandably given his terror, and laden down as he is). Nisus makes it to the vaguely defined "Alban" places (386-387 *locos . . . Albani*), where Latinus keeps his stables (probably the very departure point for Volcens' cavalry). Like Aeneas, he will rush back into danger to try to find his lost lover (and he hears the noise of the pursuing Latins, as if they were Greeks in the burning city of Troy). Unlike Aeneas, Nisus will find no ghost; he sees Euryalus surrounded by his pursuers, who do not as yet take notice of Nisus' return.

If moonlight had betrayed Euryalus, it is highly ironic for Virgil now to depict Nisus as praying to the moon goddess, Luna, for help. When Arruns kills Camilla, he will pray to Apollo that he might not only slay the Volscian girl, but also return home, however inglorious (because he has killed a woman). Apollo grants the first part of the prayer. Diana gives no answer to Nisus, and we do not know her disposition toward the two young hunters: certainly Nisus could easily have shot at the Latins from his hidden place. Nisus fatally wounds Sulmo, and then, "fiercer" (416 *acrior*) because of his success, he aims again, this time killing Tago—in a sense Nisus has started to repeat the cycle he and Euryalus began when they slaughtered the sleeping Rutulians: the first taste of blood and victory has aroused a lust for more. When Volcens decides to take his vengeance on Euryalus, Nisus is driven mad and is terrified that his lover is about to die (*exterritus, amens*). Nisus wants to save Euryalus; in his madness he thinks he can win his lover's life by swearing that all the blame for the killing is his alone (true enough in one sense, since Volcens' troop has not yet discovered the slaughter in the camp). Nisus says that Euryalus loved his friend too much; the irony is that great love for a friend is why Nisus will now die. Volcens makes no reply, and Euryalus is mortally wounded:

volvitur Euryalus leto, pulchrosque per artus
it cruor inque umeros cervix conlapsa recumbit:
purpureus veluti cum flos succisus aratro
languescit moriens, lassove papavera collo
demisere caput pluvia cum forte gravantur. (9.433-437)

Euryalus rolls over in death, and the blood goes over
his beautiful limbs, and his drooping neck falls on his shoulder,
as when a purple flower has been cut by the plough
and begins to droop as it dies, or as when the poppy sends
down its head with tired neck, when by chance it grows heavy with rain.

The simile will be evoked later, when Virgil describes the dead young Pallas, Aeneas' lover, as it were, in the Homeric scheme of Patroclus-Achilles.[18] In the Pallas simile, the young man is already dead and the description comes at his funeral, where the corpse is compared to a flower:

qualem virgineo demessum pollice florem
seu mollis violae seu languentis hyacinthi,
cui neque fulgor adhuc nec dum sua forma recessit,
non iam mater alit tellus virisque ministrat. (11.68-71)

Like a flower that has been cut down by a virgin's thumb,

either a soft violet or a drooping hyacinth,
whose gleam and beauty have not yet receded,
though no longer does its mother the earth nourish it and serve its strength.

In extant Latin literature, both similes seem to have their origin in the close of Catullus *carmen* 11, where the poet describes the effect of his girl's promiscuous behavior:

nec meum respectet, ut ante, amorem,
qui illius culpa cecidit velut prati
ultimi flos, praetereunte postquam
    tactus aratro est. (*carmen* 11.21-24)

Nor let her look on my love as she did before,
since by her fault it has fallen like a flower
at the end of the meadow, after it has been touched
by a plough passing by.

Cf. also Catullus' reflections on a girl's virginity in his celebrated nuptial hymn, *Vesper adest* (*carmen* 62):

ut flos in saeptis secretus nascitur hortis,
ignotus pecori, nullo convulsus aratro,
quem mulcent aurae, format sol, educat imber;
multi illum pueri, multae optavere puellae:
idem cum tenui carptus defloruit ungui,
nulli illum pueri, nullae optavere puellae:
sic virgo, dum intacta manet, dum cara suis est;
cum castum amisit polluto corpore florem,
nec pueris iucunda manet, nec cara puellis. (*carmen* 62.39-47)

Like a flower born apart in an enclosed garden,
unknown to the flock, cut away by no plough,
which the breezes caress, the sun forms, and the rain makes grow;
many boys have desired it, and many girls:
but the same flower, once it has been plucked by a slender nail,
no boys desire, nor do any girls:
so is a virgin, while she remains untouched, and while she is dear to her own;
but when she loses her chaste flower, once her body has been polluted,
she does not remain pleasing to boys, and she is not dear to girls.

Catullus' two flower similes have very different associations. The first compares the poet's (male) love to a flower at the edge of the meadow that has been cut by a passing plough, probably not deliberately, but rather carelessly and without notice.[19] The second compares a virgin before marriage to a flower that is cultivated, cherished, and desired: a woman is wooed, in other words, before she is obtained—the pleasure is in the wanting, not the possessing.

In Virgil's Pallas simile and Catullus' marriage poem simile, the action of cutting the flower is described in feminine terms: *virgineo pollice* in Virgil and *tenui ungui* in Catullus *carmen* 62: the image in both cases is of a young girl picking flowers (itself a symbol of destruction and even death, however innocent—Persephone was traditionally picking flowers when Hades snatched her away—was she the perfect bride for the lord of the underworld?)[20] In Catullus *carmen* 11, the flower is cut by a plough that inadvertently or carelessly sliced it down. So with respect to Euryalus and Pallas, there will be, on the one hand, no marriage for either young man: they have been cut down in death (and Virgil describes them in *feminine* terms—they are like the virgin flower that has been plucked).[21] Their unions with Nisus and Aeneas, respectively, will not come to fruition. On the other hand, Euryalus' death also recalls Catullus' careless, inadvertently destructive plough: Euryalus' capture and death deprive Nisus of his love (though very much against Euryalus' will). Nisus wants nothing else but to kill Volcens: he succeeds, though he has no chance for escape. His act of vengeance costs him his life, and he falls dead over the lifeless body of his friend. This act of revenge presages Aeneas' killing of Turnus (where there will be no Rutulian around to avenge Turnus, and, what is more, Aeneas will have a moment of calm reflection and hesitation, unlike Nisus, before he decides to kill his opponent as a sacrifice to Pallas). Virgil's two similes somewhat mirror Catullus': for Pallas' death Virgil wants to lament the fact that the young hero will not be going in procession to his marriage, but to the grave; in the case of Euryalus the emphasis is on Nisus' reaction to the slaughter of his young lover: the Latins do not realize that they are killing the beloved in the presence of the lover, and so, like Catullus' plough, they have inadvertently destroyed a love affair.[22]

Virgil's apostrophe to the two dead young friends is one of the most extraordinary moments in the epic, the most extended authorial intervention in the entire *Aeneid*:

Fortunati ambo! si quid mea carmina possunt,
nulla dies umquam memori vos eximet aevo,
dum domus Aeneae Capitoli immobile saxum
accolet imperiumque pater Romanus habebit. (9.446-449)

Fortunate pair! If my poems are able to do anything,
no day will ever delete you from a mindful age,
so long as the house of Aeneas inhabits the unmoving rock
of the Capitol, and so long as the Roman father will hold his empire.

Neither Pallas nor Camilla will receive such laudatory authorial affection; the dead Lausus, son of Mezentius, will come close, as we shall see later (10.791-793). In the latter case, there is devotion to a father; in this case, devotion to a friend and lover. Pallas' death leads directly to Aeneas' final act of madness in the last lines of the poem. Camilla's death leads directly to Turnus' critical act of madness in abandoning his sound battle plans and thereby saving Aeneas from serious harm (just as Jupiter's savage will demanded, as Virgil explicitly tells us at the end of Book 11). Nisus-Euryalus and Lausus are more peripheral characters than Pallas and Camilla. Their deaths have no effect on either Aeneas or Turnus. Virgil gives *all* of these young dead the consolation of his verse, but he is most explicit with his declaration of the eternal fame of these two young lovers. They are, in fact, the only two lovers in the *Aeneid* who enjoy a shared death: their end has a sense of closure that is missing from the Dido-Aeneas, Pallas-Aeneas, even Camilla-Turnus pairings. In a perverse sense, the fact that they die a shared death, together in their adventure and their destruction, unites them in a bond that stands forth as the only such successful union in the *Aeneid*. We do not see Aeneas and Lavinia together. We know how terribly Aeneas' relationships with Creusa, Dido, and Pallas all ended. Turnus and Camilla die apart. Latinus' marriage ends with Amata's suicide. Andromache is deprived of Hector. The *Aeneid* is loveless and devoid of positive displays of enduring romantic attachments. Nisus and Euryalus provide a tragic exception; they will be remembered together for all time.

In case the audience may have forgotten, Virgil reminds us of why Euryalus died: the Latins find the bodies of all their victims, and they find Messapus' helmet (9.457). In the case of Euryalus, the spoils were inappropriate to seize because the slaughter itself was inappropriate: he was on a mission with Nisus to get a message to Aeneas, and sleeping soldiers presented no obstacle. The idea for the slaughter was Nisus'; Euryalus was supposed to remain aloof from it, but the temptation to join his friend in the frenzy was too great for the headstrong youth to withstand (like Ascanius and Pallas, he displays great eagerness to distinguish himself as quickly as possible in war). As we shall see later, the love of spoils is part of both Turnus' and Camilla's deaths as well: in the case of Turnus, his despoiling of Pallas' corpse will spell his end, while in the case of Camilla, a moment's hesitation about what to do with Chloreus' potential spoils (she has not even killed him yet) will give Arruns the chance he needs to dispatch her (though, as we shall see, the circumstances are complicated by divine intervention). It is important to note (and often ignored by critics of Virgil) that *similarities* are not all we should take note of in related narratives: *differences* matter too. Like Camilla with Chloreus, Euryalus seeks spoils from someone he has not even killed (and, to underscore the point, his target is Messapus, an especially prominent warrior). As the dawn rises, Virgil repeats the same lines he used to describe the first light when Dido saw the Trojan fleet about to sail off (cf. 9.459-460 and 4.584-585): this dawn will see not the flight of the Trojans, but the terrible desecration of the bodies of Nisus and Euryalus (significantly, Pallas and Camilla will receive *post mortem* care, but these two warriors will suffer some of the worst indignities possible). Nisus and Euryalus are modeled after both Diomedes-Odysseus and Dolon, the Trojan spy who is unfortunately captured and killed; they have had the opportunity to play both sides, but they die as Trojans (*Iliad* 10, Homer's "Doloneia").[23] Homer's Doloneia comes after the crucial, unsuccessful embassy to Achilles in *Iliad* 9: the first third of the poem ends with confirmation of Achilles' wrath and of the continued prospect of Achaean discomfiture in his absence from the war. A night interlude then takes place before the highly significant Book 11, where Nestor urges Patroclus either to persuade Achilles to fight or to give over his arms so his young friend can fight in his place—thus setting in motion the slow march to Patroclus' death and Achilles' reaction. In Virgil, the "Doloneia" scene of Nisus and Euryalus does not occur at an obviously similar juncture. The Trojans are discomfited, to be sure, and Aeneas/Achilles is absent—but the context and circumstances are rather different. There are enough parallels to remind us of the Homeric antecedent, but the differences give pause for thought. Further, Homer's Greeks are in good spirits after Odysseus and Diomedes complete their blood-soaked night raid—the Trojans are in utter dejection after the failure of Nisus and Euryalus (Virgil's reworking of the Homeric episode is bleak and grim, with no indulgence in levity or black comedy). Virgil in particular wants us to concentrate on the parallels between Aeneas' absence from the battlefield and the withdrawal of Achilles from the Trojan War (again, a structural parallel to Homer, but in a very different context and with quite different reasons and motivations). Ascanius, for one, will be no Patroclus. No one will need to persuade Aeneas (or Turnus) to return to the fight at any point in the *Aeneid*. The Greeks in *Iliad* 9 and the Trojans in *Aeneid* 9 are both in dire straits; Virgil has taken Homer's tragic comedy of Dolon and invested it with a deep poignance that reaches its emotional climax in his powerful apostrophe to the two dead young warriors.

The connection between the Nisus and Euryalus episode and the narrative of Dido and Aeneas (the dawn formula at 9.459-460) is continued in the appearance of Rumor (473 ff.). We move from the miserable Trojans (472 *miseris*) to the miserable mother of Euryalus (475 *miserae*, 484 *miserae*, effectively repeated). Euryalus' mother (unnamed in Virgil) is weaving (like a good Roman matron) when the terrible rumors arrive; she is mindless (478 *amens*) and rushes out into the danger of the front lines, desperate to see her son.[24] We learn that she has been weaving a robe for her son; this detail will be evoked later when Pallas is buried in one of the robes Dido had apparently woven for Aeneas and Ascanius—Euryalus has a less famous weaver of his clothes. All the funeral details Euryalus' mother laments over will be fulfilled, to what end no one can say, at the burial of Pallas. Fittingly, it is Ilioneus and *Ascanius* who give the order to have Euryalus' mother taken back home to rest: Ascanius is crying (501 *multum lacrimantis Iuli*) over the whole scene that, in a very real way, his willingness to disregard his father's instructions has caused. We are very far from his lavish promises to Euryalus, his age-mate, before the young men left camp.

Once again it is the Volscians who take the initiative first, as a general attack is launched on the Latin camp: this ring will be concluded when the Volscian cavalry of Camilla are routed in Book 11 and the women of Laurentum rain down their missiles on their Trojan attackers. There is a terrible assault, and the Trojans succeed in causing many Latin casualties, but both Messapus and, for the first time in the narrative of the battle action, Mezentius is at hand with his Etruscan pine—a reminder that not all Etruscans are siding with Aeneas, who is absent securing Etruscan allies.[25] Virgil announces the general commencement of warfare with a powerful address to the muse Calliope, where he asks for her help in recounting Turnus' *aristeia* (our clue that despite Trojan success in defending their ramparts against the first assault, they will be in serious trouble quite soon). Aeneas is not present to fight the Rutulian commander, of course—though this is not Turnus' fault, either.

The first vignette of the siege is the destruction of a (counter) siege tower the Trojans had erected as a defense against attack; two men escape the crashing tower. Helenor was born of a slave woman to a Lydian king. Helenor has not yet achieved any distinction in battle (9.548 *ense levis nudo parmaque inglorius albo*); what is strange is that we are told his mother had sent him to Troy with "forbidden arms," and yet he appears to have survived the Trojan War without any battle experience—besides the mystery behind what Virgil means by "forbidden arms" (*vetitis armis*). While Servius may be right that slaves could not fight in the Roman army (though there is no indication Helenor was a slave), more likely is that Virgil has decided to increase the pathos of this pitiful escapee from the destroyed tower, right before he performs his first and final act of martial courage: like a wild animal trapped by hunters, he charges at the densest crowd of Latin soldiers, realizing he will die (551-555). The Latins are on a hunt: as it does for so many others in the poem, this mindset ultimately spells disaster. The other survivor of the tower, Lycus, is a swift runner who tries (terror-stricken) to climb up and over the ramparts to his own men (who are busily shooting weapons down at the Latins).

Turnus is faster than the swift Lycus (Greek for "wolf"), and he dispatches him just as an eagle, the bird of Jove (564), manages to catch a rabbit or a swan, and just as a wolf of Mars (*Martius . . . lupus*) catches a lamb its mother is pitifully seeking in vain. Turnus has achieved that he wanted: at the beginning of the book, he was described as a wolf seeking admission to the sheepfold (59-66)—in this case, the sheepfold (the tower) ejected its contents. Lycus is a wolf himself (by name); this passage links to Camilla's own *aristeia* later in the war (where she will be compared to a raptor that dispatches a human dove at 11.721-724), and has subtle associations with Arruns' killing of Camilla where, as we shall see, a wolf is killing another wolf.[26] Virgil's simile of Turnus' victory over a greatly inferior foe is a sort of reversal of Homer's famous simile of Achilles' pursuit of Hector (*Iliad* 22.139-142), where Achilles the raptor pursues Hector the dove (Camilla will be Achilles the dove, for a moment, in *Aeneid* 11).

Virgil delights in ambiguity as he describes the killings that ensue. "Liger" will reappear in Book 10 (576 ff.) as a foolhardy warrior who insults Aeneas; Asilas is more complicated a figure: in Book 10 (175) he is clearly an Etruscan ally of Aeneas, at Book 11 (620) he is leading a Trojan push, at 12.127 it is impossible to be certain which side he is on, while at 12.550 he is on Turnus' side. Asilas kills Corynaeus, and in the heat of battle, Virgil does not make clear who is who:

hic iaculo bonus, hic longe fallente sagitta (9.572)

this one was skilled with the javelin, this one with the arrow that deceives from afar.

It is not entirely certain who is skilled with the javelin and who with the bow. "Emathion," Liger's victim, has both Trojan and Italian associations.[27] In this essentially *civil* war, Virgil wants to capitalize on the ambiguities of who is on which side (especially once the Etruscans arrive who are allied with Aeneas), and the general confusion of battle is reflected in the confusion over who is doing what. Turnus' killing of Caeneus, which is followed by a string of half a dozen more victims, clarifies the slaughter. Privernus' death (576) reminds us of the Volscian leadership of this assault; Privernum was one of their principal towns. The appearance of Arcens, a Sicilian ally of Aeneas (the river Symaethus at 584 is in Sicily), is almost like that of Chloreus in Book 11 (768 ff.): he seems out of place, overdressed for the occasion in his embroidered Greek-style cloak and dark Iberian purple, a mere target (however noteworthy) for Mezentius to kill—and the Etruscan *contemptor divum* uses a sling (perhaps because of its association with the Spanish Balearic islands) to cut him down; we get the sense that the young Sicilian never knew he was about to die. Again, from an Augustan Roman viewpoint, this is a close to civil war: Etruscan fighting Sicilian.

The hunting imagery of this book continues now with Ascanius. Prior to this day, we are told, he was accustomed to use his bow and arrow only against wild beasts (just as he had been hunting with Dido and Aeneas in Book 4, and just as he had been hunting when he inadvertently started the whole war in Book 7). Virgil announces at once, before telling the story at length, that now Ascanius shot an arrow for the first time in combat, and that he killed Turnus' new brother-in-law, Numanus Remulus.[28] His two names (and Virgil's mention of his *cognomen* Remulus) evoke the history and traditions of early Rome (though as before, the name of *Remus* declares his short life expectancy). Virgil is conflicted about Remulus. He shouts out remarks that are both "worthy and unworthy to relate" (9.595 *digna atque indigna relatu*). He is arrogant because of his recent marriage into the royal family (*novo . . . regno*) of Turnus. Like Iarbas, the North African prince (4.198 ff.), Numanus Remulus will racially denigrate the Trojans.[29] The "Phrygians" (said with a sneer) have already been captured twice (Hercules' destruction of Laomedon's lying city, and the Greek invasion). Remulus highlights the Italians' prowess at hunting (Camilla will be the main exemplar of this), horsemanship (again, presaging Camilla) and archery. Remulus' mention of saffron and purple foreshadows Chloreus, the priest of Cybele and Camilla's last target (he will wear both colors). Remulus' explosive invective against the cult of the *Magna Mater* is reminiscent of Catullus' terrifying galliambic poem (*carmen* 63) on the fate of Attis, self-castrated man-woman eunuch for Cybele:

o vere Phrygiae, neque enim Phryges, ite per alta
Dindyma, ubi adsuetis biforem dat tibia cantum.
tympana vos buxusque vocat Berecyntia Matris
Idaeae. (9.617-620)

O truly Phrygian women, not Phrygian men, go to lofty
Dindymus, where the flute gives a double-mouthed song to those who are used to it;

the timbrel calls you, and the Berecynthian boxwood of your
Idaean mother.

If we want to accuse Remulus of being unfair in his racially charged attacks, we must find fault with the Etruscan Tarchon (not a Trojan either!) who upbraids the Trojans for their softness in the wake of the disaster they suffer at Camilla's feminine hands (11.725 ff., where Jupiter is very displeased with Camilla's brilliant performance on the battlefield and decides to stir up Tarchon to rouse his men).[30] Remulus' words come too soon after Cybele's saving of the Trojan fleet; his insults will not go unpunished. Jupiter will intervene in Book 11 to end Camilla's attacks; here he will answer Ascanius' humble prayer (9.624 *supplex per vota precatus*) to end Remulus'. Ascanius promises to sacrifice a young bull that, like him, is eager for the fight. Jupiter agrees to Ascanius' prayer by allowing him to shoot and kill Remulus.

In the *Iliad*, Apollo warns Diomedes during his great *aristeia* (in which he wounds Aphrodite) to be careful before thinking of attacking a great god (5.431 ff.). Three times Diomedes attacks Aeneas (who is protected by Apollo), and three times Apollo beats him back before taking Aeneas to a sanctuary where he and his sister Artemis heal him; Apollo stirs Ares to go and fight Diomedes in the meantime. Similarly now, though in a very different circumstance, Apollo intervenes to stop Ascanius; this is the archer god's most extended intervention in the *Aeneid* and, what is more, it is his only direct appearance "on stage," as it were (in Book 3 he speaks through an oracle). Apollo's first words are of praise, before he makes a curious prediction, of great significance in the context of the poem's racial and ethnic concerns:

... iure omnia bella
gente sub Assaraci fato ventura resident,
nec te Troia capit. (9.642-644)

... *rightly all wars about to come by fate*
will subside under the race of Assaracus;
nor does Troy contain you.

Troy is not big enough for Ascanius. Apollo's words in a sense validate Remulus' claims; Ascanius has outgrown Troy (which is quite dead, though Venus, Aeneas, and the Trojans do not as yet know it). Wars will end (the Augustan theme, this time enunciated by the patron god of the victory at Actium)—but Troy is finished (and, in a positive sense, the *fate* of Troy, being captured, is finished). Apollo disguises himself as Butes, an aged Trojan, but the god is recognized as he departs (just as Aeneas recognized his disguised mother when she left his presence): the god's bow sounds as he leaves. Apollo warns Ascanius to be content with his killing of Remulus, and to abstain from any further actions in the war. Again, this is the succession motif at work: Ascanius must remain safe, the only important young hero in the poem who will not die; the risks are too great for the heir apparent to be exposed to the dangers of war. After the Trojans ban Ascanius from fighting (662 *Ascanium prohibent*—the force of the phrase is that Ascanius did not want to be stopped), the battle rages on, like a storm, when Jupiter, the storm god, sends wind and hail over the sea (668-671). Apollo's words to Ascanius are divided in half: the first part, about the future peace and Troy's not being able to contain the young hero, comes as a voice from a cloud. The second part, about Ascanius' disengagement from battle, comes as the personal address of the god in the disguise of old Butes. The first part is the solemn prophecy of divine injunction, similar to Jupiter's speeches in Books 1 and 12 to his daughter and wife, and reflects the great momentum of Roman (and Trojan) ultimate destiny. The second part is a personal intervention of a god: would Ascanius have been killed had he stayed on the ramparts? His act was bold (though similar to Paris' killing of Achilles—archery was not always viewed as the most courageous or heroic of martial acts). Apollo was an archer god (which validates the use of the bow in warfare for any Augustan Roman); Ascanius' only two explicit acts in this war are accompanied with a bow (one of them the proximate cause of the conflict). He will be mentioned again in an extended passage at 10.132 ff., where he will be among the defenders of the Trojan ramparts—it is unclear why he is no longer out of the action there.

Of greater significance is how Apollo handles the ever-important question of ethnicity in the *Aeneid*. In Book 3 (94-98), his only other speaking appearance in the poem, he told the Trojans to seek their ancient mother (Italy, it turned out), and he referred to them as *Dardanidae duri*, "hardy Dardanians"—an image that Remulus himself invoked when he called the Italians a "hardy race" (9.603 *durum . . . genus*). Ascanius' killing of Remulus represents the end not only of one Italian's invective, but also presages the end of the justification for such invective: in Ascanius Troy will end and Rome begin. Ascanius is the appropriate killer for Remulus since in Ascanius the old Troy will finally die. Having fulfilled his symbolically crucial role, he can withdraw from the fight. It is just possible that we are meant to see in Ascanius the image of Romulus, who would kill his brother *Remus* and set Rome's foundation in fratricide and the image of civil strife.

The emphasis on archery leads directly to the mention of *Pandarus* and his brother Bitias; the former had been the famous Trojan archer in *Iliad* 4 who broke the truce by wounding Menelaus. The two giant brothers are the opposite of the now safely removed Ascanius; they invite war by deciding (foolishly) to open the gates of the camp. Ascanius opened the gates at night for the stealthy mission of Nisus and Euryalus; now removed from the action, Ascanius (a leader, and yet not a leader in the absence of his father), will not be able to approve or disapprove of these two brothers, who by their own initiative invite disaster. Virgil compares them to twin oak trees on the banks of the Po or by the River Athesis (the modern Adige in Verona).[31] The simile reminds us of the Cyclopes' menacing appearance on the Sicilian coast as the Trojans and Achaemenides sailed off to safety; the oak evokes Jupiter—though in this case the brothers will fail in their brave defense of the gates, where they stand as living towers (9.677 *pro turribus adstant*). Virgil plays with our expectations, as he so loves to do, and once again the action is not easy to disentangle: once the gates are opened we read that the Rutulians pour inside (682 *inrumpunt aditus*), and then "at once" (*continuo*) we hear that Quercens (appropriately, the "Oaken One") and Aquiculus (the "Watery One") and others are forced to flee—almost certainly we are reading the names of invading Rutulians, even if we remember the simile about Pandarus and Bitias, oak trees and rivers, and for a brief moment think these may be routed Trojans (686 *versi terga dedere*) who will die on the very threshold of the camp (their Italian-sounding names may highlight once again the civil nature of this conflict). Tmarus, too, is part of their number; his name also (that of a Greek mountain) makes us think of the giants Pandarus and Bitias. The Trojans rally (689 *iam collecti Troes*) as they face the Rutulian incursion, or the slaughter of the first invaders may make them more eager for bloodshed (like Nisus and Euryalus). The Trojans engage the Rutulians in close combat (*conferre manum*) and even dare to run ahead, past the Rutulian front line troops (*procurrere longius audent*). Whatever the case, word is brought to Turnus, who is off managing the siege operation elsewhere, that the gates to the camp are open and Pandarus and Bitias are defending the opening. His Italian spear (698 *Itala cornus*) is at once flying through the air, fatally (and gorily) wounding the son of Sarpedon.

Turnus attacks the huge Bitias. He fells the Trojan giant with a distinctly Roman weapon, the *phalarica* (705), which was a sort of wooden pike fixed with iron, usually hurled down on siege engines (Bitias is a living siege tower). His collapse is compared to the fall of huge piers at Baiae (near Cumae), the sort of piers Romans used to extend their villas out on the sea: Bitias represents the worst follies of Rome, and will be destroyed with an eminently Roman weapon (significantly, Turnus' *phalarica* is the only peculiarly Roman weapon in all of the *Aeneid*).[32] Virgil has made Turnus into a Roman giant-slayer, historically Roman, but mythologically like any other killer of the beasts of fable. As Bitias falls, even Inarime, the "hard bed" (715 *durum cubile*) trembles—Inarime, Virgil notes, was placed above Typhoeus, the monster Zeus vanquished as part of his coming to power. Virgil has powerfully compared Turnus to Jupiter, and at once, in the frenzy of battle, Mars joins the Latin cause (appropriately enough for Rome's patron), and sends Flight and Fear among the Trojans. At this critical juncture, where a complete Latin invasion is all too possible, Pandarus tries to close the gate (a wise idea), carelessly and inadvertently trapping Turnus inside (a very unwise idea). Turnus is now no wolf, but rather a tiger; his rage and madness have increased, and he is, for the moment, in complete command of the bloodshed. Turnus is, in fact, supernaturally changed by the appearance of Mars; lightning shoots from his shield, a new light shines from his eyes, and his weapons emit a terrible sound. Despite his raving appearance, Turnus is quite calm (740 *sedato pectore*) after Pandarus threatens him, warning him that he is in the midst of a camp that is personally antagonistic to him (*inimica castra*). The Rutulian camp was inimical indeed to Nisus and Euryalus; Pandarus will not be able to avenge their loss. Turnus' calm words to Pandarus are justly famous:

"incipe, si qua animo virtus, et consere dextram,
hic etiam inventum Priamo narrabis Achillem." (9.741-742)

*"Begin, if there is any courage in your heart, and join your right hand in battle:
here indeed will you tell Priam that you have found Achilles."*

This passage is the fulfillment of the Sibyl's prediction to Aeneas in Book 6; the Trojans have found another Achilles in Latium. Juno deflects Pandarus' spear; no god will intervene to save Pandarus from Turnus. Pandarus used a projectile weapon (like his Iliadic model), while Turnus relies on his sword: the wound is horrific (and it should be remembered that Pandarus is a giant), as Turnus splits his head in two, and each half rests on either shoulder (perhaps the goriest death in the *Aeneid*).

Divine intervention has been frequent and significant in these episodes. Ascanius prayed to Jupiter that he might kill Remulus, and Jupiter explicitly approved of his request. Apollo saved Ascanius from any possible harm immediately thereafter. Juno deflects Pandarus' spear from Turnus, and Mars roused the Latins to slaughter once they were in the Trojan camp. The divine action has been carefully balanced so far (Turnus, it should be noted, did not ask for Juno's help the way Ascanius did Jupiter's; appropriately, the neophyte hero prayed before his first military action, while the seasoned leader of the Rutulians assumes, rightly or wrongly, that he can handle Pandarus without supernatural help). After the scales of divine action have been balanced, Turnus fails of his own accord: he does not think to open the gates and let in his men. Virgil makes clear that if Turnus had now opened the gates, the war would have been finished that day with an Italian victory. Virgil describes Turnus' state of mind with a quite effective half-line:

sed furor ardentem caedisque insana cupido
egit in adversos. (9.760-761)

*But madness and an insane desire for slaughter
drove the burning man against those who faced him.*

Once again, a half-line pauses over a scene Virgil wants to impress on his audience. Like Nisus and Euryalus, the young and headstrong Turnus is not fully engaged in rational thought; he sees potential Trojan victims in front of him, and in the midst of the slaughter he does not stop to open the gates. The scenario is almost identical to Book 11, where Turnus will abandon his planned ambush of Aeneas once he is driven to a frenzied rage by the report of the death of Camilla. There, we shall be told that Jupiter's savage will demanded that Turnus abandon his planned operation (and the dying Camilla had sent word to Turnus that he must not give it up—she knew what effect her death might have on him). Turnus is now one man against an entire camp; Juno assists him (9.764) as he deals death to many Trojans, including a powerful hunter, Amycus, and Cretheus, a poet dear to the Muses, who, like Virgil himself, specialized in epic poetry and sang always of horses, battles, and the arms of men (777 *arma virum*)—a rare bit of self-reflection a prideful Virgil could not resist.

Turnus is only one man against an entire army, and hyperbole has its limits (even if Juno is assisting him). Mnestheus rallies the Trojans and reminds them that they have only one enemy here, and that he has allowed himself to be trapped and surrounded in their very camp. In Book 11, Jupiter will rouse Tarchon to stir up the Trojans and their allies against Camilla. There Camilla will be one of many Italians on an open plain; here there is a quite unbalanced situation, one that requires no divine intervention—or so it would seem. Turnus realizes (despite his madness) that he cannot destroy the entire Trojan assembly single-handedly, and he starts to retreat. The Trojans see how he falls back, and Virgil compares him to a lion that is surrounded by hunters. Turnus, the lion, is afraid (793 *territus*), but both his anger and his courage (*ira, virtus*) do not allow him to turn his back and run in terror. Turnus is doubtful (*dubius*), not certain what he should do (he wants to destroy the Trojans, but he sees an overwhelming number of them advancing against him)—like the lion trapped by the hunters, he is slow and does not rush; his steps are not hurried (*vestigia improperata*—and who knows, in other words, when he might spring up and attack with sudden violence). Two more times, in fact, he drives off his pursuers and they flee, confused, before his presence. The Trojans are preparing to attack him *en masse*, and, at this crucial moment, we are told that Juno did not help Turnus: Jupiter hastily sends Iris (usually Juno's messenger) to tell her that Turnus must withdraw from the Trojan camp—one gets the impression this is more to help the Trojans than to spare Turnus.

In consequence, Turnus cannot withstand the assault. Turnus had been hurling lightning bolts from his shield; now his armor cannot sustain the attack of the entire camp, and it is Mnestheus who is like lightning (812 *fulmineus Mnestheus*). We should not be surprised when the Tiber gently (*mollibus undis*, "with soft waves") takes Turnus in as he leaps to safety and is conveyed to his friends, having been cleansed by the river of all the blood and gore of the slaughter. Jupiter had, after all, demanded that Turnus leave the city; the father of gods and men had one preoccupation, and that was saving the Trojan camp from possible disaster (and it is worth noting that Virgil explicitly says that if Turnus had let his army inside, the camp would have been finished—despite Turnus' failure to do so, he still was performing manfully against the entire army even after Juno was forced to stop helping him because of Jupiter's decree that he had to withdraw.) Aeneas had a peaceful journey to his future on the Tiber; now the same river purifies Aeneas' greatest adversary, his new Achilles. Aeneas had barely escaped with his life from the first Achilles; the second will present challenges of deeper, more permanent resonance.

Not surprisingly, Book 9 will be followed immediately by the *Aeneid*'s first and last council of all the immortals. The end of the book builds up the theme of divine intervention, and forces the audience to examine another of Virgil's favorite questions: what would happen absent any sort of divine action? Who would win? Which side would conquer? What would transpire? The end of

Book 9 leads directly to some resolution of this conundrum: at the beginning of Book 10 Jupiter will, in effect, forbid any further interference in Latium's war. This edict will not be observed (least of all by its legislator), but it will offer a temporary resolution to the problems raised by the end of Book 9: Virgil must tread his ground carefully, lest he seem to be crafting a hero who constantly needs divine assistance to achieve his goals, and lest he seem to present Turnus as an enemy who could succeed in vanquishing the Trojans, if only fate, destiny, and the gods would leave things alone. The beginning of Book 10 calms those concerns and calls for a moratorium on divine action. Left to their own devices, the Trojans will lose Pallas to Turnus, and at the end of Book 12, left to his own devices, Aeneas will take his revenge on Turnus for the loss of his young friend, as Rome's progenitor becomes the poem's last victim of madness. The Jovian edict of non-intervention will force the audience to pay closer attention to every subsequent act in the poem, noting the presence or absence of the immortals. The poem's final quarter contains its three longest books, which grow longer as we move ever closer to the climax of Virgil's *maius opus*. Book 9 has served as something of an introduction to the war narrative of the poetic drama's third and final act—the bloodiest in the tragedy of the *Aeneid*. Now action on the human plane will be frozen, as Jupiter calls his council—hastily called after his recent demand to Juno that Turnus withdraw from the Trojan camp. He had come too close to winning.

Notes

1. 9.1 *Atque ea diversa penitus dum parte geruntur*, with *penitus* at midline: syntactic enactment.
2. Cf. Thucydides 2.95-101, with Hornblower's notes.
3. On this simile see further Hornsby, *op. cit.*, pp. 9-10 and 64-65.
4. Why does Jupiter save the ships at all? Why should he bother? Is there anything here beyond the mere granting of Cybele's wish?
5. Note here FANTHAM, "*Nymphas . . . e navibus esse*: Decorum and Poetic Fiction in *Aeneid* 9.77-122 and 10.215-259," *Classical Philology* 85 (1990), pp. 102-119. Fantham is right to say that Virgil is embarking on a "dangerous enterprise" in his fantastic episode of the ships; she ignores the fundamental point of Virgil's recurring, strong emphasis on how excessive divine favor redounds to Turnus' greater glory. This passage needs to be read closely with the attempted firing of the ships in Book 5.
6. Cf. *Psalms* 113.5 "Why was it, sea, that you fled, Jordan, that you turned back on your course?"
7. On Turnus' mistake in interpreting the omen, see PHILIPPS, "Seeking New Auspices: Interpreting Warfare and Religion in Virgil's *Aeneid*," *Vergilius* 43 (1997), pp. 45-55, especially p. 50.
8. The phrase *exscindere gentem* takes on a new twist in Book 12 once we learn about the sinking down" of the Trojans (836 *subsident Teucri*).
9. *Pace* Hardie's note here, I do not find Turnus' words at the end of the poem "panic-stricken."
10. He will not learn of Jupiter's agreement with Juno late in Book 12 that Aeneas' new foundation will be Italian, not Trojan.
11. For other views, see Hardie on 140-142 and Fairclough's notes in his Loeb. The point is not that the Trojans should have learned to hate all women because of what Helen had caused for them, and not that the Trojans hate everyone but women. But the passage does not read smoothly and perhaps would have been revised.
12. Nisus and Euryalus, in contrast to Camilla, are militarily insignificant in the battle narrative; their loss does not mean much to Aeneas strategically, but Camilla's death will cause Turnus to abandon his best chance to win the war with a swift rout. For the afterlife of the entire episode, see MARKUS, "Transfiguring Heroism: Nisus and Euryalus in Statius' *Thebaid*," *Vergilius* 43 (1997), pp. 56-62.
13. The difficult, crucial phrase at 9.373, *sublustri noctis in umbra*, is discussed below.
14. See further EGAN, "Euryalus' Mother and *Aeneid* 9-12," *Collection Latomus: Studies in Latin Literature and Roman History* 2 (1980), pp. 157-176.
15. See LENNOX, "Virgil's Night Episode Re-examined (*Aeneid* IX, 176-449)," *Hermes* 105 (1977), pp. 331-342, and, on the entire episode, Farron, *op. cit.*, pp. 1-26.
16. Hardie on 9.315-316 is right that the actual killers of the two young men are on a patrol—but from where does he imagine the patrol originated? The use of *castra inimica* to describe any of the encircling Rutulians causes no problem.
17. See further LEE, "*Per Nubila Lunam*: The Moon in Virgil's *Aeneid*," *Vergilius* (34) 1988, pp. 9-14, especially p. 12.
18. On all of these similes and their antecedents see further GRANSDEN, *Virgil's Iliad: An Essay on Epic Narrative*, Cambridge, 1984, pp. 114-119.
19. For the (pervasive) influence of Catullus on the *Aeneid*, especially the epic's closing movements, see PUTNAM, "The Lyric Genius of the *Aeneid*," *Arion* Ser. 3, No. 3 (1995-1996), pp. 81-101.

20. For the tradition of the flowers and Persephone's abduction, see *The Homeric Hymn to Demeter* 1-16, Ovid *Metamorphoses* 5.390-396, and especially Claudian *De Raptu Proserpinae* 2.101-136, with Gruzelier's notes.

21. The feminine terms also reflect Euryalus and Pallas' roles as *eromenoi* for Nisus and Aeneas.

22. On the deaths of Nisus and Euryalus, see further JOHNSON, *Darkness Visible: A Study of Vergil's Aeneid*, Berkeley-Los Angeles, 1976, pp. 59-66.

23. On Homer's working of the Rhesus/Dolon stories, see HAINSWORTH, *The Iliad: A Commentary, Books 9-12*, Cambridge, 1993, pp. 151-152, and, in general, FENIK, "*Iliad* X and the *Rhesus*: the Myth," *Collection Latomus* 73 (1964).

24. An excellent synthesis of this passage with the firing of the Trojan ships by the women in Book 5 is WILTSHIRE, *Public and Private in Vergil's Aeneid*, Amherst, 1989, pp. 47-53.

25. Hardie well remarks, "The monstrous Mezentius appears like some demon from an Etruscan hell."

26. The wolf-on-wolf killing also helps buttress the suspicion that Arruns and Camilla were on the same side, as we shall see in Book 11.

27. See further Hardie on 9.571.

28. On this passage see especially HORSFALL, "Numanus Remulus: Ethnography and Propaganda in *Aeneid* 9.598 ff.," *Latomus* 30 (1971), pp. 1108-1116 (reprinted in Harrison, *op. cit.*, pp. 305-315, with a 1988 afterword on later bibliography). Horsfall's point that the world depicted by Remulus is not terribly attractive is a good one; the point, though, is that Troy's effeminate world is not appealing to the native Italians either; all ethnography in the *Aeneid* is prolegomena to the final reconciliation of Juno toward the end of Book 12.

29. Hardie notes on 9.593-594 that we should be as suspicious of Remulus' words as we were of Rumor's in Book 4 (when she flew to Iarbas). But Virgil said there that Rumor was as tenacious at clinging to lies as she was an announcer of the truth (188), and her report to Iarbas could not be called mendacious, however much she editorializes Dido and Aeneas' relationship (*turpique cupidine captos*) in a negative fashion. More complicated is the charge Rumor makes that Dido and Aeneas have become forgetful of their respective kingdoms (*immemores regnorum*). When Mercury descends to Aeneas, he finds him engaged in city building (260-261). Virgil's point seems to be that the two lovers are each ignoring their *own* cities; Aeneas is building Carthage, not Rome, and Dido has forgotten all business of urban planning.

30. Is it possible that in Numanus Remulus' taunts Virgil is underscoring an opposition between Aeneas-Pallas (homoerotic) and Turnus-Camilla (heteroerotic)? In any case, neither *potential* bond will come to maturity; both relationships will be destroyed by war before coming to fruition.

31. On this simile, see further Hornsby, *op. cit.*, p. 82.

32. See further Hardie on 9.705-706.

CHAPTER X

THE HOUSE OF OLYMPUS

Book 10 begins a rising crescendo, a veritable ascending tricolon of bloodshed and turmoil. The *Aeneid* does not end happily; Virgil's poetic predecessor Lucretius had shown Latin epic a bleak ending in the abrupt close to his sixth and final book, which ends with a description of the plague that once struck Athens, and the unforgettably appalling image of human beings fighting with each other over the dearth of available funeral pyres to burn their dead: Virgil's *Aeneid* offers a not much brighter vision. Book 10 is not as episodic as its predecessor, and lacks the neat threefold vision of its successor. In consequence it has become a sort of lost book of the *Aeneid*, not much appreciated (because it is comparatively little read)—the death of Pallas is the principal exception to this lamentable neglect. The book shares a unity of vision with Books 11 and 12, and at once explores the question Book 9 bequeathed it: what of divine intervention?[1]

Stephen Harrison's Oxford D.Phil. thesis commentary on this book was published in 1991; it is a worthy companion to the great Austin-Williams-Fordyce Oxford editions of earlier books, and remains the standard guide to Virgil's most intensely martial verse.

The first book of the poem had asked if it were truly possible that the gods could ever be so angry that they might force a man of outstanding qualities to undergo tremendous trials (1.11). Jupiter opens his council by asking why war has broken out in Italy after he had forbidden it. In his great speech to Venus in Book 1, Jupiter had mentioned the war in Latium; nowhere in the *Aeneid* before now have we had any indication, however, that Jupiter had explicitly banned the outbreak of war. Jupiter notes that there will come a "just time for war" (10.11 *iustum pugnae . . . . tempus*), namely the struggle between Carthage and Rome. This reference helps explain how Juno had heard that one day a race would be born from Trojan stock that would attack her beloved Carthage and destroy it (1.19 ff). Apparently Jupiter had announced the fated conflict between the two Mediterranean powers before; the war between Rome and Carthage is sanctioned by fate, while the current war is *contra fata*. The announcement that there was never supposed to be a war in Italy is something of a surprise, though it makes complete sense in light of the poem's final revelations: since Troy is to sink down and Italy ascend to world domination, the whole issue of Trojan supremacy and Trojan victory over the Italians becomes rather a moot point: Juno loves Carthage and does not relish the thought of the loss of her favorite city, but she will be consoled by the fact that not Troy but *Rome* will destroy it—Italian Rome, not Priam's Troy rebuilt in Italy, in accordance with Jupiter's shocking promise to his sister and wife near the end of Book 12 (829 ff.). Jupiter urges the gods not to hasten (10.11 *ne arcessite*) the time of the Punic Wars. Here there is a not so veiled reference to the actions of Venus and Juno with Dido. Arguably, in the narrative of the *Aeneid*, the trouble between Rome and Carthage started because two goddesses decided to interfere with Carthage's queen (for very different reasons). War would be inevitable between two great powers vying for control of a Mediterranean they would not be willing to share in amity. But Venus and Juno have hastened that war, from Jupiter's point of view, by their actions in Books 1 and 4.

Jupiter's words have a certain naïve quality that deserves exploration. If he had forbidden war to break out in Italy, did he really expect that Turnus would gladly surrender his claims to Lavinia and Latinus' kingdom and accept a Trojan in his place? Just how much work did Juno have to do to rouse Turnus to despise Aeneas? Further, surely Jupiter realizes that his deliberate mention of the "lawful war" that is destined to erupt between Carthage and Rome is exactly the sort of thing Juno is least interested in hearing? Jupiter's definitive feelings on this entire war and the course of Italian, Trojan, and Roman destiny will not be revealed until we learn what he is willing to allow in Book 12 (and there, significantly, his great promise will be to his sister and wife Juno, not his daughter Venus). So far in the poem he has made two major interventions: in Carthage, he sent Mercury to order Aeneas to leave Carthage, and in Latium, he decreed that Turnus had to leave the Trojan camp (the two situations are roughly parallel). We have raised the possibility that Jupiter's intervention in both cases was to prevent Juno's plans from coming to fruition: in Book 4, Aeneas would gladly have stayed indefinitely with Dido, and Rome would never have been built (Carthage, in effect, would have held Rome's future prisoner indefinitely in Dido's alluring embrace), and in Book 9, Turnus was doing rather well single-handedly against the bulk of Aeneas' force. Jupiter knows the ultimate destiny of Trojans and Italians: the two races will mingle, and one will be dominant, the other recessive. But if the immortals truly did abstain from all involvement in the war, what would happen? Would Aeneas win out against Turnus? Virgil will not allow this fundamental question to be fully explored (and, like any great epic poet, he does not provide a definitive solution to every important problem), since in Book 11 Jupiter himself will not exactly abstain from involvement in Italy's war. In *Iliad* 8, when the gods meet in divine council, Zeus threatens them. Here the mood is quite different:

> nunc sinite et placitum laeti componite foedus. (10.15)
>
> *Now permit it, and, happy, establish a pleasing alliance.*

Jupiter is cajoling and pleasant; surely he realizes that at this critical moment certain of his divine family members are unlikely to be happy and cheerful.

Jupiter's delay in revealing the ultimate fate of Troy and Italy is not without consequence. It delays the inevitable fight we must imagine he will have with Venus when she finds out that Italy will most certainly not be Trojan.

Venus is the first to respond. She complains of Turnus' recent victories, and notes that Aeneas is absent and unaware of what his people are suffering (10.25 *Aeneas ignarus abest*). Venus' words about her son refer back to the end of Book 8 (730), where *ignarus* Aeneas lifted the fate of his Roman progeny on his shoulders. It is not Aeneas alone who is ignorant of the future, however. Venus complains about the Italian siege of the Trojan camp, and she describes how Turnus is attacking the very walls of "newborn Troy" (10.27 *nascentis Troiae*)—Venus fully expects that her son's destroyed city will be reborn in Italy. This theme is central to her thoughts; later in her speech she notes that Aeneas and his Teucrians have been seeking a new Pergamum, a Troy in Italy (58 *recidivaque Pergama*). Venus has been absent from the action of the poem for some time; she is aware that the Latins have sent an embassy to Diomedes in Apulia to ask for help, and she complains that he is already on his way to help Turnus—a rhetorical exaggeration, probably, an emotional complaint that contrasts nicely with Jupiter's calm detachment (though his very summoning of the divine council belies his own fears). Diomedes is the great bogeyman of the Iliadic *Aeneid*; he had nearly killed Aeneas in Homer's *Iliad*: Aeneas had to be spirited off the battlefield by Apollo after even his mother Aphrodite had been wounded by the son of Tydides (*Iliad* 5.311 ff.). Venus complains (and rightly so) that no one should be impeding the progress of fate; if her son has only been following the decrees of so many divine revelations, why should he be harassed? An answer, of course, would force Jupiter to reveal the important details of just how much of a concession to Juno he is willing to grant (concessions Fate has no objection to)—details he had left out of his speech to her in Book 1 (she had not asked for the specifics of the future Trojan foundation in Italy, after all). How—without conflict—are you supposed to bring a hero out of one city's destruction, take him to a new land where there is already a more or less stable settlement, and establish your hero as the progenitor of a new race that will have the customs, language, and characteristics of the native inhabitants, not the hero's dead culture? This quandary is the source of Jupiter's somewhat naïve opening speech. In Book 12 we shall learn that Jupiter is willing to grant his wife her final, desperate request: let Italy *not* be Trojan. He perhaps knows even now that this will be Italy's ultimate destiny: he dare not *reveal* it now to Venus. His promise to Juno in Book 12 will be devastatingly casual: *of course* Trojan customs, language, and dress can all be jettisoned from the new city: it is almost as if Juno could have had her way on those issues as early as Book 1, so easily, in the end, does she win the terms of the agreement. Rage, it seems, can have its reward: the fury of Juno will more than have its prize in the final analysis.

Venus' speech makes a lengthy and impassioned appeal for the preservation of Ascanius (again, the succession motif, which is never far from Virgil and Augustus' mind). If Aeneas is to be tormented with endless delays and troubles, Venus will at least insist on Ascanius' safety and security.

Juno, Venus' main opponent in the *Aeneid*, interrupts her speech at midline (10.62) with an angry outburst; madness (63 *furori*) has come upon her. This is the first time in the poem that we have seen Juno "in public" and not, as it were, acting in the shadows; she has engaged in conversation with Venus (Book 4), but not as yet with her husband and certainly not in a divine assembly. She asks which god it was who drove Aeneas to pursue war (66 *bella sequi*); the question is particularly ironic after Jupiter's reminder (new to us, not to the immortals) that he had banned conflict in Italy. Juno has no guilt over her use of Allecto to stir up trouble in Latium (but, again, underlying all of this debate is the more important question of what Jupiter thinks would have happened had Juno not intervened). Juno's words deserve close examination here:

> Italiam petiit fatis auctoribus (esto)
> Cassandrae impulsus furiis: num linquere castra
> hortati sumus aut vitam commitere ventis?
> num puero summam belli, num credere muros?
> Tyrrhenamque fidem aut gentis agitare quietas? (10.67-71)

> *He has sought Italy under the leadership of the fates (let it be)*
> *driven on by the madness of Cassandra: did we urge him*
> *to leave behind his camp and entrust his life to the winds?*
> *Did we urge him to entrust the issue of war to a boy, to trust*
> *in his walls, and to tamper with Etruscan faith and quiet races?*

Buried in the exaggerated rhetoric and unfair assertion is one important point: Ascanius should never have been in a position of leadership in the Trojan camp (though Virgil does not explicitly indicate that Aeneas put him there). Ascanius' decision to allow the Nisus and Euryalus expedition was an abject failure (and disobedience to his father's instructions). More difficult to construe is Juno's sarcastic reference to Aeneas' fated mission. She begins (ironically) with the future imperative of solemn, religious or legal authority: "let him go" to Italy. At once she adds, "driven on by the ravings of Cassandra." Cassandra was fated never to be believed, despite the truth of her prophecies. Juno's sarcastic reference to Cassandra refers to Anchises' words to his son (3.183) much earlier in the poem; Cassandra had often told him that the Trojans were destined to go to Italy, but, like everyone else, he had never believed her. Buried in the odd reference (the audience cannot really be expected to remember the brief mention of Priam's prophetic daughter from seven books before) is a deeper insult to Aeneas: Juno is, in effect, asking how anyone could ever believe that Aeneas was meant to be Rome's progenitor (the question is a reasonable one, given his behavior in Carthage and his damning self-indictment to Dido, where he ruefully complained of his *involuntary* departure to Italy). Juno quickly descends into rhetorical questions of false innocence, asking what she could possibly have had to do with the state of affairs in Italy (10.72-73). Again, her question has a twofold resonance. On the one hand she is being disingenuous; she has certainly had much to do with the war in Latium. On the other hand she is asking the question Virgil deliberately refuses to answer: what would have happened in the absence of any divine action? Would Turnus have agreed to accept Aeneas' rule over him with no protest? Would he have welcomed the Trojans the way Dido initially welcomed them to Carthage?

Juno quickly raises her strongest possible arguments. Why is she alone not allowed to offer assistance to anyone? Her attack is mostly aimed at Venus, the proximate cause of her provocation in this council, but also carries weight against Jupiter with its continuing theme of wonder at just what Turnus was supposed to do in the face of Aeneas' arrival. Her argument is a counterpart of her indignant question in Book 1 (37 ff.): why is she alone not permitted to avenge a slight?

Finally, and most damningly, she notes that the whole reason Aeneas was an exile in the first place was because Venus herself caused the Trojan War by her careless arrangement of the love affair between Paris and Helen. Just as Venus thoughtlessly caused so much harm to Aeneas in the first half of the *Aeneid* by her machinations with Dido (to Juno's delight), so the root cause of the whole mess, in Juno's judgment, was Venus' meddling with Menelaus' marriage. Juno's concluding words are especially damning: Venus should have been afraid for her beloved Trojans years before, when she set them on the path to destruction (10.94 *tum decuit metuisse tuis*). At once, all the gods begin to argue back and forth, some supporting Venus and others Juno. A storm is brewing in heaven, which Virgil describes with a simile that describes how trees in a forest portend trouble for sailors when they start to shake in the wind (97-99). Jupiter had opened the council calmly; now the earth shakes and the heavenly ether is silent as he makes his response: he had hoped his naïve call for happy assent to his wishes would have been followed, but Venus and Juno have frustrated his wish for peaceful settlement (though how that settlement could possibly have been achieved remains uncertain).

Jupiter prefaces his remarks by noting that it is not possible for Italians and Trojans to be joined in alliance, given the goddesses' discord. His observation is correct, but—since only he realizes the trap he is in, if he is aware of what the future Roman foundation will be like—his observation ignores the fact that the alliance is also being hindered by the (ultimate) "requirement" in the treaty that Troy sink down (12.836 *subsident*) in the new order. Jupiter makes his solemn decree:

> quae cuique est fortuna hodie, quam quisque secat spem,
> Tros Rutulusve fuat, nullo discrimine habebo,
> seu fatis Italum castra obsidione tenentur
> sive errore malo Troiae monitisque sinistris.
> nec Rutulos solvo. sua cuique exorsa laborem
> fortunamque ferent. rex Iuppiter omnibus idem.
> fata viam invenient. (10.107-113)

> *Whatever fortune there is for each one today, whatever hope each one pursues,*
> *though he is Trojan or Rutulian, I shall consider them with no distinction,*
> *whether by the fates of the Italians the camp is held under siege*

> *or by a bad error and misleading prophecies of Troy.*
> *Nor do I free the Rutulians. Each one's own beginning will bring him*
> *labor and fortune. Jupiter will be the same king for all;*
> *the fates will find a way.*

Jupiter's speech looks forward to the ultimate goal of a united Rome. He will be the same Jupiter to everyone; one gets the impression that Jupiter wishes that final goal would arrive as quickly as possible, so all the unpleasant details of how exactly it will be achieved can be forgotten—this sentiment lies behind his opening declaration that he will consider the Trojans and Rutulians "with no distinction" (108 *nullo discrimine*). As for the future of Troy, Jupiter is cagey—he knows he may incur the risk of being called to question later if he does not choose his words carefully now. He makes mention of the *fata Italiae*, the "fates of Italy"—that, of course, is a reference to the ultimate outcome, whatever that may be. Jupiter does not explicitly forbid divine intervention in this speech (which is why later he could, however pedantically, claim that he never expressly banned divine manipulation of events, just as all the other immortals who will do anything henceforth can excuse themselves). Instead, he couches what is clearly a decree of neutrality in the language of individual personal destiny. "What fortune stands forth for each one today," "what expectation each one pursues,"[2] "what labor or fortune each one's undertakings bring to him"[3]—no matter Trojan or Italian—Jupiter will make no distinction and will remain aloof. It should be noted that Jupiter technically declared his *own* neutrality and does not give the other immortals any explicit command—though his intention is clear enough. The outcome of this declaration will be most clearly seen in the fate of Camilla in the next book. Diana will correctly note that Camilla should never have left the forest to fight in Latium—but her military success is astonishing, and Jupiter will at last stir up Tarchon, and Apollo assist Arruns in bringing her down. Arguably, Camilla's fatal fortune had its *exorsa*, its beginnings, in her own decision to leave the forest. But would she have been killed without Jupiter and Apollo? When Turnus abandons his ambush plan because of his mad rage once he hears of her death, Virgil notes that the savage power of Jupiter demanded it (11.901). There is an uneasy relation between those apparent interventions and Jupiter's words here.

Jupiter's speech, in the final analysis, is feeble and weak. He is laboring under a heavy burden: as it will eventually turn out, he did not reveal the entire truth to his daughter in Book 1, and he has revealed little if anything of the entire truth to his wife.[4] He has no interest in rectifying any omissions now, in front of both angry goddesses (and the flighty Venus did not bother to pursue inquiry into specific details about the future fate of Troy / Rome with Jupiter—in the final analysis Juno is smarter in this regard). He has no interest in settling all the specifics of Rome's future. Besides these divine problems, on the human plane there is the difficult question Virgil will never answer: would Aeneas win this war without any help? Indeed, would he even have made it to Italy? These questions have no answers (as Juno noted in her angry words to Venus, one could find blame for the current mess in plenty of places). But from now on in the poem, closer attention must be paid than ever before to all divine actions. And, ultimately, these questions will be secondary for Virgil in the face of his larger concerns: the future of Rome and its slavery to Madness.

Significantly, the first human scene after the divine council shows the Rutulians in full control of the battle, with the Trojan camp besieged and "no hope of flight" for Aeneas' men (10.121 *nec spes ulla fugae*). A host of great Trojan warriors is described as they defend the walls of their besieged camp. What colors the whole passage is its introduction; they have no hope of escape, no hope of forcing their way through the Rutulian lines. Theirs is a defensive, holding action now (which is what Aeneas had ordered in case of any Italian attack). Mnestheus is there (143-144), glorious because he had driven back Turnus on the preceding day; the glory is, however, mitigated by Jupiter's decree that Turnus had to leave the camp anyway, and by the dire straits the Trojans find themselves in during this siege. Somewhat surprisingly, Ascanius is present also (132-138), in an extended description of his role in the midst of the Trojan defenders. He is Venus' "most just anxiety" (132 *iustissima cura*)—in other words, Venus is most rightly concerned for the symbol of Rome's continued stability. He is like a jewel set in yellow gold or ivory in boxwood—we might think of the *Gemma Augustea*, the large gem that was carved from onyx and probably dates to the last years of Augustus' reign: did the artist have this description of Ascanius in mind? What, though, is Ascanius doing in the midst of battle after Apollo had warned him off? These Trojan heroes are future founders of Rome: Capys, we are reminded, will give his name to Capua (145).

Finally, we hear again of Aeneas and learn that he is making his way back to camp by a night journey. We had heard an abbreviated account of his arrival at Caere to seek help from Tarchon; now we are told a more detailed version about Aeneas' new allies, the former subjects of the inhuman Mezentius; this passage begins a ring that concludes at the end of the book with Mezentius' death. Virgil reminds us that Aeneas had ships sacred to Cybele by his detail about the decoration on the ship's prow: it has a representation of the sacred Mount Ida and a pair of lions (who traditionally draw Cybele's chariot). Aeneas is still firmly entrenched in the old Trojan religion. Pallas is with him, at his very side: he is learning from Aeneas of his travels and asking about the stars. He is now established in the role of surrogate son, Virgil's very Roman modification (more or less) of the Homeric relationship between Achilles and Patroclus and its homoerotic undertones.[5]

We have wondered for some time where Aeneas was and when he was returning; even the immortals at council were commenting on the blissful ignorance of his absence from war. Now the Muses are once again summoned, this time to mark the arrival of Aeneas' Etruscan allied contingents as he arrives for battle. The invocation to the Muses marks another major stage in the war's progress: finally, for the first time, Aeneas and Turnus will be on the same battlefield at the same time. Interestingly, while this catalogue balances the one at the end of

Book 7 (cf. the invocations to the Muses at 10.163 and 7.641), the list of Aeneas' Etruscan supporters is significantly less inspiring and briefer than the previous catalogue, in reflection of the fact that these contingents are only a relatively small portion of Aeneas' complete forces. The Etruscans arrive, beginning with Massicus and his thousand men from Clusium and Cosae. Together with them is Abas, who has a ship dedicated to Apollo; perhaps Arruns, Camilla's killer (who is a devotee of Apollo) is with this contingent.

Cinyras is the leader of the Ligurians, and he is followed by Cupavo (we are proceeding more or less in alphabetical order, as we did during the catalogue at the end of Book 7). Cupavo has swan feathers on his helmet, a reference to his father Cycnus (the "Swan"), who had been changed into a swan while he lamented the death of Phaëthon.[6] Cycnus had been a king of the Ligurians; it is possible that the avian mention of this Ligurian presages the death of the Ligurian killed by Camilla (11.800 ff.), whose killing is compared to the death of a dove at the hands of a raptor. The tradition does not make clear whether Cycnus was a relative or a lover of Phaëthon; it is unlikely, though possible, that Virgil is playing on the ambiguous nature of Aeneas' relationship with Pallas. Cupavo's boat is the Centaur, which was the name of one of the ships in the boat race; much has changed since those halcyon days of athletic rest and relaxation.

Cupavo the swan comes right before Ocnus, who leads a contingent from Mantua, Virgil's birthplace, which accounts for the powerful threefold anaphora of *Mantus . . . Mantua . . . Mantua*. Virgil notes that *Mezentius* armed five hundred Mantuans against him: the Mantuans are so enraged with Mezentius' horrific rule that they have come eagerly to join Aeneas' campaign; Mincius is their leader (10.206)—neatly, "Mezentius" even maintains the alphabetic order of the catalogue). Ocnus himself is a son of the Tiber and of a prophetess (Manto, from the Greek for "seer"); Virgil has powerfully put himself on Aeneas' (winning) side. Mantua has three races, Virgil notes (Greeks, Etruscans, and Umbrians, probably), and four peoples under each race for a total of twelve cities. The division of the cities is a reference to the internecine strife that Mezentius' expulsion brought, though there is no indication that Mantua itself was divided: Mezentius' son Lausus is leading a thousand men from Agylla (7.651-653).[7] The mention that *Mezentius* armed these men against himself also highlights the civil strife in Etruria. The last figure in the catalogue, Aulestes, breaks the alphabetic pattern (just as the first, Massicus, did): his boat is the Triton, whose presence reminds us of the many times sea deities helped Aeneas' fleet in time of catastrophe.

Aeneas is met by his former ships, now sea nymphs (10.219 ff.); the ring that started at the beginning of Book 9 now closes, as Aeneas makes his return. One of the ships (charmingly, the one who is most learned in speaking!) addresses Aeneas; she is still like a boat in that she is "oaring her way" with her left hand (10.227 *laevo tacitis subremigat undis*, and cf. 247, where Virgil nicely notes that the nymph knows how to send Aeneas' ship on its way) as she treads water, talking to Aeneas, whom Virgil labels *ignarus* (228) once again: he has no idea what has happened. The ship-nymph Cymodocea reveals that Aeneas' fleet has left him unwillingly: even at this moment of innocent wonder, Virgil reminds us of a terrible moment, when Aeneas said he was leaving Dido in these very ships *unwillingly*. This meeting is a precautionary portent: unlike the usual pattern of divine revelation *ex post facto*, here Aeneas receives supernatural confirmation and assurance before he sees the dire situation in his camp. The nymph at once notes Ascanius' situation, before outlining Turnus' basic plan—he is trying to prevent Evander's Arcadian cavalry from coming to relieve the Trojan camp (they have been riding parallel to Aeneas' trip down river). Cymodocea announces that tomorrow will bring great slaughter to the Rutulians; she does not, of course, announce Pallas' forthcoming death—the impending emotional burden of which he is all too unaware; Virgil ends the fantastic episode of the sea nymphs with another reminder that Aeneas is "unknowing" (249 *inscius*).

We had left Aeneas in Book 8 with his shield; as he arrives back near his camp via the Tiber, he raises the shield in his left hand (the lucky side in Roman augury), and at once his men are roused to courage. The shout from Aeneas' men is compared to a flock of cranes that fly across the sky and drive away the south winds with their loud cry. The simile is copied from *Iliad* 3 (2-6), where it describes an onrush of Trojans. But there the simile was followed by the appearance of Paris; Menelaus sees him and frightens off the cowardly Trojan.[8] As is his wont, Virgil has invested the glorious arrival of his hero with some ominous undertones, namely his ignorance (a repeated theme) and now the reminiscence of Paris. Aeneas will not shrink away from this fight; the comparison is not followed through to any degree of completion. The overall effect of these ominous clues in the narrative is to unsettle the audience and prepare them for the great tragedy of this book, the loss of Pallas. Pallas' death will spell disaster for both Turnus *and* Aeneas. The comparison between the cranes of *Aeneid* 10 and the cranes of *Iliad* 3 works in part because Aeneas is another Paris—even if the comparison ends there, and the subsequent behavior of the two men is quite different.

Aeneas' men may shout like cranes, but the hero himself is described with a flame blazing from his helmet, a reminder, ultimately, of how his infant son's head burst into flame (2.682-684, where 683-684 *apex ... flamma* is paralleled here by 270 *apex ... flamma*), as well as how flames are erupting from Augustus' head on the shield (8.680-681). The flames are compared to comets that burn terribly (10.273 *lugubre*, of a grim portent), or to Sirius, the Dog Star of late July and early August in Rome, whose coming portended malaria and disease. This is the only explicit "comet" in the *Aeneid*; it echoes back to the comets Virgil mentions as part of the portents that accompanied Caesar' assassination in 44 B.C. (cf. *Georgics* 1.488 *nec diri totiens arsere cometae*), before he launched into a memorable lament over the martial strife that has engulfed Rome and the raging of unholy Mars (511), allegedly one of Rome's patrons. Turnus is no more moved by this portent than he was by the metamorphosis of the Trojan fleet (9.126 is virtually identical to 10.276); his encouraging words to his men form a famous half-line, "Fortune favors the brave" (284 *audentis For-*

tuna iuvat), though Virgil notes that Turnus does not have a prepared plan of battle (the siege has made him somewhat lazy)—he must quickly determine in his mind which men he should lead with him against the disembarking Trojans, and which other men he should leave behind to besiege the camp.

During the boat race in Book 5, Sergestus' ship had been wrecked when he tried to take the curve in the racecourse too sharply. Now, as Aeneas lands from the Tiber near his camp, it will be Tarchon's boat that is destroyed as it strikes a reef in the shallows (10.302-307). Turnus ignores the accident as he rushes to meet the landing Trojan and Etruscan forces. Aeneas immediately starts attacking the rustic (310 *agrestis*) Latins, and the first casualty is Theron (the "Hunter" in Greek), a continuation of the poem's theme of the coming of (urban) civilization to a primitive, rural Italy. Virgil frequently decorates his scenes of slaughter with memorable vignettes; Aeneas' victim Lichas was able to escape the knife when he was cut from his dead mother's body, but he is unable to escape Aeneas' sword (315-317). In an elaborate battle description, Cydon would have been killed by Aeneas, had not seven of his cohort attacked the Trojan hero as he targeted their friend, who for his part was distracted by his

young lover, Clytius, whom he was following amid the fray (not only the Trojans have male lovers who evoke the tradition of Greek homosexuality). Aeneas is defended by his (divine) helmet and shield (the first mention of Vulcan's work in combat), but his kindly, nurturing mother (332 *alma Venus*) deflects other weapons so that they only graze him. This is the first indication of any divine intervention after the council of the gods. As with the other interventions from now until the end of the poem, it does not technically violate Jupiter's edict (such as it was), but it is the first immortal involvement in the war *après le concile*. Aeneas goes on to attack other Latins; the mention of Numitor (342) in particular reminds us once again of how civil this war is, from the viewpoint of later Roman history.[9]

Aeneas' entry into the battle evens the struggle. The Trojans do not win a smashing victory at once; quickly enough the contest is perfectly balanced, and Virgil notes that the war was on the very threshold of Ausonia: though the two sides are locked in equal combat, Virgil has subtly shifted the scene of action from the threshold of the Trojan camp to the threshold of Italy. Three Thracians of the race of Boreas, the north wind, are killed by the Trojans; the mention of these sons of the wind leads to a simile that describes how the two clashing sides were like the raging winds (356-361).

The first explicit sign of a Latin setback comes from Pallas' Arcadian allies. This is Pallas' first action in the war; his cavalry forces have dismounted because of the rough terrain at the riverbank, and are being chased in flight by the Latins. His speech of encouragement to his men sums up powerfully and effectively why they are here: they are seeking nothing less than the praise of their country, and Pallas is hoping to show his martial courage for the honor of his father Evander. He asks his men if they would rather seek the sea or *Troy* (10.378 *Troiam*): he, too, does not understand the future, and assumes (as do Venus and Aeneas) that the Trojan camp is the first stage in building the edifice of Troy reborn. As soon as he finishes speaking, Pallas begins his *aristeia*, which leads to a fierce slaughter. One man is killed as he rages over the death of a friend; two twin brothers are gruesomely slain, one decapitated and the other horribly wounded, with his hand cut off and now twitching on the ground as it seeks its master and sword (a rare Virgilian indulgence in the sort of almost black humor that so delighted the Silver poets). The adolescent Pallas' fantastic deeds cause his Arcadians both "sorrow and shame" (10.398 *dolor et pudor*). The *dolor* is a subtle foreshadowing of the sorrow they will feel at his death; their emotions are stirred now by how ashamed they are that an extremely young warrior is proving to be braver and more courageous than his mostly older men.

Virgil compares the *aristeia* of Pallas and his Arcadians to the action of a farmer who sets fires here and there in a forest when the summer winds have come to aid him in starting a general conflagration that will clear his future land and field of trees. Virgil is again playing with the theme of the coming of urban civilization and order to the world of the forest. This invasion of what is her natural territory and home is why Diana sides not so much with the Latins *per se* in Book 11 as with anyone who would defend her sacred groves and haunts from invasion and ruination. Camilla, too, is arguably fighting for the same cause; with the coming of the Trojans, the world of unspoiled nature will yield to the rise of cities and urban development. A parallel to Camilla is the fate here of the Latin Halaesus. He begins to rise up against Pallas' Arcadians and deal death; we learn in an authorial aside that his father had once hidden his son in the forest to protect him from a prophesied death in battle. We further learn that once his father died, the Fates (10.419 *Parcae*) had thrown their hands on him and marked him for death by Evander's spear (now wielded by his son). Like Camilla, Halaesus had apparently left the safety of the woodlands at some point after the death of his father. Pallas prays to the Tiber, to whom he promises spoils; the river god assents to his prayer, and Halaesus is killed. Virgil is careful to note that it was Halaesus' fate, apparently, to die if he should ever leave the forest; the Tiber is not so much agreeing to Pallas' prayer as cooperating in the decrees of the Fates; this scenario will be replayed with greater complexity in Book 11—another good example of Virgil's tightly woven narrative and his delight in linking various episodes together to create a delicate structure of foreshadowing and reflective narrative.

Fittingly, we now meet Lausus, the son of Mezentius and the logical opponent for Pallas. The Arcadians have done very well (though not without some losses of their own); now Lausus strikes down Abas, whom Virgil calls "the knot and delay of battle" (10.428 *pugnae nodumque moramque*): Lausus' first casualty is a significant foe. At once the Arcadians, the Etruscans, and even the Teucrians themselves are slain—the Teucrians, Virgil notes, who had survived the Greeks. The balance of battle continues; Pallas may have performed manfully, but Lausus is just as good, and the two sides are depicted as equally matched (431 *viribus aequis*). Pallas and Lausus are depicted as the two leaders of the opposing sides (where are Turnus and Aeneas?), and we learn that Fortune (435 *For-*

tuna) has already denied both of them a homecoming from war. Jupiter makes his first appearance since the council of immortals: he does not allow the two to meet, since their fates (438 *sua fata*) called them to fall to greater foes (Turnus and Aeneas). Again, there is technically no violation of the non-intervention edict; neither young man is being helped—apparently their destiny is not only to die, but also to die at the hands of the poem's two main characters. Still, we may be allowed to wonder *why* this is their destiny; one answer is that Pallas must die at the hand of Turnus so Aeneas-Achilles can seek his revenge on Turnus-Hector and the *Iliad*'s great single combat can be repeated in Latium. Pallas and Lausus' avoidance of each other on the battlefield, so accidental and yet so fated, mirrors how Turnus and Aeneas have stayed apart from each other thus far, well into the third book of the war.

Virgil follows up his introduction of Lausus with Juturna, Turnus' sister.[10] Her origins are obscure; Servius thought she was Lavinian, though some scholars think she may have been Etruscan; she was apparently a water deity or nymph, who was invoked, appropriately enough, by those who used water in their occupations.[11] Juturna's first entry into the poem is difficult. She comes to warn her brother that Lausus is in jeopardy. The poem's audience knows that Jupiter has forbidden Lausus and Pallas to meet, and further that both Lausus and Pallas are doomed to die. Why does Juturna come to Turnus with worries about Lausus? It would seem that she knows Lausus' fate, though perhaps not the full details. Lausus and Camilla have strong affinities. Turnus will ruin one of his best opportunities to win the war when he emotionally overreacts to the death of Camilla (though, quite significantly, it will be Jupiter who demands his frenzied, unthinking reaction). Juturna's actions now lead directly to Pallas' death: as soon as Turnus hears that Lausus needs help (she does not mention Evander's young son), Turnus immediately thinks of Pallas:

solus ego in Pallanta feror, soli mihi Pallas
debetur. (10.442-443)

*I alone am borne against Pallas; to me alone is Pallas
owed.*

Turnus' twofold repetition of Pallas' name will be repeated (to horrible effect) by Aeneas at the end of the poem.

Juturna is the closest deity to Turnus (because of their blood relationship); like Aeneas' mother Venus, her actions are somewhat reckless. Here she is concerned only with Lausus, it seems, and ignores the logical consequence of her intervention: Turnus will come to the field where the two young men have led their opposing armies, and he will seek to cut down Lausus' greatest potential foe. As we have seen, Turnus is treading much of the same ground as Aeneas in the first half of the poem; during the sojourn in North Africa we saw the terrible results of Venus' good-intentioned but careless and unthinking attempts to manipulate events in Dido's Carthage. Now we see the same with Juturna's foolish deed. As for Aeneas, we are right to expect that he has learned much from his education in Books 5-8; he should be a more mature hero now that we have arrived at the poem's last three books.

Turnus is like a lion that has seen a bull from a high place. He leaps off his chariot to meet Pallas on foot, face to face. Now the ring that started in Book 8 will close. Pallas makes a prayer to Hercules, the patron god of Pallanteum and savior of the whole region from the bloodthirsty inhospitality of the monstrous Cacus. Pallas fancies himself a new Hercules; he will rid Latium of Turnus. His prayer here is not as neatly proper as his earlier, successful one to the Tiber (10.421-423). He wants Turnus to see his young opponent snatch away the bloodied spoils from his body. There is no mention of where those arms would be offered in dedication; Pallas is as interested in spoils as Turnus will be (it is not entirely clear whether Pallas' prayer is silent or audible to Turnus—though the latter seems probable).

Hercules is disturbed by the prayer of his beloved Pallas; he knows he cannot grant it. Jupiter consoles him. Virgil introduces Jupiter subtly and almost imperceptibly: "then the father spoke to the son" (466 *tum genitor natum*). We think of Evander and his likely reaction to Pallas' death (which Virgil will not spare us), and we hear a simple explanation from Jupiter: everyone has their appointed time to die, and the "work of virtue" (469 *hoc virtutis opus*) is to extend one's reputation and fame down through time by deeds. Jupiter turns his eyes away from the battlefield; he will not watch this death. He will not cast his eyes the other way when Camilla is slaughtering Trojans (11.725-726). He tells Hercules what we already could have guessed: not only will Pallas die, but Turnus' days are quite numbered as well. Book 10 began with a divine council, and now, in its immediate aftermath, all the battle scenes are tinged with the memory of that immortal assembly. In one sense fate can be easily considered: will a man live or die in a given conflict? On this level, the respective fates of the characters in the *Aeneid* are easy to determine. We know Aeneas will survive and win from the very opening lines of the poem. Virgil can almost never resist telling us from the outset that some other given character will, in the end, meet their death as they enter combat. There is no real mystery, either, over who will be the agent of various characters' deaths. We know far in advance that Dido was fixed on suicide. We know that if anyone is to kill Turnus, it will be Aeneas (just as Paris killed Achilles). More complicated, more difficult, and more worthy of reflection is the ramification of each individual fulfillment of destiny.

Pallas throws his spear and grazes Turnus (so far Aeneas and Turnus have both been only slightly wounded in their respective fights). Turnus throws his spear, and pierces Pallas fatally in the chest; we are perhaps surprised by how quickly it is over. Virgil had compared the young Arcadian to a bull; now the bull's hide covering of Pallas' shield will be pierced along with its iron and brass. Pallas lives long enough to pull out the weapon before he dies. Turnus' first words over the corpse are quite interesting. He begins by saying that Pallas will be returned to Evander in the state he merited by his deeds (10.492 *qualem meruit*). For Turnus, Pallas is a traitor, a native Italian who has fought on the wrong side. Next he grants burial: he will allow the Trojans to take the body at once. Turnus here is no Hector (cf. *Iliad* 16.836). The Trojan prince had taunted the dead Patroclus with the threat of leaving his body exposed to the vultures. Turnus compares favorably to Hector here; his words mark an improvement in heroic moral development from the Homeric world. More interestingly, though, we shall not see similar scenes with Aeneas' killing of both Mezentius and Turnus. Mezentius will ask for burial at the end of this book, and Aeneas will be silent; as Book 11 opens with the funerals of the Trojan and Latin dead, the disturbing question will remain unanswered.

Turnus steps on the body with his left foot (Virgil delights in playing games with the lucky and unlucky significance of the left side) as he strips off Pallas' sword-belt, which is engraved with the story of the Danaids. The myth has associations to the action of the *Aeneid* on several levels. The Danaids were punished forever in Tartarus for the unspeakable (10.497 *nefas*) act of murdering their husbands on their wedding nights. Virgil presents the death of Pallas in perversely nuptial terms; he was slain when he should have been celebrating a marriage and starting his life as a prince of Italy. The theme is a favorite of Virgil's; while Mezentius is raging over the battlefield later in this book (10.719 ff.), he will kill Acron, a Greek from Etruria who was engaged to be married and left home before the wedding to come and fight in Italy's ultimately *civil* war. Turnus has killed a fellow native Italian, with whom he should have been allied; he has acted like one of the Danaids who killed their husbands (and, indeed, in Book 11 Virgil will compare the dead Pallas to a flower that was plucked by a virgin's thumb—subtly reinforcing the connection between Turnus and Danaus' murderous daughters). As with the depiction of the terrible fate of the Athenian youths on the doors of Apollo's temple at Cumae (6.20 ff.), the slaughter of the husbands of the Danaids is also a general reflection on the untimely death of the young. Danaus was the eponymous founder of the "Danaans" (a convenient Homeric and Virgilian name for the Greeks in general); Turnus is another Greek (who also shares Argive connections with Danaus) enemy for the Trojans. When Pallas collapses, Virgil notes in a striking phrase that he struck "enemy ground" (10.489 *terram hostilem*): the ground is formally his enemy (*hostis*, not *inimica*) because it is now held by Turnus, against whom Pallas has risen up in arms. But most importantly, both Pallas and Turnus would be better off proceeding to their weddings, not to war. This connection between the belt Turnus strips off Pallas and his eventual loss of Lavinia and death is most at play in the detail about the engraving.

During this entire sequence Aeneas' whereabouts are quite uncertain. Achilles' absence from the battlefield while Patroclus fought and died was a major subject of exploration for Homer; Virgil, on the contrary, gives no explanation for the absence of his hero. Rumor does not bring Aeneas the news of Pallas' death, but a "more certain author" (510 *sed certior auctor*): someone must have sought out Aeneas immediately with the report of the loss. The death of Pallas has plunged the Arcadians and Trojans into disaster—the absence of Aeneas from his young friend's side is perhaps the result of Pallas' overly eager zest for battle, but also strikes us as troubling: why was Aeneas not taking care of Pallas on what Virgil describes as Pallas' first day in combat (508)?

Aeneas' reaction to the news of Pallas' death is violent and bloodthirsty. He cuts through the lines of Latins, seeking Turnus; we think he has killed the four sons of Sulmo and Ufens, until we reach the devastating word *viventis* (519)—he captures eight young men as living victims for Pallas' funeral pyre. Turnus had promised burial for Pallas (more than Hector had promised to Patroclus); Aeneas' first response to the news of the death is to prepare Italian victims for his young friend's future funeral pyre—we shall hear briefly of their fate later (11.81 ff.). Virgil has borrowed a grisly detail from Homer (*Iliad* 23.171), where Patroclus' funeral pyre will also have human sacrificial offerings; Aeneas' behavior here mirrors Achilles', though it comes off the worse after Turnus' granting of burial to Pallas (in contrast to Hector, and in reminiscence of Achilles in *Iliad* 24—though not *Iliad* 22, where he desecrated Hector's body). Aeneas' pursuit of Turnus is more than just; Virgil takes care to note that Turnus was haughty on account of the recent slaughter (10.514-515 *superbum/caede nova*): Anchises had solemnly enjoined the *Roman* Aeneas to be sure to vanquish the proud (*debellare superbos*). One Italian, Mago, now begs Aeneas for his life. Mago rightly notes that there is no reason he in particular must die; the outcome of the war will not be changed either way. He pleads by the shades of Anchises and the expectation of what Iulus will represent; his words echo Mercury's to Aeneas, when he urged him to think of Ascanius and flee Carthage (4.274), and also Ilioneus' words at the court of Dido (1.556), but most especially Palinurus' plea for *burial* (cf. 10.524 *spes surgentis Iuli* and 6.364 *spes surgentis Iuli*). Mago wants to be returned to his own son and father; it is a powerful appeal to Aeneas' sense of *pietas*, and it prefigures Turnus' plea at the end of the poem to be allowed to return as a consolation to his aged father Daunus. Mago is willing to pay for his life with gold and silver; Aeneas says that all such possible bargaining ended when Turnus killed Pallas—and, besides, both Anchises' shade and Iulus would agree:

hoc patris Anchisae manes, hoc sentit Iulus. (10.534)

so the ghost of my father Anchises, so Iulus judges.

While Mago is still praying for mercy (536 *orantis*), Aeneas grabs his helmet with his left hand,[12] bends back his head, and buries the sword in his neck.[13] Here the death of Turnus is foreshadowed; Mago's death comes immediately after the loss of Pallas, before Aeneas has even seen the dead body of his friend; Turnus' will come more than two books later, after Aeneas sees the fateful sword-belt spoils. Aeneas has forgotten the injunction of his father to beat down the proud and spare those who are subjected to you (6.852-853); the point will be underscored once again in the emphatic final moments of the poem, in case we missed it here. Aeneas also kills Haemon, a priest of Apollo and Diana (10.537 *Phoebi Triviaeque sacerdos*)—more accurately, he *sacrifices* Haemon (*immolat*), which is exactly what he will tell Turnus that Pallas is doing to him at the end of the poem (12.948-949 *Pallas/immolat*). Aeneas does not stop long enough to take any spoils; Serestus picks them up as a trophy for Mars. The killing of one of Apollo's own priests is a further sign of Aeneas' deranged state after Pallas' death; Aeneas also kills Tarquitus (the son of a nymph, Dryope, and Faunus—another nod to early Roman religion and history), despite prayers and pleas (cf. 554 *orantis* with 536 *orantis*, and 599 *oranti* below). Tarquitus had the misfortune of merely crossing Aeneas' path: his penalty will be taunts and threats of being left for the birds or the fish (perhaps his body will be tossed into the nearby Tiber). Virgil compares Aeneas to Aegaeon, one of the hundred-handed giants with fifty mouths and fifty breasts, who fought against Jupiter: if Turnus was like Jupiter the giant slayer, now Aeneas takes the role of the giant. The comparison well describes his total domination of the battlefield as he searches for Turnus (who is conveniently absent, just as Aeneas himself was earlier)—but it also carries an aura of impiety; we could never imagine Virgil calling Aeneas *pius* in this section of the poem. Significantly, Aeneas regains the epithet *pius*, we shall see, only after he reacts to hyperbolic insult from a Latin. He has violated his father's instructions; his education had ended in Book 8 with the glorious vision of the shield, after which he had been completely absent from Book 9—his first major experience after his return has been the loss of Pallas, and his reaction—however understandable from one point of view—does come as disobedience to Anchises' solemn injunction. Turnus, we have observed, has often reminded us of the Aeneas of the Odyssean half of the poem. In his killing of Pallas, despite the stripping away of the sword-belt that will spell his doom, Turnus surpassed his Homeric model, Hector: he was willing to grant burial. Repeatedly, the Aeneas of Book 10 fails to improve on the moral example of *his* putative Homeric model, Achilles. Like some mythical, primordial giant of the age before the coming of Jovian order, Aeneas rages victoriously over the battlefield, once he dips his sword in warm blood and gore:

sic toto Aeneas desaevit in aequore victor
ut semel intepuit mucro. (10.569-570)

So Aeneas raged over the whole plain as a victor
when once his blade was hot with blood.

The brothers Liger and Lucagus madly rush against Aeneas. Liger is especially foolhardy; he boasts that Aeneas is facing no Diomedes or Achilles, no plains of Phrygia during the Trojan War, and he predicts the end of the war and Aeneas' life. Aeneas responds with a javelin throw, which strikes and mortally wounds Lucagus, who falls from the chariot; Aeneas makes a sarcastic remark about how Lucagus has abandoned his horses—Virgil now calls him *pius* (591) in the aftermath of a killing that was in response to Liger's arrogant threats.[14] At once Aeneas seizes the moving chariot and prepares to strike down Liger, who now makes his own prayer for mercy (the third in this catalogue of raging horror). Lucagus had died in part because of his brother's boasting; now Liger is in terror. Like a raging torrent or a black whirlwind, the mad Aeneas (604 *furens*) kills the now humbled braggart. Aeneas had swept over the battlefield and killed two men who made prayerful pleas for mercy; the second especially (Tarquitus) was cruelly threatened with having his body left as food for animals on both land and sea. Only one figure in the whole *aristeia* was unsympathetic: Liger. In the heat of battle, in the face of a moving chariot, Aeneas hurls his weapon and kills Lucagus (who, significantly, is also described as the brother who is preparing to fight, while Liger is controlling the horses' reins). As aforementioned, Aeneas is now called *pius* (he is finally reacting to an actual threat, not merely conducting indiscriminate slaughter). His *pietas* here is not without irony; he is killing two brothers—this perverse sense of respect for fraternal relations is well expressed by his response to Liger's pleas:

... morere et fratrem ne desere frater. (10.600)

... die, and do not desert your brother.

Aeneas, *pius* or not, reminds us of Achilles' son Neoptolemus in Priam's palace (2.550-553).

Once Aeneas has rampaged over the battlefield, the siege of the Trojan camp is sufficiently disrupted so as to allow Ascanius and the other Trojans to burst forth and appear on the battlefield: the release of Ascanius marks this moment as a high point in Trojan fortune. There is no longer any need for Ascanius to be hidden away safely within the walls; the danger is now past.

A most interesting scene now interrupts the action on the mortal plane. Juno's name appears as a surprise (10.606); by line's end we realize Jupiter is addressing his wife, and warmly, as his sister and most pleasing wife. After Aeneas' successful (however regrettably savage) *aristeia*, Jupiter suddenly reveals that Juno was right: Venus has been sustaining the Trojans, not their own resources (*opes*), or their own right hand (*dextra*), or their own courage, however ferocious and willing to endure danger (*animusque ferox patiensque pericli*). There has been no indication that Venus was behind any of the violence we have just seen; she had kept Aeneas safe from a wound (331-332) before Pallas' death, but has otherwise been unmentioned. Juno's words to Jupiter constitute an absolute masterpiece of rhetorical splendor:

cui Iuno summissa: "quid, o pulcherrime coniunx,
sollictas aegram et tua tristia facta timentem?
si mihi, quae quondam fuerat quamque esse decebat,
vis in amore foret, non hoc mihi namque negares,
omnipotens, quin et pugnae subducere Turnum
et Dauno possem incolumem servare parenti.

nunc pereat Teucrisque pio det sanguine poenas.
ille tamen nostra deducit origine nomen
Pilumnusque illi quartus pater, et tua larga
saepe manu multisque oneravit limina donis." (10.611-620)

To whom Juno, submissive, answered: "Why, O most handsome spouse,
do you trouble a sick woman, a woman who fears your grim deeds?
If my love had the same power that it had once and that it still should have
you would not deny this thing to me,
all-powerful one, but rather I would take Turnus out of the fight and
be able to preserve him safe for his father Daunus.
Now let him perish, and let him pay the penalty to the Teucrians with his pious blood.
Nevertheless, he takes his name from our origin.
Pilumnus was his fourth father in line, and often he
weighed down your thresholds with many presents from his generous hand."

Jupiter had spoken to his wife affectionately and sympathetically (he is never directly angry with her in the *Aeneid*; the closest he comes to outright anger is when we are told obliquely that he banned her from giving any aid to Turnus when he was trapped inside the Trojan camp at the end of Book 9, when Jupiter insisted that Turnus had to leave the camp). Juno responds in kind to her brother and husband's kind words; she is remarkably calm and detached as she confesses that *she* fears her husband and his deeds: Juno is acknowledging that she at least has been respectful of Jupiter's wish for non-intervention—unlike his daughter Venus. Juno laments that if she were still treated with the same love she once knew, she would be able to save Turnus and send him home to his aged father. Here she foreshadows the very same plea Turnus himself will make to Aeneas at the end of the poem. Since she is no longer so beloved and respected on Olympus, she now surrenders: let Turnus die, even though the blood he pays will be innocent and loyal (*pio*).[15] Juno's words end with an adversative (*tamen*): despite her hypothetical willingness to let Turnus die, she reminds Jupiter that Turnus was always respectful of Jupiter, and had always showered his temples with presents. Jupiter is willing to grant the prayer (10.620 *oratur*) that Juno has made; a careful study of prayer and response to prayer in *Aeneid* 10 would be profitable.

Juno, of course, has not surrendered everything so easily. If she were forced to accept absolutely nothing else, she might be willing to settle for Turnus' safety and continued existence (however inglorious, and inconsequential to her ultimate plans for saving Carthage). Juno remains firm in her main purpose: because of Carthage's future destruction *and* the insults she suffered from the Trojans, she does not want Venus' son to rebuild Troy in Rome (and even now, as late as the second half of Book 10, that seems to be the plan everyone else is set on effecting). Jupiter sees through his wife's pleas; he realizes she has not been truly placated. But now is not the moment for him to reveal the entire future to his wife, or to make any concessions to her. Jupiter knows that Venus is helping Aeneas, while no immortal is helping Turnus. If things were left as they are, Turnus would be finished on this very day. Juno takes something of a risk here. Given Venus' open favor for Aeneas, she could have argued for permission to give succor to Turnus. Instead, in the face of Venus' disregard for Jupiter's edict of non-intervention, Juno tries the difficult strategy of presenting herself as the willing loser.

Jupiter does not take the bait. He tells Juno that he is willing to grant Turnus a brief respite from his fate; he does not need to die immediately. Jupiter warns Juno that if she is aiming at any other goal whatsoever (in other words, saving Turnus' life, let alone having Turnus' side win), she is deluded. Juno begins to cry (and we sense her tears are real). Juno argues that Turnus is innocent and undeserving of the death he is about to suffer at Aeneas' hands (is she guilty over her amplification of Turnus' rage through Allecto's fury?); she expresses her wish that Jupiter might relent and change his mind, before wasting no time in departing at once (10.633 *protinus*). She now will set in motion her plan to substitute a phantom Aeneas, so that the two heroes will not clash on this day.[16]

This divine interlude is of great importance in understanding the logic of the last books of the poem. In Book 9, when Aeneas was completely absent from the fighting, Turnus nearly destroyed the entire Trojan camp (and, by implication, Iulus was in jeopardy—the hope of the future). It was not Aeneas' fault (or Turnus' for that matter) that the Trojans were fighting without their leader. As Book 9 ended, the situation was incredibly grim for Troy. Jupiter sternly sent word to Juno that Turnus had to withdraw from the Trojan camp. At once, he called a council of all his fellow immortals; he decreed that he would not intervene, and, by implication, enjoined a similar policy on the other gods: the fate of each mortal must be worked out individually, without divine action. When next we met Jupiter, he announced to Juno that Venus had been responsible for Aeneas' *aristeia*. Significantly, Jupiter did not ask Juno anything or give her any additional instructions. He merely confirmed what Juno had already realized about Venus. Juno miscalculates Jupiter's mood and thinks she can save Turnus; Jupiter is unwilling to grant her this request. He does not yet feel it is time to make the key revelation of just how much Fate is willing to concede to Juno's wishes, to have a discussion that will result in the agreement that will finally placate Juno and make her *happy* for the first time in the poem (12.841 *laetata*, the last bit of joy in the dark concluding sections of the poem)—surely on a personal level he dreads facing Venus, and for Virgil's dramatic purposes, such a twist ending must come as late in the epic as possible. Virgil prefers to cast his twist ending as a promise Jupiter willingly grants his wife, a concession to win her favor for Rome (Silius' *Punica* will show her firmly on Carthage's side, of course, in the forthcoming Punic Wars—the reconciliation of Juno is not without lapses: the goddess is merely reconciled in *Aeneid* 12 to the idea that Rome will be born). We shall be surprised in Book 12 at how unimportant such major considerations as Trojan vs. Italian identity seem to Jupiter; the fate of Troy, however, was destruction, and destruction is what it has inherited—Rome will not be Trojan. As for Aeneas' killing of Turnus, we are certain now (if we were not already) that the Rutulian leader is doomed, both because of Jupiter's conversation with his wife and because of Aeneas' behavior in battle. At the poem's end, Aeneas will delay for a brief moment (12.940 *cunctantem*). We can argue that it is Aeneas' *fate* to kill Turnus. If we defend Aeneas' action by invoking some sort of predetermined fate, then we must note that while Turnus succumbs to his inevitable death, he understands (as does Achilles) what he is doing: he is not afraid of Aeneas, but of Jupiter and the fates the gods have decreed, and his rebellion against destiny—however foolhardy if all that matters is his life or death—contrasts greatly with the depiction of Aeneas as oftentimes a mere puppet of fate.

No, Aeneas has a chance at the end of the poem to listen to his father's advice to the *Roman* Aeneas, not the Trojan Aeneas, and to spare Turnus. But while it is quite true in the light of later Roman history that the new city will be Italian and Roman, not Phrygian and Trojan, it is also true that Aeneas (who will be dead so soon after the action of the epic), in the end, will not be a Roman, at least according to his father's definition in the underworld. Nor would many Romans of Virgil's own day be able to say that later figures in their history, indeed in their own day, had not succumbed to the same Madness that so overcame the father of their race. Perhaps Anchises was wrong, and Rome's essence and foundation is to be found in brother killing brother (Romulus and Remus, the Social War, the civil wars).

Jupiter explicitly and definitively tells Juno that Turnus' fate is to die. The sudden Olympian interlude not only makes this final outcome clear, but also offers the (gratuitous?) detail that Venus is behind the Trojan surge.

Juno has been given leave by Jupiter to delay Turnus' final reckoning with fate. She decides to create a phantom figure of Aeneas, who will delude and trick Turnus; this passage forms a sort of ring with the playful scene of Venus disguising herself to trick Aeneas in Book 1. The context here is far more serious; Juno's game to rescue Turnus contrasts greatly with her sending Allecto in the disguise of an old woman to stir him to battle, or her sending Iris to urge him to fire the Trojan fleet. Beyond the compassion the goddess might feel for her doomed favorite, what purpose does the delay of Turnus' death serve? Since we know that Aeneas could win right now, Books 11 and 12 automatically incur a certain otiose quality: why must the delay stretch out over the length of two more books? Virgil is preparing the way for the important revelations of both final chapters of his epic. Book 12 will climax with the aforementioned reconciliation of Juno and death of Turnus (peace, in other words, on the divine plane, and strife on the mortal). Book 11 will serve as a microcosm of the entire war and its character. Only after lavishing due attention (his two longest books) on all of these topics will Virgil at last close his poem. For now, we begin to feel the mood of disquiet that Virgil very much wants for the final acts of his drama: why does it not all end now? The urgent sense we might feel of wanting the poem to end as soon as possible is heightened by scenes of horrific rampage such as Aeneas' *aristeia* in this book. It is difficult to reconcile those scenes with the glorious vision of a peaceful settlement that we might crave at the poem's close (and which Maphaeus Vegius thoughtfully provided for us in his Renaissance conclusion, not to say attempted improvement, of the poem). Virgil cannot envision such calm—at least not a permanent or lasting calm—after so much apparently needless slaughter. The same fear can be transferred, by easy extension, to the Augustan regime and its succession problem. Even if the slaughter can be justified, to what end? Pallas' death, in fact, is like a shockwave through the poem; before the killing, everything pointed to Turnus' success and his control over the battlefield. Ever since the young Arcadian died, everything has pointed to Turnus' doom. Pallas is the companion piece to the phantom Aeneas we are about to meet. Like Patroclus, Pallas died as a proxy for Aeneas (again, where was Aeneas when Turnus killed his young friend?) Similarly, before the final combat at the end of Book 12, Camilla will die as a sort of proxy for Turnus, so that when the two combatants meet, they will both be seething with the desire for vengeance on account of their young loved ones (for just as Aeneas and Pallas have what the Romans would consider an honorable, father-son relationship, in contrast to any notion of Greek-style homosexuality, so Turnus and Camilla will be a celibate couple, despite Turnus' obviously emotional, not to say erotic, reaction to the beautiful Volscian heroine).

The phantom Juno conjures is appropriately eerie. Once again, Virgil has borrowed material from Lucretius, this time from Book 4 of the *De Rerum Natura*, which is concerned with sense and perception. Why is the image of Aeneas so happy (10.643 *laeta*) as it stalks before the front of the battle lines and taunts Turnus to action? Juno is happy enough to be saving Turnus from mortal danger. But the phantom is also the first of a number of eerie supernatural visions Turnus will experience before his eventual death. Juno's phantom Aeneas is a like a ghost or a dream. Turnus' waking dream has as its theme his most eager desire: the pursuit and hunting down of Aeneas; Lucretius notes (4.962 ff.) that we dream of our occupations and avocations. Perhaps we might also think of the gate of false dreams in Virgil's underworld; certainly this daytime vision differs greatly from the dream visions of Hector, Creusa, and Anchises, all of whom visited Aeneas with true reports of his forthcoming labors. The Aeneas-image runs to a nearby Etruscan boat; after Turnus boards the ship in pursuit Juno cuts the mooring rope. Here we have another evocation of the theme of the absent hero: Turnus himself is not to blame for his inability to face his foe, and, once again, Aeneas is certainly not blameworthy for not being in Turnus' path, and continues his slaughter on the battlefield as he calls out for the absent Turnus (10.661 *illum . . . absentem*). Aeneas had been absent for all of Book 9, and now both Turnus and Aeneas are simultaneously present and yet absent.

The phantom vanishes, and Turnus is given no quick chance to disembark once Juno sends a storm to propel the boat. Now it is Turnus who is unknowing and unaware (10.666 *ignarus rerum*), and, Virgil notes, ungrateful for his salvation (he does not know what actually happened). Turnus' situation is now similar to Aeneas' first appearance in the poem (1.92 ff.). He appeals to Jupiter to let the boat dash against some rocks so that he may die alone in private shame. He expresses concern for his men; he has led them into war and now he hears their cries as Aeneas cuts them down all over the battlefield. At one moment he contemplates suicide, thinking perhaps he should stab himself, and then at once he considers throwing himself overboard in an attempt to swim to shore. The crucial element in his mindset here is his ignorance; he *saw* Aeneas board the ship, and wonders how he could have escaped undetected; he has no knowledge of Juno's conjuring trick. He tries to kill himself three times; and three times he tries to jump overboard to return to the coast. Juno prevents either outcome. The boat, conveyed by Juno, takes him home to his old father Daunus—a foreshadowing of his plea to Aeneas at the end of the poem to let him return home to Ardea for his father's sake.

Jupiter returns to the poem, this time to stir Mezentius to battle.[2] This is the first of two Jovian interventions where the father of gods and men rouses up an Etruscan to battle (cf. 11.725-726)—Jupiter will at least be egalitarian with the divided Etruscans, now rousing Mezentius, and, in Book 11, Tarchon (the leader of the Etrurian faction that supports Aeneas).[3] The book will now shift its concerns to Mezentius and Lausus, another of the poem's many father and son pairings, and in some ways the most tragic of them all; Lausus loves his father with a sincere and deep filial affection, despite Mezentius' unmitigated cruelty and impiety. Mezentius was the first figure in the catalogue of native Italian warriors; he will be the first of three major casualties that serve to end the *Aeneid* at the conclusions of the final three books: Mezentius, Camilla, and lastly Turnus. Jupiter does not so much stir up Mezentius to harm the Trojans as to hasten the day of reckoning for the notorious *contemptor divum*. Virgil's simile of the boar being lured into the hunter's nets by the pursuit of dogs gives away the outcome: Mezentius is a dangerous foe, but he will fall. Camilla's father Metabus, we learn, had been driven out of their homeland; we do not learn of his ultimate fate. Mezentius forms a pairing with Metabus and Lausus with Camilla. As Mezentius begins his *aristeia* now, we learn that he hands over the spoils from the dead Palmus to his son. Lausus is to be commended for his loyalty to his father, but there are occupational hazards for one who would be so devoted to so monstrous a figure. Mezentius kills Mimas, who had been born in Troy on the same night as Paris and was a constant friend of the young prince (his name may indicate that he mimed the infamous Trojan prince). Virgil notes that Paris lies dead in his homeland, while Laurens has the "unknown Mimas" (10.706 *ignarum . . . Mimanta*). Mimas is "unknown" because he is an insignificant character in comparison to the notorious Paris, but the adjective points mostly to the difference in their respective burial places: Paris is where he belongs, and the *Trojan* Mimas should be there also. Once again, subtly (as is his wont), Virgil lays the groundwork for the eventual revelation that Troy will be suppressed: Laurens does not know Mimas.

Mezentius kills Orodes, taunting him before he dies with the sarcastic mockery that Orodes is "no mean part of the war" (10.737 *pars belli haud temnenda*). Orodes makes a prediction of Mezentius' own forthcoming end, which rouses the Etruscan to anger and a smile:

"nunc morere. ast de me divum pater atque hominum rex viderit." (10.743-744)

"Now die. But as for me, let the father of the gods and king of men see to it."

The passage is difficult to construe precisely; Virgil has once again deliberately left open quite different possibilities. Mezentius here could be arrogantly contemptuous of the gods, as befits his nature, and almost daring Jupiter to do something about his violent rampage. Jupiter had stirred him up for this battle sequence (though one imagines, once again, that the effort needed was not great); this is Mezentius' response to that divine action. Mezentius' words are a mixture of both overbearing pride and a correct analysis of the circumstances. He knows he may die, and he does not shudder from the possibility (he is one of the few figures in epic poetry that one could never imagine asking for the mercy of being spared; Turnus will do so, but Mezentius is aware that his lifestyle and personality do not allow him such a privilege). Turnus, in contrast, will ask for his life. Despite the mad frenzy that propelled him into a very welcome chance to fight against and possibly destroy Aeneas, Turnus will not mimic Mezentius when he finds himself under the point of Aeneas' blade (Turnus will be no Mimas for Mezentius). Turnus, who was willing to grant Pallas burial without hesitation or need for persuasion, will feel most acutely the need to provide living solace for his old father Daunus. Aeneas' surrender to madness is a warning to Virgil's savior Augustus: will fury ever infect you, and, if not, what of your successors?

We left Turnus in Ardea, where Juno's intervention had safely taken him. Aeneas' whereabouts are unknown, as is exactly what has been the case throughout most of the overall progress of the battle. Before Juno absconded with Turnus, Aeneas seemed to be in complete control of the war, and Turnus' doom seemed imminent. Now we learn that even with Turnus back in Ardea and Aeneas presumably on the battlefield hunting him down, the war is evenly balanced; even the immortals on Olympus take pity on the pointless slaughter. The killings are pointless because the ultimate outcome is preordained and foreknown to the gods (and to men like Aeneas, who have been assured by oracles and supernatural visitations that they will triumph); still, it is of interest to note how Virgil emphasizes the even nature of the current struggle (10.755 *aequabat*, 756 *caedebant pariter pariterque ruebant*, 757 *victores victique, neque his fuga nota neque illis*). The explanation for this balance is unclear; we are told that Venus and Juno were *watching* (760 *spectat*) the action, not that they were any longer influencing it. After Aeneas had been slaughtering everyone on the battlefield, Jupiter noted to his wife that Venus had been helping the Trojans; now, as the battle is evenly balanced, we are told that Venus, and presumably Juno, are merely observing it from opposite sides: Tisiphone, the Fury, is the one raging in the middle.[19]

Aeneas and Mezentius finally come within a spear's throw of each other. Mezentius had given spoils to his son early in his *aristeia*; now he vows that he will give Aeneas' despoiled arms to his son Lausus, who will become a living trophy (775 *tropaeum*) of Aeneas. This passage opens a ring that will finish with the trophy Aeneas sets up at the beginning of Book 11 to mark Mezentius' death. Mezentius' own sense of loyalty to his son has consisted so far of concern only about spoils and the sort of (violent) paternal generosity we might expect from such a man: he is willing to share what spoils he wins with his offspring. Mezentius is like the giant Orion or some huge ash tree (763 ff.), and he is a despiser of the gods; fittingly, it will be *pius* Aeneas (783) who now attacks him. Mezentius misses Aeneas and instead kills the Argive Antor, himself a former companion of Hercules (another mark of Mezentius' great strength is the caliber of even his accidental victim). Aeneas wounds Mezentius and advances for close combat; Lausus begins to cry as he sees his father's wound: Virgil never separates the father and son. Virgil makes clear his own authorial respect and admiration for Lausus:

hic mortis durae casum tuaque optima facta,
si qua fidem tanto est operi latura vetustas,
non equidem nec te, iuvenis memorande, silebo. (10.791-793)

Here I shall not be silent about the fate of a harsh death and your best deeds,
if antiquity is going to bring any trust to such a deed,
nor about you, O youth deserving to be remembered.

Lausus receives what is perhaps the most moving tribute Virgil gives to any of the native Italians. It is impossible for the devoted son of such a vile father to survive; Lausus' death is a tragedy that could not have been avoided. The ensuing struggle between Lausus and Aeneas evokes Pallas and Turnus' encounter earlier in the book, though it has significant differences. Pallas and Turnus engaged in a simple exchange of spear casts; Lausus is interested not so much in killing Aeneas as in defending his father and safeguarding Mezentius' withdrawal from the battlefield. He rushes against Aeneas and stays his hand, giving his father coverage and a respite of time so he can pull back. Lausus' actions stir others to begin to shower Aeneas and the Trojans with weapons; Aeneas is now no longer *pius*, but rages (802 *furit*) as the weapons fly. Lausus does much better against Aeneas than Pallas did versus Turnus; part of the difference comes from the motivation each young hero feels: Pallas wanted to bring glory home to Evander, while Lausus is concerned principally with saving his father's life. Lausus (admittedly, with the support of his Etruscan host) showers down missiles on Aeneas like a violent hailstorm that sends the ploughman and the farmer seeking hasty shelter; the simile is in part inspired by Homer's image of Hector enduring the furious storm of war (*Iliad* 17.243).[20]

Aeneas recognizes that Lausus has a strong sense of filial piety; the audience might be understandably troubled to hear Aeneas assert that such devotion can be a dangerous thing, despite the truth of his comment:

fallit te incautum pietas tua. (10.812)

your piety deceives you with your lack of caution

Lausus is out of his mind with rage (*demens*), oblivious to Aeneas' words; Aeneas too is overcome by wrath (*saevae . . . irae*). Jupiter had said that each warrior had to exercise their own fates; the Parcae, we are told, were now working with Lausus' final threads of life. Almost immediately, Aeneas stabs him to death. The death of Lausus is transformative. Like some magical epiphany, it instantly changes Aeneas. He is now the "son of Anchises" (822 *Anchisiades*), and he is overcome with emotion as he sees the dead young son, so faithful to his (undeserving) father. We are reminded of the image of the dead Marcellus in the underworld; another young worthy has been slaughtered needlessly. It may have been Lausus' fate to die in battle, but his death has cured Aeneas' madness—for the moment. Pallas' death brought Aeneas to new heights of rage hitherto unimagined in the previous long books of the poem; Lausus' death is soothing and healing. Aeneas now refers to himself as *pius* (826); he wonders what reward he can bestow on the dead Lausus that matches the young hero's extreme courage and devotion to family and duty. Just as Turnus was at once ready to grant Pallas the honor of burial, so Aeneas promises to return Lausus' body; both heroes note that there may well be no real solace in the grave (cf. 10.493 and 828). Aeneas offers one bit of grimly positive news to the dead Lausus: he can take pride in the fact that he died at the hands of Aeneas (Camilla will later express the same sentiment to one of her victims in a taunt). Lausus' companions are hesitant (*cunctantis socios*): will Aeneas strike them down as they draw near to take away his body? Aeneas upbraids them for their hesitation as he himself picks up the dead Lausus—a foreshadowing of his presence at the departure of Pallas' funeral procession in Book 11.[21]

We might think for a moment that Aeneas was now washing the blood and gore from Lausus in the Tiber; instead, Virgil suddenly changes the scene to Lausus' father Mezentius, who is nursing *his* wounds by the river. For the first time in the poem, father and son are separated; Mezentius sends his men to call Lausus out of the fight, but instead soldiers come with the dead body. The whole episode foreshadows Evander's reception of his dead son Pallas. In the *Aeneid*, in contrast to the natural order, several fathers learn that their sons have died: Priam sees Polites killed before his eyes, and Mezentius and Evander learn that their sons have died. Aeneas suffers the loss of his father Anchises. From the viewpoint of Augustan Rome, the most tragic loss of a son in the *Aeneid* is the announcement of the forthcoming death of Marcellus.

Mezentius laments that he has outlived Lausus; he knows that his own death is now not far off (and he is glad for it, we may surmise—by surviving his son, Mezentius has lived beyond the natural order). Interestingly, he confesses that he owed his guilty life to the Etruscans who drove him out in exile; he should have given his life over to "all deaths" (854 *omnis per mortis*), a reference to the vicious revenge his oppressed subjects would no doubt have taken on him and his own penchant for inventive tortures. The death of Lausus has also cured Mezentius; he acknowledges his guilt, and we wonder if a major factor in his flight from Caere was concern for Lausus' fate: what would his son have done in the face of his father's mortal danger, and what would have happened to Lausus in consequence? Was it a certain paternal piety that motivated Mezentius to flee rather than to face justice? Did similar concerns propel Metabus to flee Privernum with his infant daughter Camilla, rather than face his people's rage? Mezentius is weak from Aeneas' wound, but his heroic mindset will permit no other action than returning to fight—presumably to avenge his dead son, but more poignantly, so he can end his life now rather than live with the knowledge that he let his son die for him. Mezentius is moved by both a sense of shame (*pudor*) and insane grief (*mixtoque insania luctu*). Mezentius expresses his sentiments to his horse Rhoebus, who is mourning for its doomed master; Achilles' horse Xanthus predicted its master's death (*Iliad* 19.405-418) after Hera gave it the power of speech.[22] Mezentius does not suppose that Rhoebus will be willing to serve a Trojan master; if this is indeed to be their final contest, he assumes Rhoebus will die with him.[23] Pallas' horse Aethon will be crying as it goes riderless in the funeral cortege at the beginning of the next book (11.89-90), another of Virgil's favorite sort of close links between consecutive books.[24]

Aeneas rejoices when Mezentius returns to the fray; the reader gets the sense that Aeneas views the slaughter of the father as a sort of vengeance for the son: saving such a vicious and undeserving parent cost the innocent and admirable young man his life. With another dramatic half-line, Aeneas welcomes Mezentius' arrival with a divine invocation:

"sic pater ille deum faciat, sic altus Apollo!
incipias conferre manum." (10.875-876)

*"So let that father of the gods, so let lofty Apollo do it!
Begin to bring your hand to the fight."*

The naming of two of the most powerful gods leads directly to Mezentius' blasphemous retort. He acknowledges that Aeneas has already destroyed him, since only the death of Lausus could ruin his life. His retort is directed as much at Aeneas as at the mention of Jupiter and Apollo:

... nec divum parcimus ulli. (10.880)

... nor do we spare any of the gods.

Mezentius will attack Aeneas, despite his divine lineage and the obvious favor he enjoys from heaven. Aeneas is on foot and Mezentius on horseback; after tiring of intercepting so many javelins with his immortal shield, Aeneas finally hastens the inevitable by hurling his spear at Rhoebus' forehead. Mezentius is thrown from the mortally wounded horse and falls before Aeneas, who swiftly prepares to dispatch him with a sword, though not before taunting him. Mezentius recovers his senses (from the shock of the fall) and makes a final, powerful appeal. He refers to Aeneas as a "bitter enemy" (10.900 *hostis amare*), carefully choosing the word for a public enemy, *hostis*, that is, not someone he would personally loathe, and using it with *amare*, "bitter," to express his contempt at Aeneas' taunts. He notes that there is no unspeakable crime in Aeneas' killing him (*nullum in caede nefas*); the death of Lausus has meant that one or the other warrior must die. Mezentius' words echo Aeneas' earlier address to Mago (521 ff.), where he argued that the death of Pallas removed all chance of bargaining (and Mago was not even responsible for the loss of Pallas). He asks for one favor as a defeated enemy: burial. He knows that the Etruscans who are fighting with Aeneas would love to mutilate his corpse. He asks for burial in the same tomb as his son: the implication is that the devoted Lausus would be as grateful for this kindness as his father.

For reasons we can never know with any degree of certainty, Virgil does not reveal Aeneas' answer:

haec loquitur iuguloque haud inscius accipit ensem
undantique animam diffundit in arma cruore. (10.907-908)

He said these things, and, scarcely unknowing, he received the sword in his throat and poured forth his spirit on his weapons with with wet gore.

Does Mezentius know that his request will be denied? Is his lack of ignorance manifested in a silent acknowledgment of Aeneas' unwillingness to honor both son and father? Aeneas makes no comment in response to the father's words, in striking contrast to his generous and honorable address to the dead son; his actions at the very beginning of Book 11 will offer some indication of his mindset, though no definitive proof.

Turnus has been safely off in Ardea during this entire sequence, the city of his father Daunus. Juno had implored her husband to let Turnus return home in peace to his father and be spared death at Aeneas' hands; in the absence of his ultimate target, Aeneas has fought with both Lausus and Mezentius, a father and son pairing with some similarities to Polites and Priam in Book 2, but more differences. For the sake of the narrative, it was necessary to give significant space to Mezentius, a reasonably major figure in the traditional lore of Etruria and central Italy. In the general thrust of Aeneas' development, his treatment of son and father in this book begins the slow and steady march to the close of Book 12.

It is difficult to evaluate the relative condition of the two sides here at the end of Book 10. The Trojans have lost Pallas, the Italians Lausus and Mezentius. Both sides were fairly evenly matched in Book 10. Turnus received a fair (unfair?) amount of help over the course of the last two books from Juno, while

Venus has more than sustained Aeneas. The final outcome has been deliberately delayed thanks to Juno's removal of Turnus from the action. Book 10 is framed by two events that mark what could have been Latin victories: the storming of the Trojan camp by Turnus in Book 9 and the ambush he plans for Aeneas in Book 11. In Book 10, it is not entirely clear that either side could have won a total victory—certainly not without immortal aid, in contrast to the all too human victory Turnus seems to have had within his reach in Book 9, and which he nearly attained in Book 11. In both books, Jupiter intervenes to protect the Trojans and to prevent Turnus' triumph.

As Book 10 ends the audience has a sense that some respite is needed, some momentary pause before the inevitable final encounter between Aeneas and Turnus is staged. It is not at all clear how that encounter in single combat might be precipitated, either. The burial of the many casualties from today's carnage will offer just such a break from combat. For the duration of an entire lengthy book, the second longest in the poem, Aeneas and Turnus will remain apart, while Virgil takes the time to underscore further some points he wishes to emphasize. Virgil is now ready to explore three tragic *tableaux*: funerals, debates, and renewed warfare. Along the way he will indulge at length in reflections on the adolescent female: the central character in his penultimate book will be Camilla, Italy's heroine. Together with Turnus, she will nearly destroy the Trojans, until Jupiter decides yet again that mortals cannot be left to their own devices.

Notes

1. On Book 10 as a whole, see further BENARIO, "The Tenth Book of the *Aeneid*," *Transactions of the American Philological Association* 98 (1967), pp. 23-36. Benario misreads Aeneas' emotional state regarding Pallas, however, when he compares Aeneas' feelings for Pallas and Dido.

2. The Latin verb *secare*, "to cut," carries a reference here to the traditional action of the Fates in cutting the thread of a man's life at his death.

3. The metaphor in the Latin *exorsa* is from weaving, another reference to the traditional action of the Fates.

4. Either he knows that Rome is destined to be Italian, not Trojan, or he considers it sufficiently unimportant to preclude its use as a pawn in the negotiations with his wife in Book 12. No matter what, the audience can figure out what Venus' reaction would be.

5. On the arrival of Aeneas *and Pallas* to the war in Latium, see GILLIS, *Eros and the Death in the Aeneid*, Rome, 1983, pp. 82-83: "Pallas' scene on the ship with Aeneas (10.159-62), so easily missed, assumes in retrospect a special and ineffably sad charm: a youth anxious to learn about the world but already stalked by death."

6. Cf. Ovid *Metamorphoses* 2.333 ff., with Bömer's notes.

7. Still, there is effective pathos in Virgil's birthplace being centered amidst such war-torn, weary cities and towns, with a possible hint of Virgil's own ambivalent and conflicted feelings about this war and, by extension, Augustan Rome.

8. On this simile, see further Hornsby, *op. cit.*, pp. 34-35 and 57-58. Oddly, Hornsby does not mention the parallel passage from *Iliad* 3, which is far more apposite than the cranes of *Iliad* 2.459-466.

9. On Virgil's battle catalogues, see MAZZOCHINI, *Forme e significati della narrazione bellica nell'epos virgiliano. I cataloghi degli uccisi e le morti minori dell'Eneide*, Fasano, 2000 (with Andreola Rossi's critical review in *Bryn Mawr Classical Review* 2002.8.20). For the possible influence of gladiatorial combat on Virgil's battle scenes, see BELL, "The Popular Poetics and Politics of the *Aeneid*," *Transactions of the American Philological Association* 129 (1999), pp. 263-280, especially pp. 273 ff. For battle scenes in general, best is HORSFALL, "*Non viribus aequis*: Some Problems in Virgil's Battle-Scenes," *Greece and Rome* 34 (1987), pp. 48-55.

10. On her name (probably from *iuvare Turnum*, "Turnus' helper"), see PASCHALIS, *Vergil's Aeneid: Semantic Relations and Proper Names*, Oxford, 1997, pp. 55-57. Paschalis' work is sometimes quite valuable, sometimes very fanciful. See also TRAINA, "*Soror alma* (Verg. *Aen.* X.439)," *Maia* 43 (1991), pp. 3-7.

11. See further Dumézil, *op. cit.*, p. 388.

12. *Sinister*, the "left," referred to omens considered favorable by the Romans (and unfavorable by the Greeks). But the word is well attested in contexts where it must mean "unfavorable" (*OLD sinister* 4-5). Originally the word meant "reversed." Cf. 11.347 *moresque sinistros*, where Drances criticizes Turnus' "baleful habit" of going against the goad, as it were.

13. For a discussion of this passage and its affinities with the death of Turnus at the end of Book 12, see NIELSON, "Aeneas and the Demands of the Dead," *The Classical Journal* 79.3 (1984), pp. 200-206. Nielson argues that Aeneas could well be discharging his (pious) obligations to the dead by killing Mago and Turnus, and that, perhaps, at the end of the poem Aeneas is actually possessed by the *Manes* of Pallas, who are "locally powerful" because of the fateful sword-belt Turnus is wearing. Nielson does not discuss Anchises' words to *Roman* Aeneas in the underworld; it would seem that the principal

obligation Aeneas owes to his father is to learn the art of sparing the subjected. If *Furor* can indeed possess a hero on the battlefield as he hesitates and considers showing mercy, then indeed Jupiter's prediction about Madness in chains rings hollower than ever. If Nielson is right, then we have an explanation for why we cannot control our rage; we can perhaps absolve heroes of guilt, it seems, but the undying Madness remains.

14. Is this rationale really sufficient to credit Aeneas with *pietas*? Yes, it would seem, considering the viciousness of his previous actions, especially with Mago.

15. Juno's remark is all the more effective in the immediate aftermath of Aeneas' most impious recent behavior.

16. The episode is a reworking of the end of *Iliad* 20, where Apollo saves Agenor from Achilles and lures the hero away on a wasted mission: Turnus once again evokes Achilles, but Aeneas evokes Apollo, the principal god of the Actian victory.

17. For perceptive analysis of Mezentius, see BURKE, "The Role of Mezentius in the *Aeneid*," *The Classical Journal* 69 (1974), pp. 202-209, as well as SULLIVAN, "Mezentius: A Virgilian Creation," *Classical Philology* 64.4 (1969), pp. 219-225; GOTOFF, "The Transformation of Mezentius," *Transactions of the American Philological Association* 114 (1984), pp. 191-218; DEWAR, "Mezentius' Remorse," *The Classical Quarterly* N.S. 38 (1988), pp. 261-262; BLAIVE, "Mézence le Guerrier impie: Mythologie indo-européene et epopee romaine," *Latomus* 49 (1990), pp. 81-87; GASKIN, "Turnus, Mezentius, and the Complexity of the *Aeneid*," *Collection Latomus: Studies in Latin Literature and History* VI (1992), pp. 295-316; and KRONENBERG, "Mezentius the Epicurean," *Transactions of the American Philological Association* 135.2 (2005), pp. 403-431.

18. The double intervention with Etruscans once again highlights Etruria's divided state.

19. Was she sent down to the battlefield by Juno, *à la* Allecto?

20. See further Hornsby, *op. cit.*, pp. 40-41, who sees this simile as part of a continuing improvement in Aeneas' character: Virgil's Trojan hero moves from venting his anger against everyone, to venting it just against Turnus, to venting it against no one after Turnus is dead, and thereafter devoting himself to the works of civilization and peace (in other words, like Octavian after Actium). Naïve analysis; Virgil deliberately avoids depicting anything in Aeneas' career after his decision to kill Turnus, and his decision to kill Turnus, despite the heavy weight of the image of the *father* (a favorite theme Virgil begins to underscore heavily in the death scenes of Lausus and Mezentius), shows his surrender yet again to Madness.

21. In Lausus' valiant defence of his father, is there something of the obscure story Hyginus relates (*Fabulae* 193) about Harpalyce saving her father from Neoptolemus?

22. The horse was associated with death in the Greek conception; see Edwards on *Iliad* 19.404-417.

23. Page's praise of this whole passage is lavish (especially for a commentator who elsewhere says that the *Aeneid* lacks "vitality" and "human interest"): "the grim soldier is a pathetic figure, and the delineation of him as he mounts his old war-horse for the last time in unequalled in Latin, perhaps in any, literature."

24. For the (mostly poetic) conceit cf. also Pliny the Elder *Historia Naturalis* 8.42.64, and Silius Italicus *Punica* 10.458-471. For criticism of Virgil's other horse / death image (Pallas' riderless steed at 11.89-90), see Quinn, *op. cit.*, pp. 234-235.

Chapter XI

Dawn Left the Ocean

If the second half of the *Aeneid* has often been comparatively neglected, Book 11 is certainly one of its most ignored sections. The war actually begins in Book 7. The visit to the future site of Rome and the magnificent vision of the shield guarantee the popularity of Book 8. Book 10 has the death of Pallas, while Book 12 marks the poem's conclusion with Turnus' death. How "necessary" to the poem's actions are Books 9 and 11? The most recent published commentary on the book, Nicholas Horsfall's 2003 Brill edition, includes an appendix that asks if sometimes even Virgil sleeps, in response to the view that Book 11 does not, perhaps, represent the poet at his finest. The first consideration we should note is that Virgil himself felt Book 11 was as necessary to the final product as any other book. He composed it in the important position of penultimate book of the poem. Like Book 9, with which it has several affinities, Book 11 has a dazzling epyllion: Camilla balances Nisus and Euryalus. Book 11 looks both backward and forward in time: the funerals are a reflection on everything that has taken place already in the Latin war, while the great council of war in Latinus' halls looks both backward and forward, to the single combat between Aeneas and Turnus. As Book 11 opens, Aeneas can be certain that he will win the war. He has not been told that Turnus must die, but he knows that his victory is assured. Turnus has not been told by anyone that he must lose the war, and he has not been told that he must die. The divinities that favor Turnus (Juno, Juturna) have not shared any of this information with their champion. During Book 11, the respective knowledge of the two heroes will not change. No god or goddess, in fact, speaks to either hero through any means in Book 11: the immortals operate almost entirely on their own plane.

Book 11 is one of the most neatly divisible in the entire poem.[1] It divides into three sections of unequal length, and covers the action of three days.[2] The first section is concerned with the funerals for the dead from both sides. Preeminent among these is the requiem for Pallas. The funerals occur as part of a truce in what has been a relatively short but incredibly violent war. Aeneas had received significant support from Evander's Arcadians during the war thus far; the death of Pallas clouds their involvement, but in this book the Latins will learn that their own best chance for an external alliance, with Diomedes' Argives, will never come to fruition. The Latins will use the burial truce to hold a debate in their capitol about the progress of the war.[3] Central to the debate are the opposing figures of Turnus and Drances. We have heard remarkably little from either hero about their actual views on the conflict; most of Aeneas' words in Book 10 were taunts for the vanquished, while Turnus' comments have also been largely restricted to the circumstances of actual combat. Book 11 allows us to see both men in relative states of repose.

The last section of the book is concerned with the resumption of open hostilities between the two sides, and is dominated by the colorfully dramatic figure of the Volscian Camilla. When the book draws to its quiet close (which forms a ring with its quiet opening), in one sense the action of the narrative has not proceeded any further from where it was at the close of Book 10. In another sense, we have learned much about the ways of both men and gods. Like Book 9, Book 11 shows the Trojans in severe and potentially disastrous discomfiture.

After completing his monograph on the second half of the poem, Karl Gransden published his commentary on Book 11 in the Cambridge "green and yellow" series in 1991. Even for the standards of the series, Gransden's commentary is exceedingly brief (75 pages on 915 lines of Latin), in part because he assumes familiarity with material from both his 1984 *Virgil's Iliad* and his 1976 *Aeneid VIII*. Nicholas Horsfall's aforementioned Brill commentary (2003) is the densest guide to the book in print. The sixth and last volume in the *Reclam* series (Books 11-12) is arguably the best. On the other end of the spectrum of commentaries, Bertha Tilly's two small schoolboy editions (on Pallas and Camilla) are not without useful remarks.[4]

Book 11 is the only book of the *Aeneid* that opens with a dawn formula, which Virgil borrowed from his description of the dawn that opened the fateful day of Dido and Aeneas' hunt:

Oceanum interea surgens Aurora reliquit. (11.1 and 4.129)

Meanwhile Aurora rose and left behind the ocean.

The most relevant connection between the two episodes will be the equestrian *aristeia* of Camilla later in the book; Virgil has set the book's tone from the first line by evoking the memory of that doomed hunt.[5] Subtly, Virgil has introduced one of the main themes he will explore in the Camilla epyllion: comparison between his Volscian huntress and the Carthaginian Dido. The book at once fixes our attention on Aeneas, whose mood has been troubled by recent events. Most commentators have assumed (given the subsequent funeral rites) that Aeneas is (understandably) disturbed by Pallas' death, but the emotional upset of the loss of his young friend has been followed by the whole episode with Lausus and Mezentius, and the disturbingly unanswered question from the end of Book 10: will Aeneas grant burial to Mezentius? Virgil's refusal to provide a definitive answer to that question comes as he turns the poem's attention to the rites due to the dead. Despite his troubled mood, Aeneas performs thanksgiving rites to mark his victory over Mezentius. The first four lines of Book 11 are a masterful example of Virgilian economy and denied expectation. As we turn from the last page of Book 10 to this new chapter in the war, we are succinctly told much about Aeneas' state of mind, a little about his immediate actions, and nothing specific about what he had just been asked by his defeated foe.[6]

Aeneas now erects a trophy to mark the spot where Mezentius was defeated.[7] The passage is another classic example of Virgilian style: the details are rich, but the exact picture remains somewhat hazy. Aeneas erects a huge oak tree on a mound and dresses it with Mezentius' arms as an offering to the "one powerful in war" (11.8 *bellipotens,* who is probably, though not certainly, Mars). He binds the shield "to the left hand" (10 *sinistrae*) and hangs the ivory sword around the "neck" (11 *collo*) in a ghoulish ritual of dressing a scarecrow. The breastplate, we learn, has been struck twelve times and "thoroughly dug out in spots" (10 *perfossumque locis*). The twelve wounds correspond to the twelve cities of Etruria; it seems that the leaders of the Etruscan allies of Aeneas have come forward and stabbed the body in ritual slaughter as a sharing in the victory over the most hated of their enemies. Indeed, when Aeneas begins his address to the assembly, we are told that he was ringed by a close circle of allied leaders.

What became of Mezentius' body? Has it been hung on the tree trunk along with his arms? Is it stripped and unburied? Whatever the fate of the corpse, Virgil did not think it important for us to know. The question and wonder he has raised in our minds is only heightened by the grisly description of the conquered arms: the crests of Mezentius' helmet are dripping with blood. Aeneas views the slaughter of Mezentius as the beginning of Turnus' end, and encourages his men to take comfort from the victory and be ready for the final push against the Latins. Aeneas wants the Trojans and their allies to be ready, as he says, for when the immortals give their nod of approval to the renewal of hostilities (an interesting detail given later events in the book). There is, as yet, no formal truce for burials. Turnus is off in Ardea, and the Latins have no doubt been cowed by the loss of one of their major warriors and his son. The "proud king" (15 *rege superbo*) Aeneas mentions in his speech is most likely Turnus: Mezentius represents the first fruits (16 *primitiae*) of the ultimate victory. With a sweeping gesture toward the trophy, Aeneas declares that Mezentius is right in front of them:

... manibusque meis Mezentius hic est. (11.16)

... *and here in my hands is Mezentius.*

Once again, Virgil tempers our ability to draw a picture in our minds from the description he provides. Where is the body of the Etruscan monster who found an odd sort of redemption and peace in death? The custom of erecting a trophy of an enemy's armor set on a stake as an effigy of the defeated is well attested in both literature and art; Virgil's description here is one of the best surviving records of the practice; Aeneas' trophy of Mezentius is a makeshift, temporary dedication, in contrast to the great sculptured reliefs of later ages. Juno had spirited Turnus away, off the battlefield; both Lausus and Mezentius have fallen as preliminary sacrifices in his place. Lausus' death, further, had paralleled Pallas';

Mezentius is particularly disturbing to Aeneas because he represents the father who dies after avenging his son, and a father who dies after being saved by his son. He wants to be buried with the son who was so close to him in life. In striking contrast, Aeneas and Pallas (a Virgilian father and son image) had been deprived of any union on the battlefield in Book 10. Mezentius, once wounded, had been forced to withdraw from the field under cover from his son; where was Aeneas when Pallas faced Turnus?

Aeneas announces funeral rites for the dead, specifically for his comrades and their unburied bodies (11.22 *socios inhumataque corpora*), a hendiadys that, once again, does not answer the question of Aeneas' treatment of Mezentius' body: does he include the Etruscan chieftain in this announcement? Virgil forces our attention to focus on the unburied dead. Book 11 is a counterpoint to Book 5; the keyword then had been *laetus*, "happy," whereas the keyword now is *maestus*, "grim" or "sad," which occurs eleven times in this book out of thirty-four occurrences in the entire poem: nearly a third. Book 11 is the saddest in the *Aeneid*.[8] The first expression of that sadness will be the duty of notifying Evander of his son Pallas' fate. Aeneas had failed to protect his young charge, and the death marks the most significant loss for Aeneas during the entire war. The importance of Pallas' death to the narrative structure of the epic cannot be exaggerated, since it is the reason for Turnus' death. Aeneas' reflection on Pallas' death emphasizes its untimely nature; Virgil reuses the same line (11.28, 6.429) he had used in the underworld to describe the infants who died on the very threshold of life in the underworld—an effective hyperbole to underscore Pallas' youth.

Aeneas goes to see the body of Pallas, which is under an honor guard of both Arcadians and Trojans.[9] The smooth chest of the dead young hero is marred by a gaping wound (11.40 *levique patens in pectore vulnus*): Virgil emphasizes Pallas' youth above all (Dryden's translation of *levi pectore* as "manly breast" could not be more wrong). Aeneas himself evokes the succession motif: Pallas will not live to see Aeneas' foundation and kingdom; he will not be conveyed in some triumphal procession home to Pallanteum. Aeneas ruefully notes that this death was not the promise he had made to Pallas' father when he had gone off to his "great command" (47 *magnum imperium*); Pallas represents a partial failure of Aeneas' dream. Aeneas ends his mournful lament with the powerful declaration that both Ausonia and Iulus have lost a major bulwark in Pallas (57-58 *quantum . . . praesidium . . . quantum*). The anaphoric repetition of "how great" (*quantum*) contrasts with Pallas' youth and inexperience; like the dead Marcellus, the point is not what he accomplished in life, but what (unfulfilled) potential he had for future glories.[10]

By a brilliant trick, Virgil announces his (Catullan) simile of the cut flower (a description of the dead Pallas) with three lines (66-68) that all have a Catullan metrical phenomenon of a word of three long syllables after the caesura.[11] The metrical trick introduces the famous image of the dead flower, a simile Page considered "perhaps the most perfect in Virgil." We have already mentioned it in our analysis of the related simile that marks the death of Euryalus (9.435-437); its most striking aspect is the description of the "maiden's thumb" (11.68 *virgineo . . . pollice*) that culls the flower. Virgil has offered a bit of exquisite verse that does not entirely fit the context of Pallas' death; it would have been laughable if he had described Turnus' killing of Pallas in Book 10 as the action of a "virgin's thumb." The virgin—male or female—loses the charm and luster of youth by the transition to marriage. Pallas was at an age when he was ready for marriage, but he was still a virgin; instead of moving into a state of wedlock, he has passed into the underworld. His "partner" in this death marriage is Turnus, who is the virgin who has, in effect, deflowered him. The homosexual overtones of Achilles and Patroclus have been exchanged for a very Roman conception of the young man on the verge of nuptial union, with a horrible perversion of the wedding rites. Every marriage carries the tinge of regret that a door is closing on a part of one's youth that will be irretrievably lost; in Pallas' case, his marriage is death. Virgil will also evoke Catullus when he describes Aeneas' final words to the dead Pallas (11.97-98); his valediction recalls Catullus' powerful address to his dead brother (*carmen* 101). The evocation of his neoteric predecessor, a poet of love and the emotions of youth, serves to underscore further the deformed marriage the dead Pallas is celebrating.[12] It is possible that in Virgil's evocation of Catullan imagery we are meant to see Pallas in connection with both 1) Aeneas (who has, however unintentionally, broken faith with his quasi-lover by not protecting him) and 2) Turnus, who has cut down Pallas in a gruesome quasi-deflowering.[13]

At this moment of high emotional intensity, Virgil devastatingly reintroduces Dido to the narrative. We learn that Aeneas buries Pallas in one of *two* purple and gold cloaks (11.76 *harum unam*) that had been woven in Carthage by Dido. When Mercury had descended to earth to order Aeneas to leave Carthage, he found the Trojan hero overseeing the building projects in Dido's city and wearing one of these cloaks (cf. 4.262 and 11.75).[14] Dido had woven these two cloaks, we can assume, for Aeneas and *Ascanius*. They were the purple and gold robes of royalty (purple and gold were also the dominant colors of the hunt scene in Book 4, and will return as key colors for Camilla in the cavalry battle later in this book). The burial of Pallas (Aeneas' surrogate son) in one of the two robes represents a partial failure of Aeneas' dream and offers a profound reflection on the fragile state of the Augustan succession. Iulus' hair had burst into harmless flames as a portent of the coming glory of Rome (2.680 ff.); now Virgil notes that Aeneas uses the one cloak to veil the locks of hair that are soon to burn with a very different (and consuming) fire.[15]

Latin ambassadors arrive who request permission to bury the dead who are scattered over the no man's land between the Trojan and Italian lines. It is not clear who sent these emissaries; it is impossible to imagine that Turnus did, and in any case he has been at Ardea for much of the end of Book 10 and must be imagined as hastening back to the battlefield and Latinus' capitol. We are once again reminded of the question of Mezentius' fate; "good Aeneas" (11.106 *bo-*

nus Aeneas) agrees to their request—a request, Virgil notes, that could scarcely be spurned (*haud aspernanda*).

Aeneas uses the visit of the Latin delegates to note that he has no interest in continuing a war with them. He notes that he has arrived in their homelands by fate (quite true) and that Latinus broke faith by preferring to join himself with Turnus (an understandable conclusion on Aeneas' part, though the audience knows this is not exactly what happened in Book 7). Aeneas sums up his view of the war crisply and tersely:

> si bellum finire manu, si pellere Teucros
> apparat, his mecum decuit concurrere telis:
> vixet cui vitam deus aut sua dextra dedisset. (11.116-118)

> *If he seeks to finish the war with his hand and to drive off the Teucrians,*
> *he should have fought against these weapons of mine;*
> *that one would have lived to whom the god or his own right hand had granted life.*

Aeneas notes that the outcome of a single combat with Turnus would be decided by the "god" or "the victor's own right hand." Once again Virgil returns to the theme he finds so crucial, so worthy of frequent examination and reexamination, and yet so unanswerable: does a man succeed (or fail) by his own initiative and fault, or by the predetermined dictates of fate and the mysterious will of Jupiter, the god who is most often associated with the fulfillment of whatever is "fated"? While Virgil never sorts out the exact mechanism that controls the clash between human free will and divinely ordered destiny, he does reveal in this passage that the Latin ambassadors have learned something from the most reliable source possible: Aeneas is willing to end the war, and has no plan of invasion or conquest; the war could have ended if Turnus alone had fought Aeneas. This passage marks a crucial development in the attitude of the native Italians. Some of them, at least, are no longer the raving, frenzied crowd that had been inspired by Allecto in Book 7 and took up arms after the killing of Silvia's stag. Virgil now compresses events in the Latin capitol to turn at once to his theme of dissension and debate among the Italians. The chief orator (11.100 *oratores*) of this group now speaks to Aeneas, and another important character is now introduced: Drances, who will be the spokesman for those in Latium who are opposed to Turnus' leadership of the war.[16] Virgil introduces him with all the essential information we need to know: he does not like Turnus, in fact he hates Turnus (122-123 *odiis, infensus*, and cf. 336 *infensus*), and he is not above the crime of slander in his pursuit of that hatred (*crimine*). If Virgil wanted to present a positive view of a Latin peace party, he has once again gone about his task in the most difficult of ways. Virgil's depiction of Drances is wholly unsympathetic. The allegorical view that Virgil intended Drances to evoke Cicero is an old one, unable to be proven, but not without interest.[17] His leadership of this mission to Aeneas suddenly changes the tone of the passage; at its beginning, in the atmosphere of grief and lament for the dead, we felt nothing but sympathy and understanding for these Latins—they were the voice of peace and reason, and Aeneas' words were respectful, kind, and encouraging. Now, with the introduction of Drances, Virgil has marred the diplomatic picture. Drances has an agenda, and peace between Latins and Trojans is not its first item: he will go to any length, we realize, to discredit or harm Turnus. Drances' reasons for hating Turnus, we shall learn, are simple: Drances has significant skill with words, but little if any prowess in battle.

Aeneas' words are carefully thrown into the past tense (117-118 *decuit, vixet, dedisset*). He makes no promise that the war will end on the twelfth day with single combat. He laments that the war *should* have been settled that way before all the ensuing slaughter could take place (both Latin and Trojan—Pallas, of course, is foremost on his mind).

Like so many others in the poem, Drances is also trapped in the mindset that Aeneas is going to rebuild Troy in Italy. He lavishly declares to Aeneas that it will be a pleasure to lift up Trojan rocks on Italian shoulders and build a new city. Drances did not know what to expect when he first approached Aeneas; the message he received gave him tremendous courage and confidence in his plan to ruin Turnus, and served as proof of his hitherto unproven theories to his companions, who move from being agape with wonder at Aeneas' words (120-121) to ready agreement with Drances' sentiments (132). The whole passage is at odds with the true, ultimate destiny for Latium; it is not difficult to gain sympathy for Turnus every time Drances opens his obsequious mouth. They at once all agree to a truce of twelve days for the burial of the dead; presumably when those twelve days are finished, there will be a resumption of hostilities if there is no agreement to end the war by some others means (i.e., single combat between Turnus and Aeneas).

The sudden appearance of Drances and his fellow emissaries interrupted the grim narrative of Pallas' funeral. Aeneas was sincerely willing to grant the (legitimate) request of the Latins for a respite from combat. He has his own funeral duties to manage, however, because of his dead young friend, and the narrative makes a sudden leap again back to the reality of the deaths on both sides. Word finally reaches Pallanteum that Pallas is dead; news had only recently arrived that Evander's son had been distinguishing himself in combat. Aeneas had called Mezentius the "first fruits" in the conquest of Turnus (11.16 *primitiae*); now Evander will lament the bitter "first fruits" (156 *primitiae*) of Pallas' youth.[18] Aeneas, mercifully (conveniently?) is not present for Evander's laments; he has spoken his own words of farewell to the corpse, and does not accompany it to Pallanteum (a fact the commentators tend to gloss over by ignoring it—it is understandable, but convenient, that Aeneas is not able to leave the Trojan camp at such a crucial moment in the war). Evander does not impute any guilt for the death either to Aeneas or his Trojans (at least not explicitly). He does have a solemn request. Before his son had left him, he had expressed the wish that he might die rather than see this day, and he had made an urgent appeal to Jupiter to take pity on him (8.573-583). Now that Jupiter has denied him that wish, he enjoins Aeneas to take vengeance for him on Turnus:

> quod vitam moror invisam Pallante perempto
> dextera causa tua est, Turnum gnatoque patrique
> quam debere vides. meritis vacat hic tibi solus
> fortunaeque locus. (11.177-180)

> *Your right hand, which you see owes Turnus both to son and to father,*
> *is the reason why I prolong a life that is hateful to me now that Pallas has died.*
> *this place alone remains open to your merits*
> *and your fortune.*

Gransden's notes here are worthy of examination, since they express a view shared by many. He rightly observes that these lines "effectively seal Turnus' fate."[19] He then emphasizes that Aeneas is "reluctant" to avenge Pallas by killing Turnus. Aeneas is not present to hear these words from the father to whom he has sent home a son dead before his time. He offers no response to the request; we do not hear of it again, until that final hesitation at the end of the poem when Aeneas seems the fateful sword-belt of Pallas on Turnus' body (Turnus is a living trophy of Pallas). But the importance of Evander's words is their conclusion: "*this place alone*" remains for Aeneas' merits and fortune: the death of Turnus.[20] Incredible labor and effort have been expended in the process of making a new foundation in Italy, but there has never been any real doubt of Aeneas' future success. Whether Turnus lives or dies, Rome will be founded. No, Evander is right; this "place," this "opening," is what is left to Aeneas as he accumulates merits and fortune (i.e., it is good fortune to see your enemies vanquished, and bad fortune for your friends to die unavenged). Aeneas was right when he expressed the profound regret that Pallas would never see the new city; Evander, in contrast, can think only of Turnus' death.

These are the words of a father, and they contrast with Anchises' vision for *his* son in the underworld. Anchises progressed from an old man weary of life on the night Troy fell to a soul in Elysium with reasonably complete knowledge of the future. His journey from ignorance to enlightened education is complete. Aeneas has been engaged in a similar schooling. Evander is calling him back to the old ways, the vindictive, never ending vendettas of yore. Anchises, with his eyes on Iulus and the future, had called *Roman* Aeneas to a new sort of heroism; Evander is calling on *Trojan* Aeneas to kill the killer of his son and revisit the brutal blood for blood economy of the past.[21] Anchises spoke to an Aeneas who was alive for the future; Evander speaks for a Pallas who is dead to the past. Lausus had given his life to defend his father; Turnus will beg for his life so he can offer some solace to his aged father. Small wonder Anchises only mentioned Marcellus' soul *after* Aeneas had asked after him; Anchises is focused on the future, not the past—the "dead" Marcellus is a symbol of the past, as is Pallas.[22]

The dawn rises on the second day of the book (Virgil is very careful in Book 11 to note the progress of time, in striking contrast to elsewhere in the poem; he thereby creates a certain nervous tension in the narrative as the clock ticks for Turnus).[23] The first morning had seen the setting up of a trophy to mark the great victory over Mezentius; the day had been occupied with the preparation of Pallas' body and the journey to Pallanteum. The next dawn rises on the funerals; Aeneas and Tarchon are in charge of them, representing the union of the Trojans and their Etruscan allies. The Trojans and Etruscans spend the entire day engaged in respectful watch over the burning pyres. The actual funeral of Pallas (including the sacrifices of the sons of Sulmo and Ufens who were snatched by Aeneas in Book 10) is not described; we saw the procession set out for Pallanteum (including the unfortunate bound captives destined for the flames), but Virgil does not describe the rites.[24]

Both sides have their dead, but Virgil describes the "miserable" Latins as they erect "countless" pyres (11.203-204 *miseri / innumeras*): the stage is being set for the imminent Latin war council.[25] In the actual battle narrative of Books 9 and 10, it is not exactly clear that the Latins have the worst of the situation; certainly Turnus' view during the council is that all is not lost and, further, that the Latins still have Camilla's intact Volscian cavalry (who then, of course, dominate the rest of the book). Still, strategically the Latins are worse off than the Trojans because they cannot hope to win; everything they do is a mere delaying tactic, at least from the perspective of the final outcome. The Latins have so many dead, in fact, that they are forced to burn great heaps of undistinguished dead on their pyres; a few fortunate ones are carried off to the city for burial, while others are interred in mass graves on the battlefield. We are reminded of the end of Lucretius, with his terrifying vision of the effects of the plague on Athens and the general scene of social upheaval and disorder. Still, for the Latins the advantage of having Mezentius as your major casualty is that no one mourns for his death the way all the Trojans and Arcadians mourn for the dead Pallas; of the major Italian leaders, Messapus, Camilla, and Turnus will still have much fighting left in them.

Dawn comes again (11.210), the third and final specific mention of a new day in Book 11.[26] First light brings the grim task of sifting through the ashes of the pyres for the bones of the dead; not surprisingly, protests against the war are growing in Latinus' kingdom, and the target of the anger is Turnus (has Drances been talking about his meeting with Aeneas to everyone he meets?). Women (mothers and daughters-in-law) and children are the most poignant of protestors; they have been left bereft of husbands, fathers, and sons, and they curse the idea of Turnus' marriage to Lavinia. They want Turnus to settle the war for himself, to determine the "first honors" (11.219 *primos . . . honores*) and the "kingdom of Italy," the *regnum Italiae*. Turnus is a Rutulian foreigner in Latinus' kingdom; the weary Latins are willing to let Turnus settle his differences with Aeneas before they commit to either side. Drances emphasizes that Aeneas is willing to fight Turnus and that this single combat alone is delaying a permanent peace treaty; the (unfair) implication of this argument is that Turnus is somehow less than willing to fight alone with Aeneas: the war council will see Turnus disabuse Drances and his supporters of this falsehood. There is real division in Latium; many people support Drances' view, but many others are partisans of Turnus, both because of the support he has from Queen Amata and the fame he has won for himself in battle.

One embassy had gone off to seek a truce with the Trojans for the sake of burials; now another embassy arrives at Latinus' court to announce the failure of the mission to Diomedes that had set out for Apulia in southern Italy at the beginning of Book 8. At this point we learn that Latinus has been overcome with great grief (11.231). The Latin king has been absolutely silent thus far in the war, a largely invisible, always ineffective presence that had been unable to stop the surge of battle. Now he has had ample proof that Aeneas has indeed been brought to Italy by the will of the gods—gods who are angry (233) because of the rejection of their favorite. In view of all the dissension in his realm and the recent heavy combat losses, he declares the opening of a great council (a sort of human parallel to the divine assembly at the beginning of Book 10). Venulus is now able to give a complete report of the mission to Diomedes to the entire Latin leadership, as well as Turnus and his Rutulians.[27]

The recollection of the visit to Diomedes is a journey back in time to the early books of the *Aeneid*.[28] We traveled with Aeneas and his Trojans as they experienced their own *Odyssey* in the waters between the Troad and Italy. Diomedes begins his explanation of why he cannot help the Latins by enumerating all the trials the Greeks faced (despite their victory) after the destruction of Troy; first in his catalogue is the work of Minerva in avenging the rape of Cassandra by the Lesser Ajax (Juno had mentioned the same story at the very beginning of the poem). Much of the postwar history we hear of now from Diomedes has already been explored in Books 2-3. The Latins, of course, have no knowledge of these events; they are learning from one of the greatest and most dangerous foes Aeneas and the Trojans ever knew about just how high a price they will pay for attempting to defeat Trojans.

Diomedes' advice for the Latins is to bring their presents to Aeneas and agree to live with him in peace. Diomedes has no fighting men, in any case; in punishment for his wounding of Venus during the Trojan War, his men have been changed into birds.[29] Diomedes' mood here is quite different from his attitude in Book 5 of the *Iliad*; the report of Venulus is Virgil's commentary on Homer. Diomedes notes that if there had been only two others as powerful as Hector and Aeneas, the Trojans would have been able to cross the sea and invade Argos— hyperbole, to be sure, but understandably so; Diomedes has seen the Greeks (and, in some ways, his own fortunes) go from one extreme to the other because of Troy.

Latinus is understandably shaken by the report from the emissaries. Many Italians want to declare their view in reaction to the news; Virgil compares them to the rush of waters in a river that have been trapped by rocks and are ready to burst forth explosively. Latinus had been unable to prevent the outbreak of war, and his pleas with the Italians now are ineffective and weak, however rooted in an obvious, undeniable love for his people and a sincere desire to see their suffering end. Latinus proposes that the Trojans be given a place to settle, or be helped with resources and supplies if they want to go elsewhere. He does not mention the marriage to Lavinia, the question of rule over his own kingdom, or indeed what role Turnus would have in such an arrangement with Aeneas and the Trojans. There is no way his proposal could ever be accepted; it is the final attempt at peace of a man who agrees with the pessimistic view that everything is in ruins. Virgil will go out of his way in the last sections of Book 11 to prove Latinus wrong, at least in one sense. To be sure, if Turnus were willing to surrender and give in to Latinus' proposal here at the outset of the war council, he could perhaps save his life (though this is not at all certain, given Aeneas' reaction to Pallas' death and Evander's appeal for revenge). Aeneas will not have to face such a decision; there is no way Turnus' sense of honor will allow him to step aside and let Aeneas take what he feels is rightly his. That sense of honor will give way to filial piety at the very close of the poem, where he will subordinate any desire not to live with dishonor to a wish to return to be some sort of solace to his father.[30] The main thrust of Turnus' argument in the central section of this book will be the continuing chance the Latins have to achieve a victory despite any ill fortune heretofore. He has heard nothing to the contrary from any direct divine or supernatural revelation. And, most tellingly, he is correct. The plan he and Camilla effect in this book would have destroyed Aeneas' forces and, perhaps, forced an immediate end to the war. Jupiter, of course, whose final allegiance is always to future destiny, will not tolerate such a change of plans. His interventions are multiple and dramatic, and form a ring with his summoning of the immortal council at the beginning of Book 10. The Latin, mortal council we are about to see unfold is a human counterpoint to the assembly of the gods.

Just as Jupiter had indicated at his council that each man's undertakings will bring their own fortune (10.111-112), so now Latinus says that each man's hope or expectation is indeed his own (11.309 *spes sibi quisque*), though he at once adds that the hope for victory is, in his judgment, "narrow" (*angusta*) indeed. The offer he urges the assembly to accept is for the Trojans to take a rough tract of his western land that the Aurunci and, astonishingly, the *Rutulians* are now sowing and grazing; his ineffectual leadership is subtly indicated by how he now suggests the surrender of land being tilled by some of Turnus' own people: the plan cannot possibly succeed.

Drances at once addresses the assembly; he no doubt realizes (like any competent orator) that Latinus' speech is open to serious criticism, and he intends to lend his ample rhetorical skills to support the main line of his king's argument.[31] Drances, Virgil tells us, is wealthy (11.338 *largus opum*)—is this an indication of his willingness to bribe people to see his point of view? It is not entirely clear why Virgil notes that Drances was noble on his mother's side but of "uncertain lineage" (*genus incertum*) on his father's. Is Drances so clichéd a figure that he feels inferiority in the face of those who might outdo him, especially in deeds, if not words? Drances does not even mention Turnus' name as he speaks; he assures Latinus that many others support his position, but are afraid to speak because of Turnus' threats (and, apparently, Turnus is seething as Drances speaks and is getting ready to seize his sword to silence him). Drances gives voice to the one major omission Latinus did not have the strength or presence of mind to mention. His words are no doubt said with a smirking sneer to Turnus: Latinus should include Lavinia in the bargain he offers to Aeneas and the Trojans. Drances insults Turnus for being ready to trust in flight (11.351 *fugae fidens*), an important detail that shows well the results of some divine interventions: the Latins think Turnus ran away from Aeneas during the second half of Book 10, which is completely false—Turnus has no explanation for Juno's intervention, but he alone knows for certain that he did not flee Aeneas, and that he had been more than willing to face him on the battlefield.

Drances makes an appeal to Turnus that is a masterpiece of rhetorical effectiveness and disingenuousness. Once again, with a sneer we can almost see through Virgil's verse, Drances notes that he is the first and foremost of Turnus' suppliants (11.364-365 *primus/supplex*). He now begs his commander to free Latium from war and secure a lasting peace for Laurentum. Drances presents himself as a partisan of the peace faction: he "humbly" begs Turnus to have pity on the wretched state of the Latins; he casts himself in the role of fearful yet brave spokesman for everyone who yearns for peace. If Turnus is not willing to settle with Aeneas (by accepting Latinus' proposal), then, Drances argues, Turnus should meet Aeneas in single combat. The introduction of the issue of single combat (which will recur at the very beginning of Book 12, to set the tone for Virgil's last book) is a sequel to the phantom Aeneas sequence in Book 10. As we now learn, Turnus would like nothing more than the chance to continue the fight, and he is not unwilling to meet Aeneas in battle.

The war had begun in earnest in Book 9 with a Latin siege of the Trojan camp. Slowly, Virgil works to reverse the image in our minds; the Trojans will soon take the initiative and attack the Latin capitol. Turnus upbraids Drances for his cowardice; he notes that the enemy now surrounds their city (something of an exaggeration), and that an abundance of opportunities for valor awaits the brave. Turnus' summary of his accomplishments is unimpeachable: he notes the deaths of Pallas, Pandarus and Bitias, and all he accomplished while (ironically) trapped inside the Trojan camp as if *he* were the one under siege. Turnus subtly replies to the bad news that Diomedes has refused to come to assist the Rutulians: the great Argive warrior does not fear Aeneas, but rather is too tired and weary to get involved in a war he suspects (rightly) is being managed by the immortals. If so much tragedy could befall the Greeks after taking Troy in accord with the fated destiny of the city, what would happen to someone who sought to fight the dictates of fate and try to defeat Aeneas now, in Italy? Diomedes is unwilling to find out; Turnus, meanwhile, is not convinced all is yet lost: Diomedes had his Troy, and Turnus will have *his* Troy. Turnus is furious (though not incoherent, *pace* Gransden): he also (correctly) notes that Drances is not truly afraid of him, but rather is feigning fear and terror of Turnus for his own rhetorical agenda.

The first part of Turnus' reply to *Latinus* and his proposal follows (he is finished wasting time with the likes of Drances). His first point is agreement: the Latins should indeed surrender, if one reversal means they have truly been completely finished. He has dispensed with the coward who has no right to speak against a man of brave courage; now he addresses the specific points of Latinus' argument. After agreeing that the (truly) defeated should surrender, he expresses a wish incapable of fulfillment (imperfect subjunctive 11.415 *adesset*): *if only* the virtue and courage the Latins once knew were still present! Turnus notes that they still have tremendous resources available, and that the Trojans too have suffered heavy losses. Why, he asks, should they lose their honor and fail on the "first threshold" (423 *limine primo*)? The image is carefully chosen; it is borrowed from the lament Aeneas made over Pallas' death and, more distantly, the image of the dead infants in the underworld, lost on the very threshold of life (11.28, 6.429). Turnus reverses the image: he prefers to see the Latins on the very threshold of victory. Turnus names the forces that remain intact: foremost among them is the Volscian cavalry contingent under Camilla (the first mention of her since the catalogue at the end of Book 7, and a precursor of her dominance over the last sections of this book). Latinus had not mentioned anything about single combat; Turnus ends his speech by returning to Drances (though he does not deign to mention him). He solemnly pledges that he has no problem whatsoever in facing Aeneas alone on behalf of the Latins (and, it should be remembered, Virgil has taken care to show that not everyone in Latium, let alone elsewhere in central Italy, agrees with Latinus that the cause is lost). Turnus does not care about Aeneas' divine arms, and he does not care if Aeneas either excels Achilles or at least plays the role of Achilles:

> ibo animis contra, vel magnum praestet Achillem
> factaque Volcani manibus paria induat arma
> ille licet. (11.438-440)
>
> *I shall go against him with courage, though he is allowed*
> *to play the role of Achilles and don armor like Achilles',*
> *made by Vulcan's hands.*

The Latin verb *praestare* has two distinct meanings, which Virgil uses here to great effect. It can mean "play the role of" or "excel;" Turnus is ready for either eventuality. There is tremendous irony here, of course; in Book 6 the Sibyl had announced to Aeneas that another Achilles was waiting for him in Latium, while in Book 10 Aeneas was playing the Achilles role when he lost Patroclus-Pallas. In Book 12, Aeneas will certainly evoke Achilles in his final victory over Turnus, though the two final books of the *Iliad*, which climax with the return of

Hector's body for burial, will be ignored in Virgil's *Iliad*, which prefers to end with the moment of Turnus-Hector's death.

Turnus makes a further solemn announcement: he vows his life for the assembled Latins and his father-in-law Latinus (a bit of anticipation there, of course, since he has not yet married Lavinia).[32]

What happens next is not entirely clear:

illi haec inter se dubiis de rebus agebant
certantes: castra Aeneas aciemque movebat. (11.445-446)

Those men were arguing among themselves concerning doubtful affairs in rival strife: Aeneas began to break camp and move his battle line.[33]

A truce was ratified for twelve days of funeral rites; Virgil stopped explicitly mentioning the passage of time after the "third light" (210 *tertia lux*) had dawned. The Italians have been engaged in their war council (which has consisted of speeches by Latinus, Venulus, Drances and Turnus); now we learn that Aeneas has broken camp and has taken the field. A messenger suddenly arrives, nervous and upset, who announces that the Trojans and their Etruscan allies have descended from the Tiber riverbank to the plains before the city (an enactment of the idea of Latium's capitol under siege). What exactly happened here? Are we to imagine that the Latins have been so occupied with their war council that they have forgotten that the truce ended today? Have they really allowed themselves to be caught unaware and unprepared for Aeneas' military maneuvers? The Latins are thrown into complete disarray (Virgil effectively compares them to noisy flocks of birds) and are filled with anger; their debate now turns from almost academic considerations about how best to proceed to a frenzied rush to decide how to meet the enemy's moves. Is it possible that the Trojans have broken the truce? If not, we must assume that every last official at the war council has forgotten the day the truce ends and, what is more, has allowed the Trojans to seize the initiative once it expired.[34] In the Old French *Roman d'Enéas*, the decision to propose single combat is reached at council; envoys are sent to bring the news to Aeneas, but before they can be sent, word arrives that the Trojans have begun military operations and the city is thrown into confusion. Virgil's Turnus makes the point that while some Latins have been talking peace, Aeneas has been planning war—and indeed, we shall learn soon enough that Aeneas has a very specific battle plan.

The situation is now somewhat a reversal of the beginning of Book 9. There, Aeneas had left orders for his people to guard their camp and not engage the enemy. Turnus now issues specific orders to his men for a cavalry force (the fastest and most effective unit) to go out to the plains before the city to meet any possible assault, while men inside the walls are ordered to guard the towers and battlements and prepare for a siege attack. The change of fortune (the attackers are now the attacked) drives even the women and boys of Latium to man the walls in defense of their city: Aeneas' decision to attack has served the purpose of uniting the Latins, at least for the moment, behind Turnus. Latinus once again retires from the scene; he is cursing the day he did not insist on receiving Aeneas as a son-in-law. We shall never again hear of Drances. There is fear in Latium, but also anger (11.452 *et arrectae stimulis haud mollibus irae*): in a relatively short span of lines we have moved very far from the kindly Aeneas who agreed to a truce and expressed his wish not to make war on the Latins. We meet Amata and Lavinia for the first time since Book 7: they are making offerings at a temple of Minerva, asking her to destroy the "Phrygian robber" (11.484 *Phrygiae praedonis*) who would steal away Latinus' daughter.[35] True to her silent nature in the epic, Lavinia merely stands aloof with her beautiful eyes downcast. Virgil hauntingly refuses to reveal anything of her mindset or thoughts on the great and terrible events she has innocently and indirectly set into motion: she is the most enigmatic figure in the *Aeneid*.

Turnus arms himself for battle; Virgil uses a magnificent simile to compare him to a horse, an appropriate enough comparison given that the remainder of the book will be mostly concerned with a great cavalry battle set piece. The horse, appropriately, is ready to burst forth onto the open plain and go off into herds of mares; the point of the comparison is the eagerness of the equine Turnus to charge off against the stereotypically womanly, cowardly Phrygian halfmen so familiar from his brother-in-law Numanus Remulus' taunts (9.590 ff.). As it turns out, the simile will be somewhat arrested in its fulfillment, and quite misleading in what it portends: Virgil leads us to believe that Turnus is about to rush off onto the plain where Aeneas and his Trojans have marshaled their forces: in reality it will not be the stallion Turnus galloping off against Trojan mares, but rather the mare *Camilla*, a true female, charging off on horseback against (effeminate) Trojans who will not be able to withstand her assault: a woman to fight women.

Is the fact that Turnus is going to fail in this sound strategic plan dimly foreshadowed by Virgil's comparison of him to a horse, when he will have no part in the ensuing cavalry battle?

Deliberately, then, Virgil now introduces Camilla to the narrative after a long absence. We have heard nothing of her from the time the native Italian heroes rode into Latinus' city until the war council in this book. Camilla immediately appeals to Turnus to let *her* face the Trojan attack with her cavalry; she suggests that he stay behind and guard the city gates with infantry.[36] Turnus has his eyes fixed on the Volscian girl; Virgil does not make his feelings for her explicit, but his terrible reaction at the end of the book to the news of her death helps hint at the emotional depth of his attraction to her. Drances had lavishly lauded Aeneas, asking how he could possibly offer sufficient praise to a man of such greatness and virtue (11.125); now Turnus praises Camilla, asking how he can possibly give sufficient thanks to the girl he calls the "virgin glory of Italy" (508 *decus Italiae virgo*). Turnus admires Camilla's boldness, but he can inform her of the intelligence he has gained from reconnaissance and scouts. Aeneas, it seems, has conceived a plan of battle in the (brief?) period after the funerals. He has indeed sent a cavalry force to the plains before Latinus' city, but it is only a feint; he intends to use the horsemen to cover the real intent of his assault: he himself will lead an infantry force over difficult terrain and take the unprepared city in a surprise attack. Rumor had been the first (and unreliable) source of information about this plan; Turnus' spies have provided confirmation. We learn all of this detail from the Latin side of the war; Aeneas will not speak again in the book, and his presence at the end will be almost ghostly, an apparition that Turnus cannot exorcize in the face of Jupiter's "savage" will (11.901 *saeva*). Turnus wants Camilla to meet the Trojan cavalry feint along with Messapus (who has already been called a tamer of horses more than once) and Tiburtus. He, meanwhile, will surprise Aeneas in an ambush and cut his forces to pieces.[37]

Trickery and deceit abound in *Aeneid* 11. Both opposing heroes are open to criticism. Turnus' planned ambush is not the sort of direct, "honest" warfare and prearranged single combat we had been expecting. Aeneas' planned surprise attack is not what we had been led to believe would follow his gracious reception of the Latin emissaries. Both Aeneas and Turnus have expressed willingness to face the other to decide the outcome of the war. Why, then, does Aeneas plan this assault on the Latin capitol? No mortal knows the truth about Turnus' "flight" in pursuit of the phantom Aeneas. We must assume that Aeneas, like Drances and his supporters and sympathizers, thinks that Turnus has been running away from a fair fight. Turnus' battle plan, however "unheroic" we may (rightly) judge ambushes to be, is a reasonable reaction to Aeneas' strategy. It saves the final clash with Aeneas for Turnus: he will face Aeneas in the dense forest where the Trojan has chosen his secret path to the city. It will allow Camilla and her cavalry the use of the open plain to perform valiantly and defend the city from Trojan siege. Given the circumstances the scouts reported back to Turnus, it is difficult to see what other course of action he should have pursued. Aeneas' plan is flawed, as Virgil's ecphrasis of the location of Turnus' ambush reveals: Turnus knows the territory well, and has the ideal hidden location to keep his men on high ground where they have both mobility and defense and where they can prepare either a descent against the enemy's right or left flank or an attack with boulders.[38]

Virgil is now ready for his Camilla epyllion. Her introduction in Book 7 revealed tantalizingly little information about her. Besides her obvious affinities to Amazons, especially Penthesilea, Virgil provided only the clue in her name: *camilla*, as we have noted, is a Latin word for a female attendant of a deity. That information from Book 7 already presents some interesting material for commentary. Penthesilea is a figure from cyclic epic, not the *Iliad*; she came very late to Troy to help defend the city (in vain) against the Greeks, and was killed by Achilles. The imperial Greek poet Quintus of Smyrna, who lived some four hundred years after Virgil, made her the subject of the first book of his *Posthomerica*, where he boldly tried to "finish" Homer by telling the colorful, episodic events of the fall of Troy. Penthesilea had been the subject of the (lost) *Aethiopis* ascribed to one Arctinus (sometimes even to Homer), which was probably composed in the sixth century B.C. (though as early as 776 according to tradition). The *Aethiopis* was a five-book epic on the coming to Troy of both Penthesilea and Memnon, the child of the Dawn (from Ethiopia). In his *Punica*, a lengthy homage to Virgil that tells the story of Hannibal and the Second Punic War in dactylic hexameter complete with divine apparatus, the Silver Latin epic poet Silius Italicus (A.D. 26-101) models his Asbyte, a Libyan warrior girl and ally of Hannibal, after Virgil's Camilla (2.56-269). The Latins are now in the position of the beleaguered Trojans; like Penthesilea before her, Camilla will come too late. Curiously, Virgil will not have her face Aeneas (i.e., Achilles), but rather a strange and sinister devotee of Apollo, the Etruscan Arruns; Aeneas will never encounter Camilla. Penthesilea had been the last figure on the walls of Dido's temple to Juno in Carthage (1.488-492); the pictures had to stop before Aeneas' story of Troy's last night begins. Camilla will be the last hope for Italy before Turnus.

Diana begins to tell Camilla's background story to one of her other virgin followers, Opis. Like Lausus, we learn that Camilla had a difficult father, Metabus, who was driven out from his native Privernum.[39] The town had been one of the last holdouts against Roman rule (it was not finally subjugated until 329 B.C.).[40] Metabus ran off with his daughter and came to the raging Amasenus, which had recently been flooded with a heavy rain.[41] Metabus had to make a reasonably quick decision about what to do with his infant child; he decided to bind her to his spear and cast it over the river, vowing his daughter to Diana if the goddess would keep her safe. Just as Turnus vowed his life for Latinus and the Latins, so Metabus had vowed Camilla's to Diana if her life were safeguarded. Diana is an archery goddess, and also a natural protector of young women; the prayer was made to the right immortal. Diana notes that Camilla was *infelix*, "unlucky," as she flew over the river (11.563); the point of the powerful adjective is mostly to emphasize the unfortunate circumstance of an infant girl having to undergo such deadly risks, but also to remind the audience that Camilla had not chosen her life: from her very infancy she was ascribed to a world she had not freely chosen.[42]

After Camilla's major transition from Volscian infant princess to forest girl under Diana's protection, we learn that her father nursed her with the milk of wild animals and, as soon as she was old enough to hold them, from her very childhood he armed her with weapons. Virgil does not reveal the fate of Camilla's mother; Metabus had called his daughter "Camilla" after her mother *Casmilla*. Did her mother die in childbirth? Did the pursuing Volscians kill her? Her convenient absence from Camilla's upbringing allows the girl to be raised by wild animals in Diana's lair. Virgil had previously compared the Trojan army to Strymonian cranes as they raised their war cries (10.265); the young Camilla used to shoot the same cranes with her childish weapons—a powerful foreshadowing of how effective she will be in killing Aeneas' men. At some point in her upbringing her father vanishes, even more mysteriously than her mother; Diana simply stops talking about him in her account of Camilla's childhood. A crucial detail is emphasized, however: Camilla refused any offer of marriage, despite her attractiveness to many *mothers* who wanted her as a daughter-in-law (11.581-582). Camilla is no mannish woman who would be last on a mother's list of prospective brides for their sons; the emphasis on her desirability (which Virgil also hinted at when he showed the crowds of mothers and youths marveling over her arrival in Book 7) is an important part of Virgil's depiction: she is attractive and beautiful, but utterly devoted to the virginity that is the *sine qua non* for any devotee of Diana: an alluring enigma Virgil will take careful time to study and even celebrate in verse.[43]

The background story Diana provides introduces another problem that Virgil saw fit not to answer. How did Camilla manage to become the leader of the very people who had once exiled her father and driven him and his infant daughter away from their home under probable threat of death? Christine de Pisan offers an explanation in her 1405 prose *Le Livre de la Cité des Dames* (1.24): she relates that Camilla had heard from her father about how unjustly he had been treated in Privernum, and went off as a loyal daughter to avenge him (shades of Lausus). After a series of violent skirmishes and battles, she ended up in control of the Volscian military; de Pisan is barely interested in Camilla's *aristeia* at Latium, and prefers to focus on Camilla's infancy and eventual leadership over the Volscians. While this is all speculation, de Pisan's desire to explain Virgil's narrative is understandable. It seems safe to say that only someone of great ability and quality would be able to return to the town of her father's exile and manage to become their leader. Unlike Lausus, there is no Metabus sitting beside his daughter; the thousand Etruscans who accompanied Lausus *and* Mezentius are more representative of a civil rupture in Etruria than any particular devotion to Lausus (despite his undeniably fine qualities).

Diana laments that Camilla has been "snatched up" by warfare (11.584 *correpta*). Just as Virgil offers no clear indication of how Camilla managed to return to Privernum to lead the Volscians into battle, so he offers no definitive explanation for her decision to enter the war in Italy in the first place. The best explanation we can offer is that Camilla views the arrival of the Trojans as a threat to her sylvan way of life. Most recently, the arrival of Aeneas and his men has led to deforestation (i.e., an assault on Diana's nature haunts) as trees have been felled by both sides for funeral pyres (11.135-138); we can assume that Camilla has viewed the Trojans as a potential cause of destruction to her peaceful lifestyle as a huntress. The Trojans under Aeneas represent in part the arrival of urban order; Camilla in one sense is an image of anti-civilization, of the contrast between a solitary life in the forest and a public life in the city. But Virgil tempers this contrast with his careful depiction of Camilla's ability to lead others (at least in war), and, most importantly, with his emphasis on the rightful concern she will have at the moment of death that Turnus not abandon the plan they had formulated before the start of the battle. Camilla began her participation in the day's combat with a reckless desire to rush forth and manage everything, with Turnus staying behind to guard the gates; at the moment of her death she will function as a responsible part of a united army, not as a solitary, and she will be concerned only for the success of her side; in this sense her military abilities increase in maturity. Because Camilla has remained faithful to her virginity, she is still under Diana's protection; she may have left the forest world of Diana's followers, but she is still dear to her patroness. Diana will make sure that Camilla is buried in her native land (in other words, she will accomplish a sort of total reversal of her father's exile), and that her corpse is not despoiled— Camilla will be buried with her weapons. Opis is instructed to avenge Camilla, no matter who her killer may happen to be: the first clue in the narrative that Camilla may very well die at the hand of one of her own allies.[44]

So ends Diana's somber recollection to Opis and the audience of Camilla's history. It is a story that is not without some difficulties, though they are of the nature of missing pieces rather than inconsistencies. The most glaring possible difficulty noted by the commentators between the extended narrative in Book 11 and her appearance in the catalogue of Italian heroes at the end of Book 7 is Virgil's detail there that Camilla is a *bellatrix*, a warrior, a woman who shuns the domestic arts of Minerva, someone who is accustomed to endure harsh battles (*proelia dura pati*) and to outrace the winds with her speed. In other words, rather than the pursuit of Minerva's more peaceful aspects, Camilla is devoted to the warlike side of Minerva (the double image of Minerva is a powerful analogue to the conflict in Camilla between her sylvan existence and the life her entrance into the Latin war has brought her). Virgil's careful description in Book 7 is not so much an inconsistency in light of the fuller details of Book 11 as it is a deliberate foreshadowing of one of the fundamental problems in Camilla's life: she is caught in a world she thinks she understands (war), but unfortunately, to her doom, she thinks of war as a hunt. This is why Virgil emphasizes her tremendous *speed* in Book 7: she honed her running talents chasing all manner of wild animals in the forest. She is a *bellatrix* as she enters the Latin capitol at the end of Book 7, but at once Virgil describes her in terms that could just as easily refer to a huntress, whose "battles" are with beasts and whose ability to run after game and outpace animals is crucial to her success. Some scholars find evidence of the poem's lack of revision (or even the wholesale insertion of a separate epyllion about Camilla into Book 11, perhaps even after it had been considered for insertion into Book 7's catalogue and rejected) as they note the "inconsistency" of Camilla being an apparently seasoned veteran in Book 7 and a young novice heroine in Book 11. Rather, they have ignored Virgil's subtle artistry: her appearance in Book 7 seemed normal enough both to us and the assembly of Italians who gathered to see her—if a woman warrior can be accepted. Now, in Book 11, the reality of her life—known best to Diana—will be fully explored as she finally enters combat in Italy's war, with full evocation of Penthesilea's brave but doomed defense of Troy against the Greeks: this time the Trojans will experience the battle talents of a beautiful woman.

Despite our ability to explain away various "inconsistencies" in the portrait of Camilla we have examined thus far, we retain a vague feeling that she is a shadowy figure we cannot entirely grasp. In time, at Virgil's pace, we shall see her more clearly, in fact as she truly is, and understand something about why she must be destroyed.

The cavalry battle now begins in earnest. It offers a terrible parallel to the *lusus Troiae* in Book 5, which broke up after the Trojan ships were fired. Jupiter had agreed to help Aeneas there by sending rain; in this book, Jupiter will once again help Aeneas (who will never realize just how great a danger he evaded in this engagement). Virgil wants to set the stage for Camilla to make her entrance; he spends some thirty lines (11.618-647) describing the beginning of the action: in two even sets of encounters, twice the Latins are repulsed and driven back to their walls, and twice the Trojans are sent in flight over the plain. Finally, in the third clash (631 *tertia*) the two sides mingle their lines in horrific slaughter of both horses and humans. In the very midst of the bloodshed is Camilla, who is described as an Amazon (she is, after all, Penthesilea) who "prances" (Gransden's superb rendering of 648 *exsultat*) through the violence. Camilla very much enjoys the fray of battle; she takes pleasure in the hunt, and here, we slowly come to realize, she considers herself indulging in the same pursuits she has followed passionately since her childhood: she is comfortable in the bloodthirsty martial spirit of this day. Male human beings are now her targets, not tigresses: Diana had noted how in her youth Camilla had worn a tiger-skin cloak (probably because she killed the animal)—in Book 7, as one might expect for the leader of a contingent, animal skins are gone and the purple and gold of Volscian royalty is back. Virgil will go to great lengths to show that the clothing is irrelevant; Camilla remains what she always was, though despite her conflation of the worlds of hunting and warfare, Virgil will also go to great lengths to emphasize her ability to succeed in *either* lifestyle.

Camilla has one breast exposed to battle to facilitate archery; the detail is standard for depictions of Amazons. She has more weapons than we can realistically imagine: besides a quiver and arrows, she has a double-axe (another typical Amazon weapon) and numerous javelins. Virgil reminds us that Camilla is bearing the "arms of Diana" (11.652 *arma Dianae*), a reference to the fact that this girl should have stayed in the forest with her hunting—Diana's weapons are not used in war, but in the pursuit of animals. When Camilla is repulsed, as she retreats she fires arrows backwards against her pursuers: this favorite tactic of the Parthian archer bogeymen is immediately followed by Virgil's very Roman assortment of girls who fight alongside Camilla—a marvelous example of the poet's love for manipulating his audience and playing with their expectations: just as we begin to view Camilla critically, as if she were some Parthian banshee, Virgil thrusts us back into the world of native Italy. Virgil had noted that when the Rutulians were driven into flight by the Trojan cavalry, they would guard their exposed backs (630); Camilla, in contrast, uses flight as another chance to fight. Camilla's adopted "mother" is Diana; in contrast, Virgil explicitly points out that Penthesilea was the child of Mars (661 *Martia*). Camilla is no true Amazon. Her companions are with her both in peace and in war (658 *pacisque bonas bellique ministras*); they were probably fellow huntresses who followed her back among the Volscians and then into combat in this ill-fated enterprise. Unlike Quintus of Smyrna, who will devote many lines to the bitter deaths of Penthesilea's fellow female soldiers, Virgil will refrain from depicting any of Camilla's sisters in combat until he introduces the key figure Acca (significantly, not mentioned here) at the end of her life; Camilla will hand over her horse to an unnamed companion when she prepares to fight one of Aeneas' allies on foot (710), and she will be grabbed by her female companions as she falls off her horse after Arruns shoots her (805-806).

Larina (the name of a northern Samnite town) and Tulla (reminiscent of the warlike king Tullus Hostilius) have associations with early Roman history; so too does Tarpeia, who borrows her name from the traitorous daughter of Spurius Tarpeius, who opened a path for Titus Tatius and his Sabines so they could seize the Capitol. The names (especially Tarpeia) are not inspiring, though again Virgil confounds our assumptions at once by pointedly calling them "daughters of Italy" (657 *Italides*), a proud appellation he may have invented (it does not appear in extant literature before the *Aeneid*).[45] Virgil is ready now to begin his long description of Camilla's *aristeia*. He begins with a question modeled on Homer's address to Patroclus (*Iliad* 16.692-693):

Quem telo primum, quem postremum, aspera virgo,
deicis? (11.664-665)

*Whom first with your weapon, whom last, o fierce virgin,
did you cast down?*

Again, following his usual favorite practice, Virgil slowly builds up his narrative and lets it unfold at his leisure. The evocation of Patroclus is deliberate here; Camilla will serve as Turnus' Patroclus, and her death will spell his doom (as if he were *Hector*, not Patroclus' friend and lover Achilles). Both Camilla and Pallas will contribute to Turnus' final doom: Pallas for obvious reasons and Camilla because her death will drive Turnus to a mad frenzy that deprives him of his last, best chance to destroy Aeneas. Virgil has omitted Homer's note about a god calling Patroclus to death; this omission from his epic model is an important detail in his Camilla narrative: she is doomed, but partly because two gods decide to help in striking her down.

Euneus is first, shot through the chest with a pine shaft and left to writhe in his own blood. Liris is finished once Camilla wounds his horse underneath him; Pagasus comes to help Liris and thereby shares his death.[46] Amastrus, Tereus, Harpalycus, Demophoon and Chromis all fall as mere names in her death catalogue (Harpalycus, however, the "Snatcher Wolf," reminds us of Thracian Harpalyce from Book 1 and, in accord with Virgil's favorite trick of subtle foreshadowing, anticipates the lupine context of Camilla's *aristeia* and death—if we had forgotten Harpalyce, now we are more likely to remember her). Each weapon Camilla fires kills a Trojan (and, as we have noted, Virgil gives her quite a mass and selection of weapons). The first real vignette of one of her victims is Virgil's description of the hunter (11.678 *venator*) Ornytus, who, significantly, is a sort of mirror image of Camilla. Ornytus has an animal skin over his shoulders and a huge wolf's head helmet (which is why he towers over everyone else and is a likely target for Camilla's weapons). Camilla viciously hates Ornytus as soon as she sees him (685 *inimico pectore*); she has contempt for him because he seems to think he is hunting animals in the forest. In reality, Ornytus will be a precursor of Arruns, as we shall see later, and an important foreshadowing of Camilla's *true* nature, which Virgil (after his preferred fashion) will reveal as late as possible.

Virgil does not describe Ornytus' death, because, as he notes, it took no effort at all for Camilla to slay him. If the point is that Camilla and Ornytus are both hunters, there is no question that Camilla is more skilled in the art.

Orsilochus and Butes are a parallel to Turnus' slaying of Pandarus and Bitias. All four were Trojan giants; Camilla fatally wounds Butes in the back (he was presumably fleeing her onslaught) and then deals with Orsilochus. She flees away from him; perhaps he moved to attack her as soon as his companion was killed. He chases her in a circle, and soon we realize that the hunted will become the hunter as Camilla somehow gets behind him. The action is not altogether clear (another typical Virgilian trick to mimic the confusion of battle, which leaves us with sometimes disjointed images that form clear enough pictures): whether Camilla was chased by a furious Orsilochus *or* decided to trick Orsilochus and lead him on a hopeless hunt (most likely), she manages to wheel her horse around behind him by making a very swift change from a wider to a smaller orbit (11.695 *eludit gyro interior*). Turnus had split open the giant Pandarus' head and left him with brain halves on each shoulder (9.753-755); Camilla brings her axe down in Orsilochus' face as he prays to her—she offers no reply to his words other than the gory wound. This is one of the most grisly death scenes in the *Aeneid*, and it comes with the added horror of Orsilochus' ignored prayers for mercy.

Virgil does not name the Ligurian "son of Aunus" (11.700) who is Camilla's last victim before Jupiter reenters the war. "Aunides" wants to trick Camilla into dismounting; by reproaching her for owing all her success to her horse, he hopes to be able to goad her into agreeing to attack him on foot (so he can then escape). Virgil uses this cowardly deceiver as living proof of the incredible speed with which he had already credited Camilla (his trickster nature may be reflected in Virgil's refusal to name him—he thereby retains an aura of intrigue and stealth).[47] Aunides had decided against trying to face Camilla on horseback (a wise enough decision); he considers this trick his best chance for survival. Camilla hands over her horse in silence and stands ready to face him on the ground; the point of her "naked sword" and "undecorated shield" is that she has won no previous glory on *foot* (711 *ense pedes nudo puraque interritus parma*), though she has no lack of confidence in her ability to kill this Ligurian; she is utterly unafraid. Aunides flees off on his horse without delay; Camilla (conveniently) knows the name and provenance of this liar, and assures him that he will not survive. She hates this fraud with (yet again) a very personal hatred, and she will take vengeance for his trick by shedding his enemy blood (720 *inimico sanguine*). Once again, Virgil does not describe the actual killing; instead, he uses a celebrated simile:

> quam facile accipiter saxo sacer ales ab alto
> consequitur pennis sublimem in nube columbam
> comprensamque tenet pedibusque eviscerat uncis;
> tum cruor et vulsae labuntur ab aethere plumae. (11.721-724)

As easily as a raptor, the sacred bird, from a lofty rock
pursues a dove that is high up on its wings in a cloud,
and holds it once it has been snatched up, and disembowels it with its claws;
then gore and torn feathers glide from the upper air.

The simile of the raptor (a hawk or a falcon) and the dove is borrowed from Homer (*Iliad* 22.139-142). In Homer, the bird of prey is none other than Achilles, and the pitiable victim is Hector. In Quintus of Smyrna (*Posthomerica* 1.529-572), Penthesilea is compared to a dove in the face of the pursuing hawk as she faces Achilles soon before her death: Quintus has simply borrowed a key image from Homer.[48] In the *Aeneid*'s cavalry battle on the plains before the Latin capitol, in the absence of both Aeneas and Turnus, Camilla is the raptor.[49] The raptor is in the upper air because the bird is sacred to the gods of Olympus; the fallen dove represents an attack on Venus, one of whose sacred birds was the dove.[50] One gets the impression that the huntress Camilla is in part so contemptuous of her foes because (unlike animals in the forest), they seem too talkative and, in some cases, deceitful and scheming.

Camilla has now reached the zenith of her *aristeia*. Jupiter has been watching the entire action unfold, and he is not pleased. He stirs up Tarchon, the Etruscan king, who in turn rouses his broken and defeated ranks of horsemen.[51] Aunides and now Tarchon are not Trojans; Camilla is deeply immersed in combat with fellow native inhabitants of the peninsula, not with Trojans *per se*.[52]

Tarchon upbraids his men with their apparent lack of shame at falling before a woman. Camilla's gender had not been a problem for Turnus. We have heard no complaint from the Latins or Rutulians or seen any hesitation about fighting under a woman's leadership. It is true that Messapus and Tiburtus were appointed commanders of the cavalry battle along with Camilla, but it is unlikely this reflected any doubts about Camilla's gender; the battle was large enough to accommodate multiple separately managed cavalry units. Tarchon's criticism of Camilla's gender reflects his revulsion at seeing a girl destroy so many of his men. He reproaches his men for being more than willing to participate in love and wine (11.736-737 *Venerem / Bacchi*); the mention of Venus is ironic given her protection of the *Trojans* (Tarchon is addressing the Etruscans around him) and the taunts Priam's line has long suffered because of Paris and, now, Aeneas.

Tarchon's insult about the curved pipe of Bacchic revelry (737) also points to a criticism of the orgiastic rites associated with both Bacchus and the Phrygian Cybele; his goading insults foreshadow the imminent appearance on the battlefield of Chloreus, Cybele's eunuch devotee. Virgil had said that *Phrygians* (677) were falling before Camilla's shafts (often a contemptuous appellation for the Trojans); the image we have of the Trojans throughout the Camilla narrative is the racial stereotype of Numanus Remulus or Iarbas before him, and contrasts greatly with Camilla, the native Italian girl.

Somewhat ironically, Tarchon's first victim is Venulus, the spokesman for the emissaries to Diomedes; a character we had met in diplomatic circumstances will now be yet another casualty of war. In a dramatic equestrian feat, Tarchon snatches Venulus off his horse and carries him off in his very lap. Jupiter is now in control of the field; Tarchon's first action (though not as athletically fantastic as Camilla's outrunning of Aunides' horse and evisceration of its rider) announces the change of fortune (and, unlike Juno's occasional aid to Turnus during *his aristeia* in Book 9, Virgil never credits Camilla with *any* divine assistance whatsoever). Virgil could not resist a smile, no doubt, as he notes that Tarchon carried off Venulus "arms and all" (11.747 *arma virumque*).[53] As with two of Camilla's victims, Virgil does not offer explicit detail about Venulus' fate, preferring once again to veil gore with the perverse beauty of a simile—Tarchon is like an eagle that has snatched a serpent in its talons and carried it off. The eagle is Jupiter's bird; Tarchon, we learn, has snatched this serpent away from *Tiburtus'* sector of the field (757 *Tiburtum ex agmine*)—significantly, the first onslaught of Jovian intervention does not affect Camilla's area, but her (weaker) allied leaders, and even after Arruns is depicted stalking her, she is still described as a victorious girl (764 *victrix*).

As the Etruscans press on their attack, we meet Camilla's killer, who makes his sinister appearance at midline (759):

... tum fatis debitus Arruns
velocem iaculo et multa prior arte Camillam
circuit, et quae sit fortuna facillima temptat. (11.759-761)

... Then Arruns, owed to the fates,
circles swift Camilla with his javelin and much cunning before he strikes
and essays what would be the easiest fortune.

Camilla appears nowhere else in extant Latin literature, and neither does her killer; unlike Camilla, however, there are several other personages in history who bear the common Etruscan name *Arruns*. Lucius Arruntius was a fortunate survivor of the proscriptions of 43 B.C. who served as a naval commander for Octavian at Actium; he was consul in 22, and composed a (lost) history of the First Punic War. He had been born in Atina, a *Volscian* town (perhaps a subtle hint at Arruns' allegiance in this war); the Arruntii were quite wealthy and had Pompeian connections during the civil wars. His son was consul in A.D. 6, and had an adopted heir Lucius Arruntius *Camillus* Scribonianus, who was consul in 32.[54] Though the commentaries ignore the point, Virgil's audience would most likely have connected Arruns with the contemporary Volscian Arruntii. If Arruns is one of Aeneas' Etruscan allies, it is surprising that neither Camilla nor any of her retinue manages to notice him as he stalks the Volscian girl.[55] Ambivalence over Arruns' origins may anticipate the eventual union of Troy and Italy.

As he did with Camilla, so now with Arruns Virgil deprives us of instant knowledge, and prefers to withhold important information about just who Arruns is and why he is really hunting Camilla. We shall not have to wait over three books to learn more about Arruns, but before we return to his stalking, we meet yet another figure on this ever more complicated battlefield: Chloreus.[56]

Camilla's most recent string of enemies has had a distinctly native Italian color: Ligurian, Etruscan. Now she meets the embodiment of the worst Troy has to offer, at least according to the ethnic propaganda of a Numanus Remulus: Chloreus, a priest of Cybele. Virgil is not explicit about Chloreus' current status in the priesthood; he has either been a priest for some time now, or he was once a priest and has abandoned the vocation for unknown reasons (11.768 *olimque* is difficult to define precisely). If the latter, he has something in common with Camilla. Certainly neither a forest devotee of Diana nor a priest of Cybele belongs anywhere near this field of battle. Camilla may be defending her woodland home from a perceived invasion, but Chloreus is very far from the frenzied rites of Cybele in the Troad. Camilla is nowhere near Chloreus (769 *longe*); like a mirage, he appears far off on the battlefield, distant but clearly visible to Camilla because of his decidedly golden vesture (773 *aureus . . . auro*, 776 *auro*). Arruns has been stalking Camilla, and now Camilla will pursue Arruns. Most recently Camilla has been cutting her way through the ranks of Etruscans and native Italian allies of Aeneas; she now sees a Trojan enemy far off, and blindly (781 *caeca sequebatur*) begins to pursue him (the verb is an inceptive imperfect, with additional durative force—she can think of nothing now but the pursuit of Chloreus). Indeed, she is a *huntress* (780 *venatrix*) as she hastens off to attack Chloreus; her determined quest for a single animal might work in the sylvan world of Diana, but it will spell doom for her now in the midst of battle on the Latin plains.[57]

Why does Camilla pursue Chloreus? In the heat of combat, Chloreus appears more distinctive than any enemy she has yet seen; his clothes of purple, gold, and saffron stand out as an inviting target (just as Ornytus stood head and shoulders above everyone else because of his wolf's head helmet). In any case, Camilla is confused. As she gallops over the plain, she cannot decide what to do with Chloreus' vesture. She has already anticipated his death; the audience can accept that if Jupiter and soon Apollo were not involved in this cavalry war, she *would* be able to kill Chloreus without difficulty—but assumptions of victory can prove dangerous. Camilla's confusion over Chloreus' vesture hinges on whether she should dedicate them in a temple or wear them herself. The first option is inappropriate. Diana would properly receive the animal skins of a hunt, not the clothing of a eunuch priest of Cybele. The second option is also inappropriate; why would a huntress (or, for that matter, a Volscian military leader?) wear the saffron tunic of Cybele's priest? Despite her tremendous success in the battle so far, Camilla has slipped into exactly the same mistake she had earlier accused her victim Ornytus of making: she has reverted to the world of the hunt, and is single-minded in her pursuit of Chloreus across the plain, and has mistaken him for an animal. When she was a huntress, she wore tiger skins because it was considered appropriate to wear the skins of the animals she successfully caught; we can assume she also made proper offerings to Diana from her animal victims. When she assumed command of the Volscian contingent in the Italian war, she dressed in the purple and gold that identified her as a princess of her people, Metabus' daughter now returned to her native Privernum. Her purple and gold clothes are perfectly appropriate for use as a *warrior* in battle on behalf of Italy, though they would be utterly inappropriate for use as a *huntress* (which is precisely the ill-fated irony of Dido's purple and gold fashion during the fateful hunt in *Aeneid* 4—Dido is no true huntress). Camilla, to her doom, is hunting in the wrong costume. Chloreus' clothes are somewhat similar to Camilla's own present costume of royal purple and gold, but they are most certainly not the appropriate fashion for a huntress to don. Even if Camilla could plausibly take on Chloreus' purple and gold in place of her own, she would still be hopelessly lost in the world of the hunt. Camilla has terribly conflated the worlds of war and the hunt (which is why Virgil took the trouble to describe *two* of her costumes: the purple and gold robes of her royal station, and the tiger skin cloak of her adolescence in the forest—she is, in fact, the only character in the poem who is given a detailed description of two quite different styles of dress). Had Camilla survived the war and returned home, she would fittingly have exchanged the purple and gold of Volscian royalty for the animal skins of her earlier youth. Virgil further describes Camilla's incautious (11.781 *incauta*—in war you must be more attentive to possible enemies than in the forest) pursuit of Chloreus with a famous authorial comment:

femineo praedae et spoliorum ardebat amore. (11.782)[58]

she was burning with a woman's love for booty and spoils.

Camilla was burning with a love for booty and spoils, and her passion for them was *feminine* or *womanly*. Servius knew the adjective needed comment, though he was not sure how to define it clearly; he was satisfied with the explanation that it meant Camilla was being irrational, even impatient (Chloreus is so far off, even for the swiftest of girls). The adjective helps underscore one of the main reasons for Arruns' own obsessive stalking of Camilla. He will soon refer to her as a "disgrace" (789); he has very specific reasons for calling her that (as well as a "dire pest"), but part of the undertone of Arruns' intense distaste for Camilla is probably what Tarchon has already noted: she is a woman in a man's war (and, to the utter disgust of some, she has been slaughtering those men quite handily). The adjective *femineo* at once affirms the misogyny of her enemies and her own femininity; she is no masculine woman, but a very female heroine who happens to be quite competent in battle. When we first met Camilla, Virgil noted that her woman's hands (7.806 *femineas manus*) were not accustomed to the distaff or baskets of Minerva; she was a woman, to be sure, but her hands were not given to the traditional tasks of a dutiful (Roman) woman. The declaration of her femininity here forms a ring with that passage; Minerva is a *bellatrix* as well as a weaver, and the ambiguity fits Camilla well. Euryalus was betrayed by what was probably moonlight reflected off of a helmet he was able to strip off a dead warrior; Camilla (who is under the patronage of the moon goddess) contrasts to the other young dead fighter by her *not* living long enough to dispose of Chloreus' arms and clothing (in this she also contrasts with Turnus, who was able to strip Pallas—to his doom).

There is a wonderful contrast here: Chloreus is a eunuch priest of Cybele; he can never hope to regain his lost manhood. Camilla has been indulging in the masculine world of slaughter and martial violence, but she remains a woman—flaws and all. Women may be accused of reckless and irrational behavior in the rhetoric and thought of Romans, but *this* Volscian girl will take two male gods to destroy her. *Femineo* is not so much a chauvinistic Virgilian criticism of Camilla as a reminder that a *woman* is destroying the Trojans and Etruscans and has thereby provoked divine intervention. We are left with the sense that had Jupiter (and, soon enough, Apollo) not intervened, Camilla would have slain both Chloreus *and* Arruns. Camilla comes off as far more impressive and sympathetic than either the silent man-woman former priest of Cybele or the fanatical Arruns who once fire-walked on Soracte: recklessness is a part of her personality, for better or worse, and adds greatly to her attractive image.

So in considering Camilla and Chloreus we may consider how at the beginning of her *aristeia* Camilla saw Ornytus, and failed to see herself, while here, at the end, she sees Chloreus and thinks she sees a faint image of herself (which is part of why she is hesitant about whether she should hang his purple and gold clothes in a temple, or *wear* them).[59] Ornytus was a man and a hunter, and was dressed like a hunter; his only problem was his presence in a war. Chloreus has rejected his masculinity (he wears outlandish, effeminate clothes) *and* he is also in a war (inappropriate for a priest); in this sense he reflects Camilla, whose presence in war represents something of a rejection of her gender (besides the fact that huntresses do not belong in combat), as well as the abandonment of Diana's service. Camilla was both huntress and devotee of Diana; her occupations encompass both Ornytus and Chloreus, who frame her *aristeia*. The adjective *femineo* points to the fact that Camilla has not entirely rejected her sex (in striking contrast to the castrated Chloreus)—but she will not live long enough to appreciate the vagaries of either gender issues or the inappropriateness of conflating hunting and warfare. She will not live long enough to correct her mistakes. The lessons Camilla failed to learn when she saw Ornytus, she sees again now in Chloreus, though dimly; before she can grasp the whole picture (and connect the dots, as it were), Arruns strikes.

Once again Virgil introduces Arruns suddenly and (appropriately enough for his secret attempt to strike Camilla) unexpectedly:

> telum ex insidiis cum tandem tempore capto
> concitat et superos Arruns sic voce precatur. (11.783-784)

> *When at last, seizing the opportunity from his ambush*
> *Arruns brandished his weapon and called on the gods above in prayer.*

We think the weapon belongs to Camilla; perhaps she is sneaking up on Chloreus (*ex insidiis*), but then the illusion is quickly shattered as Arruns makes his prayer, and at long last we learn Camilla's true nature, and why Arruns wants her dead with such intensity and obsession.

> "summe deum, sancti custos Soractis Apollo,
> quem primi colimus, cui pineus ardor acervo
> pascitur, et medium freti pietate per ignem
> cultores multa premimus vestigia pruna,
> da, pater, hoc nostris abolere dedecus armis,
> omnipotens. non exuvias pulsaeve tropaeum
> virginis aut spolia ulla peto, mihi cetera laudem
> facta ferent; haec dira meo dum vulnere pestis
> pulsa cadat, patrias remeabo inglorius urbes." (11.785-793)

> *"Highest of gods, Apollo, guardian of holy Soracte,*
> *whom we above all honor, for whom the burning pine in a heap*
> *is fed, we are your votaries who, relying on our piety, walk through fire*
> *and press our steps down on many coals*
> *Grant, Father, to abolish this disgrace from our arms,*
> *omnipotent one. I do not seek any arms or trophy of*
> *the fallen virgin, nor any spoils: for me my remaining deeds*
> *will bring praise; provided that this dire pest fall by my wound,*
> *I shall return to my father's cities without glory."*

Arruns wants no spoils from Camilla (in contrast to her own pursuit of Chloreus). He wants no glory from having killed her. Camilla made the mistake (however understandable) of considering Chloreus already dead. Arruns makes the assumption that other deeds in this war will bring him fame—a bit of hubris that will manifest itself again, tellingly, soon enough. *Nostris armis* (788) further heightens the Etruscan Arruns' ambiguous allegiance. It could be an ablative of means ("by our arms") or an ablative of separation ("from our arms"); at least as early as Servius the question was raised. I suspect Arruns is indeed a partisan of

Turnus, who is sickened by Camilla's rampage for reasons Virgil will now make clear through allusion to native Italian folklore.

Arruns' prayer is to Apollo *Soranus*, Apollo as worshipped on and around Mount Soracte (the modern Soratte) north of Rome. Arruns must be from the area around Soracte; Virgil notes that he is one of the firewalkers who tread on hot coals as a sign of their devotion to the god. Just as we have seen votaries of Diana and Cybele, so now Virgil introduces a priest of Apollo.[60] Servius is one of many extant sources of information about the strange fire-walking rites on Soracte, which help explain why Arruns considers Camilla to be such a disgrace to his side. According to Servius, Soracte was a mountain of the Hirpini where rites were once being conducted to Dis Pater. Wolves suddenly appeared and snatched away the sacrificial meat offerings. Shepherds pursued the wolves a very great distance until they arrived at a cave. Suddenly, some sort of pestilential exhalation from the cave killed the shepherds, and a plague broke out. The people around Soracte were told that the only way to end the plague was to imitate the wolves, that is, to live off of plunder (*ut imitarentur lupos, id est, rapto viverent*). Servius does not make explicit exactly what was meant by this imitation of wolves. Because of the whole episode, the people were called *Hirpini*, from the Sabine word for wolves. Servius adds the further detail (he credits Varro) that the Hirpini, when they were about to do their fire-walking, used to apply some sort of ointment to their feet to protect them (in contrast to Arruns' boast that he and his fellow firewalkers relied on their piety to protect them from burns). So the Hirpini engaged in fire-walking rituals on Soracte; perhaps the wolves had stolen the offerings the Hirpini were carrying over the hot coals. Pliny the Elder connects the fire-walking Hirpini with the cult of Apollo on Soracte.[61] According to Strabo (5.2.9), there were similar rites to the mysterious goddess Feronia at the foot of Soracte.[62]

Arruns, then, is a devotee of Apollo Soranus, one of the *Hirpi Sorani*, a cult of firewalkers who are associated with the eradication of lupine pests. Camilla, then, is a lycanthrope, a she-wolf who must be destroyed as part of the coming of order. Arruns recognizes her for what she is; he is horrified and disgusted that such a creature, a werewolf only he can sense, would fight on his side against the Trojans and their Italian allies (the same sense of recognition and loathing holds true if we take Arruns to be one of Aeneas' partisans). Ornytus, with his wolf's head helmet, prefigures Arruns: the wolf-slayers on Soracte had to imitate wolves in order to destroy them (and, shortly, Arruns will be compared to a wolf in a simile where Virgil nods to those in the audience who know their native Italian folklore). Arruns, too, has been stalking Camilla like a wolf; she, for her part, has been doing the same to Chloreus.

Virgil's mention of "Thracian Harpalyce" in Book 1, where Venus was disguised like a huntress, now makes more sense. Harpalyce, whose name is Greek for "Snatcher She-Wolf," evokes the same sort of werewolf lore. According to Servius, Harpalyce was killed because she raided livestock (like a wolf); both Harpalyce and the origins of the *Hirpini Sorani* point to the protection of flocks and herds (not to mention humans) from were-creatures. Virgil has powerfully molded this native Italian (in origin Arcadian?) folklore about lycanthropes with the figure of Penthesilea from cyclic epic.[63] The Harpalyce and Penthesilea images from Book 1 have found their fulfillment in Camilla and Diana, not in Dido and Venus (the pretenders from Book 1). Camilla had a complex personality that was mirrored in both Ornytus and Chloreus; now she has a complex *Vorleben* that includes the lycanthrope Harpalyce and the Amazon Penthesilea. Now we know why Virgil had named *Harpalycus* as one of Camilla's victims; he has carefully paved the way for the climactic encounter between the "wolves" Camilla and Arruns by reminding us of the lupine lore. The embodiment in Camilla and Diana of the reality that was only fraudulently glimpsed in Dido and Venus serves as an image of the ultimate triumph of Italy over the East in Rome's future. There is no place for such a creature as the werewolf Camilla in Augustan Rome, to be sure; but there will be no place for her killer, either. In death, as we shall soon see, Camilla the lycanthrope will be known as an inspiration to patriotic virtue and fervor; the very women who once desired her as a prospective daughter-in-law will suddenly see in her death a sort of martyrdom for Italy, which will inspire them to defend their city against Trojan attack. Camilla's secret will remain hers; her killer, Arruns, will take it to his unremembered grave. The beautiful lycanthrope will be remembered, while the fanatic wolf-priest will be forgotten.[64]

Servius noted the possible conflict between Diana and Apollo; he saw in the partial fulfillment of Arruns' prayer a balanced response of a brother to his sister (*bona moderatio*).[65] Apollo was traditionally associated with the sudden death of males; given both Camilla's participation in the male world of warfare, and the obvious impossibility of having Diana involved in Camilla's death, Apollo, appropriately enough, will preside over Camilla's end. Arruns has been stalking Camilla with absolute success; when he finally launches his weapon, all the Volscians will at once turn to see the weapon as it flies through the air (the sound has attracted them). Camilla is too fixated on the pursuit of Chloreus to know what is happening; she is utterly unaware of the weapon. The weapon comes from the heavenly upper air, the ether (802 *aetheris*)—the home of Jupiter. Camilla's *aristeia* and death represent one of the longest continuous sections of the *Aeneid* where mortals are left to their own devices; unlike both Aeneas and Turnus, there is no divine aid in Camilla's exploits, but the cooperation of not one but two (male) gods in her destruction. Arruns' weapon flies straight into the nipple of her exposed breast (803-804), a viciously sexual attack on the virgin huntress:

... virgineumque alte bibit acta cruorem. (11.804)

... *and, once driven in, it drank deep of her virgin blood.*

Arruns' shaft is an instrument of sexual violation, even rape; he has made an assault on a symbol of Camilla's virginity. At once, Camilla's retinue rushes to grab her as she begins to fall from her horse. Why does Arruns now flee, thoroughly terrified (806 *exterritus*)? Part of his fear is the elation of success; Virgil notes that he was joyful and frightened at the same time. He is not entirely certain he has killed Camilla; he is afraid of the "virgin's weapons" (808 *telis . . . virginis*—and indeed a virgin's weapons will soon kill him), lest even the dying Camilla be able to take her revenge. His fear, of course, is more pointedly relevant were he one of Camilla's own allies.

Virgil compares Arruns to a wolf that has slain either a shepherd or a great steer. Arruns imitated a wolf, in accord with the tradition of the *Hirpini Sorani*, in order to hunt Camilla down in secret. Now the lupine wolf-slayer will himself be slain. If Camilla was indeed a lycanthrope, in death Virgil has freed her from her curse and rehabilitated her; she is the shepherd of the simile; the wolf-priest has indeed followed the admonition to "imitate wolves," perhaps a bit too literally, and now he will face Diana's nymph Opis (i.e., "The Avenger," probably).[66] Arruns has become the hunted wolf, and now "hateful weapons" (809 *tela inimica*) will pursue him with deeply personal (*inimica*) intent: the occupational hazards of those who would masquerade as what they are not (oracles notwithstanding). Camilla is a shepherd because she is the effective and even beloved leader of her people (both her own retinue of female companions, probably from her woodland years, and the Volscian forces from Privernum and its environs). But she is also a steer (811), a mighty (and male) animal destined for sacrifice. Despite her positive qualities, there will be no place for a living Camilla in Rome's future; she will become iconic, a protomartyr for her people, a beautiful virgin who never ages and can forever be envisioned as she was on the day she entered Latium in silent procession.

Camilla is inevitably compared to Dido. The time Aeneas spent in Carthage was a clear evocation of Antony's long sojourn in Cleopatra's Egypt. In the Camilla narrative we see nothing of Cleopatra at Actium. Virgil depicted Dido in Book 1 in decidedly inappropriate terms: her story was first told to Aeneas by his mother Venus in the disguise of Diana. The first simile describing Dido compared her to Diana, and the day she would consummate her union with Aeneas took place at a hunt, where Carthage's queen was decked out in the purple and gold of her royal station, not the animal skins or simple clothing of a forest huntress. All of this served to emphasize how Dido was living a life that did not reflect her true nature. She had lost her husband by violence and vowed to remain celibate in honor of her memory. Under the certain influence of Venus and Cupid, she began to fall in love with Aeneas (though one may imagine the gods needed to expend little effort). Camilla did not choose her lifestyle either. She did not ask to be Diana's votary. She did not ask to be consecrated for life to the goddess of the hunt and live a relatively isolated life in the forest. Like Dido, Camilla has made a change of lifestyle (*venatrix* to *bellatrix*) that, in her reckless adolescence, she does not fully understand. She treats battle as if it were a hunt.

Despite this tragic conflation, Virgil emphasizes her success (in striking contrast to Dido, whose interest in city-building seems to lessen as soon as Aeneas shares her bed). Now we shall see the most developed of Virgil's comparisons between the two women: their respective death scenes.

While stalking Camilla, Arruns had been invisible in the crowd; now he tries to lose himself in the crowd on the battlefield as he seeks safety in some out of the way place. Virgil suddenly shifts his lens back to Camilla and her final moments; throughout the sequence of Arruns' pursuit and her fatal wounding Virgil disorients us with frequent changes of scene. Acca, Camilla's closest friend, was not mentioned among the *Italides* who joined Camilla in battle. Virgil meant to evoke A*nn*a with this new character, Acca; like Anna, she will be present for the last moments of her sister's life (823 *soror*). Not blood, but an eternal loyalty to Diana, links the two women. Camilla has a simple message for Acca. She is to flee from the battlefield and take a message to Turnus (who is in ambush). He is to keep the Trojans from the city. Only after giving these final instructions to Acca does Camilla finally let go of the reins of her horse. Her last duty, she recognizes, is to make certain that Turnus will maintain the battle plan they had already outlined.[67] Did she foresee his emotionally overwrought reaction to her death? The cavalry under Camilla, Messapus, and Tiburtus had been destroying the Trojan horse until Jupiter stopped them; half the battle is now won for the Trojans. Jupiter's work is not finished: now he must stop the infantry threat that lurks in the woods, waiting for Aeneas. Camilla has done her part (823 *hactenus . . . potui*); she has no idea that Jupiter intervened in the battle (not to mention Apollo), in part because Tarchon's charge was directed against Tiburtus' sector of battle, not her own. Now she knows that Turnus must play his part (826 *succedat pugnae*).[68] Camilla's words right before her death also show an awareness of the entire struggle, not just of her personal role in it or her own Volscian contingent. The girl who had once come to war with bloodthirsty excitement and zealous eagerness for conflict and strife will now die with the quiet, careful mind of a master strategist. She prefigures, in a subtle way, the future unification of Italy—small wonder that Virgil named her Camilla, after Marcus Furius Camillus, the final *Roman* victor over the Volscians. Camilla, the exile princess, has returned to lead her Volscians in one of the first struggles of a united Italy against (Trojan) invasion.

Camilla does not want to die (828 *non sponte*, 831 *indignata*); she is no Dido ready to commit suicide. She does not die in private, either, like Carthage's queen; the whole battlefield seems to be a witness to her end, and at the moment of her death a shout goes up to the stars (832-833). Camilla's death line will be repeated as the last line of the *Aeneid*, to describe the death of Turnus:

vitaque cum gemitu fugit indignata sub umbras. (11.831)

and life fled with a groan, indignant, to the shadows below.

In a sense, Camilla dies as a proxy for Turnus (just as Pallas served as something of a proxy for Aeneas). When the two opposing heroes meet at the end of Book 12 in single combat, the ghosts of both of these young heroes weigh heavily on their minds. Turnus will find a grim union with Camilla in death; both of them will be joined in their indignant resistance to the decrees of fate and their refusal to surrender to the will of Jupiter. With Camilla dead, the three units of Aeneas' cavalry force (the Trojans, the Etruscans, and the Arcadians) all rush forward against the Italians; they have renewed vigor, obviously, once they see their deadliest foe defeated.

Opis has been carefully watching the entire spectacle unfold. No character in the *Aeneid* receives the protected, avenged, and almost antiseptic death Camilla now merits: her enemy was nowhere near her when she fell mortally wounded, there were no insults or vaunting over her corpse, there was no need for the granting of burial privileges from any foe, there will be no mortal funeral (the medieval imitations of the *Aeneid* ruin Virgil's point by indulging in grand funeral laments and rites for Camilla). Diana will not leave her mortal devotee bereft of solace. She will have a name that will be remembered through all the races of men on account of her death (846-847 *neque hoc sine nomine letum/per gentis erit*); we shall soon see the beginning of the fulfillment of Diana's assurances.

A relatively short time has brought a great emotional change to Arruns. When Opis sees him, Camilla's killer is now vainly preening himself and is swollen with pride at his act; he is rejoicing (854 *laetantem*) in his accomplishment. Opis kills Arruns with Diana's own preferred weapon, a bow and arrow (Opis ruefully notes that Arruns is really not worthy of dying by Diana's proper arms). Unlike Camilla, he will hear the noise of the arrow as it is fired (though he cannot see its origin and has no chance to address his slayer). Camilla had been shot in the nipple (803 *papillam*); Opis' right hand and the bowstring will touch her own nipple as she fires (862 *papillam*). Opis is unafraid, and hateful of Arruns; she is also a Thracian nymph, we learn—appropriate given the memory of the image of Thracian Harpalyce, and also appropriate for a warlike nymph (devotee of Diana or not). Camilla's *aristeia* began with mention of Thrace, a traditional Amazon haunt (659); now the ring closes with Thracian Opis. No companion of Arruns will know that he has died; he will remain one of the unburied dead of the war, left in unknown dust (866 *ignoto camporum in pulvere*) in complete contrast to the honored, divine burial Diana has promised Camilla; in death, Virgil has made his sympathies very clear, and Arruns' unburied corpse stands in great contrast to the solemn requiems that opened the book.[69] Apollo presided over the sudden death of Camilla; now Diana, through her proxy Opis, has presided over the sudden death of Camilla's killer. Arruns has some resemblance to Palinurus; both are destroyed by immortals (or at least near immortals, in the case of Opis) in out of the way places; Sleep throws Palinurus overboard, which leads directly to his death on the Italian coast, and now Opis shoots Arruns outright. In fact, especially given the roundabout way Sleep dispatches Palinurus,

Opis' killing of Arruns is the most dramatically direct divine intervention in the entire poem. It serves as a response to the intervention of Jupiter and Apollo during the cavalry battle. Diana cannot save Camilla, but she can make certain that Camilla will be an iconic image for future generations of Italians, a heroine of one of Italy's earliest struggles for freedom. Arruns, who stands in for Aeneas in a curious way (A-s, and, further, A*chille*s, Penthesilea's killer), will be unremembered. If there is any connection to be made between *Arruns* and *Aeneas*, it may be that Virgil's depiction of Arruns' mysterious, lonely death is meant to presage that of Aeneas.

The fortunes of the cavalry battle change dramatically after the death of Camilla. The Trojans are now in the ascendant, just as Jupiter wanted, and we see the direct results of the first half of his intervention in the turning tide of battle now as their horses charge up to the very gates of Latinus' capitol, driving the hapless Latins before them in a rout. Book 11 depicts one of the few major actions of Aeneas that was undertaken without any divine order or precept; he had decided on his own, apparently, to pursue the strategy of cavalry feint and surprise infantry attack; no god or goddess had informed Turnus of the plan. Book 11 has given us one of the lengthiest and most extensive set pieces in the *Aeneid* of entirely mortal action. Now, as the book moves quickly to its conclusion, divine action is everywhere, both in preserving Camilla's dignity and in guaranteeing a Trojan victory on the plains. The same women who had seen Camilla advancing in glory at the end of Book 7 now see the slaughter from the besieged battlements of the capitol. The gates of the city must be opened to let in the fleeing Latins, but there is tremendous fear that such an operation will also let all the pursuing Trojans in as well (a reversal of the action of Book 9, when it was Turnus who was running amok within the gates of the Trojan camp). A vicious slaughter erupts, then, right at the gates of Latinus' city; this is the worst situation the Latins have been in during the war, as men die even within their own homes (we must imagine that some Trojans make it into the city). The specter of city invasion has returned to the *Aeneid*: Troy in Book 2, the Trojan camp in Book 9, and now the Latin capitol in Book 11 all suffer the threat of imminent enemy assault.

At this worst moment for Latium, Camilla's afterlife, her *Nachleben*, begins. The women who are watching the destruction unfold directly beneath them see their sons dying horribly as they struggle on horseback to get back inside the now barred gates of the capitol. The women begin to hurl makeshift weapons down on the Trojans. Their inspiration is Camilla:

monstrat amor verus patriae, ut videre Camillam. (11.892)

True love of country shows them the way, as they see Camilla.

The syntax of the line is somewhat difficult and has occasioned comment, but the meaning is clear: Camilla's example has spurred the women of Latium to stop being mere spectators in what is now the defense of their capitol and to become its ardent defenders, who are ready, if need be, to sacrifice their lives for their country. Turnus had been right: Camilla and her Volscian cavalry were an exceedingly formidable force; even in death, Camilla continues to provide leadership and a model for heroic patriotism. We are very far indeed from the embassy to Aeneas at the beginning of the book, when Drances and his companions requested a burial truce and were assured that the war was as distasteful to Aeneas as it was to the Latins, and that Aeneas was eager for peace. That truce (perhaps broken) had been followed by a risky battle strategy that would have spelled defeat for the Trojans—had Jupiter himself not stepped in to save the day yet again. As it stands, even at this late moment, all is not lost for Italy—though only Camilla seems to have realized it.[70]

Acca brings the news of the disastrous end of the cavalry engagement to Turnus, who is waiting in ambush for Aeneas in the woods. Jupiter's work will now continue:

ille furens (et saeva Iovis sic numina poscunt)
deserit obsessos collis, nemora aspera linquit. (11.901-902)

That man, in a mad rage (and so the savage divine power of Jove demanded) abandoned the besieged hills, and left behind the rough groves.

These two lines are of tremendous significance in understanding much of Virgil's point in Book 11. Virgil could have omitted this mention of Jupiter, and the audience would have fully accepted Turnus' raging reaction to the news of Camilla's death. Indeed, once again we can accept that Jupiter probably did not have much work to do in rousing Turnus' mad frenzy. The immortals had been noticeably absent from Camilla's own *aristeia*; we now see the real reason why Jupiter finally intervened to stop her: he not only had to save the Trojan and allied cavalry in one theater of war, but he also had to work out the most effective method for ending Turnus' deadly ambush. There will be no infantry engagement, as had been planned—once again, there will be no single combat. Jupiter will not need to make a dramatic intervention to save Aeneas from what would have been a catastrophic attack in the forest. Instead, quietly and with deadly implications for Turnus, Jupiter has used Camilla's death to further the destruction of Turnus: small wonder that her death line will also be his, since her death marks the beginning of his own demise.

Virgil underscores the point of how much Turnus has lost. He just barely missed (11.903 *vix*) his opportunity to ambush Aeneas, who now advances in safety through the unguarded forest passes. Both Aeneas and Turnus are now rushing to the city in rapid flight. Aeneas and Turnus see each other at the same moment as they both advance to the city walls; Aeneas is *savage* (910 *saevum*), just as the message of Camilla's death had been (896 *saevissimus*), and just as Jupiter's divine power had been in demanding that Turnus abandon the ambush (901 *saeva*). The report of Camilla's death is *most* savage (superlative *saevis-*

simus) because it is the proximate cause of Turnus' decision to forego the infantry half of his battle plan (thus saving Aeneas); the death of Camilla has done much to ensure that Aeneas will survive this violent day.[71] Virgil has used what is, in effect, a descending tricolon of savagery: we move from the superlative of Camilla's death announcement to the lesser (positive) degree of Jupiter's will and Aeneas' arrival. Aeneas' presence in this episode of the war is of little significance: he does not realize just how close he came to complete disaster. Why is *Aeneas* so savage now? Virgil's depiction of Aeneas now contrasts greatly with the good (106 *bonus*) Aeneas who had so graciously agreed to the truce for the funerals at the beginning of the book. In one sense the adjective reflects Turnus' point of view: the news of Camilla's death, the divine power of Jupiter, and Aeneas are all *saevus* from his perspective. In another sense, we are left wondering why Aeneas needs so much help to win this war; especially after Jupiter's comment to Juno that the Trojans were not succeeding on their own, but only with Venus' help (10.606-610), we notice all too clearly how Camilla succeeds with no help from above. This constant theme of undercutting Aeneas' efforts and victory helps prepare the audience for the poem's quickly approaching climactic revelation: *Rome will be Italian*, the Italy of Camilla, not a rebirth of Aeneas' Troy. In a very real sense, Camilla's side will win this war.

Book 11 had opened with a dawn formula, and we saw how Virgil had taken particular care to delineate the arrival of a second and then a third day. Now we have an explicit note of the close of day. Turnus and Aeneas, nearer to each other than ever before in this war, *would* have joined battle had it not been so close to nightfall:

ni roseus fessos iam gurgite Phoebus Hibero
tinguat equos noctemque die labente reducat. (11.913-914)

were rosy Phoebus not dipping his tired horses in the Spanish
sea and leading back the night as day slipped away.

It was dusk, then, when Camilla died and Turnus abandoned his ambush; Aeneas would have been hampered not only by the surprise nature of the Rutulian ambush but by the added terror of darkness. Virgil says that "rosy Phoebus" was now washing his horses in the Spanish (that is, western) sea to remind us of the *dawn* formula that opened the book (Aurora is usually the rosy one, not Phoebus); the sun god is dipping his horses in the sea to remind us of the cavalry battle that has proven so fateful to both sides, and to remind us of the crucial role Apollo played in the book's battle narrative: it may have been Jupiter who stirred up Tarchon and his Etruscans, but it was Apollo who granted Arruns his wish to kill Camilla; both key divinities now appear at the quiet close of the book (whose action they have so significantly influenced). The two armies now encamp right before the gates of Laurentum. The dawn of this day had seen the weary Trojans and Latins both preparing to take stock of their losses and bury their respective dead (especially Pallas). The day now draws to an equally tired close as the two sides face each other once again, with neither side seemingly better off strategically than it was at the start of the day's military operations, but with the death of Camilla now balancing Pallas', and with a powerful Virgilian lesson for us in divine manipulation of events.

So ends the penultimate book of the *Aeneid*, the second part of the tragedy in three acts that comprises the final quarter of the epic. In one sense the thrust of the narrative has not advanced at all during the book's 915 lines; Aeneas and Turnus have yet to meet in battle, though now they are at least closer than ever before. We have learned very much, however, about the nature of the immortals and their savage will; the question Virgil asked so long ago about the anger of the celestial ones has been explored fully as we ponder the savage rage of *Jupiter*; Juno (and Venus) have been completely absent from Book 11. For now, the two sides abstain from fighting as darkness falls. But the audience knows that the end cannot be put off for much longer.

Notes

1. Mackail comments: "Book XI is in strong contrast with Book X in its finished workmanship and masterly construction. The transitions are managed with admirable skill. There are very few incompletions or superfluities, and no redundant amplifications. There are only two unfinished lines."

2. Virgil specifies the arrival of three separate dawns in this book: 11.1, 11.182, and 11.210, the "third light." The truce for the burials is supposed to last twelve days. Virgil rarely gives precise chronologies for his books (the details about the three separate dawns is unusual); in poetry, events like the great Latin war council can happen swiftly when the poet requires it. For reasons noted below, Gransden thinks the action of Book 11 occupies four days; he (correctly) refuses to assume any "extra" days for the truce. As we shall see, one reason Virgil is so careful to note the flight of time in this book is to prepare us for the immediate aftermath of the war council, where it is not entirely clear that the truce is over. Both my interpretation of the chronology and Gransden's demand an understanding that the truce was broken. Book 11 is a self-contained tragedy in three acts.

3. On the Latin war council, see HARDIE, "Fame and Defamation in the *Aeneid*: The Council of Latins, *Aeneid* 11.225-467," in Stahl, *op. cit.*, pp. 243-270.

4. *The Story of Camilla*, Cambridge, 1956, and *The Story of Pallas*, Cambridge, 1961. On Book 11 in general, see also ALESSIO, *Studies in Vergil Aeneid Eleven: An Allegorical Approach*, Laval, 1993 (a revised McMaster University dissertation).

5. Dawn imagery also abounds in the first book of Quintus of Smyrna's *Posthomerica*, which is devoted to the deeds of the Amazon queen Penthesilea; when she rides with her companions she is compared to the Dawn rising amidst the Hours (1.48-53), and she rises for battle with the dawn (1.138-141).

6. Mackail remarks well: "we move from a heavy thunderous atmosphere into a clearer though not a less tragic daylight."

7. The best extended explication of this *tropaeum* passage is NIELSON, "The Tropaion in the *Aeneid*," *Vergilius* 31 (1983), pp. 27-33. Her salient points are: 1) the arms of the slain must be disposed of properly (cf. the disposition of Pallas' arms by Turnus), 2) Mezentius was not only a threat to the nascent city of Rome, but also to "moral and spiritual" matters (i.e., he is a *contemptor divum*), and 3) Aeneas transforms the original, Homeric meaning of a trophy into a practical demonstration of his *pietas*. On this last point, I would note that the principal mystery that hangs over this passage is the unanswered request of Mezentius for burial.

8. See further ANDERSON, "*Aeneid* 11: The Saddest Book," in PERKELL, ed., *Reading Vergil's Aeneid: An Interpretive Guide*, Norman, 1999, pp. 195-209. Anderson devotes some attention at the end of his chapter to Camilla (the heroine of this book), though strangely he does not spend much time on the crucial role of divine influence in her death.

9. "Is not this scene from Book Eleven Roman Vergil at his truest and best?" (see RUTLEDGE, "*Pius Aeneas*: A Study of Vergil's Portrait," *Vergilius* 33, 1987, pp. 14-20).

10. There is also a hint of the idea that Iulus needs Pallas as a guardian because he is somewhat less than Pallas, wanting, as it were (so Evander is less than Aeneas, who was less than Anchises?) Does a single generation in Italy produce a fighter who is stronger than the son of Trojan Aeneas?

11. See further Gransden on 11.66-68.

12. Younger heroes, too, have a poignant innocence in the face of their impending doom: unlike older heroes, younger ones never have premonitions of their imminent demise.

13. Hornsby (*op. cit.*, p. 86) argues that Virgil is deliberately comparing Turnus to a young girl; just as the young girl wants flowers for self-gratification and self-adornment, so Turnus wanted Pallas' arms for self-beautification. This view is indefensible on two grounds. First, the point of the simile is that the plucking of the flower is equivalent to Pallas' murder, not the stripping of his armor. Second, unlike Camilla (11.779), who wrestles with the idea of wearing Chloreus' arms (in what is clearly a case of a woman's stereotypical interest in beautiful clothing), Turnus has no aesthetic reasons for stripping Pallas. Beyond all this, the girl in the simile does not pluck the flower with malice; she destroys life, but unknowingly. I do not think Virgil's audience would have equated Turnus and the girl of the flower simile; similes need not be pressed to their breaking point, and in the hands of great poets, they often take on a life of their own that is sometimes divorced from their immediate context.

14. On this passage see FRATANTUONO, "*Harum Unam*: Dido's Requiem for Pallas," *Latomus* 63.4 (2004), pp. 857-863, and LYNE, *Words and the Poet: Characteristic Techniques of Style in Vergil's Aeneid*, Oxford, 1989, pp. 185 ff.

15. On this passage see also GROSS, "Mantles Woven with Gold: Pallas' Shroud and the End of the *Aeneid*," *The Classical Journal* 99.2 (2003-2004), pp. 135-156. Gross misses the importance of *Ascanius* in the significance of the two cloaks Dido had prepared for Aeneas (and his son), and the poignancy of Aeneas' burial of Pallas in one of them (a symbol of the partial failure of Aeneas' dream).

16. On Drances, see further BURKE, "*Drances Infensus*: A Study in Vergilian Character Portrayal," *Transactions of the American Philological Association* 108 (1978), pp. 15-20, and SCHOLZ, "Drances," *Hermes* 127 (1999), pp. 455-466. For his unremarkable afterlife in literature, see BRUERE, "Some Recollections of Virgil's Drances in Later Epic," *Classical Philology* 66.1 (1971), pp. 30-34.

17. The extension of this view and allegory of Drances as Cicero and Turnus as Antony is one of the more perverse reflections in the history of Virgilian scholarship.

18. On both passages see further BURKE, "Mezentius and the First Fruits," *Vergilius* 20 (1974), pp. 28-30. Page has a splendid note: "He had reaped a harvest of fame, but the first-fruits were death: the lesson he learned was cruel and he had not to go far to learn it." The lessons (157 *rudimenta*, a rare word that occurs only here in the *Aeneid*) Pallas learned from Aeneas were brief and deadly; there is a subtext that Aeneas has not mastered the art of fatherhood well enough to safeguard his surrogate son, despite the powerful model of fatherhood he had in Anchises.

19. On Evander's speech over Pallas' body, see also Quinn, *op. cit.*, p. 236. Quinn considers Evander's speech a strangely unsatisfying collection of "stock points" of rhetoric. Evander says that by living, he has conquered his fate (160 *vivendo vici mea fata*): a striking phrase, in imitation of Lucretius (*De Rerum Natura* 1.202 *vivendo vincere saecla*, where the poet dismisses the idea of human beings of either immense size or great longevity). The meaning would then be that Evander has lived overly long and broken Nature's bonds (*supervivere*, in Servius' word). *Fata* is "one's allotted span of life" (*Oxford Latin Dictionary* s.v. *fatum* 4). Ogilvie and Richmond on Tacitus *Agricola* 45.3 note: "*fatum*: normally of natural, in contrast to violent, death" (with several examples); they take Tacitus' use of the word as evidence against the theory that Agricola died by poison. Dryden translates well: "Beyond the goal of Nature I have gone." Evander's *fatum*, like that of any father, is to die before his son, not after.

20. George Shea suggests that Evander's phrase *hic solus locus* may have added resonance given the fact that he utters the words on the very site of the future city.

21. And, indeed, *Trojan* Aeneas will win out over *Roman* Aeneas in Virgil's vision.

22. Note 184 *pater*; Virgil is emphasizing Aeneas' surrogate fatherhood over Pallas. As the father responsible for Pallas (both his life and, in death, his honor), Aeneas has seen to it that the trophies are (most probably) carried back in procession to Evander's Pallanteum. If Evander's Etruscans were the people who gave Mezentius twelve stab wounds at the beginning of the book, it is not impossible to imagine that they would see to it that the trophies sent home with Pallas are the slaughtered killers of Evander's son, not just their arms.

23. 11.182-3 *Aurora interea miseris mortalibus almam / extulerat lucem*. Servius has a note here citing Asinius Pollio, who argued that when Virgil describes the coming of a new day, he does it in language that anticipates the events of that day. So at 4.585 *Tithoni croceum linquens Aurora cubile*, the language presages Aeneas' abandonment of Dido. Here *extulerat* would look ahead to the somber raising of the funeral pyres. On the force of *interea*, "then" or "meanwhile," Conington argues that Virgil is using the adverb "loosely"—he posits a considerable amount of time between the Arcadian mourning and the burial of the dead. But it seems better to imagine that the events described thus far have taken up the whole night; it weakens the pathos of the passage to imagine that after the climactic speech of Evander the Trojan embassy and their Arcadian hosts have gone off to bed (or even spent the night in some nocturnal vigil). Virgil is admittedly very vague about the details of time here, but what is certain is that a burial truce of twelve days has been announced; Conington argues that several days are spent chopping wood and preparing the cremations, after which the burial mounds are raised on the third day (210 *tertia lux*). But it is more natural to take *tertia lux* as the third day *of this book*: the Trojans spend a full day with the funerals until night compels them to retire (a common conceit), while the Latins burn their dead through the night (a subtle reminder, perhaps, that they have lost more men), and then raise their mounds at dawn on the third day. In short, Virgil's chronology for what happens on each day of Book 11 is vague (as we might expect from any epic poet), but he is quite explicit in this book (as in no other) about the progression of the separate days. In handling dawn and dusk passages, Skutsch's *obiter dictum* comes to mind: "Daybreak and the approach of night were apparently described with loving care." Servius *auctus* takes 184 *tertia lux* of the custom of gathering the bones of the cremated on the third day (*mos erat tertia die ossa crematorium legi*). Conington cites Horace *Epodes* 17.48 *novendiales pulveres* (where see Watson, and Mankin), but the passage has little relevance to Virgil's.

24. Vance (*op. cit.*) captures the horror of the moment perfectly: "The Aeneas who immolates supplicants is the same Aeneas who, earlier, had recounted with horror Pyrrhus' stabbing of Priam's wounded son on Priam's own altar before the father's very eyes."

25. The chapter on Book 11 in HORSFALL, *A Companion to the Study of Virgil* (*Mnemosyne* Supplement 151), Leiden-New York, 1995, is devoted to the war council. But how could a "companion to Virgil" devote its entire treatment of Book 11 to the rhetoric of the debate and ignore Camilla? Note also FANTHAM, "Fighting Words: Turnus at Bay in the Latin Council (*Aeneid* 11.234-446)," *The American Journal of Philology* 120 (1999), pp. 259-280.

26. The mention of night at 11.201-202 does not indicate the passage of another separate day (*pace* Gransden); Virgil notes first the Trojan funerals, then the Latin, and indicates that the Trojans kept watch over their pyres until nightfall. The dawn at 11.210 (*tertia lux*) is the beginning of the long third and final day of the book.

27. Venulus first appears in the *Aeneid*; Ovid mentions him three times in his version of the Aeneas story (*Metamorphoses* 13.623-14.608). *Pace* Paschalis, there is probably no connection between "Venulus" and Diomedes' Homeric enemy "Venus."

28. In Diomedes' refusal to aid the Latins the audience sees the reversal of his tenacious refusal to abandon the fight at Troy at the beginning of *Iliad* 9 (one of the lowest points in Greek morale).

29. Papillon comments: "The story was that Diomedes' companions, for insult to Venus, were changed into sea-birds ('Diomedeae aves'), which have been identified with puffins. Ovid's vague description (Met. xiv 508) 'Si volucrum quae sit subitarum forma requiras, Ut non cycnorum sic albis proxima cycnis,' might indicate any large gull, or wild goose." See further Pseudo-Aristotle *De Mirabilibus Auscultationibus* 836, Pliny the Elder *Historia Naturalis* 10.126, besides Ovid *Metamorphoses* 14.14.483-511.

30. In a terribly appropriate sort of way, Aeneas will not allow Turnus to live in the same sort of dishonor that he ruefully speculates is Evander's only solace now: Pallas did not return home to *his* father as a source of shame, alive but defeated (11.55-58).

31. On Drances' speech see Highet, *op. cit.*, pp. 248-251. Williams notes: "Cicero would have enjoyed listening to this manipulation of rhetorical devices." Highet strangely comments that "Vergil could not create minor characters who come alive... Of Drances we can form no clear picture. Drances and Turnus are enemies, but almost equals." The view, however bizarre, has a venerable pedigree: "We must admit to ourselves that Vergil lacked the gift to create characters, real individual men," in WILAMOWITZ, "Vergil: On the Occasion of his Two-Thousandth Birthday," trans. Calder in *Vergilius* 34 (1988), pp. 115-127.

32. On Turnus' possible act of Roman *devotio*, see PASCAL, "The Dubious Devotion of Turnus," *Transactions of the American Philological Association* 120 (1990), pp. 251-268, and Oakley's notes on Livy *Ab Urbe Condita* 8.9.8.

33. The first imperfect (*agebant*) is durative, the second (*movebat*) inceptive.

34. See further FRATANTUONO, "Trickery and Deceit in *Aeneid* XI," *Maia* 17.1 (2005), pp. 33-36.

35. On the "sequence" of the word *praedo* throughout the poem, see LYNE, *Words and the Poet: Characteristic Techniques of Style in Virgil's Aeneid*, Oxford, 1989, pp. 161-162, and Putnam, *The Poetry of the Aeneid*, Cambridge, Massachusetts, 1965, pp. 154-155.

36. Highet (*op. cit.*, p. 28) notes: "Young people in the *Aeneid* say very little. The high-spirited Nisus talks most, with fifty-seven lines; but Pallas has only twenty-four, Camilla less than seventeen. Lavinia and Lausus, despite their importance to the plot, never speak at all."

37. Virgil carefully subordinated Camilla (and Messapus) to Turnus: *he* will face Aeneas, while the other leaders will manage the cavalry battle (note the incomplete analysis in VAN NORTWICK, *Somewhere I Have Never Traveled: The Hero's Journey*, Oxford, 1996, pp. 156-157, a study of the Camilla episode that, like many others, barely scratches the surface of one of Virgil's most carefully crafted and complex figures).

38. The whole episode is an evocation of the Roman disaster at the Caudine Forks (Livy *Ab Urbe Condita* 9.2-6, where see Oakley), though of course in Virgil's creative conception of history, the "Roman" Trojans will be spared an ambush: a brilliant reworking of history: because Aeneas and his Trojans are not destroyed, they are not "Roman."

39. On Metabus see KASTER, *Emotion, Restraint, and Community in Ancient Rome*, Oxford, 2005, p. 184.

40. See Livy *Ab Urbe Condita* 8.19-21, with Oakley's notes.

41. The Amasenus is also the river Camilla will be thrown across in her infancy (11.547); there is no obvious connection between the two passages.

42. On questions Virgil leaves unanswered (what happened to Camilla's mother and father?) Mandra (*op. cit.*, p. 109) deserves to be read by all students of the *Aeneid*: "Very kindly the poet leaves these and other questions to his future students. Vergil, of course, is not the only poet that has questions of this type. For example, in Sophocles' *Oedipus Tyrannus*, why should Apollo wait until Oedipus had four children with Jocasta, his mother, before revealing to him his parricide and his incest? These questions, in a sense, are a source of mystery; and in the far away hope that they may be answered, and always attract. A detective story explains everything, and is read only once."

43. For a useful example of the tracking of possible Hellenistic antecedents for a Virgilian passage, on 11.581-584 see TISSOL, "An Allusion to Callimachus' *Aetia* 3 in Vergil's *Aeneid* 11," *Harvard Studies in Classical Philology* 94 (1992), pp. 263-268.

44. See further my forthcoming article in *Collection Latomus: Studies in Latin Literature and Roman History*, "*Tros Italusque*: Arruns in the *Aeneid*" (2006). The ambiguity was already noted in Servius; Horsfall is hasty here in dismissing the possibility (749 *Maeonidae incurrunt* right before mention of Arruns does not settle the question, especially when followed by *tum*).

45. In Quintus of Smyrna, Penthesilea's companions have names appropriate for Amazons (one of them is called Antiman); Virgil's are the daughters of Italy, with both positive and negative traits.

46. For 11.671 *suffoso* or *suffuso*, see Gransden, and Horsfall; the former would mean that Camilla wounded the horse, the latter that the horse somehow went weak and lame in battle—either reading is possible (and both have strong support), since in the mayhem of a cavalry battle a horse can certainly be wounded, intentionally or not, as weapons fly. Gransden thinks it redounds little to Camilla's glory to have her attack someone's horse—but her glory is secure after killing eight men in eight lines.

47. Is there anything to Virgil's use of patronymics to describe the lying Aunides and Achaemenides, an Odyssean (i.e., trickster) doublet of Sinon?

48. Quintus also compares Penthesilea to a leopard (1.540-541). Virgil is probably thinking of the hawk, a member of the *Accipiter* family, a hunting species that feeds mainly on other birds and even small mammals. Camilla is exceedingly fast; the hawk flies with intermittent glides.

49. See further Hornsby, *op. cit.*, pp. 72-73. Servius is (as often) correct: the hawk was sacred to Mars, the war god. Hornsby emphasizes the connection of the hawk to Apollo (Diana's brother), which is hard to reconcile with the immediate context; he incorrectly notes that "in the simile the bird of prey pursues the weaker creature of its own species"—hawks (or falcons) and doves are not the same species.

50. On possible connections between birds of prey, wolves, and the avian metamorphosis of the incest victim Harpalyce, see further Lightfoot, *op. cit.*, p. 448 n. 175. But Virgil is mainly concerned with Camilla-Achilles as raptor. Is there any connection between birds of prey, snatcher she-wolves, the Harpies (Celaeno)? Note also the connection between birds of prey, Arcadia, and wolves made by Apollodorus *Library* 2.5.6, during the narrative of Heracles' defeat of the Stymphalian Birds.

51. On Jupiter's intervention Mackail notes on 727: "The intervention of Jupiter here to help one side, though not in direct contradiction of his declared purpose of neutrality (x. 108), since that only applied to the one day then passing, is rather unaccountable." Mackail's excuse for Jupiter (the application of his edict only to the "day then passing") is unconvincing as well as unnecessary; the real point is that Jupiter wanted the immortals to refrain from haggling over the fates of individual fighters, and here Jupiter does not

violate that aspect of his command, at least technically. Surely he does break the *spirit* of his decree.

52. The intervention of Jupiter to halt the Italian successes mirrors Hera's rousing of Agamemnon (despite Zeus' edict of non-intervention) to stop the Trojan rout at *Iliad* 8.212 ff.

53. Virgil is no shrinking violet, unsure of this or that and constantly fretting about the power of the poet and his project; on the contrary, he takes just pride in his work and is aware that while madness and terror may well live on forever in the hearts and minds of men, so also will the splendor of poetry, even if said poetry has no power to change human nature (any more than Lucretius' poem or Philodemus' writings converted everyone to Epicureanism). For the depressing opposite view, see SKINNER, "*Carmen Inane*" Philodemus' Aesthetics and Vergil's Artistic Vision," in Armstrong et al., *op. cit.*, pp. 231-244. We have no "fragile construct" here, then, but rather a powerful voice asking the question Lucan would revisit in a worse generation: why this madness, citizens?

54. See further Syme, *op. cit.*, p. 537.

55. Less likely, though intriguing, is the possibility that Diana's final triumph over Arruns in Book 11 is a faint echo of the accession of the Latin Servius Tullius to the Roman monarchy after a string of Etruscans. Servius was credited with the institution of the cult of Diana on the Aventine. Ovid's reworking of the Camilla story in his Atalanta narrative (*Metamorphoses* 8.316 ff.) follows the idea that Arruns is incensed at the idea of a woman carrying off the glory of the contest; Atalanta arouses the anger of Meleager's two uncles (to their doom, and Meleager's). See also MILLER, "Arruns, Ascanius, and the Vergilian Apollo," *Colby Quarterly* 30 (1994), pp. 171-178 (who well connects Arruns' prayer to Apollo with Apollo's intervention with Ascanius in Book 9), and note also his "Virgil, Apollo, and Augustus," in SOLOMON, ed., *Apollo: Origins and Influences*, Tucson-London, 1994, pp. 99-112 and 159-161.

56. On Chloreus in the *Aeneid* see especially G.S. WEST, "Chloreus and Camilla," *Vergilius* 31 (1983), pp. 13-20. Servius thought Camilla was rightly killed for attacking a priest of Cybele, a greater deity than Diana.

57. Cf. *Iliad* 10, where Homer takes care to note that Dolon arms for his espionage mission in wolf skin—only to be captured by Odysseus and Diomedes; the clothing was not appropriate, in one sense, for a military mission, though for a lone lupine marauder, it was most fitting.

58. On this needlessly difficult line see KEITH, *Engendering Rome: Women in Latin Epic*, Cambridge, 2000, pp. 27-31. Horsfall is right to note here that Virgil is not condemning Camilla by accusing her of a "feminine love" for spoils.

59. Camilla most probably viewed Ornytus contemptuously, with an attitude of derision: "I have grown up past that stage of forest games." Her behavior in pursuing Chloreus proves her wrong. Because she has conflated warfare and hunting, she fails to see that huntresses wear animal skins, not the robes of a eunuch priest.

60. Some object to calling Arruns a "priest" of Apollo (a designation accepted by numerous Virgilian critics, nonetheless), arguing somewhat pedantically over the precise meaning of 11.788 *cultores*. If Apollo's priests do not walk through fire, one wonders who does.

61. See further *Historia Naturalis* 7.2.19, with Beagon's note.

62. See also FITZGERALD, "Firewalking on Soracte: A Vergilian Note on Horace *Carmen* 1.9," *Vergilius* 31 (1985), pp. 59-60.

63. Many scholars note Camilla's "otherworldly," non-human traits, but fail to make the leap (cf. p. 77 of HARDIE, "Augustan Poets and the Mutability of Rome," in POWELL, *op. cit.*, pp. 59-82).

64. Harpalyce, like any wolf, indulged in raids on livestock. When Camilla was first described in Book 7, Virgil noted her javelin of "shepherd's myrtle" with sharp point (7.817 *et pastoralem praefixa cuspide myrtum*). Servius Danielis notes that shepherds used to fight (i.e., to defend their flocks) with such rustic weapons. Camilla—as leader of the Volscians—has shifted from lupine marauder to civilizing, pastoral guardian of her people. The shepherd's weapon symbolizes this transition. See further TARLETON, "*Pastoralem Praefixa Cuspide Myrtum*," *The Classical Quarterly* N.S. 39.1 (1989), pp. 267-270.

65. Apollo's rejection of half of Arruns' prayer may reflect the god's displeasure at his votary's presumptuous attitude: Arruns never *prayed* that he might return home, but made something of an arrogant assumption: "provided that this dire pest fall . . . *I shall return (remeabo)*, though inglorious, to my father's city." As Quinn (*op. cit.*, p. 249) observed, "it does not occur to him that he will be denied even this."

66. Opis' name is probably meant to evoke *both* the ideas of vengeance and careful sight (*pace* the quantity of the initial vowel); she is supposed to observe the battlefield carefully and take note of Camilla's killer, and then destroy him.

67. Horsfall on 11.826 says it best: "The dying Camilla returns the poem to its strategic focus." Arruns separated animal and rider: the lycanthrope finds humanity.

68. Some debate is possible over the exact point of Camilla's orders. Does she now fear for the city (because of the collapse of the cavalry engagement), and want Turnus to buttress it against attack, or does she want Turnus to remain in the woods and maintain his ambush, knowing that even with the loss of the plains, they can still win the day if Turnus ambushes and destroys Aeneas' infantry? No matter what, Virgil makes explicit that Turnus' abandoning of the ambush was what the "savage divine power of Jove" (11.901 *et saeva Iovis sic numina poscunt*) demanded. However Turnus interpreted Camilla's orders (in other words, whether he heeded them or ignored them), what matters is Jupiter's demand that he *abandon the ambush*.

69. For a more sympathetic (not to say bizarre) view of Arruns, cf. ROSENMEYER, "Virgil and Heroism: *Aeneid* XI," *The Classical Journal* 55.4 (1960), p. 163: "This man, gentle as a lamb?"

70. Shortly after her death, Camilla is already spurring the women of Laurentum on to patriotism. This is the beginning of her largely positive *Nachleben*. Despite her obvious flaws, Virgil has crafted an attractive girl with many admirable qualities. For the opposite view, see SMALL, "Virgil, Dante, and Camilla," *The Classical Journal* 54.7 (1959), pp. 295-301, an embarrassing example of chauvinism, an article where it sometimes seems that everything Camilla does is held under a microscope the author is not willing to focus just as sharply on Aeneas. Virgil is egalitarian in his presentation of savage violence.

71. Cf. the misguided view of Rosenmeyer, *op. cit.*, pp. 159-164: "We may why Camilla is introduced at all. Her contribution to the plot is nil." Like much of the negative commentary on Camilla, there is more than a hint of chauvinism here; Rosenmeyer accuses Camilla of "buxom bloodthirstiness."

So, in the end, is there a connection between Camilla/Cleopatra and Arruns/Arruntius (one of Octavian's commanders at Actium?) If so, it is strange that Virgil has Arruns die (and so ignominiously), in contrast to the divine favor shown the doomed Camilla (and from the *Italian* goddess Diana), and that the dead Camilla inspires the women of Italy to patriotic fervor. Unlike the Dido episode (a clear evocation of Cleopatra's effect on Antony, as well as Cleopatra's elaborate suicide ritual), Camilla's story presents a

Cleopatra who defies the expectations of a Roman audience. *This* Cleopatra, in contrast to Dido, becomes Italy's heroine. There is probably also, in the *Etruscan* Arruns, an evocation of Tarquinius Superbus' conflict with the *Volscians*; Camilla's rehabilitation in Virgil from violent, bloodthirsty werewolf to patriotic inspiration for Latin women, and Arruns' ignominious end, may reflect the historical reality of the eventual union of Volscians and Latins, together with the effective end of Etruscan political dominance in central Italy.

Chapter XII

As Turnus Sees

The dying Camilla had given a simple order for Turnus:

succedat pugnae Troianosque arceat urbe. (11.826)

Let him proceed to the fight and keep the Trojans from the city.

With Camilla's cavalry routed, Turnus is supposed to come and relieve her forces and keep the Trojans from the city. The command, as we have noted, is somewhat ambiguous; it could be an order to keep the Trojan and Etruscan horse from assaulting the walls, but its real point is the ambush plan Turnus has for Aeneas' infantry, which is the foremost concern on *Jupiter*'s mind, at least. Once Turnus heard the report from Acca of how the Volscian cavalry had been disrupted and the capital attacked by the Trojan and Etruscan horse, he abandoned his ambush plans and rushed back to coordinate the defense. As Book 12 begins, Turnus is burning with the implacable desire to accomplish what he had set out to do in Book 10: fight Aeneas, who is now encamped very close to the Latin city and Turnus' own forces. Virgil, however, is in no hurry to hasten that inevitable encounter. There is no doubt that the two men will meet in mortal combat; Virgil therefore, as in Book 11, is in no rush to accelerate the development of his plot. Book 12 is the longest book in the poem by almost forty lines; slowly, and with careful attention to what he wishes to emphasize, Virgil will let the story unfold. The two opposing sides deferred battle because of nightfall; the long day of blood was at last over. The last book will begin, and end, with Turnus.

Book 12, somewhat astonishingly, has never received a comprehensive English commentary; the forthcoming (as of 2006) edition of Richard Tarrant for Cambridge will remedy that inexcusable lacuna in Latin poetry studies.[1]

Virgil begins his march to the end with the earliest simile of any book of the *Aeneid*. Turnus wakes up like some wounded lion that has been struck in the breast by hunters and now, unafraid, at last rouses himself to war as he seethes with bloody mouth and breaks off the weapon of the *robber* (12.7 *latronis*, the only occurrence of the word in Virgil) from his chest. The simile is difficult.[2] It comes right after the description of Turnus' surveying of the broken forces of the Latins; they have been seriously hurt in the previous day's cavalry encounter, and the recent memory of the war council and its fractured deliberations is heavy on everyone's mind—especially after the death of Camilla. Turnus had promised that he was willing and unafraid to meet Aeneas in single combat; the book begins with a ring that will end with his death in its last lines. The lion has been wounded by the robber; the image is a startling one (are we supposed to think of Aeneas as a Paris-like thief of Lavinia?) that does not permit easy analysis. The "wound" the lion has received must be the blow delivered to his forces; the image of the hunters reminds the audience of Camilla the huntress and the severe blow *her* death has had on Turnus. He was unable, in the final analysis, to defend her and protect her from harm, just as Aeneas had been nowhere around to safeguard Pallas. Arruns, too, had been a thief; like some sinister doublet of Aeneas, he had shot down Camilla with secret treachery, just as Aeneas, in parallel, had been marching secretly over difficult terrain to try to launch a surprise and fatal attack on the Latin capital. Aeneas and Arruns were parallel figures in action (and in name, in another example of one of Virgil's favorite tricks). Arruns had killed Camilla (with help from Apollo), and Aeneas (inadvertently, since Jupiter did all the work) had killed Turnus' best chance to win the war. Arruns, then, can be the "robber"—a convenient way to shield Aeneas from the less than glorious associations the word implies. Aeneas does not have the slightest idea how close he came to destruction in Book 11, since he does not realize that Turnus had abandoned an ambush in the forest; all he knows is that when he arrived with his infantry force at the capital, Turnus was, unfortunately, racing to intercept him. The lion Turnus has had a long night to mourn both the loss of Camilla and the loss of what he surely realizes was his once great opportunity to win the war at one stroke. The lion, too, is Carthaginian (12.4 *Poenorum . . . in arvis*); we are reminded once again of Dido, perhaps even of Hannibal. Dido's emotional state was a severe threat to Aeneas' mission; he left her unwillingly, and without divine assistance she might well have kept him ensnared with her charms in North Africa indefinitely. The defeat of Turnus, too, has required help. Aeneas had faced serious threats to his future destiny in Carthage; the threat he faces in Book 12 will be just as intense. Dido committed suicide by her own choice; Turnus, too, could leave and follow Latinus' forthcoming advice to retire from his claims to Lavinia and the throne.

Turnus at once goes to Latinus to state his case. He notes that there is no need for the "cowardly sons of Aeneas" (12 *ignavi Aeneadae*) to take back their words and retract their pledges. On one level this is a reference to the agreement Aeneas more or less made to end the war willingly with single combat during his audience with Drances and the other Latin emissaries (11.100-121). On another level, it looks back with contempt (*ignavi*, of pusillanimous cowards) to the probable breaking of the truce that triggered the combat in Book 11. Virgil follows his usual style; he does not use a bludgeon on the reader to emphasize his points. In the context of the cavalry battle's immediate aftermath, Turnus is more contemptuous than ever of Aeneas and the Trojans, and states succinctly his willingness to end the war now. Turnus says that he will use his sword to refute the nation's "common crime" (16 *crimen commune*), a difficult expression that must be a reference to the apparent outcome of the previous day's engagements. The Latins had been in serious discomfiture before the cavalry battle (so, too, the Trojans); now they appear to everyone (especially themselves) to have suffered a serious loss. No mortals are aware of the role the immortals played in the battle, and the Trojans certainly do not realize how close they came to complete disaster. The "common crime" also refers to the charge (about to be enunciated by Latinus) that the Trojans have come by solemn divine ordinance, and that the Latins have incurred the disfavor of the immortals by attacking the chosen of heaven. If Turnus wins and defeats Aeneas, he will "refute that common crime."

Latinus' mood is one of concern and anxiety on behalf of Turnus. He realizes what happened in Book 11 with the surprise news from scouts about what the Trojans were doing; he terribly regrets and laments that affairs have gone so far down the path to destruction, and he has a certain loyalty to Turnus, whom he now addresses as a "young man outstanding in courage" (12.19). His loyalty, however, is not blind. In Book 11 he had suggested at the war council that the Trojans be offered a tract of land from his western territories, or perhaps resources and aid in outfitting ships for a journey elsewhere. The events of Book 11 have changed his outlook. Now he realizes that it is by a powerfully overwhelming divine decree that Aeneas has come to marry his daughter. Latinus now makes a proposal to Turnus. He offers him an arrangement similar to what he had proposed in Book 11 for the Trojans: land, gold, even some unmarried girl from Latium to replace the lost Lavinia. Most of all, Latinus is concerned for Turnus' safety (he knows the Rutulian cannot win). Latinus' mention of Turnus' aged father in Ardea foreshadows Turnus' own plea to Aeneas at the end of the book, and prepares the audience for the poem's final reflection on the nature of the father-son relationship.

Turnus will hear nothing of Latinus' appeals. In the immediate aftermath of Camilla's death *and* his lost chance to win everything at one stroke, he is similar to Aeneas just after the death of Pallas. He will listen to no pleas for his withdrawal from combat at this late stage. Just as Aeneas will make his choice at the end of the book, so Turnus makes his decision here; his fatal mistake is observing that when he fights Aeneas, there will be no Venus to come and snatch her son out of combat (a reference to Aeneas' combat at Troy with Diomedes, where his goddess mother saved his life, and to how Apollo saved Aeneas from Achilles with a cloud of mist).[3] Turnus is sick with rage, and Latinus' attempts at a cure for the disease only make the condition worse (12.46). As the slow progress to the end of the epic continues, Turnus is catching up to Aeneas; his reaction to Camilla's death here is akin to Aeneas' behavior in Book 10. The decisions of the two heroes frame this last book of the poem; the book begins and ends, moreover, with Turnus (cf. also the beginning of Books 8 and 9).

Amata now appears to join her prayers to Latinus'. She has recovered something of her senses from the emotional frenzy she experienced in Book 7; she makes an urgent appeal to Turnus: abstain from combat with the Teucrians (12.60 *desiste manum committere Teucris*). At first her petition seems eminently reasonable, rational and sensible (especially given what we have seen of her overwrought attitude earlier in the poem). But then a strange and troubling tone enters her speech:

qui te cumque manent isto certamine casus

> et me, Turne, manent; simul haec invisa relinquam
> lumina nec generum Aenean captiva videbo. (12.61-63)

Whatever fortunes await you in this struggle,
the same fortunes await me, Turnus: at the same time I shall leave
this hateful light, and I shall not as a captive see Aeneas as my son-in-law.

Immediately after urging Turnus not to fight, Amata acts almost as if she knows her plea is hopeless. Amata casts herself in the role of captive *Trojan* queen after the Greek sack of the city, as if Turnus were now Hector and she Hecuba or Andromache. All of this presages Amata's imminent suicide. Her mind is not quite as clear as we initially thought; like Dido, she is very close to a most irrational end. The silent and mysterious Lavinia knows full well what her mother intends. Lavinia is crying, a blush coming over her face that is at once uncomfortably embarrassing and alluringly beautiful, like roses among the lilies or the staining of ivory with scarlet (12.67-69).[4] The image is borrowed from Homer (*Iliad* 4.141-147), where it described the stain of blood on Menelaus' thighs after Pandarus had been driven by Athena to break the truce and shoot Helen's husband. In Homer, a woman stained a cheek-piece for a royal horse, but it was left in some treasure chamber where it remained more as an object of desire than a regularly used ornament. So Lavinia has been left under lock and key, as it were, in the treasure house of Laurentum; she is a civilizing restraint on potentially violent heroes and, ironically, the very source of violence for the warriors who fight for her (symbolized by the allusion to Homer's cheek-piece for a war horse), but she is also a beautiful object of desire. Turnus, unlike Aeneas, is in the emotionally painful position of being locked inside the city with the unattainable cause of his frenzy. He can see Lavinia's blush and be stirred by desire for her to arms and violence, but he cannot possess her, though she is so near. Unlike Helen, Lavinia is completely innocent, one of the most innocent characters in the *Aeneid*, in fact; she is never overcome by any divinely inspired madness that drives her to some terrible deed, never guilty of any crime or misdeed. She is also one of the most pitiable figures in the poem, aware (as here) of how she is the unwilling cause of so much sadness and strife, now most especially the likely suicide of her mother. Just as Camilla's death had brought Turnus such turmoil, so now Lavinia's tears and blush stir him to arousal and violence: he orders a herald to send word to the *Phrygian* (12.75 *Phrygio*, said with a sneer as usual; cf. 99-100 below) that he will face him on the plains before Laurentum at first light.

Lavinia's blush, with Virgil's allusion to Menelaus and the breaking of the truce in the *Iliad*, refocuses the mood of the beginning of Book 12 on the old issue: the arrival in a foreign land of a Trojan who seeks a bride someone else either had or was at least expecting to have. These scenes in Latinus' palace are the first (relatively) calm moments after the renewed outbreak of hostilities in Book 11; they serve as commentary after the fact. Turnus' instructions to the herald Idmon include both an invitation to single combat and a request that the

Trojans and Rutulians halt their current military operations (interrupted by nightfall).[5] What remains unclear (Virgil does not provide detailed information) is what Aeneas had planned by his strategy of cavalry feint and infantry attack. Did he intend to reenact the siege of Troy (where his cavalry feint would be a living Wooden Horse) and take *his* Helen, Lavinia, by force? Pandarus had broken the truce between Trojans and Greeks; had Aeneas broken his truce in order to strike quickly and win an immediate victory? He had no idea that Juno had deluded Turnus with a phantom Aeneas; he thinks, understandably, that Turnus has been scared to meet him face to face.

Turnus arms himself for battle. We feel a palpable sense of impatience as Virgil lingers over the details of the armor and weaponry. Turnus' madness and wrath is at its height, though he is curiously sedate; in the immediate aftermath of Pallas' death, Aeneas had raced over the battlefield in a frenzy of gory slaughter, while Turnus—despite the sparks that are seen to shoot from his face and the fire that flashes from his eyes—seems completely self-possessed. He is compared to a bull that is eager for the fight; the image is ominous, since it at once reminds us of a sacrificial victim (Laocoon was sacrificing a bull before Minerva's serpents destroyed him). His confidence and determination are misguided; Latinus, Amata (and Lavinia?) know that he is doomed if he meets Aeneas in battle. Virgil's model for the bull simile is a famous passage in his *Georgics* (3.210 ff., especially 232-234) where he describes the effects of amorous passions on animals. Turnus has been watching Lavinia as she blushes and cries; he is stung by an intense desire both to calm her and to possess her.

The image from the *Georgics* helps us to appreciate the rich complexity of Virgil's image of Turnus here. In the *Georgics*, the bull has lost its combat for a fair heifer. The conquered bull does not remain in the same stable as the winner, but must, sadly, go into exile in a foreign land, far from his ancestral home. Once in exile the bull is overcome with anger on account of his lost love, and, unavenged, is filled with bitter resentment. Therefore, Virgil says, the bull practices for battle in rough terrain, in sleepless nights, and prepares to charge against his "forgetful foe" (*Georgics* 3.238 *oblitum . . . hostem*), "forgetful" because he thinks he has won. This bull simile brilliantly sums up Turnus' reaction both to the Trojans and his own people. The audience alone has complete knowledge of everything that has transpired since the end of Book 10 and Juno's phantom Aeneas. Turnus, despite his ignorance of the full reality, knows that he is no coward and that he has not sought flight from combat with Aeneas; he would have a difficult time, however, convincing some people (especially Drances' supporters) of this point. The image of the bulls at war for the sake of a heifer will appear again as Aeneas and Turnus clash later in the book (12.715-724)

If anger is a crime, Aeneas shares in it with Turnus. Just as he appeared "savage" (*saevus*) at the end of Book 11, so now he appears savage and angry, though also happy (12.109 *gaudens*) at the prospect of finally meeting Turnus. It was not Aeneas' fault that the two warriors did not meet at the end of Book 10; it is more difficult to say what was on Aeneas' mind as he planned his military operations in Book 11 (where deciding the war by a single combat did not seem to be the first item on his agenda). In a poignant detail, Iulus is worried and fearful as his father prepares to do battle with Turnus; Aeneas consoles his son by teaching him about fate (12.111 *fata docens*)—he knows he cannot lose.

As if in preparation for some spectacle entertainment or gladiatorial combat, the two opposing armies advance to the open plain as soon as dawn arrives (barely at dawn, in fact, as Virgil notes—there is an excited state of eagerness as the climax of the war finally approaches). The women are once again watching from the walls of the city; they are no longer raining down weapons on attackers, but rather standing in observation of the contest about to unfold.

Juno is also watching the action on the plain. She addresses Juturna, Turnus' divine sister, who, we now learn, won her divinity as a consolation for her lost virginity: Jupiter had raped her. The detail is significant; the father of gods and men has abused both brother and sister. Juno usually feels nothing but anger and contempt for the women her husband either seduced or forcibly abducted; her cooperation with Juturna reflects Virgil's desire to emphasize Jupiter's violation of the nymph: she was no willing participant, and she shares her brother's resentments.[6] Juno remarks that only Juturna has won any favor with her out of all the women who ever shared Jupiter's bed. She has a powerful lesson for the sister of the doomed hero:

disce tuum, ne me incuses, Iuturna, dolorem. (12.146)

Learn your sorrow, Juturna, lest you blame me.

Juturna has good reason to think Juno would be angry with her over Jupiter's rape (despite her innocence); Juno begins by reassuring Juturna of her friendship. Juno's message is hauntingly simple: she can do no more. She had moved even hell with her entreaties; now she quietly nods to Juturna and invites the nymph to do anything she can to help her brother. Juno remarks that perhaps better things will come for those who are wretched (12.153 *forsan miseros meliora sequentur*); we are reminded of Aeneas' words in Book 1, where he expressed the optimistic view that one day, perhaps, it might be pleasant to recall even such terrible straits as his Trojans had just experienced in shipwreck (1.203). Aeneas had been faking his optimism then, and Juno is no doubt faking her optimism now; what she does not realize is that "better things" are indeed soon to come her way.

Juturna begins to cry. Juno feels the same rush of emotion on seeing her tears as Turnus experienced when Lavinia cried. Suddenly her words are more forceful and direct, and for a brief moment we are reminded of the powerful goddess who had sought the help of Allecto. Her sudden change of tone leaves Juturna confused (12.160 *incertam*): Juno now orders her to go and snatch Turnus from death, to incite warfare and to break the agreement the two sides have made to decide everything by single combat.

The solemn arrival of Turnus and Aeneas is full of Roman foreshadowing. Aeneas is identified explicitly as the "origin of the Roman stock" (166 *Romanae stirpis origo*), and Ascanius, who is at his side, is the "second hope of great Rome" (167 *magnae spes altera Romae*). After a long absence, Ascanius has been quietly reintroduced in the early scenes of this last book; the return of the succession motif comes as the final contest is scheduled to commence.

Aeneas makes a solemn prayer, which includes a petition to Juno to look more hospitably on the Trojans.[7] The prayer is full of appropriate addresses of reverence and respect for the gods in heaven, on earth, and in the sea; Aeneas makes an invocation of the very land for which he has been enduring so many labors, now into a twelfth book. Aeneas announces that if Turnus should win, then he and Iulus will withdraw to Evander's Pallanteum and never again bother the Latins. If he wins (and he declares that he suspects that this will be the case, and, humbly, he asks that the gods confirm this suspicion by their power), he will not order the Italians to obey the Trojans, not seek a kingdom for himself (a nod to the anti-monarchical sensibilities of later Romans, and to Augustus Caesar himself), but instead join the two peoples together under equal laws. The sentiment is noble and admirable; Aeneas adds the detail that he will give the Italians "sacred things and gods" (12.192 *sacra deosque dabo*). Aeneas' prediction of what life would be like after a Trojan victory will, of course, have to be revisited in light of Jupiter's final revelations and agreement with Juno. Aeneas makes no request for himself; he does not define the issue of his own fate in the event that he should lose the fight; instead he focuses on Iulus and his survival: if Aeneas loses, Iulus will lead the Trojan exiles to Pallanteum.

Latinus makes an equally solemn promise in return. He raises his scepter, which is made out of wood that had been encircled with bronze by some master craftsman, and remarks that his oath will stand firm forever just as the scepter will never again grow leaves or flower (12.206-211). The image is borrowed from Achilles' speech to Agamemnon in front of the assembled Greeks (*Iliad* 1.234 ff.), where the great hero declares that he will withdraw from the fight against Troy, and that a great longing will come upon the Greeks once they realize how badly they need the warrior they had so dishonored. The image, therefore, is ominous; it comes from the very beginning of Homer's *Iliad*, even as the clock ticks so quickly for Virgil's version (revision?) of the wrath of Achilles. Latinus' personal oath may perhaps remain firm forever (once the truce is broken and war resumes he will flee the battlefield), but the truce that has now been officially ratified will have a life of about fifty lines and not much chronological time in the narrative.[8]

At this point Virgil inserts an interesting detail, in a passage that leaves more to the imagination than it expresses plainly. The Rutulians, we learn, had long been thinking that the contest was not evenly matched. This could either mean that they feel Turnus is not strong enough to face Aeneas, or that Aeneas has too much support from the immortals on his side, and that Turnus is, in effect, a mere mortal fighting gods. These feelings, Virgil notes, are not new (12.217 *iamdudum*); now, as the two sides watch the coming contest, they once again sense the unfairness of the struggle. Their feelings of sympathy are increased when they see Turnus approaching the altar to make his own offerings. He is silent (as opposed to making any proud boast), suppliant, and mindful of the honor owed to the gods (220 *venerans*). His eyes are cast down (again, humbly). Most manuscripts say that his cheeks were youthful (221 *pubentes*); some manuscripts (and Donatus' commentary) read *tabescentes*, meaning that his cheeks were wasted ("his cheeks drawn," as Fitzgerald translates), much as we might note that someone does not look particularly healthy (Servius does not comment on the line).[9] His youthful body is pale (221 *pallor*), as if he were wan and weak. He is younger than Aeneas, we can assume; Virgil does not say that he is afraid to advance against Aeneas, but he is quite weak and weary. The support Turnus has from his Rutulians—and, soon enough, from Laurentines and Latins—is a link to the war council and the calumny of Drances (who has disappeared from the narrative since the burial truce ended, never to return). While at the beginning of Book 11 it seemed that a good number of Latins were eager to see Turnus either surrender or fight alone, now (probably in large part due to the events of Book 11) he has gained more supporters.

Juturna had been left unaware of what exactly she might do to help her brother. Now she sees how the Rutulians are beginning to speak openly about the impending struggle, and how they are unsure whether they should stand by idly while Turnus risks his life against Aeneas. She takes the opportunity their wavering minds allow her, in a strikingly clear example of Virgil's fondness for having the gods intervene in situations where circumstances seem ideally suited for their involvement (as with Dido in Carthage). Juturna disguises herself as Camers, one of the more respected and powerful of the Rutulians, and points out how the Latins could still overpower and outnumber the Trojans, even with their Etruscan and Arcadian allies—especially since the Arcadians are *fatales manus* (12.232), "fated" bands, "destined," that is, to be able to face Turnus only if they have a suitable foreign leader (cf. 8.499 and 11.232). Juturna follows the example of her brother Turnus, who had told the Latin war council that they still had sufficient forces with which to launch a successful attack on the Trojans (11.428-433). Juturna also recalls her brother's act of *devotio* on behalf of his people (11.440-442); if Turnus loses, she notes, he will achieve eternal fame and honors, while they will be forced to serve Trojan masters (exactly what Aeneas had shortly before said would *not* happen—"Camers" does not trust Trojan words).

Virgil has now set into motion Book 12's companion to the possible breaking of the truce in Book 11. There he left us in mystery and confusion: we were not certain exactly what had happened to the twelve days set aside for burial. Here we see Juturna engaged in direct instigation of the Rutulians—and, soon, the Laurentes and Latins change their mind about the truce as well (12.239-240). The Rutulians already had the idea of objecting to this truce; we may assume that they were still bitterly stung by the Trojan cavalry attack during the *last* truce. Just to ensure that the Rutulians will fight, Juturna sends an omen: the eagle and the swans. The eagle is the bird of Jupiter (though the swan is associated with Venus); the eagle snatches a swan and carries it off, but finally the other swans so harass the eagle that it is forced to drop the swan back into a river. (The eagle chases the swan through a red sky because the Trojans and Latins have assembled at dawn; it is still very early in the morning). The augur Tolumnius at once rouses everyone to defend Turnus from attack and fight the Trojans as an army, not by the single combat of leaders. Tolumnius now breaks the truce, not by any surprise march over difficult terrain, but standing directly opposite the amassed Trojans, Etruscans, and Arcadians. He hurls his spear, which fatally wounds one of the nine sons of Arcadian Gylippus.

Tolumnius' breaking of the truce at once sends the entire battlefield into motion. The anger, resentment, and bitter feelings of the previous engagement are still fresh on everyone's minds; one weapon is enough to rekindle the fires of total war. Once again, Juno has entered the poem with violence and madness. In Book 10, during her last appearance (she was completely absent from Book 11), Juno had been at her calmest in the entire poem as she appealed to Jupiter to spare Turnus' life. Jupiter had been willing to grant Turnus only a brief respite and nothing more. We heard nothing from Juno as the dramatic events of Book 11 unfolded, including Jupiter's not so subtle interventions. Her actions in the first third of Book 12 are a horrible version of what she had sought in Book 10: there she was willing to settle for spiriting Turnus away from danger, while here she is willing to use Juturna (whom she can later conveniently blame, if need be), just as she had previously used Aeolus, Allecto, and Iris to incite trouble and mayhem. This time, though, as we have seen, Juno is wondering if there is some better fortune awaiting Turnus' side. Her optimism will be rewarded, for once.

Tolumnius' breaking of the truce is modeled on Pandarus' similar action in the *Iliad* (4.85-219). Books 11 and 12, then, both contain elements of truce breaking; in Book 11, the narrative is ambiguous, while in Book 12, the direct evocation of Homer's episode of Trojan violation of the truce foreshadows Turnus' defeat. He is now the Paris who has stolen Aeneas' rightful bride, in another complication of the twisted Homeric heroic parallels Virgil presents continually throughout his epic. But, also, there is the fact that in Homer the *Trojans* break the truce early in the epic, while in Virgil, the same tradition of Trojan malfeasance is echoed in Book 11, even if the more formal imitation of Homer comes later and is ascribed to the Latins. It should also be noted that divine action precipitates the breaking of the truce in Book 12; Virgil is deliciously ambiguous about the same issue in Book 11.

The slaughter that now ensues on the battlefield is horribly impious and an affront to the immortals, since it takes place in the midst of the altars that had been set up to mark the solemnity of the single combat. Messapus sacrifices one man on an altar, while one unlucky Trojan has his flowing beard set on fire by an altar torch (the sort of macabre black humor that would later become a favorite trick of the Silver epic poets—Virgil is usually sparing with such grisly cleverness). In one sense, though she has no idea as yet, Juno's instigation of the destruction of the religious milieu represents something of a divine rejection of

Aeneas' announcement that in the event of Trojan victory there would be equality between Trojans and Latins, and the introduction of Trojan gods and sacred rites. The war could not end with single combat under those announced terms; the war cannot end until after Jupiter has had his chance to decide the reality of the future more precisely, and in league with Juno. Juno's rage will most definitely serve the future; while the audience was perhaps impatient for immediate single combat, Jupiter and Juno still have decisions to make that force a deferral of quick and immediate resolution. Juno had told Juturna to "dash the treaty" to pieces (12.158 *excute foedus*), entirely out of hatred for the Trojans and the wish to delay the inevitable death of Turnus: she does not yet realize how much her action serves the ultimate destiny of both Trojans and Italians.

Juno and Juturna are pawns, then, in the planning of the future settlement. The groundwork has already been established; no peace will be struck on the terms that were enunciated at first light on the battlefield. Aeneas cannot realize this any more than Juno, Juturna, or Turnus (only Jupiter knows just how much tinkering with the future destiny will allow); his actions are admirable as he calls to his Trojans and their allies, asking why they are fighting after an agreement had been struck. He feels that the terms were fair and just, and that Turnus is owed only to him according to the sacred rites that have witnessed the ratification of the treaty (12.317 *Turnum debent haec iam mihi sacra*). At this moment, Aeneas is struck with an arrow.[10]

Virgil notes that no one would ever boast of having been the one to wound Aeneas. It could well have been a chance arrow, though perhaps it was even an immortal (321 *casusne deusne*). The deed is noteworthy and carries much glory (322 *insignis gloria*), but the glory will be claimed by no one, either human or divine (one might well suspect Juturna was responsible, though the real issue is whether Juno either encouraged it or actually did it; cf. below on 12.796). Jupiter later asks Juno if it is right for a mortal to be able to wound a god (12.797), an apparent reference to Aeneas' wound (since he is destined for deification). It seems Jupiter is making a comparison between the future high rank of the divine Aeneas and the comparatively low rank of the Italian nymph Juturna (who may be immortal, but who is hardly a significant figure in any pantheon). In any case, once again, the single combat will be delayed. Aeneas will need to recover from this wound (it is not a mere glancing blow, but will in fact require divine healing). Virgil at once mentions *Turnus'* reaction to the wounding because Turnus is, presumably, marking out his opportunity to fight Aeneas: he has been silent throughout the entire resumption of hostilities.

Turnus is at once driven to hopeful frenzy by the departure of the wounded Aeneas from the battlefield. He perverts the dawn of the last day of his life by kicking up bloody dew (12.339-340 *spargit rapida ungula rores/sanguineos*, and cf. 512 below) with his horse as he charges off; Virgil compares him to the war god Mars with his retinue of horrific personifications (Fear, Anger, etc.). Virgil will now repeat one of his favorite patterns in the poem's war narrative; when the two heroes are separated (as they usually are), the one triumphs in the absence of the other. The war in Latium has three main phases: the outbreak of hostilities during the siege of the Trojan camp, the cavalry battle before the Latin capital, and now the final clashes on the same plain before the inevitable single combat. In the first sequence, Pallas died. In the second, Camilla perished and her death drove Turnus to the same sort of madness Aeneas had suffered in Book 10—though this time, the consequences will be far more significant. Now the final slaughter begins to rage; the last third of the *Aeneid* is indeed an epic of blood.

One of the longest vignettes of violence in Turnus' new *aristeia* is his killing of the son of Dolon, the Trojan spy who had aspired to win the very horses of Achilles as a reward for his bravery (*Iliad* 10.314 ff., the "Doloneia"). In Virgil's *Iliad*, the Doloneia is his depiction of the night raid of Nisus and Euryalus (a very different context, but essentially the same story). Diomedes had killed Dolon, as Virgil reminds us (12.351-352); we are reminded, however, of how the son of Tydeus has refused to come and fight the Trojans one last time. The image of Diomedes is a terrifying one in the *Aeneid* for Aeneas; the Greek hero had almost killed him years before, and his refusal to come and fight in Latium is a key indication that Turnus' side is doomed to lose. The Greeks had won at Troy and then suffered untold miseries on the return voyage; the Italians will lose in Latium, but win in the unfolding of Rome's history.

Turnus' *aristeia* affords a good example of later poetic borrowing. Turnus kills Asbytes and Chloreus; Asbytes was a companion of Eumedes', while Chloreus merely helps build a powerful four-word hexameter of casualties:

Chloreaque Sybarimque Daretaque Thersilochumque (12.363)

and Chloreus and Sybaris and Dares and Thersilochus.

It is probable that Turnus here kills the same Chloreus whose clothing so tempted Camilla (and that this is the Dares from the boxing match in Book 5). In the narrative of the *Aeneid*, this is the completion of the "revenge" for Camilla's death; now both Arruns and Chloreus are dead. The mention of Asbytes and then Chloreus gave the idea to the Silver Latin poet Silius Italicus to name *his* virgin heroine Asbyte after Asbytes (Silius was also playing with Virgil's note that Camilla derived her name from Casmilla). Asbyte is killed by a priest of Hercules ("Theron," the "Hunter"); her body, in great contrast to Camilla's, is desecrated: Theron decapitates her and puts her head on a pike. Hannibal avenges her by killing Theron; Asbyte's body is burned on a funeral pyre, while Theron's is left for vultures.[11]

The death of Phegeus balances the long description of Eumedes; Phegeus has a reckless sense of bravery as he throws himself at Turnus' chariot and tries to wrench aside the horses' heads as they foam at the bits. While Turnus is dealing death to everyone he encounters on the battlefield, Aeneas is raging (12.387 *saevit*; cf. 107 *saevus*) as he limps off the battlefield with the usual retinue of key Trojan leaders: Achates, Mnestheus, and of course Ascanius. It is not entirely clear what we are to make of the scene of Aeneas' healing. Iapyx had been a beloved of Apollo; he had been offered the gifts of prophecy, musical talent, or archery skill, but had chosen medical knowledge so he could heal his sick father (a fine example of Virgilian filial piety). His divinely inspired healing arts, however, are unable to cure Aeneas' wounds, which helps point to a divine origin for the arrow shot (again, probably Juturna). Fortunes are low for the Trojans; their leader is apparently seriously injured, and Turnus is sweeping their forces over the battlefield in headlong rout. Fairly balancing the likely divine cause of the grave wound, Venus secretly descends to the battlefield with a healing remedy from Mount Ida in the Troad (appropriately enough). This secret appearance of Venus balances her disguised visit so long ago in Carthage; Aeneas had recognized his mother as she departed, in part because of her ambrosial locks of hair (1.403) and their intoxicating scent. Here the juice of divine ambrosia is part of the curative potion (12.419), and Iapyx recognizes that he had nothing to do with this cure; it must have been divine (Aeneas does not respond to Iapyx's observation, but arms himself for his reentry into combat). Virgil seems to be using the episode of Aeneas' mysterious divine cure to provide a context for Aeneas' address to his son as he departs for battle:

> "disce, puer, virtutem ex me verumque laborem,
> fortunam ex aliis. nunc te mea dextera bello
> defensum dabit et magna inter praemia ducet.
> tu facito, mox cum matura adoleverit aetas,
> sis memor et te animo repetentem exempla tuorum
> et pater Aeneas et avunculus excitet Hector." (12.435-440)

> "Learn, boy, virtue and true labor from me,
> fortune from others. Now my right hand in battle
> will provide defense for you and will lead you to great rewards.
> As for you, see to it that when a mature age has come upon you,
> you remain mindful and, as you recall the examples of your forebears in your mind,
> let your father Aeneas and your uncle Hector stir your soul."

The passage shows the poem's usual concern for the fate of the anointed successor; Aeneas views his return to battle first and foremost as a defense of his son and a path to his son's future reward of glory. Stranger is Aeneas' admonition that Ascanius learn courage and true labor from him and fortune from others. Aeneas is once again ignorant; it was Iapyx who noted that the wound was cured by divine intervention, not Aeneas. We have just seen yet another example of the benefits Aeneas receives from his divine ancestry and his divinely inspired destiny. The force of "true labor" does not sit easily with us given Aeneas' continued receipt of help from Venus. We have noted that this recurring undercutting of the hero serves to pave the way for the now very imminent revelation about Rome's Italian destiny. But it also serves as a reminder to any leader—especially Augustus—that he cannot know the future, anymore than he can know how many of his accomplishments came through fortune and luck rather than virtue and labor. Aeneas fittingly links himself here with Hector, who had been the single best hope for Troy's survival against the Greeks; Aeneas is a sort of latter day Hector, with all the attendant Hesiodic imagery of the decline of the ages (an idea that would also appeal to Lucretius). Diomedes is not fighting in this war in part because it is not a war for his generation; he belongs to the past (as does Hector), not the present. Aeneas had been saved from Diomedes and Achilles in the Trojan War, and he has been saved just now by his mother from a potentially fatal or at least crippling wound. Virgil consistently does not let us know whether or not Turnus could defeat Aeneas in a contest utterly devoid of divine apparatus (the closest we get to such a scenario is Book 11, and even there the picture is clouded by the fact that Turnus is responding to Aeneas' plans for surprise attack and not to any solo appearance of the hero before the gates of the capital). The immortals never let us explore the issue too far without imposing some check on mortal affairs.

Juturna has been with her brother on the battlefield, and she above all recognizes Aeneas as she hears him coming (12.449 *adgnovitque sonum*). She flees away from the sound in terror (again, probably in shock after thinking she had seriously sidetracked him with her arrow shot). Turnus and his Ausonians now know fear. They had last seen Aeneas only a short time before, hobbled and weakly exiting the battle; now they see him returning in full panoply and with fierce readiness for the fight. Fittingly, Tolumnius the augur, who had broken the truce, will be among Aeneas' casualties (460). Aeneas returns like a storm that brings fear to the hearts of farmers and destroys both trees and crops; the image is a parallel to the storm off the northern coast of Africa in Book 1, and reminds us yet again of the image of urban encroachment on rural life: Aeneas is viewed as a destructive force, bringing ruin to agriculture and disturbing peaceful agrarian life. Once the Rutulians are driven into flight, Aeneas is seeks only Turnus; he advances against the Rutulian leader and ignores the fleeing soldiers.

Now Juturna plays the same role as Juno in Book 10: she seeks to save Turnus, even if it is only a delay of the inevitable. Juno had told the Italian nymph to do anything she could to salvage the doomed situation; Juturna had helped stir up combat, she probably wounded Aeneas, and now she assumes the role of Metiscus, Turnus' charioteer, throwing him off the car as if he were Palinurus, Turnus' helmsman on land. Juturna is compared to a small black swallow that flies around the home of a wealthy man, seeking some small nourishment (12.475 *pabula parva*) for her noisy nestlings (who are hungry for food, and chirping for their parent). The point of the comparison is not easy to construe in every detail. Juturna has assumed an almost maternal role in Turnus' life, seeking to protect him. She is a like a bird in that no one else on the battlefield can match her swift speed; there is no phantom Aeneas for Turnus to chase after now, but Aeneas quickly grows frustrated when he tries to outpace his foe's divinely guided chariot. The bird is black, because Juturna is seeking to help a doomed cause, and is a sort of grim wraith for Aeneas: she may well have wounded him, she certainly roused up the two armies to renewed war, and now she is keeping him from facing his enemy. The small crumbs of food the bird seeks for its nestlings must correspond to the meager fragments of time Juturna can seek out for Turnus to prolong his life. The house of the rich man is the most difficult part of the simile to explicate; it may point to the house of Dis, the wealthiest of the gods: Juturna is seeking some brief respite from Turnus' eternal sojourn there.

Aeneas had been fixated on the pursuit of Turnus, but (as Camilla so recently discovered) in battle one cannot have exclusive control over the choice of enemies. Messapus, one of Turnus' strongest allies, sends the top of Aeneas' helmet (with its crests) flying off as he hurls a weapon at him, forcing Aeneas to duck down on his knee behind his shield. Aeneas is roused to anger and finally commences a savage, general slaughter (12.498 *saevam . . . caedem*); a recurring theme in the *Aeneid* is that the constant divine action of Juno and Juturna to save Turnus from Aeneas results in the death of so many more who otherwise might well have survived the war. Virgil does not completely understand the need for such slaughter; he makes a powerful apostrophe to Jupiter:

> . . . tanton placuit concurrere motu,
> Iuppiter, aeterna gentis in pace futuras? (12.503-504)

> . . . *was it pleasing to you, Jupiter, that nations should run*
> *together in such tumult, nations about to be joined in everlasting peace?*

The poet looks ahead to the final reconciliation of Troy and Italy, while keeping the poem's ultimate revelation secret for a little longer: first more blood must be shed, and then Jupiter will negotiate with Juno to achieve her reconciliation. Significantly, as Virgil wonders who would be able to tell fully the story of great slaughter that he is about to try to relate, he calls Aeneas a *Trojan hero* (502 *Troius heros*), which emphasizes the contrast as yet between Turnus and Aeneas. Their respective peoples are soon to be united, which points again to the theme of civil war: the bloodshed about to unfold is internecine strife in the light of future history. This morning will continue its bloody progress; Aeneas and Turnus will now launch an indiscriminate slaughter, and Turnus will be so savage as to hang two Trojan heads on his chariot: the heads are "dewy" with blood (12.512 *capita . . . rorantia sanguine*), a further development of the perversion of this morning's dew with blood on both sides. The war does not cost the lives only of those who sought glory in vain, but even of men like the poor Arcadian fisherman, Menoetes, whose father had been a tenant farmer (517-520). This scene marks the most balanced presentation in the *Aeneid* of the anger and strength of Aeneas and Turnus. Juturna is keeping them apart, and separately they are both compared to fire in a dry forest (their victims are mere kindling) and rushing rivers that destroy everything in their paths. Both men are full of wrath (527 *ira*), and neither man knows how to yield to the other. We are now more than halfway through the poem's final book, and no rest from fury and madness is at hand. Cretheus, a Greek, is killed by Turnus, and Cupencus, a Sabine (as Servius' note about the divine favor he enjoyed indicates), was not saved from Aeneas, even though he was apparently a priest. The battle is perfectly balanced and even; neither side is able to gain the advantage.

Aeneas now conceives of a plan that is reminiscent of his shadowy strategy in Book 11. The idea is put into his mind, we are told, by his mother (12.554 *genetrix pulcherrima*), who had last been seen when she cured his serious wound. Did Venus have anything to do with the strategy in Book 11? Venus/Aeneas' idea is once again to attack the Latin capital. The idea is born out of frustration; the slaughter is equal, and Juturna is driving Turnus' chariot fast enough and far enough away to keep her brother from Aeneas' spear. Venus may be "most beautiful," but she is capable of conceiving violent plots; there is a deliberate contrast between her loveliness and her capacity for involving herself in wars when it suits her (an idea that Virgil also plays with in the Camilla epyllion). The logic behind Venus' idea is not easy to grasp; Virgil notes that Aeneas was set aflame by the desire for even greater slaughter:

continuo pugnae accendit maioris imago. (12.560)

At once the image of a greater fight set his mind on fire.

This attack on the city will be the companion to Aeneas' foiled plan in Book 11. There the city was guarded both by Camilla's Volscian cavalry and Turnus' infantry ambush; now it has been left unprotected (a reminder of how suddenly the war erupted on this morning once Tolumnius was roused to break the truce). As Aeneas urges his men to launch the attack on Laurentum, he notes that Jupiter is on their side (12.565 *Iuppiter hac stat*); this correct analysis of the battle situation as they prepare to strike the city reminds us of Jupiter's control over the war at the end of Book 11. We get something of a clue as to Venus' true motivation for inspiring this attack in some of the most shocking words Aeneas utters in the poem. Unless the Latins are ready to accept the yoke and confess that they are ready to obey the Trojans as conquered foes (12.568 *ni frenum accipere et victim parere fatentur*), Aeneas will on this very day raze their city to the ground just as the Greeks once destroyed Priam's Troy (569 *eruam et aequa solo fumantia culmina ponam*). These lines represent the second part of the divine action that began when Juno and Juturna started their interference in the war earlier in this book. There, as we observed, Juturna's plan to prolong her brother's life (and accomplish who knows what else) by rekindling the war and renewing hostilities served the purpose of shattering a treaty that had been struck on terms that would prove contrary to destiny. Now Venus has interfered in the war, and Aeneas makes a boast that will not be fulfilled. He will not destroy Laurentum on this day or any other, *and* the Laurentines will not accept the Trojan yoke or obey new masters. From the viewpoint of Aeneas' character development, these lines represent a horrible reversal of his earlier promises not to make the Latins obey Trojan masters. Just as the treaty Latinus and Aeneas struck earlier in Book 12 was destroyed and declared null and void by the resurgence of violence, so Venus' inspiration here and her son's vaunting will come to naught in the end. Jupiter's ultimate agreement with Juno has not yet been ratified. Aeneas views this attack on the city with fire as a way to "reclaim the treaty" (12.573 *foedusque reposcite flammis*); the "treaty" of which he speaks was the agreement to settle the war by single combat. Aeneas feels that since Turnus refuses to fight him (again, he is unaware of how Juturna is keeping her brother away), all promises are declared null and void: the "treaty" will now be regained by fire, and if the Latins are willing to engage in slaughter rather than witness a single combat between Turnus and Aeneas, then their capital will burn. Venus' intention, it would seem, is to destroy the Latins completely: in her son's word *eruam*, "I shall destroy," both a city and its way of life is to be understood. Venus, as we have noted, will be absent from the imminent decisions Jupiter will make in league with Juno (her last partner in "crime," as it were, will be her most successful ally). Jupiter's words to Juno will be, in effect, a reply to Venus' intentions here. Juturna is fighting mainly for the salvation of her beloved brother; Venus wants her beloved Troy to be reborn in Italy as the future ruler of the world (something Priam's Troy never was). She seeks both recompense for past losses and the glory of increased power in the future.

Aeneas is present among the first warriors who attack the gates of the Latin capital. He calls out for Latinus, and summons the gods to witness that he has been compelled to fight (12.581 *se ad proelia cogi*), and that twice now the Italians have broken their treaties (582 *bis iam Italos hostis, haec altera foedera rumpi*). The reference is to the original agreement in Book 7, and to the solemn ratification of a treaty this very morning on the plains that are now drenched with blood (no mention, of course, is made of Book 11 and what may have happened there with the burial truce). The Latins themselves are once again torn. Some want Aeneas to be escorted into the city to be crowned as king; others want to defend the walls against attack: the capital is torn by civil strife. All the inhabitants of the city are like bees whose secret lair has been discovered by a shepherd who sends "bitter smoke" (12.588 *fumo . . . amaro*) to fumigate them.[12] The simile concludes a ring that started in Book 7 with the portent of a swarm of bees that came from the direction of the sea and settled on a laurel tree in Latinus' palace (7.55 ff.). In Book 7 the bees described Aeneas and the Trojans, who had come to Italy to find a new foundation and a new bride in Lavinia; now in Book 12 the bees describe the beleaguered inhabitants of the city. The portent has been perverted; bees, for one thing, represent an ordered, social society, and here the confusion occasioned by the sudden attack on the gates is reflected in the bees under attack: they rush about like a mad swarm because of the smoke the shepherd has used to drive them out of their rocky home. The more peaceful omen of Book 7 has been replaced by the violent circumstances of Book 12. Bees, of course, can be an image both of social harmony and of terrible violence, depending on the context; here the bees are being disturbed by a shepherd who wants to eradicate them (569 *eruam*). The shepherd will not succeed in invading Laurentum; his planned purpose will fail. The bees of Book 7 and of Book 12 alike represent a successful order, just as the bees of Book 1 (430-436) represent the *successful* development of Carthage, which, despite its doomed future, will raise up to strong enough heights to be one of Rome's greatest threats. The slow, even leisurely exposition of Book 12's first half, with its emphasis on rival divine intervention, serves only to prepare the audience for the revelations of the book's second half. Here those preparations crystallize in the announcement of a destruction that will not take place (unlike the Greek sack of Troy, or even the predestined ruin of Carthage). The bees of Laurentum *and* the bees of the nascent Carthage both represent future urban glory. The bees that settled in the shelter of *Latinus'* house represent the absorption of Troy by *Italy*: the Trojan bees will be safe and protected, but under the cover of an *Italian* Rome. We begin to see more clearly why Virgil invests such mystery in Latinus' city (we never learn its name, even; it can conveniently be called *Laurentum*, as most commentators label it, but it remains a mythical symbol of the future, not a city that can be lamented for ever having been sacked in battle).

The attack on the city will fail, but Latinus' wife and queen Amata thinks it signals Turnus' death. She blames herself for what she perceives to be the end of the war and the disaster of an invasion. Her suicide has several affinities to the death of Dido, but these should not be pressed too far; the circumstances are very different, though what they have in common is a failure on the part of a queen to recognize that her city will have continued life, indeed a vigorous and powerful life, without her. Dido's death did not mark the end of Carthage, and Amata's does not signal Laurentum's fall. Dido had Anna in her final moments; Amata's end will be lonely and desolate. Hanging was one of the most shameful methods of suicide; we think of a crazed tragic figure like Phaedra or perhaps Jocasta. Lavinia makes another of her rare appearances; once again the ostensible cause of the war is stricken with grief. As with her previous lament, Lavinia is all too aware that she is the proximate reason for all this suffering. In one sense she is like Helen in the grip of fear on the night Troy fell; she does not know if this day will signal the conquest of Laurentum and the destruction of her old life. Even if she can anticipate an honored nuptial union to a victorious Aeneas, Virgil never allows us to think happily or in celebratory tones of the prospective marriage between Aeneas and this young girl, who remains Virgil's most elusive and mysterious character. Dissertations and books can be written on Camilla, but Lavinia remains an enigma, a masterful creation of Virgil at his most shadowy and obscure. This is the final appearance of Lavinia in the *Aeneid*; once again we can see what would motivate later poetasters to invent a "better" ending for the poem, complete with marriage between Aeneas and Latinus' daughter. The death of Amata is another work of madness (12.601 *furorem*); Amata's justifications for her suicide are irrational, since 1) Turnus is still alive, 2) she is hardly the cause of the war, and 3) her city is not being invaded. She and Dido are the only suicides in the poem; the death of Carthage's queen portended future doom for the Romans, while the death of Amata, in the final analysis, is all the more tragic because of its negligible impact on destiny.

Juturna had been keeping Turnus away from the battlefield; she had no way of knowing that Venus would counter her with a full-scale Trojan attack on the Latin capital. Turnus has fewer and fewer enemies before him as he surveys the very edges of the open plain (12.614-616); most of the Trojans and their allies have either fled his onslaught or been killed. Juturna notwithstanding, Turnus can hear the uproar of calamity and lament from the city. We have been led to think that he has no awareness of the fact that his divine sister is steering him clear of Aeneas; as with his pursuit of Aeneas' phantom, he seems not fully unaware of how far away from his enemy he has been led by divine power. Juturna, of course, does not want her brother to rush over to the city out of concern for his safety, which has been her sole motivation for everything she has done so far. Interestingly, Turnus announces suddenly that he has long recognized his sister with him in his chariot. This revelation comes in contrast to Aeneas' late recognition of his mother Venus in Book 1. Turnus begins his address to sister by asking which Olympian god willed Juturna to come down to the battlefield; he does not mention Juno. He wonders which immortal would have sent his sister down to see him die (perhaps, he thinks, Juno would not do this, given her fondness for both him and his sister). Turnus' speech to his sister reveals succinctly and poignantly his current state of emotions as the book moves rapidly to its conclusion. Juturna wants nothing more than to save Turnus' life; for Turnus, there are fates worse than death. To the bitter end, he does not think he was wrong in waging war against Aeneas and the Trojans.

Turnus' address to his sister is a companion to Aeneas' brief remarks to his son after the curing of his wound. The two scenes balance each other and offer quiet reflections from Virgil's major characters before they meet together in battle. Ascanius and Juturna are the most trusted and beloved figures Aeneas and Turnus have as they prepare for their climactic encounter. Turnus has no illusions about his chances for victory; he knows that his last, best hope had been the military engagements of Book 11. Turnus mentions the charges brought against him by Drances during the war council; since Book 9, Turnus' main burden has been trying to convince the Latins (especially in times of disaster and setback) that he is willing to fight Aeneas. Just as Italy had been so elusive for Aeneas in the first half of the poem, so Aeneas has been elusive for Turnus; the two heroes continue to parallel each other. When Saces arrives with the news of Aeneas' assault on the city (and he appears as a living witness to disaster, with an arrow wound in his face), he gives confirmation to Turnus' worst fears: Aeneas is planning to destroy the capital. Now there is once again an unavoidable delay of the single combat. Some (Drances for one) have been arguing that everything could be solved between Turnus and Aeneas. Why, then, has Venus put it in her son's mind to threaten Laurentum with fire? Saces reports that even Latinus is beginning to wonder who should be his son-in-law (12.658 *quos generos vocet*). For one thing, Latinus has no sons to defend his embattled empire. One prospective son-in-law is hurling fire at his walls. The other is off somewhere on the very edge of the battlefield, far from the disaster about to befall his prospective parents.

Aeneas had admonished his son to learn virtue and true labor from him, and fortune from others. In light of Turnus' words to his sister Juturna, who will be grief-stricken as he prepares to rush off to relieve the capital, we see a great sense of irony. "Fortune" has abandoned Turnus; no one could learn of fortune or chance from Turnus, at least not any positive sort of luck.

Turnus' reaction to Saces' words is understandable. He feels a strong sense of shame (667 *pudor*) that he is not standing as the final defense before the city. He feels grief (*luctu*) once he hears of Amata's suicide. He feels a sense of courageous virtue (*virtus*), because he feels called to rush to the city, even if the battle there proves hopeless. He feels love (*amor*) mixed with madness (*furiis*), because Lavinia is in the city, and he wonders (as do we) how an assault on the very city that houses the allegedly beloved object of desire for both himself *and* Aeneas can possibly be a good thing. Paris had won Helen by romantic stealth; is Aeneas going to seize Lavinia by force, perhaps over the dead bodies of her parents? We are, again, reminded of Troy on its final night and the plight of the women of that wrecked city. At this moment, as Saces finishes reporting the news of Aeneas' attack on the city, we are told that the light was restored to Turnus' mind:

ut primum discussae umbrae et lux reddita menti,
ardentis oculorum orbis ad moenia torsit
turbidus eque rotis magnam respexit ad urbem. (12.669-671)

As soon as the shadows were scattered and the light returned to his mind,
he turned the burning orbs of his eyes to the walls
and, greatly disturbed, from his chariot gazed back on the mighty city.

Turnus is not suddenly calm and free from all madness. Quite the contrary, in fact: he soon asks Juturna, his temporary charioteer, to let him rage one more time before the end (680 *hunc, oro, sine me furere ante furorem*). His eyes are burning as he gazes at the city (which is under fiery assault). What does it mean, then, that the shadows have been dispelled and the light returned to his mind? Venus' act of inspiring her son to attack the city has seriously hampered Aeneas' public relations campaign in Latium. Before the attack, Troy's hero had repeatedly assured the Latins that he had no plans for conquest, no aspirations to destroy their city and way of life. All of that now seems to be a lie. Turnus had earlier been confronted with the message from both Trojans *and* some of his own beleaguered people that he and Aeneas could settle everything alone. To his incredible frustration, Aeneas was ever receding, ever distant, ever out of his reach (thanks mostly to Juno and Juturna). He felt thoughts of self-recrimination, even: maybe I am wrong. Now he feels vindicated: the groans of misery from the city and Saces' plea for help (as he stands bloody and mutilated) validate every prejudice he ever felt against the Trojans. Now he is certain that they are invaders, bent on the destruction of the Italians. The light has indeed been returned to his mind; Venus has no concern for the fate of the Italians (she is fixated only on her son, grandson, and his people). Her willingness to let Laurentum be burned is telling; she will not have her way, though, as the settlement of the ultimate destiny of both races draws nearer.

Turnus rushes to the city, and Aeneas instantly gives up the attack as he rejoices that he can at last meet the man who is the object of his rage. Turnus is compared to a huge stone that has been dislodged from a height because of wind or storm; Aeneas, in terrible contrast, is compared to Athos, Eryx, or the Apennines: Virgil leaves no doubt who will win. The two heroes had been close by each other at the end of Book 11, but here the context is very different: all the raging armies stop in their tracks as their respective leaders have eyes only for each other. Turnus orders all the Rutulians and Latins to cease operations as he appears (he has had enough shame from seeing others die for what he is willing to consider his personal cause), and there is an amazing freeze in the action: battering rams and siege defense all stop their martial action at once. The two men finally clash, and Virgil makes a fabulously ambiguous remark, very much in his usual style, one of his most moving descriptions of combat:

... fors et virtus miscentur in unum. (12.714)

... *chance and virtue are mixed into one.*

The laconic comment on the two heroes and their fight hearkens back to Aeneas' words to Ascanius and Turnus' to Juturna. Fortune and courage are the two qualities that mingle and become one mass on the battlefield. Does Aeneas represent the former, and Turnus the latter? Do both Aeneas and Turnus have both chance and virtue? Turnus is like Hector (indeed, the simile of the rock is borrowed from *Iliad* 13.136-141, where it describes the Trojan hero in battle), but he is also Achilles, who knew full well that he would die soon after he returned to battle to avenge Patroclus' death (unlike Aeneas' entry into battle after Pallas' death, which had none of the Achillean image of the hero who knows he will die). Turnus is both Hector *and Achilles* as the last book of the epic unfolds (exactly as the Sibyl predicted). Aeneas could realize that Turnus' death had affinities to Hector's, and, besides his personal ties to Hector, he had heard the Sibyl predict the presence of "another Achilles" in Latium; Turnus, then, will have a surfeit of Homeric heroism. This surfeit allows Aeneas to forge new ground for himself as a peculiarly *Roman* hero: such was the point of the solemn injunction from Anchises to his *Roman* son in the underworld of Book 6. Aeneas, to be sure, plays the roles of both Hector and Achilles at various points in the poem (he is like Hector in that he is the strength of his people and that he is consistently linked with Hector as the bulwark of Troy, while he is like Achilles in his killing of Turnus/Hector). But the principal point of comparison between Aeneas and Achilles is the fact that like his Greek predecessor, the Trojan hero will kill his enemy. As we have noted, there is nothing in the *Aeneid* of the Achilles of *Iliad* 24, no scene in Virgil's *Iliad* to balance that moving visit of Priam to Achilles' camp. The omission is glaring.

Jupiter weighs the fates of both Aeneas and Turnus in a scale to see whose fate sinks down in death; the image is Homeric (*Iliad* 22.209-212), where it describes the fate of the doomed Hector. Which of the two heroes does the labor damn (12.727 *quem damnet labor*)? Now Virgil reintroduces the concept of *labor*, another of the ideas Aeneas told his son to learn from him, not from others. The labor, it seems, is on both sides; Aeneas must engage in an effort to fight Turnus, and Turnus must do the same on his side. If there is labor on both sides, there is also fortune and luck: Turnus strikes first, and his sword mysteriously breaks with a snap as he raises it, leaving him unarmed and forced to run away quickly in flight. The beginning of the combat is inauspicious for Turnus; the sword breaks just after we learned of Jupiter's weighing of the two men's fates in the balance. Virgil gives a reason for the breaking of the sword. In his haste to do battle, Turnus had picked up the wrong sword. Instead of his divine weapon, he had grabbed the sword of Metiscus, his charioteer (whose place his sister Juturna had taken). At least, Virgil says, this is the report (735 *Fama est*); some explanation is owed for why the hero's sword would suddenly snap. Virgil's description of the commencement of the combat continues all the themes he has already used in his portrait of Aeneas and Turnus at war. Turnus has been desperate to meet Aeneas, who has always seemed just out of reach for one reason or another. Now, at the last minute, he has forgotten his sword, and as he runs around the battlefield in flight, he calls out to his men and asks them to bring it to him so that he can face Aeneas with a divine weapon. Turnus was a fool to forget his weapon in haste, but the scene of the two men facing off, one armed with a sword of Vulcan and the other with a mere mortal sword of Metiscus, provides a powerful commentary on the nature of their combat. Turnus cannot hope to fight against the fated victory of Aeneas. He has no chance, and yet still he fights. Some might call this madness. But in one important sense, Turnus has more to fight for than Aeneas: he is close to the territory of his own native land in Ardea, and, thanks to Venus' intervention, his hasty rush into battle comes as a perceived defense of the Latin capital against a siege. He rushed off to defend the capital so quickly that he forgot his sword: Venus' action has had far-reaching consequences. Aeneas hears Turnus as he calls to his men, and he utters threats. If *anyone* should come to aid Turnus by giving him his divine sword, he will destroy the capital. Even now Aeneas is fixed on the idea of destruction. Surely an even battle would call for even weapons (we are reminded of Aeneas' concern for fairness during the boxing match, where Entellus did not fight Dares with his Herculean boxing gloves). Turnus' mortal sword has broken, and Aeneas threatens to raze the city if anyone arms Turnus against him. Curiously, Virgil notes that Aeneas is a bit limp from his arrow wound earlier (12.746-747, 762). His wounded state is aggravated as he is forced to chase Turnus; the aggravation causes him to be angrier and angrier as he feels delayed from taking his vengeance for Pallas and ending the war. What happens next is fascinating.

There was a wild olive tree (766 *oleaster*) that was sacred to Faunus and invested with ancient religious awe.[13] The Trojans had cut it down so that they could have an unimpeded plain to advance over in marshaled ranks. Aeneas' spear was lodged in it (an affront to Faunus and to the tree's nymph). Since he found it impossible to chase Turnus down (because of the arrow wound), he decided to try to wrest the spear from the oak stump. Turnus, in terror, called on Faunus to protect him by refusing to allow Aeneas to pull the spear from the desecrated tree. Faunus agreed, and the delay allowed Juturna time to bring Turnus his divine sword. Juturna's action evens the contest (since no one could have reasonably argued that Turnus should be deprived of a divine weapon against Aeneas'). Venus, however, is enraged. She immediately plucks the spear from the tree for Aeneas (so now he has two weapons instead of one), and the two men stand a bit more evenly balanced. Had Aeneas not received the spear, the two men would still have been equal; Juturna's action so angers Venus that she feels the need to increase Aeneas' odds.

The failed attempt to pull the spear from the oak is reminiscent in these final scenes of the poem of the (successful) attempt to secure the Golden Bough. There, we saw that Aeneas faced a hesitant Bough because he disregarded the Sibyl's instructions to pluck it, and instead tried to wrench it from the ground using the same action Catullus once used to describe a rampaging lion of Cybele (no doubt the connection to the Trojan Aeneas was in Virgil's mind when he carefully chose his verb). Here, Aeneas feels frustration because of Turnus' flight. Turnus is not being divinely aided as he runs away, but Aeneas *was* wounded: strangely, the wound still hurts enough to dull his step, even after Venus' ambrosial divine healing. His frustration finds expression in threats to destroy the Latin capital if anyone gives Turnus his sword. Of course, Turnus would not be fleeing *if* he had his own sword.

Once the weapon problem is solved, the scene changes to the divine realm. Jupiter approaches Juno, who has been watching the contest unfold. He complains that she has caused enough delay; she was allowed to send storms and start wars, but now nothing more can be allowed to prevent the destined, fated outcome. He upbraids her for allowing Juturna to return Turnus' divine sword; he accuses Juno of being the source of the nymph's audacity (a reference to Juno's earlier instructions to Juturna to do whatever she thought necessary to help her brother—one gets the impression Juturna needed little prompting). Aeneas will be a god, Jupiter reminds his wife, and there is nothing she can do about it. Jupiter already envisions Aeneas as a god; he asks if it was right for a mortal to be able to wound an immortal.[14] The reference is apparently to the arrow that struck Aeneas earlier; the nymph Juturna is immortal (cf. 12.879-881), though in mythology nymphs typically lived to spectacular, though not infinite, ages. Juno, for her part, denies that she told Juturna to do anything against Aeneas with a bow (12.815 *non ut contenderet arcum*), and she swears by the Styx that this is the truth; Juturna, of course, could have acted independently, and Virgil leaves the whole matter somewhat cloudy (we probably should believe Juno's Stygian oath, after all—but who can really say?). Virgil refuses to tell us who shot Aeneas. Juno freely admits defeat; she could be down on the battlefield, fighting on behalf of Turnus and his Rutulians, but instead she is only a spectator, watching the contest from a cloudy perch (792 *fulva . . . de nube*).

Venus, significantly, is nowhere; the two spouse-siblings are alone. Juno has one plea for her brother and husband. Her plea is a response to his emphasis on Aeneas' divinity and Turnus' doomed future:

> illud te nulla fati quod lege tenetur,
> pro Latio obtestor, pro maiestate tuorum:
> cum iam conubiis pacem felicibus, (esto)
> component, cum iam leges et foedera iungent,
> ne vetus indigenas nomen mutare Latinos
> neu Troas fieri iubeas Teucrosque vocari
> aut vocem mutare viros aut vertere vestem.
> sit Latium, sint Albani per saecula reges,
> sit Romana potens Itala virtute propago:
> occidit, occideritque sinas cum nomine Troia. (12.819-828)

> *This I beg from you, which is bound by no law of fate,*
> *for Latium, for the majesty of your own children:*
> *when soon they establish peace with a happy marriage—let it be so,*
> *when soon they join their laws and alliances,*
> *do not order the indigenous Latins to change their name*
> *or to become Trojans and be called Teucrians*
> *or change their language or their style of dress.*
> *Let it be Latium, let the Alban kings reign through the ages,*
> *let the Roman offspring be powerful with Italian courage;*
> *Troy has died, so now let her die together with her name.*

When the poem started, Juno had wanted nothing more than the destruction of the Trojans. She hated them already, even without any prophecy or oracle about how one day the Romans, born from Trojan stock, would destroy her beloved Carthage. Here she makes very specific requests. First, she wants the old Latin name to remain the same. She does not want the Latins renamed "Trojans" or "Teucrians." She does not want the Trojan language or Trojan dress (the object of so much derision throughout the poem) to be adopted by the Latins. She wants Troy dead, together with the very name of Troy. She favored the Rutulians and Latins; she is willing to continue that favor, even though it means that one day Carthage will fall to them (though the peaceful reconciliation of this book will not prevent her from taking up the cause of the Carthaginians later in history, as ponderously depicted by Silius Italicus in his *Punica*!) She is willing to settle for the death of Troy, even at the price of Carthage's eventual destruction. Juno's solemn future imperative *esto* hearkens back to the same decree of her husband during the divine council in Book 10 (67 *esto*): Juno here asks for a codicil, as it were, to be added to what Jupiter had so firmly announced earlier.

Juno's wish for the abolition of Trojan customs and way of life is not a surprise *per se*. From the poem's very beginning she sought the total destruction of the Trojan race. The Greeks had been allowed by fate to sack Troy and deal it its second and most lasting devastation. Venus had been consoled from the outset of the *Aeneid* with the promise (at least as she understood it) that Troy would be reborn in Italy, and, in fact, one day grow so powerful that it would take its vengeance on the Greeks who had long ago sacked the mother city in the Troad. Throughout the poem, the clear understanding of Aeneas and his men is that they are going to reestablish in Italy the city they lost in Asia Minor. Jupiter had not explicitly told his daughter in Book 1 that Trojan customs, language, and dress would be preserved in the new foundation. But no one would criticize Venus (or Aeneas) too strongly for their expectations. Virgil faced a difficult problem, though, in composing his *Aeneid*. Italy was *Italian*, not Trojan. Here, in Juno's plea to Jupiter and his reply, we find Virgil's solution to the conundrum.[15]

Jupiter's response is immediate and gracious:

sermonem Ausonii patrium moresque tenebunt,
utque est nomen erit; commixti corpore tantum
subsident Teucri. morem ritusque sacrorum
adiciam faciamque omnis uno ore Latinos. (12.834-837)

*The Ausonians will retain their native speech and customs,
and their name will remain as it is; mixed with them only in body
the Teucrians will sink down. Customs and sacred rites
I shall add and I shall make them all Latins with one voice.*

The first consideration we might make in reaction to Jupiter's promise here, his revelation of the future Roman reality, is why only now? Would Juno's anger and rage have been quelled much earlier if this news were given sometime before the last hundred or so lines of the poem? How many Italian and Trojan lives have been lost because Juno—and Turnus—thought that the victory of Aeneas would, in the end, mean the death of Italian custom and the imposition of the Trojan way of life?[16] Aeneas had promised much the same (cf. 12.189-194) before he reached such a point of madness that he threatened to burn down the capital (courtesy of Venus, mostly, and to a lesser extent Juturna). The Ausonians, we now learn, will keep their language and customs, and their name (they will not be called "Trojans" at any time). The Trojans will be mixed in with the Italians in body (they will intermarry and have children together), and they will "sink down" (836 *subsident*)—not a verb that would, one suspects, please Venus or Aeneas.[17] They will all become Latins, with one language (the pride of the poet in the Latin language is palpable throughout this passage). Aeneas had said that he would grant the Latins their gods and their sacred rites (192 *sacra deosque dabo*); Jupiter here says that he will let the Latins have their customs and their sacred rites. Both Aeneas' and Jupiter's choice of words is a bit vague on one point; Aeneas says "I shall give sacred rites and gods" in the sense of "I shall grant (the Latins) their gods," though there is also a tinge of "I shall give them *my* gods" (a delicious ambiguity, whereby Aeneas can be seen to defend both the native Italian deities *and* the cults of, for example, the household gods he brought with him from Troy). Here, too, Jupiter follows up his declaration that the Trojans will sink down with the announcement that he will "add customs and the rites of sacred things and make them all Latins with one voice." Contextually, especially after "the Teucrians will be mixed in body *only*," the force of Jupiter's words is that he will grant the Latins their way of life and religious practices, more than it implies that he will add *Trojan* customs and religious practices to Latin ones, though it does also cover such "Trojan" customs as the Penates Aeneas brought from Troy. Small wonder, then, that the worship of the *Magna Mater*, which would have needed no explanation or excuse were Rome Trojan, only entered Roman life late (204 B.C.), during a time of national calamity (the Second Punic War), and was not open freely to all Roman citizens. In any case, as we saw especially at the beginning of Book 7, it is Italy, not Troy, which holds most of the future symbols of Roman religious and legal tradition (7.170 ff.); this makes perfect sense, of course, since a main point of Books 7 and 8 is how the future Rome will exist on the very site of central Italy where Latinus and Evander (and even Turnus) have their dominions (in some sense, Rome is more Greek than Trojan!) No, Troy is finished, Jupiter grants; Carthage is too, of course (the basic dictates of destined history remain completely valid and operable)—but now Juno is more than happy.[18] The city she so hated will be truly and finally dead. We shall never see her again in the *Aeneid*; she leaves her husband's presence as the happiest character in Book 12:

adnuit his Iuno et mentem laetata retorsit.
interea excedit caelo nubemque relinquit. (12.841-842)

Juno nodded to these things, and, now happy, changed her mind.
Then she departed from the heavens and left the cloud behind.

The great classicist Eduard Fraenkel felt that Juno had scored "a modest point" in Book 12.[19] But there is nothing modest or minor about Juno's victory here. Venus is absent (she too will not reappear in the poem). Juno has won a great triumph over her rival; she may not have saved Carthage, but she has destroyed Troy finally and definitively. Virgil has brilliantly allowed Aeneas to remain firm and unchallenged in his role as Roman progenitor and father of the future, but he has significantly muddied the waters of that future, at least from the Trojan point of view. Jupiter could never have announced to Venus in Book 1 that the Teucrians would sink down. The agreement that Trojan dress will disappear is an answer that would have pleased Iarbas, or Numanus Remulus: a major source of contempt has been removed from the Trojan remnant's future. We are left so near to the end of the *Aeneid* with a happy *Juno*; Venus had her chance for a happy departure in Book 1—sometimes, it would seem, impetuous caprice brings quick but only partial gratification, while patient bitterness reaps great rewards. Small wonder that Jupiter assures Juno that the future Romans will outdo even the gods in *pietas* (12.839 *supra ire deos pietate*): the gods and goddesses of the *Aeneid* have not necessarily been the best exemplars of *pietas*, any more than the Homeric gods are. *Pietas*, the great quality of Aeneas (typified in his rescue of father and son from the burning city of Troy), is destined to be the defining trait of the Roman people. And, of course, Juno can be comforted for the future loss of Carthage by the assurance that no nation will cultivate her rites more than the Romans (840): she will find in the Romans her most earnest devotees (a nod to her future place in the Capitoline Triad). Juno does not make any mention of Turnus and his fate; she lacks the sisterly love for him we find in Juturna, and, in any case, her feelings for Turnus are quite similar to her feelings for Aeneas: she has no real concern for the individual, only for what the individual represents. Now that she sees how Turnus' side will be in the ascendant, and Aeneas' Teucrians will be sinking down, she has no reason to pursue the one hero with hate and defend the other with her favor. Both men are now irrelevant to her.[20]

Interestingly, in the version Livy records (*Ab Urbe Condita* 1.2), it is *Aeneas*, not any god, who determines that both the Trojans and the original inhabitants of Latium (the *Aborigines*) will be called *Latini*. In Livy's account, Aeneas' intention was thereby to rally Latinus and his men against the threat from Turnus and Mezentius, by creating a united, *Latin* front against the Rutulians and Etrurians.

The poem has slightly more than a hundred lines left, but its climax on the divine level has now come and gone. The immortals—at least the ones we hear about—are content with the settlement that has been reached through the reconciliation of Juno. Now the mortals must settle their differences. Juno's wrath and rage, in effect, will soon be passed on to Aeneas. The madness that had driven her on in anger and rage so needlessly (given the final revelations of Jupiter) will now infect Aeneas. He will not be made aware of the agreement just sealed between Jupiter and Juno.

Jupiter is now closer to Juno than he has ever been in the chronology of the *Aeneid*. Just as Juno used the Fury Allecto to pursue her goals in Book 7, so now Jupiter will also invoke darker powers. The fiendish powers he now calls upon are not the same as the traditional Furies of Tartarus, but they evoke the same hellish world. The twin *Dirae*, Virgil notes, are the daughters of the Fury Megaera (Allecto's sister) and Night. Jupiter wants to remove Juturna (once a victim of his amorous advances) from the battlefield and her brother. He was clearly incensed that such a lesser figure in the cosmic hierarchy decided to attack Aeneas (ironically, she displays a sort of *pietas* in her constant loyalty to her doomed brother). Juno's summoning of Allecto had been designed to instigate a war; Jupiter's summons of one of the two daughters of Megaera and Night is designed to hasten this war's conclusion by removing Juturna from the fight. The calling of "one of the two" (12.853 *harum unam*) is perhaps an unconscious echo of Aeneas' use of one of the two cloaks (11.76 *harum unam*) Dido had made for him (and probably Ascanius) to bury Pallas. The Fury descends to earth like an arrow shot by a Parthian or a Cydonian (i.e., Cretan); the reference to Crete is a nod to Jupiter's connection with the island (he was said to have been safely smuggled there as a newborn, to escape his father Saturn's desire to swallow him), while the reference to the Parthians is more difficult to construe. No mention of one of Rome's bitterest foes is positive—and neither are the Furies ever benign. In mentioning them immediately after the reconciliation of Juno, who so prominently invoked a Fury at the outset of this war, Virgil closes the ring started in Book 7 and once again muddies the waters: Jupiter is not very different in the end from the sister he acknowledged to be not unlike her brother:

> "es germana Iovis Saturniaque altera proles,
> irarum tantos volvis sub pectore fluctus!" (12.830-831)
>
> *"You are the sister of Jove and the other child of Saturn:
> what great waves of wrath you turn over in your heart!"*

It is difficult to determine the correct punctuation: a question, an exclamation, or a declarative sentence (as the Oxford texts print)? I prefer an exclamation; Jupiter's mood here is one of casual consolation; at once he tells Juno to let go of her madness (*submitte furorem*), since he assents to her wish (*do quod vis*) with no objection or protest, no codicil or exchange. Jupiter's words here probably mean that as the sister and wife of the father of gods and men, Jupiter sees no reason why Juno should be so upset and angry (after all, she need only ask, it seems, and she receives). Underlying this is the notion that if there are immortals, they do not care about our suffering. Virgil does not make clear whether Jupiter's agreement with Juno came only after all the rage and madness she exercised through the last twelve books. Could Juno have received what she wins here all the way back in Book 1? Perhaps yes, though more likely we see in Juno's transformation from angry, bitter goddess to joyful future patroness of Rome a parallel to Aeneas' own journey: she has won much by her madness, while Aeneas will lose much when he surrenders to madness. Juno opened the poem with furious wrath; Aeneas will end the poem in the same way.

The Fury transforms herself into a small bird of ill omen (probably a screech owl, traditionally associated with cemeteries and portents of death). Turnus is driven numb with fear when it appears; the bird beats against his shield as if Jupiter himself, its master, is fighting the Rutulian champion. Juturna at once recognizes the Jovian origin of the hellish bird. She is resentful: Jupiter stole her virginity by rape, and now her "reward" of immortality means that she can never hope to go with her beloved brother to the lower world. Juturna is immortal, and her bitterness will be eternal. She covers herself in the gray cloak of a river deity (cf. 8.31-34) and buries herself in her spring (12.886 *et se fluvio dea condidit alto*)—an image of her perpetual death.

Aeneas now assures Turnus that nothing can save him; he brandishes his weapon and calls him to the final combat. Juturna had recognized Jupiter's Fury; Turnus, too, understands what he is facing:

> ille caput quassans: "non me tua fervida dicta terrent
> dicta, ferox; di me terrent et Iuppiter hostis." (12.894-895)
>
> *That one shaking his head said, "Your hot words do not terrify me,*

fierce one: the gods terrify me, and Jupiter is my enemy."

Turnus is not contemptuous of the gods; he is no Mezentius. He understands that the powers that be have ordained his death in battle against Aeneas, just as his Greek predecessor and heroic model Achilles knew that fighting Hector and avenging the loss of Patroclus would be followed by his own doom. Turnus has come to the full realization that Jupiter has blocked him at every juncture of the path. Turnus had been compared earlier to a stone crashing down from a height; now he picks up a boundary stone that, we are told, scarcely twelve men of Virgil's day would have been able to pick up—another evocation of one of the poet's favorite themes, namely the decline of the ages and the heroic (902 *heros*) glory of a lost world. Turnus hopes to cast the mighty boulder at Aeneas, but he is unable to throw it far enough; his knees go weak and his blood freezes in his veins. He does not recognize himself (903 *se nec cognoscit*) as he runs forward with the rock held high. The stone he is using as a weapon was a boundary stone, a dividing mark to make clear the division of land. With the unification of Trojans and Italians, the removal of this huge stone signifies the end of division; such a stone could never be used by an Italian to kill a Trojan, or to mark where Trojan land started and Italian land ended. The stone had been set up to decide a point of contention (898 *litem ut discerneret*); here Turnus uses it to the same end (he does not, after all, know anything of what Juno has learned from Jupiter), and he is doomed to fail: all contention is now settled and finished, at least so far as the immortals are concerned. Virgil compares Turnus to a man in a dream; everything he tries seems impossible for him. He is unable to speak. He lacks all of his customary strength. Virgil gives an explanation for the sudden enervation of the hero's body: the "dread goddess" (914 *dea dira*), Jupiter's Fury, denied him success (*successum . . . negat*). Allecto had roused Turnus to war; now this daughter of the Night prevents him from fighting with his usual ability. Turnus sees his Rutulians, and the city; once again, he feels tremendous frustration, since *he* knows that there is some divine explanation for his faltering step and weak performance, but—just as no one else really understood the episode of the phantom Aeneas, or the role of Juturna in steering him away from Aeneas earlier on this day, so now he suspects that he appears to be a failure in the eyes of his men. He may also be afraid for his people and Latinus' city—there have been threats from Aeneas to burn it—and he may suspect that even his death will not really satisfy Aeneas' rage, despite all the promises to the contrary. He sees no escape: he has no strength to face his opponent, thanks to Jupiter's Fury. And, indeed, as Aeneas casts his weapon at Turnus, we see a glimpse of divine help: the spear he throws carries with it "dire destruction" (12.924 *exitium dirum*), an echo of the power of the Jovian Fury. The help Aeneas has received is the Fury's weakening of Turnus' body; Virgil will once again deprive us of the chance to see the two men fight on equal terms, without any divine interference. Turnus is seriously wounded in the thigh, and falls to the ground with a huge crash. The last lines of the poem deserve to be quoted at length:

ille humilis supplexque oculos dextramque precantem
protendens "equidem merui, nec deprecor" inquit;
"utere sorte tua. miseri te si qua parentis
tangere cura potest, oro (fuit et tibi talis
Anchises genitor) Dauni miserere senectae
et me, seu corpus spoliatum lumine mavis,
redde meis. vicisti et victum tendere palmas
Ausonii videre; tua est Lavinia coniunx,
ulterius ne tende odiis." stetit acer in armis
Aeneas volvens oculos, dextramque repressit;
et iam iamque magis cunctantem flectere sermo
coeperat, infelix umero cum apparuit alto
balteus et notis fulserunt cingula bullis
Pallantis pueri, victum quem vulnere Turnus
straverat atque umeris inimicum insigne gerebat.
ille, oculis postquam saevi monimenta doloris
exuviasque hausit, furiis accensus et ira
terribilis: "tune hinc spoliis indute meorum
eripiare mihi? Pallas te hoc vulnere, Pallas
immolat et poenam scelerato ex sanguine sumit."
hoc dicens ferrum adverso sub pectore condit
fervidus. ast illi solvuntur frigore membra
vitaque cum gemitu fugit indignata sub umbras. (12.930-952)

*That one, humble and a suppliant, raised up his eyes and his
right hand in prayer and said, "Indeed I have deserved it, and I do not beg;
exercise now your lot. If any concern for my miserable
father is able to touch you, I pray (and you had such a father in Anchises)—
take pity on the old age of Daunus and send me back to my own people,
or, perhaps, send back my corpse,
deprived of the light. You have conquered and the Ausonians see
that the conquered one raises his hands; Lavinia is your wife:
do not persist any longer in hatred." Aeneas stood fierce in arms,
turning his eyes over him, and he stayed his right hand;
and now more and more as he hesitated, the words began to
bend him, when on Turnus' shoulder there appeared the unlucky baldric,
and the sword-belt with its well-known studs of the boy Pallas
shone forth, whom Turnus had struck down, vanquished with a wound,
the sword-belt Turnus was now wearing on his shoulders as his enemy's insignia.
Aeneas, after he had drunk deep of the memory of his savage sorrow
and the spoils, grew hot with madness and anger and said terribly:
"Are you now to be snatched away from me, clad in the spoils of my own?
Pallas, Pallas sacrifices you with his wound
and takes the penalty from your criminal blood."
After saying this, hot with rage he buried the sword full in the chest.
But for that one the limbs are dissolved with a chill
and life fled with a groan, indignant, to the shadows below.*

The situation is almost identical to the end of Book 10 and the death of Mezentius. Turnus does not necessarily beg for his life. He asks either to be sent back alive to his aged father Daunus (to provide some comfort for the old man in his last years) or to be sent back as a corpse (that is, for burial). He asks either for life or for burial. Aeneas did not answer Mezentius' request for burial; he will offer no reply to Turnus' request either.[21] We can assume all we want about Aeneas' behavior after the killing of Turnus, but the image we are left with by Virgil is one of wrath, anger, the fever of hatred, and madness. In some sense Turnus is like Jupiter in his address to Juno; he urges Aeneas to give up his hatred and accept what is clearly and undeniably a victory. He makes specific mention of Lavinia: she is now Aeneas', and there is no longer any question or contest, any struggle or fighting. Aeneas' limbs had grown slack with the chill of fear in Book 1 (92), when first we saw Troy's hero on the deck of his flagship; now Virgil uses exactly the same language to describe Turnus' limbs as they grow slack with the chill of death. Virgil could not have created a more perfect scenario for Aeneas to test his understanding of the education he received in the climactic revelations from Anchises (whom Turnus introduces into the scene) in the underworld. Turnus is humble, not defiant. He is a suppliant at the feet of Aeneas' mercy. Juno had given up her anger and wrath once she had received what she realized was a major victory. Aeneas, too, realizes the advantage in keeping Turnus alive; though Virgil does not mention it, the very same Rutulians Turnus saw watching are now all in full view of Aeneas' actions here. Their opinion of the decision Aeneas makes is not recorded. Aeneas perhaps realizes that killing Turnus is objectionable; he makes *Pallas* the killer with his powerful twofold repetition of his young friend's name. Some have seen a sort of supernatural possession here; the ghost of Pallas takes over Aeneas in a final illustration of Aeneas' frequent role as conduit for the will of others. In this reading, the question is not what Aeneas decides to do (even in a fit of madness), but what someone else (in this case, a shade) wants Aeneas to do at his behest. In either case, the end of the *Aeneid* is the triumph of madness and the victory of wrath. Homer's *Iliad* ends with the quiet victory of Achilles over his fury; Virgil's *Iliad* ends with the surrender of Aeneas to his.[22] Aeneas has won Lavinia; he has won the *Lavinian shores* (1.2-3)—but at a great cost.[23]

The *Aeneid*, strangely, has rarely received any treatment in film (unlike both of Homer's epics, and even Apollonius' *Argonautica*).[24] One filmmaker, however, has captured exactly the point of Virgil's great epic of madness and its horrifying conclusion. The British director Michael Reeves (1943-1969) made only three films before his untimely death from a barbiturate overdose. His last and most famous film, *Witchfinder General* (1968), is a fictionalized account of Matthew Hopkins, a brutal witch hunter in mid-seventeenth century England. Hopkins executes the aged father of a beautiful young woman—even after the young woman had agreed to submit to his sexual advances in the hope of saving her father. The young woman's soldier fiancé, away fighting a (civil) war during all the horror, returns to find his beloved Sarah an emotional wreck, devastated by the loss of her father and her virginity. He vows to hunt down the Witchfinder. He successfully tracks down Hopkins and, at great personal risk, finally kills him in a terrible act of brutal vengeance. As he rains down blows on his dying enemy, a friend of his finally intervenes and fires his gun, killing Hopkins and ending the sadistic revenge. The soldier looks up at his friend, bloody axe still in hand, and cries out repeatedly in furious rage that his enemy has been snatched from him, that his revenge is not sated. As Sarah watches her beloved's final and complete descent into an insanity of madness, she can only scream, and the film closes with her screams of horror and a frozen frame on her terrified face. For its American release, the film was renamed *The Conqueror Worm* (from the Poe poem) and given a short voiceover prelude and postlude from Poe's verse. As we see the frozen face of Sarah's horrified recognition that her lover has been overcome by unconquered madness, we hear Poe's words:

> "Out, out are the lights, out all!
>   And, over each quivering form,
>   The curtain, a funeral pall,
>   Comes down with the rush of a storm,
>   While the angels, all pallid and wan,
>   Uprising, unveiling, affirm
> That the play is the tragedy, 'Man,'
> And its hero the Conqueror Worm."

The sentiments are very Virgilian. Works as long and complex as the *Aeneid* defy simple schemas and easy analysis, but if Virgil's epic has any one overarching theme, it is the questioning of Jupiter's announcement that Madness, *Furor*, would be chained up (1.294-296). Madness is certainly alive and well at the end of Book 12; the hope expressed in Book 1 points forward to the Augustan Age and Virgil's own time. Would Madness finally cease to work its horrors under the new Golden Age of Caesar Octavian? Virgil and his contemporaries could not be sure; Rome would have to wait a generation or so for the poet Lucan to write his epic on Madness during the height of Nero's reign. Lucan's poem is the true sequel to Virgil; the young poet of Nero's day had the benefit of seeing the aftermath of the Augustan program. What would have been speculative prediction for Virgil was dread reality for Lucan. Fears for the actual Augustan reign might well have been very real, but the most intense fear in Virgil's day was for the succession. So we have a second, related theme at the heart of the *Aeneid*. The deaths of Marcellus, Nisus and Euryalus, Pallas, Lausus, Camilla, and finally Turnus all reflect the tragic loss of young heroes. A third theme is the undercutting of the poem's ostensible hero, Aeneas, which in the narrative context reflects the poem's revelation that Rome will not be Trojan, but will possess the customs and language of the apparently defeated side. Here Virgil finds room to celebrate the primitive Italy of rural countryside and simple, humble lifestyle, in contrast to a more decadent urban life (Aeneas comes from the oriental city of Troy). While the *Aeneid* often celebrates the (sometimes fictionalized) triumphs of Augustus over the barbarian powers of the East, the poet also calls the reader (and Augustus was first among all contemporary readers of the *Aeneid*) to the devoted preservation of the past and its more homegrown pleasures: Augustus would, in the end, advise future Romans not to seek expansion of the borders of the empire, but to maintain what they already had—not exactly "empire without end," but a wiser course. In the Augustan logic, if you are not at war with your neighbor, you can just as well claim a victory over them, since if they did not fear you, no doubt they would fight you. Virgil has respected, then, the general thrust of the tradition of Aeneas' arrival in Italy—but he has sanitized Rome's origins, in a sense, and made them unquestionably Italian, at least in their dominant strain. For this reason, Aeneas is no Augustan precursor; Augustus' birth into Roman history is solemnly announced in the underworld, but he will not be a reincarnation of Aeneas. Further, since Aeneas and Turnus are the leaders of two sides Jupiter has just decreed will unite to form one future Roman race, the death of Turnus is the first in a long history of *civil* bloodshed at Rome.

Like Lucretius' *De Rerum Natura* (and Lucan's *Bellum Civile*), Virgil's *Aeneid* ends somewhat abruptly (barring any questions of unfinished or unrevised composition for any of the three poems in question).[25] It leaves us with a resounding yes in answer to the question posed at the poem's beginning about the possibility of the existence of such great divine anger (and, it should be remembered, Jupiter emphasizes the future *divinity* of Aeneas in his conversation with Juno so soon before Aeneas gives in to his fury and kills Turnus). Can the immortals have such great wrath? Aeneas . . . explicitly identified before the end of the *Aeneid* as a future god . . . provides Virgil's answer: yes. But, in the end, as the climactic vision in the underworld may well have shown, Virgil was probably in full agreement with Lucretius: there are, most likely, no gods, and, if they did exist, they would not be concerned with mortal affairs. Rome had seen horrible days before the time of Augustus, but her history was soon to become far worse. It would be another poet of the age of Nero, Seneca (who had been so involved in the education of the madman), who would end his *Medea* with Jason (whose children have just been slaughtered by their mother) calling on the Eastern sorceress to be witness to the fact that there are no gods:

per alta vade spatia sublime aetheris,
testare nullos esse, qua veheris, deos. (1026-1027)

Go aloft through the deep spaces of the heavenly air,
and wherever you go, give witness that there are no gods.

Seneca's final word, *deos*, is perhaps the most crushing concluding word of any classical drama.[26] It expresses sentiments that might have been easy to believe during Nero's reign. The *Aeneid* belongs to a far calmer and more peaceful period in Roman history, where the future seemed at last *somewhat* assured (not to say guaranteed) in a way that nervous men had not dared to dream during the long preceding century of blood. Virgil's contemporary and close friend Horace concluded his great Augustan ode (*carmen* 1.2) with the no doubt sincere and heartfelt plea that Rome's savior be slow in ascending to his well-deserved heavenly honors:

> serus in caelum redeas (*carmen* 1.2.45)
> *Late may you return to heaven*

Virgil's *Aeneid* does not condemn Augustus. It does not express any particular fear about the *princeps* himself. But, on the other extreme of the spectrum, it is no mere vehicle for imperial propaganda either. The *Aeneid*, though firmly rooted in the reality of Augustan Rome and only properly understood in its historical context, concerns itself principally with a universal fear: madness never dies; whether there are really gods and goddesses or not is irrelevant in the face of this terrible reality. Virgil could hope that one day *Furor* would be chained in the temple of Janus, the doors of war closed forever. While these reflections on Book 12 were being revised, missiles and rockets were flying back and forth between Israel and Lebanon. Nicholas Horsfall notes in the preface to his commentary on *Aeneid* 7 that Roger Mynors advised him to prepare a commentary on Virgil's opening battle book on 5 June, 1967, the first day of the Arab-Israeli Six Day War, nearly forty years ago. Virgil's same hauntingly enigmatic vision remains with us. It comes with the lament that our most fervent hopes might be scattered among the breezes, never to be heard by the gods. It comes also as a testament to the poet's own unique brand of courage. The most pessimistic poets make the most eloquent witnesses to humanity's dreams for a better world.

Notes

1. But, for those with Italian, note TRAINA, *L'utopia e la storia. Il libro XII dell'Eneide e antologia delle opere*, Torino, 1997. For sensitive, sympathetic commentary, FOWLER, *The Death of Turnus: Observations on the Twelfth Book of the Aeneid*, Oxford, 1919, remains unmatched. There is a school commentary by Maguinness (London, 1964), which is cited more often than its scale warrants because of the lack of available editions of the book. Note also the outstanding *Reclam* edition of Binder and Binder (Stuttgart, 2005), with translation and notes.

2. See further Hornsby, *op. cit.*, pp. 119-120, who notes that Turnus is "at last" accepting the challenge of single combat. This is a grossly unfair analysis; Turnus has had no problem with the idea of fighting Aeneas. It is not his fault that the immortals, and Aeneas' plans for secret attack, have kept preventing it. Better analysis is found in THOMAS, "The Isolation of Turnus," in Stahl, *op. cit.*, pp. 288-291.

3. See *Iliad* 20.443 ff., with Edwards' notes.

4. This is the only blush in Virgil, an expression of Lavinia's "shy love" for Turnus (see LATEINER, "Blushes and Pallor in Ancient Fictions," *Helios* 25.2 (1998), pp. 163-189). See also LYNE, "Lavinia's Blush: Vergil, Aeneid 12.64-70," *Greece and Rome* 30 (1983), pp. 55-64.

5. For a sensitive examination of this seemingly mundane detail about the herald Idmon, see CASALI, The Messenger Idmon and the Foreknowledge of Turnus' Death: A Note on the Poetics of Names in the *Aeneid*," *Vergilius* 46 (2000), pp. 114-124.

6. Rape is not always a sufficient reason for Juno to "forgive" one of her husband's playthings (cf. Callisto); Juno cooperates with Juturna principally because they both favor Turnus, but there is also a tone of mutual empathy: both women know Jupiter all too well.

7. For detailed analysis of this scene, see CALLAWAY, "The Typical Oath-Scene in Vergil," *Vergilius* 40 (1994), pp. 37-48, especially pp. 41 ff., and HAHN, "Vergilian Transformation of an Oath Ritual: *Aeneid* 12.169-174, 213-215," *Vergilius* 45 (1999), pp. 22-38.

8. The omen of the swans and the eagle (12.244-256) apparently reflects the early hour of the morning (247 *rubra . . . in aethra*). For the significance of different passages of time in the *Aeneid*, see especially MACK, *Patterns of Time in Time in Vergil*, Hamden, Connecticut, 1978.

9. See further Camps, *op. cit.*, p. 161.

10. On the wounding of Aeneas see especially Gillis, *op. cit.*, pp. 89-92, who explores the (ancient) theory that Aeneas was wounded in the thigh as part of a conflict over sexual territorial rights. Gillis notes that the thigh may have had homosexual overtones—another evocation of the Trojan sodomite theme.

11. In "Theron" Silius may be alluding to Camilla's own possibly lycanthropic origins.

12. On this simile see Hornsby, *op. cit.*, pp. 128-129.

13. On the "wild olive" (*olea silvestris*) see SARGEAUNT, *The Trees, Shrubs, and Plants of Virgil*, Oxford, 1920, pp. 86-88. "The oleaster was used as a stock on which to graft the olive."

14. Jupiter's detail about a "mortal" is not so much an inconsistency with Virgil's clear statement later that Juturna is actually immortal, but rather works as 1) a comparison between Juturna, an insignificant figure (immortal or not), and the future Roman god Aeneas, and especially as 2) a useful trap to set for Juno: Jupiter surely knows who shot

Aeneas, but his reference to a "mortal" wound allows him to pretend some Rutulian was responsible for Juno/Juturna's action.

15. Fowler remarks (*op. cit.*, p. 137) that "to some it may seem that Jupiter and Juno are too homely in their talk to be presiding over the destiny of the world."

16. A fruitful area for Virgilian scholars to explore further would be the connection, if any, between Jupiter's colloquy with Juno (and its results) and the issue of predestined fate vs. free will (with due attention to Lucretius' explication of the "swerve" of atoms and the place of free will in Epicurean philosophy). Essentially, the unalterable "fate" Juno spends so much time railing against is the founding of Rome. This founding is unstoppable (as is Carthage's inevitable destruction). While some (major) "fated" events cannot be altered by anyone (even Jupiter), other outcomes can be changed or are at least negotiable, as it were. Such is the question about the ethnography of the fated city: will it be Italian or Trojan? The question did not arise in Book 1 between Jupiter and Venus (why should it?), but the important points are 1) we cannot imagine Venus being present with Jupiter and Juno now and keeping silent, 2) we cannot imagine Jupiter's revelation of the future city's ethnography to his daughter in Book 1, and 3) the apparent negotiability of Rome's ethnography can be viewed as either "fated" (i.e., Rome was always destined to be Italian, and we only see it decided here and now), or Rome's ethnography is a matter that is open to the free will of free agents, in this case the enraged Juno. Have Troy's atoms swerved just a bit? In any case, the lesson is that some things cannot be changed—others can. See further FOWLER, *Lucretius on Atomic Motion: A Commentary on De Rerum Natura 2.1-332*, Oxford, 2002, pp. 322-339. "If there is no *clinamen* [swerve], there is no *voluntas* [will]; but we can see that theer is *voluntas*; therefore the *clinamen* exists."

17. For the possible ominous idea that just as Troy could sink down, so also could Rome, see EDWARDS, *Writing Rome: Textual Approaches to the City*, Cambridge, 1996, pp. 63-66. An interesting detail in the *Aeneid* that deserves further study is the meaning/extent of Jupiter's *imperium sine fine* promise from his speech to his daughter in Book 1. It could well be taken at face value in Virgil's time; history would, of course, prove it false.

18. Papillon and Haigh on 4.615-620 connect Dido's imprecation there with Jupiter's revelation here: Aeneas and the Trojans will be forced to endure a *pax iniqua*.

19. See further Fraenkel, *op. cit.*, pp. 267 ff., and Nisbet and Rudd, *op. cit.*, pp. 35-38, for information on the possible revival of Julius Caesar's old idea (Suetonius *Divus Iulius* 79.3) of moving the imperial capital from Rome to Troy. Fraenkel (and Gordon Williams) do not think Augustus ever seriously contemplated the idea; we have no proof either way. On the ethnographic question of Roman/Trojan, see also Hardie on 595 ff., Gransden on 11.676-677, and Thomas, *op. cit.*, pp. 98 ff. On the whole topic of Juno's reconciliation, see FEENEY, "The Reconciliations of Juno," *The Classical Quarterly* N.S. 34 (1984), pp. 179-194 (reprinted in Harrison, *op. cit.*, pp. 339-362). Jupiter announces to Juno that the Romans will even surpass the gods in piety (839 *supra . . . deos pietate*). Mackail notes here that Virgil's immortals are capricious and unreliable in their response to mortal prayers: "Juno in the *Aeneid* is not won over by the prayers and oblations of Aeneas, but by her own reluctant submission to the divine will . . . " True enough, except for Juno's reluctance: her effort over the twelve books of the poem has accomplished much.

20. I see little or no connection between Juno's reconciliation and the war between Rome and Veii that ended with the *evocatio* of Juno from Veii to Rome after Camillus' victory in 396 B.C. (see Livy *Ab Urbe Condita* 5.19-23, with Ogilvie's notes).

21. For a summary of the various scholarly opinions on Turnus' act of supplication, see NAIDEN, *Ancient Supplication*, Oxford, 2006, pp. 166 and 274-276. Naiden does not note in his schema of Virgilian supplications that Turnus please for the alternatives of life or burial; oddly, Naiden does not consider Mezentius' request for burial at the end of Book 10. Note also the arguments of DYSON, *King of the Wood: The Sacrificial Victor in Vergil's Aeneid*, Norman, 2003. On Dyson's thesis that the death of Turnus is required by the religious, cult framework of the *Aeneid*, Leah Kronenberg is right: "For the most part, D.'s careful marshalling of evidence convinces that this cult not only lurks behind several key passages in the *Aeneid*, including the infamous Golden Bough, but also that it is more subtly embedded into the texture of the epic through allusions to Diana, tree violation, and reciprocal violence. It is less clear, however, how many important problems of interpretation the recognition of these allusions solves. D.'s hypothesis about the centrality of this cult for the *Aeneid* does make sense of several perceived inconsistencies in Virgil's text and usefully connects and highlights important themes in the poem. D. wants it to do more than that, however: she suggests that the sacrificial logic of the cult provides the definitive explanation for why Aeneas must kill Turnus at the end of the poem. In placing so great an emphasis on the religious and metaphysical implications of this cult for the plot of *Aeneid*, D. risks flattening the complexity of the poem by ignoring the more properly human factors driving the poem to its *telos*." (*Bryn Mawr Classical Review*, 2002.07.06). Kronenberg is also right in emphasizing that any ambivalence Virgil has about the very existence of the immortals compels us to blame mortals for their own actions, rather than ascribe divine excuses for seemingly questionable deeds: " . . . in her eagerness to remain out of the optimist/pessimist, pro-Augustan/anti-Augustan debate and to avoid judging Aeneas' actions, D. makes it difficult to distinguish meaningfully between Virgil's characters. They all become equally culpable and equally innocent, all are priests and murderers."

22. Tyler Travillian is right here: "Both heroes lose their humanity, but unlike Achilles, who regains his with the help of the gods and a visit from Priam, and unlike Odysseus, who must spend ten years relearning his, Aeneas gains no such redemption in the *Aeneid*. Virgil leaves us with a vision of the man-at-war as a beast who has set aside his higher ideals (the ghost of Anchises), who merely wars for supremacy, driven by his passions, and who wins. It is in this soil that the Roman race which was so hard to found (1.33 *condere*) is planted (12.950 *condit*)" (*A Commentary on Aeneid XII, Selections*, unpublished Dallas thesis, 2005). Virgil's trick with *condere . . . condit* is the last ring in the *Aeneid*, which stretches from the poem's proem to its close. For an oddly lackluster reading of the poem's last line (which barely acknowledges its highly significant repetition from Camilla's death scene), see SPRINGER, "The Last line of the *Aeneid*," *The Classical Journal* 82.4 (1987), pp. 310-313. SPENCE, "Clinching the Text: The Danaids and the End of the *Aeneid*," *Vergilius* 37 (1991), pp. 11-19, is an insightful study, though the point of Pallas' *balteus* with its depiction of the Danaids was probably to evoke the interrupted nuptials of Pallas and Turnus (especially the latter given his loss of Lavinia)—Pallas should have processed to his marriage, not his funeral. On the poem's conclusion, useful *inter alios* are FEENEY, "How the *Aeneid* Ends," *Omnibus* 12 (1986), pp. 11-13; BURNELL, "The Death of Turnus and Roman Morality," *Greece and Rome* 34 (1987), pp. 186-200; POTZ, "*Pius Furor* und der Tod des Turnus," *Gymnasium* 99 (1992), pp. 248-262; NOONAN, "Daunus/Faunus in the *Aeneid*," *Classical Antiquity* 12 (1993), pp. 111-125; and NICOLL, "The Death of Turnus," *The Classical Quarterly* N.S. 51 (2001), pp. 190-200. Aeneas' killing of Turnus is a reversion to the madness he displayed during the worst moments of Books 2 and 4 (not to mention the immediate aftermath of Pallas' death in Book 10). Aeneas fails his lessons; arguably Camilla and

even Turnus do not (both of them die quietly and peacefully, however indignantly; they may rail against the injustices of fate, but they have put aside the fury Aeneas displays in his final moments in the poem. For the opposing view, see HORNSBY, "The Refracted Past," *Vergilius* 33 (1987), pp. 6-13. For the possible influence of Philodemus on the end of the poem (along with analysis of the Homeric antecedents), see GALINSKY, "How to be Philosophical about the End of the *Aeneid*," *Illinois Classical Studies* 19 (1994), pp. 191-201.

23. The whole poem has been centered on Lavinia, even from its opening (1.2-3 *Laviniaque . . . litora*); she has been the prize. Virgil's refusal to delineate her character clearly is part of his point; we do not feel as if we know Lavinia, and Aeneas is with us in that ignorance. He has lost his soul, as it were, for a woman he does not even know. *Lavinia* and not *Lavina* is the true reading at 1.2; Virgil wants to highlight the poem's most important female character *ab initio*.

24. Franco Rossi directed an obscure 1971 *Eneide* for Italian television (watchable, if not memorable); Purcell's Dido and Aeneas opera has been produced for television at least twice.

25. See further ROBERTS, DUNN, and FOWLER, eds., *Classical Closure: Reading the End in Greek and Latin Literature*, Princeton, 1997, pp. 112-138, and 142-151.

26. "*Nullos esse deos* is not a characteristic complaint in Greek tragedy, even in Euripides; rather the sufferer asks 'How can the gods allow these things to happen?'. On this ending T.S. Eliot remarked: 'In the verbal *coup de théâtre* no one has ever excelled him. The final cry of Jason to Medea departing in her car is unique; I can think of no other play which reserves such a shock for the last word." (COSTA, *Seneca Medea*, Oxford, 1973, pp. 159-160).

SELECT BIBLIOGRAPHY

No Latin author has enjoyed (or suffered) such a huge bibliography of secondary scholarship as Virgil. The best available survey of the history of Virgilian scholarship is Stephen Harrison's introduction to his edited volume of "classic" articles on the *Aeneid* in the *Oxford Readings* series. His article is a sane and reasonable attempt to summarize a complicated history of scholarship. I have listed here the majority of the English language (and some other) commentaries on the *Aeneid* and its individual books (excluding "schoolboy" editions). The commentator has a more difficult time ignoring problems (and lines) than the monograph author (though this difficulty does not keep even the best of commentators from avoiding some thornier issues and maintaining their silence as they see fit). I urge the preservation of Virgilian virginity for as long as possible: given the vast quantities of ink that have been spilled over almost every scene (if not line) in the poem, it is refreshing to avoid what Mackail once decried as the timidity of scholars who are afraid to say anything about the poem, given the likelihood someone has either said it already or refuted it. An individual's ideas on the poem need to be developed privately and personally, before any examination of the criticism of others should be attempted. For this reason, I highly recommend that readers of the poem spend as much time as possible buried in the commentary tradition (including the "readings" of the poem offered by Dante, Milton, and the medieval *Aeneid* poets!), and be as immersed as possible in Homer, before they worry too much about the views of critics (myself included). Commentaries provide necessary historical, mythological, literary, metrical, syntactical and morphological information; they can (and, I would argue, should) offer literary criticism, but the very nature of a lemmatized, line by line structure creates a wonderful stricture on flights of fancy, a stricture that keeps the reader fixed always on the text. The student of the *Aeneid* should eschew any tendency to forget writing any thoughts of their own on Virgil. Much work remains to be done on the *Aeneid*—and, thanks to the greatness of the poem, much work will always remain undone. Virgil's spring never runs dry.

For students of the original Latin, the standard college commentary on the entire poem remains R.D. Williams' London "Macmillan Red" edition of 1972-1973. Williams' commentary (he also prepared a volume on the *Eclogues* and *Georgics*) was meant to "replace" T.E. Page's *fin de siècle* Virgil. Williams came to his *Aeneid* project with much experience in explicating his poet: he had also completed Books 3 (1962) and 5 (1960) for the "Oxford Virgil" project. By the mid-1970s, he and Roland Austin had finished separate commentaries on Books 1-6. Williams' edition of the complete *Aeneid* does not replace Page, but rather supplements its venerable predecessor; Williams tries to offer more in the way of literary criticism than Page's workmanlike, "schoolboy" commentary. But Page has stood the test of time better; Williams looks duller on every read. The Oxford Virgil project (interrupted by the deaths of Roland Austin and

Christian Fordyce) never finished the Iliadic *Aeneid*. The (posthumous) Fordyce commentary on Books 7-8 (1977) is on a smaller scale than the Austin-Williams volumes (and its brevity, together with the idea of putting two books in one volume, actually contributes to the mistaken notion that the poem's second half is less important or interesting than the first). Cambridge's undergraduate/"sixth form" series of "green and yellow" commentaries has taken over where the Oxford project left off: Gransden on Books 8 (1976) and 11 (1991) and Hardie on Book 9 (1994). Stephen Harrison's Oxford D.Phil. thesis commentary on Book 10 (1990) has been published in their "Classical Monographs" series. More recently, Books 3 (2006), 7 (2000), and 11 (2003) have received large scale Brill commentaries by Nicholas Horsfall (massive, learned, idiosyncratic). Alongside Austin, the other Oxford commentaries on Book 6 (Butler, 1920, and Fletcher, 1941) still contain much useful and valuable material.

The only other English scholarly commentary in the twentieth century is Mackail's highly selective but praiseworthy single volume edition (*The Aeneid of Virgil*, Oxford, 1930), issued on the occasion of the bimilleniary of Virgil's birth. Even when wrong, Mackail is worthwhile reading. The two-volume complete edition of Virgil's *opera* by Papillon and Haigh (Oxford, 1892—a rival to Page's Macmillan reds) is a sane and judicious guide to the poems, with fine analysis of Virgil's grammar and syntax. All of these English commentaries are deeply indebted to the magisterial three-volume edition of Conington and Nettleship, *The Works of Virgil* (London, 1858-1883)—the first truly great work of Virgilian scholarship in England.

The *Reclam* (Stuttgart) pocket editions of Virgil's *Aeneid* in six volumes (ed. Binder and Binder) constitute a fine addition to the commentary tradition: a faithful translation is accompanied by refreshingly sane notes, with much useful supplemental material (including illustrations). They have provided a generally underappreciated and quite value summary of the scholarship and major problems for a late 20th and early 21st century Virgilian audience, and frequently repay consultation.

Tiberius Claudius Donatus (late fourth - early fifth century A.D. wrote a lengthy *Interpretationes Vergilianae*, dedicated to his son. We lack the main body of the "other" Donatus' (Aelius) Virgil commentary (only the dedicatory letter, the *Vita* of Virgil, and the introduction to the *Eclogues* survives), but it was the basis for the great and immensely learned fourth century A.D. commentary of the grammarian Marius (or Maurus) Servius Honoratus. The Donatus commentary itself may have provided the supplementary notes that appear in the so-called *Servius auctus* or *Servius Danielis* commentary, named after its French publisher Pierre Daniel (1600), which is most probably a medieval (eighth century? ninth?) compilation of "fuller" Virgil commentary notes. The only complete edition of Servius is the monumental Thilo-Hagen edition (Leipzig, 1881-1902); the so-called Harvard Servius is the standard text for the commentary on the first five books of the *Aeneid* (Books 1-2, 1946, and Books 3-5, 1965). As of the printing of this book discussion continues in the American Philological Association on the continuation of the long-neglected Harvard Servius project.

Scholarship on the *Aeneid* is vast and dense, as befits so beloved and spellbinding a poem; I have tried to be comprehensive in my notes, so interested parties can pursue favorite problems to their hearts' content; citation of a book or paper does not equal endorsement of its views, and in fact I have consciously tried to give opposing arguments. A monograph on the *Aeneid* can never be completely original; this book contains some ideas scattered here and there that have never been noted in the scholarly tradition, to the best of my knowledge, but in a book like this, which attempts to explicate every last scene of the poem, many important ideas have already been observed multiple times along the vast *catena* of Virgilian criticism. I have tried to err on the side of over-documentation. Still, *pereant qui ante nos nostra dixerunt*. The sources referenced in the notes try to represent many and diverse viewpoints on Virgil; this bibliography offers a guide to my own suggested diet of Virgilian secondary scholarship, along with some favorites (especially in French, German, and Italian) that I have found particularly helpful in my own Virgil work. When are there not "holes" in any Virgilian bibliography? I would note that some of the finest commentary on the *Aeneid* can be found in the literary works that to varying degrees can call it parent: Ovid's *Metamorphoses*, Lucan's *Bellum Civile*, even Silius' *Punica* and the medieval French *Roman d'Enéas*. The notes and bibliography, then, do not aim at providing comprehensive references to every relevant secondary source (nor could they), but they do seek to offer the reader a guide both to the highly frequented and the more obscure avenues of Virgiliana.

Nota bene: I have not listed every existing reprint; a large number of Virgil titles have been reissued, sometimes more than once, by different publishers. Nor have I noted paperback reissues (sometimes with corrections and minor supplements, usually bibliographical). Standard commentaries on Greek and Latin authors, even when cited in the notes, are not listed here. Some of these are cited in the notes by author name alone; those interested in pursuing the matter in question will know the commentary. In general, I have not been able to take into consideration any scholarship published after the summer of 2006.

Adler, E. *Vergil's Empire: Political Thought in the Aeneid*. Lanham: Rowman and Littlefield, 2003.

Alessio, M. *Studies in Vergil: Aeneid Eleven, an Allegorical Approach*. Laval, Québec: Montfort & Villeroy, 1993.

Anderson, W. *The Art of the Aeneid*. Englewood Cliffs, NJ: Prentice-Hall, 1969.

A brief survey of the entire epic, by the editor of the Teubner Ovid *Matamorphoses* and many publications on Latin poetry: sensible, laconic, unobjectionable.

Armstrong, D., et al. *Vergil, Philodemus, and the Augustans*. Austin: University of Texas Press, 2004.

Work on Philodemus on Gadara, the Epicurean poet and philospher, and his connection to Virgil is one of the most promising modern areas of inquiry in Virgilian scholarship. The essays of Jeffrey Fish and Michael Wigodsky in this collection are especially valuable.

Arrigoni, G. *Camilla: Amazzone e Sacerdotessa di Diana*. Milan: Cisalpino-Goliardica, 1982.

Austin, R. *P. Vergili Maronis Aeneidos Liber Primus*. Oxford: Clarendon Press, 1971.

———. *P. Vergili Maronis Aeneidos Liber Secundus*. Oxford: Clarendon Press, 1964.

———. *P. Vergili Maronis Aeneidos Liber Quartus*. Oxford: Clarendon Press, 1955.

———. *P. Vergili Maronis Aeneidos Liber Sextus*. Oxford: Clarendon Press, 1977.

The Austin commentaries provide the most reliable and usable guides to Books 1, 2, 4, and 6. The only lacuna is an introduction to Book 6 (owing to Austin's untimely death). Austin's commentaries are full of measured, judicious appraisals of various Virgilian problems. They suffer, however (due to their concentration only on single books), from a lack of comprehensive literary criticism of the poem, despite their fundamental usefulness in explicating difficult passages. Beautifully written and soberly critical, Austin's commentaries are a lasting achievement of twentieth-century English Virgilian scholarship.

Bailey, C. *Religion in Virgil*. Oxford: Clarendon Press, 1935.

Despite its age and the tremendous advancement in the study of Roman religion since the 1930s, Bailey's book remains a standard guide to the subject.

Bartelink, G.J.M. *Etymologisering bij Vergilius*. Amsterdam: Noord-Hollandsche Uitg. Mij., 1965.

Basson, W. *Pivotal Catalogues in the Aeneid*. Amsterdam: A. M. Hakkert, 1975.

Bellesort, A. *Virgile: son oeuvre et son temps*. Paris: Perrin, 1949.

Benoist, E. *Oeuvres de Virgile* (3 volumes). Paris: Hachette, 1867-1872.

For decades the standard French commentary; the first volume of the second edition (1884) has a valuable survey of nineteenth-century Virgil scholarship. Somewhat underappreciated by English (and American) classicists; Benoist was sometimes wrong, but never careless and always sensitive to the poet.

Binder, E., and Binder, G., *Vergil Aeneis* (6 volumes). Stuttgart: Reclam, 1994-2005.

Binder, G. *Aeneas und Augustus.* Meisenheim am Glan: A. Hain, 1971.

Bowra, C.M. *From Virgil to Milton.* London: Macmillan & Co., 1945.

Boyancé, P. *La Religion de Virgile.* Paris: Presses Universitaires de France, 1963.

Boyle, A. *The Chaonian Dove: Studies in the Eclogues, Georgics, and Aeneid* (*Mnemosyne* Supplement 95). Leiden: E. J. Brill, 1986.

Brill, A. *Die Gestalt der Camilla bei Vergil.* Heidelberg, 1972.

Butler, H. *The Sixth Book of the Aeneid.* Oxford: B. Blackwell, 1920.

Cairns, F. *Virgil's Augustan Epic.* Cambridge: Cambridge University Press, 1989.

Camps, W. *An Introduction to Virgil's Aeneid."* London: Oxford University Press, 1969.

A lucid, thoughtful *prolegomenon* to the poem: Camps' volume retains its usefulness as a primer in Virgilian literary criticism. Virgilians of the late 1960s were busy absorbing the work of Pöschl (and Putnam); a flood of survey books on the poem was part of the fruit of their busy labors (Otis first, then Quinn, Camps, Anderson).

Cartault, A. *L'Art de Virgile dans l'Eneide* (2 volumes). Paris: Les Presses universitaires de France, 1926.

A marvelous delight: Cartault provides a comprehensive, scene-by-scene study of Virgil's *Aeneid*, with a healthy amount of prolegomena. One of the finer examples of French Virgilian scholarship, with very sensible analyses of numerous difficult passages, Cartault is not so much "hypercritical" (Highet) as attentive to nuance and detail.

Commager, S. *Virgil: A Collection of Critical Essays.* Englewood Cliffs, NJ: Prentice-Hall, 1966.

Commager's edited collection was the Harrison (see below) of its day. Together, the two volumes offer foundational articles of modern Virgilian criticism.

Conington, J., and Nettleship, H. *The Works of Virgil* (3 volumes). London,: Whitaker, 1858-1883.

Constans, L. A. *L'Eneide de Virgile*. Paris: Librairie Mellottée, 1938.

Conway, R. *P. Vergili Maronis Aeneidos Liber Primus*. Cambridge: Cambridge University Press, 1935.

Crump, M. *The Growth of the Aeneid: A Study of the Stages of Composition as Revealed by the Evidences of Incompletion*. Oxford: B. Blackwell, 1920.

Cruttwell, R. *Virgil's Mind at Work: An Analysis of the Symbolism of the Aeneid*. Oxford: B. Blackwell, 1946.

Della Corte, F. *La mappa dell'Eneide*. Florence: La Nuova Italia, 1985.

Desmond, M. *Reading Dido: Gender, Textuality, and the Medieval Aeneid*. Minneapolis-London: University of Minnesota Press, 1994.

Di Cesare, M. *The Altar and the City: A Reading of Virgil's Aeneid*. New York: Columbia University Press, 1974.

Duckworth, G. *Structural Patterns and Proportions in Vergil's Aeneid*. Ann Arbor: University of Michigan Press, 1962.

Eden, P.T. *A Commentary on Aeneid VIII* (*Mnemosyne* Supplement 35). Leiden: Brill, 1975.

Edgeworth, R.J. *The Colors of the Aeneid*. New York: P. Lang, 1992.

Fairclough, H. *Virgil* (2 volumes). Cambridge, Mass.: Harvard University Press, 1999-2000.

George Goold's revision of the World War I era Loeb Classical Library original Virgil set (1916, 1918).

Farron, S. *Vergil's Æneid: A Poem of Grief and Love*. (*Mnemosyne* Supplement 122). Leiden-New York-Cologne: E. J. Brill, 1993.

Feeney, D. *The Gods in Epic*. Oxford: Clarendon Press, 1991.

Fletcher, F. *Virgil: Aeneid VI*. Oxford: Clarendon Press, 1948.

Forbiger, A. *P. Virgili Maronis Opera* (3 volumes). Leipzig: Hinrichs, 1872-1875.

The fourth edition of the Latin commentary on the *Aeneid*; the best of the post-Heyne / Wagner nineteenth-century editions, which always repays consultation.

Fordyce, C. P. *Vergili Maronis Aeneidos Libri VII-VIII*. Oxford: Oxford University Press for the University of Glasgow, 1977.

Fowler, W. *Virgil's Gathering of the Clans: Being Observations on Aeneid VII.601-817*. Oxford: Blackwell, 1916.

———. *Aeneas at the Site of Rome: Observations on the Eighth Book of the Aeneid*. Oxford: B. H. Blackwell, 1917 (2nd edition 1918).

———. *The Death of Turnus: Observations on the Twelfth Book of the Aeneid*. Oxford: B. H. Blackwell, 1921.

Galinsky, G. *Aeneas, Sicily, and Rome*. Princeton: Princeton University Press, 1969.

———. *Augustan Culture: An Interpretive Introduction*, Princeton: Princeton University Press, 1998.

George, H., ed. *T. Claudii Donati Interpretationes Vergilianae* (2 vols.). Leipzig, 1905-1906.

Geymonat, M. *P. Vergili Maronis Opera*. Turin: In aedibus I.B. Paraviae, 1973.

Gillis, D. *Eros and Death in the Aeneid*. Rome: "L'Erma" di Bretschneider, 1983.

Gossrau, G. G. *Publii Virgilii Maronis Aeneis*. Quedlinburg: Bassi, 1876.

Latin notes that have retained their usefulness; it is essential to use the second edition, which has the names of scholars appended to their cited ideas.

Gransden, K. *Virgil: Aeneid VIII*. Cambridge: Cambridge University Press, 1976.

———. *Virgil: Aeneid XI*. Cambridge: Cambridge University Press, 1991.

———. *Virgil's Iliad: An Essay on Epic Narrative*. Cambridge: Cambridge University Press, 1984.

Gransden's monograph on the second half of the *Iliad* is an important overview of Virgil's war books. Much work has been done in the years since it appeared, but it remains a useful survey of Books 7-12, even if it sometimes glosses over complex issues for the sake of brevity (also a major weakness of his *Aeneid* 11). The commentary on *Aeneid* 8 is solid and useful; the edition of *Aeneid* 11 is not only woefully brief, but also lamentably derivative and oftentimes either misguided or simply wrong. On Gransden's *Aeneid* 11, see Farrell (*Bryn Mawr Classical Review* 04.01.14) for a positive/neutral view, and "T.L. Calder" (Nicholas Horsfall), *Vergilius* 38, 1992, pp. 144-146, for a very negative appraisal ("The logic of publishing ever shorter commentaries aimed at 'school and undergraduate level' is, one imagines, that the whole class will be able to buy the wretched little book.") Significantly (?), Farrell's review is more of a supplement to his more detailed review of Harrison's *Aeneid* 10; I would argue that it is almost an insult to Harrison's commentary to link it with Gransden's.

Grassman-Fischer, B. *Die Prodigien in Vergils Aeneis*. Munich: Fink, 1966.

Griffin, J. *Virgil*. Oxford: Oxford University Press, 1986.

Guillemin, A. *L'Originalité de Virgile*. Paris: Société d'édition "Les Belles lettres," 1931.

———. *Virgile: Poète, Ariste, et Penseur*. Paris: Michel, 1951.

Halter, T. *Form und Gehalt in Vergils Aeneis*. Munich: T. Halter, 1963.

Hardie, C. *Vitae Vergilianae Antiquae*. Oxford: Oxford University Press, 1966.

Hardie, P. *Virgil: Aeneid IX*. Cambridge: Cambridge University Press, 1994.

The best of the Cambridge "green and yellow" editions for "sixth formers and undergraduates," Hardie's book contains a valuable introductory section on Nisus and Euryalus and the death of young heroes in the poem. Nicholas Horsfall is right: Hardie's IX puts the other Cambridge Virgil green and yellows "to shame."

———. *Virgil's Aeneid: Cosmos and Imperium*. Oxford: Clarendon Press, 1986.

Harrison, S. *Vergil: Aeneid 10*. Oxford: Clarendon Press, 1991.

———. *Oxford Readings in Vergil's Aeneid*. Oxford: Oxford University Press, 1990.

Heinze, R. *Virgils epische Technik*. Leipzig: B. G. Teubner, 1903 (4th edition 1928). (Note Harvey, H. and D., and Robertson, F., trans., *Virgil's Epic Technique*, Berkeley-Los Angeles, 1993.)

Heinze is foundational to the modern study of Virgil. All subsequent Virgilian scholarship is indebted to his work that, in effect, gave birth to the twentieth century in Virgiliana.

Henry, E. *The Vigor of Prophecy: A Study of Vergil's Aeneid*. Carbondale-Edwardsville, 1989.

Henry, J. *Aeneidea* (4 volumes). London-Dublin, 1873-1892.

A fascinating, sublime, eccentric, monumental guide to Virgil's *Aeneid*: Henry's four volumes have never been matched for their ardent love of detail and nuance. Every student of Virgil should at least timidly explore the vast riches of the *Aeneidea,* or "*Critical, Exegetical, and Aesthetical Remarks on the Aeneis, with a personal collation of all the first class Mss., upwards of one hundred second class Mss., and all the principal editions.*"

Heuze, P. *L'image du corps dans l'oeuvre de Virgile.* Rome: Ecole française de Rome, 1985.

Highet, G. *The Speeches in Vergil's Aeneid.* Princeton: Princeton University, Press, 1972.

Hirtzel, F. *P. Vergili Maronis Opera.* Oxford: Clarendon Press, 1900.

The "original" Oxford Classical Text of Virgil; not very different from Mynors' text, as one might expect with an author whose text is relatively stable and free from numerous serious difficulties.

Hornsby, R. *Patterns of Action in the Aeneid: An Interpretation of Vergil's Epic Similes.* Iowa City: University of Iowa Press, 1970.

An important critical work because it remains the only book devoted entirely to the similes of the *Aeneid*, but marred by a maze-like style of presentation that forces the reader to view the similes (and related scenes) as Hornsby wants them to be seen, not necessarily as Virgil might. The book is not sympathetic to any positive reading of Turnus or Camilla. The similes await another general, systematic study.

Horsfall, N. *A Companion to the Study of Virgil (Mnemosyne* Supplement 151). Leiden- New York: E. J Brill, 1995.

———. *Virgil: Aeneid 7, A Commentary.* Leiden-Boston-Cologne: Brill, 2000.

———. *Virgil: Aeneid 11, A Commentary (Mnemosyne* Supplement 244). Leiden-Boston: Brill, 2003.

———. *Virgil: Aeneid 3, A Commentary (Mnemosyne* Supplement 273). Leiden-Boston: Brill, 2006.

Hügi, M. *Vergils Aeneis und die hellenistiche Dichtung.* Bern-Stuttgart, 1952.

Jackson-Knight, W. *Roman Vergil.* Harmondsworth, 1944.

Jenkyns, R. *Virgil's Experience. Nature and History: Times, Names, and Places.* Oxford: Clarendon Press, 1998.

Johnson, W. *Darkness Visible: A Study of Vergil's Aeneid.* Berkeley-Los Angeles: University of California Press, 1976.

Klingner, F. *Virgil: Bucolica, Georgica, Aeneis.* Zürich-Stuttgart: Artemis Verlag, 1967.

Knauer, G. *Die Aeneis und Homer: Studien zur poetischen Technik Vergils mit Listen der Homerzitate in der Aeneis* (*Hypomnemata* 7). Göttingen: Vandenhoeck & Ruprecht, 1964.

Kragelund, P. *Dream and Prediction in the Aeneid: A Semiotic Interpretation of the Dreams of Aeneas and Turnus* (*Opuscula Graecolatina* 7). Copenhagen: Museum Tusculanum, 1976.

Kraggerud, E. *Aeneisstudien* (*Symbolae Osloenses* Fasc. Supp. XXI). Oslo: Universitetsforlaget, 1968.

Kühn, W. *Götterszenen bei Vergil.* Heidelberg: C. Winter, 1971.

Kvíĉala, J. *Neue Beiträge zur Erklärung der Aeneis.* Prague, 1881.

Lesueur, R. *L'Enéide de Virgile.* Toulouse, 1975.

Lundströn, S. *Acht Reden in der Aeneis* (*Studia Latina Upsaliensia* 10). Uppsala: Univ., 1977.

Lyne, R. *Further Voices in Vergil's Aeneid.* Oxford: Clarendon Press, 1987.

———. *Words and the Poet: Characteristic Techniques of Style in the Aeneid.* Oxford: Clarendon Press, 1989.

Mack, S. *Patterns of Time in Vergil.* Hamden, Conn.: Archon Books, 1978.

Mackail, J. *The Aeneid of Virgil.* Oxford, 1930.

One of the most sensible and enjoyable of Virgilian commentaries, Mackail's edition in honor of the 1930 bimillenium deserves to be studied by everyone interested in the *Aeneid*. Despite some flawed analyses of difficult passages, Mackail's work remains a wise guide to several vexed readings.

Maguinness, W. *Virgil Aeneid XII.* London: Methuen, 1953.

Mandra, R. *The Time Element in the Aeneid of Vergil.* Williamsport, Penn.: The Bayard Press, 1934.

Martindale, C. *Virgil and his Influence.* London, 1984.

———, ed. *The Cambridge Companion to Virgil.* Cambridge: Cambridge University Press, 1997.

McAuslan, I., and Walcot, P. *Greece & Rome Studies: Virgil.* Oxford: Oxford University Press on behalf of the Classical Association, 1990.

A collection of fifteen articles on Virgil from the *Greece and Rome* journal Oxford publishes for the Classical Association.

McKay, A. *Vergil's Italy.* Greenwich, Conn.: New York Graphic Society, 1970.

Monti, R. *The Dido Episode and the Aeneid: Roman Social and Political Values in the Epic* (*Mnemosyne* Supplement 66). Leiden: Brill, 1981.

Moskalew, W. *Formular Design and Poetic Language in the Aeneid* (*Mnemosyne* Supplement 73). Leiden: Brill, 1982.

Mynors, R. *P. Vergili Maronis Opera Omnia.* Oxford: Clarendon Press, 1969 (corrected 1972).

The most accessible standard critical edition of the poem, a replacement of Hirtzel's 1900 Oxford text, is lamentably laconic (after the fashion of the series) on certain points where we would very much have appreciated a "companion" volume (like Diggle's praiseworthy *Euripidea*) explaining Mynors' views on certain textual problems.

Nagy, G. *The Best of the Achaeans.* Baltimore, 1979: Johns Hopkins University Press (2nd edition 1999).

Since one cannot fully come to terms with Virgil without a deep and abiding familiarity with Homer, and since Nagy's book is the most important single work of modern Homeric scholarship (and is aimed at both specialist and nonspecialist in Homeric studies), I have included it as recommended reading.

Norden, E. *P. Vergilius Maro Aeneis Buch VI.* Leipzig-Berlin: B. G. Teubner, 1903 (3rd edition 1927).

———. *Ennius und Vergilius.* Leipzig: B. G. Teubner, 1912.

O'Hara, J. *Death and the Optimistic Prophecy.* Princeton: Princeton University Press, 1990.

———. *True Names: Vergil and the Alexandrian Tradition of Etymological Wordplay.* Ann Arbor: University of Michigan Press, 1996.

Otis, B. *Virgil: A Study in Civilized Poetry.* Oxford: Clarendon Press, 1964.

Page, T. *The Aeneid of Virgil* (2 volumes). London: Macmillan, 1894-1900.

Papillon, T., and Haigh, E. *P. Vergili Maronis Opera: Virgil, with an Introduction and Notes* (2 volumes). Oxford: Clarendon Press, 1892.

Paschalis, M. *Vergil's Aeneid: Semantic Relations and Proper Names.* Oxford: Clarendon Press, 1997.

Pease, A. *P. Vergili Maronis Aeneidos Liber Quartus.* Cambridge, Mass.: Harvard University Press, 1935.

Peerlkamp, P. *P. Virgilli Maronis Aeneidos Libri*. Leiden: apud H.W. Hazenberg et socios, 1843.

An often perceptive, sometimes quite valuable Latin commentary on the entire poem, with a valuable collection of parallel passages.

Perkell, C., ed. *Reading Vergil's Aeneid: An Interpretive Guide*. Norman: University of Oklahoma Press, 1999.

Perret, J. *Virgile, l'homme et l'œuvre*. Paris: Boivin, 1952 (2nd edition 1965).

———. *Les Origines de la légende troyenne de Rome*. Paris: Société d'édition "Les Belles lettres," 1942.

Pöschl, V. *Die Dichtkunst Virgils: Bild und Symbol in der Aeneis*. Innsbruck-Vienna, 1950 (3rd edition Berlin-New York, 1977).
(Note Seligson, G., trans., *The Art of Vergil: Image and Symbol in the Aeneid*, Ann Arbor: University of Michigan Press, 1962.)

Along with Heinze and Norden, this is the book that motivated many a young Virgilian to learn German; Pöschl is essential reading for understanding the modern era in literary criticism of the *Aeneid*.

Prescott, H. *The Development of Virgil's Art*. Chicago: University of Chicago Press, 1927.

Putnam, M. *The Poetry of the Aeneid: Four Studies in Imaginative Unity and Design*. Cambridge, Mass.: Harvard University Press, 1965.

For Books 2, 5, 8, and 12, Putnam's chapters in this book are essential reading. They are fundamental to the "Harvard School" reading of the poem, and they provide sensitive supplement to commentaries on the individual books.

———. *Virgil's Aeneid: Interpretation and Influence*. Chapel Hill: University of North Carolina Press, 1995.

———. *Virgil's Epic Designs: Ekphrasis in the Aeneid*. New Haven: Yale University Press, 1998.

Quinn, K. *Virgil's Aeneid: A Critical Description*. Ann Arbor: University of Michigan Press, 1968.

Quinn's book attempts much of what the present work hopes to provide: a careful reading of the poem that moves or more or less straight through the epic book by book and scene by scene. Though sometimes reluctant to make synthesizing arguments, Quinn's book has stood the test of time.

Quinn, S. *Why Vergil? A Collection of Interpretations.* Wauconda, Ill.: Bolchazy-Carducci Publishers, 2000.

More articles on Virgil than any other Latin author have been reprinted (sometimes more than once) in different collections. I have noted some, though not all, of these reprints; besides the "standard" collections of Commager and Harrison, Quinn's volume is a useful compilation of essays on a wide range of Virgilian topics, along with some newly published material by Michael Putnam.

Rand, E. *The Magical Art of Virgil.* Cambridge, Mass.: Harvard University Press, 1931.

Rand, E., et al. *Serviani in Vergilii Carmina Commentarii Vol. II (Aeneid 1-2),* Lancaster, 1946.

Reed, J. D. *Virgil's Gaze: Nation an Poetry in the Aeneid.* Princeton: Princeton University Press, 2007.

Sargeaunt, J. *The Trees, Shrubs, and Plants of Virgil.* Oxford: B. H. Blackwell, 1920.

Schlunk, R. *The Homeric Scholia and the Aeneid: A Study of the Influence of Ancient Homeric Literary Criticism on Vergil.* Ann Arbor: University of Michigan Press, 1974.

Sellar, W. *The Roman Poets of the Augustan Age: Virgil.* Oxford: Clarendon Press, 1908.

Sidgwick, A. *P. Vergili Maronis Opera* (2 volumes). Cambridge: At the University Press, 1890.

A complete text and commentary on Virgil; Sidgwick's two volume set is a compilation of his separate *Aeneid* commentaries, with revisions, expanded introduction, and the removal of some lexical and metrical aids. Sidgwick's notes (like their Oxford sister edition by Papillon and Haigh) contain many gems of important observations.

Spargo, J. *Virgil the Necromancer.* Cambridge, Mass.: Harvard University Press, 1934.

Sparrow, H. *Half-lines and Repetitions in Virgil.* Oxford: Clarendon Press, 1931.

Stahl, H-P., ed. *Vergil's Aeneid: Augustan Epic and Political Context.* London: Duckworth, in association with the Classical Press of Wales, 1998.

Stocke, A., Travis, A., et al. *Serviani in Vergilii Carmina Commentarii Vol. III (Aeneid 3-5).* Oxford, 1965.

Thilo, G., and Hagen, H. *Servii Grammatici qui feruntur in Vergilii carmina commentarii* (3 volumes). Leipzig: B. G. Teubner, 1878-1902.

Thomas, J. *Structures de l'Imaginaire dans l'Eneide*. Paris: "Belles Lettres," 1981.

Thomas, R. *Virgil and the Augustan Reception*. Cambridge: Cambridge University Press, 2001.

Thornton, A. *The Living Universe: Gods and Men in Virgil's Aeneid* (*Mnemosyne* Supplement 46). Leiden: Brill, 1976.

Tilly, B. *Vergil's Latium*. Oxford: B. Blackwell, 1947.

Warwick, H. *A Vergil Concordance*. Minneapolis: University of Minnesota Press, 1975.

Wetmore, M. *Index Verborum Vergilianus*. New Haven: Yale University Press, 1930.

Wigodsky, M. *Virgil and Early Latin Poetry*. Wiesbaden, 1972.

Wilhelm, R., and Jones, H., *The Two Worlds of the Poet: New Perspectives on Vergil*. Detroit: Wayne State University Press, 1992.

Williams, G. *Tradition and Originality in Roman Poetry*. Oxford: Clarendon Press, 1968.

———. *Technique and Ideas in the Aeneid*. New Haven, NJ: Yale University Press, 1983.

Williams, R. *The Aeneid of Virgil* (2 volumes). London, 1972-1973.

———. *P. Vergili Maronis Aeneidos Liber Tertius*. Oxford: Oxford University Press, 1962.

———. *P. Vergili Maronis Aeneidos Liber Quintus*. Oxford: At the Clarendon Press, 1960.

———. *Virgil* (*Greece and Rome*: New Surveys in the Classics, No. 1). Oxford: Clarendon Press, 1967.

Wiltshire, S. *Public and Private in Vergil's Aeneid*. Amherst: University of Massachusetts Press, 1989.

INDEX

Acca, 124, 341, 352, 355
Acestes, 21, 65, 133-134, 140, 142-146, 148, 150-153
Achaemenides, 89-90
Achates, 6-7, 14, 17-18, 20-22, 164, 166, 171, 235, 245-246, 248-249, 377
Achilles, 1-4, 11-12, 18-19, 26, 164, 166, 168-169, 181, 194, 197, 207-208, 214, 229, 233, 237, 243, 245, 249, 269-270, 276, 279-281, 284, 286-287, 297, 302-307, 310, 316, 235, 333, 336-337, 341, 343, 354, 363n50, 369, 373, 377, 379, 386, 394, 396
Actium: Aeneas' stopover at, xv, 4, 7, 80-81, 84, 96n14; on the shield, 254-256;
Aeneas, 62-65, 77-78, 80, 82, 85-87, 92-93, 151-152, 185-197; assurances to his men in Carthage, 7-8; combat with Lausus and Mezentius, 314-317; and Creusa, 63-64, 66-71; death traditions, 10, 31n16; and Dido, 21-22, 26-27, 99-115, 121, 124, 132-134, 179-181, 204, 206, 211-213; first appearance, 5-6; funerals for the war dead, 321-329; journey through Dido's city, 17-21; and Liger and Lucagus, 306-307; and Odysseus, 2, 75, 81, 88-91; and Pallas, 248-249, 321-325, 327-329; phantom Aeneas, 309-312; quality of *pietas*, 9, 16, 21-22, 59, 114-115, 306-307, 314-315; reaction to Pallas' death, 304-307; and Turnus, 59, 247-248, 355-357, 386-399; wounded in battle, 376-379
Aeolus, 5-7, 16
Aethiopis, 336-337
Allecto, fury, 213-220, 372, 375, 392, 394
Amata, 214-215, 330, 369-371, 383, 385
Anchises, 47, 62-68, 63, 74n38, 77-78, 80, 82, 85-87, 92-93, 112, 115-116, 125, 131-135, 138, 142, 146-149, 153, 157, 185-197, 205, 207, 305
Androgeos, 50, 73n21
Andromache, 82-83, 86
Anna, 101-102, 115-118, 123-124
Antenor, 9, 31n15
Antony (Marcus Antonius), 4, 23, 56, 72n4, 81, 84, 99, 113, 146, 254-255
Apollo, 42-43, 80-81, 106, 164-168, 176, 179, 183, 185, 209, 218, 298; invoked by Arruns, 166, 348-349; role in the victory at Actium, 254-255; warning to Ascanius, 97n33, 283-284
Apollonius Rhodius, 78, 100, 106, 141, 206, 234
Arma virumque cano acrostic, 1, 29n1
Arruns, 49-50, 60, 106, 155-156, 166, 264, 272, 276, 279, 281, 290n26, 298, 337, 341-342, 344-354, 356
Ascanius, 10, 21-22, 24, 26, 49-50, 61, 64-65, 67-68, 75, 83, 86-87, 106-107, 132, 134-135, 146-151, 154, 189-190, 197, 201n32, 217-218, 230n3, 235, 237-238, 245, 248-250, 254,

264, 268, 272-274, 279-280, 282-284, 286, 293, 299, 305, 307, 373, 377-378, 384, 386, 392
Atlas, 25, 109-110, 190-191, 237
Augustus (Gaius Julius Caesar Octavianus), xiv-xvii, 2, 4-5, 7, 11-13, 22, 27, 29n1, 75, 81, 85-86, 88, 90, 92-93, 99-100, 119, 146, 158, 167, 190-193, 195-197, 221-222, 253-254, 265, 293, 297, 299, 313, 344
Austin, R. G., 37, 40, 47-48, 66, 72n10, 99, 101, 105, 114, 163, 166, 172, 175, 188, 196, 205

bears, Libyan, 133-134
Bellona, 214, 230n12, 255, 261n39
Bergman, Ingmar, 72n14

Cacus, Virgil's "Bad Man," 235, 237-240, 242-243
Caeneus / Caenis, 179, 183, 200n25
Caesar, Gaius Iulius, 12-13, 57, 65, 128n15, 145-146, 160n24, 190-194, 201n34, 213, 299
Callimachus, 15, 56, 180, 207, 225, 245, 362n43
Callisto, 26, 35n58
Camilla, 140, 147, 150, 232n29, 236, 242, 244, 246, 251, 263, 278-283, 286-287, 296, 298, 301-303, 311-312, 315-316, 318, 367-370, 377, 380-381, 383, 397; and Arruns, her killer, 49, 60, 166, 264, 344-345, 352; in catalogue of native Italian heroes, 226-229; charming childhood epyllion, 336-338; and Chloreus, 345-348; death scene, 352-353; and Diana, 336-339; and Dido, 99-100, 105-106, 120, 124-125, 127n7; and Harpalyce, 15, 32-33nn27-30, 95n12; as hawk or bird of prey, 343; inspiration of heroism in women, 150, 192, 354-355; and Lausus, 301-302; as lycanthrope, 349-350; and the lying son of Aunus, 342-343; and Nisus and Euryalus, 140, 270-274, 276, 278, 321, 347; and Ornytus, her *alter ego*, 342, 347-348; and Penthesilea, 15, 19, 228-229, 340; and Turnus, 335-336, 355-357
Camillus (Marcus Furius), 192, 229, 251, 352
Cassandra, 43-44, 51-52
Catalogues: of Aeneas' Etruscan allies, 297-298; of Italian heroes, 222-229
Catullus (Gaius Valerius), 57, 136, 156, 165, 173, 180, 240, 277-278, 282, 289n19, 324-325
Celaeno, Harpy, 79-80, 83, 95n12, 210
Chloreus, 225, 279, 282, 345-350, 377
Cicero (Marcus Tullius), 136, 159n8, 326
Circe, 205, 207, 209, 212-213, 226, 236
Cleopatra, xv, 4, 23-24, 27, 56, 81, 84, 99-100, 115, 118-119, 122, 128n24, 167, 253-256, 261nn35-36, 265-266, 271, 351
Condere (1.5 *conderet* and 12.950 *condit*): *to found* and *to bury*, xiii, xviiin3
Coroebus, 48-52, 61
Creusa, 10, 61, 63-64, 66-71, 83-84, 268, 273-274, 279
Cybele, 69-71, 77, 108, 148, 173, 189, 259-260nn13-14, 268, 282-283, 289n4, 297, 344-347, 349, 388
Cyclopes, 5, 8, 89-91, 183-184,

238, 243, 245, 284
Cypress, 66, 76, 90-91, 125, 173

Daedalus, 164-165, 199nn4-5
Dardanus, 75-78, 109, 212, 237
Dares, 141-144, 377, 387
death at the ends of books, 92-93, 124-126, 155-158, 208, 312, 352-353, 393-396
Deiphobus, 47, 58, 181-182, 189
Diana, 14-15, 19-20, 32n27, 42-43, 90-91, 100, 103, 105-106, 119-120, 124, 164, 166-167, 170, 173-174, 180, 183, 228-229, 236, 251, 296, 301, 306, 337-340, 345-347, 350-354
Dido, or Elissa: with Aeneas at the fateful hunt, 104-107, 346; background story, 15-16; and Camilla, 99-100, 105-107, 120, 126-127, 127n7, 322, 337, 346, 350-352; Carthage's queen, 19-28; as Cleopatra, 23-24, 99-100, 118-119; and the dead Pallas, 237, 325; as false Diana, 19-20, 26; first assault on by Venus and Cupid, 23-25, 100-101, 107; first speech to Aeneas, 111; gifts of Dido mentioned in connection with Ascanius, 147-148; second speech, 113-114, 128n17; secret plans for suicide, 117-121; suicide, 123-125; in the underworld, 178, 180-181
Diomedes, 36n60, 40, 136, 142, 234-235, 238, 259n3, 270, 279-280, 283, 293, 321, 330, 332-333, 344, 361n29, 369, 377
Dionysius of Halicarnassus, 27, 75-76, 81-82, 86, 88, 155, 223
Dolon, 270, 279-280, 377
dolphins, 148, 252-253

Drances, 136, 159n8, 321, 326-327, 329-336, 355, 359n16, 384

Elissa. *See* Dido
Elysium, 182-196, 249
Ennius, 44, 123, 171, 224
Entellus, 141-144
Erato and the invocation at the beginning of Book 7, 205-209
Eurydice, 70-71, 169-170, 184
Evander, 169, 176, 235-239, 241-242, 245-246, 248, 321, 324, 327-328, 331

Fate, 38-39
funeral rites: for Misenus, 171-175; for Polydorus in Thrace, 76; for the Trojan and Italian war dead, 321-329

Gates of Sleep, Virgilian enigma, 163, 170, 196-198, 200n21, 202n47
Golden Bough, 127n7, 170-173, 175, 177, 183, 243
Gransden, K.W., 233, 322, 328, 333, 340, 358n2

half-lines, purposeful, non-purposeful, 34n46, 39, 83, 112, 140, 154, 193, 216, 224, 239, 286, 299-300
Hannibal, 100, 123-124
Harpalyce, 14-15, 32n28, 100n12, 236, 320n21, 341, 349-350, 353
harpies, 95nn9-12, 112; curse of the eating of the tables, 79-80, 210-211; episode in Book 3, 78-80
Harrison, S.J., 291
Hector, 19, 26, 44-45, 52-56, 63, 67-69, 76, 78, 82, 84, 207, 302, 304, 306, 370, 378-379, 386, 394

Helen, 22, 34n50, 57-61
Helen-episode, disputed lines in Book 2, 57-62, 74n33
Helenus, xvii, 81-86
Hercules, 169-170, 177, 191, 223, 237-240, 243, 303, 314
Homer, 1-5, 44-45, 78, 85, 89-90, 99, 131-132, 134-136, 138, 140-141, 144, 147, 163, 171, 174, 177-179, 181-187, 189, 194, 197, 207-209, 212, 214, 222, 224, 229, 270, 279-281, 330, 336, 341, 343, 370, 373, 375, 386, 391, 396
homosexuality, Roman attitudes to, 139-140, 159-160nn13-14, 325
Horace, Virgil's close friend and Rome's poet laureate, xiv-xvi, xixn14, 4, 62,119, 158, 410
horses, 147-148, 316, 335, 362n46
human sacrifice, 235-236, 305

Iarbas, 108, 140, 282
Ilias Parva, 30n2, 53, 82, 96n23, 200n28
Ilioneus, a Trojan, 6, 20-21, 212-213, 280
Iopas (from Joppa?), 25-26
Iulus. *See* Ascanius

Juno: with Aeolus, instigating the storm in Book 1, 5-6; with Allecto, 213-214, 219-220; at the divine council, 291-296; instigating the burning of the Trojan fleet, 149-150; with Jupiter, pleading for a respite for Turnus and sending a phantom Aeneas to trick him, 307-310; with Jupiter, settling the future fate of Rome, 388-393; with Juturna, 372; taking pity on Dido's death agony, 124-125; with Venus, orchestrating the fateful union of Dido and Aeneas, 104-105, 112, 115

Jupiter: at the divine council, 291-296; with Hercules before the death of Pallas, 303; with Juno, discussing her pleas for Turnus, 307-310; with Juno, during the great reconciliation scene, 388-393; orchestrating the death of Camilla and its consequences for Turnus, 343, 355-357; prophetic speech to his daughter Venus, xvi, 8-13; sending Mercury to fetch Aeneas from Carthage, 109-110; summoning of the *Dirae* before Turnus' death, 392-393; weighing the respective fates of Aeneas and Turnus, 396-387
Juturna, 302-303, 319n10, 372, 374-376, 378-388, 390, 392-394

Laocoon, 37-38, 41-43, 50, 54, 137, 216, 266, 371
Latinus, 209-214,220-222, 321, 325-326, 329-337, 354, 368-371, 373, 381-384, 391-392, 394
Lausus, 222-223, 301-302, 312, 314-317, 320n21
Lavinia, 64, 66, 206, 208-210, 213-216, 221, 329, 331-332, 334-335, 368-372, 382-383, 385, 395-396
Livy, 13, 244, 250-251, 392
Lucan (Marcus Annaeus), xvii, 150, 156, 193, 397-398
Lucretius (Titus Lucretius Carus), 3, 10, 26, 34 n. 43, 52, 74n42, 96nn20-21, 102, 136-137, 163, 172-174, 183, 187, 193, 197, 202-203n49, 221, 242, 291, 311, 379, 398
Lupercalia, 241-242
Lusus Troiae, 147-149

INDEX

Macrobius, 27
Mago, 305
Mapheius Vegius, xiv, xviii n. 9, 206, 311
Marcellus (Marcus Claudius), 92-93, 165, 184, 194-195, 197, 201-202n45, 248-249
Mars, 10, 30n6, 32n19, 206, 212, 245, 252, 255, 281, 285-286
Mercury, 13, 25, 32n2, 100, 104, 108-112, 115, 117, 121, 164, 191, 306, 376
Messapus, 222, 224, 231n24, 233, 265, 268, 275, 279-280, 329, 336, 343, 352, 375, 380
Metabus, 337-338, 346
Mezentius, 177, 208, 222-223, 229, 233, 246, 248, 257, 278, 280, 282, 297, 312-317, 320n17, 332-325, 327, 329, 338
Minerva (Pallas Athena), 18, 33n38, 40, 42-44, 50, 54, 88, 227-228, 244, 255, 330, 335, 339, 347, 371
Misenus, 79, 87, 171, 173-174, 177, 184, 195
Mnestheus, 136-138, 144, 270, 287, 297
Musaeus, 185, 188

Naevius, 27, 99
Nausicaa, 20
Neoptolemus. *See* Pyrrhus
Neptune, 6-7, 41-42, 132-133, 136, 141, 149, 151, 153-157, 205, 219, 224
Nisus and Euryalus, 139; in the foot race, 139-141; night raid on the Rutulian camp, 270-280
Numanus Remulus, 108, 140, 282, 290nn28-30, 335, 344-345
Numa Pompilius, 191

Odysseus, 1-3, 5, 8, 39-40, 43, 45, 78-79, 81-82, 85, 89-91, 99, 107, 110, 113, 140-141, 155-157, 163, 168, 170, 174, 178-179, 197, 207, 209, 226, 241, 270, 279-280
omens. *See* portents
Opis, 337, 339, 351, 353-354
Orcus, 200 n. 18
Orpheus, 70-71, 169-170, 175, 182, 184-185, 189
Ovid (Publius Ovidius Naso), xv, 101, 134, 207, 226, 228, 236, 361n29, 363n55

Palinurus, 79-80, 87, 93, 131-133, 136, 139, 151, 155-158; thrown overboard by Sleep, 155-158; underworld shade, 171, 174-177
Pallanteum, 241-242
Pallas, 71, 237, 246, 248-250, 300-306, 321-325, 327-328, 377, 386-387, 392, 395-397
Pandarus and Bitias, 284-286
Panthus, 47-48, 52, 55
Parcae. *See* Fate
Parentalia, 135
Penates, 5, 16, 47-48, 55, 66-67, 77-78, 84, 234, 236, 254, 391
Penthesilea, 19, 99, 140, 228-229, 336-337, 350, 358n5
Pentheus, 117
Persephone. *See* Proserpina
Phaëthon, 135, 159n6
pictures on the walls of Dido's temple to Juno in Carthage, 18-29
Polites, 55-56
Polydorus, 69, 76
portents: in Book 1, of the horse's head at Carthage, 17, 214; in Book 2, of Ascanius' head bursting into flame (confirmed by lightning), 64-65, 254, and

cf. 209-210; in Book 3, of the white horses in Italy, 86, 88; in Book 5, of Acestes' flaming arrow, 65, 144-146, 150; in Book 5, of the rainstorm that saves the Trojan fleet, 150-151; in Book 7, of the "eating of the tables," 79-80, 210-211; in Book 7, of the swarm of bees and Lavinia's fiery hair, 64, 209-210; in Book 8, of the sow and her thirty offspring, 87, 236; in Book 8, of the thunder and lightning before the revelation of the shield, 246-247; in Book 9, of the ships turning into sea nymphs, 267-269; in Book 12, of the evil bird sent to frighten Turnus, 393
Priam, 52-57, 73n30, 181-182, 189-190
Propertius (Sextus), xvi, 4, 207, 261n40
prophecies: in Book 1, of Jupiter to Venus about Rome's future greatness, 8-13; in Book 2, of Creusa's ghost to Aeneas, 69-70; in Book 3, of Apollo's oracle on Delos, 76-77; in Book 3, of the Harpy Celaeno to the Trojans, 79-80, 210-211; in Book 3, of Helenus to Aeneas at Buthrotum, 83-85; in Book 3, of the Penates to Aeneas, 77-78, 234; in Book 4, mysterious prophecies from Grynean Apollo and Lycian oracles, 112; in Book 5, dream visit of Anchises to Aeneas in Sicily, 151-152; in Book 6, prophecy of the Sibyl to Aeneas, 168-171; in Book 8, Evander's recollection of prophetic utterances about the Aneadae, 241;

in Book 8, of Tiberinus to Aeneas, 234-235
Proserpina, 66, 70, 120, 124-125, 170, 177, 278, 290n20
Pyrrhus ("Fire"), or *Neoptolemus*, 53-56, 63, 73n25, 82-83, 132, 134, 140, 147, 149

Quintus Smyrnaeus, 37, 49, 228, 232n32, 336, 341, 343, 358n5, 362n45

Reeves, Michael, 396-397
Religio, 83
ring composition, xiii, 26-27, 29-30n4, 37, 76, 80, 82, 85, 87, 115, 132, 147, 152, 164, 184, 196, 250, 257, 268, 280, 297, 322, 331 347, 353, 388
Roman d'Enéas, 206, 230n5
Rome: the city's bloody founding and the *Aeneid*, xiii; ethnography of the future city, 69-70, 95nn3-4, 107-108, 259-260nn13-14, 260n16, 290n28, 293, 312, 389-392, 401n17
Romulus, 10, 146, 189, 212, 241-242, 250, 252
rumor, 108, 110, 112, 124, 210, 280

Saeculum and the Secular Games, 167
Servius, 57-58, 60, 66, 83, 115, 155, 182, 212, 225, 275, 281, 302, 346, 348-350, 360n23
shield: Aeneas' divinely forged, decorated armor, 64, 250-257
Sibyl, the Cumaean Sibyl Deiphobe, 62, 84, 152, 154, 164, 166-175, 177-178, 182, 184-185, 196-197, 214
Sicily, 75, 85, 87-89, 91-92
Silius Italicus, 226, 311, 337, 377, 389
Silvia, 217-218, 231n18

similes: in Book 1, describing Neptune's quelling of the storm, 7; in Book 1, Dido as Diana, 19-20; in Book 2, Andrgeos compared to a man who steps on a snake, 50; in Book 2, the gods destroying Troy as farmers felling an ancient tree, 61; in Book 2, Laocoon becomes the bull he was sacrificing, 41-42; in Book 2, Pyrrhus as a snake, 53-54; in Book 2, shepherd Aeneas, 46; in Book 2, Trojan heroes on the city's last night as wolves, 49-50; in Book 3, Cyclopes as cypress trees, 90-91; in Book 4, Aeneas as Apollo, 106-107, 221; in Book 4, Aeneas as buffeted tree, 116; in Book 4, Dido as a raging Bacchant, 100, 111, 117-118, 126; in Book 4, Dido as wounded deer, and Aeneas as shepherd, 100, 102-103, 105-106, 117, 127n4, 221-222; in Book 4, Trojans as ants, 115, 123; in Book 5, the *lusus Troiae* as the Cretan labyrinth and the swimming of dolphins, 148; in Book 5, Mnestheus' ship as dove, 137; in Book 5, Sergestus' broken ship as wounded snake, 138, 159n12; in Book 5, ship race as chariot race, 136; in Book 6, Charon's pitiable souls as leaves in autumn and birds in winter flight, 175; in Book 6, the Golden Bough as mistletoe, 172-173; in Book 6, the Sibyl and Aeneas as travelers under an "uncertain" moon, 174; in Book 6, the souls of the blessed as bees, 186-187; in Book 7, Amata as a spinning top, 215, 231n13; in Book 7, beginning of the Italian war as windswept sea, 219; in Book 7, Messapus' men as birds, 224; in Book 7, Turnus as cauldron of boiling water, 216; in Book 8, Pallas as Morning Star, 248-259; in Book 8, Venus' seduction of Vulcan as lightning cutting through a cloud, 243; in Book 8, Vulcan as humble female laborer, 244-245; in Book 9, the death of Euryalus and flower imagery, 276-278; in Book 9, the doomed Italians as Nile or Ganges, 265-266; in Book 9, Pandarus and Bitias as oak trees, 284-285; in Book 9, Turnus as wolf stalking a sheepfold, 266-267; in Book 9, Turnus as eagle, and wolf, 281; in Book 10, Aeneas' men as flock of cranes, 299; in Book 10, forest trees as harbingers of a storm describe the divine council, 295; in Book 10, Lausus as violent hailstorm, 314; in Book 10, Mezentius as wild boar, 312; in Book 10, Pallas and the Arcadians as farmers setting fires, 301; in Book 10, Turnus as lion, 303; in Book 11, Arruns as wolf, 351; in Book 11, Camilla as hawk, 343; in Book 11, the dead Pallas as cut flower, 324-325, 359n13; in Book 11, Tarchon as eagle, 344; in Book 11, Turnus as majestic horse preparing for battle, 335; in Book 12, Aeneas returns to battle like a storm, 379; in Book 12, Juturna as bird seek-

ing food for her nestlings, 379-380; in Book 12, inhabitants of Laurentum as bees that have been smoked out by a shepherd, 382; in Book 12, Turnus as bull preparing for combat, 371; in Book 12, Turnus as a man in a dream, 394; in Book 12, Turnus as rock, Aeneas as mountain, 386; in Book 12, Turnus as wounded lion, 367-368
Sinon, 39-44, 72n6, 89
Sirens, 157
snakes, 41-44, 50, 53-54, 73n27, 135, 138-139, 152, 177, 214, 216, 223, 225, 240, 255
Sortes Vergilianae, 167, 199n1
Sychaeus, 15-16, 101, 107, 109, 114, 117-118, 120, 181

Tarchon, 246-248, 283, 287, 296-297, 300, 312, 329, 343-344, 347, 352, 356
Theseus, 165, 169-170, 177, 183
transformation of the Trojan fleet into sea nymphs, 267-269
trophy: Mezentius' defeat as *locus classicus* for trophies, 322-324
Turnus, Aeneas' rival, hero (or anti-hero?) of the epic, 59; in Book 6, Sibyl's prophecy of the "new Achilles," 168, 214; in Book 7, Allecto's attack on, 215-217; in Book 7, entrance in the procession of Italian warriors, 226; in Book 9, attack on the Trojan camp in Aeneas' absence, 265-270, 281-282, 285-288; in Book 9, attempt to fire the Trojan fleet, 267-269; in Book 9, visited by Iris in Pilumnus' grove, 263-265; in Book 10, slaughter of Pallas, 303-304; in Book 11, during the great Latin war council, 330-334; in Book 11, reaction to the death of Camilla and abandonment of the ambush, 355-357; in Book 12, death of, 59, 177, 194, 208, 223, 249-250, 352-353, 394-397nn19-20

Ucalegon, 47, 73n17
Umbro, 225, 231n26
Underworld: vision of souls of future Roman worthies, 189-196

Venulus, 238, 330, 334, 344
Venus: absence from the end of the poem, 86, 389; colloquy with her father Jupiter, xvi, 9-14; at the divine council, 291-296; instigation of Dido's love for Aeneas, 23-25; with Juno before the fateful hunt in Carthage, 100-104; mockery of Diana, 14-15; with Neptune before the death of Palinurus, 153-155; saving Helen from Aeneas' wrath during the fall of Troy, 61-62; with Vulcan to beg arms for Aeneas, 243-245
Virbius, 225-226, 229, 236
Virgil: brief biographical outline, xiv-xvi, xixn16
Vulcan, Roman god of fire and the forge, craftsman of Aeneas' divine arms, 243-245
wolves (Virgil's favorite animal?), 10, 15, 49-50, 235-236, 241-242, 250, 264, 266-267, 274, 281, 285, 341-342, 345, 349-351

ABOUT THE AUTHOR

Lee Fratantuono completed the Bachelor of Arts in Classics at The College of the Holy Cross in Worcester, Massachusetts; the Master of Arts in Classics at Boston College in Chestnut Hill, Massachusetts; and the doctorate in Classics at Fordham University in New York City, New York, where he finished a thesis commentary on Book 11 of the *Aeneid* under the direction of the late Professor Robert Carrubba. In 2005 he was appointed Assistant Professor of Classics in Ohio Wesleyan University, where in 2006 he was named the William Francis Whitlock Professor of Latin. He has published numerous articles on Virgil, Horace, and Ovid, and is the forthcoming editor (with Stephen Maddux) of a critical edition (with text and commentary) of the sermons of Peter the Lombard. His next project will be a full-scale commentary on Book 11 of the *Aeneid*. Besides his work in teaching Latin language and literature and Roman history at Ohio Wesleyan, he also serves as academic advisor to the Delta Upsilon Chapter of Delta Delta Delta. Lee Fratantuono resides in Delaware, Ohio.